A TWENTIETH CENTURY FUND SURVEY

THE TRUSTEES of the Fund choose subjects for Fund investigations, underwrite the expenses of each project and appoint special committees which formulate programs for action based on the findings. The Trustees, however, assume no responsibility for the findings or the recommendations for action that result.

INTERNATIONAL CARTELS SURVEY OF THE TWENTIETH CENTURY FUND

THIS VOLUME contains the factual findings of an extended survey of international cartels made by a special research staff of the Fund. The report and recommendations for action by the special committee will appear in a later volume on this survey.

THE COMMITTEE

JAMES M. LANDIS, *Chairman*

Chairman, Civil Aeronautics Board; formerly Dean, Harvard Law School; formerly Chairman, Securities and Exchange Commission

A. S. GOSS

Master, The National Grange

MARION HEDGES

Director of Research, International Brotherhood of Electrical Workers

DONALD M. NELSON

President, Society of Independent Motion Picture Producers; formerly Chairman, War Production Board

JACOB VINER

Professor of Economics, Princeton University

J. RAYMOND WALSH

Chairman, New York Citizens Political Action Committee

A. D. WHITESIDE

President, Dun & Bradstreet, Inc.

THE RESEARCH STAFF

GEORGE W. STOCKING, *Co-Director*
MYRON W. WATKINS, *Co-Director*
ALFRED E. KAHN   GERTRUDE OXENFELDT

CARTELS IN ACTION

*Case Studies in International
Business Diplomacy*

BY

GEORGE W. STOCKING

AND

MYRON W. WATKINS

with the assistance of
ALFRED E. KAHN *and* GERTRUDE OXENFELDT

New York
THE TWENTIETH CENTURY FUND
1946

MANUFACTURED IN THE UNITED STATES OF AMERICA
BY AMERICAN BOOK–STRATFORD PRESS, NEW YORK

55

FOREWORD

DURING THE WAR it became clear that the problems of monopoly—both national and international—which had been temporarily submerged under the urgent necessities of armed conflict, would rise up to plague the world again after the fighting stopped. Newspaper accounts of the relation between certain cartels and Germany's economic preparation for war had sharpened the determination of the public eventually to come to grips with these problems as part of any sound program to keep the peace.

Early in 1944 the Fund selected this field as one of those most in need of an impartial factual review and in which constructive policies in the public interest would be most urgently called for. The Fund therefore appointed a special research staff under the direction of George W. Stocking and Myron W. Watkins, both seasoned authorities on cartels and monopolies, to prepare reports on both of these subjects, designed to give the general public the essential facts necessary to understand the issues involved. The Fund also appointed a special committee, under the chairmanship of James M. Landis, to formulate an affirmative program of action to deal with these problems.

This volume is the first to come out of this investigation. It is a sort of "case book" on international cartels: a factual account of the origins and operations of cartel arrangements in eight fields in which they have played an important role. These include: sugar, rubber, nitrogen, iron and steel, aluminum, magnesium, incandescent electric lamps, and chemicals.

A second volume on the subject will follow in a few months. This will describe and appraise the methods and the economic effects of cartels in every field. It will also include the report of the special committee, with its conclusions and recommendations for action.

When the two reports on cartels are finished the staff and the committee will turn their attention to the problems of domestic monopoly. Present plans call for the publication of a single volume on this subject which will contain both the factual findings of the staff and the policy report of the special committee.

EVANS CLARK, *Executive Director*
The Twentieth Century Fund

330 WEST 42D STREET
NEW YORK 18, N. Y.
JUNE 15, 1946

THIS BOOK is the first of three volumes dealing with the closely inter-related problems of domestic monopoly and international cartels. Our approach to these problems in the present study, surveying con-crete experience with international business diplomacy in particular fields, reflects the main object of the whole inquiry.

We view monopolistic tendencies and the cartel movement, not as isolated phenomena, but as manifestations of a trend involving modifications in the pattern, and changes in the bases, of the tradi-tional system of economic control. Changes in public economic policy parallel these developments in the field of business practice. Though the shift in the actual and the formal bases of industrial control is everywhere evident, it has gone farther and become plainer in some countries than elsewhere.

The trend toward concerted action or collective controls in eco-nomic affairs, with or without government sanction or direction, is unmistakable. But it is not, in our view, inevitable. Although time is running out, democratic societies still have room for choice. If they have the will to do it, they can shape their own destinies. Science, and in particular nuclear physics (see, for example, Irwin Schroe-dinger, *What Is Life?*, Macmillan, New York, 1946), now comes to the support of politics and economics in the view that freedom is not an illusion. Our purpose here is to explore the grounds and limits of social choice in the sphere of economic organization.

In a very real sense this volume represents a cooperative study. Our research assistants have contributed vitally to several chapters. No one of us is solely responsible for a single chapter. Discussion and criticism have flowed back and forth, freely and continuously. Furthermore, the study in its present form owes much to the incisive criticisms and cogent suggestions of several members of the special committee for this survey appointed by the Fund. In addition, we have enlisted the aid of a number of persons not connected in any way with the Fund, each of whom by reason of training and experience is exceptionally familiar with the technical development, commercial organization, and business practices of one or more of the specific industries treated. Without associating these individuals in the least degree with our views or methods, we wish to acknowledge here our indebtedness to Messrs. Leon Falk, Jr., Williams Haynes, and Earl Wilson for their generous assistance.

Finally, the constant encouragement, unfailing courtesy, and unstinted cooperation of Mr. Evans Clark, the Fund's Director, of Dr. J. Frederic Dewhurst, the Fund's Economist, and of the Fund's editorial staff have contributed immeasurably to whatever merits the book may have. For the deficiencies that remain, as well as for the judgments and viewpoints it embodies, we accept full responsibility.

GEORGE W. STOCKING
MYRON W. WATKINS

CONTENTS

TABLES

CHARTS

FIGURE

CARTELS IN ACTION

Chapter 1

INTRODUCTION

THE TERM CARTEL was virtually unknown to the American language a generation ago. Like most borrowed words, when first taken over it meant different things to different persons. Time was required to crystallize its meaning. In this country it now commonly refers to international marketing arrangements. In a companion study we have defined such a cartel as an arrangement among, or on behalf of, producers [1] engaged in the same line of business designed to limit or eliminate competition among them.

Cartels as thus defined include a wide variety of business arrangements. They range from loosely defined gentlemen's agreements or informal understandings among business rivals—by which any one of the numerous elements affecting the flow of goods to market, and hence market price, are brought under joint producer control—to formal compacts providing administrative machinery for regulating output, sharing markets, and fixing prices. The loose arrangements may be so honored in the breach that they affect market prices only slightly or for short periods. In their more highly perfected forms, however, cartels may eliminate all competition among their members, for example, by using a single selling agency to supply the market, or by financial consolidation.

Cartels differ not only in form and structure but in legal status. National governments occasionally have established them through negotiation of international treaties or, where producers are located in a single country, by statute or decree. At the other extreme, private producers have entered into secret cartel arrangements, many of which violate the laws of their own countries.

But, however much cartels may differ in their structure or legal status, they have one element in common. They seek to free pro-

---

1. The term producers as used here and throughout this report refers to business units. Wage earners are producers, of course, but in a discussion of business problems it is common usage to limit the term to producer-sellers.

3

ducers from the influence of market forces and to subject the market to deliberate, concerted control, by and for producers. They represent a type of economic planning—planning primarily for the protection and promotion of producer interests.

Extent of Cartel Movement

Such producer planning became a marked, if not the outstanding, characteristic of business between the two world wars. In certain countries, notably Germany and Japan, scarcely a major product came to market free from cartel controls. Even in those countries where economic liberalism had taken firm hold, notably England and the United States, businessmen were rejecting competition as a regulator of economic activity and turning with increasing frequency to cartels to temper competitive forces and diminish business risks.

Nor were cartels confined to those areas of economic activity ordinarily regarded as "business." Farmers, planters, and small-scale producers of raw materials endeavored to improve their lot by collective marketing controls. Since producers in these fields were generally small, they sought state aid. With a frequency not seen since the heyday of mercantilism and on a scale without precedent, national states responded through governmentally devised control schemes. Governments, from the most totalitarian to the most democratic, have resorted to compulsory cartelization of many fields not adapted to joint control through voluntary action of private producers.

It is impossible to measure accurately the extent to which cartel controls have been imposed on industry, commerce, mining, and agriculture. Suggestive of the scope and impact of international cartels on the American economy, however, are calculations which we have made of the ratio of 1939 United States sales of those mineral, agricultural, and manufactured products which have been directly affected by cartel regulation to total sales in that year.[2] The ratio was

2. The "domestic sales" of both the "cartelized" portion and the total volume of these products marketed were computed by adding imports to, and subtracting exports from, domestic production. In general, the source of the domestic production figures was the 1939 Census reports, and the source of import and export data was the 1939 Foreign Commerce and Navigation reports. In certain cases in which domestic production is insignificant—for example, coffee and rubber—"domestic sales" represent simply imports minus exports.

This kind of survey encounters many statistical hurdles, but it would serve no useful purpose to enumerate them here and discuss the methods employed to surmount them. A detailed description of the sources of the data used and of the method of computation is included in an appendix to the companion study mentioned above.

computed separately for each of these three major classes of products. Our tentative findings indicate that 87 per cent by value of mineral products sold in this country in 1939, 60 per cent of agricultural products, and 42 per cent of manufactured products were cartelized.

Scope of the Study

Why has the cartel movement gained such momentum since World War I? What are the springs of cartel action, the factors shaping cartel policies on prices, volume of production, quality of products, and technological innovation? How do cartels tend to affect the operation of a business economy—its efficiency and productivity, its resiliency in adaptation to ever-changing conditions, and its power of dynamic growth? Does the cartelization of industry threaten political democracy? Are cartels—whether syndicalistic "self-government in industry" programs or intergovernmental pacts providing for administrative regulation of specific industries—compatible with democratic diffusion of power and equality of opportunity?

To answer these broad questions requires both historical interpretation and economic analysis. But it also requires a solid factual foundation. Discrimination and appraisal are needed to abstract from the myriad forces shaping industrial organization those which have been most effective in spurring cartelization, and to distinguish the influence of cartels from other economic forces. Generalizations and judgments to be sound must be grounded on concrete data. To provide this factual foundation from actual cartel experience in specific industries is the primary object of this volume. The companion study will deal with the broader questions outlined above.

But, even in a survey of "cartels in action," description is not enough. The facts speak for themselves, but they speak with many tongues. Selection, analysis, and evaluation are also necessary to determine why cartels have developed in a particular industry, what methods have been used to make them effective, and what the results have been.

In this volume we develop case histories of international cartels in eight industrial fields: sugar, rubber, nitrogen, iron and steel, aluminum, magnesium, electric lamps, and chemicals. The span covered ranges from more than half a century in nitrogen to less than two decades in sugar and magnesium. Partly because of the prominent role of German industry in most international cartels, but mainly because of governmental intervention in putting industry on an "all out" production basis, World War II brought general suspension of cartel activities. We have made no attempt, therefore, to carry our surveys beyond 1940. Several of the studies, however, include a brief sketch of wartime changes for their bearing on the prospects of the resumption of cartel activities.

The scope of these eight studies varies widely. For example, three chapters are given to "chemicals" and only one to each of the other fields. The chemicals group embraces numerous branches of manufacture, while magnesium represents less than a single branch, as the metal is ordinarily a joint product of chemical operations, or one supplementary to other metallurgical operations. Incandescent electric lamps are only a single product of electrical equipment manufacturers, while iron and steel embrace the entire range of products manufactured by blast furnaces and rolling mills, from pig iron to steel wire. Moreover, some overlapping of subject matter occurs, as in the separate chapter on nitrogen and the subdivision on synthetics in the rubber chapter, both of which are parts of the chemical field.

Basis for Selecting Cases

We have not chosen the industries at random, but to show the wide range of economic activities subjected to cartel controls, the diversity of circumstances out of which cartels have grown, and the differences among cartels in objectives, structure, methods, power, and results. The list is a representative cross section of the cartel movement.

The survey includes agricultural products (sugar and rubber), raw materials (nitrates and rubber), intermediate goods (iron and steel, aluminum, magnesium, and chemicals), and finished products (electric lamps). Included are cartels based on agreements negotiated by numerous independent producers, whose methods of production and commercial relationships vary widely (sugar and nitrates), as well as some resting partly on financial interconnections among a few large enterprises of a more or less homogeneous character (electric lamps and aluminum). Some of the cartels cover almost all the business interests of the members (chemicals and iron and steel) and others a single product representing a minor business interest of each participant (magnesium and electric lamps).

The studies also show the diverse structures of cartels and the variety of devices used in making them effective. The sugar and rubber cartels were relatively simple export restriction schemes backed by state authority and administered by international committees. Neither exercised any direct control over prices. The iron and steel cartel, on the other hand, had a relatively complicated structure. It was a sort of federation of specific commodity syndicates. The steel cartel regulated both exports and prices, and most of the separate syndicates had joint sales agencies. It used various arrangements to insure stability in world markets, including export quotas, with penalties and compensations for over- or underselling, and division of markets. The aluminum and incandescent electric lamp cartels were even more closely knit than the iron and steel cartel. Both were governed by corporations in which the stock was held by cartel members, in proportion to their respective annual capacities in the aluminum cartel, and in proportion to their basic sales quotas in the lamp cartel.

Defensive and Aggressive Cartels

Despite the marked dissimilarities among these cartels and the wide range of industrial situations which they reflect, one can readily recognize two broad, but not always sharply differentiated, categories: defensive and aggressive. At one extreme stands sugar, an industry long wracked by surplus capacity and a chronically depressed market. As *The Economist* (London) said on June 16, 1945, "Before the war the world's sugar markets suffered from a perennial glut." The persistent, long unavailing, and still imperfectly realized efforts to establish cartel controls in this industry sprang from conditions which threatened serious economic and political readjustments. The industry was badly out of balance, and more than the financial security of business interests was at stake. In the island sugar empires the livelihood of large sections of the population was menaced and in Cuba, at least, the stability of government itself was endangered. The successive sugar cartels were almost purely defensive: designed primarily to avert worse disasters than those which the industry had already met.

At the other extreme is aluminum, which has never in its half-century history known ruinous prices or faced a serious problem of excess capacity or dislocated markets. The successive aluminum cartels, from 1896 to the present, were not the product of economic distress. They were not defensive measures to protect an overexpanded industry from the "ravages" of economic readjustment. They have been instruments of economic aggression. The financial record of aluminum companies, through good times and bad, at home and abroad, attests the efficacy of cartel controls to insure a high rate of earnings.

Between these two extremes range the other cartels in the survey. Of the aggressive type, "born with a silver spoon in its mouth"—and reaching always for a bigger ladle—is the electric lamp cartel. Profits in this industry have been as high and as continuous as in aluminum. But it has occasionally faced a real threat of competition, for example, by Japanese producers using semihandicraft methods or by the producers of fluorescent electric lamps. Nearer to the opposite extreme, but still far from the almost purely defensive sugar cartel, are the nitrogen and rubber cartels. Serious maladjustments confronted both these industries after World War I, but in overcoming their difficulties producers learned techniques and acquired habits which have been used for aggressive ends.

Obviously, no sharp dividing line separates the defensive and aggressive types. Every cartel is defensive to the extent that it need be. Most cartels probably are as aggressive as opportunity permits. "When the devil was sick, the devil a saint would be. When the devil was well, the devil a saint was he." Circumstances alter cases, and many cartels find themselves in, or are formed in response to, circumstances which preclude monopolistic exploitation of consumers.

Nevertheless, the balance of defensive and aggressive elements in cartel motivation is often so steeply tilted to one side or the other that there is no real difficulty in distinguishing one type from the other. And it is certainly useful for understanding the cartel problem and devising public policies to meet it, to distinguish between cartels which have grown out of conditions generally regarded as intolerable, and those based on aggressive business policies by producers who are in no position to plead that the community owes them special privileges.

State-Sponsored and Privately Contrived Cartels

Just as we can classify cartels in a general way as defensive or aggressive, so they fall into two roughly corresponding categories—governmentally sponsored and privately contrived. Here again the distinction is not always clear cut. But by and large, to take well-known examples, coffee valorization and the tin consortium illustrate the governmentally sponsored, and the glass and copper cartels, the privately contrived.

The sugar and natural rubber cartels are also instances of intervention of sovereign states to help producers establish reasonably enduring and effective controls. Sugar and rubber producers are so numerous and their interests so diverse that concerted action to regulate markets proved ineffectual without resort to the coercive powers of governments. A kind of commercial treaty was the alternative adopted. Governmental sponsorship of these cartels reflects both public concern for the welfare of those dependent on the industry and the political influence of the interests involved.

Private producers promoted the nitrogen and the iron and steel cartels, but negotiations were of a quasi-public character. Government representatives were privy to, and carefully watched, the maneuvers of the European iron and steel producers leading to the first cartel, and the agreement was made contingent on the conclusion of a commercial treaty between France and Germany. When the English industry joined the second cartel the British Government cooperated with it, lending its tariff-making power as a bargaining weapon to the British Iron and Steel Federation. While governments generally played a less important role in forming the nitrogen cartel, the Chilean Government was represented in negotiations and other groups of producers had informal governmental approval, if not official sanction.

In contrast, the aluminum, magnesium, and electric lamp cartels have been primarily private business arrangements. The number of business units in these industries has been relatively small, and the economic conditions have given no basis for active governmental assistance. Businessmen conducted their cartel negotiations in private and the agreements they reached were private, and generally secret, contracts. Many of them have run afoul of American antitrust laws and have been vigorously prosecuted. But indirectly and probably unwittingly, governments have frequently lent a helping hand to cartels by their patent laws.

Patent and Process Agreements

Not all patents and processes agreements are illegal, of course, nor do they necessarily constitute cartels or reinforce cartels. Only when they go beyond the recognized and legitimate scope of patent privileges duly conferred, and impose mutual restrictions or create contractual rights which impair freedom of opportunity in trade and impede competitive adjustments in open markets, do they take on the character of a cartel arrangement. The patent cross-licensing agreement has been an important device used by American and foreign firms to establish a degree of control over international markets much greater than would have been possible under a separate and independent exercise of their respective monopoly privileges based on patent grants. Through these agreements the parties have divided world markets, allocated output, and fixed prices, and they have done this not simply on a temporary basis during the term of patent rights actually exchanged and concerning presently patented products or the products of presently patented processes. They have frequently extended the scope of these arrangements to products and processes not at the moment subject to patents, and they have made these arrangements for technological—and market—cooperation on a permanent basis. In brief, when, as has often happened, patents and processes agreements substitute concerted for competitive control of the market, they are cartel agreements. Only confusion and misunderstanding can result from allowing a euphemism to obscure this plain fact.

In chemicals and electronics, especially, the practice of exchanging patent rights—with reservations and limitations adapted to contingencies—has become a fine art if not an exact science. No Gulliver was ever more firmly enmeshed in a network of restrictions than these youthful industrial giants have been by "patents and processes" agreements.

In chemicals no single world-wide cartel rules the market. But the number of international patent-licensing agreements is legion. In part, doubtless, these agreements have served well-accredited ends.

managers, like the king's jesters, do not let them—or us—forget these heart-warming anachronisms.

What was once a way of life in the business world is fast becoming a way of rumination—or oratory. If competition is to survive, it must be more than a shibboleth or a slogan. The discrepancy between the truths which men live by—in business—and the truths which they profess but do not live by, is one of the most significant, and disturbing, revelations of this survey.

Chapter 2

INTERNATIONAL SUGAR CONTROLS

BEFORE WORLD WAR II, Americans consumed on the average over 100 pounds of sugar annually, or more than a quarter of a pound daily. The entire world consumption was roughly 31 million short tons in 1938,[1] or about 29 pounds per capita. Assuming rather arbitrarily that this sugar sold at an average retail price of 6 cents a pound,[2] consumers paid almost $4 billion for their sugar in that year. An esoteric luxury when introduced to Western civilization at about the time of the Crusades, sugar has become an everyday necessity and the basis of a vast industry.

The sugar industry illustrates the world economic trend toward progressive abandonment of competition as a regulator of investment, output, and price. Almost every country regulates, in one way or another, its production, imports, and exports of sugar.[3] Almost every sugar producer has taken part willingly or unwillingly, with or without governmental sanction, in some scheme substituting control by conscious direction for impersonal control by the forces of a free market. The consumer, in whose diet sugar has become an indispensable element, has a direct interest in the operation and consequences of this kind of economic "planning."

Structure and Processes of the Industry

The sugar industry is divided into three rather distinct stages that

1. Unless otherwise indicated, all tons are short tons of 2,000 pounds.
2. Prices in the United States and United Kingdom, the world's first and third largest consumers, respectively (India is in second place, with a huge consumption of low-grade domestic *gur*), were somewhat below this level, and in other major consuming countries they were well above it. Cf. Myer Lynsky, *Sugar Economics, Statistics and Documents, Supplement,* U.S. Cane Sugar Refiners' Association, New York, 1939, p. 306.
3. See League of Nations, Publications, Series II, *Sugar,* 1929, No. 20, pp. 37-47; Oswin Willcox, *Can Industry Govern Itself?*, Norton, New York, 1936, *passim.* (The former of these works will hereinafter be cited simply: L. of N., *Sugar.*)

differ in techniques and in business organization: first, the agricultural stage—the growing of plants containing commercially recoverable sugar; second, the "milling" or crude processing of these natural products, involving, mainly, a grinding or crushing operation; and third, refining the raw sugar.

The first two stages of production are of chief interest in a study of cartels—those which center on and near the farms and plantations where sugar-yielding plants are grown and converted into the raw, or crude, product. Though these two operations usually are carried on close to one another, they are technologically very different. One is an agricultural process, utilizing the arts of husbandry. The other is a manufacturing process, even though a preliminary one, utilizing the mechanic and chemical arts in expensively equipped and highly specialized plants.

Nevertheless, in spite of their differences, the productive facilities in these two stages of the industry are often operated under a common ownership and management. In the United States, it is true, mills ordinarily purchase their cane or beets from independent farmers in the vicinity, especially in the beet branch of the industry, in which extraction of sucrose and refining are commonly conducted in a single establishment. But in the major cane-producing regions—for example, in Cuba and still more so in Java and Hawaii—plantations and local crushing mills have tended to be integrated. Perhaps the established pattern of land ownership and the traditional plantation system in colonial areas help to explain this tendency. Thus, in the beet sugar industry the first of the three major processes—beet culture—frequently is carried on by independent units and the last two operations, crushing and refining, are integrated, while in the cane branch the two preliminary processes tend to be combined and the third stands alone.

But, in either case, this study need not include the refining branch of the industry. For sugar refining does not have to be conducted in the cane or beet growing regions. Beet refineries are commonly so located, it is true, because beet culture is feasible near the large markets. But sugar cane is a tropical or semitropical product, and refiners generally prefer to locate their highly specialized plants, which require large capital investments, in politically more stable regions.[4] The availability of skilled labor and tariff discrimination against imports of refined sugar have also influenced this separation of cane sugar refining from the preliminary processes.[5] Though the opposing forces of competition and centralized control have battled also in the refining phase of the industry, that is another story, for the field of battle is domestic rather than international.

Beet v. Cane

The two major sources of raw sugar—beet and cane—together make production possible almost anywhere in the more habitable parts of the world. Cane thrives best in subtropical and tropical regions. A belt of cane plantations girdles the earth near the equator, embracing the island sugar empires of the West Indies, the Dutch East Indies, Hawaii, the Philippines, and the continental regions of India and South America. The temperate zones, which consume most of the world's sugar, have a local source of supply in the sugar beet, which is cultivated widely throughout Europe and continental United States. The completely refined products of cane and beet are practically indistinguishable, and when international or nationalistic restrictions do not interfere, cane and beet producers vie strenuously for the privilege of filling the world's sugar bowls.

Beet sugar generally costs more to produce than cane.[6] Even the

4. There apparently is very slight advantage, freight-wise, in transporting the raw rather than the refined product, or vice versa. While the raw sugar is bulkier (though by less than 4 per cent, ordinarily), the refined has a tendency to "cake" during a long sea passage and it also requires somewhat greater care to prevent contamination.

5. The United States tariff has always discriminated against foreign refined sugar, though the differential between the rates on raw and refined sugar has never been prohibitory. Cf. Frank W. Taussig, *Some Aspects of the Tariff Question*, 3rd ed., Harvard University Press, Cambridge, 1931, Chap. 8. However, the sugar controls instituted under the Jones-Costigan Act of 1934 placed severe restrictions (exceptionally low quotas) on the importation of "direct-consumption" (i.e., refined) sugar. They halted a tendency of recent years toward the development of refining facilities in Cuba for supplying the near-by United States market, and more especially their establishment as sources of supply for large sugar-consuming enterprises bent on industrial integration.

6. It was estimated during the late twenties that the average cost of producing beet sugar, f.o.b. mills, in Germany, where local growers are heavily protected and subsidized, was more than twice that in Java, the site of probably the lowest-cost cane plantations in the world. These estimates included interest costs in both cases. League of Nations, Publications, Series II, *The World Sugar Situation*, 1929, No. 30, p. 11 f. (This work will hereinafter be cited simply: L. of N., *World Sugar Situation*.)

The United States Tariff Commission reported to the President in 1926 that the average (1917–1922) cost of production of domestic (beet) sugar exceeded that of the Cuban (cane) product by either 1.23 cents or 1.85 cents a pound. (The members of the Commission were unable to agree unanimously, and hence reported these two esti-

advantage of closeness of markets to sources of supply does not, as a general rule, offset the cost handicap of beet sugar. There are few market areas, however remote, that cane producers could not supply more cheaply than beet producers could, however near they were— under conditions of free competition. Large-scale beet culture has been able to survive and grow only by means of governmental assistance—protective tariffs or subsidies.[7]

Because of its higher cost, beet sugar never has been exported regularly and in large volume except with the aid of export bounties. It is sold primarily within the protected domestic markets of its producers. Conversely, the cheaper cane sugar—which, except in India, is usually produced in far greater quantity than native demand requires—finds its market mainly through international trade. Beet sugar accounted for only 12 per cent of the net international trade in sugar, which averaged 11,048,000 tons, in 1925–1929.[8] On the other hand, average annual net exports of cane sugar from Cuba and the Netherlands Indies (mainly Java) alone amounted to 7,410,000 tons in this period, with 5,030,000 for Cuba, 2,380,000 for the Dutch colonies—or two thirds of all the world's sugar exports. On the receiv-

mates.) *Sugar*, Washington, 1926, pp. 69 f., 107. Since estimates of the cost of Cuban raw sugar delivered to North Atlantic ports at that time ranged between 2.25 cents and 3 cents a pound, this represented a sizable discrepancy, in percentage terms.

A later study, based on Tariff Commission figures for the years 1929–1931, estimates the average total costs of refined Cuban sugar (including interest), f.o.b. Atlantic and Gulf Coast refineries, at 2.74 cents, as compared with 3.93 cents for domestic beet, f.o.b. factory. Works Progress Administration, National Research Project on Reemployment Opportunities and Recent Changes in Industrial Techniques, Report No. N-1, *Studies of Productivity and Employment in Selected Industries: Beet Sugar*, Philadelphia, 1938, p. 50; see also pp. 49, 55, 60, 70.

Of course, these data do not negate the possibility that in exceptional situations a fractional part of the beet output may cost less than that part of the cane supply produced under the most disadvantageous conditions or by the least efficient units. Cf. Philip G. Wright, *Sugar in Relation to the Tariff*, McGraw-Hill, New York, 1924, and J. W. F. Rowe, *Sugar*, Studies in the Artificial Control of Raw Material Supplies, No. 1, Memorandum No. 23, Royal Economic Society, October 1930, p. 18. (This study will hereinafter be cited simply: Rowe, *Sugar*.) See also L. of N., *Sugar*, p. 9.

7. Of course, elimination of all artificial trade barriers might not result in complete disappearance of beet sugar. Total unit costs of both cane and beet vary greatly as between different producers and regions, and probably the total unit cost of a cane production large enough to supply the world's total requirements would exceed the total unit cost of the more efficient beet producers, particularly at the outset. Undoubtedly, however, the degree of displacement would be substantial, and cane would, in time, become by far the leading source of the world's supply.

8. U.S. Department of Agriculture, *Agricultural Statistics*, Washington, 1937. The world total represents net exports of both raw and refined sugars, in terms of net sugar content, of those countries with export balances. Gross world export figures cannot be used because they involve double counting of sugar exported by one country and re-exported by the recipient; some countries import raw sugar, and re-export it in the refined state.

ing end, two consuming countries—the United States and Great Britain—took most of the exported sugar: 4,260,000 and 2,030,000 tons, respectively. The remaining purchases, supplementing local supplies, were scattered over both hemispheres. India, China, Japan, and Canada all took substantial quantities.

Beet-Cane Rivalry on the World Market

But one should not infer that beet sugar is a minor factor in the world market. For though in the export trade the beet branch of the industry cuts little figure on the side of supply, it exerts a potent influence on the demand for imports, both directly and indirectly. To the extent that consuming countries effectively foster local production of beet sugar, the product displaces cane supplies. In other words, it reduces the demand for imported sugar. Indirectly, too, beet production affects adversely the demand for cane sugar because it depends on tariffs and similar devices which raise the price and thereby tend to curtail cane sugar consumption.

Furthermore, these measures for protecting the high-cost beet industry require political action and this adds a highly variable factor to the numerous other uncertainties with which producers must contend. Political decisions are notoriously erratic and unpredictable. Thus beet sugar has a greater bearing on the world market than its share in net exports might suggest—a factor in the instability of the sugar market as a whole.

Until 1800 sugar came almost exclusively from the cane plantations of the New World and the islands of southeastern Asia. The newly discovered sugar beet received its initial stimulus from the continental blockade during the Napoleonic Wars, when Napoleon offered subsidies to encourage its growth on the continent. By the end of those wars, the new industry had taken sufficient root to demand and receive various forms of state aid. With this protection, beet culture expanded throughout the nineteenth century. Before World War II, 35 to 40 per cent of the world's sugar came from this source.

Why Beet Sugar Persists

The beet sugar industry, born out of wartime exigencies, got another boost from the "sugar famine" during and following the first world war. The blockade and shipping shortages, which cut off or reduced supplies of cane sugar, led major consuming countries to adopt a program of sugar self-sufficiency.

The serious plight of farmers all over the world during the twenties and thirties made governments unusually responsive to the clamor, for protection by local beet growers and refiners. The fact that under common methods of beet cultivation the labor cost is higher in relation to the value of the product than for virtually any other crop made the encouragement of beet culture particularly attractive in some areas as a partial solution of the unemployment problem as well as the farm problem.[9] Moreover, sugar beet production affords an excellent means of scientific crop rotation, resulting in improvement of the soil, and the byproducts make good cattle feed.

These factors have been considered adequate to justify protection of the sugar beet industry in a great many countries. However, although governments sought self-sufficiency by protecting the producers of high-cost beet sugar, the "sugar famine" of the first world war was the result far less of the curtailment of cane sugar imports than of a drop in European beet production from 9,104,000 tons in 1913–1914 to 2,831,000 in 1919–1920.[10] Labor shortages, insufficiency of fertilizers, and sheer physical devastation of the land contributed to this decline. Government-stimulated local outputs declined drastically during the very period when they were supposed to step into the breach created by military operations.

National security considerations would not seem to justify the protection of a beet sugar industry in peacetime. Warring countries can scarcely afford the luxury of uneconomic production of sugar. Modern warfare requires effective mobilization of manpower "behind the

9. The record does not indicate that this has been a pressing consideration in protecting the American industry, where migratory Mexican labor has frequently been used.

10. Europe as a whole was, on balance, an exporter of sugar in the calendar year 1913—by roughly 500,000 tons, according to the Department of Agriculture, *op. cit.* Even gross imports of sugar by European countries—a large part of which represented merely intra-European trade in beet sugar—amounted to less than 2.7 million tons in that year.

In the text above, the figures are for crop years, which in the sugar industry run from September first. In order to simplify the exposition we shall hereinafter omit the first of the two calendar years linked to designate a single crop year. For example, instead of referring to European beet production from September 1, 1919 through August 31, 1920 as the output of 1919–1920, we shall describe it as the 1920 production. This rule applies to both cane and beet figures. Since the crop year in Java is the calendar year, this mode of designating the conventional crop year actually conforms to established practice in that exceptional case.

front" no less than in the military theater. Beet culture requires an exceptionally high expenditure of labor per unit of output. Minimum wartime requirements could be assured at less cost by maintaining stand-by facilities geared to an emergency output of, say, 25 per cent of normal consumption (as in Europe in 1917–1918), than by continuously subsidizing local (beet) production on a scale of domestic self-sufficiency.

As for the strictly economic arguments, if beet cultivation were an economical method of crop rotation, soil improvement, and cattle-fodder production, the cost (supply price) of beet sugar would be low enough to permit it to be produced and sold in competition with cane sugar, without subvention.[11] The persistent requests in all beet-growing countries for governmental assistance have cast some doubt on the reality, or at any rate on the extent, of the alleged collateral advantages of beet culture.[12]

The fact remains that, largely because of governmental intervention, beet sugar producers supply a large share of the world's demand, most of which cane producers would otherwise supply. Cane producers have also sought to advance their interests by enlisting the aid of their governments. But the struggle is an unequal one. Since it is easier to induce national governments to discriminate against foreign producers than to defend the interests of domestic consumers, "the brunt of the battle is borne by the exporting countries"[13]—predominantly by Cuba and Java.

Rivalry Among Cane Producers

In spite of their common struggle against beet sugar, the producers of cane themselves have divergent interests. The bulk of the exports of Cuba and Java do not directly compete. At least 75 to 80 per cent of Cuba's exports in the late twenties went to the United States,

11. This argument assumes (1) that farmers evaluate the byproducts in accordance with competitive market standards, and (2) that they take account of their own long-run interests (e.g., in soil conservation) as fully as they take account of their short-run interests.

12. However, in so far as the community at large might obtain collateral benefits from the cultivation of sugar beets—benefits not reflected in cost savings or value yields to the individual farmer—"protection" of the industry could logically be justified. This assumes, however, that the community could obtain no corresponding collateral benefits from the production of the alternative goods, which a protected sugar industry displaces. See A. C. Pigou, *Economics of Welfare*, P. S. King, London, 1920, Pt. II, in particular, Chap. 6, pp. 149-79.

13. L. of N., *World Sugar Situation*, p. 9.

aided by geography and by a 20 per cent tariff preference under the Reciprocity Treaty of 1902.[14] Most of Java's sales were in near-by India, China, and Japan. Nevertheless, they both produced more than adjacent markets could buy. These surpluses competed in the world market, especially in Europe, with each other and with the beet surpluses of Germany, Poland, and Czechoslovakia.

The conflict of interest between Cuban and Javanese cane producers came into the open during the late twenties, when the Javanese refused to cooperate in restricting output to support the sagging world market. The Javanese producers were introducing a new variety of cane that yielded as much as 30 per cent more sugar. They probably were, or at any rate seemed likely soon to be, the lowest-cost producers, and could withstand better than others any temporary price decline. The encouraging growth of their Asiatic markets reinforced their refusal to cooperate with their Cuban competitors.

Moreover, the Javanese producers were confident that their strong organization would shield them from a drastic decline in price. A single-seller handled the marketing of their output. This was the Vereenigde Javasuiker Producenten (VJP), which was organized in 1918 to prevent weak selling when Javanese stocks were at an unprecedented level due to the wartime shipping shortage. Individual producers, lacking finances to hold the stocks even briefly, had begun to dump them, thus severely depressing prices. The VJP, dominated by a few large banking-trading concerns, was able to hold such temporary surpluses off the market, and thus to check the price decline.

Javanese Costs Low

Because of their low costs and the expanding Asiatic market, the Javanese producers felt secure until the very late twenties. Even in 1928—when, with a record crop in prospect, it seemed unlikely that Java's markets could take the whole output—VJP's quasi monopoly in the Far East enabled it to protect its members from serious loss. It shipped large consignments to Europe at net realization prices substantially lower than those on concurrent sales in its far eastern domain. This discriminatory pricing policy, by helping to prevent

14. This tariff preference applies to all Cuban exports to the United States. Cuba made similar concessions on American exports to its markets. The special political and military relationship between the two countries which evolved out of the Spanish-American War helps to account for these commercial clauses of the treaty.

accumulation of large stocks, may have tended to check the decline of prices in the world's sugar markets generally.[15] But the dumping in markets normally served by both Javanese and Cuban producers emphasized the threat of increasingly intense competition between them, even in years of normal crops.

Another area of conflict among sugar cane producers is the United States, which absorbs more "offshore" sugar than any other country. Although Cuba since 1902 has had tariff preference, even the preferential rate offers a substantial protection to United States domestic producers.[16] And the latter group comprises not merely the continental United States beet growers and the relatively small cane plantations in Louisiana and Florida. It includes every sugar producer within the United States customs area, which embraces Hawaii (since 1875), Puerto Rico (since 1901), and the Philippines (up to July 4, 1946).

The real competition between these interests has taken place far more in congressional cloakrooms than on the open market, and the struggle has been intense, at times even bitter. The propagandist and lobbyist are important elements in the sugar industries which vie for a share in the United States market. Though they operate behind the lines, as tacticians and strategists, their role in the campaign is even more decisive than that of the generals and the infantrymen who wage the actual battle of the markets.

15. This can neither be verified nor disproved on the basis of available data. But in spite of the heavy Javanese shipments to Europe, the average London price declined slightly less in 1928 from the 1927 level than did the average New York price. (See Table 2.) Of course, the movement of sugar prices in continental (European) markets may not in every case, or even on the average, have coincided with the price movement on the London market. In fact, the basic ground for the hypothesis advanced in the text is precisely the insulation of the sugar markets in most European countries from world market forces. To the extent that the increased Javanese exports to Europe were concentrated in particular countries where their price-depressing influence could be impounded, the discriminatory pricing policy may, as stated, have been advantageous. Monopolistic price discrimination always depends on this condition. If some sections of a market cannot be cut off (in a measure) from other sections, price discrimination is impossible.

16. This rate was 1.0048 cents a pound until 1921, when it was raised to 1.6 cents by the Emergency Tariff of that year. The protective policy was intensified with the Fordney-McCumber Tariff of 1922 and the Hawley-Smoot Act of 1930, which lifted the duty, successively, to 1.7648 cents and 2 cents. The rate was reduced to 1.5 cents by presidential proclamation in 1934 and again to 0.9 cents under a trade agreement with Cuba in the same year. Except for a brief interlude at the outbreak of war, the tariff remained at the latter level until January 1942, when it was dropped once more, to 0.75 cents. However, as we shall see below, the lower rates after 1934 were contingent on Cuba's accepting a limited quota share in the United States market.

Regional Clashes

Sharp differences among various groups of producers have appeared even within individual producing countries. In particular, conflict in Cuba between native growers, dealers, and processors, on the one hand, and American-owned plantations and mills, on the other, has had important political and economic implications. Before 1900 the Cuban industry operated on a relatively small scale. The tariff preference extended to Cuban sugar in 1902 attracted a huge influx of American capital. Along with these ample funds came the American flair for big business. Thus the Cuban sugar industry, in the last half century, has changed from subsistence farming and small-scale milling, often powered by animals, to large-scale corporate enterprise powered by machines. Sugar cane cultivation and processing have become mechanized to an extent rarely encountered in agricultural industries.

This system of large plantations and modern mills operating under "remote control" today dominates the island's economy. Locally owned mills, whose share of total production has gradually declined until it was only about one fifth in 1935–1940,[17] have remained small and generally less efficient than the American, which have the advantage of size and up-to-date equipment. Moreover, American interests have opened plantations in the richer, relatively virgin, eastern sections of the island. Production costs of these newer American plantations and mills are estimated to be at least one half cent a pound, and probably nearer one cent, less than those of the older plantations and mills in the west.[18]

The native Cubans soon realized that, if the price of sugar fell, the burdens of bankruptcy and unemployment would fall first on them because of the foreign companies' lower costs and far greater financial resources. Consequently, whenever sugar prices have fallen it has been the native producers—that is, the generally high-cost producers—who have exerted the greater pressure for governmental restrictions to cut the output of all producers uniformly, or at least in a way to save the weaker elements in the industry. A similar, though less sharp, cleavage of interest is found in Java, between large

17. See tables in *Anuario Azucarero de Cuba,* Cuba económica y financiera, Havana.
18. Rowe, *Sugar,* p. 14.

European-owned enterprises with heavy fixed capital investments and a few Chinese producers operating on a smaller scale.

Roots of Sugar Cartels

The industry has been generally in serious straits since the first world war. A decline in the rate of expansion of international trade during these years, the business depression after 1929, and the spread and intensification of economic nationalism between the two world wars, all contributed to the difficulties of the sugar industry. However, sugar producers have met grave problems of their own. Deeply embedded structural maladjustments resisted correction by such free market forces as unilateral national controls have permitted to operate. Stocks have tended persistently to accumulate and prices to fall below the costs of even the low-cost producers. The sugar problem has been not merely to protect a few inefficient producers, doomed ultimately to bankruptcy, but to restore the whole industry to economic health.[19]

The world-wide maladjustment between sugar supply and demand in the postwar period cannot be laid to any abnormal weakness of demand. In the decade between World War I and the depression, the world's consumption grew at a rate of about 4.5 per cent yearly.[20] The difficulty arose from an even more rapid expansion of productive capacity.

World War I certainly gave the initial impetus to disruption of the world sugar trade. And the radical dislocation of the industry and convulsive disturbance of market relationships occasioned by the war have been largely responsible for subsequent difficulties. Europe's production of beet sugar declined from 9,104,000 tons in 1914 to 2,831,000 tons in 1920. From that low level it recovered only gradually to 5,654,000 tons in 1924, though by 1928 it had expanded to 8,827,000 tons, virtually the prewar level.

This large-scale abandonment of beet culture gave an enormous stimulus to cane production. The world output of cane sugar rose from 11,997,000 tons in 1914 to a plateau of about 14,600,000 tons

19. It may well be, of course, that, had the forces of competition been permitted complete freedom, low-cost producers in particular, and the industry in general, not only would have survived, but would have been better off. We shall discuss this question at a later point. In fact, the forces of the market were never permitted to be effective.

20. L. of N., *World Sugar Situation*, p. 6.

annually in 1917–1921; and then, in the face of the government-sponsored re-establishment of the European beet industry, soared even more rapidly to 18,262,000 tons in 1925, and reached 20,787,-000 tons in 1929. As a result of continued expansion of cane production while European beet production was mounting to prewar levels, the world's sugar output climbed from 18,654,000 tons in 1920 to a peak of 32,028,000 tons in 1929.[21]

Production Costs Reduced

The rapid expansion of supply was clearly not due solely to the war. Cane sugar output reached a definite plateau between 1917 and 1921, and then increased more in the six years from 1923 to 1929 than in the preceding decade. The most important reason for the 1923–1929 increase was the rapid progress in applying scientific methods to cane cultivation. A new and more productive species of cane was widely adopted in Java. More intensive methods, such as a wider use of irrigation and fertilizers, were applied (largely by American-owned companies) in Hawaii and Puerto Rico. American capital, exploiting the more fertile provinces of Cuba, introduced cost-reducing techniques of large-scale production, efficient organization, and modernized equipment. All these developments contributed to a rapid and long-sustained expansion of cane production.

Though these improvements were not directly traceable to the war, they were undoubtedly stimulated by the temporary eclipse of the European beet sugar industry in the world market—and that was beyond any doubt one of the "economic consequences of the war." Moreover, the reductions in cost that accompanied and spurred on these developments in the cane industry gave an illusion of economic security which persisted for some time. Planters in Java and the American interests in Cuba continued to increase output after 1922, evidently in the belief that the high-cost beet industry in Europe would recover but slowly, and that their own low costs would, in any event, shield them from the harmful effects of general over-supply.

Meanwhile, the beet-producing countries of Europe, determined

21. Statistics from L. of N., *World Sugar Situation*. The available estimates of world sugar production show considerable variation; the reader will note, however, that these figures are reasonably close to those given in Table 1 for the period 1920–1921 to 1939–1940.

to grow their own sugar at any cost because of the war and postwar sugar famine, renewed and reinvigorated their policies of subsidy and protection to local growers. These nationalistic measures in time restored the high-cost production in spite of the rapid increase in cane supplies. Similarly, the 1921–1922 changes in the United States tariff, raising the rate of duty on Cuban sugar from 1.0048 cents to 1.7648 cents a pound, not only encouraged the domestic beet growers but also stimulated expansion by cane producers in Puerto Rico, Hawaii, and the Philippines, whose combined output rose from 1,646,000 tons in 1921 to 2,789,000 tons in 1930. (See Table 1.)

Sugar Supply and Demand

Under ordinary competitive conditions, any long and serious maladjustment between supply and demand cannot last. The decline of price due to a continued oversupply must tend both to reduce output, by eliminating high-cost producers, and to increase the quantity demanded, until the two come into balance. However, the nature of the sugar market is such that these adjustments are difficult. The demand for sugar is relatively unresponsive to changes in price.[22] Consequently, as the price of raw sugar in the world market sagged after 1923 under the impact of steadily expanding supplies, that decline was not appreciably arrested by increased purchases.

The supply of sugar seems also to be relatively inelastic in the short run.[23] In agriculture, producers cannot figure the unit cost of marginal output close enough to adjust that output promptly to price changes. Indeed, because of the relatively large "fixed capital" investment, the farmer tends to produce the single cash crop to capacity at all times. Heavy taxes—and, when the land is mortgaged, interest charges and debt amortization—force him to produce "up to the hilt" even though price may not cover total unit costs. Moreover, the chief direct cost is for labor, which—apart from that of the farmer and his family—is supplied largely by hired laborers who have few

22. Henry Schultz concludes from a study of the period 1890–1914 that "under normal conditions, an increase of one per cent in the price of sugar is associated with a decrease in consumption of only one-half of one per cent. The demand for sugar may, therefore, be designated as quite inelastic." *Statistical Laws of Demand and Supply*, University of Chicago Press, Chicago, 1928, p. 92.

23. "The world's supply of sugar is also inelastic . . . That is to say, a 1 per cent increase in the New York price for any year will call forth an increase of only 0.6 of 1 per cent in the world's production for the following year." *Ibid.*, p. 187 f.

TABLE 1

WORLD SUGAR PRODUCTION, 1921–1940

(In Thousands of Short Tons of Raw Sugar) [a]

Year [b]	Cuba	Java [b]	India [a]	Europe [c]	Conti-nental U.S.A.	Hawaii, Puerto Rico, Philippines	Estimated World Total Cane	Beet	Total
1921	4,469	1,681	2,825	4,091	1,345	1,646	14,415	5,306	19,721
1922	4,581	1,853	2,952	4,327	1,425	1,557	15,400	5,517	20,917
1923	4,141	1,994	3,437	4,988	1,024	1,409	15,215	5,739	20,954
1924	4,671	1,981	3,746	5,634	1,111	1,692	16,575	6,526	23,101
1925	5,894	2,201	3,059	7,669	1,256	2,221	18,305	8,920	27,225
1926	5,602	2,535	3,529	7,990	1,119	2,015	19,007	9,041	28,048
1927	5,121	2,140	3,725	7,442	1,008	2,228	18,936	8,397	27,333
1928	4,591	2,592	3,788	8,574	1,242	2,477	19,784	9,747	29,531
1929	5,857	3,223	3,208	9,133	1,271	2,446	20,920	10,220	31,140
1930	5,305	3,165	3,231	8,982	1,307	2,789	21,037	10,005	31,042
1931	3,545	3,214	3,754	11,356	1,508	2,759	19,561	12,251	31,812
1932	2,956	3,056	4,610	8,213	1,421	3,224	20,287	9,190	29,477
1933	2,266	2,822	5,402	6,964	1,717	3,223	18,984	8,386	27,370
1934	2,583	1,513	5,681	7,741	2,007	3,716	19,580	9,632	29,212
1935	2,883	701	5,964	9,168	1,508	2,515	19,296	10,507	29,803
1936	2,904	562	6,864	9,313	1,651	3,011	21,409	10,721	32,130
1937	3,375	646	7,494	9,652	1,832	3,127	23,995	11,197	35,192
1938	3,380	1,546	6,143	10,602	1,840	3,134	22,831	12,136	34,967
1939	3,094	1,542	4,581	9,601	2,386	2,996	21,718	11,574	33,292
1940	3,128	1,730	5,977	10,762	2,262	3,137	23,010	12,698	35,708

Source: U.S. Department of Agriculture, *Yearbooks* and *Agricultural Statistics.*

a. Indian cane sugar output, included in the world total, is in terms of *gur*, a low-grade sugar polarizing between 50° and 60°.

b. Production figures are for crop years 1920–1921 to 1939–1940, except in certain cane-producing countries (notably Java) where the crop year coincides with the calendar year.

c. Data for 1921–1936, beet sugar only; 1937–1940 figures include relatively small Spanish cane sugar crops. Figures for all years include Turkey in Asia.

other opportunities. Hence labor cost is unusually flexible. Such a combination of rigid indirect costs with flexible direct costs contributes to the unresponsiveness of production to price changes.[24] Finally, as in agriculture generally, fortuitous changes in the weather affect the supply of sugar independently of demand.

24. There are other reasons for the inadaptability of supply, particularly on the downward side. Sugar cane is a perennial plant, and in the West Indies many years' harvests are customarily obtained without replanting; thus costs in any given year may be greatly reduced by restricting new plantings, without immediately reducing supply.

"Moreover, in Java, where plantings are annual, the growing of cane has been part of an elaborate six-year cycle of crop rotation, linked with the supply of food for the inhabitants, sugar being planted eighteen to twenty months before the harvest. Thus the law of supply and demand is materially impeded in its functioning . . ." Foreign Policy Association, Commission on Cuban Affairs, *Problems of the New Cuba,* New York, 1935, p. 237.

Because sugar supply and demand are so little affected in the short run by price changes, price movements in either direction are more protracted and intense than they would be otherwise. These factors help to account both for the sustained abnormally high prices of 1919–1920 and for the continued depression of prices during the latter half of the twenties.

However, even more than this inherent inflexibility, it was the feverish epidemic of nationalistic policies of economic self-sufficiency which was primarily responsible for the world sugar problem. The pursuit of national self-sufficiency encouraged expansion of high-cost output beyond any economically justifiable limits. It not only hampered normal competitive adjustments—the displacement of high-cost producers—but, by "protecting" home markets against cheap foreign supplies, it tended to curtail consumption, which would otherwise have expanded somewhat in response to declining world market prices. The resurgence of militant nationalism and neomercantilism was quickened by the patriotic passions of the first world war.

Market Out of Balance

Sugar production ran regularly ahead of consumption during the twenties. Stocks accumulated steadily, increasing from 4,997,000 tons on September 1, 1923 to 10,360,000 tons six years later,[25] and their growth contributed to an almost unbroken decline of prices. The annual average price of Cuban sugar delivered in New York declined from 5.24 cents a pound in 1923 to 2.56 cents in both 1925 and 1926, and, after a short-lived recovery, to 2.46 cents in 1928 and 1.99 cents in 1929. (See Table 2.)

The expansion of output by the low-cost cane producers during the twenties was, under the circumstances, clearly a business error. In a competitive market other producers—in the main, high-cost beet growers—would eventually have borne the brunt of the readjustments required. But economic nationalism was steadily narrowing the range of competitive adjustments, putting increasing pressure on cane producers, high- and low-cost alike.

The native planters of Cuba experienced the greatest difficulties.

25. According to estimates by Lamborn & Company, Inc., published in *Lamborn Sugar Statistical Bulletins*. Estimates of sugar stocks vary considerably, as Table 2 clearly demonstrates. Nevertheless, all available figures indicate an increase on some such scale.

Their costs were generally higher than those of the local American plantations and mills, and also probably higher than those of the Javanese growers. Virtually all their competitors enjoyed preferential

TABLE 2

RAW SUGAR STOCKS AND PRICES, 1920–1939

Year [a]	Stocks [b]			Prices [c]	
	Lamborn	Mikusch	Czarnikow	New York	London
	(Thousands of Short Tons)			(Cents Per Pound)	
1920	—	—	—	11.35	—
1921	—	—	—	3.15	—
1922	5,691	—	—	2.85	3.01
1923	4,997	—	—	5.24	5.26
1924	5,901	1,407	—	4.20	4.28
1925	8,014	2,186	—	2.56	2.75
1926	8,736	2,603	—	2.56	2.66
1927	8,559	2,887	—	2.95	2.98
1928	9,139	2,727	3,520	2.46	2.53
1929	10,360	3,665	4,461	1.99	1.96
1930	11,834	4,661	6,087	1.47	1.43
1931	13,845	7,194	7,457	1.33	1.27
1932	13,517	8,056	7,815	0.93	0.91
1933	11,836	7,858	6,905	1.22	1.02
1934	11,189	—	5,968	1.50	1.06
1935	10,072	—	4,550	2.33	1.01
1936	9,641	—	3,288	2.69	1.04
1937	9,942	—	3,104	2.54	1.40
1938	11,421	—	3,969	2.04	1.10
1939	11,501	—	4,321	1.91	—

a. Price figures are calendar year averages. Estimates of stocks: Lamborn for September 1, Czarnikow, September 30. The Mikusch figures are given with year captions "1923–4," "1924–5," etc., with no indication as to whether they pertain to the beginning or end of the crop year. It is assumed here they pertain to the end of the crop year: hence the 1923–4 figures appear here in 1924, the 1924–5 in 1925, etc.

b. Three series of estimates are shown because a full explanation of the wide discrepancies among them is lacking. However, Lamborn & Company states that its figures are for "practically every country in the world" which supplies stock data, and this series probably has a wider coverage than either of the others. The Lamborn estimates appear in the *Lamborn Sugar Statistical Bulletins*, the Mikusch (Gustav) in his article "Sugar," *Encyclopaedia of the Social Sciences*, Macmillan, New York, 1937, Vol. XIV, p. 454, and the Czarnikow in *The Economist*'s (London) annual "Commercial Histories and Reviews."

c. The prices are of Cuban raw sugar, 96°, delivered to the respective markets. London prices converted at average annual rates of exchange. New York prices from Czarnikow-Rionda Co., New York, *Annual Sugar Review*, and Department of Agriculture, *Agricultural Statistics*; London prices from League of Nations, Publications, Series II, *The World Sugar Situation*, 1929, No. 30, p. 26, and "Commercial Histories and Reviews."

advantages over them in one form or another: Puerto Rican, Hawaiian, and Philippine planters, in the United States market; the beet producers of the United States and Europe, in their respective home markets; and the Javanese, in their far eastern domain.

The impact of the progressive postwar maladjustment between supply and demand was first felt acutely in the marketing of the 1925 crop. Cuban production, which had hovered near 4.5 million tons annually in 1919–1924, jumped to 5,894,000 tons. At the same time European beet production mounted from 5,634,000 tons in 1924 to 7,669,000 tons the next year.[26] Besides, the output of the cane producers of Hawaii, Puerto Rico, and the Philippines, operating behind the recently raised United States tariff walls, continued to expand, rising from 1,692,000 tons to 2,221,000 tons in the same period. So the outlets for Cuban sugar in both the American and European markets were sharply reduced just when the supply from this source reached record levels. As a result, the New York price for Cuban sugar toppled, hitting a low of 1.94 cents a pound in October 1925.

When a sugar-starved world purchased all it could obtain and was still unsatiated in 1920, the Cuban sugar industry realized an estimated gross income of $774 million. The natives danced "the dance of the millions," as the boom was popularly termed. A 25 per cent larger crop in 1925 yielded but $311 million.[27] With good reason, the Cubans were alarmed by this turn of events.

The Cuban Dilemma

The only means of avoiding disaster, in the view of most native growers, was to restrict output to match the shrinking free market. This called for governmental authority, for most American producers in Cuba were lukewarm or openly hostile to such a program, and they controlled the bulk of Cuban capacity. They had made heavy investments to insure their own competitive superiority, and they were well aware that their unit costs would be increased as output was curtailed.

Cuban restriction represented the first of a series of attempts to

26. Department of Agriculture estimates, reproduced in Table 1.
27. The 1932 crop, restricted to one half the 1925 output, brought $68 million, according to the same source. Myer Lynsky, *Sugar Economics, Statistics and Documents*, U.S. Cane Sugar Refiners' Association, New York, 1938, p. 71. These figures suggest the devastation of the Cuban economy which resulted.

correct maladjustment in the world's sugar industry by keeping supply from outrunning demand at prevailing price levels. It is fair to
ask whether any alternative policy might have been pursued. Of
course, if Cuba had been able to prevail on the major importing
countries to abandon their discriminatory policies and to throw their
markets open to foreign sugar, doubtless the problem would have
disappeared—for Cuba!

But this was asking too much of Cuba's erstwhile customers. The
governments of the principal European countries and of the United
States represented not only millions of consumers but also thousands
of sugar beet growers and scores of beet sugar factories. Though the
consumers vastly outnumbered the beet sugar groups, the producers
were far more articulate and politically active. Neither diplomacy
nor propaganda seemed likely to secure a fair, competitive opportunity for the export of Cuban sugar to the only markets which could
economically absorb it. Nor did there appear to be any alternative
way of disposing of the Cuban product without loss. The only real
alternative to restriction, therefore, was to do nothing—to leave the
determination of Cuban output and price to the impersonal forces
of the market. But this market would not have been a competitive
world market; it would have been a market "cut to pieces" by the
protective policies of the principal consuming countries.

Eventually equilibrium would have been attained in this way.
High-cost plantations and mills might have hung on stubbornly, continuing to produce as long as out-of-pocket expenses were met.
Plantation labor's wages would have been drastically reduced, and
doubtless an excess of world supply over demand would have continued for some time. But the resultant continued downward pressure on prices would inevitably have driven out the relatively higher-
cost producers of cane, until the contracting supply was restored to
balance with the effective demand at a price covering the survivors'
long-run costs of production. The basic problem might have been
solved in this way, but as long as high-cost cane producers were kept
alive restriction would continue to be necessary to prevent oversupply.

However, the Cuban Government could scarcely have been expected to resist the clamor of its people for some form of state-
enforced restriction. For sugar was the backbone of the island's
economy. It accounted for 78.8 per cent of total Cuban exports in

1927. A continued fall in its price, such as seemed probable, would have prostrated the entire national economy. There was no reason to suppose that the higher-cost cane producers could be easily driven into other lines, for such alternatives were few in what had become largely a one-crop economy. The fall in price would inevitably have brought financial loss to all producers, high- and low-cost alike. The decision to hold back the oversupply of Cuban sugar was also prompted by local distrust of the American segment of the industry. These restrictions were designed to retard the growth of American output at the expense of native.[28]

Cuban Restriction Begins

A series of laws and presidential decrees, beginning May 3, 1926, sharply curtailed the harvests of 1926, 1927, and 1928. In the first two seasons a simple 10 per cent restriction was imposed, with a prohibitive tax ($5 a bag) on excess production. The restriction was applied at the milling level; each mill was required to reduce its output of raw sugar to 90 per cent of a standard output, determined by administrative authorities. This standard "grind," or output, was to be based in part on scale of operations in the recent past, in part on anticipated yield of acreage normally tributary to the mill, and in part on "other factors." The plan contemplated that the 10 per cent reduction in permitted mill production would lead to a roughly equivalent cut in the harvest on the plantations.[29] Future expansion in plantation capacity was likewise curtailed by a prohibition against further cutting of virgin forest for new planting.

The law of October 4, 1927 stipulated a more detailed system of crop control. It empowered the President to estimate, for the coming year, the requirements of the United States, Cuba, and the rest of the world for Cuban sugar, to fix production quotas to meet those requirements, and to allot each mill the amount which it might sell

28. The precedent of Brazilian coffee valorization may well have fortified the Cuban Government in its decision to intervene. The Brazilian Government had adopted marketing regulation for the coffee industry, which provided the bulk of national export trade, on the ground that the prosperity of that industry was of crucial significance to the entire economy. However, Brazil designed her 1923 valorization scheme primarily to offset extreme, year-to-year fluctuations in output—to equalize rather than to restrict. Not until 1931 did Brazil attempt directly to curtail total sales—by the expedient of burning a certain percentage of the crop.

29. In the first crop year, restriction was not fully effective because many of the mills had already surpassed their permitted production by the time the law was passed.

to the American market. To prevent "weak selling," the Cuban Sugar Export Corporation was set up to handle all other sales.

The vagueness of the legal provisions, particularly those for determining each mill's standard output, was an open invitation to arbitrary and discriminatory administration. But even with scrupulous fairness in administration, the latitude of discretion exercised by the officials made for dissatisfaction among the mills. Of course, more definite criteria might not have avoided such vexations. More explicit legal provisions could not have resolved to the satisfaction of everyone the ineradicable conflicts of interest between high- and low-cost producers. For example, a hard and fast requirement that quotas be fixed strictly on the basis of past production would have discriminated against the many producers who had recently expanded their capacities.

The invitation to the executive agencies to consider all relevant factors was a kind of compromise between the proponents of "past production" and "present capacity" as criteria. The continuous complaints, notably by American interests, against allegedly discriminatory administrative decisions show that not everyone was satisfied with the "compromise." These grievances doubtless contributed to the ultimate abandonment of the restriction program. But the basic reason was its failure to raise prices.

Market Effects of Cuban Restriction

Cuban restriction had some temporary bullish effect, contributing, along with poor crops in Europe and Java, to temporary recovery and stability of prices in late 1926 and early 1927. But it was powerless to reverse the persistent tendency for world output to exceed consumption, for stocks to accumulate, and for sugar prices to decline. The production of Java and Europe, as well as that of the favored suppliers to the American market, continued to increase rapidly under the impact of forces already mentioned—notably nationalistic encouragement and technological progress—and perhaps also in response to the temporarily more stable prices to which the restriction of Cuban output contributed. Nevertheless, the steady reduction of the Cuban crop, from 5,894,000 tons in 1925 to 4,591,000 tons in 1928, undoubtedly retarded the price decline. In view of the extremely depressing effect of small sugar surpluses, 5.9-million-ton Cuban crops during these years would have been disastrous.

As the price continued to decline Cubans were understandably disappointed in restriction. It seemed to them that foreign growers were taking advantage of Cuban self-denial to expand operations, although actually Cuban restriction was not the primary cause of the continued upward trend of production elsewhere.

Cuba's outlook was dark. Cane left uncut in the fields was drying up and creating an obstacle to the resumption of production, if and when that might seem desirable. Curtailed harvesting had caused unemployment among farm workers. Inasmuch as decreased crops had brought increased unit costs, the 2.5 cent price of mid-1928 meant profits to only a few very large and modern American-owned mills. Since these mills had always opposed restriction, the growing disaffection of the native producers spelled the doom of this initial scheme and it was abandoned at the end of 1928.

"Out of the Frying Pan Into the Fire"

Cuba quickly learned what a 5.9-million-ton crop would do to the sugar market; for the unrestricted 1929 crop fell short of that figure by only 43,000 tons. Native mills in particular, lacking credit to store the unmarketable portion of their output, undercut each other furiously, and the average New York price slumped to 1.75 cents a pound in June 1929. The government once more intervened, this time by establishing a Cooperative Export Agency to take over the marketing of the entire crop.

This move represented simply a renewal of the effort to keep up prices by "orderly marketing." The scope of activities of the single-seller agency was broader than under the 1927 law; it handled all export sales. But the centralized sales scheme was not buttressed by even the stopgap device of crop restriction, as had been the scheme of 1926.

Moreover, the Agency was inadequately implemented to attain its limited objective. For, "the prevention of weak selling demands some means of financing those producers whose want of finance is the reason for the weak selling . . ." [30] The Export Agency had no

---

30. Rowe, *Sugar*, p. 9. Our discussion of the history of the Cuban experiments owes much to this penetrating study.

resources of its own and it was unable to obtain credit, either locally or from the United States, particularly after the Wall Street crash in October. Purchasers, aware of its lack of finances, refused to meet the price of 2 cents to which the Agency stubbornly clung and waited for the time when it would have to dump supplies. As a result, stocks accumulated at a growing rate; and, as incipient world depression reduced consumption, the price fell to record lows.

Disillusioned once more, the native producers clamored for an end to governmental intervention. They were in desperate straits for lack of credit or ready cash, and were anxious to sell for whatever they might get. The American-owned mills, with ample credit, did not object to enforced withholding of supplies from the market. For in a few more months, it appeared, their high-cost competitors would at last be eliminated by bankruptcy. But the Cuban interests had their way with the Cuban Government, and in April 1930 this second scheme, too, was abandoned. 611091

It had by now been proved—as should have been clear from the outset—that Cuban restriction alone could not insure Cuban cane producers a profitable price for sugar. On the contrary, it tended to prolong the life of high-cost cane producers, whose disappearance alone might have helped greatly to solve the problem—provided nationalistic beet sugar subventions remained, and, with them, the curb which higher prices exercised on demand in the major consuming countries. By postponing the withdrawal of high-cost producers from a time of world prosperity to a time of world depression, Cuban restriction increased the difficulties and hardships of an unavoidable readjustment. But this judgment is made with the benefit of hindsight. Probably few observers realized at the time that the economic, political, and social "costs" of readjustment were bound to be high, in whatever manner it might be made. Certainly no one prominent in the industry gave any sign of awareness of this fact.

The problem obviously called for drastic retrenchment in the Cuban cane sugar industry. Whether retrenchment were left to the pressure of market forces or enforced by governmental action, heavy sacrifices were inevitable. Competition might distribute the costs of the required readjustment in a different way from that in which a statute or an administrative authority would. So, in a certain sense, a planned retrenchment might mitigate the economic penalties. But to attempt to avoid readjustment—that is, the shift of productive resources out of the industry—merely by holding off the market excess Cuban sugar, was to court disaster.

Such an expedient might temporarily stop the fall of prices, but it could not remove its cause. For the strategy of price-supporting measures does nothing to abate the conditions which generate such price-depressing forces. Curtailment schemes predicated on the false assumption that persistent price declines are the cause of threatening ruin, instead of the symptom of underlying maladjustments, tend to aggravate the basic difficulty rather than to correct it.

Attempts at International Cooperation

The Cuban restrictive schemes of the twenties had two fatal drawbacks. The first was Cuba's failure to enlist the cooperation of other exporting countries with which she competed in what was left of the free world market. The second, and probably more important in the long run, was her inability even to retard, let alone to reverse, national protective policies which were gradually constricting this "free" market by encouraging continued expansion of domestic beet output.

Cuban interests made several attempts to remedy the first deficiency during the late twenties. Colonel Tarafa, motivating spirit, administrator, and guiding genius of Cuban restriction, conferred in 1927 with representatives of the sugar industries of Czechoslovakia, Germany, and Poland, the major beet exporters. He found them receptive to his proposals for concerted limitation of plantings to balance world production with prospective consumption. However, a tentative agreement to restrict the 1929 crop was never put into effect because of the refusal of the Dutch companies owning plantations in Java to cooperate. Similar attempts late in 1929, on the initiative of the European producers, proved abortive for the same reason. The Dutch still took the position that their lower costs and favorable location near Asiatic markets would shield them from loss.

But anxiety continued among the less fortunately situated elements in the industry. Appealing to the League of Nations for a diagnosis of their ills, they were told, in the 1929 report, *The World Sugar Situation,* merely that "the difficulties with which the industry is at present beset are such as can, to a large extent, either remedy themselves or be remedied by those responsible for the conduct of business." This prescription was too equivocal to encourage forthright action in any direction, and the sugar situation went from bad to worse.

The world depression halted the steady progress of sugar consumption; but, in the absence of agreement, production continued for a time to advance. In 1931 world output reached the record level of 31,812,000 tons, 670,000 tons more than the previous peak of 1929. This rise was traceable entirely to the striking expansion of beet production—from 10,220,000 tons in 1929 to 12,251,000 in 1931. This expansion in the face of a declining world market price was the consequence of reinvigorated governmental efforts to protect domestic producers against the inroads of cheap imported sugar—or perhaps to protect domestic consumers against the diabetic risks of overindulgence! A good example of this prudential, paternalistic strategy was the increase in the American duty on Cuban sugar from 1.7648 to 2 cents a pound in the Hawley-Smoot Tariff of 1930. This new rate was equivalent to an ad valorem duty of 136 per cent on the average ex-duty price in that year (1.47 cents a pound) for Cuban sugar delivered in New York.

Also mirroring a progressive maladjustment between supply and demand, world stocks on September 1, 1931, after an unprecedented increase during the year, reached an all-time record high of 13,845,-000 tons. This was equal to half of current annual consumption.[31] Prices, accordingly, reached new lows, the New York price, for example, averaging 1.47 cents a pound in 1930, 1.33 cents in 1931, and 0.93 cents in 1932, with a monthly average of only 0.59 cents in May 1932.[32]

The Chadbourne Plan Launched

By this time even the Javanese producers were prepared to cooperate. Late in 1930 conferences began which culminated in an agreement signed in Brussels in May 1931 by representatives of the sugar industries of Cuba, Java, Czechoslovakia, Poland, Germany,

31. Estimates of stocks vary, and these particular estimates are much higher than others. (See Table 2.) However, we consider them the most reliable.

32. This price of 0.59 cents includes the cost of shipping sugar to New York! The Havana price reached its lowest monthly average in April 1932, when it was 0.487 cents a pound.

Belgium, and Hungary, and soon after by Peru and Yugoslavia—all the major sugar-exporting countries. The resultant program, scheduled to cover the period to September 1, 1935, was called the "Chadbourne Plan" after an American lawyer who with other representatives of the Cuban industry had taken the initiative in organizing the conference.

Its purpose was to bring about a recovery of the price of sugar from its disastrously low levels. To this end, the annual supply had to be brought more nearly into line with world consumption requirements. Since the continental and insular producers of the United States, as well as those in all parts of the British Empire, were not represented, the parties were in no position to control world production, and they were either unwilling or unauthorized to limit their own production for domestic consumption. All they could do was to temper competition among themselves in markets outside their own countries.

So the signatories undertook to restrict their exports during the next five years to specified tonnages, varying in some cases from year to year. Also, to neutralize the depressing effects of enormous stocks, particularly in Cuba and Java, each country with excess stocks agreed to centralize and segregate them. Their release was authorized only in specified annual amounts, distributed over the life of the agreement. The Plan did not provide for any direct agreement on prices. The authors of the Plan believed the pricing problem would be cared for by restricting the flow of supply. However, they provided for gradual percentage increases in quotas in case the daily average price of raw sugar in the London market rose above the equivalent of 2 cents a pound, f.o.b. Cuba, for thirty consecutive days.

The Chadbourne agreements were not treaties or intergovernmental contracts. They were negotiated by the producers themselves. However, the governments stood in the background. The several national producers' organizations were in most cases the outgrowth of previous governmental intervention, and in some cases their agreement to control exports had behind it the explicit promise of governmental support. Cuba's quota limitations were enforced by law. When the association of Javanese producers could not obtain the cooperation of one leading company, the Netherlands Government also enacted enforcement legislation. In fact only in Belgium was there no enforcement legislation—because it was unnecessary.[33]

In terms of positive, demonstrable results, the Chadbourne Plan was a failure. The annual average price of sugar imported into Great Britain, the best indication of a "free" world price, declined to 0.91 cents a pound in 1932 from an average of 1.27 cents in the year preceding (see Table 2) and hovered about the one cent level during the entire period 1931–1935. The monthly average price, ex-duty, paid in New York for Cuban sugar, declined to a low of 0.59 cents for May 1932, one year after the signing of the agreements. It then recovered slightly. But the notable advance to more than 2 cents a pound in 1935 was the result of preferential reductions in the United States custom duty on Cuban sugar—amounting to more than 50 per cent.

The first of two reductions was made by presidential proclamation in June (under authority conferred by Section 336 of the Tariff Act of 1930), whereby the duty on Cuban raw sugar was lowered from 2 cents to 1.5 cents a pound. The second was under the Reciprocal Trade Agreement with Cuba, which cut the duty on the Cuban product to only 0.9 cents a pound. From the Cuban standpoint, however, these gains were partly offset by limitation of American imports under the Jones-Costigan Act of 1934. Thus, the rise of prices in the New York market after the middle of 1934 was due to strictly "local" factors. The "free" world price remained at the one cent level until the outbreak of World War II.

Appraisal of Chadbourne Plan

The Chadbourne Plan did achieve some reduction of the heavy excess stocks which had been an important factor depressing the world price of sugar. However, the reduction in the "carry-over" was far less than had been hoped for. World stocks were reduced from the September 1, 1931 peak of 13,845,000 tons to 10,072,000 tons four years later, when the Plan expired—a reduction of only 27 per cent.

The signatory countries faithfully adhered to severe limitation of

33. Kurt Wilk, "The International Sugar Regime," *American Political Science Review,* October 1939, Vol. XXXIII, p. 872.

their sugar exports and in doing so curtailed production. Their output in 1935 was 6.7 million tons, almost 50 per cent lower than their 1929 peak. The brunt of the curtailment—more than four fifths of it—was borne by the two chief exporters, Cuba and Java, which reduced outputs 51 and 82 per cent, respectively. The Javanese reduction showed a determined effort to cut accumulated stocks,[34] and probably reflects, in part, the greater ease of reducing production where an annual crop is grown.

On the other hand, the production of nonsignatory countries, almost exclusively for protected domestic markets, had risen by almost exactly the same amount—6.9 million tons—during the same period, although part of this advance (2.6 million tons) was recorded by 1931, before the launching of the Chadbourne Plan. The greatest gainer was India. Other notable advances occurred in the rest of the British Empire, aided by various forms of protection and Imperial tariff preference; in nonsignatory producers on the European continent—France, the USSR, Spain, Austria, and Sweden; in Japan; and, finally, in the United States and its favored offshore suppliers, Hawaii and Puerto Rico. As a result, the net sugar exports by the Chadbourne countries made up only 62.5 per cent of the world's total in the period 1932–1935, as compared with 82 per cent in the years 1925–1929. Their share of world production declined even more sharply—from 45 per cent in 1925–1929 to but 26 per cent in 1931–1935.[35]

The increased output of countries not in the Chadbourne Plan and the corresponding reduction in their import requirements negated the export limitations imposed on its participants by the Plan and hence doomed any agreement adopted by exporting countries alone. Nor, as one might guess, were the restrictions of the Chadbourne Plan indirectly responsible, in any appreciable degree, for the increased production of outsiders. For one thing, a substantial part of the increase was recorded before 1931. For another, while the Chadbourne

34. The Chadbourne agreement limited the exports of the countries represented among the signatories, not their production. In view of the ceiling on exports, Javanese producers evidently saw no point in maintaining output, as long as huge stocks remained unsold.
35. In these computations, the net total of world exports is measured by the net exports of those countries enjoying active balances of trade in sugar; the trade of Yugoslavia, a Chadbourne signatory, is excluded from the computations because that country was an importer of sugar on balance during both periods.

Plan apparently was a real influence in the recovery of prices during the period of its operation, the prices were not high enough to encourage greatly the expansion of output in nonrestricted areas. This expansion was, rather, mainly a result of the intensified programs of numerous consuming countries for fostering domestic production in spite of the fact that sugar could have been imported more cheaply than ever—gauged either by minimum monthly average price within the five-year period or by the quinquennial average price itself. These developments help to explain why the Chadbourne agreement was not renewed upon its expiration in September 1935.

American Sugar Control Measures

Meanwhile, as part of its general domestic program to hasten recovery of agricultural prices and incomes, the United States had independently adopted a thoroughgoing control of the flow of sugar supplies, domestic and foreign, into the American market. Since this country took 38.6 per cent of the world's net exports in the period 1925–1929,[36] such controls affected a substantial portion of the world's industry. Under the new plan, the influence of free competition in allocating sales (and indirectly output) among competing producers was superseded, in this important sector of the world market, even more fully than it had been under the tariff system.

By the terms of the Jones-Costigan Act of 1934, and the Sugar Act of 1937 which followed it, the Secretary of Agriculture was required to estimate in advance the annual sugar requirements of continental United States, and to allot quotas in the market to the various supplying regions according to ratios set forth in the act. The law provided that 55.59 per cent of estimated consumption be allotted to domestic areas—that is, to continental beet and cane producers, and to the cane growers of Hawaii, Puerto Rico, and the Virgin Islands. The remaining 44.41 per cent was to be the share of the Philippines and foreign producers (almost exclusively Cuba). In addition, absolute minimum quotas were prescribed for the domestic areas (3,715,000 tons) and for the Philippines (800,000 long tons of unrefined sugar plus 50,000 tons of refined).

These quotas gave more than adequate protection to domestic

36. This does not include the sugar exports of Hawaii and Puerto Rico. If their sales were considered international trade, the American proportion would have been about 45 per cent.

producers. Continental American farmers supplied about 18 per cent of apparent national sugar consumption in 1929; by 1933, behind the Hawley-Smoot tariff, their participation had increased to 29 per cent. Under the Jones-Costigan and Sugar Acts their share was raised to 32 per cent in 1938, and they also received direct subsidies (under the Agricultural Adjustment Act) for "restricting" output to the levels authorized.

The quotas allotted to Hawaii, Puerto Rico, and the Philippines were likewise fixed at levels well above their respective participations in the American market in the late twenties. Together, these insular suppliers furnished roughly 39 per cent in 1938 and 41 per cent in 1939, as against 30 per cent in 1929. But these quotas were less than their collective share in the early thirties. In 1933, for example, thanks largely to the tightening of restrictions on imports by the Hawley-Smoot tariff, their share rose to 46.5 per cent. These insular "dependencies" or "protectorates" likewise received AAA benefit payments. On the other hand, the quotas assigned to Cuba have virtually frozen its position in the American market at the drastically curtailed level of the early thirties. Although Cuba had supplied 52 per cent of United States sugar consumption in 1929, its share in 1933 and 1938 was only 24 and 27 per cent respectively.

Preference for Cuba

The sugar controls developed by the United States in the thirties combined novel policies of relief for domestic agriculture with a new form of protection against imports of the foreign product.[37] The high-cost American producers continued to be protected at the expense of the American consumer and subsidized at the expense of the American taxpayer. At the same time, as the chief foreign producer for this market, Cuba got the substantial benefit of a preferential reduction of the customs duty on her sugar by executive order and trade agreement in 1934. But the preferential duty was contingent upon, and subsidiary to, the maintenance of quota limitations. The Cuban exporter got a share in the benefits from the high price

37. Moreover, the traditional policy was extended, for the first time, to include special protection for domestic cane sugar refineries, in the form of quota limitations upon imports of "direct-consumption" sugars. In this way the Atlantic Coast refineries, in particular, put a check to the increasing tendency for Cuban sugar to be refined in Cuba, where milling and refining operations were increasingly becoming one continuous process.

of sugar in the American market, a high price now maintained by strict limitation of supply, but his market was drastically cut.

While Cuban growers got assurance of a greater income from the American market than under the 1930 tariff, this higher income was not from a greater volume of sales at lower prices, with benefits to the American consumer, but from continued low volume of sales at higher prices. They have enjoyed a larger income at the expense of the American consumer. Moreover, though these benefits for both the American and the Cuban producers have all come ultimately out of the pockets of domestic consumers, the United States Treasury has sacrificed a portion of the revenue formerly obtained from customs duties.

Although the Chadbourne Plan halted the persistent growth of relatively low-cost cane production, it failed to correct the basic maladjustment caused by the government-stimulated expansion of relatively high-cost beet production in the face of an arrested growth of world demand. Of the factors tending to retard the increase in sugar consumption, not the least important have been the incidence of "protective" measures on prices in sheltered markets and the contraction of general purchasing power in the Great Depression. The spread of protectionism was, of course, closely related to the onset and intensification of the depression.

The Chadbourne Plan showed that private exporters alone could not prevent the progressive shrinkage of the world's "free" market in the face of the autarchic policies adopted by the governments of importing countries. Accordingly, at the World Monetary and Economic Conference of 1933, and again a year later, the countries represented in the Chadbourne agreement, and Cuba in particular, attempted to enlist the aid of the world's sugar-importing countries as well as other exporting countries. Eventually, in the International Sugar Agreement of 1937, their cooperation was obtained.

International Sugar Control

By the 1937 cartel agreement twenty-one governments joined in a systematic regulation of the world's sugar industry. These countries accounted for 85 to 90 per cent of the world's sugar production and consumption.[38]

38. Lynsky, op. cit. (1938), p. 274.

First, and most important, the Agreement provided assurances against further contraction of the "free" world market for sugar. The United States, its market already completely under government allocation, agreed that the proportion of its supplies purchased from world exporters would be no smaller than their quota in 1937. Great Britain undertook to limit domestic output and its purchases from other Empire sources to the proportion of its requirements obtained from these sources in 1937. Similar obligations were assumed by other importing countries. It now became possible, within these limits, to plan exports with some degree of assurance.

Second, in spite of these efforts to preserve what was left of a free world market, the plan provided an effective control of exports. Basic quotas in the "free" market were fixed for the several countries normally occupying a net export position. Small reserve quotas were set aside for occasional exporting countries. Furthermore, effective production control was established by a provision that, in general, stocks should not exceed 25 per cent of annual production.

From the viewpoint of foreign cane producers, the negotiators of the International Sugar Agreement were not guilty of inconsistency in these two major provisions. From the economist's standpoint, however, the provisions were contradictive. The "free market" which the negotiators sought to preserve was not the economist's free competitive market, but a market "free" from *additional* governmental barriers to importation.

In managing or planning the world's sugar economy so as to exclude further inroads on the "free market" (in the narrow, technical sense defined above), the basic aim was to preserve—and perhaps even gradually enlarge—the market outlets for low-cost supply, chiefly cane. This was certainly an economically defensible and salutary objective. On the other hand, by setting up this so-called "free market" on a prearranged quota basis, the aim was to freeze the shares of the producing areas in the market *in disregard of cost considerations.* In view of the chronic indigestion from which the sugar economy had been suffering, it may be that a diet of this sort was the only hope. But if industry-wide planning is feasible only in so far as it preserves inviolate the vested interests in the status quo ante, are the advantages of stabilization worth what they cost in the risks of stagnation?

The Sugar Council

The Sugar Agreement entrusted administration to a representative International Sugar Council with narrowly limited powers. The Council was to include up to three representatives from each country.[39] But the number of representatives a country might send to the Council was unimportant since the Agreement fixed the voting strength of each delegation. Out of a total of one hundred votes on the Council, forty-five were allotted to the governments of importing countries, including seventeen votes each to the United States and Great Britain. The remaining fifty-five votes were distributed among the exporting countries, Cuba receiving ten of these and the Netherlands (Java) nine.[40]

The task of the Council was to make annual estimates of the requirements of the "free market," in advance, and to see that these requirements were met in line with the provisions of the covenant. It was empowered to reduce all export quotas proportionately, if it thought this necessary to prevent supply from "breaking the market." But this power was granted only for the first two years, and the reduction was not to exceed 5 per cent in either year. While these

39. The Agreement expressly provided for the appointment of "advisers," likewise up to a maximum of three. The document contemplated that each country's delegation should be composed of a like number of (1) government officials, presumably members of the civil service, and (2) industry representatives, at least in the case of the exporting countries. Conceivably, of course, a government might select men from the industry to serve as its "representatives," as well as to serve as "advisers" in its delegation. This may have happened among some of the exporting countries, but so far as we have been able to ascertain the "representatives" of the importing countries have consistently been drawn from the diplomatic ranks, from other branches of the civil service, or from the armed services.

The precise relationship between the "representatives" and the "advisers" in the actual functioning of the Council is obscure. Perhaps the best guess, or most promising hypothesis, would be that the relative strength of personalities in the two "orders" of a delegation has much to do with the determination of their respective shares in the responsibility for decision making. But does the distribution of power and influence between the two "orders" differ among the importing-country delegations, on the one hand, and those of exporting countries, on the other? Again, is there any correlation between the voting strength of delegations and the extent of effective participation in policy formulation by the "adviser" group? We cannot answer questions of this kind on the basis of information at hand, but they might well repay investigation.

40. A direct comparison of the vote allotments, country by country, gives a rather misleading impression of the relative "stake," and the relative actual influence, of the several signatories in the deliberations and decisions of the Council. That Cuba was allotted only ten votes, as against seventeen for Great Britain, for example, might appear rather anomalous. But the vote distribution by countries has to be interpreted in the light of the fact that, collectively, the exporting countries, of which there were a score, obtained a "working majority" in the Council, while the four importing countries had to accept a minority position in that body. The United States and Great Britain had seventeen votes each, but their real power in the Council was presumably subordinate to that of Cuba and Java, which between them had only nineteen votes. For on the

limited reductions might be put into effect by a simple majority vote, a license to increase exports beyond the standard quotas required the approval of three fifths of the Council votes.

In other words, the exporting countries commanded among themselves sufficient voting power (1) to reduce quotas within the authorized limits, and (2) to block an increase of quotas, however small, at any time. Moreover, even transfers of quota rights among exporting countries—in the event, for example, that one had a poor crop and another a yield high enough to fill the deficiency of the first in a given year—might be made only by a majority vote. Finally, the application of sanctions against any member required seventy-five votes (three quarters of the total). Beyond these limits, any action looking to the regulation of the flow of supplies required unanimous consent.

Experience of the Cartel

By exercising its power to reduce quotas pro rata during the first two years, and by forestalling transfers (in some cases) of those portions of their quotas which certain exporting countries were unable to fill, the Council was able to balance supply and demand at prices about 30 per cent over the 1935–1936 average.[41] While in

crucial issues of divergent group interests the latter could count on the support of other exporting countries and, with their help, easily outvote the importing countries.

Technically there was no distinction between the votes of importing countries and those of exporting countries. Nor did the members of either group vote as a unit. Indeed, the division of interest among the exporting countries was at the root of the entire Agreement and it was one of the principal responsibilities of the Council continuously to resolve their differences.

It was the main purpose of the Agreement to divide exports to the "free" world market so that each exporting country could count on a definite share. Council votes were allotted *among the exporting countries* roughly in proportion to their export quotas. Cuba's vote allotment was apparently "out of line," because her exports to the United States were excluded in calculating her export quota. But even if they had been included, and Cuba's voting power thus raised to correspond more closely with her actual "weight" as a sugar-exporting country, the change would have made little difference in the "balance of power" in the Council. Specifically, it would not have meant any alteration in the agreed 55 to 45 ratio of voting power between the exporting countries as a group and the importing countries. For *that* ratio clearly rested on strategic considerations and had nothing whatever to do with productive capacity or potentiality.

41. This assumes an average price of 1.34 cents a pound for the two years ending September 1, 1939. That is our estimate of the average price during the cartel period. In making this estimate, only the 1938 annual average could be taken from Table 2. It was necessary to compute an average for the last four months of 1937 and the first eight months of 1939. We made a rough approximation of monthly averages for these two periods by scanning the daily averages on the London market. These figures, in shillings and pence per cwt., have been converted into cents per pound at prevailing exchange rates, likewise roughly estimated. The resultant "average prices" are 1.38 cents a pound in the last four months of 1937 and 1.68 cents a pound in the first eight months of 1939. These figures combined with the 1938 average of 1.10 cents a pound give 1.34 cents for the two-year period ending September 1, 1939.

percentage terms this was a substantial rise, the actual price level of about 1.34 cents a pound was roughly one cent below what it had been a decade earlier. Probably neither the average nor the marginal costs of production of sugar had declined proportionately during these years. The average London price was lower by a cent than the New York price. However, this differential resulted from the difference between the British and American methods of "protecting" domestic sugar producers, not from cartel price discrimination.

The restrictions imposed on the flow of supplies under the International Agreement might seem no greater than reasonable for all the interests at stake. The importing countries were in a minority on the Council and could easily be outvoted by the producing interests. On a showdown, the exporting countries had the final say, and, once assured of this, they may well have decided that "moderation is the best policy." More specifically, the actual course of the market suggests that the exporting countries, which had a clear majority on the Council, hesitated to override the views or impair the interests of the minority.

It would be unrealistic, however, to overlook other influences which helped to shape Council policy—in particular, the divisive tendencies among the exporting countries. Each hesitated to accept a lower quota, indeed demanded its "full rights"—even at lower prices —in order to find an outlet not only for current supplies but for a larger output. While we have no clue to the motives that inspired the majority, one ground for its forbearance may well have been to hold the importing countries to their part of the bargain.[42] Obviously the interests of the exporting countries would have been injured if the importing countries had walked out and resumed aggressive promotion of domestic beet production.

From the record, it appears the Council shaped its policy, in part, to placate the consuming countries. For example, when an acute sugar shortage developed in Great Britain in 1939, the Council promptly readjusted quotas, over the protests of a minority of the exporting countries. In May 1939, the British Government, which

42. The Council was severely limited by the Agreement in restricting the flow of supplies (5 per cent each year). But it might readily have administered the provisions governing transfer of quotas so as to have curtailed sugar supplies more stringently than it did. Moreover, it might have diverted available supplies from the market into secret stocks if it had chosen to do so.

had been accumulating stocks in anticipation of war, asked the Executive Committee of the Council for an increase of quotas. Two proposals were submitted: (1) that 239,000 tons be added to current export quotas, and (2) that the (calculated) 153,000 tons increase in preferential Empire supplies which Britain would presumably have been authorized to import in the following year (based on current rate of absorption) be released immediately.

The Council approved both measures by telegraphic vote, the first by eighty votes and the second by seventy-six. But the Cuban Sugar Institute is reported to have been opposed to these concessions,[43] and both Cuba and Germany protested that the second proposal would violate the basic agreement. Nevertheless, the first proposal was put into effect at once, and the second in June, after a full meeting of the Council, when it was determined that the measure was within its powers.[44]

Appraisal of the Cartel

During the brief period of peace in which it operated, the International Sugar Agreement showed serious shortcomings. The compromises which gave it birth came only after "jockeying and haggling." On the one hand, the Agreement gave an extremely narrow range of discretion to the administrative authority in adjusting the flow of supplies to the current market. Doubtless the demands—or fears—of the importing countries prompted this limitation. On the other hand, the quotas of the several exporting countries were high, in some cases more than current "capacity." This feature was probably the result of demands by the more aggressive exporting countries based on their prospects of growth.

As a stabilization mechanism, the scheme lacked the elasticity and adaptability essential to effective "management" of a market subject to as many variables as the sugar market. On the side of supply, the unpredictable weather is important. On the side of demand, the fluc-

---

43. As Willett and Gray expressed it: "Cuba's attitude is based on the argument that, after a decade of working with sugar prices not fully covering costs of production, the world's producers should not be begrudged a short spell of comparative prosperity." *Weekly Statistical Sugar Trade Journal*, May 25, 1939, p. 214.

44. *Ibid.*, June 1, 1939, p. 227, June 8, 1939, p. 233 f.; *International Sugar Journal*, July 1939, p. 249.

tuations of the business cycle upset calculations. During the first few months of the Agreement, for example, the world price of sugar declined rather sharply. In part this may have been simply a reaction of the market in weighing the limited powers of the Sugar Council to restrict exports against the contingency of a sudden decline in demand. However, the sharp business slump during these months would seem more responsible.

In 1939 events again demonstrated the inadequate flexibility in the scheme. This time it was a question of the power of the Council to avert a threatened sugar shortage. Poor European beet and Indian cane crops, coinciding with a rise in demand stimulated by growing fears of another world war, caused a marked rise in prices in late 1938 and early 1939. Though the Council responded promptly and conciliatingly to the specific applications of importing countries that experienced the first sugar shortage in nearly two decades, such as Great Britain, it is doubtful whether its powers or wisdom were adequate to meet the rapidly developing emergency.

Had the war not halted this experiment in international sugar control, the Council's work within the limited range of its authority would soon have shown the need for radical revision of the whole plan. Effective "management" of the world's sugar economy, assuming administrative capacity and good judgment of the body entrusted with that responsibility, certainly requires more direct control of stocks and wider discretion in regulating exports than the Council possessed. No market control scheme can possibly be economical and enduring that does not provide for flexibility in administration. But solution of "the sugar problem" depended, above all, on direct intergovernmental agreement or indirect action by an international authority to reduce gradually the special favors (tariff protection, subsidies, and the like) to local, high-cost sugar producers.

World War II brought such a disruption of the world sugar industry that the limited operations of the cartel after September 1939 need not concern us. The Agreement was technically alive until August 31, 1942, and its term was at that time extended for another two years by those countries that were in position to make this declaration, except India and the Polish Government-in-Exile. The prospects are that it will be resumed now that the war is over.

CONCLUSIONS

The steady eclipse of competition in the world sugar industry has been due less to international cartel agreements than unilateral national policies involving protection and subsidization of local producers. The rise of economic nationalism has both fostered and balked cartel organization by exporting countries.

The various attempts at cartelization have been too feeble to alter radically the course of sugar prices. Virtually every major consuming country is an importer on balance, or would be in the absence of artificial controls, and every one controls its imports. Whether these limitations are in the form of simple tariffs or complicated quota arrangements, the prices paid by most consumers have been determined mainly by the policies of their own governments rather than by international concerts of producers.

The consumers—or the taxpayers—have ample ground for complaint. The ordinary household purchaser in the United States paid about 2 cents a pound more than world market prices for his sugar during the last decade.[45] This 2 cent differential multiplied by an annual consumption averaging about 6.5 million tons during the decade of the thirties comes to $260 million—taken out of consumers' pockets each year to support an uneconomic domestic production.[46]

45. The world market price of sugar (c.i.f. London) has averaged about 1.19 cents a pound during the thirties (1.16 cents excluding 1930). These figures are computed from the data in Table 2, supplemented by the estimated average price of 1.68 cents a pound for the first eight months of 1939. According to Department of Agriculture statistics the wholesale price of raw sugar in New York, on the basis of duty paid, averaged 3.2 cents a pound in the years 1931–1939.
In Great Britain the cost of subsidy is borne directly by the taxpayer, consumers paying a free competitive market price. Under this plan, inaugurated in 1925, the Exchequer had paid subsidies totalling £41 million up to October 1939 which resulted in a total production of nearly 100 million cwt. of beet sugar. In addition, the Exchequer lost during this period some £20 million of import duties which it would have collected had the sugar been imported. Thus, the total cost to the taxpayer was roughly $300 million in fifteen years, or about $20 million annually, equivalent to 2.7 cents a pound of sugar consumed. "Sugar Supplies," *The Economist*, October 7, 1939, Vol. CXXXVII, p. 14. See also Rowe, *Markets and Men*, Macmillan, New York, 1936, p. 86. Meanwhile raw sugar was being delivered to British ports at a price averaging 1.19 cents a pound during the thirties. See Table 2.
46. Henry A. Wallace, then Secretary of Agriculture, in a letter of March 1, 1938, to Senator Buckley (reproduced in Lynsky, *op. cit., Supplement*, 1939, pp. 416-18), cites an estimate that American consumers pay over $350 million annually in excess of the world price for their sugar supply. As the Secretary pointed out, the few added pennies per pound come to $10 a year for the average family—a serious tax burden for many. Of course, as the Wallace letter admits, such estimates take no account of what the world price would be if Americans purchased all their sugar from abroad. In the long run, probably the world's cane sugar growers would require in these circumstances a price of more than one cent a pound to cover average unit costs.

While with one hand the United States Government levies this toll on the consumer, with the other it tries to enforce competition among American sugar refiners and thus to reduce the final price to the consumer.[47] These policies are not necessarily contradictory, of course, but the average margin of the refiner, the entire spread between the cost to him of raw sugar and the price at which he sells the refined product—omitting the processing tax payments to the United States Treasury under the Sugar Control Acts of 1934 and 1937 described above—was less than one cent a pound during the last decade.[48] Since a large part of this spread represented refining costs, the possible extent of its reduction by enforcement of the antitrust laws was extraordinarily small as compared with the possible price saving to the consumer by relaxing sugar protective policies.

Public Interest Not Adversely Affected by Cartel

In view of high tariffs in the United States and other sugar-importing countries, the "public interest" in these countries has not been adversely affected to any appreciable extent by the operations of the international sugar cartel. Consumers in those countries which were not insulated from the world sugar market by "protective" measures bore the chief burden of the restriction schemes. These countries were comparatively few and small; and, even for them, the disadvantage was more apparent than real. For though they had to pay more for sugar than they would have had to pay in the absence of concerted restriction, *they probably paid no more* than they would have had to pay in the long run in a freely competitive world market. About all that the restrictive schemes accomplished was to prevent a more drastic fall in the price of exported sugar.

The cartel was unable to raise the price of sugar much above what it brought at the bottom of the depression. The 1938 annual average price in the London market was only 1.10 cents as against 0.91 cents in 1932 and a range from 1.01 to 1.06 during the years 1933–1936. It is unlikely that this price could have covered average unit costs of even the more efficient producers. Nevertheless, the cartel temporarily bolstered the position of high-cost producers in the cane branch

47. See, for example, *Sugar Institute* v. *U.S.*, 297 U.S. 553 (1936).
48. Indeed, the annual average refiners' margin did not exceed 1.5 cents either during the twenties or in the entire period from 1890 (when the Sherman Antitrust Act was passed) to 1914.

of the industry, and kept the consumers in a few countries which avoided heavy taxes on sugar imports from getting a "windfall"—buying their sugar at distress prices. But the prices charged most consumers of sugar, including American consumers, have all along been much higher than "free" world market prices. They were higher because, with or without restriction, the tariff rates boosted domestic prices to levels that encouraged local beet production in spite of its high-cost handicap.[49]

Restrictions Failed

If the restriction schemes of the twenties and thirties were undertaken to correct the basic difficulties of cane growers, they were doomed to failure. Cartel arrangements represented a device ill adapted for a long-run solution of a problem of this kind. For essentially the problem was overexpansion of sugar production resources, traceable partly to technological advances but mainly to actions of industry and government and to wartime exigencies.

Ultimately what was plainly needed to restore the health of the

49. This statement requires no qualification, upon the basis of the experience surveyed in this chapter. However, under the stimulus of wartime labor shortages, mechanization of beet sugar culture has recently made rapid progress and this is probably significant for the future.

The greatest competitive drawback of beet sugar in the past has been its high labor cost, a function both of its heavier requirement of man-hours than any other basic crop and of the relatively high cost of labor in temperate regions, where beet cultivation is practiced. In the opinion of many observers the widespread adoption of mechanical planting, thinning, and harvesting in the United States has already gone far to put beet sugar on a competitive basis with cane, without governmental aid.

Mechanical planting and thinning are made possible by the development of a process known as seed shearing, whereby the cluster of seeds is broken apart before planting. The individual seeds are treated with a protective coating. The rows not being so thickly planted, the thinning operation may be done fairly satisfactorily by mechanical means, with a great saving in labor. Tests of mechanical thinning by the Colorado Experiment Station obtained the same yield from an expenditure of 2.45 man-hours an acre as was previously secured from 27.2 man-hours. (Cited by Roy Bainer, "New Developments in Sugar Beet Production," *Agricultural Engineering*, August 1943, Vol. XXIV, pp. 255-58.) One grower is reported by the *Wall Street Journal* (January 26, 1945) to have had his harvesting costs reduced from $1.60 to 37 cents a ton by the introduction of a mechanical harvester—the latter figure including depreciation and amortization on his equipment. These examples do not, of course, constitute reliable, adequate, cost comparisons; nevertheless, they are illustrative of the high hopes held out for a very substantial reduction of the cost of beet sugar in the very near future. See O. W. Willcox, "Sugar Agriculture and Technology in 1943–1944," *Sugar Reference Book and Directory*, 1944, Vol. XIII, pp. 4-6; "Sugar and the Wars," *Industry Record* (National Industrial Conference Board), February 23, 1945, Vol. IV, No. 2, p. 4.

These developments may indicate that cheaper sugar need not wait on tariff reduction. This may be good news for the consumer, but cane producers might face even more drastic readjustments than those traceable to wartime trade disruption.

world sugar industry was a reduction of these sugar-making resources. This involved a shift of the resources commanded by high-
cost producers to other lines of industry, where they could be used
more economically. These high-cost producers were, in general, the
beet sugar producers. If they had not received subsidies for producing beet sugar, they would have had to take up production of other
goods. But none of the cartel schemes was designed to bring about
such a shift.

This does not imply censure of the Cubans and other participants
in sugar restrictive schemes for the course they followed—in the exigencies that confronted them. These exigencies were current and they
were pressing. The producers were not in position to wait for a long-
run solution of their dilemma. Return of prosperity for them, and
restoration of the world sugar industry to a sound economic basis,
depended above all on an abandonment of the policy of beet sugar
subvention and a reversal of the trend toward national self-sufficiency.
Since the cane producers could do nothing in this direction, the answer lay in restricting cane supplies. The production of Cuba and
Java together declined from 9,080,000 tons in 1929 to 4,858,000 tons
in 1940. But even if no controls had been instituted, other than those
designed to protect high-cost domestic producers in the leading consuming countries, output in Cuba and Java still would have been
adjusted inevitably to shrinking "free market" outlets and falling
world market prices.

The practical question was how the burden of curtailing production might most fairly and conveniently be distributed among the
cane producers. Would it be "better," "sounder," "safer" to let the
artificially restricted market wield the axe of bankruptcy and unemployment on the unprotected "weaker" elements of the low-cost
branch of the world sugar industry? Or would a more humane conception of *political* economy sanction concerted measures for cutting
output in fairly uniform proportion among cane sugar suppliers, regardless of their relative efficiency or staying power? The governments of Cuba and the Netherlands (Java) chose the latter course
and only a doctrinaire judge would condemn them for it. They could
scarcely be expected to sit by and look dispassionately on the disin-
tegration of an important segment of their economies, with all it
would mean in social and political instability.

As a method of lowering many of the insular producers gently into their graves, and of preventing others from succumbing at all, the schemes may perhaps be defended. Since the successive sugar cartels did little more than reduce capital losses for investors and wage losses for employees by spreading them out,[50] neither common sense nor economic principles afford much ground for condemning them. If that is to be the measure of successful cartelization, these schemes were probably "successful."

On the other hand, since the cartel made cane sugar production less unprofitable than it would otherwise have been, it became less urgent that capital resources be shifted or that their capitalized values be written down, thereby reducing costs. This applies likewise to beet production. For precisely in the measure that the cane-producing countries restricted *their* output and retarded the fall of prices, the incentive to shift resources out of the beet sugar industry was weakened. This restrictive policy not only discouraged the voluntary withdrawal of sugar beet growers; more important, it reduced the amount of subsidy necessary to maintain the domestic beet sugar production and thus made it easier for governments to justify their "protective" policies.

Defensible Only as a Necessary Evil

The cane producers' strategy of restriction may be defended on the ground that there was little prospect that the protective policies of consuming countries would be abandoned and the beet sugar producers forced to shift into other lines. But it was defensible solely as a necessary evil.[51] Though it tended actually to retard correction of the basic maladjustment in the industry, consumers, by and large, were

50. For example, Cuban restriction apparently accomplished little more for the relatively high-cost, local producers than a retardation of their continued decline relative to the lower-cost, financially stronger, American-controlled mills. The continually rising share of total Cuban output supplied by mills owned or controlled by American capital has been estimated to have reached 68 per cent in 1934. Compare Leland H. Jenks, *Our Cuban Colony,* Vanguard Press, New York, 1928, pp. 281-84; Foreign Policy Association, *op. cit.,* p. 227; Rowe, *Sugar,* p. 11; and estimates in *Anuario Azucarero de Cuba.*

51. An analogous situation confronted many countries in the twenties and thirties which would have preferred to work out the necessary adjustments in their foreign trade position through a free-market mechanism, but which found themselves at a disadvantage in trying to do so in view of the bilateral and even unilateral policies currently being followed elsewhere (most signally and aggressively by Germany). *In the circumstances,* they found no acceptable alternative to embarking on similar policies themselves. Cf. Jacob Viner, *Trade Relations between Free Market and Controlled Econ-*

adversely affected to only a slight degree. The high prices they paid were primarily the result of actions by their own governments; tariffs kept prices well above the level that sugar-exporting countries could have hoped to achieve by concerted restriction.

The agreements of the thirties may have paved the way for more fundamental correctives. By accepting export quotas under the Chadbourne Plan, the European signatories were, in effect, setting a limit to the subsidization of the local beet producers who had been exporting with the aid of governmental subsidies. By agreeing in 1937 to reserve for low-cost cane at least as large a share of their domestic markets as it then had, the United States and the British Empire displayed their willingness to cooperate with other countries in working out a more economical system of sugar supply. Even though this action came late and represented a small concession, it provides a basis for hope of more forthright action along the same line in future.

When nations persist in unilateral protection of high-cost producers at the expense of domestic consumers, and when the forces of free competition are in this way greatly hampered and unable to adjust supply to demand promptly—without severe losses to high- and low-cost producers alike—then an export restriction mechanism like the International Sugar Agreement of 1937 may be "a necessary evil." But it cannot provide a solvent for deep-seated problems of economic maladjustment such as those that have harassed the world's sugar industry for the last quarter century.

---

omies, L. of N., Geneva, 1943, pp. 41-44. As Professor Viner comments (p. 43), "The adoption [of this *sauve qui peut* policy, in the instance he was discussing 'partial exchange control,' in this instance, sugar production control] on their own part is not an acceptable long-run solution for countries which are anxious not to . . . add to the extent to which world trade in general is lastingly subject to [as the case may be, exchange control or production restriction]."

Chapter 3

RUBBER RESTRICTION SCHEMES

THE NATURAL RUBBER CARTEL

PEARL HARBOR signalled a setback on the economic front scarcely less disturbing than on the military front. Japan's staggering blow cut us off from the sources of supply of more than 95 per cent of our crude rubber—indispensable to modern industry and modern warfare. One brief weekend, and an economic crisis was upon us.

The dependence of automotive transport, including aviation, on rubber tires is obvious. Its dependence on rubber hose, belting, and miscellanous items of equipment is less well understood but equally vital. America customarily imported its rubber from the Far East. Of a domestic consumption in 1940 of about 757,000 tons, domestic sources supplied less than 15 per cent—4,500 tons of synthetic rubber and reclaimed rubber equivalent to 105,000 tons of crude rubber.[1] In the five years ending with 1940, 60 per cent of world net exports went to the United States.

On the day of Pearl Harbor, synthetic rubber supplied less than one per cent of our requirements. To meet the war emergency, we have since built up domestic productive capacity to approximately 900,000 tons. Although our output has fallen far short of our combined war and customary peacetime requirements, we have supplied our Allies with substantial amounts of this strategic material.

Pearl Harbor brought into sharp focus the vulnerability of the American economy, remote from geographical sources of natural rubber and inexperienced in the making of synthetic rubber. But it did

1. The actual absorption of reclaimed rubber in 1940 was 190,000 tons. According to estimates generally accepted in the trade, 1.82 pounds of reclaim is equivalent in utility to a pound of new crude rubber.

While "more than 95 per cent" of the world's (and of our own) supply of virgin natural rubber comes from the Far East, in 1940 only 85 per cent of the rubber and rubber substitutes consumed in the United States came from this source.

more than this. The rubber crisis has probably defined public opinion on the cartel problem more sharply and colored it more indelibly than any other single development. With paralysis threatening more than half of its transportation system and the national economy in danger of being literally "stalled," the nation quickly cast off its customary indifference to "business politics." Faced with a rubber shortage and lack of technical experience in synthetic rubber, and awakened to the implications of this situation by an aggressive Assistant Attorney General, the public wondered if the arsenal of democracy had not been caught in the crossfire of two sharpshooting cartels—the international rubber restriction scheme and cartel controls in the synthetic branch of the industry.

Beginnings of the Natural Rubber Industry

Gums from various plants have been used for waterproofing since prehistoric times. The aborigines in pre-Columbian America apparently knew the elastic properties of certain natural gums. Columbus reported that the Indians used crude "rubber" to make bouncing balls. It was not until the middle eighteenth century, however, that two French scientists aroused widespread interest in Europe in this novel material [2] by the accounts of their explorations in the Amazon Valley. Fresneau and Condamine exhibited specimens of their "discovery" before the French Academy in 1751, and investigators studied its properties from time to time thereafter. They made little progress in adapting it to everyday use, however, until three quarters of a century later.

In 1823 a Scotsman, Macintosh, found that cloth could be made water-repellent by impregnating it with rubber. In the same year a sea captain brought to New England a few pairs of rubber shoes of crude Indian manufacture. This started a vogue. Businessmen promptly founded numerous companies for manufacturing footwear, clothing, and other articles of rubber. All these articles proved unsatisfactory, however, because natural rubber becomes viscous in warm weather and stiff and hard when the temperature falls. Initial pur-

2. The material was called *caoutchouc* after the name by which it was known among the Tupi Indians who had first shown it to the explorers. This word also forms the root of the German, Spanish, and Italian names for the commodity which we call rubber. The English name "rubber" derives from the discovery by Joseph Priestly in 1770 that the new substance would rub out the marks made by lead pencils on paper.

chasers seldom renewed their patronage, and most of the early business ventures had failed by 1837.[3]

Charles Goodyear was the founder of the modern rubber industry. After several years of persistent experimentation, he obtained his first patent in 1837.[4] It covered a process for treating rubber with nitric acid to give it a hard smooth surface. Two years later, Goodyear as assignee of the inventor, Nathaniel Hayward, obtained a patent on treating rubber with sulphur. Neither of these processes proved commercially successful, however, because ordinary atmospheric temperature changes affected the rubber adversely: on hot days it got sticky, on cold days, brittle. Undismayed by repeated disappointments, Goodyear finally discovered, in 1839, the basic elements of the vulcanization process. He found that rubber mixed with sulphur, when subjected to heat, undergoes a chemical change which enables it, if cooled in a mold, to retain its molded shape. At the same time its elastic property actually may be increased by vulcanization. Goodyear's discovery opened the way for the everyday use of rubber.

Before 1890, vulcanization increased the popularity of rubber in its conventional uses but led to no radical shift in the directions of consumption.[5] But vulcanization did open some promising new fields to rubber—hose and tubing, mechanical and surgical goods. Though consumption of rubber in established uses was expanding and minor outlets were being steadily added—for example, in electrical insulation—total requirements remained comparatively small. Domestic consumption rose from about 4,000 tons in 1870 to perhaps 15,000 tons in 1890.

Growth of Rubber Industry

The transportation revolution, inaugurated by the automobile, made rubber an industrial raw material of primary importance. In 1890 world production was only about 30,000 tons, about half of which the United States imported. This was all wild rubber and most

3. Charles R. Whittlesey, *Governmental Control of Crude Rubber*, Princeton University Press, Princeton, 1931, p. 1.

4. P. W. Barker, *Charles Goodyear, Connecticut Yankee and Rubber Pioneer*, G. L. Cabot, Inc. [Private Printing], Boston, 1940, p. 29. On the details of the development of vulcanization, consult also: R. P. Wolf, *Charles Goodyear*, Caxton Printers, Caldwell (Idaho), 1939; and Sir Harry Lindsay, "Remarks," *Journal of the Royal Statistical Society*, 1938, Vol. CI, Pt. II, p. 366.

5. Cf. James C. Lawrence, *The World's Struggle with Rubber*, Harper, New York, 1931, Chap. 1.

of it came from Brazil, the native habitat of *Hevea braziliensis.* This plant has proved the most economical source of the latex from which rubber is made.[6] By 1900 world production had risen to about 44,000 tons, most of it still coming from Brazil.[7] This growth was mainly traceable to the rapid increase in the output of pneumatic tires for bicycles. With the development of the automobile in the following decade, the consumption of rubber doubled, reaching 94,000 tons in 1910.

A phenomenal rise in price, which reached a peak of more than $3 a pound in 1910, accompanied this rapid expansion. Rubber consumption probably would have far more than doubled during the first decade of the century had additional supplies been available at customary prices, say about 50 cents a pound. Two principal factors prevented output from expanding as fast as demand. First, the supply came from remote sections of the Amazon Valley. The only practical access to new sources of supply in the dense jungle was along natural waterways, not always navigable nor readily made so. Second, the wild rubber trees must be regularly "tapped" to recover the latex, but the native Indian tribes of the Amazon region, which provide the sole practical source of labor, cannot easily be induced by wages or other stimuli to put forth extra effort. They are not business minded. Higher wages, instead of stimulating larger output, may in some cases even reduce it; though the main factor in continuing low productivity is probably undernourishment and all that follows in its train. It is perhaps more surprising that Brazilian exports doubled in the decade ending with 1910 than that they failed to rise as rapidly as demand.

The inelastic demand for rubber contributed to the phenomenal rise of prices.[8] Tires and tubes for the rapidly developing automobile industry provided the major source of demand for rubber. In these uses rubber has no substitute. Tires and tubes are only a minor part

6. Latex is a milky secretion from the cortex layer of the tree, just inside the bark. It should not be confused with sap. It is obtained by cutting off diagonal strips of bark on one side of the tree and inserting a spout at the base of the cut, from which the latex drips into a receptacle. After evaporation of the water (about 60 per cent of contents) a soft coagulum remains; this is the crude rubber of commerce.

7. See Table 3 for data on exports, stocks, absorption, and prices of crude rubber, 1900–1941.

8. Before the advent of the automobile, consumption of rubber was no doubt much more responsive to price changes. At least the demand for rubber footgear and apparel probably was more elastic than that for tires and tubes.

TABLE 3

RUBBER STATISTICS: SELECTED YEARS, 1900–1941

Year	World Exports	Far East Exports	Principal World Stocks [a]	U.S. Imports [b]	Ratio of U.S. Absorption to World Net Export	N.Y. Price [c]
	(Thousands of Long Tons)					(Cents Per Pound)
1900	44	1	4	20	45.4	—
1906	63	3	3	29	46.0	86–150
1910	94	11	4	42	44.7	141–288
1911	94	17	6	42	44.7	114–184
1912	114	32	6	56	49.1	108–140
1913	120	54	4	52	43.3	59–113
1914	123	75	d	62	50.4	56– 93
1915	171	116	d	99	57.9	58– 79
1916	214	161	d	118	55.1	55–102
1917	278	218	d	157	56.5	52– 90
1918	219	182	d	160	73.1	40– 70
1919	400	349	119	215	53.8	38– 57
1920	342	311	198	206	60.2	16– 57
1921	302	277	219	178	58.9	16.35
1922	406	378	223	301	74.1	17.34
1923	409	380	221	319	78.0	29.55
1924	426	396	163	329	77.2	26.07

of the cost of the motor vehicle, and the crude rubber required for their manufacture a much smaller part. Even doubling the price of crude rubber would scarcely deter a prospective purchaser from buying an automobile. A rapidly growing demand for automobiles made the demand for rubber exceptionally insistent, and the price of rubber skyrocketed.

A revolution in the organization of the crude rubber industry resulted. Rubber producers established a plantation industry in the East Indies, using seeds transferred from Brazil.[9] Though many

9. A romantic story, long current, ascribed the establishment of the plantation industry to "high politics." Historical investigation has disproved many features of this traditional account, such as the alleged smuggling of the seeds out of Brazil by Edward Wickham. The seeds were obtained stealthily and germinated in the Royal Botanical Gardens in London in 1877, a full quarter of a century before any serious effort was made to start a plantation industry in Malaya. Cf. P. W. Barker, *Rubber: History, Production, and Manufacture*, Trade Promotion Series, No. 209, Bureau of Foreign and Domestic Commerce, Department of Commerce, 1940, p. 4 f.

TABLE 3 *(continued)*

RUBBER STATISTICS: SELECTED YEARS, 1900–1941

Year	World Exports	Far East Exports	Principal World Stocks [a]	U.S. Imports [b]	Ratio of U.S. Absorption to World Net Export	N.Y. Price [c]
	(Thousands of Long Tons)					*(Cents Per Pound)*
1925	528	486	144	388	73.5	72.46
1926	622	587	227	366	58.8	49.36
1927	607	568	261	373	61.4	37.81
1928	654	626	244	437	66.8	22.33
1929	863	837	330	467	54.1	20.48
1930	822	804	493	376	45.7	10.24
1931	798	783	614	355	44.5	6.12
1932	708	700	630	337	50.4	3.43
1933	851	839	655	412	48.4	5.90
1934	1,017	1,004	706	462	45.4	12.94
1935	872	854	624	491	56.3	12.32
1936	856	832	467	575	67.2	16.43
1937	1,135	1,107	546	544	47.9	19.37
1938	895	863	587	437	48.8	14.6
1939	1,004	969	448	592	59.0	17.5
1940	1,390	1,348	570	648	46.6	19.9
1941	1,500	1,452	859	663	52.7	22.2

Sources: U.S. Department of Commerce, Bureau of Foreign and Domestic Commerce, *Rubber Statistics: 1900–1937*, Washington, 1938; *Statistical Bulletins* of the International Rubber Regulation Committee, London, 1935–1941, Vols. I-VII; George Rae, "Statistics of the Rubber Industry," *Journal of the Royal Statistical Society*, 1938, Vol. CI, Pt. II, p. 335; Sir Andrew MacFadyean, *The History of Rubber Regulation 1934–1943*, Allen & Unwin, London, 1944, Table III of Statistical Supplement.

a. At end of year, except for 1941, which is for October 31.
b. 1900, 1906–1916—net imports; 1917 and thereafter—consumption. The 1941 figure is for ten months ending October 31.
c. From 1906 to 1920, inclusive, annual low and high on the first day of month; for 1906–1910, "Ceylon plantation fine sheet"; 1911–1913, "plantation fine smoked sheet"; 1914–1920, "plantation ribbed smoked sheet." For 1921 and later years, annual average prices for "plantation ribbed smoked sheet."
d. Not available.

planters of the Far East were at first disinclined to substitute rubber cultivation for the extensive and well-established coffee culture, a destructive coffee blight in 1903 and a rapidly mounting price for rubber overcame their reluctance. By 1910 the East Indies were experiencing a veritable boom in rubber planting. Though in that year Indonesian plantations contributed less than 12 per cent to the

world's output of rubber, extensive plantings had laid the basis for
an expanding supply. This opened the way for the stupendous
growth of the automobile industry, destined to play such a dynamic
role in the economic evolution of the ensuing decades. Meanwhile, as
far eastern plantation output increased and prices dropped, production of wild rubber steadily declined. In the thirties it reached an insignificant trickle of from 10,000 to 20,000 tons a year, about 2 to 3
per cent of world rubber output.

Far East Production Systems

Rubber in the Far East is produced under two radically different
systems. Most of the output comes from relatively large plantations
owned by Dutch and British investors and to a less extent by Chinese.
This branch of the industry is a business venture involving substantial capital investments. Plantation production relies on scientific
agriculture. To increase yields, plantation managers have resorted to
cross-budding and grafting. They have grafted trees of suitable root
stocks with shoots from the more prolific trees. They try to preserve
the vitality of rubber trees by a carefully devised system of intermit-
tent tapping and resting, and to prolong their useful life by scientific
treatment of disease, establishment of proper drainage conditions,
and similar precautions. Among plantation producers, the cost of
production varies considerably, reflecting differences in managerial
skill and the extent to which science has been successfully applied.

The output of these large rubber plantations has been supplemented by another system of production; small-scale operations carried on by a large number of natives in both the Dutch East Indies
and the Malay Archipelago. Methods and practices differ widely between these two groups. The natives of the Dutch islands produce
rubber as a sort of byproduct of their normal agricultural operations,
frequently in areas remote from the major markets. Rice production
is usually their main source of livelihood: produced on small plots,
which they clear from time to time and which they frequently abandon in a year or two when they make new clearings. Since the introduction of rubber culture, the native has followed the practice of
planting rubber seeds on the abandoned rice paddies. Until the rubber tree gets a start, the plants must be kept clear of weeds. Thereafter they take care of themselves. When prices are high enough to

remunerate him for his effort and to cover transportation costs, which frequently are high because of the remoteness of the native "gardens" from the market, the native taps his trees, often with little regard for their health. When prices fail to cover transportation costs, the trees are left alone.

Although the Malayan natives operate like the Dutch on small plots, as a rule they depend primarily upon rubber as a source of income. As a cash crop it provides their livelihood. Since they usually produce no alternative marketable products and for the most part live from hand to mouth, price reductions may actually stimulate output, even at the expense of the health of the trees.

The spectacular growth of the rubber industry, which was of boom proportions as early as 1910, continued throughout the next decade. In the ten years ending with 1920, world production soared from 94,000 tons to 342,000 tons, and United States consumption rose from 42,000 tons to 206,000 tons. On top of this decade's fivefold increase in the use of rubber in this country, came a threefold increase in the next twenty years. In 1940 the United States took nearly 650,000 tons of crude rubber out of total world exports of 1,390,000 tons.

Approximately three fourths of all the crude rubber consumed in the United States goes into tires and tubes. Mechanical goods, footgear and clothing, shock-cushioning and electrical insulation materials represent, in the order named, the more important other uses. These products indicate the range of rubber's services to modern civilization. The vast consumption of rubber in the ordinary course of civil life makes the organization of rubber supply a matter of national concern.

Genesis of First Rubber Cartel

Since the *Hevea* rubber-bearing tree takes about six years to reach maturity, the effects of the large-scale planting about 1910 were not fully realized until World War I. At that time, unfortunately for the growers, and indeed for the consumers also, shipping space was at a premium. Nevertheless, by 1917 plantation rubber shipments had increased to 218,000 tons, or twenty times the 1910 exports! Though the New York price had fallen to about 25 per cent of its 1910 peak, the purchasing programs of the Allied governments and a rigorous allotment of shipping space stabilized it at about 65 to 70 cents. Nevertheless, stocks continued to pile up in East Indian ports.

Since the obstacles to disposal of current supplies were temporary, growers not only maintained but expanded their plantations. This strategy apparently was sound, for the close of the war released ample shipping, and, in 1919, producers disposed of accumulated stocks at moderately rising prices. However, with the business recession of 1920 came drastic price declines. Demand fell off sharply just when many trees, planted during the first year of the war (when adequate shipping was still available), were beginning to bear. This aggravated the price decline.

Producers sought relief from this situation through concerted control measures. The history of the market through the next two decades is largely a record of the "ups and downs" of restrictive devices and of changes in cartel policy. In 1920 the Rubber Grower's Association, composed of British plantation companies with headquarters in London, sought a voluntary 25 per cent restriction of output for the ensuing year.[10] Rowe states that "This restriction was well supported by the members of the Association, and also by many Dutch and other foreign producers." [11]

Prices failed to respond, however, because rubber manufacturers, particularly in the United States, were heavily overstocked, and because Malayan production outside the control of the plantation companies continued to rise. The influence of the native growers upon the market was particularly pronounced in 1920, since native planting had constituted a large part of the acreage expansion during 1914–1916, when the war curtailed the flow of investment funds from the London and Amsterdam capital markets.

Toward the end of 1921 the business outlook brightened consid-

10. A large part of far eastern rubber supplies comes from extensive estates owned by Dutch and English companies. These "rubber growers" have been the principal sponsors (and beneficiaries) of the cartel schemes—the London and Amsterdam stockholders of the plantation companies are in no proper sense of the term "planters," much less farmers. Most of these "absentee owners" have probably never seen a rubber plantation.

11. J. W. F. Rowe, *Rubber,* Studies in the Artificial Control of Raw Material Supplies, No. 2, Memorandum No. 29, Royal Economic Society, London, April 1931, p. 4. This excellent monograph will hereinafter be cited as Rowe, *Rubber.* We have used it extensively in the preparation of this section, together with Chapter 6 in the author's *Markets and Men,* Macmillan, New York, 1936, and Professor C. R. Whittlesey's scholarly study cited above.

erably, and the price of rubber rose to more than 30 cents a pound, virtually 100 per cent above the low mark of the 1920–1921 depression. Although this was almost certainly a very profitable price for most plantation rubber, the Rubber Grower's Association continued to urge the advantages of output restriction. It tried to renew the voluntary scheme, but its efforts failed. Attracted by high prices, many producers preferred to expand their output.

The Stevenson Committee

Lacking the support of its whole membership, the Association appealed to the British Government to compel curtailment. Although the situation of the rubber growers was far from desperate, on October 24, 1921 the Secretary of State for the Colonies, Mr. Winston Churchill, appointed a committee—named, after its chairman, the Stevenson Committee—to draft a plan for enforcing restriction. World politics, quite as much as a desire to relieve the rubber industry, prompted this move. Mr. Churchill is reported to have declared that the projected scheme was "one of the principal means of paying the debt to America." [12]

The Stevenson Committee sought the cooperation of the Dutch Government in the contemplated venture, but its approaches were rebuffed. After six months of deliberation the Committee made a report on May 19, 1922, advising against any restriction scheme without Dutch cooperation. The Committee pointed out that the British colonies held only about 72 per cent of the world's rubber-producing capacity, but with the Dutch support fully 97 per cent could be brought under control.

The Committee was convinced that, barring Dutch aid, "no scheme, however excellent in itself, could properly be recommended." [13] It did recommend, however, "further representations" to the Dutch Government on the advantages of a joint control of rubber supply. Again the Dutch Government declined to negotiate. Then the Stevenson Committee, on the urgent solicitation of the Rubber Grower's

12. Quoted by Whittlesey, *op. cit.*, p. 39. The implication of this statement was that the scheme facilitated Britain's effort to meet its war debt obligation to America by building up dollar credits through enhancement of the prices of a major British export to the United States.
13. Quoted by Rowe, *Rubber*, p. 7.

Association, decided to disregard its own earlier advice. On October 2, 1922 it brought in a second report recommending export control by the British dependencies. Bills were promptly rushed through the colonial legislatures and the Stevenson Plan became law on November 1, 1922.[14]

Outline of Stevenson Plan

The Stevenson Plan contained two basic features: (1) it assigned quotas (called "standard assessments") to the plantations, and issued negotiable permits quarterly for exportation, without tax penalty,[15] of a certain percentage of the assigned quotas; and (2) it regulated the permissible exports for any quarter automatically according to the average price of standard crude rubber (in the London market) for the preceding quarter.[16]

The discretionary power of the administrative authorities was limited, in effect, to the establishment of the "standard assessments." These were supposed to be based on the actual output of the year ending October 31, 1920. Since the records of output two years earlier were often not available, the assessors exercised a rather wide discretion in determining quotas. Because the Plan authorized adjustments principally on the basis of plantings reaching maturity after the base period, their administrative discretion was further widened. Committees of planters had authority to make assessments for areas of more than one hundred acres, whereas the regular civil service administrators in each district made assessments for smaller holdings (mostly Chinese and native). Only growers cultivating more than twenty-five acres could appeal their assessments. The appellate tri-

14. The Plan was officially adopted only in Ceylon, the Federated Malay States, and the Straits Settlements. However, these areas were estimated to produce some 70 per cent of the world's rubber supply. See *ibid.*, p. 6.

15. Licensed exports were not duty-free but bore a nominal tax of 2 cents (Straits money, equivalent to about one cent United States currency). Exports beyond the amount licensed were taxed at a prohibitive rate.

16. During the initial quarter beginning November 1, 1922, permits were authorized for the export of 60 per cent of one fourth of the assigned annual quota, or "standard assessments." Thereafter the percentage exportable was to be increased by 10 per cent of "standard" above the rate of the preceding quarter if the average London price in the preceding quarter was above 18 pence, and by 5 per cent if it was between 15 and 18 pence. The percentage exportable was to remain unchanged if the average price was between 12 pence and 15 pence, and it was to be decreased by 5 per cent if it was below 12 pence or if the price, having been below 12 pence, had not recovered to 15 pence. These regulations governed operations under the Plan until April 30, 1926, when the terms were modified in the manner discussed below.

bunal was a Central Advisory Committee set up in each colony to administer the Plan.

Annals of First Cartel

The cartel encountered many practical problems. Rivalries developed among the colonies or dependencies and among different districts, each seeking more liberal assessments for its plantations at the cost of the others. Similar controversies developed between large estates and small estates, between corporation-owned estates and native and Chinese holdings. Problems of license counterfeiting and of smuggling plagued the cartel administrators. Although these practical difficulties did not wreck the scheme, they were never satisfactorily resolved, and the measures to repress them were costly. Disputes over the Plan's administration were acrimonious and left an aftermath of bitterness, particularly among the native and Chinese cultivators, which tended to undermine the "good will" of the colonial governments.

Nevertheless, the Stevenson Plan, as judged by its short-run market effects and from the business point of view, was a "great success" —as it was from Mr. Churchill's broader point of view. It certainly was a favorable factor in the British balance of international payments; by raising the price of an important British Empire export it helped to offset the heavy demand for dollars to meet British import and war debt obligations. But if the sponsors and proponents of the scheme intended to stabilize the rubber market, they chose a poor method to do so. In actual operation the Stevenson Plan led to feverish fluctuations in rubber prices and further upset the relation of supply to demand.

The scheme lasted six years. During its first year, demand was fairly steady, with a slight tendency to rise.[17] The temporary steadiness of demand concealed the defects in the restriction machinery. All went well until a minor recession in demand in the spring of 1924 was followed by a quick recovery, which lasted two years. During this period the slight increase in exports allowed under the Plan, coupled apparently with some market manipulation to keep the

17. For the course of prices and the (dependent) changes in export percentages, together with price relatives, from quarter to quarter, 1922–1928, see Table 4.

average price for the quarter from rising to a level which would permit release of additional rubber for export, brought about an acute shortage of rubber.[18] The movement culminated in a peak price of $1.23 a pound in July 1925.

The development of a stringency of rubber supplies, in kind if not in degree like that of 1925, might have been foreseen. The narrow range of adjustments (5 or 10 per cent quarterly) in the rate of exports authorized by the Plan was plainly insufficient to cope with the sharp changes in demand to which the rubber market was subject. Moreover, the comparative infrequency (once every three months) of revision of the export rate crippled the Plan as a stabilizing device. A great deal can happen in ninety days to upset the balance of rubber supply and demand.

So rigid were the mechanics of the scheme that exports of rubber were almost certain to respond tardily to any major swing of demand. The Plan made no provision for such a contingency, by building up a buffer stock or otherwise. The economic justification of a "pivotal price" of 15 pence, roughly 30 cents, is also questionable.[19] Even if a price of 15 pence were required for high-cost producers to recover costs, it is doubtful that the best interests of the industry were served by holding back low-cost producers in order that these marginal, or submarginal, producers might survive.

Causes for High Prices

The spectacular advance in the price of rubber from 1922 to 1925 was not caused entirely by the arbitrary constriction of supply, of course. Important factors affecting demand also tended to boost prices. General business recovery both in Europe and America ex-

18. Whittlesey notes (pp. 181-82): "At the end of the ninth quarter . . . January 1925, a 10 per cent increase [in export rate] was expected. In the last few days of the quarter, however, price remained low so that the quarterly average fell short of one shilling, six pence by 0.0017 of a penny . . . Some 3400 tons of rubber per quarter were thus withheld just at the time when the panic in the rubber market was developing."

19. A judgment on this issue hinges on one's estimate of the cost of producing rubber—in 1922. Such an estimate is bound to be highly speculative and none will be attempted here. Unquestionably, however, some estates were poorly managed after a decade of rapid expansion and easy profits, and 15 pence may have been no more than a cost-indemnifying price for them. Nevertheless, after thorough studies, both Rowe and Whittlesey reached the conclusion that a pivotal price of 15 pence was probably excessive.

TABLE 4

Exportable Percentages, Prices, and Price Relatives of Rubber
Under Stevenson Plan

Period	Exportable Percentage	London Average Price (In Pence)	Per Cent of 11/1/22 to 1/31/23 Average Price
First year of restriction			
Nov. 1, 1922 to Jan. 31, 1923	60	14.285	100.00
Feb. 1, 1923 to Apr. 30, 1923	60	16.858	118.01
May 1, 1923 to July 31, 1923	65	14.242	99.70
Aug. 1, 1923 to Oct. 31, 1923	60	14.994	104.96
Second year of restriction			
Nov. 1, 1923 to Jan. 31, 1924	60	14.175	99.23
Feb. 1, 1924 to Apr. 30, 1924	60	12.917	90.42
May 1, 1924 to July 31, 1924	60	10.974	76.82
Aug. 1, 1924 to Oct. 31, 1924	55	14.632	102.43
Third year of restriction			
Nov. 1, 1924 to Jan. 31, 1925	50	17.998	125.99
Feb. 1, 1925 to Apr. 30, 1925	55	19.356	135.50
May 1, 1925 to July 31, 1925	65	38.469	269.23
Aug. 1, 1925 to Oct. 31, 1925	75	43.269	302.90
Fourth year of restriction			
Nov. 1, 1925 to Jan. 31, 1926	85	46.709	326.98
Feb. 1, 1926 to Apr. 30, 1926	100	28.013	196.10
May 1, 1926 to July 31, 1926	100	21.0017	147.02
Aug. 1, 1926 to Oct. 31, 1926	100	20.199	141.40
Fifth year of restriction			
Nov. 1, 1926 to Jan. 31, 1927	80	19.265	134.86
Feb. 1, 1927 to Apr. 30, 1927	70	19.697	137.89
May 1, 1927 to July 31, 1927	60	18.165	127.16
Aug. 1, 1927 to Oct. 31, 1927	60	16.620	116.35
Sixth year of restriction			
Nov. 1, 1927 to Jan. 31, 1928	60	19.023	133.17
Feb. 1, 1928 to Apr. 30, 1928	60	12.604	88.23
May 1, 1928 to July 31, 1928	60	9.154	64.08
Aug. 1, 1928 to Oct. 31, 1928	60	8.866	62.07

Sources: Charles R. Whittlesey, *Governmental Control of Crude Rubber,* Princeton University Press, Princeton, 1931; J. W. F. Rowe, *Rubber,* Royal Economic Society, London, April 1931.

panded consumer purchasing power and increased the demand for
automobiles and rubber. The rapidly increasing number of automobiles in operation added cumulatively to the tire replacement demand. Moreover, a technical development spurred the demand for
rubber. The introduction of balloon tires increased rubber consumption per tire by some 30 per cent.[20] Nevertheless, the severity of export restriction under the Stevenson Plan and the rigidity of the
scheme certainly accentuated the rubber crisis.

The stringency of supplies provoked vehement agitation in consuming countries, especially in America.[21] The cartel strategy was denounced in nonofficial quarters as a sheer "holdup." In response to
these protests, the Stevenson Committee increased allowable exports
from 85 per cent to 100 per cent of standard assessment for the
quarter beginning February 1, 1926 instead of the 10 per cent increase required under the Plan.[22] But in authorizing an extra "allowable" [23] the Committee changed the general provisions governing
adjustments by raising the pivotal price nearly 50 per cent from 15
pence to 21 pence a pound. Rowe has commented on this move as
follows:

The previous standard of 1 shilling, 3 pence, had been sufficiently profitable:
the new standard meant enormous profits to all producers outside the scheme,
and therefore a direct incentive to them to increase their output to the greatest

20. Whittlesey, *op. cit.*, pp. 35-37. Accompanying this innovation, improvements
were being effected in rubber compounding and in casing construction. Although these
developments lengthened the service life of tires and tended in the long run to decrease
the consumption of rubber, in the short run the introduction of balloon tires unquestionably increased demand.

21. Department of Commerce, Bureau of Foreign and Domestic Commerce, Trade
Information Bulletin No. 385, 1926. On the measures adopted to counteract the restriction of exports, see below.

22. The cartel administrators made other attempts to ease the price panic. In August
1925 and May 1926 assessment regulations were tempered somewhat, and in September
1925 part of the accumulated stocks in the Far East were made available for export
under certain conditions, regardless of quota limitations.

These measures were wholly inadequate for an economical solution of the rubber
shortage. Smuggling continued, and as Whittlesey observes (*op. cit.*, p. 40): "At the
very height of the panic, with buyers clamoring for more rubber, a quantity of rubber
amounting to 57,000 pounds which had been confiscated by the customs authorities in
the Middle East was burned instead of being released for sale."

23. These modifications of the Plan were not simultaneous. The authorization of the
15 per cent increase in permitted exports was announced on January 31, 1926 and the
changes in the basic mechanism were announced on April 26, 1926. See Rowe, *Rubber*, p. 10. But they were "contemporaneous"; both were the outcome of a review of the
terms of the Plan upon which the Colonial Office had been engaged for some time.

possible extent, which they naturally did. Looking back, it is hard to conceive how such a blunder could ever have been made by a British Government.[24]

Abandonment of Unilateral Restriction

The market price of rubber steadily declined despite this revision, which resulted in the reduction of the rate of permitted exports to 60 per cent of "standard" by May 1, 1927 and held it at this low level for the last year and a half before repeal of the legislation. Apart from the "psychological" influence which its anticipated expiration exerted on the market in the latter stages of the scheme's operation, three factors were primarily responsible for its diminishing efficacy and final abandonment: (1) the growth of rubber production outside the restricted areas; (2) the development of substitutes for and economy in the use of crude rubber; and (3) defection and smuggling among those subject to the restrictive scheme.

Growth of Nonrestricted Production

The British share in the world rubber market declined persistently during the period of the Stevenson Plan, 1922–1928. It dropped from 67.5 per cent in 1922 to 54.1 per cent in 1927, the last full year of restriction under the Plan.[25] Rubber exports from the Dutch East Indies (and other far eastern sources) rose phenomenally in direct response to the market opportunities created by British restriction. In the six years 1922–1927 inclusive, the Dutch exports rose from 94,000 tons to 229,000 tons, or some 143 per cent, and their share of the world market increased from 23.2 per cent to 37.7 per cent.[26]

24. Rowe, *Markets and Men,* p. 135. This expresses the considered judgment of a British economist whose attitude toward cartel controls in general, and toward valorization schemes for agricultural commodities in particular, is that of a dispassionate eclectic. He is persuaded that, in so far as cartels adopt, or can be held to, a defensive strategy aiming to mitigate the severity of price declines in periods of business depression, they play a legitimate role in a business economy. His conclusion is that "there is no clear-cut issue between artificial or conscious control and so-called *laissez faire,* because their relative merits and demerits depend upon the particular kind of control which under given circumstances is proposed as an alternative to *laissez faire,* and how it will be administered in practice." *Ibid.,* p. 253.

25. See Table 5. The heavy exports from British territories in the last quarter of 1928 after the removal of restrictions helped to raise the British share in that year to 59.1 per cent. Probably, too, in anticipation of the lifting of restrictions considerable British-grown rubber found its way into the world market. Furthermore, the Stevenson Committee estimated the British proportion *in 1920* at not less than 70 per cent of the total.

26. While expansion of the Dutch output at a rate sufficient to increase its relative share in the world rubber trade began prior to the restriction scheme, the stimulating effect of British restriction on Dutch expansion can hardly be questioned.

TABLE 5

BRITISH AND DUTCH RUBBER EXPORTS, 1920–1940

Year	British [a]		Dutch [b]	
	(Long Tons in Thousands)	(Per Cent of World Total)	(Long Tons in Thousands)	(Per Cent of World Total)
1920	232.7	68.0	80.0	23.4
1921	201.9	66.9	71.0	23.5
1922	274.2	67.5	94.0	23.2
1923	254.9	62.3	117.0	28.6
1924	240.0	56.3	149.0	35.0
1925	281.2	53.3	189.0	36.0
1926	371.5	59.7	204.0	32.8
1927	328.1	54.1	229.0	37.7
1928	386.6	59.1	229.0	35.0
1929	569.3	66.0	255.0	29.5
1930	548.3	66.7	242.0	29.4
1931	511.8	64.1	257.0	32.2
1932	471.9	66.7	211.0	29.8
1933	533.3	62.7	282.3	33.2
1934	588.0	57.8	379.4	37.3
1935	513.5	58.9	282.9	32.4
1936	447.1	52.2	309.6	36.2
1937	596.5	52.6	431.6	38.0
1938	492.0	55.0	300.9	33.6
1939	519.0	51.7	369.9	36.8
1940	710.0	51.1	537.5	38.7

Sources: G. Rae, "Statistics of the Rubber Industry," *Journal of the Royal Statistical Society,* 1938, Vol. CI, Pt. II, p. 335; Sir Andrew MacFadyean, *The History of Rubber Regulation 1934–1943,* Allen & Unwin, London, 1944, Table III of Statistical Supplement.

a. British Malaya, Ceylon, India, Burma, North Borneo, and Sarawak.
b. Netherlands East Indies.

This rise in Dutch exports had three principal causes. (1) The advance in price encouraged more intensive tapping of trees. (2) It also stimulated the natives to restore and expand production on their small, half wild, overgrown "gardens" on the edge of the jungle, many of which had been abandoned after the pre–World War I boom.[27] (3) But new plantings on the large European-owned plantations were the prime factor. New plantings were in part traceable to

27. See George Rae, "Statistics of the Rubber Industry," *Journal of the Royal Statistical Society,* 1938, Vol. CI, Pt. II, p. 317.

higher prices, in part to a technological advance. Dutch planters developed an improvement in horticultural methods, known as "bud grafting," which shortened the growing period and increased greatly the yield per acre.[28] But because of the cartel's "invitation" to expand, undoubtedly the planters "stepped up" their operations more rapidly than they would otherwise have done.

The initiation of plantation projects in other areas, mainly by American rubber companies, was also important, though doubtless far less disturbing from the British point of view. The most notable of these was the large-scale Firestone project in Liberia.[29] These enterprises had no immediate effect on the rubber market during the period in which the Stevenson Plan was in operation. Indeed, for a variety of reasons, they have contributed little to world supply to date. But they emphasized the significance of the Dutch East Indian expansion.

Development of Substitutes

Both the high price of the natural product and the arbitrary way it had been brought about spurred the development of substitutes for crude rubber. Although it is impossible to determine how far the Stevenson Plan intensified research and experimentation on synthetic rubber, the search for a substitute was vigorously renewed in this period of artificially high prices.

28. Bud-grafted stock has variable yields and entails some additional expense for estate maintenance. It is generally estimated, however, that a properly bud-grafted estate will yield, on the average, three times as much or more rubber per acre as estates relying on plantings of selected seeds. See British Department of Overseas Trade, *Report on Economic Conditions in British Malaya*, London, February 28, 1931, p. 55; *India Rubber World*, October 1, 1935, p. 60; and U.S. Bureau of Foreign and Domestic Commerce, Trade Promotion Series, No. 159, *Rubber Regulation and the Malayan Plantation Industry*, Washington, 1935, pp. 25-26.

29. Firestone's entry in the plantation industry came in 1925, immediately following the rubber crisis of that year. It leased 200,000 acres from the Liberian Government and obtained a 99-year option on an additional 800,000 acres. By October 1943 the company had planted over 75,000 acres, of which 45,000 acres had matured. Scale of the investment is indicated roughly by a book value on October 31, 1943, of $6,853,276, over and above development costs in the first eight years amounting to $7,705,842, which were charged to current profit and loss account. The property includes two local processing plants and a hydroelectric power plant. *Moody's Manual of Investments* (Industrials), 1944, p. 1254.

Production data are not reported, but rubber exports from Liberia probably furnish a fair measure of the growth in output. These more than doubled from 1937 to 1939, when they reached 5,400 tons. In 1940, shipments were at the rate of 7,500 tons a year, representing about 7.5 per cent of Firestone's annual consumption. However, most of the company's Liberian rubber output goes to its factories abroad. U.S. Tariff Commission, *Crude Rubber* (revised), Washington, 1940, pp. 3, 14, 17.

Rapid progress was made around 1925 in both Germany and the United States. Indeed, the technical foundation was then laid for a synthetic rubber industry which eventually yielded products which could be substituted for rubber in all its major uses and are actually superior for many purposes. Regardless of whether synthetic rubbers can displace the natural product on a strictly economic basis, they will continue to limit monopolistic natural rubber restriction schemes and safeguard consumer interests.

Another substitute for crude rubber imports was reclaimed rubber. In meeting the rubber crisis in the mid-twenties, and in weakening the grip of the cartel on the market, the development of the reclaimed rubber industry was far more important than the beginnings of the synthetic rubber industry. Rubber reclamation in the United States reached its peak in 1928, the last year of restriction under the Stevenson Plan. In that year this country used 223,000 tons of reclaimed rubber. (See Table 6.) This represented a fourfold increase from 1922.

Reclaimed rubber supplied one third of all rubber used in 1927 and again in 1928. Although before World War II the rate of output was not maintained, the proportion of reclaimed to crude rubber has varied directly with the price of imported crude. The increase in consumption of reclaimed rubber is the more significant, since maintaining the quality of finished products made of a mixture of crude and reclaimed rubber requires technical changes in compounding and manufacturing processes. This apparently represented a permanent improvement in rubber technology. After the end of the Stevenson Plan, the proportion of reclaim to crude used by American rubber manufacturers never fell below one fifth.

British Government Abandons the Plan

The Stevenson Plan encouraged smuggling and aroused discontent among planters.[30] Both these influences were undoubtedly real, though neither was decisive. Smuggling apparently was kept within fairly narrow limits, but it was never stopped altogether. Widespread disaffection developed among the planters, because of allegedly inequitable "assessments," corruption among local administrators, and

---

30. Cf. Whittlesey, *op. cit.,* Chap. 4, where the difficulties encountered in administration of the Plan are canvassed and analyzed in detail.

TABLE 6

ABSORPTION OF RECLAIMED RUBBER:
UNITED STATES, 1919–1941

Year	Reclaim Used	Per Cent of Reclaim to Crude
	(Thousands of Long Tons)	
1919	74	32.7
1920	75	35.0
1921	41	24.3
1922	54	19.1
1923	70	22.8
1924	76	22.7
1925	137	35.2
1926	164	45.1
1927	190	50.5
1928	223	50.7
1929	213	45.3
1930	153	40.8
1931	123	35.1
1932	78	23.3
1933	85	21.2
1934	101	22.2
1935	118	23.9
1936	142	24.6
1937	162	29.8
1938	121	27.6
1939	170	28.7
1940	190	29.3
1941	213	32.1

Sources: Statistical Bulletins of the International Rubber Regulation Committee, London, 1935–1941, Vols. I-VII; Bureau of Foreign and Domestic Commerce, *Rubber Statistics: 1900–1937,* Washington, 1938. The figures for 1941 cover only the ten months ending October 31.

above all, divergent views on restriction. In particular, the so-called "unused coupon" problem became increasingly vexatious.[31]

The British Government finally concluded that the Stevenson Plan

31. This problem concerned the period of validity of export licenses. The question was whether a grower whose sales in a given quarter did not exhaust his allotment could "carry over" the deficiency into a later period. This issue was tied up, of course, with the whole question of restriction policy: how severe it should be, how speculative it should be, and who should participate in determining it. Cf. Rowe, *Rubber,* pp. 34-42.

was prejudicial to the very interests it was designed to serve.[32] Accordingly, in 1928 it abandoned the whole scheme. Resentment by American automobile users against the "tax" imposed on them by the cartel caused a progressive deterioration in British-American relations and contributed to the abandonment of the Plan. Most sponsors of the rubber restriction scheme recognized that its continuation, at least on an independent, British Empire basis, would be a mistake.

The final decision to end restriction and the way it was executed provoked hardly less bitterness among various elements in the British industry than had its operation among foreigners. Cartel control had certainly not lessened the conflict of economic interests, especially between native producers and the absentee owners of large estates.

Effects of the Depression

In 1929, the year after the Stevenson Plan ended, net exports of rubber from the Far East increased by 211,000 tons while from other sources exports declined slightly. The restriction had been so severe that prices held firm in spite of an increase of almost exactly one third in exports. The New York price declined only 10 per cent to an annual average in 1929 of 20.48 cents a pound.

An increase in world consumption absorbed the bulk of the new supplies. While world stocks increased by 86,000 tons, 63,000 tons of this went to replenish the severely depleted working stocks of the United States rubber manufacturers. At the 1929 rate of consumption, stocks were nowhere excessive. Unhappily, with the onset of the Great Depression, consumption declined and stocks mounted rapidly. By 1933 world stocks were twice as large as in 1929, reaching the unprecedented level of 655,000 tons. This was three times the volume of the carry-over in the depression year 1921. Prices promptly declined.

The Rubber Grower's Association arranged a "tapping holiday" for May 1930 but it proved inadequate. The annual average price for 1930 fell to 10.24 cents a pound, exactly half that of the preceding year. World rubber consumption held up remarkably well during the depression, however, falling to a rate in 1932 only about 15 per cent

32. Cf. Rowe, *Markets and Men*, pp. 135-36.

below that of 1929. Even in the United States, where consumption declined more than the average, the amount of rubber used in the "worst" year of the depression was about the same as the seven-year annual average under the Stevenson Plan. An all-time-low annual average price of 3.43 cents was reached in 1932. This was just 10 per cent of the average price in 1927.

Even this drastic decline in price curtailed supply only slightly. From 1929 to 1932, exports declined only 155,000 tons and in 1933 were back almost to the 1929 level. Three factors helped to explain the marked inelasticity of rubber supply during this period. First, the trees planted during the boom in the mid-twenties were just beginning to yield. Second, bud grafting was being widely adopted.[33] Third, under pressure of declining prices, noteworthy reductions in operating costs were effected. In part these consisted of simple wage and salary cuts, but in part, also, they represented improvements in efficiency.[34] Nevertheless, the cascading prices in the early thirties undoubtedly occasioned distress in the rubber industry—as they did in other industries.

Distress in the industry stimulated official and unofficial discussions of a renewal of rubber restriction. By 1933 even the Dutch were ready to consider concerted measures for counteracting the depression in rubber—and perhaps for capitalizing on a strategic position in the industry gained through their canny tactics in the twenties.[35]

The International Rubber Regulation Scheme

After negotiations extending over a year, on May 7, 1934 the governments of the United Kingdom, India, the Netherlands, France, and Siam reached an accord—the International Rubber Regulation Agreement (hereinafter IRRA). The signatories established the International Rubber Regulation Committee (hereinafter IRRC) as the governing body of the new cartel. The Agreement was to run to De-

33. See contemporary issues of *India Rubber World*. While the bud-grafted area was larger on the Dutch islands than elsewhere, its proportion to total acreage was higher in French Indo-China (28 per cent by 1935) than in any other jurisdiction.

34. Cf. Rowe, *Markets and Men*, p. 140.

35. By 1934 the Netherlands East Indies proportion of the world exports of crude rubber had risen to 38.4 per cent. Though this was only slightly above the proportion which they sold in 1928, the last year of the first cartel, it suggests why they were more amenable to a proposal to "freeze" the status quo than they had been in 1921, when they had supplied barely a quarter of the total world exports.

cember 31, 1938, but, by a protocol signed on October 6, 1938, was extended for another five years.[36] It was subsequently extended once more, for a "final period" of four months. On April 30, 1944, IRRC came to an end.[37]

Articles IV, VI, and XV fixed basic quotas for each year for each of the nine rubber-producing regions into which the territories of the signatories were divided.[38] Only eight delegations were represented in IRRC, however, India and Burma having a joint representative on the Committee. Votes were apportioned among the several delegations on the basis of "one vote for each complete 1,000 tons . . . of basic quota." Rubber manufacturers were invited to nominate three representatives, including one American, to serve as a sort of "consumer's counsel." Their function was entirely advisory.

IRRC was empowered to fix periodically a uniform percentage of the basic quotas of the several producing regions which could be exported without penalty, and each of the signatories undertook to limit exports from the territories under its control to this amount. Article XI tied production closely to exports by prohibiting the accumulation of surplus stocks within the areas covered by the Agreement. Moreover, Article XII "absolutely prohibited" new planting during the period of the pact, except in strictly limited amounts for experimental purposes and save for a special concession to Siam of 31,000 acres. Article XIII also forbade the exportation of "leaves, flowers, seeds, buds, twigs, branches, roots or any living portion of the rubber plant that may be used to propagate it." These provisions were clearly designed to prevent any further expansion of productive capacity, either within or outside the regulated areas, *regardless of the growth of demand.*

36. The text of the principal documents may be found in TNEC *Hearings,* 76th Cong., 2d sess., pursuant to Public Resolution No. 113 (75th Cong.), Pt. XXV, Ex. 2080, pp. 13369-77. In addition to extending the Agreement, the 1938 protocol contained other minor amendments.

37. Sir Andrew MacFadyean, *The History of Rubber Regulation 1934–1943,* Allen & Unwin, London, 1944, Introduction.

38. See Table 7. Special terms were accorded French Indo-China and Siam to get their adherence to the pact. Indo-China was permitted to export to France practically without limit. Siam was guaranteed specified minimum limits for its "permissible exports," limits which represented no actual curtailment of its output.

All basic quotas referred to annual exports. But these quotas were solely for the purpose of insuring a proportionate degree of restriction on the several members. IRRC generally fixed the permissible rate of exportation (percentages of quotas) quarterly, as under the Stevenson Plan.

Comparison of First and Second Cartels

Both cartels froze quotas, fixing each area's share in the market. The IRRA program showed even more solicitude for vested interests than did the Stevenson Plan. Under the Stevenson Plan the maintenance of independent assessment agencies provided for flexibility in the adjustment of quotas, whereas the IRRA prescribed the territorial quotas in advance. The scope of regulation under IRRA was broader than under the Stevenson Plan, which controlled exports only. IRRA controlled exports, and in addition restricted output and limited new investments.

Both cartel arrangements showed the same indifference to the impact of output restrictions on production costs. Limitation of production to an amount less than would be yielded if trees were tapped at the highest rate consistent with sound horticultural practice presumably raised unit costs for all rubber growers. However, the resultant increase in cost was probably not uniform for all producers; in general, the restrictions were relatively more severe on the low-cost plantations.[39] Neither plan provided that the gains realized by producers from occasional operation at full-capacity or minimum-unit-cost rates should be used to offset losses (or lower profits) from operations at other times at less-than-capacity rates. Both plans weakened incentives to reduce costs by fixing basic quotas without regard to differences in unit costs. Because these differences were so wide, this common feature of the two plans tended to generate internal friction and external complaint.

Since it provided for greater flexibility in regulating the flow of supplies, IRRA represented a decided improvement over the Stevenson Plan, from the administrative standpoint. This certainly tended to promote its efficacy. No rigid formula, as under the Stevenson Plan, bound IRRC in determining the volume of exports. It had discretionary power to control rubber exports directly and production indirectly. From the standpoint of the rubber producers, this was a sensible and expedient arrangement. Assuming wisdom in its exercise, administrative discretion in adjusting the flow of rubber supplies to current market developments may be desirable even from the standpoint of the consumer. While nothing in the car-

39. Cf. K. E. Knorr, *World Rubber and Its Regulation,* Stanford University Press, Stanford University, 1945, p. 160 and, on this subject generally, Chap. 9.

tel agreement insured IRRC's exercising sound judgment in administering the cartel, nothing in the agreement precluded it. How did the cartel fulfill its responsibility?

Record of IRRC

When IRRC began operating, the price of rubber had been on the upgrade for nearly two years. From June 1932 to May 1934 the New York price had risen fourfold—or from 3 cents to 12 cents a pound. Because of abnormally low prices in the immediately preceding years, native production was still at a comparatively low rate, especially in the Dutch East Indies.[40] The Committee allowed 100 per cent of the basic quotas to be exported, therefore, during the first two months. (See Table 8.) By the end of the year, however, the Committee had reduced the percentage of permissible exports by stages to 70 per cent. World stocks amounting to 706,000 tons as of December 31, 1934 were equivalent to nine months' supply at the current rate of absorption. Though six months' supply is considered normal, this stock position represented a distinct improvement over that of any other year back to 1930.

With prices advancing rapidly, the Committee raised the permissible export rate to 75 per cent of basic quotas for the first quarter of 1935, but as price reacted the Committee reduced it and the average for the year was 67.5 per cent.[41] In 1936, in spite of mounting prices, the Committee reduced the rate still further to an average of 62.5 per cent. As the Committee reduced exports, world rubber stocks declined until by the end of 1936 they represented only 5.3 months'

40. Many of the natives on the larger islands, such as Sumatra and Borneo, live far inland. They find unremunerative a price below about 6 pence a pound. When such a price level persists for an extended period, the natives, particularly those on the Dutch islands who have alternative sources of livelihood, tend to discontinue tapping. Cf. Rowe, *Markets and Men*, pp. 149-51; and Knorr, *op. cit.*, p. 123.

41. The Committee, in endeavoring to maintain a price of not less than 8 pence, or 16 cents a pound, encountered the ever-present "menace" of expanding native production. As *The Economist* (London) reported (October 19, 1935, p. 764): "In order to check exports of native-produced rubber, which have been running this year from 20,000 T. to 25,000 T. above their quota, the Dutch Government has imposed an export tax, which, on Wednesday last, was raised to the present level of 24 guilders per 100 kilograms. At this figure, . . . equivalent to approximately 4 *d.* per pound, it is a question whether the return to many native growers has not been forced down below subsistence level."

Of the equity of this policy, the Dutch Government evidently had misgivings. At any rate, to forestall "native trouble," the government decided, on October 15, 1935, to purchase up to 20,000 tons of export licenses from estate growers. These were to be used for covering the "excess" native exports. Cf. Knorr, *op. cit.*, pp. 127-28.

TABLE 7

BASIC RUBBER EXPORT QUOTAS, 1934–1943 [a]

(In Long Tons)

	1934 [b]	1935	1936	1937	1938	1939	1940	1941	1942	1943
Total		1,118,500	1,254,000	1,298,500	1,335,250	1,519,000	1,541,550	1,554,700	1,563,000	1,569,000
Malaya	504,000	538,000	569,000	589,000	602,000	632,000	642,500	648,000	651,000	651,500
Dutch Indies	352,000	400,000	500,000	520,000	540,000	631,500	640,000	645,500	650,000	651,000
Ceylon	77,500	79,000	80,000	81,000	82,500	106,000	107,500	109,000	109,500	110,000
India	6,850	12,500	12,500	13,000	17,500	17,750	17,750	17,750	17,750	17,750
Burma	5,150	8,000	8,500	9,000	9,250	13,500	13,750	13,750	13,750	13,750
N. Borneo	12,000	13,000	14,000	15,500	16,500	21,000	21,000	21,000	21,000	21,000
Sarawak	24,000	28,000	30,000	31,500	32,000	43,000	43,750	44,000	44,000	44,000
Thailand	15,000	40,000	40,000	40,000	40,000	54,500	55,300	55,700	56,000	60,000

a. As set out in the text of the International Agreement. The limitation on Indo-Chinese exports came into effect only if and when total exports from this French colony rose above 30,000 tons a year and at the same time were less than total French imports of crude rubber.
b. Seven months.

TABLE 8

"PERMISSIBLE EXPORTABLE" RUBBER, AS FIXED BY IRRC

(Percentages of Basic Export Quotas)

	1934			1935	1936	1937	1938	1939	1940	1941
Average	87 1/7			67½	62½	83¾	55	58¾	83¾	105
June–July	100	1st	Quarter	75	60	75	70	50	80	100
Aug.–Sept.	90	2nd	Quarter	70	60	80	60	50	80	100
Oct.–Nov.	80	3rd	Quarter	65	65	90	45	60	85	100
December	70	4th	Quarter	60	65	90	45	75	90	120

Source: Statistical Bulletin of the International Rubber Regulation Committee, London, November 1941, Vol. VII, No. 11, p. 1.

supply. This rigorous restriction contributed to a sharp advance in the price of rubber in the spring of 1937.[42] By March rubber was selling for about 25 cents a pound, a 100 per cent increase over the price just prior to the renewal of restriction three years before.

Permissible Exports Increased

After this rapid rise in price the Committee increased permissible exports to 75 per cent of quotas for the first quarter of 1937, to 80 per cent for the second quarter, and to 90 per cent for the third. In spite of this increase in allowable exports, year-end stocks had not recovered to their normal level; they represented only 5.7 months' supply. This level was not improved during 1938, in spite of a 20 per cent decline in consumption, because the IRRC reduced the rate of permissible export to 45 per cent in the last half of the year. The result was an average price for the final quarter of 16.4 cents compared to an average for the year of only 14.6 cents. Although the

42. A "war scare" boom of considerable proportions about this time also contributed to the increase in prices. Raw material prices generally rose, many of them reaching postdepression highs for the decade in March or April of 1937. But the Bureau of Labor Statistics general index of raw material prices advanced during this three-year period only 37 per cent while the price of crude rubber rose 100 per cent.

In defense of its policy during this period, the Committee has argued that: "By raising the quota to 75 per cent and 80 per cent for the first two quarters and 90 per cent for the last half of 1937, the Committee showed its determination to defeat speculation and maintain ample supplies and a moderate price policy. The Committee rejected the advice of the Advisory Panel to grant still higher quotas because it feared that a too sudden expansion might lead to labor difficulties, less rubber, more speculation and higher prices." MacFadyean, *op. cit.,* p. 113.

This explanation may be accepted for whatever it may be worth. However, clear implications of this official statement are: (1) that "speculation" in rubber was confined to outside parties—IRRC never indulged in that putatively reprehensible practice; and (2) that the "speculation" in the spring of 1937 developed out of "thin air"—had no connection with the antecedent course of restriction policy, of stocks, and of prices.

year-end price was one third lower than the peak reached in the spring of 1937, it was one third higher than the prevailing price at the inception of the restriction program. The price rise continued during 1939; although, with the outbreak of war, the permissible export rate was advanced to 75 per cent from the 50 per cent level maintained through the first half of the year, the average price for the year was 17.5 cents—20 per cent above the 1938 average.

In spite of the outbreak of war in 1939 and the increased strategic importance of rubber, the Committee held the permissible export rate to an average of 83.75 per cent in 1940. World stocks at the end of the year were reduced to the critical level of less than five months' supply. Prices continued to advance, rising 15 per cent to better than 20 cents a pound during the year. Nevertheless, the Committee did not authorize the release of supplies up to 100 per cent of quotas until the first quarter of 1941.[43] Moreover, in releasing rubber to the United States Government for reserve stocks, as insurance against the contingency of its being cut off from its sources of supply, the Committee stipulated that, barring the contingency of American entrance into the war, none of this tonnage should be released for consumption within a specified term of years following the sale.[44]

43. The attitude of IRRC was reflected not only in its checking the flow of crude rubber supplies but also in its efforts to discourage the precautionary synthetic rubber program. As reported in a memorandum of February 21, 1941 by Mr. Frank Howard of the Standard Oil Company: "On top of these inherent difficulties, Sir John Hay, representing the British Rubber Control, has been very persuasive in his arguments that the production of synthetic rubber is uneconomical, that the construction of plants will impose a drain on the American productive power at a time when it is badly needed, and that in any case the plants could not be completed until the emergency is past. In view of the above situation, Mr. Schram admitted last Tuesday that the rubber program of the Reconstruction Finance Corporation is in a state of suspended animation and that it is impossible to say when any action may be taken." See *Investigation of the National Defense Program*, Hearings before a Special Committee of the U.S. Senate, 77th Cong., 1st sess., pursuant to S.Res. 71, Pt. XI, Washington, 1942, p. 4490. (These hearings will hereinafter be cited: Truman, Pt. —. The committee is commonly referred to as the Truman Committee, after the name of its original chairman.)

MacFadyean states that Sir John Hay was a representative in this country of IRRC. *Op. cit.*, p. 139.

44. Under the cotton-rubber barter exchange agreement between Great Britain and the United States of June 23, 1939, the latter was required to withhold from the market for seven years, barring an emergency, the 90,000 tons of rubber acquired. See U.S. State Department, Treaty Series, No. 947, Washington, 1939; also, *The Economist* (London), July 1, 1939, p. 8.

On June 28, 1940, RFC organized the Rubber Reserve Company, and the very next day this agency concluded an agreement with IRRC for the purchase of 150,000 tons of rubber. This amount later in that year was increased to 430,000 tons. The agreement provided that, barring an emergency, none of this rubber could be released for use prior to 1944, and then only in amounts not exceeding 100,000 tons annually. See *The Economist* (London), August 24, 1940, p. 259; and MacFadyean, *op. cit.*, pp. 129-42.

While the figures on world stocks and absorption of rubber are not available for the war years, it is significant that the market price rose steadily to a level in May 1941 only slightly below the peak reached in the 1937 boom. Prices were stabilized at this level when Rubber Reserve took over the control of all rubber supplies in this country and became the sole importer of crude rubber.[45]

Appraisal of IRRC Policy

The IRRA plan clearly has operated less perversely as a market "stabilizing" device than did the Stevenson Plan. Prices have fluctuated less violently during its operation than under the previous plan. Whether prices have been more erratic than they would have been in the absence of concerted restriction and the wartime imposition of even more rigid governmental controls, no one can say positively. But such cost and profit data as are available indicate that prices have been at all times since 1934 remunerative, and at most times highly profitable.

The United States Bureau of Foreign and Domestic Commerce has found that, in 1934, "The all-in costs for rubber produced on estates ranges from a little over $0.036 (U.S. currency) to almost $0.084 per pound. . . . It is estimated that the . . . average price received . . . [1934] is approximately $0.1221; average all-in cost is $0.0525; and the gross profit for estates is $0.067 per pound." [46] The Bureau's all-in cost figures contain no allowance for a return on invested capital; but they do provide for depreciation and for amortization in addition to direct operating costs. However, a margin of 126 per cent above average all-in cost in an agricultural industry probably yields a better than "fair" return on the investment. The chairman of an important plantation company has estimated that "The average Malayan estate . . . breaks even at 4.5 pence [per pound]." [47]

According to a later survey, average all-in cost per pound in 1940 for a representative group of Malayan plantations was 7.13 pence, equivalent to about 13 cents in United States currency at then prevail-

45. The proscription of private rubber imports applied only to new contracts. Private imports continued to be received for some months after June 21, 1941, the date of the Rubber Reserve order. After September 11, 1941 the ceiling price of crude rubber remained fixed at 22.5 cents a pound, but its use was subject to rigorous control by the War Production Board and later by the Rubber Coordinator.
46. *Rubber Regulation and the Malayan Plantation Industry*, pp. 35 ff.
47. Eric MacFayden, quoted in *India Rubber World*, October 1, 1935, p. 60.

ing exchange rates.[48] Cost for the estates surveyed ranged from 5.66 to 9.04 pence a pound. These cost figures include an average depreciation charge of 1.24 pence a pound. For the same year the average price of ribbed smoked sheets at Singapore was 10.514 pence. Thus the gross profit margin for this group of plantations was equivalent to nearly 50 per cent of their average unit cost.

In the absence of definite accounting standards, cost studies, of course, are bound to show variable results. While expenses had undoubtedly risen along with the general price level between 1934 and 1940, it is doubtful that this fully explains the difference between the average cost estimates reached by these two surveys. But even if we accept without qualification the higher estimate and assume that it reflected conditions throughout the whole active period of IRRC, rubber growers would have had on the average a gross profit margin of 3.25 cents a pound.[49] The average New York price in the eight years preceding our entrance into the war (1934–1941, inclusive) was 16.9 cents a pound. Allowing 0.7 cents a pound for delivery costs, this leaves an average net realization price to growers of 16.2 cents. On a most generous estimate of the costs of rubber growing, the industry was certainly operating on a remunerative basis under the IRRA scheme.[50]

Attitude of Rubber Manufacturers

Although the rubber control programs restricted output and raised prices, rubber manufacturers generally have remained indifferent to their operation. On its face, this is surprising since they are the sole immediate consumers of rubber and presumably would be "incon-

48. This estimate corresponds closely with one given by George Rae, *op. cit.,* p. 333. He estimated on the basis of data collected by the Rubber Grower's Association that in 1937 the average all-in costs in Malaya were about 6.15 pence a pound. Knorr (*op. cit.,* p. 158) reached a similar conclusion.

49. Of course, the return on invested capital afforded by such a margin might be high, reasonable, or low. But that a 16 cent price was acceptable even to the growers themselves is indicated by a statement of IRRC. Speaking of conditions in 1937, the Committee has said that: "Assuming a modest return for tropical enterprises of 7.5 per cent on invested capital, a price of over 8 pence was indicated as the lowest reasonably remunerative level for the average estate." Sir Andrew MacFadyean, *op. cit.,* p. 112.

50. Available data on the course of rubber plantation profits, while too scattered and fragmentary to afford a basis for a reliable statistical study, at least confirm this cautious conclusion. See *The Economist* (London), April 13, 1935, Vol. CXX, No. 4781, pp. 862-63; January 29, 1938, Vol. CXXX, No. 4927, p. 241; May 4, 1940, Vol. CXXXVIII, No. 5045, p. 824. See also Knorr, *op. cit.,* pp. 143-44.

venienced" by a market control managed by "outsiders" primarily in the outsiders' interests. Since the control programs have apparently insured a substantial profit margin in crude rubber production, and since the raw material cost of the manufacturer represents about one third of the price he obtains for a tire, it would presumably have paid the manufacturer to develop his own source of supply. Why has he not done so? [51]

In the first place, since the demand for rubber products in its principal use is inelastic, a high price for crude rubber matters little to the manufacturer, as long as his competitors pay the same price. Secondly the cartel is none too strong, even with government support. The potential expansion of native production creates a highly unstable situation.[52] In the Dutch colonies small native holdings represent well over half the total acreage,[53] and wherever large foreign-financed plantations can be established, native cultivation is also possible—indeed, probable. Thirdly the waiting period (five to seven years) before one can obtain any return on the capital sunk in a rubber plantation is a deterrent to investment. This might not be decisive by itself; but, coupled with the comparative insecurity of investments in far-distant tropical countries with a reputation for political instability, it has hindered the development of integration by rubber manufacturers.

Finally, in canvassing the advantages and disadvantages of rubber growing on his own account, a manufacturer could scarcely ignore the possibility of natural rubber's being displaced by a synthetic product. Before the thirties this contingency might have appeared remote to practical businessmen, even though the Germans in World War I had demonstrated that it was technically possible to make a substitute for rubber. But the appearance on the market in the first half of the thirties of at least half a dozen varieties of artificial rub-

51. Although Firestone, U.S. Rubber, Goodyear, Ford, Raybestos-Manhattan, and Intercontinental Rubber maintain rubber plantations abroad, their combined production amounted in a normal prewar year to a bare 6 per cent of the yearly imports of crude rubber. The U.S. Rubber Company supplied more of its requirements from its own plantations than any other manufacturer, but it obtained only about one fifth of its supplies from this source. Moreover, Firestone (in Liberia) and Ford (in Brazil) are the only manufacturers whose plantation interests are all located outside of the Far East. See Tariff Commission, *Crude Rubber.*
52. See the series of reviews of "The Rubber Situation" appearing irregularly, but every few months, in *The Economist* (London). See also Rowe, *Markets and Men,* pp. 143-51; and Knorr, *op. cit.,* p. 131.
53. See Rae, *op. cit.,* p. 319.

ber was a token of what the chemists' "magic in a bottle" might do to the plantation rubber industry.

If, because of their special qualities, these synthetic compounds were salable in direct competition with the natural product even when it was selling at record low prices, was it safe to invest in a rubber plantation? Or, once concerted restriction was resumed, was it worth while to buck the cartel? If one had to gamble, was it not safer to bet one's money on synthetic rubber than on natural rubber? For a long time rubber manufacturers were content to rely on natural rubber produced by outsiders. Although they eventually became interested in synthetic rubber, for the most part they entered the field too late to secure a commanding position in synthetic rubber technology. It was the chemical industry that undertook the technological pioneering in synthetic rubber. Thereby it won a strategic position for controlling the development of this new industry.

THE SYNTHETIC RUBBER CARTEL

The first step in the development of synthetic rubber was the investigation of the chemical properties of natural rubber. Before 1885, chemists had isolated and identified isoprene as natural rubber's basic constituent.[54] Early research concentrated on discovery of an alternative source of this compound.[55] This line of investigation proved a blind alley. However, chemical research, in which British scientists took a leading part, revealed that numerous other monomers could be polymerized into a coagulated compound with properties similar to those of natural rubber.[56] The monomers bearing the closest chemical relation to that of the natural product are

54. Isoprene is a diolefin with the formula C_5H_8. The diolefins are a family of hydrocarbons in which the two elements are united according to the formula C_nH_{2n-2}.

55. On the historical development of synthetic rubber techniques, see: Bureau of Foreign and Domestic Commerce, Trade Promotion Series, No. 209, *Rubber: History, Production, and Manufacture*, Washington, 1940; article on "Synthetic Rubber," *Fortune*, August 1940, p. 112; Harry Barron, "Synthetic Rubbers," a series of articles in *Rubber Age* (London), April-August 1941; and Tariff Commission, *Preliminary Report on Rubber*, January 1942.

56. A monomer is any chemical which can be polymerized. Polymerization is the generic name of any process which fuses or links a monomer's molecules to yield a product of the same chemical composition but of different molecular weight and with very different properties. The resultant product is called a polymer. Polymerization requires certain conditions among which as a rule, though not invariably, is the presence of a suitable catalyst. When the conversion is made in conjunction with one or more other reactants, the process is termed co-polymerization.

the diolefins. These are readily obtainable from a wide variety of common materials, notably grains, coal, and oil.

Inventions of Synthetic Rubber

The scientists of several countries have conducted intensive research to discover monomers suitable for making synthetic rubber, but German and American scientists have made the most signal achievements in this direction. The Germans took the lead in synthetic rubber research around 1910, and were the first to develop a suitable substitute for rubber:[57] the so-called methyl rubber. Its monomer was dimethyl butadiene, a diolefin containing two methyl radicals, in contrast to the one in isoprene and none in butadiene.

Though this first successful synthetic rubber was produced on a commercial scale during World War I, its manufacture was discontinued after 1918, because of poor quality and comparative costliness. Search for a better monomer continued, however, particularly in the laboratories of the great German chemical combine, I. G. Farbenindustrie A. G. (hereinafter IG). In the late twenties IG technicians settled upon butadiene as the most promising basis for synthetic rubber manufacture. Butadiene is the basic constituent of the German Buna rubbers, the Russian SK rubbers, and the bulk of the synthetics now being produced in the United States.

At about the time German scientists discovered the adaptability of butadiene for rubber making, an American scientist discovered that chloroprene, another diolefin monomer, was also a promising basis for synthetic rubber manufacture.[58] From this discovery, made by Father Nieuwland of Notre Dame University, came the first commercial synthetic rubber development in this country. The du Pont Company, which acquired patent rights in the original Nieuwland discovery and in various features of the polymerization process which it developed, manufactures the product, first called Duprene and later renamed Neoprene. More recently (1937), technicians of the Standard Oil Company of New Jersey discovered by experimental research the suitability of isobutene as a basic monomer in synthetic

57. See Law Voge, "German Patents Relating to Synthetic Rubber Materials," *India Rubber World,* April 1940, pp. 48-50; also, the works cited in n. 52.
58. Chloroprene is sometimes called chlor-butadiene. It differs from butadiene only in having one less hydrogen atom, which is replaced by a chlorine atom.

rubber manufacture.[59] The product which is called Butyl is the first vulcanizable synthetic rubber to be derived mainly from a simple olefin monomer.[60] Hence it is one step removed, as it were, from the vulcanizable synthetics previously developed, which bear a closer chemical relationship to natural rubber.[61]

The leading synthetic rubber monomers—butadiene, chloroprene, isobutene, styrene, acrylonitrile—may be obtained from a variety of source materials. And usually they may be produced in a number of different ways by a series of fairly simple and well-understood chemical reactions. This does not mean that in particular circumstances one source material does not have a decisive advantage over another or that no opportunity exists for simplifying processes or inventing new ones. A wide range of choice exists, but the technical problems of monomer production present no serious obstacle to enterprise in synthetic rubber manufacture.

It is the second step, that of transforming the monomer into a coagulated rubber-like compound, which presented real opportunities for effectively controlling the development of the synthetic rubber industry. Polymerization processes are not fully understood even today, and those in use have been developed, in the main, empirically. Patents blanket virtually the entire field; and partly perhaps to eliminate the obstructive effects of conflicting claims and to bring together advances in different directions, but certainly also to assure unified control of the industry, the principal interests concluded a

59. Isobutene is an isomer (or variant form) of the olefin butene (or butylene). In the polymerization of the isobutene a small amount (less than 5 per cent) of butadiene is included as a minor reactant. Thus Butyl is a co-polymer, like the Bunas (butadiene, 60-85 per cent, and styrene or acrylonitrile). This slight difference in the composition of Standard's Butyl and its Vistanex, a simple isobutene polymer, may account for the fact that the former alone is vulcanizable.

60. Olefins are hydrocarbons containing two atoms of hydrogen for each carbon atom.

61. A number of other substitutes for rubber have been developed, but they are much less like the natural product in chemical or physical characteristics. They fall into three principal classes. The organic polysulphides are represented by Thiokol (American), Perduren (German), Vulcaplas (British), and Ethanite (Belgian). Though they are vulcanizable, they have a limited range of uses. The plasticized vinylchloride polymers include Vinylite, Koroseal, Korogel, and Flamenol. Their elastic properties are poor but they are widely used in waterproofing and electrical insulation. The polyisobutenes, such as Standard Oil's Vistanex and I. G. Farben's Oppanol, have a narrow range of uses, chiefly as an admixture to other rubbers for improving certain properties. Neither of the latter two classes of rubber substitutes is vulcanizable.

See Lawrence A. Wood, *Synthetic Rubbers*, Circular No. C427, National Bureau of Standards, 1940; J. W. Schade, "Rubber, Natural and Synthetic," *Purchasing*, April 1941, p. 54; J. Delmonte, "Properties of Synthetic Rubber-like Materials," *Product Engineering*, March 1941, p. 151.

series of patent exchange agreements. The major participants in these cartel arrangements were Standard Oil, du Pont, and IG.

Pattern of Patent Controls

For many reasons, but primarily because of its urgent strategic need in case of war, Germany took the lead in developing synthetic rubber. For two decades, the German chemical industry held its technical and commercial leadership in this field. This was partly due to its head start, but even more to continuing subsidization by the German Government.[62] For the Weimar Republic, no less than the Empire of Kaiser Wilhelm and the Third Reich, desired to establish rubber autonomy. From the standpoint of industrial control the German chemical industry is virtually synonymous with IG.[63]

Fortified by governmental favors at home, IG undertook to extend monopolistic control over synthetic rubber production beyond the German borders. For this purpose its formidable patent position provided effective leverage. In Soviet Russia, which recognizes no private property in technology, this was impossible.[64] Elsewhere the prospects were more promising. IG had learned from experience the inexpediency of undertaking production abroad through directly owned subsidiaries. It favored "alliances." For one reason or another, it preferred to develop its patented processes in foreign countries by licensing concerns of each country to use them.[65]

Du Pont, as the largest American chemical firm and the nearest industrial counterpart to IG in this hemisphere, apparently was a natural ally. However, certain obstacles blocked such an alliance. Du

62. See E. G. Holt, "Rubber Conservation Methods in Germany," *Rubber Age*, November 1940, p. 99; V. A. Cosler, "Commercial Application of Chloroprene and Butadiene Rubbers," *India Rubber World*, December 1936, p. 44; and Harry Barron, *op. cit.*, August 1941, p. 150.

63. Cf. Joseph Borkin and Charles A. Welsh, *Germany's Master Plan*, Duell, Sloan & Pearce, New York, 1942.

64. The USSR has been making synthetic rubber in quantity since 1933. The Bureau of Foreign and Domestic Commerce offers the following estimates of the course of production: 1933, 5,000 T.; 1934, 12,000 T.; 1935, 20,000 T.; 1936, 24,000 T.; 1937, 40,000 T.; and "thereafter" 40,000-60,000 T. annually. *Rubber: History, Production, and Manufacture*, p. 42. Soviet output includes all the principal types of synthetics, except possibly Butyl. Whether the processes employed are original Russian developments or were simply "lifted" out of published patent specifications filed in Germany, the United States, and other countries is not clear. The question is perhaps academic, since the Soviet product is not offered on world markets.

65. One obvious advantage was the trade good will it thus enlisted. Moreover, a patent controlled by a domestically owned corporation may be less subject to attack, and less vulnerable if attacked, than one exploited by a foreign corporation.

Pont's developments in synthetics were, at the end of the twenties, at least as promising as IG's. Moreover, du Pont had shown a singularly independent attitude in negotiations with IG covering a variety of subjects of common interest during the decade following World War I.[66] This had not prevented agreements of limited scope on certain specific matters, such as explosives and dyestuffs. But it had stood in the way, as indeed it continued to stand in the way throughout the thirties, of any comprehensive formal agreement, or *entente cordiale,* between these German and American chemical leaders.

Negotiations With New Jersey Standard

Meanwhile, IG's negotiations with another potential American partner, the Standard Oil Company of New Jersey, had gone more smoothly. Since Standard had no "going concern" stake in the production of synthetic rubber, no conflicting competitive interests hampered negotiations. But, as the leading American producer and distributor of petroleum and its products, it had a direct and immediate interest in the spectacular technological advances which IG had made in the production of synthetic gasoline from coal by the hydrogenation process. An alarming "scare" of early exhaustion of American petroleum reserves reached its height in the mid-twenties and accentuated Standard's interests in these developments.[67]

Standard, recognizing the advantages of an alliance with IG, was

66. See letter of April 15, 1930 from Dr. C. Bosch, head of IG, to W. C. Teagle, head of Standard, in which Dr. Bosch states: "I believe that as a result of your intervention the deadlock of the negotiations between du Pont and IG has now been overcome and that thereby our desire will be realized to reach a cooperation with this very energetic and cleverly proceeding firm, which we have tried to bring about for years." See Truman, Pt. XI, Ex. 419, pp. 4647-48.

The "deadlock" in negotiations apparently referred to the relationship of du Pont's interests in the field to a joint enterprise by Standard and IG in the production of synthetic ammonia. See *ibid.,* Ex. 418, pp. 4646-47. The "cooperation" referred to a hoped-for (but never realized) general, comprehensive, cartel agreement covering the entire range of interests of both companies in the chemical industries.

67. The threat of an imminent oil shortage led to the establishment of the Federal Oil Conservation Board in 1925. See Myron W. Watkins, *Oil: Stabilization or Conservation?,* Harper, New York, 1937, p. 42. See also *U.S.* v. *Standard Oil Co., et al.,* in the District of New Jersey, Civil Action No. 2091, Complaint, March 25, 1942. Reproduced in Truman, Pt. XI, as Ex. 441, p. 4693, is a criminal information of the same tenor.

Also, on the direct connection between the oil shortage and Standard's initial interest in the hydrogenation process, see the testimony of the late W. S. Farish, then president of Standard, in *Patents,* Hearings before the Committee on Patents, 77th Cong., 2d sess., on S. 2303 and S. 2491, Pt. IX, p. 5036 f. (These hearings will hereinafter be cited as Bone, Pt. —, after the chairman of the committee.)

For a contemporary view of the importance of IG's technological achievements to Standard, see the letter of Frank Howard to Walter Teagle dated March 28, 1926. Mr.

in a bargaining mood. While negotiating an alliance with Standard
Oil providing for a joint development of certain fields and a division
of others, IG did not break with du Pont. It continued its efforts to
reach an agreement which would insure a development of the organic
chemical industry in a manner compatible with its interests. By holding out to du Pont the prospect of (1) eventual participation in an
inclusive (IG–Standard–du Pont) joint enterprise for synthetic rubber, or (2) having the field reserved for its own Neoprene, or (3)
obtaining other concessions in the organic chemical field, IG was able
to hold du Pont in line.

For convenience, we shall treat separately these two "arms" of the
synthetic rubber cartel—the IG-Standard alliance and the IG–du
Pont *entente cordiale*. However, the negotiations were not conducted
wholly independently. Indeed, it was of the essence of IG's strategy
to play off one American company against the other. For a full decade this strategy worked. It worked so well, in fact, that when the
United States became involved in the war and was cut off from crude
rubber supplies, it found itself with only the rudiments of a synthetic
rubber industry.

The Standard-IG "Marriage"

On November 9, 1929, IG and Standard concluded four agreements under the terms of which, as Dr. Bosch of IG has declared,
the two parties were "married." These agreements were the Four-
Party Agreement, the Division of Fields Agreement, the German
Sales Agreement, and the Coordination Agreement.[68]

The Four-Party Agreement transferred to a jointly owned company, Standard-IG, rights in the hydrogenation process in all coun-

---

Howard was reporting from Germany the results of a fact-finding trip. He wrote:
"Based upon my observations and discussion today, I think that *this matter is the most
important which has ever faced the company since the dissolution.*

"The Badische can make high grade motor fuel from lignite and other low quality
coals in amounts up to half the weight of the coal. This means absolutely the independence of Europe on the matter of gasoline supply. *Straight price competition is all
that is left.* . . .

"They can make up to 100% by weight from any liquid hydro-carbon, tar, fuel oil,
or crude oil. This means that refining of oil will have as a competitive industry in
America and elsewhere, catalytic conversion of the crude into motor fuel."
Quoted from statement of Wendell Berge, Assistant Attorney General, before the
Senate Judiciary Committee (Hearings on S. 11, 79th Cong., 1st sess.), May 18, 1945.
Italics supplied.

68. These Agreements are reproduced in Truman, Pt. XI, as respectively, Exs. 360,
362, 363, and 367, pp. 4561-84.

tries of the world, except Germany.[69] The German Sales Agreement fixed the shares of the parties in the German market for "oil products." The Coordination Agreement simply provided for the amicable adjustment of the interests of the parties in unforeseen contingencies. As a consideration for the benefits received under these four Agreements, Standard transferred 546,000 shares of its stock, valued at more than $30 million to IG.[70]

The Division of Fields Agreement was the basic accord. A Standard vice-president in 1936 accurately summarized it as follows: "I. G. are going to stay out of the oil business proper and we are going to stay out of the chemical business insofar as that has no bearing on the oil business." [71] In the terms of the contract, each party disavowed "any plan or policy" of "so far expanding its existing business in the direction of the other party's industry as to become a serious competitor of that other party . . ." [72]

The Agreement recognized, however, that "a certain overlapping

69. This supplemented a 1927 contract by which Standard had obtained United States rights in the process. The 1929 contract was broader in subject matter, also; it defined the parties' relations in the entire "hydrocarbon field," including future developments.

70. Bone, Pt. VII, p. 3333, and Ex. 9, pp. 3460-61.

71. Letter of Frank Howard to E. F. Johnson, July 27, 1936. See Truman, Pt. XI, Ex. 372, p. 4590. Translated into legal terminology, this was a simple contract in restraint of trade. In effect, each party undertook not to compete with the other, in consideration of the other's undertaking not to compete with it. Such covenants may or may not be unlawful.

72. *Ibid.*, Ex. 362, p. 4573. This passage sets forth the basic consideration underlying the whole arrangement. Standard was intent on fortifying its dominant position in the world oil industry. Its main interest was in securing control of the hydrogenation process, which was a potential threat to that position; all other matters, such as synthetic rubber, were quite incidental. Its acquisition of preferential rights in all IG technical developments in "the hydrocarbon field" served it well in the course of the next fifteen years. Through a period of revolutionary technical developments, convulsive business readjustments, and violent political turmoil, Standard has managed to more than hold its own. Its liaison with IG and its ground-floor monopoly on the hydrogenation process have contributed to its success in maintaining its dominant position in oil.

The three most signal technical advances in the production of synthetic gasoline in the decade of the thirties came primarily from other sources. These were: hydrocarbon synthesis (the Fischer process); sulphuric acid alkylation; and catalytic cracking (including hydroforming). In the development of these processes the research activities of at least a score of industrial laboratories besides those of Standard, including those of Shell, Texaco, Kellogg, Anglo-Iranian, Ruhrchemie, Phillips, Houdry, Universal, and Standard of Indiana, made signal contributions and, collectively, the major contributions. The prestige and financial power represented by the Standard-IG coalition and the similarity of some of the essential features of the new processes to the original high-pressure "hydrogenation process" developed by IG may have been partly responsible for the fact that none of them except the Houdry process was independently and competitively developed. A series of agreements and maneuvers, e.g., the USAC arrangement (Hydrocarbon Synthesis Corporation, 1938), the Polyco pool (Polymerization Processes Corporation, 1935), the Sulphuric Acid Alkylation Agreement (1939), and the CRA alliance (Catalytic Research Associates, 1940), all pointed toward non-

of activities will exist." In order to avoid "mutual irritation" the parties agreed on the following policies:

1. "If the Company [Standard] shall desire to initiate *anywhere in the world* a new chemical development not closely related to its then business," e.g., production of fuels and lubricants from oil and natural gas, "it will offer to I. G. control of such new enterprise (including the patent rights thereto) on fair and reasonable terms."

2. "If I. G. shall desire to initiate *outside of Germany* . . . a new chemical development which cannot be advantageously carried on except as a department of an oil or natural gas business, it will offer control thereof (including the patent rights thereto) to the Company [Standard] on fair and reasonable terms."

3. "If I. G. shall desire to initiate *outside of Germany* . . . a new chemical development" other than of the character described above "but related to the then business of the Company, as for example by use of natural gas or petroleum products, I. G. will offer to the Company [Standard] a substantial but not controlling participation." [73]

The Jasco Agreement

These definitions of policy showed that the parties intended to renounce all competition, but hardly provided an objective measure of just what was reserved to each. To clear up the ambiguity and to implement the Division of Fields Agreement, the parties concluded a supplemental agreement on September 13, 1930.[74] This was known as the Jasco (Joint American Study Company) Agreement. It supplemented but did not supersede the basic 1929 Agreement. The Jasco Agreement was of narrower scope. It covered only "new chemical processes" which employ as a "starting material crude petroleum, natural bitumen or natural gas or products made therefrom." On the other hand, the "new chemical developments" embraced in the basic Division of Fields Agreement covered all new chemical processes regardless of the nature of the raw materials.

competitive exploitation of synthetic gasoline technology. Truman, Pt. XI, Ex. 441, pp. 4704-10, and Bone, Pt. VII, pp. 3325-4170, give a detailed account of these transactions. For a discussion of technical developments and commercial relationships in synthetic gasoline production, see Bone, Pt. IX, pp. 5088-5113.

In sum, then, from the strictly business standpoint Standard probably made "a fast, smart deal" with IG in 1929, as *Fortune* (August 1940, p. 119) tersely asserts. Whether this justifies the concessions to IG on "chemical" matters, and specifically on the synthetic rubber project throughout the thirties, the reader may judge for himself from the facts presented in the text.

73. Truman, Pt. XI, Ex. 362, p. 4573. Italics supplied.
74. Bone, Pt. VI, Ex. 15, p. 2879.

The Jasco Agreement provided that when either party developed "a new chemical process" it should offer the other an option to have rights in the process assigned to a jointly owned company (Jasco, Inc.). Jasco was to make experiments and to act as a licensing agency for the exploitation of patents on promising "new chemical processes." Though the stockholding interests of Standard and IG in Jasco, Inc., were equal, the profits (from royalties) were to be divided in the proportion of 62.5 per cent for the originator of a process and 37.5 per cent for the other partner.

The Agreement committed the parties, when either of them originated a process within the Jasco field, to negotiate with the other the specific terms on which Jasco might have the licensing rights. According to the interpretation which Standard officials have placed on these agreements this left Standard in control of any new chemical process which it might originate in the borderline zone between the oil business and the chemical field.[75]

The Electric Arc Process

IG promptly turned over three "processes" to Jasco. One was the so-called "electric arc" process.[76] It involved the conversion of hydro-

---

75. They declare it was the accepted practice in Jasco undertakings to leave control with the party responsible for the original development. However, since IG alone ever actually transferred any new processes to Jasco, all Jasco ventures were in fact IG-controlled. See Bone, Pt. IX, pp. 5119-20, 5193-99. See also *ibid.*, Pt. III, 1409-10. For the views of Department of Justice representatives, see *ibid.*, Pt. III, pp. 1366-72, Pt. VI, pp. 2650-54, 2716-22, and Pt. VII, p. 3331.

Moreover, in adjudicating the issue of the extent of the interests Standard acquired in IG patents and processes by or under the Jasco Agreement, a federal court has held that the Agreement gave Standard no "equitable interests enforceable by a court . . . in short, imposed upon IG no more than an obligation in good faith to seek to negotiate with the Jersey group a supplementary agreement for each new Jasco process." *Standard Oil Co.* (New Jersey) v. *Markham, Alien Property Custodian,* 64 Fed.Supp. 656, 663 (1945).

76. The other two processes transferred to Jasco were the conversion of paraffin wax to fatty acids by oxidation and the production of polyisobutenes (Vistanex and Paratone). The latter was not formally brought into Jasco until February 1933. A fourth process, the chlorination of paraffin wax, yielding a pour-point depressant for paraffin-base lubricating oils, called Paraflow, was on the border line between a "chemical development" and a petroleum-refining process. Accordingly, by special agreement in March 1932, it was transferred to Standard-IG, instead of to Jasco.

All these processes proved commercially profitable. Indeed, the Paraflow development was extraordinarily lucrative. It brought about signal advances in the quality of lubricants. By preserving their fluidity at low temperatures, it facilitated the development of high-altitude flying. The fatty acid oxidation process was developed in cooperation with Procter & Gamble, which used the product as a substitute for vegetable oils in soap-making. See Truman, Pt. XI, pp. 4711-13; Bone, Pt. IV, pp. 1750-69, Pt. VI, p. 2904, and Pt. IX, pp. 5135-53.

carbon gases into acetylene. Acetylene was then the source of both butadiene (for Buna) and chloroprene (for Neoprene). Both Jasco partners anticipated that this "electric arc" process would become the initial stage of a synthetic rubber project, though the only product ever made from the acetylene so produced was acetic acid. IG and Standard technicians carried on intensive experimentation for several years on this process, and from 1932 to 1935 acetic acid was produced and sold on a scale sufficient to show that the process was both practical and profitable.[77] However, because the marketing of the acid disturbed the friendly relations of IG with Union Carbide & Carbon Company, the dominant concern in that field, IG insisted on suspension of the Jasco acetylene–acetic acid project.[78]

IG was unwilling to undertake the conversion of acetylene into butadiene until it had "perfected" its Buna technique. Apparently IG desired to reserve every technical process closely related to synthetic rubber production for use as counters in bargaining with du Pont.[79] It feared that du Pont's Neoprene might prove superior to its Bunas; and, if so, it wanted to be well stocked with techniques, free from prior commitments, to offer in exchange for it. As Fritz ter Meer wrote to Dr. C. Krauch, a director of I. G. Farbenindustrie, on December 20, 1934:

Finally, I want to remind you that until such time as the synthetic rubber question will be clarified (the question being whether butadiene or Duprene is the better product) I want to reserve the field of vinylchloride, in the event that Duprene should prove to be the superior product. In that event Dupont would no longer be interested in an exchange of experience in the narrow field of synthetic rubber and we would have to have available another bargaining object in order to induce Dupont to license its German Duprene patents.[80]

77. See Bone, Pt. III, p. 1375 f.; Ex. 4, p. 1423; and Ex. 28, p. 1463.

78. See ibid., pp. 1383-1403, and Exs. 27, 64-66. Standard had a high opinion of the value of this development, the so-called "E" project. As expressed by Frank Howard in a letter to W. C. Teagle, October 9, 1935, "we believe that the Baton Rouge E project has a good chance of turning out to be the lowest cost acetylene producer in the world." Ibid., Pt. VI, p. 2896. Nevertheless, no further use was made of the equipment after 1935 (ibid., Pt. III, pp. 1385 and 1468), and in 1939, on IG's initiative, the plant was dismantled. Ibid., Pt. III, Exs. 64 and 65, p. 1509. The expedition with which this was achieved is significant. Within a week of the outbreak of war in Europe, IG had arranged to liquidate the E project.

79. See letter of Dr. Krauch to Fritz ter Meer, February 28, 1934, ibid., Pt. VI, pp. 2890-91.

80. Ibid., Pt. III, p. 1499.

IG Holds Up Synthetic Rubber

IG did not turn over the butadiene polymerization process to Jasco until after war broke out, in spite of the fact that it was operating a Buna pilot plant in Germany at least as early as 1932 and began large-scale production in 1934.[81]

Nevertheless, Standard regarded the Buna development as coming properly within the scope of the Jasco Agreement, certainly by 1932 if not earlier.[82] At that time the Goodrich Company sought to obtain rights under the IG patents on Buna processes.[83] Standard offered Goodrich a license but on terms so onerous that Goodrich indignantly rejected them.[84] Standard and Jasco continued to receive similar inquiries from rubber manufacturers intermittently throughout the thirties.[85] Without exception they were met with what Goodyear denounced as "stalling tactics."

The major obstacle preventing IG from releasing Buna rights and technical information was the attitude of the German Government. Nazi officials regarded Buna rubber as a strategic material, and declined to authorize IG to proceed with its commercial development outside Germany.[86] Standard gradually became aware of what was balking its efforts to get Buna into Jasco. As Dr. Hopkins of Standard expressed it on July 23, 1937: "So far as I know, foreign rights to the product outside of Germany . . . have not been released to anyone by I. G., probably because the Hitler government does not look with favor upon turning the invention over to foreign countries . . ."[87]

A few months later Frank Howard explained to Standard's Execu-

81. See testimony of R. T. Haslam, a Standard vice-president, *ibid.*, Pt. IX, p. 5108.
82. See letter of Clark, Standard vice-president, to Krauch of IG, April 30, 1930, *ibid.*, Pt. VI, Ex. 14, p. 2879. Even as early as 1928 Standard had expressed an interest in "our being 'in' on the synthetic rubber picture here in America." *Ibid.*, Ex. 12, p. 2878.
83. *Ibid.*, Ex. 16, pp. 2884-88.
84. The proffered license was subject to the condition that Goodrich would assign to Jasco all patents resulting, up to 1965, from its own research and development work in this field.
85. See, e.g., Bone, Pt. VI, Exs. 17, 19, 20, 21, 36, 40, 51, 54, 55, 65-68, pp. 2888-2919. Goodrich, General, Atlas, Goodyear, U.S. Rubber (which made tires for Atlas), were eager to gain access to the Buna techniques. Typical of the "stalling tactics" was the advice which Frank Howard of Standard gave to Mr. Davis of U.S. Rubber, as reported by the former in a letter of November 6, 1936 to Hochschwender of IG. "I told Mr. Davis . . . that the I. G. were very actively pushing . . . the work . . . in Germany, and . . . to discuss the matter directly with the I. G." Ex. 36, above, p. 2898.
86. In a cablegram of May 4, 1938, Fritz ter Meer of IG warned: "There must be absolutely no publicity in regard to the steps we want to take in U.S.A., before our Government has given its permission." *Ibid.*, Ex. 59, p. 2913.
87. *Ibid.*, Ex. 40, p. 2902.

tive Committee that technical information on Buna "has not been
forthcoming as a result of the German Government's refusal, because
of military expediency, to permit I. G. to reveal such information to
anyone outside Germany." Mr. Howard "deplored the fact that the
German Government's restrictions on I. G.'s freedom of action had
prevented our making material progress in the American field, particularly as there is some indication that the American rubber companies are making independent progress along these lines." [88]

Standard Gives Its Butyl to IG

Despite IG's persistence in withholding the Buna techniques from
Jasco and Standard's knowledge of the actual grounds for this
strategy, Standard in March 1938 sent IG samples and complete
information on Butyl.[89] This was done on the recommendation of
Frank Howard, who seems to have carried the ball on nearly every
play in the friendly game with IG—and, just as consistently, to have
been thrown for a loss. Addressing another Standard official, from
London, on March 15, 1938, he reported:

At my meeting with the I. G. gentlemen in Berlin on the Buna question, it
developed that very rapid strides were being made in all phases of the Buna
development, and there is even a prospect that this development will very
soon stand on its own feet economically in competition with natural rubber
under manufacturing conditions and costs in the United States. This is not
only in the specialty field of high-priced products, but in the main field of tyre

88. *Ibid.*, Ex. 44, p. 2904. Another obstacle to the transfer of Buna to Standard was
IG's cartel aspirations and commitments, in numerous directions, with du Pont. Prior
to 1936, IG regarded du Pont's Neoprene development as more promising than its own
Buna technique. Howard stated that "The gist of the matter, therefore, is that the I. G.
would like to take over Du Pont's Duprene development for Germany and push it on
a larger scale in place of their own process." *Ibid.*, Ex. 33, p. 2896.
   Even after IG became convinced of the limited competitive threat of Neoprene to
Buna, it was interested in preserving du Pont's good will in connection with numerous
other cartel relationships between the two companies. In dyes, plastics, solvents, nitrogen, and many other fields, du Pont had interests, jointly with IG, which the latter
could scarcely afford to ignore. Standard knew in a general way of IG's desire to preserve du Pont's friendship, but it was not fully informed of the extent and character of
their cartel connections. Standard's vice-president, Frank Howard, writing to his associate, F. H. Bedford, on April 20, 1938, tried to explain IG's slowness in turning over
Buna to Jasco. He stated: "We know some of the difficulties they have, both from
business complications and inter-relations with the rubber and chemical trades in the
United States, and from a national standpoint in Germany, but we do not know the
whole situation. . . ." *Ibid.*, p. 2912 f.
89. *Ibid.*, pp. 2906-07. The development of this co-polymer had by then reached a
stage where the technicians, and indeed the business executives, who had had most to
do with it were convinced that it was "ripe" for commercial introduction. See *ibid.*,
Exs. 46, 144a, and 146, pp. 2905-06 and 3032-33.

manufacture. Certain difficulties still exist which prevent our I. G. friends from giving us full technical information and proceeding in the normal manner with the commercial development in the United States. It is to be hoped that these difficulties will be surmounted in the near future, and we here desire to do everything possible to bring about that result.

In view of the very genuine spirit of cooperation which Dr. ter Meer displayed, I am convinced that it is not only the right thing to do, but the best thing from every standpoint to pass on to them full information on the copolymer at this time. I do not believe we have anything to lose by this which is comparable with the possible benefit to all of our interests.[90]

Standard's loyal observance of its Jasco obligations after eight years of frustration in its quest of Buna techniques for Jasco, when it had plain evidence of the commercial and political significance of those techniques, raises several nice questions in business diplomacy. Of course, under the Jasco Agreement, Standard was only a "junior partner" and was not in position to insist on transfer to Jasco, Inc., of any IG processes. The only obligation IG had assumed was to turn over to Jasco such of its "intermediate zone" processes as it might "desire" to exploit "outside of Germany."

Nevertheless, it was certainly contemplated in the Agreement that commercially promising "chemical developments" in this intermediate zone would be made available to Jasco. If, for political reasons, IG was not in position to carry out its, shall we say, moral obligations under the Agreement, would not ordinary business prudence have justified abrogation of the Agreement? Ordinarily, the intervention of *force majeure* (or its equivalent) preventing one party from full performance of a contract relieves the other.

In the light of the obligations it had assumed, the investments it had made, and the benefits it had already received, Standard's judgment on the issue of the expediency of abrogation is obviously better than that of an outsider. But it is fairly clear even to an outsider that the considerations at stake were broader than those immediately at issue. Several circumstances help to explain the tactics Standard actually followed, however maladroit they might appear on their face. Most important is the one referred to by implication in Frank Howard's letter quoted above. The phrase "all of our interests" covers a great deal, but it includes, first of all, Standard's interests as an oil refiner. In that sphere it had already obtained substan-

90. *Ibid.*, Ex. 47, p. 2906.

tial benefits from its cartel alliance with IG; and it stood to gain additionally from consummation of the comprehensive CRA (Catalytic Research Associates) agreement then under negotiation.[91] Second, by divulging Butyl information to IG in the face of IG's refusal to divulge information on Buna, Standard might strengthen its claim for eventual participation in an American synthetic rubber monopoly. For IG had not categorically refused to release Buna information and rights; it was only waiting for "permission" to do so.

Standard Renews Pleas for Buna

Standard still had hopes of getting Buna, and continued to urge IG to deliver the information. On April 20, 1938 Mr. Howard wrote Dr. ter Meer:

> My view is that we cannot safely delay definite steps looking toward the organization of our [Buna] business in the United States, with the cooperation of the people here [rubber manufacturers] who would be our strongest allies, beyond next fall—and even to obtain this much delay may not be too easy.[92]

He gave assurance, however, that "Dr. Hochschwender [of IG] and myself will do our very best to keep the situation here under control. . . ." On the same day he wrote to his associate, F. H. Bedford, who had requested direct action on Buna, advising him:

> Until we have this permission, however, there is absolutely nothing we can do, and we must be especially careful not to *make any move whatever* . . . *without the consent of our friends.* We know some of the difficulties they have both from business . . . interrelations with the rubber and chemical trades in the United States and from a national standpoint in Germany, but we do not know the whole situation. . . . The only thing we can do is to continue to press for authority to act, but in the meantime loyally preserve the restrictions they have put upon us.[93]

But the frustration of Standard's efforts to get IG's permission to proceed with the Buna development, and thus at least lay the groundwork for a domestic synthetic rubber industry, is not the only, or indeed the most significant, aspect of these Buna negotiations. The Jasco cartel agreement had so tied Standard's hands that it felt that

91. For a full story of the CRA episode, see *ibid.*, Pt. VII, pp. 3375-3426.
92. Truman, Pt. XI, Ex. 381, p. 4602.
93. *Ibid.*, Ex. 379, p. 4600. Italics supplied.

it could not, without IG's consent, undertake the commercial development, even in the United States, of Butyl, a product of its own laboratories.

In the spring of 1939, on the eve of one of Mr. Howard's periodic trips to Germany, one of his associates asked him to make suitable arrangements with IG to enable Standard to proceed with development of its co-polymer through "contact with . . . rubber companies." [94] Upon his return to the United States he reported, June 15, 1939, that "Dr. ter Meer has no objection to our taking up the copolymer [Butyl] with rubber manufacturers." [95] Mr. Howard seemed to interpret this as a concession, although under the express terms of the Jasco Agreement IG had forfeited any rights whatsoever in Butyl, either in the United States or elsewhere, by its failure to exercise its option within four months of March 15, 1938 when Standard had turned over to IG the Butyl technical data.[96]

Nevertheless, Mr. Howard was so impressed by his IG friends and so anxious "to give most careful consideration to their views" that he recommended delaying "for some two or three months . . . decision on taking the matter up with any rubber manufacturers." [97] His counsel prevailed in spite of the opposition of several other Standard officials.[98] Actually, it was not until fifteen months later, in September 1940, after the fall of France and on the solicitation of the Army and Navy Munitions Board, that Standard released its Butyl product to the rubber trade generally.[99]

The Hague Agreement

With the outbreak of war in Europe, the IG strategy in withholding Buna techniques from Standard had served its purpose in part. "Stalling" tactics could no longer prevent the use of IG's patent specifications in the countries at war with Germany. These countries were now free to seize these patents as enemy property. Moreover, it

94. Letter of H. W. Fisher to Frank Howard, May 5, 1939, Bone, Pt. VI, Ex. 148, p. 3034. Nine months earlier, Murphree had urged upon Russell (and other Standard executives) "the desirability of tying up with some rubber company in order to carry this development along more rapidly." *Ibid.*, Ex. 147, p. 3033.
95. *Ibid.*, Ex. 150, p. 3035.
96. Cf. testimony of Robert M. Hunter, *ibid.*, p. 2718.
97. *Ibid.*, Ex. 151, p. 3035.
98. See letters of June 19 and 22, 1939 to Howard from Murphree and Russell, respectively, *ibid.*, Exs. 151 and 152, p. 3035 f.
99. *Ibid.*, pp. 2722-46; Ex. 165, p. 3058; and Ex. 230, p. 3143. Firestone and U.S. Rubber were furnished samples for testing, however, in June 1940.

looked as if the United States would soon be drawn into the war. IG was prepared, in this situation, at last to release the Buna rights to Standard—for a consideration. But the value of the "know-how" was not affected by this turn of events. On that, IG continued to stall.

IG and Standard opened negotiations, and on September 25, 1939 they signed an agreement at the Hague providing for a *"modus vivendi"* during the war.[100] By this Agreement IG assigned to Standard, among other things, its patent rights on the Buna products and processes for use in the United States and the British and French empires and Irak.[101] IG retained exclusive rights to these processes in all the rest of the world.

Two features of the Hague Agreement stand out. First, Standard obtained no technical information on the compounding or manufacture of Buna rubbers.[102] Second, Article IV provided that "the parties shall exchange reports of their respective returns from the promotion of the said processes."

Standard's failure to get technical information is significant in the light of the general agreement among technicians that novel technical processes are likely to be so complicated that patents without the "know-how" ordinarily represent little more than a right to experiment. Apparently Standard at first assumed that, because the Jasco Agreement expressly stipulated that "know-how" should accompany all patents or processes transferred to Jasco, IG would supply this essential information. However, IG soon dissipated this illusion. On October 16, 1939 it cabled to Standard, "Referring to your question with respect to technical information about buna, we have to inform you that under present conditions we will not be able to give such information." [103]

---

100. By its express terms, as well as according to the interpretation placed upon it by Frank Howard, who conducted the negotiations for Standard, the Hague Agreement represented only a "readjustment" of the relations of the parties. It was not a divorce of Standard and IG, who by their own account had been "married" in 1929. As Mr. Howard stated in reporting the transaction to his chief, W. S. Farish, on October 12, 1939, "They delivered to me assignments of some 2000 foreign patents and we did our best to work out complete plans for a *modus vivendi* which would operate through the term of the war, *whether or not the US came in."* Truman, Pt. XI, Ex. 368, p. 4585. Italics supplied.

101. For text of the Agreement, see *ibid.,* Ex. 366, p. 4583.

102. As Dr. M. B. Hopkins, a Standard official, explained: "When Jasco took over the Buna development for the United States, the IG was not permitted by its government to give any technical information regarding the process except that contained in the patent disclosures." *Ibid.,* Ex. 382, p. 4605.

103. *Ibid.,* Ex. 412, p. 4639.

The object of the provision to exchange reports on returns was not left in doubt. The Hague Agreement explicitly declared that

. . . if it shall appear from such reports that the division of territory . . . between the parties . . . have [sic] not been equitable in its financial results *as judged by the agreement of September 30, 1930,* then the parties shall correct the inequity in such manner as may seem most fair and advantageous at the time.[104]

Plainly, the Hague Agreement did not end the basic relations of the parties. It merely changed temporarily control in exploiting the pooled processes in the intermediate zone between oil and chemicals. According to the Federal District Court, under the "real agreement" Standard was obligated to reconvey the Jasco patents at the end of World War II, or on demand, to IG.[105]

Standard to Consult du Pont on Buna Program

Although the express terms of the Hague Agreement did not include it, Standard had agreed to consult with du Pont, producer of Neoprene, before shaping its policies on the Buna development. IG's ter Meer reminded Standard's Howard of this on October 16, 1939: "As discussed between us we ask you to approach Wilmington before starting to exploit Buna patents." [106] Mr. Howard was somewhat more explicit in an interoffice memorandum of November 6, 1939. He declared: "We have assumed to the I. G. the obligation to discuss with the Du Pont Company the entire situation before deciding on our policy here." [107] Apparently Standard meticulously complied with this obligation. On November 14, 1939, Mr. Howard cabled to Dr. ter Meer, "Pursuant to my promise have discussed buna question with du Ponts before talking to others . . . We shall continue to keep in

---

104. *Ibid.*, p. 4583. Italics supplied.
105. The District Court for the Southern District of New York held that ". . . the so-called Hague Memorandum . . . was neither an accurate summary of the past dealings of [the] companies, nor a complete or faithful representation of the agreements made at the Hague. Its purported division of the world of Jasco patents upon a territorial basis *was not intended to be a binding agreement.*" Italics supplied. *Standard Oil Co.* v. *Markham* (*op. cit.,* p. 659). The court further stated: ". . . these transfers both of legal title and equitable interest [in Jasco and certain other patents] were to be null and void at the pleasure of IG, and the parties intended that after the War they would make whatever deal then seemed appropriate." *Ibid.*, p. 664.
106. Truman, Pt. XI, p. 4639.
107. *Ibid.*, p. 4640.

contact with them." [108] In judging the significance of this voluntary assumption by Standard of an obligation "to consult" du Pont, the reader should note (1) that du Pont was the established producer of a synthetic rubber technically comparable and potentially competitive with the Bunas, (2) that, according to Standard's own account, the ownership and control of Buna patents in the United States rested exclusively in its hands after September 1939,[109] and (3) that the licenses later offered by Standard were apparently designed to limit the use of these patents to the production of a relatively high-cost specialty rubber.[110]

While Standard at long last had obtained the Buna rights, it did not obtain them free from strings. IG retained a stake in any Buna development program in the United States.[111] First, it retained a contingent interest in any profits which might result therefrom. Second, it stood to gain indirectly from the stipulation that whatever program was worked out by Standard should not impair IG's relations with du Pont by prejudicing the latter's vested interest in the American synthetic rubber market.

Standard's Licensing Policy

To dominate this new industry, Standard formulated a licensing policy for rubber manufacturers that would have compelled them to forfeit to Standard all their own technical developments and to sell synthetic rubber at a price that would prevent its use except for high-cost specialty products. As outlined by Dr. Hopkins, a Standard official:

1. The rubber company takes a license to produce for consumption in its own products but not for sale otherwise. It gives us an option to buy one-fourth of its plant capacity for distribution to the trade generally.

108. See Bone, Pt. VI, p. 2933.
109. See *ibid.*, Pt. IX, p. 5065. Question: "You said you broke off relations with I. G. Farben in September 1939." Answer (by W. S. Farish): "My interpretation of the Hague agreement is that all official relations with the I. G. were severed at that time."
110. On the significance of the restrictive terms of the original Buna licenses which Standard offered the rubber companies, from the standpoint of the fulfillment of its "obligation" to du Pont (via IG), see text below.
111. Notwithstanding the statement to the contrary by Frank Howard, in announcing Standard's acquisition of Buna rights, to the American rubber manufacturers on November 6, 1939. He then flatly stated that "I. G. Farbenindustrie has withdrawn completely from participation in this Buna development in the United States." Bone, Pt. VI, p. 2678, and Ex. 79, p. 2933. Cf. also Exs. 80 B, C, and D, pp. 2933-35.

2. A high royalty rate (7.5 cents per pound) is fixed so as to make the operation practical for the rubber company only so long as the product is used as a relatively high-cost specialty.

3. The rubber company agrees to license back to us its improvements.[112]

These proposals were characterized by W. E. Currie, Standard's patent attorney, as follows:

The agreement as it is now drafted will lead to the centering of all patent rights of licensees in the hands of licensor, with no outflow of those rights except to customers of licensor. . . . All manufacturing patent rights of licensees will help to build up licensor's dominating position, but as licensee will get the benefit of any other licensee's manufacturing patent rights. In other words, this is not a cross licensing agreement, but one in which patents are piled on patents in the hands of one centralizing company.[113]

Goodyear and Goodrich appear to have reached a similar conclusion on their own account.[114] They declined to accept such onerous license terms. Eventually Standard brought an infringement suit against Goodrich in an effort to force the company to sign up.[115] The immediate purpose of Standard in adopting such a restrictive li-

---

112. Truman, Pt. XI, p. 4604; and Bone, Pt. VI, p. 2689. Dr. Hopkins added that in his opinion: "The effect of these terms is to limit rather drastically what the rubber companies may do under their license and to leave Jersey free to itself manufacture and sell, . . . or confine its activities to licensing and supplying raw materials."
Even these stringent licensing provisions were regarded by Standard as only a "stopgap." Frank Howard, in particular, was intent on drawing the "big four" rubber companies into a joint corporate enterprise for Buna production which would be under Standard's control. See Bone, Pt. VI, pp. 2963 and 2988; also, Truman, Pt. XI, p. 4608.

113. Truman, Pt. XI, Ex. 383, p. 4605. Frank Howard expressed a like view more tersely. Referring to the reluctance of the rubber companies to sign the proffered license, he said, "One cannot blame them for being critical of many of its provisions. . . ." Bone, Pt. VI, p. 2963.

114. On the other hand, Firestone in March 1940, and U.S. Rubber in June 1940, accepted the license. But these companies had less to lose by such a course than Goodyear and Goodrich. The former two were far less advanced in synthetic rubber technology than the latter two. Bone, Pt. VI, p. 2690, and Exs. 100-03, pp. 2965-67.

115. See *Rubber Age*, December 1941, p. 215; and Truman, Pt. XI, Ex. 387, p. 4609.
About a month before bringing suit, Standard's Hopkins advised Goodrich's Graham that formal notice of infringement would shortly be filed. He pointedly added: "I am writing to you personally in advance of this notice in the hope that the matter may be adjusted amicably through a completion of the earlier negotiations." Bone, Pt. VI, p. 3019.
The patent infringement suit was filed in October 1941, but never came to trial. With the outbreak of war in the Pacific, the government insisted on pooling technical experience and expediting the synthetic rubber program. The Patent Exchange Agreement of December 19, 1941, sponsored by Rubber Reserve, included a provision for the withdrawal of Standard's infringement suit. The issue became moot, in any case, after the consent decree was filed in the antitrust suit against Standard on March 25, 1942.

censing policy for Buna rubber was admitted by Dr. M. B. Hopkins in a letter of January 10, 1940 to the Goodrich Company.[116] He said: "Quite frankly, it was our intention that the license would not be a suitable one under which to operate if the licensee expected to go beyond producing a relatively high-cost specialty product." Apparently the ultimate purpose of this policy was to fulfill Standard's obligation to IG to respect du Pont's vested interest in the synthetic rubber market.

Pearl Harbor upset Standard's cartel-orientated policy for synthetic rubber development. To meet American war needs as expeditiously and as fully as possible, the Rubber Reserve Company, an RFC subsidiary, sponsored a patent exchange agreement, effective December 19, 1941. This arrangement made available to the principle rubber manufacturers, in addition to the techniques which several of them had developed, all Buna (but not Butyl) patents on more reasonable terms than Standard had previously offered them.[117] Shortly afterward the Department of Justice brought an antitrust action based on its investigation of the Standard-IG cartel agreements.[118] This proceeding was settled by a consent decree after the defendants had plead *nolo contendere* and paid fines. The decree released both Buna and Butyl processes for use by anyone, royalty-free during the emergency and subject to judicially determined "reasonable" royalties thereafter. Freed from cartel restrictions, the wartime synthetic rubber program overcame all obstacles and expanded production of rubber substitutes at a rate which was sufficient eventually to meet emergency needs.

116. Truman, Pt. XI, Ex. 385, p. 4608.
117. Even so, the royalty rate exacted by Standard, amounting to three quarters of one cent a pound, was high enough to have yielded, potentially, on a 400,000-tons-a-year output, $12 million annually. This is based on the assumption of double-royalty liability, which was implicit in the terms of Article II, Section 5, and Article IV, Section 2, of the Patent Exchange Agreement. This construction of these provisions is borne out by a press release of Standard itself on June 21, 1942. See *N.Y. Journal of Commerce*, June 22, 1942, p. 17.
118. *U.S.* v. *Standard Oil Co., et al.*, in U.S. District Court for the District of New Jersey, November Term, 1941, Criminal Action No. 682, Information filed March 25, 1942. On the same day, the defendants pleaded *nolo contendere* and paid fines. Thereupon the court entered final judgment in the form of a consent decree. The Information and the Final Judgment are reproduced in Truman, Pt. XI, at pp. 4693-4721 and pp. 4676-92, respectively. The text of the decree is also printed in Bone, Pt. VI, Ex. 10, p. 2862. Had it not been for the forfeiture of royalties on these processes, the American people might have been paying tribute to IG on virtually the entire synthetic rubber program developed to meet the exigencies of the war.

Du Pont–IG Relations

Like the Standard-IG relationship, du Pont's connection with the big German chemical combine had many facets. The common interest of the two companies in synthetic rubbers has been only one phase of their cartel tie-up, and indeed a minor one. Du Pont had a longer background of concerted arrangements with IG, or IG's predecessors, than had Standard. Long before du Pont had become a well-rounded chemical enterprise, when its interests were still centered almost exclusively in the manufacture of explosives, it had entered into cartel arrangements with Köln-Rottweil, one of the constituent concerns of the IG consolidation.[119]

These pacts were renewed from time to time, and as the range of du Pont's interests in the chemical industry expanded after World War I, similar adjustments with IG were worked out covering other products.[120] In seeking an accord mutually delimiting their respective interests in synthetic rubber, therefore, du Pont and IG were treading a familiar path.

Nevertheless, while they did not meet as strangers to compose rival interests, they did meet as traders jockeying for position. The du Pont–IG relationship differed from that of Standard and IG chiefly in the absence of any underlying foundation agreement uniting the parties in "marriage." Neither du Pont nor IG displayed such trustfulness toward the other as have Standard and IG. Nevertheless, through its relations with du Pont, IG succeeded in keeping the door open and except for the war might have eventually taken part in the American synthetic rubber industry on favorable terms.

Du Pont was a pioneer in the domestic synthetic rubber industry. After five years of intensive experimentation, it introduced Neoprene commercially in 1931.[121] Since then it has steadily expanded its productive capacity. According to du Pont, output has increased at an

119. Apparently the first comprehensive international cartel in this field was the so-called Jamesburg Agreement of 1897. See W. H. S. Stevens, "The Powder Trust," *Quarterly Journal of Economics* (Harvard University Press), Vol. XXVI (1912), p. 444.
The "IG consolidation" started as a restrictive sales agreement among a limited number of German chemical companies in 1905. It passed through many transformations and extensions in the next twenty years and was finally incorporated in 1925.

120. For example, in dyestuffs, nitrogen, celluloid, and artificial leather. Many of these cartel arrangements are reviewed in the chapters on chemicals.

121. Originally called Duprene, the co-polymer was renamed Neoprene in 1935. According to testimony before the Bone Committee, Duprene was brought out in 1932. Bone, Pt. VI, p. 2657. However, this is not in accord with our information.

average rate of 100 per cent annually with the exception of 1938.[122] It reached a rate of 10,000 tons annually a decade after the introduction of the new product and 20,000 tons annually at the end of 1942.

In spite of this quantity production, du Pont has sold its Neoprene at a relatively high price. In 1934, Neoprene sold for one dollar a pound, in 1938, 75 cents, and in 1942, 65 cents.[123] The product has commanded these high prices because of its superiority over natural rubber in a limited range of uses.[124] Du Pont apparently found it more profitable to concentrate on this high-price specialty market than to compete in a larger market with natural rubber.

Ordinarily the high price of Neoprene would have stimulated the competition of IG's Buna. The Nazi Government blocked this potential competition. Whether or not this embargo on Buna was disconcerting to it, IG certainly had a vital interest in preventing the growth of the American synthetic rubber market pending Buna's introduction here, either on a competitive or a cartel basis. Du Pont's price policy, by severely restricting the sales of Neoprene, kept open the potential market for Buna and limited IG's sacrifice in withholding its techniques. IG could afford, in this situation, to keep both Standard and du Pont "in suspense." [125]

IG Fears Neoprene

But to do this safely IG had to be sure that its Buna was technically on a par, at least, with du Pont's Neoprene. Lacking an intimate tie-up with du Pont, IG had recurring misgivings on this score. In the spring of 1934 and again in 1935, it became fearful of its position in synthetic rubber technology. IG's ter Meer declared in an interoffice letter of February 24, 1934 that

122. See testimony of E. R. Bridgewater in *Defense of the United States,* Hearings before Committee on Naval Affairs, U.S. Senate, 76th Cong., 3d sess., on S. 4082, p. 23 f. In 1938 an explosion in du Pont's plant, at Deepwater, New Jersey, stopped Neoprene production entirely for several months. American imports of IG's comparable synthetic, Perbunan, increased greatly during this period. This was not a competitive gesture by IG, however; it was an accommodation to du Pont's customers. Truman, Pt. XI, p. 4858; and Bone, Pt. VI, p. 2670.

123. See Bone, Pt. VI, p. 2892; Truman, Pt. XI, p. 4857.

124. See Bone, Pt. VI, p. 2892. The outstanding advantage of Neoprene is its oil-resistant property, adapting it to such incidental uses as gasoline-pump hose. *Ibid.,* p. 2896. In 1942, in response to war demands, du Pont expanded its capacity greatly by building a new plant at Louisville.

125. The phrase is IG's in an interoffice letter of November 12, 1934, referring to negotiations with du Pont. Truman, Pt. XI, p. 4848.

. . . it can be said even today that Duprene will be a much cheaper product, so that, assuming that the qualities of the two products are alike, it will emerge victorious from the competitive struggle. . . . This situation, it seems to me, compels us to continue the negotiations initiated by Dupont . . . and to conduct them with a view to reach a broad agreement in the field of synthetic rubber, exchange of licenses being the final aim.[126]

A letter of March 1, 1934 from IG to its American representative, Dr. Hochschwender, says: "Our position in relation to Du Pont is considered unfavorable in the field of synthetic rubber products. We should try, therefore, to reach a broad understanding in this field." [127]

The key to IG's apprehension was du Pont's patented technique for converting acetylene to chloroprene, the monomer of Neoprene. Chloroprene is one form of butadiene, the basic monomer of all Buna-type rubbers. Dr. Krauch of IG has aptly described this process as "the short and elegant way, discovered by Du Pont, from acetylene to Butadiene." [128] IG in turn had an improved process for the production of acetylene in which du Pont was keenly interested.[129] IG was aware of this interest and used it as leverage in negotiations with du Pont, which began early in 1934. An IG memorandum reporting a conference in Germany with two du Pont executives (Ewing and Wardenburg) on May 18, 1934 states:

Du Pont was looking for a process of manufacturing acetylene as cheaply as possible, because Du Pont believed that acetylene was steadily increasing in importance in synthetic chemistry. He mentioned the part which acetylene had recently begun to play as the basic product for Duprene and for acid to be used in the manufacture of acetylcellulose . . . Dr. Krauch pointed out that the process of manufacture of acetylene from coal hydrogen by way of the luminous arc—which process IG was trying out in Baton Rouge in an experimental plant in conjunction with Standard—had been developed to such an extent that it was now available for practical use.[130]

126. Bone, Pt. VI, p. 2890. See also the reply to this letter, from Dr. Krauch. "I regret very much, as you do, that despite the great effort that it has exerted in this field, IG is apparently limping behind Du Pont." *Ibid.* This letter was dated February 28, 1934 on the very eve of the public announcement by IG of its Buna rubber!
127. *Ibid.,* p. 2891.
128. Letter of February 28, 1934 to ter Meer, *ibid.,* p. 2891.
129. IG had turned this process over to Jasco in 1930. It was the main element in the so-called E project which Standard and IG had developed at Baton Rouge. In spite of its demonstrated economy, they abandoned it in 1935, as we have seen, because of the objections of Union Carbide & Carbon, with which IG had cartel connections in other chemical fields. The process, sometimes referred to as the luminous-arc process, converted natural or refinery gases into acetylene by passing them through an electric arc. The older and more costly process used by UC&C derives acetylene from carbide.
130. Bone, Pt. VI, p. 2892.

The negotiations thus inaugurated continued intermittently during the next four years, waxing and waning principally with IG's interest in du Pont's monovinylacetylene (MVA) process for the production of chloroprene. In the fall of 1935, IG sent its Buna specialist, Dr. ter Meer, to this country to "work out a deal." Initially, Dr. ter Meer acquainted IG's "junior partner" with his plans. Frank Howard of Standard has reported the view of "one of the strongest men in the I. G. executive organization" as follows:

> Our I. G. friends have been following closely the development of the Du Pont's synthetic rubber product, Duprene, or chloroprene. . . . The opinion of our I. G. friends is that for immediate purposes chloroprene is a more promising commercial synthetic product than their own product . . . Dr. ter Meer proposes to endeavor to work out a deal with the du Ponts to take over the Duprene development for Germany. His hope is to substitute the Duprene development for the projected thousand-ton per month development of his own process. . . .
> There is a possibility of finding some common ground between du Pont and ourselves on the Duprene development in the United States through the Jasco arc acetylene process. Acetylene is the raw material for Duprene and we believe that the Baton Rouge E project has a good chance of turning out to be the lowest cost acetylene producer in the world. . . . du Ponts are very much interested in this process of ours and recognize its possibilities.[131]

In a conference of November 5, 1935 with du Pont officials, Dr. ter Meer reached an amicable understanding on a synthetic rubber program. This procedure was in line with a "gentlemen's agreement" of March 6, 1930, one part of which an IG official summarized as follows:

> If . . . products or chemicals will be produced that are now commercially manufactured by the Du Pont interests, the Standard and IG would discuss same with the Du Pont Co. and endeavor to find a way in which the commercial exploitation of such processes and products would best be carried on to the greatest benefit of each of the three parties.[132]

Du Pont–IG Reach a Compromise

The outcome of the 1935 conference was a compromise. Neither

131. Letter of Frank Howard to W. C. Teagle, October 9, 1935, *ibid.*, pp. 2895-97.
It is possible, of course, that Dr. ter Meer was insincere in his statements. Conceivably, he may have been trying to provide a plausible excuse for the persistent IG "stalling" on the transfer of Buna processes to Jasco. However, he had expressed almost identical views eighteen months earlier in a letter to another IG official, when he could have had no possible motive for dissimulation.
132. Truman, Pt. XI, p. 4647. For a slightly different version, see Bone, Pt. V, p. 2350.

party got just what it wanted. IG offered du Pont the arc acetylene process on condition that it merge its Neoprene development with IG's Buna techniques in a joint enterprise with Standard and IG, each party taking a one-third interest.[133] Du Pont rejected this minority status. The accord reached apparently represented simply a renunciation by both parties of any program or policy calculated to disturb the status quo.[134]

Negotiations continued, however, looking toward a broad agreement for exchange of patents and processes. Throughout the negotiations du Pont insisted on the protection of its "prior preferred" position in the domestic market as the pioneer commercial producer of synthetic rubber in the United States. IG wanted to obtain as much as it could for its Buna processes but it was committed by the gentlemen's agreement not to offer Buna-type rubber competitively in the American market, to the prejudice of du Pont's Neoprene rights. Apparently the negotiators had reached a stalemate. On one point only were they fully agreed: to keep the promising synthetic rubber market from getting out of control. The unresolved issues were: who should control what, and where?

Eventually, in 1938, IG obtained the German rights to "the short and elegant way, developed by Du Pont" for producing butadiene, the monovinylacetylene process.[135] This MVA agreement provided for an exchange of licenses covering basic processes for making monovinylacetylene and certain derivatives, including butadiene. Neither party licensed the other, however, to use these processes in the production of rubber-like substances comparable to its own co-polymers. In other words, du Pont received licenses under IG's United States patents in this field for use, among other things, in producing Neoprene, but not Buna; and IG received licenses under du Pont's Ger-

133. See letter of Dr. ter Meer to Mr. Howard, November 8, 1935, Bone, Pt. VI, p. 2897.

134. This conclusion follows from the whole course of dealing of the parties in the next five years. One specific reference to the arrangement is in a note by Frank Howard on a conference with IG in Frankfort, Germany, September 8, 1937. "I. G. cannot very well export Buna N without clearing with Du Pont who withdrew Isoprene in late 1935." *Ibid.*, p. 2903.

Apparently, Mr. Howard wrote "Isoprene" by mistake. He is obviously referring to Neoprene.

135. See *U.S.* v. *Imperial Chemical Industries*, in U.S. District Court for the Southern District of New York, Civil Action No. 24-13, Complaint filed January 6, 1944, Appendix, Agreement of June 30, 1939, Schedule A, p. 20. The original contract was dated June 23, 1938; but the final agreement was signed September 14, 1938.

man patents (on MVA) for use, among other things, in producing
Buna, but not Neoprene. Royalties were payable to du Pont alone.
This apparently indicates agreement by both parties that the du Pont
rights were more valuable than IG's.

Presumably, in view of du Pont's settled policy in patent bargaining, it received something more than mere royalty payments in consideration of the transfer to IG of its basic monovinylacetylene
process. What was the real *quid pro quo?* No precise answer is
possible.

But the large number of points of contact between the business
interests of the parties suggests that the compensating advantages
may have been made up of several elements. The bargaining points
raised at one time or another during the extended negotiations leading to the MVA agreement, and the continuous adjustment of
operating policies not only between du Pont and IG but also between
IG and other American chemical companies, offer some clues to the
broader considerations involved in this transaction—as in other
phases of their gentlemen's agreement. Over and above royalty payments, du Pont received benefits from: (1) continued postponement
of Buna production in the United States;[136] (2) continued abstention
from the American synthetic nitrogen market by IG;[137] (3) access to
IG's developments in the field of plastics;[138] and (4) recognition of

---

136. On April 4, 1938 Frank Howard wrote Mr. Bedford of Standard regarding
IG's commitments to du Pont: "Our partners have had certain discussions with the
Du Pont Company concerning the licensing of Duprene in Germany, and it may be as
a result of this situation that some arrangement will have to be made with the Du
Pont Company." Truman, Pt. XI, p. 4601. This was two months prior to the conclusion of the MVA agreement.
   Eighteen months later when Standard secured the Buna patent rights on the outbreak
of war, it was bound by IG's prior commitments to "consult" du Pont before ventur-
ing to use them. *Ibid.,* p. 4640 f.
   137. See Chapter 4 on nitrogen. On the 1930 episode, in particular, see Truman,
Pt. XI, pp. 4646-47.
   138. See Chapter 9. Before the gentlemen's agreement of November 1935, du Pont
apparently worked in the plastics field quite independently of IG. The latter had an
American "partner" in one sector of this field in which du Pont had a keen interest as
a producer of lucite plastics. By a contract of October 30, 1934, Röhm & Haas, of
Philadelphia, had secured exclusive American rights from IG in the acrylate field, with
a strict limitation of product fields, in accordance with the usual custom. Truman, Pt.
XI, p. 4654. In March 1936, du Pont concluded a cross-licensing agreement with Röhm
& Haas whereby the parties shared on an agreed basis certain methyl-methacrylate
techniques. Bone, Pt. II, p. 819. While this agreement excluded rights in the Plexi-
glas field, du Pont acquired a share in this important field also by a supplementary agreement of November 17, 1939. *Ibid.,* p. 836.
   Walter Hutchinson testified before the Bone Committee that this 1939 contract also
provided for du Pont's access to another IG plastics process, relating to mixtures of
vinylchlorides and methyl-methacrylates. See *ibid.,* p. 672. Possibly this contract was

its prior claims in the acetic acid field.[139] Numerous other phases of du Pont–IG technical collaboration are developed in the chapter on chemical cartels, but the above list indicates the wide range of fields in which du Pont may have found compensation for its release to IG of the basic technique in Neoprene production.

CONCLUSIONS

Two aspects of the synthetic rubber cartel differentiate it from ordinary cartel arrangements: its amorphous character and its dynamic thrust. The restrictions worked out by the parties were not confined merely to limitations mutually imposed upon their respective activities *in the synthetic rubber industry*. The consideration for privileges obtained or concessions made took the form, more often than otherwise, of commitments relating to other fields of enterprise in which the parties were engaged. Unlike the ordinary cartel—which is concerned simply with investment, output, and pricing policies in some specific field—the operations of the synthetic rubber cartel affected at almost every step the business of one or another of the parties in spheres having only slight connection with synthetic rubber.

---

preliminary to du Pont's polyvinylchlorides agreement with IG in 1940. See Corwin D. Edwards, *Economic and Political Aspects of International Cartels*, Monograph No. 1 of the Subcommittee on War Mobilization, Committee on Military Affairs, U.S. Senate, pursuant to S.Res. 107, 78th Cong., 2d sess. (Washington, 1944), p. 63. However, the formal contract of November 1939 contains no reference to this purported settlement.

Patent interference proceedings in the methyl-methacrylate plastics field were pending between Röhm & Haas and du Pont in 1936, and settlement of this controversy was the ostensible occasion for the original cross-licensing agreement. Whether Röhm & Haas as exclusive licensee made these concessions without subtle pressure from IG is not clear. It is clear, however, that as early as July 1935 Mr. Haas had indicated an unwillingness to share the field with du Pont. Mr. Haas said that, in conference with Mr. Wardenburg of du Pont, "I told him the history of our Acrylic and Methacrylic development and told him quite frankly that we have spent a lot of money and effort in several fields, for instance in the laminated glass field, and that we would not like to see Du Ponts come in under a license." See Bone, Pt. II, pp. 816-17.

139. This was revealed in the negotiations between IG and Hercules on a license for the latter, to use IG's process to produce acetic anhydride. An IG letter of April 1, 1936, states: "In the course of the negotiations which ter Meer had recently in the United States with du Pont concerning Duprene rubber, the question was discussed as to whether du Pont was interested in our experience in the field of acetic acid anhydride and acetyl cellulose. After a relatively superficial examination, du Pont answered this question in the negative and said they had no objection to I. G. licensing its patents in the United States. . . . Dr. ter Meer thinks that another conference with du Pont should be held. Ter Meer feels that when du Pont said they had no objection to our granting licenses to third parties in the field of acetyl cellulose and acetic acid anhydride, du Pont did not have in mind that we would grant licenses . . . to . . . companies which had not theretofore been active in this field." See Bone, Pt. III, p. 1505.

Standard's position in the cartel was conditioned throughout by its primary interest in oil refining, du Pont's by its primary interest in the chemical industries, and IG's by its business interests in both fields, but also by a desire to promote German nationalism. These widely diverse interests of each of the parties outside of synthetic rubber were so intricately tied together that every transaction among them almost had to take into consideration incidental or contingent effects upon other matters. As a rule these "side reactions" came from technical interdependence or from commercial integration.

The dynamic thrust of the cartel is shown, in the case of du Pont–IG relations, by the steady succession of mutual accommodations—in the absence of anything corresponding to the usual foundation agreement. No document set the "metes and bounds" of the cartel. The parties did not specify in advance what should go into the common pool or their shares in control. The rights and obligations of the parties were defined in a series of steps, as exigencies demanded. These arrangements had direct antecedents reaching as far back as 1897, in the case of du Pont, and at least to 1927 in the case of Standard. Standard Oil has all along emphasized that the essence of the cartel was in the "genuine spirit of cooperation" among the partners.[140] Thus the cartel was a growing enterprise, not a static condition. It changed from year to year, not only under the impact of new technical discoveries, but also in response to subtle changes in the strategic business position of the parties and in the political conditions in which they operated.

The Final Score: U.S. v. Germany

As the ultimate outcome of this decade-long series of interlacing cartel activities, IG had obtained, by playing off one American enterprise against another:

(1) the basic Neoprene process (from du Pont)
(2) the Butyl process (from Standard)
(3) the retardation of Buna development in the United States
(4) the postponement of Butyl development in the United States
(5) the curtailment of output and capacity in a number of other

---

140. See letter of Frank Howard to R. P. Russell, March 15, 1938, *ibid.*, Pt. VI, Ex. 47, p. 2906; letter of Frank Howard to A. C. Minton, October 16, 1939, *ibid.*, Ex. 70, p. 2921; and letter of Frank Howard to F. H. Bedford, April 20, 1938, Truman, Pt. XI, Ex. 379, p. 4600.

branches of the chemical industries, including especially those of acetic acid and synthetic nitrogen

As against these tangible benefits to the German partner, the American associates could claim certain benefits for themselves. The du Pont score included, at a minimum:

(1) protection of its domestic Neoprene market
(2) protection of its synthetic nitrogen interests
(3) acquisition of "preferential options" and "special participations" in certain segments of the general field of plastics

The Standard score included:

(1) control of hydrogenation and catalytic-cracking processes in oil refining, outside of Germany
(2) exclusive licenses for Buna, Vistanex, and Paratone processes in the United States and the British and French empires
(3) control of Butyl development in these same territories

Standard claims that, had it not been for its agreements with IG, the United States would not have got the use of many important patented processes and the essential "know-how," and that industrial progress in the chemical and petroleum fields would have been seriously retarded.[141] But this is conjecture. In evaluating it, one should take account of the fact that the American market is the largest in the world. Barring the opposition of its government, IG could scarcely have afforded to keep out of it.[142] That IG did actually release some of its processes to Standard (hydrogenation, catalytic cracking, Paraflow, synthetic methanol), under a broad arrangement dividing markets and fields and restricting competition, does not mean that it would have barred their use in America if it had not found a partner willing to use them on the terms to which Standard agreed.

141. See *ibid.*, Pt. IX, p. 5038 f.
142. It might be argued, of course, that IG could have exploited the American market on a straight export basis. By selling its German-made products here through American distributors, instead of through its own subsidiaries or agencies, IG might develop a substantial trade, while holding its techniques entirely to itself.
Several factors work against such a strategy in this sphere. (1) IG had no important petroleum holdings either in the United States or elsewhere. If it was to utilize effectively its know-how in petroleum technology, from a practical standpoint, an alliance with an oil company was necessary. (2) Tariff barriers were obstacles to exploiting the American market from abroad, and they were subject to sudden and drastic changes which made the risk of such a strategy formidable. Moreover, political disadvantages attend the exploitation of patents by corporations not domiciled in the land where the patented product is sold.

Presumably such terms as Standard accepted were essential to insure Standard such control as it did obtain of the patents and "know-how" released by IG. Presumably also they would have come to America through other hands and on other terms if Standard had not got them. Undoubtedly IG tried to drive the best bargain possible. With almost equal certainty, if it had not reached an agreement with Standard, IG would have accepted the best alternative.

The dye industry is a case in point. In the early twenties du Pont had planned to extend its operations in the dye field, and wanted rights to IG's patents and processes. When du Pont found unacceptable the terms on which IG offered them, it went ahead in its own way. IG also proceeded independently to utilize its "know-how" in the rich American market. [143]

Americans at a Disadvantage

The advantages obtained by du Pont and Standard were all in the nature of monopolistic privileges. Aside from any limitations imposed by the antitrust laws,[144] they stood to profit from these cartel maneuvers, perhaps as much as IG stood to gain, from the purely commercial standpoint. But from the military strategic standpoint, the score was plainly lopsided. This is not to say that these American business representatives were personally unpatriotic. It is simply to recognize that they were the exponents of a system which in theory fostered the competitive interests of business, subject mainly to private responsibility, but which in practice gave paramount consideration to the monopolistic interests of business, subject to a minimum of public responsibility. The men with whom they dealt were not simon-pure businessmen, like themselves, intent predominantly on advancing their private interests. A totalitarian state in

143. For a detailed discussion of the effects of these cartel arrangements on the pattern of control and the course of American development in the petroleum and chemical fields, see Chapter 11.

144. The antitrust action against Standard for taking part in the cartel led to pleas of *nolo contendere*, payment of fines, and the entry of a consent decree on March 25, 1942 that enjoined similar activities in the future and deprived Standard of some of its privileges as a patentee under the patents exchanged with IG. (Cited above.) The Department of Justice has not directly attacked the du Pont–IG agreements. However, several phases of du Pont–IG relations are indirectly involved in the ICI case (cited above) and in the Röhm & Haas case (*U.S.* v. *Röhm & Haas,* in U.S. District Court for the District of New Jersey, Criminal Action No. 877-C, Indictment returned August 10, 1942). In both of these cases du Pont was one of the defendants. The latter was a criminal prosecution and the trial resulted in a verdict of acquittal on June 20, 1945. See New York *Times,* June 21, 1945, p. 1.

Germany had effectively subordinated private business interests to its aggressive nationalistic designs.[145] Standard's German partner was, in fact if not in law, an arm of the state, and was deliberately used as an instrument of economic warfare.

Standard Oil and du Pont officials, acting as the "plenipotentiaries" of American business but having no direct responsibility to protect or advance the interests of national defense, were severely handicapped in dealing with the business representatives of a foreign totalitarian state. They were at an obvious disadvantage. Under American law they could not speak with one voice. Though technologically and financially strong, strategically they were vulnerable. The Americans, like the Germans, put first things first; but what was first to one—a good business bargain—was only second to the other.

So far as synthetic rubber developments alone are concerned, the Americans gave the fruits of American technical progress, such as they were, to their German cartel partner but received only empty promises and barren patent specifications in return.[146] The record is plain: the cartel system retarded the development of a domestic synthetic rubber industry, and, in so doing, jeopardized national security.

145. The full scope and degree of the participation of the leaders of German industry in the Nazi program of political and military aggression is only gradually coming to light. AMG has recently disclosed some significant information on this subject obtained in the course of its investigations in the American area of occupation. See the testimony of Colonel Bernard Bernstein, director of the AMG division of investigation of cartels and external assets, before the Senate (Kilgore) Subcommittee of the Committee on Military Affairs, December 11, 1945. New York *Times,* December 12, 1945, p. 3; and New York *World-Telegram,* December 13, 1945, Financial Section.

146. This statement is limited specifically to the synthetic rubber field. Regarding Butyl, Standard officials have sometimes asserted it was a purely American development "entirely independent of any other synthetic rubber development from this country or abroad." (Dr. Per K. Frolich, head of Esso Laboratories, in an article in the *India Rubber World* of July 1, 1940, quoted in Bone, Pt. IX, p. 5233.) Mr. Asbury has testified to the same effect. "I would not say that we got Butyl from I. G." Bone, Pt. IX, p. 5163. On the other hand, W. S. Farish flatly declares, "From I. G. we also got Butyl rubber, potentially the most important of all synthetic rubbers." *Ibid.,* p. 5159.

The truth would seem to be somewhere between these contradictory contentions. IG apparently had not recognized its isobutylene-polymerizing techniques as a basis for a vulcanizable synthetic rubber.

Chapter 4

NITROGEN: A PROBLEM IN POLITICAL AND ECONOMIC CONTROL

LEGEND HAS IT that the nitrate beds of what is now northern Chile were discovered by a Peruvian Indian who observed that the ground melted and ran like a stream where he had made a fire on the salty earth of the desert. Awed by this strange and unaccountable behavior, he hastened to report it to his curé. This man of God promptly called it the work of the devil—a revelation of the fires of hell. Nevertheless, good seems immediately to have come of it, for the priest, after having examined a sample of this bedeviled soil, threw it into his garden. To his great surprise, he found that his plants flourished as never before.

Whether or not this legend is true, Chilean nitrate deposits, the sole source of natural sodium nitrate, became the basis of both life-giving and death-dealing activities. As an essential plant food, nitrogen has greatly increased crop yields and has permitted a growing population to be continuously better fed and better clothed. In high explosives and propellants it has permitted warring nations to bring death and destruction on an unprecedented scale. In peace it has also served industry well. It is used in modern refrigerants, industrial explosives, nitric acid, dyes, plastics, and a score of other industrial products.

Until World War I the natural deposits of Chile and byproduct ammonia, from the manufacture of coke and coal gas, were the chief sources of nitrogen. Of these two major sources, Chilean nitrate was the more important. In spite of the phenomenal growth of the iron and steel industry (a principal source of byproduct ammonia) in the last half of the nineteenth century, Chile accounted for approximately two thirds of the world's output of chemical nitrogen during the first decade of the present century.

Natural Nitrate Deposits

Chilean nitrogen occurs as nitrate of soda ($NaNO_3$) mixed with other chemical compounds, chief of which is common salt with smaller amounts of magnesium, calcium, and iodine. Only the nitrogen and iodine are commercially recoverable. These mixed constituents, together with insoluble clays and sands amounting to about 45 per cent, make up the deposits which are locally known as *caliche*. They are found in an area about 400 miles long and from 50 to 90 miles wide at elevations varying from 4,000 to 9,000 feet in northern Chile. The *caliche* forms a rocky layer usually from one to four feet below the surface and from one to fifteen feet thick with perhaps an average thickness of four feet. The sodium nitrate content has sometimes run as high as 60 per cent in handpicked specimens, but its usual range in recent years has been from 10 to 30 per cent.

Until World War I the *caliche* was mined by hand, without preliminary stripping of the overlying materials. The miner simply drilled a hole into the deposit, inserted a charge of black powder, and set off the blast. He then sorted the *caliche* out of the rubble, broke up the larger chunks, and stacked the stuff or loaded it directly into mule carts or small pit cars for transportation to the near-by refinery. Refining methods were only slightly less primitive. Using the so-called Shanks process, each proprietor of a mining lease ordinarily operated his own refinery. The *caliche* was first crushed and then dumped into an iron tank containing water with a capacity, ordinarily, of about 65 tons. The salt solution in the tank was heated by steam, which was circulated under low pressure in coiled pipes. The solution passed through a series of such tanks with gradually diminishing temperatures, which resulted in the separation and purification of the sodium nitrate and sodium iodide. In its essence, the Shanks process depended simply on the differences in solubility of the various salts and impurities and on the tendency of the former to crystallize at different temperatures. After separation, the nitrate of soda was stacked for further drying by evaporation and then sacked for shipment.

Development of the Chilean Industry

Commercial exploitation of the Chilean deposits began early in the nineteenth century. The first shipment for foreign markets was made in 1830 but the industry remained relatively unimportant until about 1880. During the next three decades production multiplied tenfold. World War I, with its insatiable demand for munitions, further swelled output. During the first half century of the industry, Peru, Bolivia, and Chile shared control of the deposits. Progress in scientific knowledge of plant food requirements enhanced the economic significance of the deposits and generated international disputes over their control. Friction, between Chile on the one hand and Bolivia and Peru on the other, finally culminated in the War of the Pacific (1870–1882). Victor in the conflict, Chile eventually established undisputed sovereignty over the world's sole source of sodium nitrate.[1] These vast deposits of readily accessible *caliche* became the basis for Chile's most important industry, gave to her a unique position in world trade, and for more than a half century were her principal source of national revenue.

Shortly after Chile had won the War of the Pacific, the government levied an export tax equivalent to approximately $12 a metric ton on all nitrate shipments. From its inauguration to World War I, the export tax represented from 30 to 70 per cent of the selling price of nitrate of soda at Chilean ports. As long as the Chilean producers met little competition in world markets no organized groups urged modification of the tax, and it remained unchanged for almost fifty years. During this period it yielded the government the equivalent of about one billion dollars in gold. From 1880 to 1930 receipts from the tax averaged 42.8 per cent of the government's ordinary revenue. The proportion was highest in 1894, when 68 per cent of public revenues came from this source.[2]

Competition Gives Way to Cartels

In spite of the export tax the demand for Chilean nitrate of soda continued to expand with only occasional interruptions until the close of World War I. Output tended to expand even more rapidly. Although the Chilean Government exercised its monopoly power to tax foreign consumers of its nitrate of soda, at first it encouraged

1. A series of treaties extending from 1884 to 1896 extended Chilean sovereignty over all nitrate-producing areas. *Nitrate Facts and Figures,* compiled by A. F. B. James, London, 1904, p. 5. This is primarily a statistical review of the Chilean industry, published annually from 1904 to 1929.
2. U.S. Tariff Commission, Report No. 114, Ser. II, *Chemical Nitrogen,* Washington, 1937, p. 107.

decentralization in production. The *caliche* deposits were readily accessible and large enough to supply world demands for many decades. Shortly after securing undisputed possession of them Chile opened its nitrate lands to private exploitation and periodically auctioned off many blocks to producers who independently exploited them. Neither technology nor capital requirements offered a serious obstacle to new enterprisers. The result was a continuous increase in the number of nitrate-producing establishments.[3] By 1901 the producers numbered seventy-eight. A decade later the number of establishments had doubled.

Although exports of nitrate of soda showed an almost uninterrupted increase, productive capacity of refineries expanded more rapidly than world consumption. To cope with this situation the Chilean producers entered into a series of agreements to restrict output. Between June 1884 and January 1914 they made six such agreements.[4] While these agreements differed in details, the essential features of all were: (1) allocating a basic quota to each establishment; (2) determining annually the total amount of nitrate of soda to be exported; (3) determining for each establishment allowable exports as a percentage of its basic quotas (as the number of quota-bearing establishments increased, to hold exports within total allowable it was necessary to reduce each establishment's percentage share); (4) penalties for exceeding quotas; (5) reduction of quota of any producer who failed to produce amount allowed; (6) permission to an owner of more than one establishment to apportion allowables among his several establishments as he wished.[5]

Restrictions Self-Defeating

Although these early loose cartel arrangements were designed primarily to raise prices by restricting output, they proved self-defeating and were periodically dissolved. By raising prices above a competitive level, they tended to prevent disappearance of high-cost pro-

---

3. An establishment denotes a refinery for the separation of nitrate of soda from other salts which are intermixed with it and the refinery's complement of nitrate deposits, which are ordinarily under the same ownership.

4. The periods covered by these agreements were as follows: June 1884 to December 31, 1886; January 1, 1891 to March 31, 1894; January 1, 1896 to October 1, 1897; April 1, 1901 to March 31, 1906; April 1, 1906 to March 31, 1909; August 31, 1913 to January 31, 1914. See Federal Trade Commission, *The Fertilizer Industry*, Washington, 1916, p. 23.

5. *Ibid.*, pp. 23-24.

ducers. By guaranteeing to every establishment an export quota, they brought an influx of new producers and encouraged old producers to construct new plants and expand capacity.

The fragmentary statistical material available on the Chilean industry before World War I bears out these generalizations. Except for the short-lived cartel of 1913–1914, the organization of each cartel before the first world war signalled an advance in prices. Not all the cartels were equally successful in maintaining the higher price schedules, but in every instance the ending of a cartel was followed by lower prices. Average annual prices reached a record low in 1898 at $22.34 a ton f.a.s. Chilean ports after the third cartel had ended in 1897. With the fourth cartel average annual prices advanced from $25.05 for 1900 to $40.53 a ton for 1906— more than 60 per cent. During the fifth cartel they reached a twenty-five-year high in 1907 at $41.40. The cartel was unable to hold prices at this level, however, and average annual prices declined to $36.15 for 1908.

As prices advanced during the fourth cartel the number of quota-bearing establishments increased sharply. For the fertilizer year ending March 1902, seventy-eight establishments had received quotas. When the agreement expired in 1906 the number had risen to 112. Before the end of the first year of the fifth agreement, the number of quota-bearing establishments had increased further to 124, only 105 of which were in operation. In March 1909, when the fifth agreement expired, 146 establishments held quotas, only 118 of which were operating. During the last year of this agreement allowable exports represented only 48 per cent of the basic quotas. Potential supply had become so great as to preclude a renewal of the agreement.[6]

As the number of establishments increased it became more difficult to enforce cartel regulations. Cartel prices declined sharply in the latter part of 1907 with the advent of world-wide depression. The decline continued throughout the cartel's life. Average prices for 1909 were 21 per cent below the 1907 peak. A sixth cartel formed just before World War I lasted only a few months. The results of the comparatively free market after collapse of the fifth cartel were salutary from the point of view of both consumers and low-cost pro-

6. For price data see Table 9. Data on the number of establishments from James, *op. cit., passim.*

TABLE 9

AVERAGE ANNUAL PRICE, CHILEAN NITRATE OF SODA, F.A.S. CHILEAN PORTS

1880–1918 and 1919/20–1933/34 [a]

(Price in U.S. Dollars Per Ton of 2,000 Pounds)

Calendar Year	Price	Calendar Year	Price	Calendar Year	Price	Nitrate Year Ending June 30	Price
1880	$47.05	1893	$28.40	1906	$40.53	1919/20	$49.66
1881	49.53	1894	28.71	1907	41.40	1920/21	78.49
1882	37.68	1895	25.92	1908	36.15	1921/22	51.88
1883	32.27	1896	26.81	1909	32.70	1922/23	43.91
1884	31.06	1897	24.97	1910	32.93	1923/24	44.60
1885	33.68	1898	22.34	1911	35.14	1924/25	44.55
1886	39.25	1899	23.41	1912	38.20	1925/26	43.12
1887	26.53	1900	25.05	1913	37.55	1926/27	42.59
1888	28.80	1901	30.07	1914	33.40	1927/28	37.18
1889	27.35	1902	31.12	1915	33.12	1928/29	36.78
1890	23.88	1903	31.20	1916	36.74	1929/30	34.20
1891	26.22	1904	34.60	1917	60.13	1930/31	28.82
1892	28.32	1905	36.40	1918	58.21	1931/32	22.32
						1932/33	18.87
						1933/34	18.80

Sources: *Sinopsis Geográfico-Estadística de la República de Chile*, 1933, p. 205, and U.S. Tariff Commission, Report No. 114, Ser. II, *Chemical Nitrogen*, Washington, 1937, p. 116.

a. Converted from Chilean pesos of 6 pence gold per hundred kilos to U.S. dollars per ton of 2,000 pounds by U.S. Tariff Commission.

ducers. Exports during 1910, the first year of the free market, expanded by about 20 per cent.[7] The number of establishments in operation decreased. Since this presumably meant closing down high-cost plants, average production costs in operating establishments must have declined sharply.

Cartels Made for Inefficiency

For almost half a century a continually expanding demand for nitrogenous fertilizers and control schemes designed to insure monopoly prices brought a prosperity to the Chilean nitrate industry, only temporarily interrupted by market glut and severe price de-

7. Data are derived from statistical material compiled by James, *op. cit., passim.*

clines.[8] These same influences, however, had developed serious structural weaknesses within the industry. They had offered little incentive to improve methods of production. On the contrary, they had perpetuated an inefficient technique, encouraged waste, and saddled the industry with obsolete and redundant productive facilities.

Under the prevailing methods of mining by hand, from 15 to 25 per cent of the total nitrate in the *caliche* was lost—left in the field, mixed up with the rubble of blasted overburden. Moreover, it was profitable to work by hand methods only the richer deposits. Those containing no more than 10 per cent of nitrate of soda, those having a relatively thin layer of *caliche,* and those overlaid with a relatively thick cover of barren rock might be wasted even though adjacent to an operating refinery. Refining by the Shanks process was likewise wasteful.[9] Experts have characterized this process as "technically weak and inefficient." The refining resulted in recovery of only about 65 per cent of the processed nitrate. Thus out of every ton of available nitrate in the *caliche* worked, with about 20 per cent of the nitrate unclaimed in the mining process and a 35 per cent loss in the refining process, barely half of the contained nitrogen was recovered. Waste of heat energy in the refining process also contributed to high production costs. A mining engineer associated with Guggenheim Brothers described these wastes and their causes at the Institute of Politics, Williamstown, Massachusetts, in August 1926, as follows:

This exceedingly low recovery is undoubtedly due to the fact that the method used today, both in mining and in recovery, is essentially the method used fifty years ago. In dealing with *caliche* containing 50 per cent of nitrate, it was economically possible to discard low grade and fine material on the

8. For data on capital, earnings, and dividends, consult *ibid., passim;* see also B. B. Wallace and L. R. Edminster, *International Control of Raw Materials,* The Brookings Institution, Washington, 1930, Chap. 2; Bureau of Foreign and Domestic Commerce, Trade Information Bulletin No. 170, *Nitrogen Survey,* Pt. I, "The Cost of Chilean Nitrate," Washington, 1924, p. 40.

9. Since the middle twenties, the Shanks process has been in part superseded by the Guggenheim process. For a discussion of the technical aspects of the Chilean nitrate industry, consult: H. A. Curtis (ed.), *Fixed Nitrogen,* Monograph Series, No. 59, American Chemical Society, Chemical Catalogue Co., New York, 1932, Chap. 3, "The Chilean Nitrate Industry"; Bureau of Foreign and Domestic Commerce, *Nitrogen Survey,* Pt. I; J. R. Partington and L. H. Parker, *The Nitrogen Industry,* Constable & Co., London, 1922, rev. ed. 1940; M. B. Donald, "History of the Chilean Nitrate Industry," *Annals of Science,* London, Vol. I, pp. 29-47 and 193-216; National Fertilizer Association, *World Conditions as to Mineral Raw Materials for the Fertilizer Industry,* Addresses delivered at the Meeting of Institute of Politics, Williamstown (Mass.), August 12-14, 1926, sections on nitrogen, particularly the paper by P. Mayer, "The Technology of Chilean Nitrate," and that by B. Cohen, "Chilean Nitrate World Trade."

pampa and to discharge to the tailings dumps 6 per cent of the nitrate and still make a creditable technical and economic showing, but with materials of as low grade as that worked today this method of work is no longer profitable.

Until very recently the Chilean nitrate industry, though not enjoying an absolute monopoly of the world's supply of inorganic nitrogenous material, nevertheless furnished so large a proportion thereof that it was able to fix the price for such material. It was consequently able to discount its loss in technical efficiency by increasing the price of its product, and the result of this advantage has been that, except in minor details, it has made no great technical progress.[10]

Byproduct Nitrogen

Paradoxically, World War I brought to the Chilean industry a new prosperity and at the same time laid the basis for its decay. During the war, demand increased sharply and prices rose abruptly. At the same time, however, the production of byproduct ammonia [11] expanded greatly and the exigent demand and high prices accelerated the commercial development of synthetic nitrogen. Scientists turned to the inexhaustible atmosphere, of which nitrogen constitutes 75.5 per cent by weight, as a new source of supply.

The world output of byproduct nitrogen, derived from the destructive distillation of coal in the manufacture of coke and in the production of artificial gas, was 312,500 tons in 1913. This represented slightly over 36 per cent of total world production of nitrogen. It compared with 472,700 tons of nitrogen, representing 55 per cent of total world output, produced by Chile as nitrate of soda. (See Table 10.) The world war not only hastened the substitution of byproduct coke ovens for the wasteful beehive oven, but it greatly expanded the production of coke and hence that of byproduct nitrogen.

By 1918 the output of byproduct nitrogen had increased to 402,400 tons while Chilean nitrogen had increased to only 487,500 tons. This trend continued throughout the twenties. It accompanied an increase in the percentage of American coke made in byproduct ovens from 5.2 in 1900 to more than 94 in 1930.[12] As fertilizer consumption was sharply reduced with the depression in 1921–1922 the world output

10. Mayer, *op. cit.*, pp. 157-58.
11. Ammonia (NH_3) is a colorless gas composed of nitrogen and hydrogen. It is easily reduced to a liquid by cold and pressure, or when treated with sulphuric acid is readily converted to sulphate of ammonia.
12. Tariff Commission, *op. cit.*, p. 179.

TABLE 10

WORLD PRODUCTION OF CHEMICAL NITROGEN BY TYPES OF
PROCESS AND WORLD CAPACITY

1900–1937

(In Thousands of Tons of 2,000 Pounds of Nitrogen)

Year	Chilean Nitrate	Byproduct Nitrogen	Cyanamide Nitrogen	Synthetic Nitrogen [a]	Total Production	World Capacity
1900	220.0	110.0	—	—	330.0	379.5
1901	234.3	110.0	—	—	344.3	385.0
1902	236.5	115.5	—	—	352.0	396.0
1903	253.4	124.2	—	—	377.6	412.5
1904	265.8	136.7	—	—	402.5	456.5
1905	299.2	147.3	—	—	446.5	484.0
1906	310.6	164.7	0.1	—	475.4	577.5
1907	314.8	205.8	.3	0.2	521.1	616.0
1908	337.4	197.2	.5	1.1	536.2	671.0
1909	359.9	209.0	2.5	1.8	573.2	715.0
1910	420.3	226.6	4.5	5.1	656.5	896.5
1911	429.9	246.8	12.0	8.1	696.8	902.0
1912	440.8	277.2	28.3	9.8	756.1	935.0
1913	472.7	312.5	42.0	24.2	851.4	962.5
1914	420.0	283.7	45.6	29.6	778.9	1,001.0
1915	299.3	301.3	55.5	38.5	694.6	1,067.0
1916	496.6	336.9	87.7	76.8	998.0	1,232.0
1917	511.7	365.7	95.0	124.0	1,096.4	1,342.0
1918	487.5	402.4	98.0	171.7	1,159.6	1,507.0
1919	290.4	287.9	100.2	147.4	825.9	1,562.0
1920	430.2	318.3	103.5	141.8	993.8	1,551.0
1921	223.3	275.3	113.0	186.2	797.8	1,540.0
1922	182.6	324.3	116.2	248.8	871.9	1,523.5
1923	324.5	356.9	112.5	270.6	1,064.5	1,617.0
1924	412.4	352.3	120.5	355.5	1,240.7	1,715.0
1925	433.4	368.6	145.7	432.3	1,380.0	1,900.0
1926	346.1	397.6	181.5	552.4	1,477.6	2,065.0
1927	277.0	440.3	207.9	703.1	1,628.3	2,392.0
1928	543.1	466.9	214.5	944.9	2,169.4	2,757.0
1929	554.8	496.6	250.7	1,102.1	2,404.2	3,278.0
1930	419.7	476.5	255.6	1,019.0	2,170.8	3,917.0
1931	193.2	397.2	184.6	991.0	1,766.0	4,448.0
1932	120.1	345.9	166.7	1,149.1	1,781.8	4,788.0
1933	75.6	356.6	198.5	1,264.1	1,894.8	4,955.0
1934	144.8	396.7	235.0	1,347.7	2,124.2	5,082.3
1935	205.0	434.3	275.6	1,545.4	2,460.3	—
1936	219.4	498.2	308.6	1,779.1	2,805.3	—
1937	237.0	519.2	328.5	1,988.5	3,073.2	—

Sources: U.S. Tariff Commission, Report No. 114, Ser. II, *Chemical Nitrogen,* Washington, 1937, p. 60, and by letter.

a. Includes the output of arc process and synthetic ammonia plants.

of byproduct nitrogen exceeded for the first time Chilean output.[13] Although Chile's output of nitrate of soda exceeded world production of byproduct nitrogen during the middle twenties, this initial shift in primacy signalized Chile's eclipse as the dominant element in the fixed nitrogen market. At the bottom of the Great Depression in 1933, the world output of byproduct nitrogen was almost five times Chilean nitrogen production.

Synthetic Nitrogen

The role of synthetic nitrogen in displacing Chilean nitrate is even more striking. During the first decade of the twentieth century circumstances were peculiarly favorable for the birth of this new industry. Dismal predictions by Sir William Crookes had spread the false notion that the Chilean deposits, although immediately adequate to meet world demand, would soon be exhausted.[14] The Chilean export tax and control schemes had raised the prices of Chilean nitrate. The cartels had perpetuated an inefficient technique. National leaders, particularly those of Germany, were reluctant to depend on a single distant source of supply of nitrates, indispensable for modern warfare. Finally, businessmen were beginning to appreciate the importance of scientific research, particularly electrochemical research, as a means of expanding industrial horizons and increasing business profits. All these circumstances stimulated search for a new source of nitrogen.[15]

This search had made substantial progress by the outbreak of World War I. In 1913 world production of synthetic nitrogen by all processes reached 66,200 tons—about 7.7 per cent of the total fixed nitrogen output. (See Table 10.) By 1918 synthetic production had

13. Byproduct nitrogen from the coking ovens of the steel industry tends to fluctuate with general business activity. The output from public utility gas works is far more stable. This accounts largely for the comparatively slight decline in byproduct output during depression years. From the standpoint of potential expansibility of supplies both sources of byproduct nitrogen are extremely inelastic, once the limit of installed coking ovens capacity has been reached.

14. Bureau of Foreign and Domestic Commerce, *Nitrogen Survey*, Pt. I, p. 41.

15. For a more complete discussion of technical developments in the nitrogen industry, see: Partington and Parker, *op. cit.;* J. Enrique Zanetti, *The Significance of Nitrogen,* The Chemical Foundation, Inc., New York, 1932; Bureau of Foreign and Domestic Commerce, Trade Information Bulletin No. 266, *Nitrogen Survey,* Pt. II, "General Review of the Nitrogen Situation in the United States"; Trade Information Bulletin No. 240, Pt. III, "The Air Nitrogen Process"; Trade Information Bulletin No. 270, Pt. IV, "The Nitrogen Situation in European Countries"; and Tariff Commission, *op. cit.* The last represents the most recent and most comprehensive available study of developments in the world nitrogen industry.

expanded to 269,700 tons and was 23 per cent of total output.

Germany was the major producer. The Allied blockade had cut off its Chilean supply. Germany's munitions requirements and increased reliance on domestic agriculture for food supplies had virtually forced it to expand domestic capacity for the production of synthetic nitrogen. Though at the outset Germany's synthetic nitrogen industry received substantial government subsidies, it soon became self-sustaining. Private enterprise pushed to completion the plants under construction when the Armistice was signed, and in 1925 Germany produced more than 560,000 tons of synthetic and byproduct nitrogen, 30 per cent more than Chilean output in the same year. German consumption in 1925 was over 413,557 tons, while German exports were 152,000 tons. Germany's imports were negligible.[16] Not only had Chile lost its most important prewar market, but it now had to meet German competition elsewhere in the world market.

Although during World War I all the major warring countries had taken steps to supplement their supplies of Chilean nitrate by domestically produced synthetic nitrogen, only Germany succeeded in achieving national self-sufficiency. After the war, German producers aggressively entered export markets. Chilean producers had previously supplied these markets at noncompetitive prices. Instead of meeting German competition by a reduction of the export tax and pricing nitrate of soda on a competitive basis, thereby checking further expansion of the German industry and discouraging similar developments in other countries, Chile clung tenaciously to its prewar policy. The government refused to reduce the export tax. Private producers promptly resumed the controls which they had temporarily abandoned during the war.

The Chilean Nitrate Producer's Association

In 1919 the Chilean Nitrate Producer's Association was organized, embracing all the major Chilean producers. Through the Association producers undertook to limit and allocate output and fix the price in world markets. The Chilean Government played an active role both in inaugurating and supporting this program. The statutes of the Association received official approval on July 2, 1919 and again on February 10, 1921. They provided that the President of Chile should

16. Tariff Commission, *op. cit.*, p. 131.

appoint four of the Association's eighteen directors. Since the law required an affirmative vote of 80 per cent of directors present in determining prices, the government could veto price action if it so desired.[17]

The Association owned no plants, shipped no nitrate, and made no profits. It acted, however, as a selling agent for all producers, who, in turn, were bound to make no sales except through the Association or at the price determined by it. Every producer was assigned a sales quota in accordance with which orders were distributed. Producers could sell their quotas to other producers, and this seems to have been a common practice. Many plants were shut down, but their owners continued to receive an income from the sale of their quotas. Payments for the nonuse of capacity became a part of production costs. After a sharp drop in prices following World War I during the depression of 1921–1922, the price of nitrate of soda was stabilized through 1927 at a level somewhat higher than the highest price at which it had sold during any prewar year since the eighties, although below that of the war period. (See Table 9.)

The "Nitrogen Rush"

This policy inevitably encouraged a further expansion of synthetic capacity, not only in Germany but throughout the industrial world. Expanding demand and relatively high prices, caused in part by the Chilean export tax and the restriction of output, contributed to a "nitrogen rush." During 1926–1934, additions to world nitrogen capacity, almost wholly synthetic, were more than 150 per cent greater than the total annual capacity developed in the industry's first hundred years. (See Table 10.)

Two other factors besides Chilean price policy contributed powerfully to this development: (1) the rapid advance of chemical technology, and (2) the determination of national governments, spurred by the example of Germany, to rid themselves from dependence on foreign sources of supply for this indispensable war material.

The advance in chemical technology was along a broad front. Three processes for deriving nitrogen from the air had been developed before World War I—the arc process, the cyanamide process,

17. Price agreements were temporarily abandoned in February 1927. A new agreement was made on September 21, 1928 on the initiative of the government.

and the synthetic ammonia process. First, but ultimately of least importance, was the arc process. It consisted of passing an electric spark through the air, causing a combination between the oxygen and nitrogen which was absorbed in water to yield nitric acid. By 1902 a plant was in operation at Niagara Falls for the production of nitrogen by this process. But it proved costly, and the promoters abandoned the enterprise.

Second, and of far greater commercial importance after World War I, was the production of cyanamide by passing atmospheric nitrogen over calcium carbide at high temperature in an electric furnace. Since the commercial success of this process depends on cheap electric power, it has been employed primarily in conjunction with large-scale hydroelectric developments. Norway was a pioneer in the process, the Odda Smeltewerk A. S. having begun operations in 1908. However, by 1937 this concern had a reported annual capacity of only 16,500 short tons of nitrogen.[18]

Another early cyanamide project was that of the American Cyanamid Company. This company constructed a plant at Niagara Falls, Canada, which has operated continuously since 1909. Production by this process has also developed in a limited way in other countries, even without benefit of cheap power—for example, in Germany, Japan, France, and Poland. Immediately before World War I, total world capacity for the production of nitrogen as cyanamide was about 70,000 tons. By 1924, primarily as a result of expansion during the war, capacity had increased to 250,000 tons.[19] In the next decade, the cyanamide branch of the industry shared in the "nitrogen rush," and capacity was again more than doubled.

Synthetic Ammonia

Last in point of time, but destined to contribute most to the "nitrogen rush" and ultimately to top world output, was the process for producing synthetic ammonia (NH_3) by combining nitrogen and hydrogen at high temperatures under great pressure in the presence of a catalyst. Germany had relied primarily on this technique—the Haber-Bosch process—for overcoming the military handicap of the blockade and providing itself with nitrogen for World War I.

18. Tariff Commission, *op. cit.*, pp. 24, 38, 162-65; Bureau of Foreign and Domestic Commerce, *Nitrogen Survey*, Pt. IV, pp. 39-40,
19. Tariff Commission, *op. cit.*, p. 62,

While German scientists were pioneers in the search for newer and cheaper ways of obtaining nitrogen, scientists in other countries were not idle. Many roads, and more numerous bypaths, might lead to a chemical nitrogen industry with the atmosphere as source of supply. As technical knowledge and industrial experience advanced along a broad front, as scientists learned more of the behavior of chemicals under diverse conditions of pressure, temperature, and catalysis, as they became better acquainted with the caprice of molecules, they discovered several ways to domesticate atmospheric nitrogen. Before the "nitrogen rush" was over, at least six commercially successful variants of the original Haber-Bosch process were in use. While basically alike, they differ as to: (1) source of hydrogen,[20] (2) method of separating the nitrogen from the air, (3) pressure and temperature in the reaction chamber, (4) method of removing ammonia from the system, and, perhaps above all, (5) the type of catalyst used.

Governments Promote Synthetic Industry

National states bent upon economic self-sufficiency to achieve national survival and political security assisted the scientists and businessmen. The role of the governments differed, of course, from country to country. Assistance to the nitrogen industry has been both direct and indirect. In some instances nitrogen plants are state owned: wholly so in Russia; in large part in Hungary, Poland, and Czechoslovakia; and to a lesser extent in the Netherlands and France. Most of the more important industrial countries have utilized tariffs to promote domestic production, and some have granted direct subsidies, notably for the completion by private capital of nitrogen ventures undertaken by the government during World War I.[21]

20. Hydrogen may be obtained from (1) the electrolysis of brine, (2) coke oven gas, (3) water gas, or (4) natural or refinery gases. The cost of hydrogen, an important element in the cost of nitrogen fixation, may vary greatly depending on its source. Companies obtaining hydrogen as a byproduct in electrolytic production of chlorine or in petroleum refining apparently have a distinct advantage over other synthetic producers.

21. For example, the British Government made capital advances for plant construction and granted subsidies for research. It assisted Synthetic Ammonia & Nitrates, Ltd., in completing the synthetic ammonia plant begun by the government during the war at Billingham-on-Tees near Stockton. This plant was acquired by Imperial Chemical Industries, Ltd., upon its formation in 1926, and it has since become the second largest chemical plant in the world. It was designed not merely to produce nitrogen but to convert its five primary raw materials, coal, water, air, salt, and anhydrite, into some fifteen or twenty heavy chemicals essential to the fertilizer, munitions, dyestuffs, glass, fuel, and a wide array of other industries.

In the United States, on the other hand, the synthetic nitrogen industry developed without special state aid, direct or indirect.[22]

Capacity Outruns Consumption

Although national governments, for political reasons, assisted the nitrogen expansion program of the late twenties directly and indirectly, businessmen for the most part carried out the program apparently upon the assumption that the manufacture and sale of synthetic nitrogen would be profitable at the prevailing level of prices. The apparent success of the German industry supported this view. Germany had not only become self-sufficient but was an important exporter. Businessmen seem to have recognized that in domestic markets they would have a great advantage in transportation costs over Chilean production, remote from the major consuming areas.

Moreover, in many countries this expansion was part of a more extensive program involving developments over a broad chemical field. The sale of nitrogen was not its sole aim. In some instances chemical companies wished to provide a market for a chemical by-product already being produced; in others, to control the source of materials that they used in their related manufacturing operations. In general they sought to fortify their commercial position as producers of a wide variety of products under diverse chemical processes.[23] Numerous independent business units each making its own estimates, under a wide variety of cost and marketing conditions, of the probable gains from making nitrogen took part in the expansion program. No over-all supervisory or control agency planned it. By the time it was completed, world productive capacity had far out-

22. Under the National Defense Act of June 1916 the government constructed a cyanamide plant and a smaller synthetic ammonia plant at Muscle Shoals at a cost of over $80 million exclusive of hydroelectric facilities. However, the plants were only partially completed before the end of the war and, after a two-week trial run in January 1919, were placed in a stand-by condition. Thereafter they remained idle until recent modernization. See Tariff Commission, op. cit., p. 183.

The Fixed Nitrogen Laboratory of the Department of Agriculture also developed the "American" process for making synthetic nitrogen. Despite this government interest, largely war-inspired, in synthetic nitrogen production, businessmen in search of profits developed the American industry on their own responsibility with neither direct state subsidies nor tariff protection, except for byproduct ammonium sulphate, which was protected by a tariff duty of $5 a ton from 1922 to 1930.

23. E.g., Allied Chemical & Dye Corporation by making sodium nitrate broadened the market for its sodium; du Pont by entering the nitrogen field got a source of nitrogen, free of foreign controls, for its lacquers and explosives; Pennsylvania Salt Manufacturing Company by producing nitrogen got an outlet for the byproduct hydrogen from its electrolytic chlorine plant.

stripped consumption, the upward trend of which was temporarily reversed during the Great Depression. By 1929 total world capacity for the production of nitrogen by all processes was 3,278,000 tons, while total consumption of nitrogen was only 2,102,584 tons. In 1934 world productive capacity had increased to 5,082,300 tons, whereas world consumption, after a dip during the period 1930 to 1933, was only slightly above the 1929 figure. (See Tables 10 and 11.)

In 1934, 64 per cent of world capacity, 3,231,800 tons, was for the production of nitrogen as synthetic ammonia. This, together with cyanamide capacity (539,000 tons), represented almost 75 per cent of world total.[24] When the "nitrogen rush" had subsided, Chile had to meet the competition of Germany, Great Britain, Belgium, Norway, Canada, and the Netherlands, all net exporters of nitrogen. The United States, France, Japan, Russia, and Italy had made substantial progress toward economic self-sufficiency. Poland, Yugoslavia, Czechoslovakia, and Manchuria were also important producers. Switzerland, Sweden, Spain, South Africa, Hungary, and Roumania had made beginnings.

The Guggenheim Process

Not only had the Chilean control program encouraged new sources outside of Chile, but it had perpetuated at home an inefficient, wasteful, high-cost method of production. No producer had introduced a major technological innovation in the Chilean industry from its birth until the "nitrogen rush." It would be difficult to find a better illustration of how monopoly may retard technological advance. As world capacity outside of Chilean control expanded, the natural nitrate industry faced the necessity of adopting new techniques if it was to survive.

A new technique was at hand. Guggenheim Brothers, whose interest in the nitrate industry dates back to the early twenties, had developed at much expense an improved process for treating copper ores. Having determined that the process could be adapted to the refining of Chilean nitrate ores, they acquired extensive interests in the Chilean nitrate industry through the Anglo-Chilean Consolidated Nitrate Corporation (Delaware) and the Lautaro Nitrate Company,

24. Tariff Commission, op. cit., p. 62.

TABLE 11

ESTIMATED WORLD CONSUMPTION OF CHEMICAL NITROGEN
FOR SPECIFIED YEARS

1913–1937

(In Tons of 2,000 Pounds of Nitrogen Content)

Year	Amount	Year	Amount
1913	808,030	1931	1,747,152
1924	1,214,840	1932	1,816,252
1925	1,324,565	1933	1,984,982
1926	1,443,662	1934	2,171,730
1927	1,654,800	1935	2,481,600
1928	1,932,959	1936	2,844,600
1929	2,102,584	1937	3,081,100
1930	1,964,655		

Sources: Tariff Commission, Report No. 114, Ser. II, *Chemical Nitrogen*, Washington, 1937, p. 63, and by letter.

Ltd. In November 1926 they completed a plant, with an annual capacity of 540,000 tons, the Maria Elena, for producing nitrate of soda by this new process. Later they constructed a second plant with an annual capacity of about 750,000 tons.[25]

Although it involves a larger capital investment per unit of capacity than the Shanks process, the Guggenheim process costs less per unit of product—when plant operations are close to capacity. It overcomes the outstanding shortcomings of the Shanks process: excessive heat requirements, heavy losses of nitrate, and much manual labor. Under the Guggenheim process, the ore, after having been pulverized, is treated in a series of tanks with graduated strengths of mother liquor circulated at a temperature of about 40° C. The nitrate, which has gone into solution, is then precipitated in two stages in a series of tanks in which the temperature is finally reduced to about 5° C. The heat energy is derived from heat interchangers, operated in connection with the ammonia condensers which cool the crystallizing tanks, and from the exhaust gases and radiator water from the Diesel engines which supply electric power for plant operations.

With more efficient recovery the Guggenheim process permits the

25. *Ibid.*, p. 121. These capacity figures are in terms of metric tons of nitrate of soda. Approximately equivalent figures in terms of short tons of contained nitrogen would be, respectively, 93,000 tons and 129,000 tons.

use of lower-grade ores, and this in turn permits the utilization of mechanical techniques in mining and handling the ore. The labor cost per unit of output is estimated to be less than one sixth of that required for hand mining. The unit cost of production, exclusive of capital costs, is reported to be from 50 to 60 per cent of that by the Shanks process.[26]

The Guggenheim process came too late, however, to stem the "nitrogen rush." It served merely to swell still further the industry's over-all capacity. In the face of world-wide expansion, the Chilean price control program proved ineffective. A bunghole might have been stopped but the gates had been opened. The flood swept prices rapidly to new low levels. Despite an increase in annual world consumption of nitrogen of about 900,000 tons, or 75 per cent, from 1924 to 1929 (see Table 11), the price of Chilean nitrate of soda declined 20 per cent, from $44.60 for the fertilizer year ending in June 1924 to $36.78 five years later. By 1934 the price had sunk to $18.80. (See Table 9.)

Chile Reorganizes Its Nitrate Industry

Although Imperial Chemical Industries, Ltd., leading British synthetic nitrogen producer, and I. G. Farbenindustrie A. G., leading German producer, had entered a cartel agreement in 1929 to which the Chilean producers subscribed, in an effort to reverse the price trend, Chile's situation continued to deteriorate. By the spring of 1930 it had become so bad that the Chilean Government undertook to reorganize completely the domestic industry. The Guggenheim interests cooperated closely with the government in this venture, if indeed they did not initiate it.[27]

The Guggenheims had an important stake in the Chilean indus-

26. A report to the British and French preferred shareholders of the Lautaro Nitrate Company, Ltd., on June 27, 1932 indicated that the cost at the Maria Elena plant was $8.00 a metric ton and at the Pedro de Valdivia plant, $7.00 a metric ton. This compared with a cost at the Brac plant, using the Shanks process, of $14.40 a ton, at Prosperidad of $15.05 a ton, and an average cost at nine other Shanks plants of $13.60. Of the plants using the Shanks process only the Condo plant utilizing exceptionally rich ores had a cost approaching that of the Guggenheim process. Cost at this plant was $9.60 a metric ton. *Ibid.,* p. 121.

27. See the report of the subcommittee of the Chilean congressional committee investigating acts of the Ibañez dictatorship, published in *El Mercurio* (Santiago), November 8, 1931, and translated in *Hearings on Sale of Foreign Bonds or Securities in the United States,* before the Senate Finance Committee, 72d Cong., 1st sess., Pt. IV, pp. 2051-67.

try. They had backed the Anglo-Chilean Consolidated Nitrate Corporation, which began operations in 1926 with a heavy capitalization, including a bonded indebtedness of $34 million.[28] It had promptly fallen upon evil days. With a productive capacity far in excess of its annual output and with prices of nitrate of soda rapidly declining, it had accumulated a deficit by June 1930 of nearly $11 million.[29] Although it had been able to reduce its funded debt during this period by some $3.5 million, its balance sheet showed cash advances by Guggenheim Brothers of over $25 million.

Under these circumstances the Guggenheim interests naturally welcomed a reorganization of the industry which promised to place the obligations of Anglo-Chilean on a sounder basis. The Chilean Government also had reasons to favor reorganization. The industry had demanded that the export tax be reduced so as to improve its competitive position in world markets. Moreover, government representatives recognized the generally unstable situation confronting the world nitrogen industry with capacity far in excess of consumption and prices rapidly declining. If Chile were to maintain her place in world markets, production costs must be lowered. While total world consumption of nitrogen reached a new peak during the 1929–1930 fertilizer year, world consumption of Chilean nitrogen reached its postwar peak a year earlier and by 1930 had declined by about 13 per cent.[30]

Whether the Guggenheim interests or the Chilean Government took the initiative in reorganizing the Chilean nitrate industry is not clear. In any event Pablo Ramirez, representing the Chilean Government, and E. A. Cappelen Smith, president of the Anglo-Chilean Consolidated Nitrate Corporation, jointly pushed the undertaking in the spring of 1930.

Cosach Is Organized

The reorganization plan as finally approved by government statute provided for a single, gigantic corporation to control the industry.[31]

28. *Moody's Manual of Investments* (Industrials), 1927, p. 2283.
29. *Ibid.*, 1931, p. 2889.
30. Tariff Commission, *op. cit.*, p. 68.
31. See Chilean Law No. 4863 of July 21, 1930. The charter was to run for sixty years, subject to extension by legislative approval. See Charles A. Thompson, "Chile Struggles for National Recovery," *Foreign Policy Reports*, Foreign Policy Association, New York, February 14, 1934, Vol. IX, No. 25, p. 289; also, Tariff Commission, *op. cit.*, p. 118.

Compañía de Salitre de Chile, popularly known as Cosach, was incorporated on March 20, 1931. It acquired control of about 95 per cent of all Chilean nitrate production facilities. The equity in the major part of these assets was represented by the shares of the two large Guggenheim companies, Anglo-Chilean Consolidated and Lautaro; a smaller part, by the shares of thirty-four independent companies. Cosach obtained all the share capital of these thirty-six companies in exchange for part of its own capital stock. It also obtained from the Chilean Government, in exchange for another part of its capital stock, nitrate reserves estimated to contain 150 million tons of recoverable nitrate, which, added to the deposits owned by the private companies it absorbed, gave it control of upwards of 250 million tons in all. Only fourteen small companies remained outside the consolidation.

Cosach's authorized capitalization consisted of 5 million shares of preferred stock and 25 million shares of common stock, divided into two classes, Series A (15 million shares) and Series B (10 million shares).[32] Since each class of stock had a par value of 100 pesos, the total nominal capitalization amounted to the equivalent of $365 million. In addition, Cosach was authorized to issue approximately $50 million of prior-lien bonds and $70 million of junior bonds.[33] The consolidation also guaranteed outstanding bonds of its constituent companies, amounting to $77,205,193.[34] The par value of securities issued or guaranteed by Cosach amounted to nearly $600 million. This was a transaction in high finance, even as judged by the standards of more highly industrialized countries.

32. The preferred stock and the Series B common stock all went to the constituent companies, in exchange for their shares. The Series A stock was issued to the Chilean Government in consideration of its transfer of mining rights in the public domain and of its undertaking to substitute for the traditional export tax a tax on Cosach's net income. This income tax was limited, moreover, to a rate of 6 per cent annually.

33. The senior issue was for working capital, organization expenses, and the acquisition from Guggenheim Brothers of $27 million of notes of Anglo-Chilean Consolidated Nitrate Corporation, representing cash advances they had made to that company. Of the junior issue, slightly over $40 million went to the Chilean Government in settlement of tax liabilities of the underlying companies. These claims rested on the government's deferment of export tax collections during the two-year period of declining markets before the organization of Cosach. The remainder of the junior bonds provided the means of paying certain debts of the constituent companies and of acquiring other properties.

All of these bonds were protected by a tax on nitrate production, amounting to sixty gold pesos a ton. See *Hearings on Sale of Foreign Bonds or Securities*, pp. 2045 and 2059; also, *Moody's Manual of Investments* (Industrials), 1931, p. 2888.

34. See Guillermo A. Suro, "The Reorganization of the Chilean Nitrate Industry," *Bulletin of the Pan-American Union*, May 1931, p. 515.

In organizing Cosach, private and public interests had joined to form a state monopoly. Under the law creating it, Cosach was to be administered by a board of directors composed of twelve members, of whom four, representing the holders of A shares (i.e., the Chilean Government), were to be selected by the President of Chile and the remaining eight by the holders of B shares.[35] Nominally, control apparently rested with private shareholders, the owners of B stock. The law provided, however, that in matters affecting the national interest the directors representing the government could veto any resolution supported by the representatives of B shares. More specifically, it required the support of government representatives in fixing the prices of nitrate of soda and in approving a limitation of production to less than the average of total sales during the preceding three years.[36]

Cosach Fails

Cosach came upon unhappy days from the outset. It could hardly have turned out otherwise. It was launched at the beginning of the Great Depression. Cosach promptly encountered shrunken markets and a severe drop in prices. The decline in the volume and value of nitrate exports and in state revenues had serious repercussions on the whole Chilean economy, contributed to acute political instability, and stirred bitter and vigorous denunciation of Cosach.

Its critics claimed that Chile had sold its birthright for a mess of pottage. They charged that Cosach was designed primarily to pull Guggenheim chestnuts out of the fire. They pointed out that the Guggenheim venture had accumulated nothing but deficits from the outset, that these had grown to tremendous amounts, that the Guggenheims had found it necessary to make cash advances to Anglo-Chilean of approximately $25 million, and that these obligations had been assumed by Cosach and been given priority in its capital structure. They alleged that Cosach had been heavily overcapitalized, with excessive valuation of the Guggenheim process and of other assets whose profit-producing potentialities had been grossly overrated.

35. The office of president and general manager was to be filled by a vote of three fourths of the directors. This official need not be a member of the board, but if he was not, he had no right to vote.
36. See Article XIX of Law No. 4863, translated in *Hearings on Sale of Foreign Bonds or Securities,* p. 2072. In computing the sales in the base period, the amount sold by plants not controlled by Cosach was to be deducted.

The critics contended that the plan could yield no revenue to the government, and that the fixed charges were so heavy they could only result in Cosach's ultimate bankruptcy. To cover fixed charges alone would require exports of from 2.5 to 3 million tons (contained nitrogen equivalent, 175,000-205,000 tons) and a price of not less than $40 a ton, whereas in 1930–1931, the year of Cosach's organization, actual sales had totalled only 1.6 million tons (contained nitrogen equivalent, 113,000 tons) and price had fallen to $28.81. The critics argued that concentration of production on the highly mechanized Guggenheim plants was socially undesirable, creating as it did an acute unemployment problem. They vigorously denounced the plan as sacrificing human values to material considerations.[37]

By 1932 Chilean production of nitrate of soda had declined to 120,100 tons of nitrogen—less than one fourth of 1929 output, and price had sunk by almost 40 per cent. (See Tables 9 and 10.) The political and economic burden was heavier than Cosach could bear. In fact, it seems to have been heavier than the Chilean Government could bear. Chilean economic life is dependent to an unusual degree upon its foreign trade.[38] This trade has been dominated by mineral products, chiefly nitrates and copper, which together normally constitute from 70 to 80 per cent of the country's exports. In value, Chilean exports had declined by more than 60 per cent between 1929 and 1931 and its imports had declined by almost as much.[39]

Cosach Is Dissolved

The political repercussions of this development are reflected in seven changes of president in Chile between July 1931 and January 1933, generally without benefit of election. In October 1932, however, Arturo Alessandri, former President, was elected again for a six-year term [40] on a program committing him to Cosach's dissolution. The new government's Decree No. 1, January 2, 1933, fulfilled

37. See report of subcommittee of Chilean congressional committee, November 5, 1931, on the organization of Cosach, translation in *ibid.*, pp. 2050-67. See also Carlos Keller, *Un País al Carete* (Santiago Editorial Nascimento, 1932), pp. 35-36; José Tercero, "Chile Revamps the Nitrate Industry," *Bulletin of the Pan-American Union*, May 1934, pp. 334-42.

38. The Corporation of Foreign Bondholders has estimated that in Chile "for every $100 per capita of domestic commerce there is $90 per capita of external commerce, whereas similar figures for the USA would be $750 and $75 respectively." See Corporation of Foreign Bondholders, *Fifty-ninth Annual Report*, London, 1932, p. 139.

39. Department of Commerce, *Commerce Yearbook*, 1932, Washington, Pt. II, p. 381.

40. See Thompson, *op. cit.*, for an excellent account of these developments.

this campaign pledge. Cosach was ordered to be dissolved on the legal ground that it had exceeded its authorized powers, particularly with regard to capitalization.[41]

In compliance with the dissolution order Cosach returned to the state title to the national nitrate lands, which it had taken over. All other assets, including mining concessions previously obtained by constituent concerns, were vested in three major companies—the old Anglo-Chilean Nitrate Corporation and Lautaro Nitrate Company, Ltd. (both Guggenheim controlled), and a new company, Compañía Salitrera de Tarapaca y Antofagasta. The latter took over the thirty-four independent companies which Cosach had acquired. The reorganization was accompanied by a substantial writing down of capital values and fixed charges.[42]

The Chilean Nitrate & Iodine Sales Corporation

Although centralized control over the Chilean industry was temporarily relinquished with the dissolution of Cosach, official policy did not encourage the sale of nitrates in the world markets on a competitive basis. On the contrary, the government promptly considered various control schemes to insure a united front by Chilean producers in meeting the competition of synthetic nitrogen, to protect state revenues that came from nitrogen, and to insure the operation of plants scattered throughout the several nitrate zones as a re-employment measure.

A statute (Law No. 5350) of January 8, 1934 embodied the government program. It provided for a state monopoly for thirty-five years in foreign sales of Chilean nitrate, through a Chilean Nitrate & Iodine Sales Corporation. The law authorized the Sales Corporation to purchase from domestic producers such quantities of nitrate of soda as it required to cover its export sales, and to determine the purchase price from time to time. The pricing standard set up was "industrial cost" alongside ship, plus $1.50 (U.S. currency) a metric ton, but the Corporation could pay lower prices if market

41. Tercero, *op. cit.,* p. 338.
42. These reductions included cancellation of $40 million secured gold bonds held by the Chilean Government, conversion of $16,964,990 bonds held by Guggenheim Brothers into certificates of indebtedness of Anglo-Chilean Nitrate Corporation, and conversion of $10,510,000 bonds into income bonds of Tarapaca y Antofagasta. Interest rates on other bonds were later reduced and arrears of interest cancelled. *Moody's Manual of Investments* (Industrials), 1936, p. 2659.

conditions necessitated a reduction. Industrial cost was to include, besides direct operating expenses, the cost of transportation to port and outlays for necessary repairs on plant and equipment. Excluded from the standard were interest and amortization on capital investments and ore depletion allowances. The producers could use the extra $1.50 a ton which the Sales Corporation paid them over and above the computed "industrial cost" only to supplement their working capital or to finance plant improvements. The Corporation might reduce the scale of these "extra" disbursements—analagous in some ways to AAA "benefit payments" in the United States—when market conditions abroad affecting adversely its revenues made such a reduction expedient.

The law defined the profits of the Sales Corporation as the difference between what it paid the producers and what it realized from sales, minus expenses. Twenty-five per cent of profits was to be paid to the Chilean treasury in lieu of the old export tax. From the remaining 75 per cent, representing the producers' share, the Corporation was to deduct interest and amortization on the debt substituted for Cosach's prior-lien bonds and on the indebtedness of the several private companies. The remainder, if any, was to go to producers on the basis of their allotted sales quotas.

The law also provided for allotment of sales quotas among the domestic producers. No person, company, enterprise or consortium of enterprises was to be allowed a sales quota larger than 65 per cent of the aggregate allotments. Quotas were allotted for the first five years as follows: Lautaro, 36 per cent; Tarapaca y Antofagasta, 31 per cent; Anglo-Chilean, 26.1 per cent; and the remaining companies, all small, 6.9 per cent. Tarapaca's substantial quota apparently reflected the government's intention to insure continued operation, despite their relatively high unit cost, of plants using the Shanks process, thereby providing employment for a larger labor force than would otherwise be required.

Germany Takes Lead in Establishing World Nitrogen Cartel

While Chile was setting her house in order, German nitrogen producers were trying to bring the industry's several branches under a common, world-wide, cartel control. German industry was well qualified by organization and experience for this role. Essential to the effective functioning of an international cartel is the collective organization on a national basis of producers within the several participating countries. In Germany control either through ownership or cartel arrangements was highly concentrated in each of the three major branches of the nitrogen industry. Although numerous, the byproduct ammonia producers had organized effectively into three control groups, each with a single sales agency—the Ruhr byproduct ammonia cartel, the Silesian byproduct ammonia cartel, and the gas works cartel. Production of cyanamide had developed in only four large plants. The production of synthetic ammonia was concentrated almost entirely under I. G. Farbenindustrie A. G., the German chemical trust.[43]

These three major groups were further organized as the Deutsche Stickstoffsyndikat G. m. b. H., better known as the German Nitrogen Syndicate. Although actively engaged in propaganda to increase the sale of nitrogen, the Syndicate was primarily a marketing agency. It sold all but about 2 per cent of Germany's nitrogen output in 1934. Competition in the German market had been almost completely eliminated. Moreover, I. G. Farben by acquiring a substantial interest in the Norwegian Hydro-Electric Nitrogen Company had gained control of all Norwegian exports.

The British nitrogen industry had been subjected to similar centralization. Production of synthetic ammonia and its various derivatives before World War II was concentrated largely in Imperial Chemical Industries, Ltd., organized in 1926, representing a merger of Brunner, Mond & Company, Nobel Industries, Ltd., British Dyestuffs Corporation, and United Alkali Company, Ltd. The numerous byproduct ammonia producers, together with Imperial Chemical Industries, were associated through the British Sulphate of Ammonia Federation, Ltd., which under various titles has been in existence for almost half a century. The Federation regulates all prices and handles

43. IG's production was carried on principally in two plants—the Leuna plant near Merseburg, the largest plant in the world, with a capacity of 715,000 tons of nitrogen a year, and the Oppau plant, until 1929 the world's second largest plant. The Billingham plant of Imperial Chemical Industries and the Solvay Process Company's plant at Hopewell, Virginia, had become before World War II, respectively, the second and third in size.

The Leuna capacity alone exceeded the estimated capacity of the entire Chilean nitrogen industry in the twenties, which in 1929 was at a maximum, for the decade, of 660,000 tons a year. Even at the all-time peak of Chilean capacity in 1932—725,000 tons a year—the potential output of the Leuna plant was virtually identical. Tariff Commission, op. cit., Chap. 6, particularly p. 62, and Chap. 9, particularly p. 124.

all sales of British sulphate of ammonia. Under these arrangements competition among British producers of nitrogen had been effectively eliminated.

Both Germany and Great Britain are important exporters of nitrogen. In 1929 they ranked second and third, after Chile, as the leading world exporters. In that year these three countries accounted, if the Norwegian exports subject to German control are included, for 88 per cent by volume of total world exports.[44] The task of stabilizing the world's nitrogen markets rested, therefore, primarily in their hands.

Germany took the lead in a series of nitrogen conferences during the decade 1929–1938 which resulted in a succession of cartel agreements through which the competitive interests of the leading world producers of nitrogen were reconciled by the allocation of markets and the collective determination of prices. Although these agreements differed in their scope and details, their common aim was elimination of competition among sellers of nitrogen in world markets, and regulation of the market by administrative decisions jointly arrived at by cartel members. With the passage of time and the accumulation of experience, the successive cartels became more effective instruments of market control. Their scope was progressively widened and their life extended. They were expanded not only to cover additional producing countries and more producers but a larger proportion of total production.

Early Cartels Fail

The 1929 cartel embraced the German Nitrogen Syndicate, Imperial Chemical Industries, Ltd., and the Chilean producers. The agreements, separately executed, provided for cooperation among the three contracting groups for one year on propaganda and prices. This loose consortium was more the expression of a hope than the attainment of a goal. On its expiration a new agreement was made in August 1930, known as the Convention Internationale de l'Azote, or International Nitrogen Cartel. It included producers in Germany, Great Britain, Norway, France, Belgium, the Netherlands, Italy, Poland, Czechoslovakia, the Irish Free State. An agreement between the cartel group and the Chilean producers brought in the Chileans.

44. *Ibid.,* p. 95.

Of the major world producers only those of the United States and Canada were outside. The arrangement was to continue for one year.

As the depression deepened and world consumption of nitrogen declined, the conflict of interest among different branches of the industry and among the producers in different countries became so bitter that the cartel agreement was not renewed. A price war followed the termination of the agreement in July 1931. It was so severe that in some markets within thirty days prices were cut almost in half.[45]

These developments shifted negotiations from the business to the political forum. With the breakdown of private negotiations, the German Government imposed a tariff on Chilean nitrate of 120 Reichsmarks a ton (equivalent to $28.60) effective July 15, 1931; France, Poland, and Czechoslovakia prohibited imports of several nitrogenous products; Italy increased import duties on all these products; while Belgium and Japan issued decrees requiring licenses to import them. In 1932 Chile set up exchange controls which were used to force the purchase of Chilean nitrate. By so-called compensation agreements with France, Germany, Denmark, Belgium, and Czechoslovakia, Chile "compelled" these countries, some of which were self-sufficient in nitrogen, to purchase 300,000 tons of nitrates by June 30, 1934.

Price wars and political recrimination developed a more conciliatory attitude among the business leaders. After prolonged negotiations conducted in an atmosphere of secrecy, they made a new agreement, to run for two years from July 1932. This cartel eventually embraced all the leading producers except those of the United States. Except for Chile's temporary withdrawal in 1933, the cartel continued until World War II, though the details were now and again revised. The last agreement was signed in 1938 and was ended by the war.

Structure of the World Cartel

The later cartels were patterned after that of 1930—the Convention Internationale de l'Azote (CIA)—and bore the same title. (See Chart 1.) Participants in CIA fell into two categories: (1) a major

45. For example, the price of sulphate of ammonia in Great Britain, delivered to farmer's nearest station, was reduced from £9 10s. a long ton in June to £5 10s. in July. *Ibid.*, p. 93.

CHART 1. INTERNATIONAL NITROGEN CARTEL, 1939

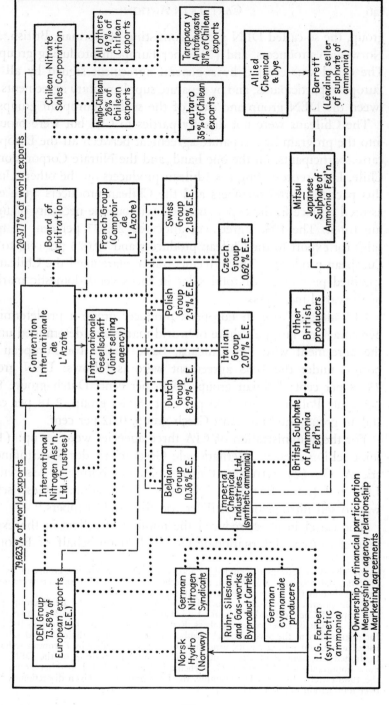

group, the so-called DEN group, consisting of German, British, and Norwegian producers, and (2) other European producing groups.[46] The cartel was created by a general agreement signed by all the European participants, and by separate supplementary agreements between the DEN group and each of the several European groups.

The Chileans were not directly parties to CIA but were brought into the program by a separate agreement between all the European cartel participants, on the one hand, and the Nitrate Corporation of Chile, Ltd., representing the Chilean producers on the other. Under this pact the cartel members and the Chilean producers were each assured a place in the export markets without the necessity of fighting for it. The 1938 agreement allocated 20.377 per cent of total sales for export to the Chilean producers and 79.623 per cent to the European producers. The agreement also guaranteed the Chileans a specified percentage of total sales in the several domestic markets of the cartel members.

CIA allotted to each European producer group a predetermined percentage of Europe's share of world markets as determined under the agreement with the Chileans. Basic quotas for European exporters under the 1938 agreement were as follows: DEN group, 73.58 per cent; Belgian group, 10.36 per cent; Dutch group, 8.29 per cent; Polish group, 2.90 per cent; Swiss group, 2.18 per cent; Italian group, 2.07 per cent; Czech group, 0.62 per cent.

For the administration of CIA three agencies were set up: (1) a joint selling agency, Internationale Gesellschaft der Stickstoffindustrie A. G., (2) a trustee, the International Nitrogen Association, Ltd., and (3) a Board of Arbitration. Internationale Gesellschaft was to sell nitrogenous fertilizer for all cartel members.[47]

The cartel in effect reduced the number of sellers in the export market to two—Internationale Gesellschaft on behalf of European

46. The 1938 agreement included, in addition to DEN, producing groups of Belgium, Holland, Italy, Switzerland, Poland, and Czechoslovakia. French producers were not signatories, but in fact were active participants in this fourth cartel.

47. In practice, sales were conducted largely by members of the DEN group, primarily Imperial Chemical Industries and I. G. Farbenindustrie, both on their own account and on account of other cartel members. Receipts for nitrogen sold went to the trustee for distribution to the several cartel members in proportion to their allowed sales. The use of a common selling agency insured a common price policy by European sellers and facilitated enforcement of export quotas. The dominant position of the DEN group, most important of which was I. G. Farbenindustrie, is reflected in other provisions of the 1938 cartel agreement. For example, the DEN group was given discretionary power over termination of the cartel.

producers and the Chilean Nitrate & Iodine Sales Corporation on behalf of Chilean producers. The agreement between them provided for a common price policy. Each undertook to sell at prices such as not to prejudice the declared purpose of the agreement.[48] The agreement also provided for cash penalties on all sales by either group in excess of its quota. The several national groups, most of which were organized into tightly controlled domestic cartels, were responsible for stabilization of prices in their home markets. However, CIA expressly prohibited sales or deliveries of nitrogenous fertilizers by any member in the home market of any other cartel member. Under the 1938 agreement a cartel member accused of violating this provision was considered guilty until he had proved his innocence.

American Producers Contribute to Cartel's Instability

Thus in the early thirties, although world capacity greatly exceeded world consumption, even at the comparatively moderate prices then prevailing, the Chilean and European producers reconciled their differences. However, the cartel had one serious defect. It did not include American producers. So long as they were not parties to the cartel the whole scheme was vulnerable. Although up to the late twenties the American market had been continuously on an import basis, American capacity rose to a level well above normal consumption with the completion of the synthetic nitrogen plants then under construction. For example, in 1934 total domestic capacity was approximately 541,000 tons, while domestic consumption was only 360,705 tons. Nevertheless, domestic net imports were 98,181 tons.[49]

Excess capacity made for instability in the American market, and hence also in world markets. As long as American producers faced the competition of foreign sellers in the American market, it was natural that they should look to foreign markets, where prices were subject to cartel control, to dispose of their surplus. By far the largest foreign supplier of the American nitrogen market was the Chilean Sales Corporation. As nitrogen production in the United States expanded, the Chileans were gradually losing the American market. This made the Chileans bring pressure on the other cartel members

48. The 1938 agreement provided that prices in export markets should be maintained at levels to discourage development of capacity in importing countries.
49. Tariff Commission, *op. cit.,* p. 188.

for larger quotas in the controlled markets. Stabilization of the American market was essential, therefore, to continued stabilization of world markets.

But two formidable obstacles made this difficult. First, formal cartel arrangements among domestic producers are banned under our antitrust laws. Second, the diversified and decentralized conditions under which chemical nitrogen is produced in America make it difficult for producers to cooperate, regardless of antitrust statutes.

The Organization of American Byproduct Producers

The two main sources of chemical nitrogen in the United States are byproduct nitrogen (ammonia) and synthetic nitrogen. The byproduct nitrogen industry, a branch of the coal-processing industry, also falls into two divisions—the so-called furnace plants and the merchant plants. The main business of furnace plants is to supply coke for pig iron blast furnaces. The output of byproduct ammonia from furnace plants tends, therefore, to vary directly with the production of pig iron. The main business of merchant plants is either to produce coke for the solid fuel market or, as public utility enterprises, to produce gas for industrial and domestic consumers. Their output of byproduct ammonia tends to fluctuate directly with general economic conditions, though less violently.

Since ammonia is released as a gas in the distillation of coal, its cost of production is a necessary item of cost in the coking of coal or the production of coal gas. Reducing it to a commercial form involves either "scrubbing" the ammonia gas with water to form liquid ammonia or treating it with sulphuric acid to form ammonium sulphate.[50] Ordinarily, therefore, byproduct ammonia would not be produced commercially unless its price promised to cover the added cost.

However, ammonia released in the manufacture of coke and coal gas really has an economic status below that of a byproduct. It is corrosive and must ordinarily be removed from fuel gas to prevent damage to metal equipment. To dispose of it as waste is generally more expensive than to prepare it for the market. Thus byproduct

50. See Curtis, *op. cit.*, Chap. 4, "A History of Fixed Nitrogen Fixation Processes," *passim;* also Tariff Commission, *op. cit.*, p. 181.

ammonia practically forces its way on the market for what it will bring.

In the United States the number of byproduct producers is quite large: 65 companies and 108 plants in 1934. Their total investment at that time in equipment for the recovery of ammonia is estimated to have been $40 million, and their annual capacity about 200,000 tons.[51] Although production is widely scattered, it tends to concentrate in several local geographic areas. The tri-state area within a radius of 125 miles of Pittsburgh, Pennsylvania, and the Chicago area including Gary, Indiana, and Joliet, Illinois, are the most important producing centers. The districts around Birmingham, Alabama, and Philadelphia, Pennsylvania, rank next. Aside from the Alabama district these areas are all remote from the most important consuming section of the country: the southeastern states, where ammonium sulphate is used extensively as a fertilizer.

Although in 1934 eight domestic plants produced synthetic nitrogen, those of E. I. du Pont de Nemours & Co., at Belle, West Virginia, and of the Solvay Process Company, at Hopewell, Virginia, accounted for almost 90 per cent of the domestic capacity. The Hopewell plant produced nitrate of soda primarily for the fertilizer market, where it directly faced Chilean competition. Next to the whole of Europe, the United States was the largest Chilean customer. Although the du Pont plant produced some nitrogenous fertilizers, its chief market was industrial, where it met the competition of both domestic byproduct nitrogen and imported nitrogen.

Barrett Company Organizes Ammonium Sulphate Market

Stabilization of the American market required the harmonizing of these diverse and conflicting interests. The Barrett Company appears to have played a key role in this undertaking. The Barrett Company, wholly owned subsidiary of Allied Chemical & Dye Corporation, is the distributor of the synthetic nitrogen products (chiefly nitrate of soda) of the Solvay Process Company, another Allied subsidiary. It also acts both as sales agent and as purchaser of sulphate of ammonia produced in the numerous byproduct plants. Its sales are mostly to fertilizer manufacturers. It has from time to time made

51. Tariff Commission, op. cit., p. 182.

exclusive sales agency contracts with many of the byproduct ammonia producers and it has purchased for resale on its own account much of the byproduct supply not handled by it on a commission basis.[52]

Barrett's proportion of the domestic sales of sulphate of ammonia has varied from time to time. According to the indictment returned by a federal grand jury against the Barrett Company on September 1, 1939 charging that this arrangement constituted a violation of the antitrust laws, the Barrett Company sold, either as agent or as pur-chaser for resale, 425,000 tons (contained nitrogen equivalent, 85,000 tons) of an estimated domestic production of about 525,000 tons (contained nitrogen equivalent, 105,000 tons), or about four fifths of the total in the fertilizer year 1938–1939.[53] A few large producers, including the United States Steel Corporation, the Republic Steel Corporation, and the New England Coke Company, sold most of the balance.

Barrett Sets Up Basing Point System

In selling ammonium sulphate Barrett charges the same price f.o.b. any coke oven or Atlantic seaboard port.[54] That is, a buyer would pay $x a ton at New York or at Pittsburgh, or Podunk, if an oven is located there. But Barrett has also set up a system by which the price delivered to the buyer at any point other than at the oven or port equals the regular oven or port price plus the freight charges from the *nearest* oven or port—no matter where the shipment originates. If it actually comes from farther off than the nearest oven or port, the producer absorbs the additional freight. For example, a purchaser in Kewanee, Illinois, buys ammonium sulphate which comes from ovens in Pittsburgh, although the nearest ovens are in Chicago. The price he pays is the uniform base oven price plus the freight charges, not from Pittsburgh, but from Chicago. The seller pays the difference between the actual freight bill and the Chicago-Kewanee rate.

The net price realized by the producer varies inversely with the

52. The Barrett Company, incorporated on January 31, 1916, is the successor of the American Coal Products Company. The practice of engrossing the byproduct supply is as old as Barrett's predecessor.

53. *U.S.* v. *The Barrett Company, et al.,* in U.S. District Court for the Southern District of New York, Criminal Action No. 106-13, September 1, 1939.

54. In the interest of clarity we have simplified our account of the basing point system. Beginning in 1938, Barrett's quoted price at inland ovens was one dollar less than its seaboard prices. This price differential was to stimulate the use of ammonium sulphate fertilizer in north central states.

freight charges absorbed. The net price will be equal to the f.o.b. oven or port price only when the freight charge from the oven or port to a particular destination is less than the freight rate from any other oven or port to that destination.

The purpose of a basing point system is to stabilize prices in all parts of the market. It removes or reduces the incentive of the producers in any given district to "invade" the market areas adjoining other production centers. However, it enables producers in areas of surplus production to invade other markets without disturbing the price structure or provoking retaliation. Any competitive seller producing less ammonium sulphate than can be consumed at prevailing prices in the area contiguous to his plant would find it more profitable to sell in his "home market area," even if he had to shade his prices slightly, than to ship to more distant markets and absorb freight. Under a basing point system he may be dissuaded from concentrating his sales in the near-by markets. Since the sellers of sulphate of ammonia are numerous in the major surplus-producing areas, and since shipments to buyers located at long distances from the seller's plant involve heavy freight absorption, it is doubtful that 'an equalized delivered pricing system could survive in the absence of collusion, either through a stabilizing mechanism of the sort which Barrett has created or otherwise.

Barrett's mechanism thus had three noteworthy features: (1) Barrett acted as sales agent for most of the output; (2) Barrett, and other sellers following its lead, quoted uniform f.o.b. oven and seaboard prices; (3) all sellers, under Barrett's leadership, absorbed freight in excess of the lowest freight from any oven to the destination. The result was a uniform delivered price at destination regardless of point of origin. By this mechanism, effective competition in the sale of ammonium sulphate was eliminated.[55]

Chileans and Barrett Adopt Common Marketing Policies

By itself, of course, this arrangement did not relieve sulphate of

55. See *U.S.* v. *Allied Chemical & Dye Corporation, et al.,* in U.S. District Court for the Southern District of New York, October Term, 1940, Civil Action No. 14-320. The consent decree entered in this case on May 29, 1941 enjoined Barrett from entering into contracts or arrangements whereby it acts as an exclusive agent for the sale of sulphate of ammonia, from selling ammonium sulphate in any fertilizer year (for consumption in the United States) in excess of 35 per cent of total domestic production, plus imports minus exports, and from agreeing, or conspiring, with any producer of sulphate of ammonia to fix its price.

ammonia from the competition of other forms of fertilizer nitrogen, chiefly nitrate of soda. But the Barrett Company apparently took part in arrangements to stabilize directly the market for nitrate of soda.

The Solvay Process Company completed its nitrate of soda plant at Hopewell, Virginia, in 1928. At that time, Chilean producers sold their nitrate of soda in the United States exclusively through the Chilean Nitrate Sales Corporation. The Barrett Company was the sole distributor of Solvay's synthetic nitrate of soda. At the outset the Barrett Company competed vigorously and successfully with the Chilean producers in the United States market. By the early thirties it was supplying from one fourth to one third of the domestic consumption of this particular nitrogenous product. Barrett's campaign took place during a period of generally declining prices. It was brought to a halt by an arrangement initiated by the Chilean Nitrate Sales Corporation and afterwards adopted by Barrett.

Under this arrangement the Chilean Nitrate Sales Corporation sold nitrate of soda at prices f.o.b. certain designated Atlantic and Gulf ports. The Barrett Company sold on a similar basis, regardless of whether it shipped nitrate of soda from these ports or direct from Hopewell.[56] To the base price each company added identical charges for handling, bagging, and storage, and a fixed railroad "freight charge," regardless of the mode of delivery and the actual cost of transportation. To control prices from producer to ultimate consumer and insure a uniform delivered price to consumers in the same area, all middlemen were designated as "producer agents," even though they assumed obligations and responsibilities ordinarily attached to ownership, and were required to adhere to a stipulated price schedule. Moreover, the Chilean Corporation and Barrett allowed "agents" an identical "commission," graduated with volume of sales.

Finally, a distributor frequently occupied the anomalous position of serving as "agent" simultaneously for both these nominally competitive principals. When he did so, the distributor could count his sales for both companies in computing the commission rate to which his sales volume entitled him. By such devices the Chilean Corpora-

---

56. The arrangements differed somewhat in different sections of the country. Those described applied to the most important nitrogen-consuming area, viz., the southeastern states.

tion and Barrett restricted price competition and controlled nitrate prices from producer to consumer.[57]

American Firms Cooperate With World Cartel

As the principal sellers of sulphate of ammonia and nitrate of soda restricted competition in the American market, members of the International Nitrogen Cartel apparently took steps to bring that market within the sphere of its influence. In any event a federal grand jury returned an indictment in 1939, naming as defendants Allied Chemical & Dye Corporation and its three subsidiaries (the Barrett Company, Semet-Solvay Company, and Solvay Process Company), Imperial Chemical Industries, Ltd., and the Chilean Nitrate Sales Corporation and certain associated companies, together with twenty-five individuals, and also naming as co-conspirators forty-two foreign firms (including I. G. Farbenindustrie, the German Nitrogen Syndicate, and the International Nitrogen Cartel) and sixty-two individuals. The indictment charged that American firms participated in the international arrangements; that the defendants unlawfully agreed to restrict American imports and exports of sulphate of ammonia and other nitrogenous products; that American firms operated in certain markets on a quota basis; that American firms cooperated in maintaining prices in foreign countries, and that they maintained a fixed relationship between unit prices for various nitrogenous products in both American and foreign markets. The indictment in effect

---

57. For these practices Allied Chemical & Dye Corporation, the Barrett Company, Solvay Process Company, the Chilean Nitrate Sales Corporation, and certain associated companies, and a large number of individual officers and directors of the companies, were indicted by a federal grand jury September 1, 1939 for having conspired to restrain trade in violation of the antitrust statutes. See *U.S. v. Chilean Nitrate Sales Corporation, et al.*, in U.S. District Court for the Southern District of New York, October Term, 1939, Criminal Action No. 106-14. The criminal proceedings against Allied Chemical & Dye Corporation, the Barrett Company, Solvay Process Company, and associated individual defendants were later *nolle prossed*. A complaint was then filed (*U.S. v. Allied Chemical & Dye Corporation, et al.*, cited above) and a consent decree entered May 29, 1941. The final judgment enjoined a continuation of the alleged conspiracy and specifically prohibited the producer agency arrangement and resale price maintenance agreements.

Probably some economists and perhaps some businessmen would argue that such an arrangement between the only two sellers of nitrate of soda reflects merely independent rational behavior of sellers under conditions of imperfect competition. The complexity of the arrangements, the pattern of the relationship, and the articulation between the programs of the two companies indicate strongly that, however rationally they behaved, the two companies did not act independently.

charged that American firms were parties to the international cartel and the cartel had extended its control to the American market.[58]

Although the details of these allegations have not been legally substantiated, it is clear that both at home and abroad producers have been unwilling to trust their fortunes entirely to the unrestricted play of competition. Both in world and domestic markets businessmen have sought security by substituting collective controls for the free play of market forces.

Results of Chilean Monopoly

Until 1929 the effort to subject nitrogen production to collective controls was primarily a Chilean enterprise. It had two major objectives: to insure the Chilean Government a convenient and lucrative source of state revenue and to insure producers higher prices for nitrate of soda than would have prevailed in a free market. It achieved the first objective continuously for more than half a century, and, at times, both.

Both deductive and inductive analysis supports this conclusion. Presumably the Chilean producers acting collectively tried to adjust output and set prices so as to maximize their profits. To do this they had to take account of the effect of output on costs and of prices on demand. The government's interest in securing revenue from the export tax conflicted with the interests of producers in maximizing profits. The tax in effect increased production costs per ton of nitrogen by the amount of the levy. It was added to the selling price, but it yielded nothing to the producers. It tended to restrict demand and curtail sales. Consumers and producers shared the tax burden. Although the tax was a burden to producers, their problem of maximizing profits was not changed by it. The problem was to adjust output and prices so that net revenue per unit of output times the number of units sold would be maximized.

Chilean control in practice did not, of course, always achieve this

58. The indictment specifically charged that the cartel was made applicable to the United States by a supplementary agreement and an exchange of letters on April 17, 1939, between Imperial Chemical Industries, Ltd., and the German Nitrogen Syndicate representing I. G. Farben and about fourteen other German producers of fertilizer nitrogen. The Barrett Company was charged with having agreed to refrain from shipping sulphate of ammonia to various countries, including Japan, and with having accepted quotas for sulphate and other nitrogenous materials for other countries. *U.S.* v. *Allied Chemical & Dye Corporation, et al.*, in U.S. District Court for the Southern District of New York, Criminal Action No. 106-12, September 1, 1939.

end. The producers' knowledge of the effect of price changes on consumption and cost was imperfect and their joint control of nitrate
exports far from complete and continuous. In a general way, however, the producers sought to increase profits by raising prices, and in
part they succeeded. Before World War I with a single exception—
the short-lived cartel of 1913—when a cartel was set up, prices
advanced; when it terminated, prices declined.[59]

In the years immediately after World War I, when the government placed its power behind the Chilean Nitrate Producer's Association, the cartel met with greater success in stabilizing prices—except
during the 1920–1922 depression. The average annual price of
Chilean nitrate per metric ton at Chilean ports had risen from $33.40
for 1914 to $78.49 for the fertilizer year 1920–1921. Prices fell
sharply during the depression, averaging $43.91 for the fertilizer
year 1922–1923. Thereafter the controls exercised by the Chilean
Nitrate Producer's Association kept the price of nitrate of soda
relatively stable until the middle of 1927 at levels well above the
highest reached before World War I. During the period 1924 to
1927 average annual prices varied around $44.

Prices Above Competitive Levels

That prices at times during this period were above competitive
levels is clearly indicated by the discrepancy between Chilean output
and productive capacity. During the six years from 1921 to 1927
Chilean production of nitrate of soda varied from a low of 182,600
tons of contained nitrogen to 433,400. This reflected changes in
percentage of capacity operated ranging from less than 40 to about
87. Average annual output during this period represented only 60
per cent of average annual capacity.[60]

Such production and price behavior is not compatible with a free
market. In a free market a decline in demand would ordinarily be
accompanied by a decline in price. With a continuing excess of
capacity in a competitive market, price trends will be downward.
Continued stability of prices in the face of sharp fluctuations in
demand and continuing excess capacity reflect the cartel's control

59. At times the cyclical upward trend of prices aided cartel strategy, but the movement of prices correlates so closely with cartel organization as to indicate a causal relationship. See text, pp. 122-23.
60. Calculated from data presented in Tariff Commission, *op. cit.,* pp. 60 and 62.

over the market. As world capacity to produce nitrogen increased greatly during the second half of the twenties, the Chilean control scheme proved futile and prices broke sharply. With controls relaxed in 1928 and 1929, Chilean output rose sharply despite lower prices. There can be little doubt that lower price levels would have prevailed at an earlier date in the absence of the artificial Chilean control scheme.

A survey made by the Chilean Government indicates that nitrate prices during 1920–1927 yielded monopoly returns. After provision for general expense, depreciation, depletion, amortization, and service on loans, the average annual rate of return on invested capital for this period by a group of the larger nitrate companies was over 50 per cent.[61] For a group of medium-sized companies the net rate of return varied from 25 per cent to 30 per cent; and for the remainder of the companies it varied from 10 per cent to 25 per cent.

Chile's Problem of Economic Readjustment

The two objectives—high profits for the producers and lucrative revenues for the government—were achieved primarily at the expense of the world's nitrogen consumers, most of whom belonged to a relatively low income group—the farmers. Both Chilean producers and the Chilean Government were, of course, more concerned with their immediate economic problems than with welfare of foreign consumers. Although producers, whose primary interest was to increase profits, had sponsored the earlier control schemes, the government had given them its blessing. After World War I the government played an increasingly important role in the control of nitrate production. It assumed increasing responsibility both for the industry's "health" and for the social welfare of those dependent upon it.

The government's problem was difficult. By the middle twenties it was apparent that the Chilean monopoly had protected inefficiency and subsidized high costs. Meanwhile technological progress in the chemical field had opened an unlimited commercial source of nitrogen outside of Chile. Unrestricted competition under these circumstances would have entailed serious economic readjustments, disturb-

61. See Pablo Ramirez, "The Government and the Nitrate Problem," *Chile,* Vol. III, pp. 133-35, cited in Wallace and Edminster, *op. cit.,* p. 50.

ing to the whole social and political fabric of Chile. To the business interests concerned, it threatened an immediate reduction in profits and a writing down of capital values. Unless the costs of producing Chilean nitrate could be lowered sufficiently to eliminate foreign competition, Chile was confronted with the necessity of shifting resources from uneconomic to economic uses.

Importance of Nitrate to the Chilean Economy

To appreciate the significance to the Chileans of such readjustments it is necessary to review briefly Chilean economy and nitrate's dominant role in it. Chile consists of a narrow strip of land extending more than 2,600 miles along the Pacific coast of South America. Much of it is unfit for agriculture. The northern third is a vast desert. Much of the southern third is too broken or too bleak for farming. Only about 10 per cent of the Republic's area is well fitted for agriculture, and most of that is owned by a relatively few large landowners. As late as 1925, approximately 2,500 landowners are said to have held almost 80 per cent of all Chilean rural properties. In the central province of Santiago fifty-one property owners controlled three fourths of the rural holdings.[62] Employment opportunities in agriculture for those who might be forced to leave the nitrate industry were apparently limited.

An estimate of the United States Department of Agriculture placed the total value of Chilean agricultural and pastoral products in 1928–1929 at $146 million. Official data showed the value of manufactured products to be $173,218,000, the value of products of the mine to be $153,585,000. Nitrate of soda alone, with a total value of $72,225,000, accounted for nearly one half the value of mineral products and was almost one half the value of all agricultural and pastoral products.[63] During 1926–1928, nitrate of soda and iodine (obtained as a byproduct in the production of nitrate) represented about 50 per cent, by value, of all Chilean exports. Chile's capacity to buy foreign goods depended largely upon the amount of nitrogen Chile could sell and the price at which she could sell it.

Although a substantial reduction in the value of Chilean nitrate

62. See Thompson, op. cit., p. 286.
63. Wallace and Edminster, op. cit., p. 29.

threatened stability of the whole of the Chilean economy, its impact was more serious in some localities than in others. The production of nitrate is confined entirely to the northern provinces. The population of this area is directly or indirectly dependent almost exclusively on mining, largely nitrate mining, for its livelihood. During the twenties the nitrate industry directly employed approximately 60,000 employees. It also furnished employment indirectly to a large group of individuals who supplied goods or services to those who worked in the nitrate industry. Any permanent decrease in employment in the nitrate industry involved a shifting of whole populations to new industries and to new areas.

Chilean Control Ignores Basic Problems

Those remote from the Chilean problem may be inclined to view a competitive struggle in the world's nitrogen market as a battle of the giants—Big Business controlling the Chilean industry and Big Business controlling the synthetic and byproduct industries. To the Chilean officeholder it was a battle involving the Chilean Government and the economic and social basis upon which it rested. From this point of view it is easy to understand the government's concern with Chilean nitrate and its willingness to sponsor control schemes.

Whatever their apparent justification, however, the control schemes have failed to reach the basic problem—that of directing resources into channels where they can be economically employed and, conversely, of diverting or redirecting them from uneconomic uses. On the contrary, they have given resources a scarcity value by withholding them from use. To the extent that the control schemes have succeeded they have done so largely at the expense of consumers. But, unfortunately from the Chilean point of view, their success in recent years has by no means been complete. Nor is it likely to prove so in the future.

Despite persistent efforts of the government and the nitrate producers to stabilize prices during the twenties, an increase in production not under Chilean control had forced the price of Chilean nitrate by the early thirties to levels about half those of 1921 to 1926. The average annual price at Chilean ports declined from $43.12 in 1926 to $18.87 in 1932. (See Table 9.) Chilean exports of (contained) nitrogen declined from a high of 498,155 tons in 1929 to a low of

41,538 tons in 1932. The number of employees of nitrate plants in 1928–1929 averaged 60,000 yearly; in 1932–1933, 12,000.[64] Afterwards, revival in world trade and Chile's participation in the world cartel improved at least temporarily the position of Chile's nitrate industry. But it is probable that in the aftermath of World War II only low-cost mechanized Chilean production can survive. Chile's effort to bring prosperity by perpetuating inefficiency seems doomed to failure.

Objectives and Achievement of the International Nitrogen Cartel

When the International Nitrogen Cartel was organized in July 1929, the nitrogen rush was drawing to a close. World capacity was almost twice what it had been five years earlier and exceeded world consumption by about 50 per cent. The average annual price of nitrate of soda (at Chilean ports) had decreased by about 20 per cent during this period. A year later when the cartel was renewed, world capacity had further increased and consumption had declined slightly. Capacity then exceeded consumption by more than 100 per cent. (See Tables 10 and 11.)

Confronted with surplus capacity and declining prices, nitrogen producers sought refuge in cartel controls. By dividing markets, allocating exports, and centralizing sales, they tried to raise prices to more remunerative levels. The German Nitrogen Syndicate announced the objectives of the cartel as follows:

The Syndicate [cartel] just concluded aims at bringing the production of nitrogen fertilizers, which has lately risen out of proportion to requirements, back to a level of consumption. By eliminating unsound competition on the nitrogen market, it is intended to prevent losses both in production and distribution of nitrogenous fertilizers and thus enable the industry to supply agriculture with cheaper fertilizers in the future.[65]

64. Tariff Commission, *op. cit.*, p. 116.
65. *Ibid.*, p. 83.
The German Syndicate argued that "the consolidation of the nitrogen market resulting from international agreements will bring agriculture greater advantages in the long run, than a temporary fall in prices which may have been expected from a competitive action between the manufacturers, since in the latter case the industry would be compelled to regain the losses suffered from such competition through price advances during a longer period of time to follow."
The validity of this argument rests upon two assumptions: (1) that, if competition temporarily drives prices below normal, long-run, competitive levels in an industry of surplus capacity, prices must subsequently rise above such levels in order to insure a long-run equilibrium between demand and supply; and (2) that, given the power to

Cartel Restricts Output

How successful was the cartel in its avowed objectives of (1) "bringing production of nitrogen fertilizers, which has lately risen out of proportion to requirements, back to a level of consumption," and (2) in raising prices? These two objectives are obviously in conflict. An increase in price tends to check consumption. It also tends to encourage the development of additional capacity and raise output. However, the cartel took positive measures to reduce world output. The 1930 agreement, for example, provided for reductions in output by cartel members varying from 10 per cent for the French industry to 50 per cent for the British. Under the 1932 agreement certain members were indemnified for restricting output. Thus the Internationale Gesellschaft der Stickstoffindustrie A. G. paid 4.5 million RM to the Compagnie Néerlandaise de l'Azote for closing down a portion of its Sluiskil plant in the Netherlands and limiting its output to 15,000 metric tons of nitrogen for the year ending June 30, 1933.[66]

Later agreements continued to restrict output of the Sluiskil plant. The 1938 agreement provided for annual payments to Sluiskil of 11d. for every 100 kg. of nitrogen which cartel members sold in their home and export markets to compensate it for restricting sales to 15,000 metric tons a year.[67]

The 1938 agreement also provided for an annual payment of 12d. to the Belgian group of producers for every 100 kg. of nitrogen which cartel members sold in their home and foreign markets to compensate the Belgian producers for restricting output under a supplementary agreement made between the DEN group and the Belgian group.[68]

---

control prices, cartels will not use it to exploit consumers. We believe both these assumptions are false. We will discuss the principles underlying the first in some detail in a companion study. Neither common sense nor cartel experience justifies the second assumption.

66. *Ibid.*, p. 85. This sum was equivalent to one million dollars.

67. Sluiskil was permitted, however, to manufacture all or a part of the export quota of the Italian group and a part of the quota of certain Belgian producers—both of which groups are said to have had an ownership interest in Sluiskil.

The "compensation" for nonproduction in this instance was equivalent to a surcharge of $20 a ton on the output of all other cartel members.

68. These payments were made quarterly out of a common fund set up in the cartel agreement. The Chileans contributed £150,000 to the fund plus 1.5d. for every 100 kg. of nitrogen which they sold. The balance came from European cartel members (with the exception of the French and Italian groups) in proportion to their sales.

Despite the specific measures which the cartel took to reduce production, its efforts were not strikingly successful. Nitrogen stocks had risen continuously during the five years before the organization of the world cartel—from 420,000 metric tons on July 1, 1925 to 980,-000 tons on July 1, 1929. During the first year of the cartel they rose to 1,040,000 tons. By the middle of 1934 they had been reduced only to 870,000 tons.[69]

Cartel Tries to Restrict Capacity

Although the cartel did not publicly acknowledge curtailment of capacity as an objective, the dominant cartel members took positive steps to stop expansion of capacity. In 1932 the DEN group paid substantial sums to the uncompleted Ressaix-Laval Plant in Belgium to stop construction.[70] Under the 1938 cartel the International Nitrogen Association, Ltd. (the cartel trustee) was to pay 75 million Belgian francs, in quarter-year payments of 3,750,000 francs over a period of five years, to the corporate owners of Ressaix-Laval for its liquidation, with the understanding that, if a third party bought the plants, buildings, or equipment, the property would not be used to produce synthetic ammonia for eight years.

I. G. Farben, which dominated the DEN group, tried persistently to block expansion of capacity in the United States, apparently in part because of its commitments to other American producers. In 1933 IG refused to grant the Hercules Powder Company a license under its patents. In doing so IG advised Hercules that "because of our other nitrogen interests we were not in a position to permit your firm to use our process and experience for the production of hydrogen and ammonia synthesis." Again in 1936 IG advised Hercules, "We have again reached the conclusion that, because of our other interests in the nitrogen field, we are not in a position to put at your disposal the experience you desire."

After the outbreak of World War II, the Atlas Powder Company had developed plans for the construction of a synthetic nitrogen plant and had sought a license from IG through its American agency, Chemnyco. The latter wrote to IG as follows:

69. Tariff Commission, *op. cit.,* p. 72.
70. Hearings before a Special Committee Investigating the Munitions Industry, U.S. Senate, 73d Cong., in response to S.Res. 206, Pt. XII, pp. 2812-13.

The project of Atlas Powder Company is analogous to the project of Hercules. It will be carried out irrespective of whether or not you will give Atlas a license and technical advice. We do not know whether under these circumstances you would still refuse to promote in any way the building of basic nitrogen plants in the United States.

Confronted with this situation, IG began negotiations with Atlas. After six months it terminated them abruptly with the advice to Atlas that "I. G., for the time being, are not in a position to grant a license. To their regret they are also not able to indicate at what future time negotiations on this matter might possibly be resumed." [71]

World Capacity Expands Despite Cartel

Although the cartel and its leading members bought off particular producers and blocked others from entering the industry, their effort to check the growth of capacity was not successful.

World capacity in 1929 was 3,278,000 tons. It had increased to 4,448,000 tons by 1931—almost 40 per cent. It steadily increased thereafter, reaching 5,082,300 tons by 1934. (See Table 10.) Expansion of synthetic capacity in the United States was great during the cartel's early life. Domestic capacity in 1929, when the cartel was organized, was only 171,500 tons. By 1934 it had increased to 341,350 tons.[72]

Businessmen built this new capacity for business reasons. Their having built it in the face of rapidly declining prices throws grave doubt on the economic validity of the cartel's output restriction and price control program. When the cartel was organized prices were still sufficiently high to attract capital in large amounts. The 1938 agreement apparently recognized the cartel's failure to check expansion of capacity in providing that prices in export markets should be maintained at a level low enough to discourage the development of domestic production.

Cartel's Control of Prices

In judging the cartel's effort to stem the decline in nitrogen prices,

71. Not until it became evident that Hercules would proceed independently did IG grant it a license. It finally refused Atlas a license when it learned that Atlas planned to construct an explosives plant for the British Government. See Chapter 10. See also Corwin D. Edwards, *Economic and Political Aspects of International Cartels,* Monograph No. 1 of the Subcommittee on War Mobilization, Committee on Military Affairs, U.S. Senate, pursuant to S.Res. 107, 78th Cong., 2d sess. (Washington, 1944), p. 30.
72. Tariff Commission, *op. cit.,* p. 188.

it must be borne in mind that from 1925 to 1929 competition became increasingly severe. The trend of prices was sharply downward. It was out of this situation that the first international cartel had originated. It was this situation that the cartel was designed to remedy. The cartel was inaugurated just as the depression began.

The cartel was endeavoring to reverse a price trend actuated by two powerful forces—a large and growing capacity for the production of nitrogen, and a decline in demand occasioned by a recession in business and a decline in farm incomes. These forces combined were too powerful for the cartel. The downward trend of sulphate of ammonia prices was not reversed until 1932, of nitrate of soda until 1934–1935.

Nevertheless, the cartel apparently retarded price declines during the first two years of the depression. This is clearly shown by the course of ammonium sulphate prices—the most important cartel-controlled nitrogen product—in the British market. Before the cartel collapsed in 1931, sulphate of ammonia sold in the United Kingdom for £9 10s. a long ton. Except for a slight increase in February, the quoted price had been unchanged for six months. With the breakdown of the cartel, prices—like Humpty Dumpty—had a great fall. They declined over 43 per cent within 30 days;[73] and "all the king's horses and all the king's men couldn't put Humpty Dumpty back again." Sulphate prices reached their low during 1932, the average annual price for that year being £6 3s. 10d. as compared with £9 14s. during 1930 when the cartel was still operating. The cartel was reorganized at the bottom of the depression and has operated continuously since. Neither the cartel nor expanding demand raised nitrogen prices to their predepression levels. The trend throughout the second half of the thirties was distinctly upward, however. The rise both for sulphate of ammonia and for nitrate of soda was marked. (See Tables 12 and 13.) Average annual prices for sulphate of ammonia in the United States rose about 33 per cent between 1932 and 1939; in the United Kingdom they increased about 20 per cent. The course of nitrate prices was similar except that the decline was more prolonged—the low annual average having been reached in 1935 in both the United States and the United Kingdom—and the increase less sharp.

73. To £5 10s. for July. See Ibid., p. 93.

TABLE 12

AVERAGE ANNUAL PRICES OF SULPHATE OF AMMONIA AND NITRATE OF
SODA IN LONDON, ENGLAND, 1913 AND 1924–1939

(In Pounds Sterling Per Long Ton)

Year	Sulphate of Ammonia			Nitrate of Soda (15.5%)		
	£	s.	d.	£	s.	d.
1913	12	8	4	—	—	—
1924	14	9	1	13	12	11
1925	13	4	8	12	19	2
1926	12	19	11 a (Jan.-Aug.)	13	2	3
	11	12	6 a (Sept.-Dec.)			
1927	11	7	2	12	15	5
1928	10	9	3	10	9	8
1929	10	4	1	10	3	7
1930	9	14	—	9	16	9
1931	8	2	6	9	9	10
1932	6	3	10	8	15	9
1933	6	12	3	8	5	4
1934	7	1	6	7	15	—
1935	7	1	—	7	12	—
1936	7	1	—	7	12	—
1937	7	5	—	7	15	—
1938	7	10	—	8	—	—
1939	7	10	—	8	3	—

Sources: Data from International Institute of Agriculture, Statistics Bureau, *International Yearbook of Agricultural Statistics,* 1926–1927, pp. 548-49; 1928–1929, pp. 551-52; 1933–1934, pp. 764-65; 1934–1935, pp. 840-41; 1939–1940, pp. 1061-62.

a. Monthly average. The table does not include an average annual price for 1926 because through August of that year prices listed by the *International Yearbook of Agricultural Statistics* were for sulphate of ammonia 21.1 per cent, whereas from September 1926 prices listed were for sulphate of ammonia 20.6 per cent. This change also means that sulphate of ammonia prices for the period before September 1926 are not strictly comparable with the prices given for September 1926 through 1939.

Prices rose in the face of potential capacity more than 100 per cent in excess of peacetime world consumption. This reflects the influence both of the cartel and of general economic recovery.

Nitrogen prices are low, however, as compared with nitrogen prices before the "nitrogen rush." Moreover, they declined much further than the general price level between 1919 and 1939. Despite substantial recovery in the late thirties, nitrogen was relatively cheap.

TABLE 13

Prices of Sulphate of Ammonia and Nitrate of Soda in the
United States Expressed as Relatives, 1913 and 1924–1939

(1926 = 100)

Year	Sulphate of Ammonia	Nitrate of Soda
1913	118.9	96.8
1924	104.8	97.7
1925	108.9	101.1
1926	100.0	100.0
1927	92.4	97.9
1928	94.5	87.5
1929	84.2	84.6
1930	68.2	81.4
1931	55.0	77.7
1932	33.9	62.2
1933	36.9	51.2
1934	40.0	51.9
1935	39.0	50.0
1936	41.2	52.2
1937	45.5	55.3
1938	46.8	56.9
1939	45.1	56.9

Sources: Data from U.S. Bureau of Labor Statistics, Bulletins 440, 493, 521 and 542, for
the years 1913 and 1924–1930, and from the December issues of the monthly reports of
Wholesale Prices for 1931 through 1939.

Nevertheless, nitrogen prices were no doubt higher than they would
have been without the cartel.

Nitrogen Prices and Consumption

Although nitrogen prices in the second half of the thirties were
well above the depression levels, the demand for nitrogen increased.
Declining soil fertility, a more widespread recognition of the advantages of fertilizers, the growth of population, an increase in
world food requirements, an expansion in industry and trade, and
higher farm incomes increased consumption despite rising prices.

Consumption would no doubt have been even greater, however,
had lower prices prevailed. The chief peacetime use for nitrogen is
as a fertilizer. According to studies made by the United States De-

partment of Agriculture in determining the effects of changes in the price of fertilizers,

Two principles are now well established. One—Farmers in the United States spend a definite percentage of income for fertilizers, regardless of plant-food prices. . . . Two—The retail price of a ton of fertilizer in any year tends to be the wholesale cost of the plant food contained plus a uniform amount per ton to cover the cost of transportation, processing and distribution.[74]

Any given percentage reduction in the price of plant foods will reduce the price of fertilizers by a much smaller percentage, since transportation, processing, and distribution costs are independent of the cost of fertilizers. During the years 1925–1941 they made up a little less than 50 per cent of the retail price of fertilizers. A 10 per cent reduction in the cost of plant foods during this period would have reduced the price of fertilizer by only about 5 per cent.

Nitrogen is generally used with other plant foods in mixed fertilizers. A reduction in the price of nitrogen tends to increase its consumption at the expense of other plant foods. Regardless of this tendency, however, a reduction in the price of nitrogen will of itself reduce the price of mixed fertilizers—although by a very much smaller percentage than the nitrogen price reduction, since the price of the other plant foods may change less or not at all.

Since farmers tend to spend a fixed percentage of their income for fertilizer, any reduction in the price of nitrogen will increase its consumption although the percentage increase in consumption will be less than the percentage decrease in price. Shaw and his associates, after painstaking statistical analysis, have concluded that a 20 per cent reduction in the price of chemical nitrogen in 1937 would have increased its consumption for plant food by 13.8 per cent.[75]

We can safely conclude, therefore, that farmers bought less nitrogen than they would have bought had prices been lower. While the cartel by curbing production brought it more nearly in line with consumption, to the extent that it kept prices above the levels to which

74. U.S. Department of Agriculture, Bureau of Plant Industry, Soils and Agricultural Engineering, *Plant Food Memorandum Report No. 9*, "The Influence of Wholesale Prices of Nitrogen, Phosphoric Acid and Potash on the Consumption of Those Materials in Fertilizer," by B. T. Shaw, Mordecai J. B. Ezekiel, and F. W. Parker, Beltsville (Md.), 1944, pp. 1-2.
75. *Ibid.*, p. 67.

they would have otherwise fallen, it encouraged expansion of capacity and retarded consumption. The cartel tended to increase rather than diminish the basic imbalance of the industry.

Cartel and Costs

But not only have prices been higher and production lower than they would have been in the absence of restrictions; costs have likewise been higher.

Chilean control policies have been designed to permit outmoded processes to survive. A specific objective of the Chilean law of 1934 was to prevent disappearance of the Shanks process. By providing for distribution of quotas by nitrogen zones, the law has prevented concentration of production on the low-cost plants. Cartel policy has had a similar effect on synthetic producers. When the second international cartel was organized, quotas apparently were distributed so as to compensate high-cost producers for their relative cost disadvantage. A representative of du Pont has said:

Information obtained from I. C. I. was to the effect that the agreement was based on each producer limiting his production to what he stated was the minimum required for economic operation. This minimum was determined separately for each producing unit and rested solely on the merits of each individual case. That is, one unit with an actual capacity of 50,000 pounds might have a rated economic capacity of 25,000 pounds, while a second unit of the same actual capacity, because of higher overhead or operating cost, will have an economic capacity of say 35,000 pounds. Each unit is allowed to produce up to the stated economic capacity and an outlet for this production is assured.[76]

The cartel raised production costs not only by fixing prices and quotas to insure survival of high-cost producers, but by preventing low-cost producers from operating on the most economical scale. The latter have been forced to distribute fixed charges over a smaller output and hence to increase fixed charges per unit of output.[77]

In brief, the cartel apparently made for lower output, higher costs,

76. Edwards, *op. cit.,* p. 40.
77. This disadvantage may have been overcome in part through the sale of quotas by cartel members. Once a cartel has burdened costs by output restrictions, the transfer of quotas, which permits a reduction in unit costs by fuller utilization of the quota purchaser's facilities, may have an ameliorating influence, even though the quotas have to be paid for. The 1938 agreement provides, however, that except by special agreement with the DEN group, quotas may be ceded in whole or in part only to members of that group. (Art. III, par. 3.)

somewhat higher prices and lower consumption. Consumers have bought less nitrogen than they would otherwise have purchased, and they have paid more for it. The cartel has raised production costs and subsidized idle capacity.

Postwar Outlook

The war brought at least a temporary end to the cartel's operations. It did not eliminate the conditions out of which the cartel arose. On the contrary, it greatly aggravated them. World capacity for the production of nitrogen in 1934 was about 5 million short tons.[78] By 1939 it had expanded to approximately 6 million tons. This expansion represented primarily an increase in the capacity to produce synthetic ammonia. Italy and Germany accounted for almost half the increase. This presumably reflects preparations for war. And the war further increased world capacity.

Complete data are not available on the expansion of capacity since 1939. The greatest expansion undoubtedly took place in the United States. American capacity and output before the war originated in response to economic rather than military factors. Our production and capacity were geared to peace, not war. Although we were the world's largest importer of nitrogen, most of which came from Chile, our total domestic capacity exceeded total domestic consumption. Nevertheless, domestic synthetic, byproduct, and organic capacities combined were quite inadequate to the requirements of total war.

Between 1940 and 1944 domestic nitrogen capacity was increased from 615,300 to 1,451,000 tons—an increase of about 135 per cent. Of the total increase of 835,700 tons, 755,000 tons represents government plants. Increases in other countries were much smaller. On the other hand, Allied bombing no doubt destroyed a considerable part of the installed capacity in Axis and Axis-occupied countries. How complete this destruction will prove to be, we do not know.[79]

78. Of this total, 621,500 tons was represented by byproduct nitrogen, 690,000 by Chilean nitrate of soda, 539,000 by cyanamide, and the balance by synthetic ammonia. Tariff Commission, *op. cit.*, p. 62.

79. First postwar reports indicate the damage to nitrogen plants was less than might have been expected. Moreover, apparently such damage as was done was not irreparable. A Berlin dispatch of December 28, 1945 reported that the great Leuna synthetic ammonia plant had resumed production and at that time was employing 18,000 workmen, or about half its normal working force. See New York *Herald Tribune*, December 29, 1945.

Vigorous Potential Competition

Furthermore, current peace plans apparently contemplate the destruction of additional capacity in Axis countries. Such a program obviously has an important bearing upon postwar competition in nitrogen. But even if we destroy all the nitrogen plants, including by-product nitrogen, in the lands of the two major warmakers—Germany and Japan—world capacity would still greatly exceed the highest rate of world consumption in any prewar year.

This would seem to promise cheap nitrogen. If permitted, vigorous competition might readily develop. On the other hand, surplus capacity and low prices may breed control schemes. Over half the American capacity is represented by government plants. The pressure to keep these out of production may be great. Already representatives of the Chilean industry and of the Chilean Government are insisting that disposition of these plants under terms which subsidize private producers would constitute a violation of the good-neighbor policy.[80] Already businessmen are insisting that war plants be held in reserve for future military emergencies.

Other countries have also expanded capacity for military rather than economic ends, and they will doubtless want to preserve domestic sources of nitrogen adequate for war emergencies. National states

80. In the spring of 1945 the United States and Chilean delegates to the Inter-American Conference on Problems of War and Peace, held in Mexico City, discussed the problem of the operation and disposal of the synthetic nitrogen plants owned by the United States Government. The Department of State, in a press release of April 3, 1945, summarized the results of the discussions as follows:

". . . the Secretary of State informed the Minister of Foreign Affairs of Chile that it was not the intention of the Government of the United States that the production by the Government of synthetic nitrogen in plants owned by it and constructed for war purposes should be continued beyond the period necessitated by the conditions or consequences of the war, except as might be necessary in order to maintain the plants in efficient operating condition for national security from the point of view not only of physical condition but also for the purpose of continuing scientific research and technological progress. The Chilean Minister of Foreign Affairs was also informed that should it be necessary for the Government of the United States to modify this position, there would be consultation with the Government of Chile before action was taken."

The Secretary also advised the Chilean Foreign Minister that the U.S. Government would consult with the Chilean Government before disposing of government-owned plants "if the terms or conditions of cession, sale, or lease of such plants to private interests might create serious problems affecting the production or exportation of Chilean nitrates."

In August 1944 the Inter-Bureau Committee on Postwar Programs recommended to the Department of Agriculture that the government should convert government-owned plants with a capacity of 300,000 tons of nitrogen to meet civilian needs, and the Secretary of Agriculture later submitted this recommendation to Congress. The Surplus Property Administration has since also recommended this program to Congress. See Report of the Surplus Property Administration to the Congress on *Chemical Plants and Facilities,* November 12, 1945, p. 52, and Supplement III, December 5, 1945, pp. 2-3.

will be reluctant to risk the future of these plants to the play of competitive business rivalry.[81] Nor is it likely that the businessmen will be willing to leave their position in the industry to the determination of free market forces. What constitutes wise policy with respect to these issues will depend on whether the immediate objective of policy is the promotion of political ends, the protection of vested interests, and the preservation of economic values, or the satisfaction of consumer needs.

81. Undoubtedly the atomic bomb has lessened greatly the military importance of nitrogen. But until its use and significance are more widely known nations are unlikely to abandon their policy of protecting domestic nitrogen plants.

Chapter 5

THE INTERNATIONAL STEEL CARTEL

IRON AND STEEL are basic not only to modern industry, but to modern warfare. World War I stimulated an expansion of productive capacity beyond peacetime needs. It did more than this: it disorganized the intricately interdependent elements of the Ruhr-Saar-Lorraine region, the center of the European industry. These disturbances led to the first international steel cartel. After months of negotiation, the steel producers of Germany, France, Belgium, Luxemburg, and the Saar signed an agreement on September 30, 1926 establishing the Entente Internationale de l'Acier (EIA). Although the countries represented in the cartel produced less than one third of the world output of steel in 1926, they accounted for about two thirds of all exports. The cartel's immediate objective was to eliminate competition among steel producers of the participating countries, and thereby insure a better price in world markets.

Before the steel cartel was organized in 1926, the European industry had conducted a reorganization and expansion which raised its capacity far above prewar levels. Meanwhile, the European demand for steel actually had declined. As a result, plant capacity exceeded the average rate of consumption. In 1925, when output was larger than in any other postwar year before the cartel's formation, steel ingot plants in Germany, France, Belgium, Luxemburg, and the United Kingdom operated on the average at only about 70 per cent of capacity.[1] Confronted with excess plant capacity and shrunken demand, the major European producers organized the cartel to avoid a costly competitive struggle in world markets.

World War I Disturbs Postwar Markets

The European steel industry's troubles began largely with World War I. Before 1913, world production of iron and steel had increased

1. See Walter S. Tower, "The New Steel Cartel," *Foreign Affairs* (New York), January 1927, pp. 255-56.

about 50 per cent every ten years. World production of steel ingots and castings reached a new high of more than 80 million long tons in 1917. In the early postwar years, however, production slumped sharply. During the six years 1919–1924, world production ranged from a low of 43.51 million tons in 1921 to a high of 77.23 million tons in 1924.[2] Although in the United States demand recovered promptly and soon reached new peaks, it expanded far more slowly throughout the rest of the world. In 1925 our consumption of iron and steel products exceeded that of 1913 by about 50 per cent. In the same year the combined consumption of the United Kingdom, Belgium, Luxemburg, Germany, the Saar, France, and Italy was about 5 per cent less than in 1913.[3] This contrasts sharply with other basic commodities. By 1925 both production and European consumption of cereals, textiles, rubber, and coal exceeded the prewar figures.

Two major factors, both growing out of the war, explain the failure of the demand for steel to expand in spite of an increase in world population and a general increase in production. The shipbuilding industry, which normally consumes large amounts of steel, had been continuously depressed in the postwar period because of its abnormal expansion during the war. Meanwhile, the impoverishment of Europe had decreased greatly capital investment in durable producers' goods. American lending, which later made good this deficit, had not yet got well under way.

The European steel industry is far more dependent on foreign markets than the American industry. Export markets grew rapidly before World War I. Between 1904 and 1913, iron and steel exports of the four leading exporting countries—Germany, United Kingdom, Belgium, and the United States—had increased from 7.8 million tons to 15.7 million tons, 100 per cent.[4] Germany exported about one

2. U.S. Tariff Commission, Report No. 128, Ser. II, *Iron and Steel*, Washington, 1938, p. 487 f. The figures are in long tons. Throughout this chapter unless otherwise noted, long tons are used. A long ton equals 2,240 pounds, a metric ton, 2,204.6 pounds.

3. League of Nations, International Economic Conference, May 1927, *Memorandum on the Iron and Steel Industry*, Geneva, 1927, p. 32. (This work will hereinafter be cited simply: L. of N., *Steel*.) The League's figures on consumption of iron and steel for the countries mentioned were calculated by adding to the production of raw steel that part of pig iron production not used for the manufacture of steel (wrought and cast iron), and combining this total with the import or export balance of raw steel and semifinished iron and steel.

4. D. L. Burn, *The Economic History of Steelmaking, 1867–1939*, The University Press, Cambridge, 1940, Table XXIV, p. 330.

third of its steel in 1913, and Great Britain and Belgium each exported about half. In contrast, the United States exported less than 10 per cent.

Moreover, export markets were seriously disrupted after the war. Stagnation in 1921 followed speculative buying in 1920. Labor troubles in Great Britain and Belgium, collapse of German currency, depreciation of French and Belgian currencies, French occupation of the Ruhr, and political disorders in Russia and China, all made for confusion in world trade. These developments aggravated the depression of the European industry.

Effect of World War I on the German Steel Industry

Economic and political disturbances growing out of the war, the Versailles Treaty, and national rivalries, which the war intensified, were largely responsible for overexpansion of the European iron and steel industry. The war and the peace settlement necessitated serious readjustments in the steel industries of all European countries, but their impact on the German industry was most serious. Germany had built its steel industry largely on Ruhr coal and Lorraine ore. Indeed, the whole closely knit and intricate Ruhr industrial machine rested on this foundation. A basic interdependence and sensitive balance had developed between the coal of the Ruhr and the ore of Lorraine.[5]

Both areas engaged in the full range of activities that turn ore into steel, but the Lorraine area specialized in pig iron and heavy steel, the Ruhr in coke, steel, and finished products. Ruhr coal, unexcelled for its coking qualities, moved as coke from the Ruhr to blast furnaces in the Lorraine area. On the return trip pig iron, as well as some ore, moved from Lorraine to the steel plants of the Ruhr.

Under the Versailles Treaty, Germany lost the whole Lorraine and Upper Silesian sectors of its steel industry and altogether relinquished territory (including the Saar and Luxemburg, which were separated from the German customs union) accounting for 75 to 80 per cent of its blast furnace capacity, about 45 per cent of its pig iron production, and about 24 per cent of its rolling mill capacity.[6] The most

5. See Guy Greer, *The Lorraine Industrial Problem*, Macmillan, New York, 1925, pp. 12-14, 20-21, 27-29.
6. C. E. Herring, *German Iron and Steel Industry*, Trade Information Bulletin No. 96, U.S. Department of Commerce, Washington, 1923, p. 1.

serious blow was the loss of the ore deposits of Alsace-Lorraine, together with sixty-five blast furnaces and nine steel works.[7]

The plants in the lost areas were among Germany's newest and
most modern. The loss not only strengthened the competitive position of the French, Belgian, and Polish industries, but disturbed
seriously the industrial balance and organic unity that previously had
characterized the German industry. Ore deposits, blast furnaces, steel
plants, and rolling mills previously under common political control,
and frequently common ownership, were disintegrated. Blast furnaces were separated from their source of ore or from the steel mills
they customarily supplied. Steel plants were separated from rolling
mills, and rolling mills from machine-manufacturing establishments.
In general, the Lorraine-Luxemburg steel industry was separated
from its coal and coke supply, the Ruhr industry from its principal
ore and pig iron supply.

Postwar Reorganization of German Industry

German iron and steel producers, anxious to fortify their position
in world markets and to integrate their operations, purchased new
properties or constructed new facilities within the new Reich. The
German Government encouraged and assisted them by indemnifying
the former German owners for their loss of private property, stipu-
lating that the funds be used to reorganize the industry or construct
new plants.[8] As a result, steelmaking capacity within the new German boundaries expanded rapidly. The expansion was not well
planned or coordinated, however, and it failed to correct the industry's imbalance.

Germany's postwar inflation further accentuated the tendency toward unbalanced expansion. Industrial leaders, fearful of the loss of
purchasing power, converted liquid capital promptly into physical
assets. They launched many industrial combines, often without regard to the diverse character of properties amalgamated. The gigantic Stinnes-controlled Siemens-Rhein-Elbe-Schukert-Union is an illustration. The Stinnes combine, which covered a wide range of

7. L. of N., *Steel*, p. 102. The disturbances in Upper Silesia, although on a somewhat
smaller scale, were of an equally serious nature.
8. Robert A. Brady, *The Rationalization Movement in German Industry*, University
of California Press, Berkeley, 1933, pp. 103-07.

industrial activities, including iron and steelmaking, proved so unwieldy that it collapsed in 1925.

After the Dawes plan stabilized the German monetary and banking system in 1924, the German steel industry further reorganized and expanded along more rational business lines. This reorganization was not merely to integrate more closely the physical processes of steelmaking, but to reduce market risks by bringing larger segments of the industry under common management. A few large fully integrated companies, chief of which was the United Steel Works (Vereinigte Stahlwerke A. G.) emerged in control of the industry.

Organization of United

United, organized in 1926, merged the properties of four of the largest German steel companies. The combine is comparable in size and scope, in relation to its more limited domestic market, to the United States Steel Corporation. Like the latter, it was a combination of combinations, controlling 40 to 50 per cent of the principal steel products manufactured in Germany. It merged: (1) the Rhein-Elbe-Union, formerly a part of the Stinnes combine and representing a community of interests among three integrated concerns—the Gelsenkirchener Bergwerks A. G., the Deutsch-Luxemburgische Bergwerks und Hütten A. G., and the Bochumer Verein für Bergbau und Gusstahlfabrikation; (2) the Thyssen Group, consisting of six iron and steel enterprises controlled by the Thyssen family; (3) Phoenix A. G., and some half-dozen affiliates; and (4) the Rheinische Stahlwerke A. G., about one half of the stock of which was owned by I. G. Farbenindustrie. United, together with five other combines—Friedrich Krupp A. G., the Gutehoffnungshütte Oberhausen A. G., the Hösch Eisen und Stahlwerke A. G., the Klöckner Werke A. G., and the Mannesmann Röhrenwerke—controlled most of the German output of iron and steel products.[9]

Rationalization and Cartelization

"Rationalization" of the iron and steel industry went hand in hand

9. The combined production quotas of these six concerns in the principal domestic iron and steel cartels in 1929 were: pig iron, 55 per cent; steel ingots, 77.4 per cent; semifinished steel products, 87.9 per cent; steel plates, 91.1 per cent; railroad structural steel, 84 per cent. See National Industrial Conference Board, *Rationalization of German Industry*, New York, 1931, p. 93.

with reorganization. Rationalization involved regrouping and modernization of existing plants and equipment, improvement in layout, closer integration of technical processes to economize fuel and handling costs, construction of new plants to establish a better balance among the several stages of production under concentrated control, and replacement of plants technically obsolete or badly located for raw materials or markets.[10]

The rationalization program, which required a sharp increase in capital investment, was financed partly by loans floated by American bankers.[11] The indebtedness of eight German iron and steel firms increased by more than 600 million marks from 1925 to 1928. During the same period, steel companies plowed back large sums from earnings. Vereinigte Stahlwerke alone reinvested some 400 million marks from 1926 to 1929.[12]

Domestic cartelization went hand in hand with rationalization. Domestic cartels were not new to the German steel industry, but of the many prewar cartels only Roheisenverband G. m. b. H., regulating the marketing of pig iron, had survived the war and the inflation. After the German currency was stabilized and the German banking system reorganized, a brief period of severe price competition ensued. Organization of the crude steel cartel (Rohstahlgemeinschaft) in October 1924, followed by seventy-odd other domestic cartels covering iron and steel products, ended the price wars. The cartels in crude steel, "A products" or semifinished steel, structural shapes and heavy rails (A-Produkten-Verband), merchant bars (Stabeisen-Verband), bands and strips (Bandeisen-Vereinigung), heavy plates (Grobblech-Verband), rolled wire (Walzdraht-Verband), and drawn wire (Draht-Verband) were combined under common management as the Stahlwerke-Verband A. G., a corporation with stock held by the

10. Rationalization was partly the industrialists' response to trade-union demands. Although the average percentage of unemployment among German trade-union members (all industries) was 11.5 in 1924–1929 and employment in iron and steel showed a slight decrease, wage rates in this industry increased 25 per cent. Businessmen invested in improved equipment to lower labor costs. See Frederic Benham, *The Iron and Steel Industry of Germany, France, Belgium, Luxemburg and the Saar*, Special Memorandum No. 39, London and Cambridge Economic Service, 1934, p. 23. A more important factor was the German turnover tax on all money sales. This was at the rate of 2 per cent in 1924. Although reduced gradually to three fourths of one per cent by 1930, it no doubt encouraged integration in the iron and steel industry as a means of avoiding the tax.

11. See *Iron Trade Review*, January 29, 1925, Vol. LXXVI, No. 5, p. 339 f.; also Benham, *op. cit.*, p. 22 f.

12. Benham, *op. cit.*, p. 22 f.

cartel members. These together with the other German cartels established effective control over output and prices of iron and steel products in the domestic market.[13]

Results of "Rationalization"

Rationalization and domestic cartelization of German steel brought temporary prosperity to the leading producers. The industry earned an average return of 8 to 9 per cent on capital stock during the twenties and paid dividends of 5 to 6 per cent.[14] United did somewhat better. During its first three fiscal years it not only paid dividends of 6 per cent on its capital stock of 800 million Reichsmarks, but spent more than 300 million Reichsmarks in improving its plant and equipment. It also increased its investment in other concerns by 90 million Reichsmarks, and reduced the book value of its plant and equipment by 20 million Reichsmarks.[15]

Although rationalization and domestic cartelization brought prosperity to the German steel industry, apparently they did not result in its efficient organization or an economical utilization of its resources. Their primary aim was to improve the commercial position of the leading producers and to establish centralized control over the domestic market. Economy in production was subordinated to market control. Leading producers acquired marginal firms to stifle competition. They paid for these properties prices representing their nuisance value to the cartel, rather than values based on their independent earning power. For example, in 1930, during negotiations for renewal of the domestic cartel, members bought plants of numerous independents threatening competition at an estimated cost of 60 to 70 million marks—far more than their market value on the Berlin stock exchange.[16]

"Rationalization" saddled an excessive overhead on the industry. It expanded productive capacity far more than was necessary to supply the peacetime domestic and export markets at prevailing

13. For a fuller discussion of these developments, consult Rudolf K. Michels, *Cartels, Combines and Trusts in Post-War Germany,* Columbia University Press, New York, 1928, Chap. 7; National Industrial Conference Board, *op. cit.,* Chap. 4; and Brady, *op. cit.,* Chap. 6.

14. Estimates made by J. W. Angell, *The Recovery of Germany,* Yale University Press, New Haven, 1932, p. 127 f.

15. National Industrial Conference Board, *op. cit.,* p. 99. See also "Das Neue Stahl-Jahrzehnt," *Frankfurter Zeitung,* February 16, 1930.

16. Benham, *op. cit.,* p. 25.

prices. "Capacity" in the steel industry is a loose and relative term, and data on capacity may be somewhat misleading. But investigators of the German steel industry, using available materials, agree that the industry was greatly overexpanded.[17]

In 1928, when output was close to its postwar high, productive capacity for pig iron exceeded actual output by about 30 per cent, according to Angell. Palmer estimated that productive capacity of all German plants producing steel ingots and castings in 1925 and 1926 was 17.5 million metric tons. Output in these years was only 12.294 million metric tons and 12.342 million tons, respectively.[18] Plants apparently operated on the average at about 70 per cent of capacity.

Enquête Ausschuss

Enquête Ausschuss, an official commission set up by the German Government to investigate production and marketing conditions in the whole German economy, held extensive hearings in which experts and industrial leaders thoroughly familiar with conditions within the iron and steel industry took part. The commission concluded that the industry was greatly overexpanded, its investments badly planned, and its structural organization cumbersome and uneconomic. In 1930, the commission summarized its judgment in these words: "The difficult conditions under which most of the German steel industry is laboring today are not occasioned by the cyclical fluctuations in business, but stem from the structural upbuilding of the industry and are therefore determined by permanent factors." [19]

Rival business groups "put through" the postwar reorganization of the German steel industry to fortify their position in the market. They received, however, the active support of the German Government, which was anxious to make good the loss in productive capac-

17. See L. of N., *Steel*, p. 87 f.; J. W. Angell, *op. cit.*, pp. 118-21; National Industrial Conference Board, *op. cit.*, pp. 102-04; Ausschuss zur Untersuchung der Erzeugungs-und-Absatzbedingungen der deutschen Wirtschaft, III, Arbeitsgruppe 3, Band 2, *Die deutsche eisenerzeugende Industrie, passim* (hereinafter referred to as Enquête Ausschuss); *Frankfurter Zeitung*, December 16, 1930, "Eisen-Ueberkapazität, Das Urteil des Enquête-Ausschusses"; J. Joseph W. Palmer, *Origin and Development of the Continental Steel Entente*, Trade Information Bulletin No. 484, U.S. Bureau of Foreign and Domestic Commerce, Washington, 1927.

18. Palmer, *op. cit.*, p. 3.

19. Enquête Ausschuss, p. 122. Leading German steel producers vigorously denounced the findings of the commission. They contended that the industry's troubles were largely the result of the general decline in business activity and excessive burdens imposed on it by the government through taxation and social legislation. See Brady, *op. cit.*, p. 125, and National Industrial Conference Board, *op. cit.*, p. 103.

ity resulting from the Versailles Treaty and to regain, if indeed not to enlarge, Germany's prewar industrial power. German industrialists and the state planned not merely to meet the requirements of the domestic market but to regain and even strengthen their premier position in export markets. Before the war, Germany ranked second only to the United States as a producer of iron and steel products; [20] and as an exporter she led the world.

Reconstruction of the French Industry

But in the struggle for postwar markets German producers met far more vigorous competition than in the last prewar decade. While territorial losses had curtailed Germany's immediate productive capacity, they expanded correspondingly that of her continental competitors. France and Belgium were the chief beneficiaries. France gained directly the blast furnaces, steel mills, and ore deposits of Lorraine. France gained indirectly by inclusion of the Saar in her customs area, and Belgium through inclusion of Luxemburg in her customs area.

By the recovery of Alsace-Lorraine, France virtually doubled her capacity for producing iron ore, increased pig iron capacity by about two thirds, and ingots and castings by about one half. The blast furnaces in the ceded area produced an average of 2.9 million metric tons of pig iron during the four years 1909–1913, while in 1913 steel plants produced 2.3 million metric tons of steel ingots and castings. This compared with average production in France during the same years of 4.4 million metric tons of pig iron and 4.7 million [21] of steel ingots and castings.

Three other factors further increased France's postwar productive capacity. First, iron and steel plants had been built in other districts during the war to compensate for those captured or destroyed by the Germans in the industrial areas of northern and eastern France.

20. From 1909 to 1913, the United States produced an annual average of 27.9 million metric tons of pig iron and 27.7 million metric tons of steel ingots and castings. Germany's average annual production of pig iron for the same period was 14.0 million metric tons and her average annual production of steel ingots and castings was 14.5 million. The United Kingdom, ranking third, produced an average of 9.8 million metric tons of pig iron and an average of 6.7 million metric tons of steel ingots. Germany, including Luxemburg, ranked first in exports, with a total of 6.3 million metric tons of iron and steel products in 1913; the United Kingdom ranked second with 5.0 million metric tons; and the United States third with 3.0 million metric tons. L. of N., *Steel*, pp. 29, 40-43.

21. *Ibid.*, pp. 40-42.

Second, plants in the devastated areas had been rebuilt, enlarged, and modernized in the postwar reconstruction. Third, French iron and steelmaking facilities were expanded in reorganization of the industry after acquisition of the German properties, incorporation of the Saar into the French customs area, and severance of ownership and political ties between the properties of the ceded areas and those of the Ruhr. This expansion was directed primarily toward a better balance between domestic capacity for pig iron and crude steel, on the one hand, and for finished rolled products, on the other. The blast furnaces and steel plants acquired by French concerns lost part of their customary market and had to look for outlets elsewhere. Expansion of finished iron and steel plants within France provided a partial outlet.[22]

With the cession of Alsace-Lorraine to France, the French Government took over the properties formerly owned by German industrialists and credited them to the German Government as a payment on reparations. Five groups of French iron and steel companies subsequently acquired these properties.[23]

Increases in Productive Capacity

French productive capacity had increased between 1913 and 1925 far more than domestic consumption. In 1913 French exports of iron and steel totalled only 630,000 metric tons; by 1925 they had multiplied more than sixfold, to 3,875,000 metric tons.[24] Although the postwar expansion established a somewhat better balance of productive facilities under common ownership and political control, it did not destroy completely the basic interdependence between the French and German industries. French plants continued to receive some Ruhr coke credited as payments on reparations under the Versailles

22. Figures are not available showing changes in French capacity for the production of finished rolled steel products. Production figures throw some light on the problem, however. Maximum prewar production of finished steel in French postwar areas was 4.7 million metric tons in 1913. Production in 1925 had increased to 4.9 million metric tons. See *ibid.*, p. 50. Moreover, the industry presumably was operating much closer to capacity in 1913 than in 1925.

23. Schneider-de-Wendel; Société de la Marine-Homécourt; Société Lorraine Minière et Métallurgique; La Société des Aciéries du Nord et de Lorraine; and Société Cooperative des Consommateurs. See U.S. Bureau of Foreign and Domestic Commerce, Trade Information Bulletin No. 367, *The French Iron and Steel Industry*, Washington, 1925, p. 33 f.

24. L. of N., *Steel*, p. 29.

Treaty. Until January 10, 1925, Lorraine blast furnaces and steel plants also sold large quantities of iron and steel products in Germany free of duty under a provision of the Treaty. In spite of the help of the Versailles Treaty, France was forced to find markets outside of Germany for much of her iron and steel.

Moreover, German producers needed Lorraine ore so badly that they continued for a while to import substantial amounts. Germany soon took measures, however, to find alternative sources of iron ore. When the French occupied the Ruhr in 1923, the German industry entered into contracts with Swedish producers for large quantities of ore.[25] Thereafter the German industry looked more and more to Sweden and to Spain for its ore.

Similar postwar readjustments in the iron and steel industry of Luxemburg and Belgium, occasioned by similar influences, contributed to an increase in their productive capacity. The combined capacities of Germany, the Saar, France, Luxemburg, and Belgium increased sharply between 1913 and 1925. Although no data are available on the prewar pig iron capacity of these areas, their combined output of pig iron in 1913 (when output was not far short of capacity) was 26 million tons. This compares with an estimated capacity of 34 million tons in 1925.[26] The combined capacities of these areas for steel ingots and castings in 1925 was about 32 million tons, compared with a 1913 output of 24.8 million tons.

England Also Expands Capacity

Expansion of the British industry further aggravated the competitive situation. Most of the increase in British capacity took place during the war, although capacity increased somewhat in the postwar reconstruction. During the war, shipping losses from the German submarine campaign necessitated a substantial increase in crude steel and heavy plates manufacturing facilities. The shipbuilding boom in 1920 further expanded capacity. Between 1913 and 1927, British pig iron capacity increased from 11 million to 12 million tons; crude steel, from 8 million to 12 million; rolled and forged products, from

25. British Parliamentary Committee on Industry and Trade, *Survey of Metal Industries*, Part IV of a survey of industries, London, 1928, p. 80. (Hereafter referred to as the Balfour Committee, after its chairman.)
26. *Ibid.*, p. 79 f.

7 or 8 million to 10 or 12 million.[27] But British pig iron production in 1925 was only 52 per cent of capacity and steel ingots only 61.5 per cent of capacity.[28] With postwar European consumption of iron and steel below that of the best prewar year and the total productive capacity of the principal European producers greatly above the prewar levels, competition in world markets was severe and price cutting was the rule.

Influence of Depreciated Currencies and Tariff Barriers

Two other factors aggravated the struggle for international markets. First, the depreciation in national currencies intensified competition in the world market and injected into it new elements of uncertainty and speculation. Germany's postwar inflation, especially, gave German exporters a temporary advantage. After the Dawes plan and the stabilization of the German mark, the situation was reversed. German exporters were then at a disadvantage in competing with French and Belgian producers whose national currencies had not yet been stabilized. Second, after January 1925, Germany, no longer required under the reparations settlement to accept French and Saar iron and steel duty-free, erected prohibitive tariff barriers. Other countries followed suit.

The First International Steel Cartel

In 1926 the iron and steel producers of Germany, Luxemburg, Belgium, the Saar, and France began negotiations to bring their combined production under concerted control and to harmonize their conflicting interests. German industrialists, accustomed to group action and familiar with machinery for stabilizing markets, took the lead in these negotiations. On September 30, 1926, the organized steel producers of the five areas signed an accord, establishing the first international steel cartel.[29] The agreement was to last until

27. *Ibid.,* p. 18.
28. L. of N., *Steel,* p. 107.
29. This was the first comprehensive international steel cartel attempting to control, although indirectly, all semifinished and finished steel products. Cartels to control the marketing of specific steel products had been organized at a much earlier date. The oldest of these was the International Rail Makers Association (IRMA), first organized toward the end of the nineteenth century and reorganized from time to time thereafter. Ervin Hexner, *The International Steel Cartel,* University of North Carolina Press, Chapel Hill, 1943, pp. 69-71, 154, 203.

March 31, 1931, unless ended at an earlier date in accordance with a prescribed procedure.[30]

The first steel cartel tried to stabilize steel markets by: (1) determining the total amount of crude steel to be produced by the countries represented in the cartel, (2) dividing allowable production among these countries in accordance with predetermined quotas, and (3) penalizing cartel members whose country exceeded its allowance. The basis of quota allotment was relative production during the first quarter of 1926. Initial quotas were: Germany, 40.45 per cent; France, 31.89 per cent; Belgium, 12.57 per cent; Luxemburg, 8.55 per cent; Saar Territory, 6.54 per cent.[31] A management committee, composed of a representative from each of the four major participating groups,[32] determined quarterly the total tonnage to be produced.

The cartel created a system of penalties and compensations. If any country exceeded its allotted quarterly production, the cartel required that country's producers to pay into the cartel's common fund a fine of $4 per metric ton of excess (Article VI).[33] If any country fell short of its allowable production, the cartel paid its national group

30. Various publications give the text of the agreement. See Palmer, *op. cit.*, p. 15 f. Also L. of N., *Steel*, pp. 109-12. These two studies reproduce what purports to be the whole of the agreement. According to Ervin Hexner, who participated as a representative of the Czechoslovakian steel industry in the second international steel cartel, both accounts omit Article XV of the agreement and produce only parts of Articles XII and XIII. Hexner reproduces the text including these omissions. While indicating that his own reproduction is incomplete, he does not state in what respects. See Hexner, *op. cit.*, p. 72 and Appendix III, pp. 289-95.

31. The determination of quotas was perhaps the most difficult problem confronting the cartel organizers. Its settlement took months of negotiation. Belgian producers, who were the least well organized of any national group and whose production had been curtailed in the first quarter of 1926 by a strike, offered the chief stumbling block. See Palmer, *op. cit.*, p. 9. To get Belgian agreement, the cartel granted the Belgians a quota larger than that based on their 1926 first-quarter output. Germany's quota was cut with the understanding that, as allowable production was expanded, Germany's quota would be increased at the expense of the other participants, primarily Belgium, until it reached a maximum of 43.18 per cent. L. of N., *Steel*, p. 113; also Hexner, p. 294 f.

32. Germany, France, Belgium, and Luxemburg. Germany and France together represented the Saar producers.

33. Although the cartel was a contractual arrangement between "national groups" representing the steel producers of the several countries, it resembled an official commercial treaty. According to its strict language, the accord required the "country" that exceeded its quota to pay the fines. The governments of the participating groups approved, if indeed they did not sponsor, the negotiations for setting up the cartel. See Palmer, *op. cit.*, p. 21. Difficulties which the French and German Governments had in negotiating a commercial treaty delayed the cartel agreement. Article X of the cartel accord provides for its termination if Germany should increase its tariff on iron and steel or if the "Government of one of the Contracting Parties objects to it on the ground that, in the absence of a commercial treaty, one of the other countries is applying unfavorable treatment to the products as a whole."

$2 a metric ton for every ton of deficit (Article VII) up to 10 per cent of the allowable production.[34] The cartel made each national group responsible for production in excess of its country's quota, even though the excess was caused by the refusal of nonmembers to go along with the cartel program.

In short, the cartel determined to what extent each country's steel plants could be utilized without payment of a fine. This gave a strong incentive to cartel members to perfect their domestic organization in closely knit, cohesive national groups. Although the object of the arrangement was to limit competition in international markets, the procedure was to restrict the output of crude steel domestically.

Contemporary Opinion of the Cartel

In spite of the limited membership and scope of the cartel, industrialists, politicians, and students of economic affairs all heralded it as an industrial event of historical significance. They differed widely, however, as to just what it signified. Mindful of the disturbing effects of the Versailles Treaty on the industrial interdependence of the Ruhr-Lorraine area, the London *Economist* saw in the arrangements "from one point of view . . . simply a repairing of one of the fissures in the European economic structure made by the Peace Treaty." [35] A representative of the American Department of Commerce in London said: "The conclusion of the European steel agreement has been hailed by some of its sponsors as the greatest recent economic development and a first step toward the formation of an 'Economic United States of Europe.' " [36]

Others, taking a narrower view, thought it might place nonintegrated producers, who bought their steel from cartel members, at a disadvantage or that its power might be directed toward domination of the world's markets. Still others, while taking a similar

34. The cartel also required its members monthly to pay into the common fund one dollar for every metric ton of steel produced (Art. I). Penalty accounts were balanced quarterly and fines and bonuses paid immediately. After deducting general expenses, the cartel liquidated the common fund semiannually. It distributed among its members, in proportion to their actual production, an amount equal to the total tonnage payments for the six months. It distributed the remainder among members in proportion to their quotas (Art. VIII). Under this arrangement, a portion of the penalties paid for overproduction might be returned to the offenders.
35. *The Economist,* October 9, 1926, p. 572. Trade Commissioner David J. Reagan at Paris expressed a similar point of view in a report dated October 23, 1926. See Palmer, *op. cit.,* p. 30 f.
36. See Palmer, *op. cit.,* p. 41.

approach, doubted the cartel's ability to dominate world markets, but believed it might alleviate cutthroat competition, insure a more remunerative adjustment between world output of steel and world consumption, and benefit all steel producers, whether or not members of the cartel.[37]

The Cartel, an Instrument of Market Control

The cartel, as judged by subsequent developments, was the first step in a program to substitute collective control for competition in international steel markets. Under this program an individual producer no longer was free to determine how much steel he would produce, where he would sell it, and at what prices. The principal sellers of steel were jointly to decide these matters. Confronted by vigorous competition, which was aggravated by surplus capacity and a temporarily slackened uptrend in steel consumption, European steel producers tried to improve their cost-price relationships by centralizing control of crude steel production.

As a fair-weather device for stabilizing steel markets, the plan early showed serious defects. The cartel controlled directly neither the price of crude steel nor the output or price of any rolled steel product. Non–cartel members produced about two thirds of the world exports. The cartel's coverage industry-wise was limited. Although designed primarily to stabilize export markets, the cartel tried to control total crude steel output of the participating countries, whether intended for domestic or foreign markets. But the only check on output of crude steel was the fine for excess production. Since total unit costs tended to drop as existing facilities were more fully utilized, some individual producers found advantage in expanding production—the fines were less than the additions to net income.

Collapse of the Cartel

Although with mounting prosperity demand for steel improved during the early life of the cartel, and although the cartel raised allowable output from time to time, producers persistently exceeded their quotas. The worst offenders were the Germans. As their fines mounted in 1926 and early in 1927, they demanded revision of

37. See Walter S. Tower, *op. cit.,* pp. 249-66, *passim;* Hexner, *op. cit., passim;* and Palmer, *op. cit., passim.*

quotas and reduction of fines as a price of continued adherence to the cartel.[38] After protracted negotiations, the cartel raised Germany's quota and broke it into two parts—domestic and export. They then reduced the fines for exceeding the domestic quota, first to two dollars and later to one dollar a metric ton.[39]

With the world-wide recession in demand during 1930, the cartel found it increasingly difficult to stabilize the price of rolled steel products by its direct but ineffectual control over the output of crude steel. It therefore suspended control over crude steel production from February 1 to July 17, 1930, and instituted direct controls over certain steel products. Syndicates were set up to sell semifinished steel, structural steel, merchant bars, hoops and strips, and plates in export markets for all cartel members at uniform prices. The syndicates distributed the orders in accordance with predetermined quotas.

This belated attempt to salvage the cartel proved inadequate. It failed utterly to stem the decline in steel prices. By March 1, 1931, the cartel had abandoned all pretense of controlling prices, and by the middle of the year the organization dissolved.

The Second International Steel Cartel

After a year and a half of unregulated competition, during which steel prices reached their lowest ebb, the charter members of the original cartel began negotiations which culminated in a more comprehensive and far-reaching scheme for controlling world markets. During these negotiations, certain principles crystallized for avoiding the pitfalls of the earlier venture.

A general agreement regulated the export of all crude or semifinished steel, and six special agreements regulated the export of certain classes of steel products. The general agreement provided over-all quotas for each national group. The special agreements fixed specific quotas for particular classes of steel products—bars, rods, structural shapes, and the like—which might or might not correspond to the over-all quotas of the several national groups. In addition,

38. In the first year of the cartel the German groups paid in fines the equivalent of $10,381,000, 95 per cent of the total penalties incurred by the original cartel members. See Wm. F. Notz, *Representative International Cartels, Combines and Trusts,* Trade Promotion Series, No. 81, Bureau of Foreign and Domestic Commerce, p. 51 f. An increase in demand for steel in German markets and an improvement of Germany's position in world markets, as the franc currencies were stabilized and world business expanded, apparently made the Germans less favorable to the cartel.

39. See Hexner, *op. cit.,* p. 78. See also Notz, *op. cit.,* p. 51 f.

each of these special agreements established a selling syndicate for a given class of products and made it the exclusive agency of members for export sales. The cartel supervised and coordinated the activities of the several syndicates.

The new agreement became effective June 1, 1933. It was to have ended on June 30, 1938, but, before it expired, was renewed. However, the outbreak of World War II disrupted it. Between the date of its organization and its termination, the cartel greatly expanded its scope, modified its procedures and structure, and tightened its market controls. Eventually it embraced, besides the organizing groups of Germany, France, Belgium, and Luxemburg, the major steel-producing groups of Czechoslovakia, Poland, Austria, the United Kingdom, and the United States. It brought within its jurisdiction about 90 per cent of all the iron and steel entering international trade in 1937.[40] This expansion transformed it from a European steel cartel into a world steel cartel.

Structure of the Second International Steel Cartel

The cartel's structure is presented in a simplified form in Chart 2. A management committee consisting of representatives of each of the national groups and a *comptoir* committee consisting of the managing directors of each of the export syndicates were the cartel policy-making bodies. Although no sharp functional division existed between these two committees, the management committee, as the general over-all administrative agency, was concerned primarily with broad questions of general policy and with matters of organization. The *comptoir* committee's functions were narrower. The two committees were jointly responsible for coordinating the programs of the several selling syndicates. The *comptoir* committee dealt primarily with prices, distribution, elimination of outside competition, and other practical problems.

Since producers in some finishing branches were not well enough organized to operate a sales syndicate effectively, the cartel provided temporarily for dual control over exports of steel products. First, it determined periodically the total tonnage of steel to be exported. Most of this was exported as finished products. For this part the

40. This figure was derived from export statistics included in *Statistics of the Iron and Steel Industries*, 1937, published by the British Iron and Steel Federation.

cartel translated allowable exports into tons of crude steel required to manufacture the specified products.[41] It then distributed the total among the national groups in accordance with their quotas. Second, the cartel determined periodically an export tonnage for each product for which a selling syndicate had been organized. The selling syndicate then allocated this tonnage among the several national groups in accordance with specific quotas which it established.

When the cartel began operations in 1933, it organized six special selling syndicates. The activities of several others, previously formed, were later articulated with the cartel program, and the cartel sponsored some additional syndicates. Eventually the cartel supervised and coordinated the market-regulating activities of seventeen affiliated selling syndicates.[42] (See Chart 2.)

As the cartel thus brought export of specific steel products more completely under control, it gradually relinquished its over-all limitations on the amount of crude steel that members could use for the manufacture of products for export markets. The cartel suspended limitations on crude steel production on July 1, 1936, and formally abolished them when it was renewed as of July 1, 1938.[43]

Special Product-Selling Syndicates

Cartel experience showed that export steel markets could be most effectively controlled by separate marketing organizations for each particular product. Although the several selling syndicates differed in structure, scope, administration, and effectiveness, they had certain common features and conducted similar activities. The structure and functions of the merchant-bar syndicate are fairly typical. This syndicate was formed when the general cartel agreement was signed in June 1933. Its original members were the Steel-Works Union of Germany, the French Iron and Steel Comptoir, and similar groups representing the steel producers of Belgium and Luxemburg. The purpose of the organization (Article I)[44] was "to regulate the export sales of merchant bars and effectively to adjust the supply to the consumers' demand."

41. For this purpose cartel members had agreed upon appropriate conversion factors. See Hexner, op. cit., p. 83.
42. The International Scrap Convention was a buying syndicate designed to centralize the buying power of cartel members in the purchase of scrap iron.
43. See Hexner, op. cit., p. 85.
44. The agreement is reproduced as Appendix V, Hexner, op. cit.

CHART 2. INTERNATIONAL STEEL CARTEL AND ASSOCIATED EXPORT SYNDICATES

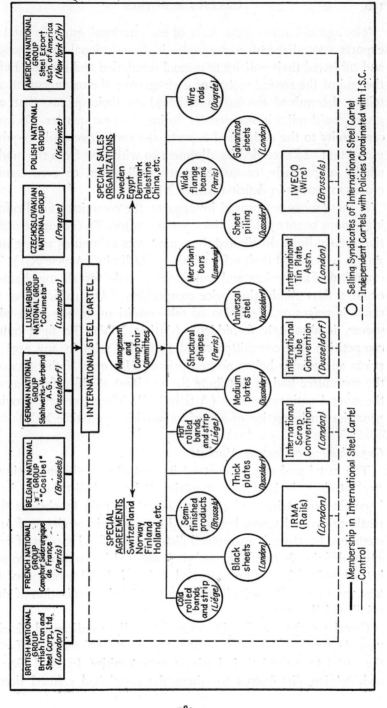

BRITISH NATIONAL GROUP British Iron and Steel Corp., Ltd. *(London)*

FRENCH NATIONAL GROUP Comptoir Sidérurgique de France *(Paris)*

BELGIAN NATIONAL GROUP "Cosibel" *(Brussels)*

GERMAN NATIONAL GROUP Stahlwerks-Verband A.G. *(Düsseldorf)*

LUXEMBURG NATIONAL GROUP "Columeta" *(Luxemburg)*

CZECHOSLOVAKIAN NATIONAL GROUP *(Prague)*

POLISH NATIONAL GROUP *(Katowice)*

AMERICAN NATIONAL GROUP Steel Export Ass'n. of America *(New York City)*

INTERNATIONAL STEEL CARTEL

Management and Comptoir Committees

SPECIAL AGREEMENTS Switzerland Norway Finland Holland, etc.

SPECIAL SALES ORGANIZATIONS Sweden Egypt Denmark Palestine China, etc.

Cold rolled bands and strip *(Liège)*

Black sheets *(London)*

Semi-finished products *(Brussels)*

Thick plates *(Düsseldorf)*

Hot rolled bands and strip *(Liège)*

Medium plates *(Düsseldorf)*

Structural shapes *(Paris)*

Universal steel *(Düsseldorf)*

Merchant bars *(Luxemburg)*

Sheet piling *(Düsseldorf)*

Wide flange beams *(Paris)*

Galvanized sheets *(London)*

Wire rods *(Augrée)*

IRMA (Rails) *(London)*

International Scrap Convention *(London)*

International Tube Convention *(Düsseldorf)*

International Tin Plate Ass'n. *(London)*

IWECO (Wire) *(Brussels)*

Membership in International Steel Cartel
—— Control
○ Selling Syndicates of International Steel Cartel
--- Independent Cartels with Policies Coordinated with I.S.C.

189

The agreement fixed the share of each national group in total bar exports, centralized all export sales in four national sales agencies, and subjected their policies to mutual regulation and control. Before the end of the second month of each quarter, the management committee determined the tonnage, based on their quotas, that each group could sell without penalty during the next quarter. To insure conformity to the authorized exports, the committee could require a group that had exceeded its allotment to withdraw from the market, wholly or partially, or quote "protective" prices, or even transfer orders to groups in deficit (Article XII).

If these measures proved inadequate, the committee fined offending groups twenty gold shillings per excess ton. To encourage restriction the syndicate distributed these payments as bonuses among those groups which kept their sales within quota limits (Article XII). The committee fixed prices and conditions of sale for all merchant-bar exports, thus eliminating price competition. "Any reduction or discount in prices or alleviation of sale conditions, in any form whatsoever, is absolutely forbidden" (Article XIV). To fight outside competition, the committee could authorize sales in any area "at prices appreciably below normal prices." However, if this occurred, the committee had to distribute the resultant sacrifice fairly among the several national groups (Article XV). The agreement provided penalties for infraction of any of its provisions (Article XIX).

Organization of Import Markets

The cartel undertook to extend its control over the marketing of steel products in importing countries. It licensed distributors in the importing countries, and required them not only to observe fixed resale prices and terms, but to handle exclusively products of cartel members. In return it guaranteed distributors a fixed margin of profit and a definite share of the market. It allotted import quotas to markets organized in this manner, and assigned the distribution of this tonnage among domestic distributors to a local organization of those privileged licensees.

Cartel members ordinarily refused to sell to unlicensed distributors. At times independent sellers strenuously resisted the effort of the cartel to control their business opportunities. In 1934 German and Belgian distributors to whom the cartel had refused licenses protested so vigorously—even endeavoring to elicit the support of their respective governments in the controversy—that the cartel compromised by setting up a second category of distributors and allowing them half the customary commission. However, the cartel required merchants in the new category to buy through licensed distributors.[45]

Since such "organized markets" proved exceptionally profitable, the cartel persistently tried to expand the areas and to increase the number of products subject to these elaborate distributive controls. It eventually set up similar controls for one or more products in Denmark, Sweden, Norway, Portugal, Bulgaria, Greece, Japan, China, Egypt, Syria, Palestine, and India.[46] Where a local steel industry operated in such an "organized" area, the cartel tried to bring the domestic industry under the control scheme. It concluded special agreements for this purpose with Swiss, Norwegian, Dutch, Finnish, and South African steel producers.[47]

Significance and Importance of National Groups

Throughout the entire life of the second international steel cartel, the national groups that composed its primary membership played a role of peculiar importance. Each national group comprised the leading domestic steel-producing companies. The continental groups were generally incorporated. Ordinarily, group membership was identical with that of the domestic steel cartel.[48] Home markets were generally reserved to the national groups, though the cartel and supplementary syndicate agreements provided for some specific exceptions. A cartel quota applied to a country as a unit, and each national group divided its quota among its members, making such allowance for nonmembers as it saw fit. In return for protecting its home markets, the second cartel like the first held each national group responsible for keeping exports from its territory within its quota.

45. *Ibid.*, p. 165. For a further discussion of the organization of distribution, see Tariff Commission, *op. cit.*, p. 401 f., and Hexner, Chap. 7.
46. See Hexner, *op. cit.*, p. 170.
47. Tariff Commission, *op. cit.*, p. 401.
48. American participation in the cartel was through the Steel Export Association of America, organized in 1928 under the Webb-Pomerene Act. Polish participation was through an export cartel closely affiliated with the domestic cartel. The national groups of the other participants were organizations designed both to control the domestic market and to regulate exports.

Each national group was responsible for control of its home market. The cartel's success depended largely on the effectiveness with which the several national groups discharged this responsibility. Weakness of the Belgian group had prevented an earlier renewal of the cartel. Eventually, as the depression deepened and as the financial stake of Belgian bankers in the steel companies increased, their influence overcame the separatist tendencies in the industry and in 1933 Belgian producers organized Comptoir de Vente de la Sidérurgique Belge. Better known by its more picturesque name of Cosibel, this cooperative commercial company with a nominal capital of 5 million francs operated as a selling agency on both the domestic and export markets.[49]

Organization of the British Market

The British industry affords the best illustration of the necessity of tight control over the domestic market to insure effective participation. Developments in the British steel industry also signalize the radical departure of British industrial practice in recent years from the principles of economic liberalism.

When the first steel cartel was organized in 1926, British steel producers were invited to join. The British industry at that time was at a competitive disadvantage in foreign markets, partly because of unfavorable exchange rates. It stood to gain, therefore, from cooperating in a plan to raise prices in export markets. Nevertheless, the British did not join. The London *Economist* commented: "Even if Great Britain wished to join, the British steel industry is not yet accustomed to co-operative working, and has not developed the internal machinery for limiting production in accordance with such a plan." [50]

The difficulties of the British industry were of long standing. Control of the industry was decentralized. Both the ownership unit and the operating plant were relatively small. Traditional family ownership was the rule, and it is said to have resulted in rigidity and lack of adaptability. Operations in plants technically interdependent but separately owned were not well articulated. Nor was geographic

---

49. Cosibel's direct control was limited to semifinished steel, structural steel, merchant bars, thick plates, medium plates, universal steel, and black sheets. Separately administered *comptoirs* controlled other steel products. See Hexner, *op. cit.,* p. 120.
50. *The Economist,* October 2, 1926, p. 539.

coordination of the several branches of the industry highly developed. Many of the plant units were antiquated and inefficient.[51]

Although the British industry had made some progress toward amalgamation, integration, and modernization of equipment particularly in the postwar years, it was far behind the American and the German industry in the use of mass production techniques and continuous processes. In the main, steel production in the British Isles was still geared to a "special order" type of operation. Production costs remained relatively high, and the industry continued to lose ground in world markets.

World War I aggravated the competitive disadvantage of the British steel industry. In response to war demands, the industry had shown a marked but uneven expansion in capacity. Pig iron capacity increased between 1913 and 1926 by about 10 per cent, while that for steel ingots and castings increased by about 50 per cent.[52] Although expansion had resulted in some individual plants of modern design and great technical efficiency, according to the Balfour Committee

. . . few British works, if any, [were] modern throughout in equipment and practice, with coking ovens, blast furnaces, steel furnaces and rolling mills adjacent to one another, and making full use of waste gases. Moreover, there [was] not infrequently a lack of balance between the productive capacity at different stages, e.g., deficient coking oven or blast furnace capacity.[53]

Moreover, as a result of extensions constructed at inflated wartime price levels, heavy capitalization burdened the industry.

In contrast, the German, French, and Belgian industries had undergone a comprehensive businesslike reorganization both in their structure and in their physical plant and equipment. More important, the German industry (and to a less extent the French), by reason of closely knit cartel control of its domestic market, was able to follow a persistent policy of price discrimination. This gave it a tremendous

51. The Balfour Committee reported in 1928: "Regarding the iron and steel industry itself, there seems no doubt that the efficiency of plant is less uniform in the heavy branches of the British industry than it is in Germany or America. This is primarily a result of the earlier development of the industry in this country, and the survival of plant which is not in accordance with modern designs" (p. 26). For a further discussion of the prewar status of the British industry, consult Burn, *op. cit., passim;* also T. H. Burnham and G. O. Haskins, *Iron and Steel in Britain, 1870–1930,* Allen & Unwin, London, 1943, *passim.*
52. L. of N., *Steel,* p. 107.
53. Balfour Committee, p. 27.

competitive advantage over the British industry in world markets. By selling at cost-plus prices to domestic consumers, the Germans and French if need be could sell to foreign buyers at cost-minus prices and still make a net profit on over-all operations.

Moreover, the continental producers generally had an additional advantage over British steelmakers after Britain's restoration of the gold standard because the pound sterling was overvalued. The monetary policies of the continental countries did not follow a uniform pattern, but in general they tended to make for favorable exchange rates and encourage exports.

By the end of the twenties, not only had the British steel industry suffered a loss of position in world markets, but its home markets had been invaded by continental sellers. British imports of iron and steel reached 2,231,000 tons in 1913. In the decade after the war, they showed a persistent upward trend. Steel imports in 1929 exceeded 1913 imports by more than 25 per cent. On the other hand, steel exports failed to reach the volume of 1913 in any postwar year.[54]

Britain Abandons Free Trade

As the Great Depression aggravated the impact of these developments, Britain abandoned its traditional individualism and free trade. British iron and steel policy reflected, of course, the general changes in British commercial policy. As unemployment increased, as exports declined, and as its balance of payments grew progressively more unfavorable, Britain went off the gold standard and turned from free trade to a policy of protection. On March 1, 1932 a general duty of 10 per cent was levied on imports of iron and steel. Two months later the duty was raised to 32 per cent on pig iron, semifinished steel, girders, sheets, and similar items, and to 20 per cent on finished items. "For perhaps the first time in British tariff history a higher duty had been put upon the raw material than on the finished product." [55]

As a price for its support of the industry's demand for protection, the British Import Duties Advisory Committee (IDAC), a governmental agency, exacted a promise from the National Committee for the Iron and Steel Industry to formulate and execute a plan for the

---

54. Burn, op. cit., p. 394.
55. "Ingot," The Socialization of Iron and Steel, quoted in Frederic Benham, Great Britain Under Protection, Macmillan, New York, 1941, p. 181.

reorganization of the industry.[56] The plan drastically suppressed competitive freedom of action in the industry. It established a cartel-like arrangement to control the marketing of iron and steel products.

Under this plan, the British Iron and Steel Federation occupies a key position in the industry's structure.[57] Many trade associations of producers in the several stages and branches of steel production are affiliated with the Federation. These associations are designed as "effective instruments for the control of production in the several main divisions of the industry, . . ." One object of the Federation is to "support and co-ordinate the activities of the associations and to give effect to the will of the industry in matters of general policy extending beyond the sphere of any one association." [58]

The associations' duties have been to fix minimum prices and to allot production and sales quotas among their members. The Federation and IDAC review prices as fixed by the associations. Their power is only advisory; but, since IDAC has great influence in determining iron and steel tariff rates, it has virtually exercised a veto power over prices.

To insure affiliation by all producers with the appropriate association and adherence to its "principles of mutual support and stability," the Federation has encouraged the associations to grant so-called "loyalty rebates" to those consumers who agree to "buy all their requirements from members of an association of producers at the previous stage." [59] Stripped of all euphemism, this means price discrimination designed to promote the monopoly power of the association. Such practices by individual sellers in this country would violate the Robinson-Patman Act and the Clayton Act; if followed by mutual agreement among otherwise competing sellers, they would violate the Sherman Act.

Functions of the British Federation

In general, the Federation makes and coordinates policies for its affiliated associations and acts as a sort of over-all planning agency

56. See correspondence between the National Committee for the Iron and Steel Industry and IDAC, *The Iron and Steel Reorganization Scheme,* White Paper 63-9999, London, 1930, p. 5.

57. The British Iron and Steel Federation, established in April 1934, represented a reorganization of the older National Federation of Iron and Steel Manufacturers.

58. Report of IDAC on the *Present Position and Future Development of the Iron and Steel Industry,* Cmd. 5507, London, 1937, p. 18.

59. *Ibid.,* p. 55.

for the British industry. It reviews programs for expanding existing plants or for building new ones.[60] Although the Federation lacks mandatory power to compel revision or abandonment of such plans, its influence is so great that in practice it has been able to block new construction.[61]

In its 1937 report on the iron and steel industry, IDAC reviewed at length the Federation's activities, and sketched the outlines of a future program. IDAC foresees the Federation exercising, subject to administrative review, a steadily more comprehensive and detailed control over the flow of investment into the industry and over operating policies. In the opinion of IDAC:

> There cannot be a return to the lack of organisation, . . . and the competition largely unrestricted at home and almost wholly unrestricted from abroad, . . . before 1932.

IDAC recognizes, however, that

> . . . the State cannot divest itself of responsibility as to the conduct of a protected industry so far-reaching in its scope, so vital to the national well-

60. In December 1936 the Federation's council adopted this resolution: "That all proposals in regard to the expansion of plant should be submitted to a Committee of the Federation; that the Chairman of the Executive Committee should be the Chairman of the Committee and the President be an ex-officio member of it; and that [they] should select from the membership of the Council (which would, for this purpose, constitute the full panel) 5 members to sit with them in each case, regard always being paid to the nature of the case when the selection was made; that the Committee should have power to call upon expert or technical assistance when they thought it desirable to do so; that the Import Duties Advisory Committee be afforded the opportunity of sending a representative to act on the Committee when they thought it desirable." *Ibid.*, pp. 35-36. The last provision was subsequently abandoned.

61. In 1936, in spite of a rapidly expanding demand for steel, the Federation refused to approve a plan for a Bessemer steel plant with an annual capacity of from 350,000 to 400,000 tons and finishing mills of coordinate capacity at Jarrow-on-the-Tyneside. Producers in the Middlesbrough area opposed the project and it was abandoned.

The Economist laid bare the implications of this episode with rapier thrusts: "The story of Jarrow throws a particularly vivid light upon the degree to which British industry is already in the strait jacket . . . The facts . . . ought to blow sky-high the strange delusions of those who believe in the 'self-government of industry.' The plain fact is that if an industry is elevated to a monopoly . . . it will . . . refuse entry to newcomers. . . . It will put its own interests above those of . . . the community as a whole. It will exploit the market for all it is worth . . . it is an ossification of inefficiency, an endowment of selfishness." "The Lessons of Jarrow," *The Economist* (London), July 18, 1936, Vol. CXXIV, p. 105.

IDAC was more complacent. See its Report, pp. 24 ff. On the whole, IDAC warmly supports the entire control scheme. Although recognizing that the concentration in private hands of power to determine capacity, output, quotas, and prices in such a basic industry may endanger the public welfare, IDAC expresses the view that the Federation has exercised its power with a commendable sense of responsibility. It is confident that, with Federation decisions subject to official review, public interests are adequately safeguarded.

being, so largely affected by state fiscal policy, and now being brought into a closely-knit organisation . . . The problem is, therefore, to secure the systematic planning of the industry as a whole . . . whilst at the same time avoiding the evils of monopoly, safeguarding the public interest and fostering efficiency.[62]

British Join the Cartel

Meanwhile, the Federation has made great strides toward centralized control of the market. On July 31, 1935, it subscribed to the international steel cartel. The British Government gave official support to this move. When negotiations were about to fail because the parties could not agree on the maximum British import tonnage to be reserved for continental steel producers, Parliament obligingly raised the customs duty to 50 per cent on recommendation of IDAC. In requesting this action, the Federation stressed the "importance of placing the industry in a position to negotiate satisfactory agreements with competitors overseas." [63]

Confronted with a tariff wall so high that they were bound to lose a substantial portion of their British markets, the continental members acquiesced in the Federation's demand that imports be restricted to 670,000 tons for the first year of the agreement and thereafter to 525,000.[64] After Parliament had ratified the agreement, the Federation inaugurated a licensing system under which imports within the agreed quotas are admitted on payment of duties of only 20 per cent.[65] Imports not coming within the agreed quotas are subject to a standard duty of 33 1/3 per cent. The Federation, which has assumed "responsibility for ensuring adequate supplies of suitable steel," [66] has discretionary power to increase the volume of imports permitted to enter at the preferred rate. By this anomalous arrangement, the Federation has become a quasi-public administrative agency

62. Report, p. 77.
63. See *Memorandum on Clause 6 of the Finance Bill, 1936,* presented by the President of the Board of Trade to Parliament, June 1936, Cmd. 5201, London, p. 3.
64. *Ibid.* These figures compare with annual British imports ranging from 881,000 tons to 4,406,000 tons during the decade 1921–1930. Burn, *op. cit.,* p. 394.
65. After the objective for which the duties had been raised to the 50 per cent level had been achieved, these rates were rescinded, and the rates previously in effect were restored, for imports within quota limits. Article II of the agreement provided that the accord would become effective on August 8, 1935, only if "in the meantime arrangements shall have been made by the United Kingdom Government whereby the rate of duty applicable to imports covered by the agreement may be reduced wherever practicable to not more than 20 per cent ad valorem."
66. *Memorandum on Clause 6 of the Finance Bill, 1936,* p. 7.

exercising tariff-making authority within the limits set by Parliament. As previously, however, it is still composed solely of private, profit-seeking business enterprises.

When the Federation joined the cartel, EIA organized several new selling syndicates to regulate exports of products in which British producers were particularly interested. British producers also joined EIA's several selling syndicates already in operation, and received stipulated quotas.

More effectively to control imports and exports, the Federation organized the British Iron & Steel Corporation, Ltd., as a central agency for the purchase and sale abroad of steel products. The Corporation purchases all authorized cartel imports and "then in effect hands their imports back to the [domestic] cartels for distribution" to British steel consumers, "in consultation with the Federation." [67] The Corporation also purchases most of the steel for export and resells it in accordance with cartel regulations.[68] The Federation and continental groups share foreign markets in the same proportions as in 1934.[69]

America Enters the Cartel

After the British Federation had joined the cartel, the European industry encountered competition in world markets from the exporters of only a single important country—the United States. American exports, which had averaged more than 2 million tons annually during 1925–1929, declined to a low of 367,000 tons in 1932. The downward trend was reversed, however, with the general recovery of business. An uninterrupted increase in American steel exports after 1933 culminated in a peacetime high of 3,472,000 tons in 1937.[70] As American exports threatened the cartel's control of world markets, steps were taken to bring them under concerted regulation.[71]

67. *Ibid.*, p. 6.
68. Exceptions include the Welsh Plate and Sheet Manufacturers Association, which has continued to function as a central selling agency for its members in export markets; the Oriental Steel Company, which handles exports of galvanized sheets to India; and British Sheet Marketing Company, Ltd., which controls sales in New Zealand. Hexner, *op. cit.*, p. 115 f.
69. The agreement has been published as Annex I in the *Memorandum on Clause 6 of the Finance Bill, 1936*, pp. 8-11.
70. *Iron Trade Review* (Cleveland) and *Steel* (Cleveland), various January issues.
71. See the testimony of S. M. Bash, member of the Board of Directors of the Steel Export Association of America, TNEC *Hearings*, 76th Cong., 2d sess., pursuant to Public Resolution No. 113 (75th Cong.), Pt. XX, p. 10939 f.

In 1928 United States Steel and Bethlehem Steel had obtained a corporate charter for the Steel Export Association of America, a Webb-Pomerene association.[72] It included in its membership not only numerous independent steel companies operating in the export market, but also United States Steel's export subsidiary. A major objective of the Association was to conduct export operations in such a manner as to disturb foreign markets as little as possible. The Association itself has reported its chief advantages to be the "ability to meet foreign competition through establishing uniform terms and contracts for export sales, standardizing weights and qualities and the collection and exchange of information regarding foreign markets." Before 1938, collaboration between the Export Association and the steel cartel was limited to price and quota agreements with three of the cartel's selling syndicates. These agreements covered exports of tin plate, rails, and tubular products.

Experience in these fields proving mutually satisfactory, the cartel undertook to broaden the area of collaboration. In the second quarter of 1936 it opened negotiations with the Export Association looking to stabilization of export markets, generally, and its adherence to additional selling syndicates, specifically. By 1938 they had reached a basic understanding and had concluded specific agreements insuring American participation in the syndicates regulating the sales of "heavy products" and "sheet products." [73] In accordance with arrangements, representatives of the Export Association took part in the policy-making decisions of both the cartel and its affiliated syndicates.

The Export Association agreed, on behalf of its members, to recognize the domestic markets of other cartel members as their exclusive marketing territory. In return, the cartel recognized certain areas as American spheres of influence.[74] American exporters received quotas based on their share of certain export markets during the year

72. An earlier Webb-Pomerene association, the short-lived Consolidated Steel Corporation, had been organized in 1919. It included in its membership Bethlehem, Republic, Youngstown, and several smaller independent steel companies. United States Steel was not a member. One of its major objects was the reduction of selling costs through cooperative marketing. In 1922 Consolidated reported that "no one of our member companies could maintain foreign agencies individually, as economically as we maintain them acting for all." Nevertheless, it was dissolved in 1923.
The Steel Export Association was organized on a broader basis than Consolidated. See TNEC Monograph No. 6, *Export Prices and Export Cartels*, pp. 175 and 218 f.
73. Heavy products included bars, plates, shapes, wire rods, and semifinished material; sheets included hoops and strips, and black and galvanized sheets.
74. TNEC *Hearings*, Pt. XX, p. 10930.

1936. The Export Association assumed responsibility at the outset for keeping American exports within the assigned quotas. Should total American exports of any particular product exceed the American quota, the Association obligated itself to pay penalties even though the excess resulted from failure of independents to cooperate in the program.

Relation of Association Activities to Webb-Pomerene Act

Although the Webb-Pomerene Act authorizes cooperation among business rivals in export trade, it prohibits an association of exporters from entering "either in the United States or elsewhere . . . into any agreement, understanding, or conspiracy," or doing any "act which artificially or intentionally enhances or depresses prices within the United States of commodities of the class exported by such association, or which substantially lessens competition within the United States or otherwise restrains trade therein." [75]

Each of the agreements between the Export Association and the several selling syndicates accordingly contained a provision formally indicating the Association's compliance with the Webb-Pomerene Act. For example, the agreement of August 1, 1937, covering the export of rails, provided:

Materials sold in the United States other than for export and sold for export to the United States shall not be covered by this agreement, and this agreement shall not be construed as in any way referring to trade in materials so sold and shall not be allowed directly or indirectly to restrain trade within the United States or the export trade of any domestic competitor of the American group or to enhance or to depress prices of such material or to lessen competition therein within the United States.[76]

In spite of the Association's formal adherence to the principles of the Webb-Pomerene Act, its participation in the cartel apparently tended both to lessen competition in the American market and to curtail the export trade of domestic producers not members of the Association. A basic principle of the steel cartel was preservation of domestic markets for domestic producers. In entering the cartel, American producers agreed to respect the domestic markets of other

75. Act of April 10, 1918, 40 Stat. 516, Sec. 2. TNEC Monograph No. 6, Appendix, Ex. 1. In 1921 the Federal Trade Commission ruled that "an incidental and inconsequential effect upon domestic prices is not unlawful." *Ibid.*, p. 128.
76. TNEC *Hearings*, Pt. XX, p. 10933.

cartel members and to limit their sales in neutral markets. What was the *quid pro quo?* What did the American steelmakers gain under the agreement by restricting their foreign sales? One possible gain is obvious—better prices for steel exports. As S. M. Bash, a member of the Board of Managers of the Steel Export Association, expressed it, the Association entered the cartel "to get a fair return, a reasonable return, and not have to sell at ridiculous prices brought about by competition." [77]

There is another bird, however, at which the stone may have been aimed. Cartel representatives made clear to the American group that, if they failed to implement effectively their general understanding with the cartel, the cartel would lower steel prices drastically and ship large quantities of foreign steel into the higher-priced American market. The Export Association's Board of Managers warned executives of the affiliated companies of this danger.[78] H. W. Schroeder, of the Wheeling Steel Corporation, has testified that while he negotiated with the cartel on behalf of the Export Association he kept in mind the possible consequence of failure to reach full agreement. But he was able, he said, to make a clear distinction between "doing anything because of something and realizing that something might be an inferential result." [79]

However skillful Mr. Schroeder may have been at such mental gymnastics, American participation in the cartel apparently tended to forestall invasion of the American market by foreign producers. Whether or not affiliation of the American group with the cartel was accompanied by an understanding, express or implied, that its domestic market would be reserved for domestic producers, the European members refrained from aggressive selling in the United States.

Cartel Restricts Competition of Unaffiliated American Companies

American participation in the cartel affected American trade in a second way. The Association had guaranteed that total American exports of specific steel products would not exceed American quotas. As prices mounted during the second half of the thirties, Association members confined their exports to their quotas. Nonmembers, however, increased greatly their share of American foreign trade.

77. *Ibid.*, p. 10935.
78. *Ibid.*, pp. 10948 ff.; Ex. 1447, p. 11018.
79. *Ibid.*, p. 10979.

Since the cartel required Association members to pay heavy penalties on sales in excess of American quotas, even though the excess might have resulted from an increase in sales by nonmembers, they urged their European colleagues to cut prices in certain export markets to eliminate American nonmembers from the trade.[80] As one Association member expressed it, "the sooner these mills are eliminated from taking [export] business the better our chances will be of bringing them under control in our own group." [81]

American membership in the steel cartel ended with World War II, which disrupted the cartel. It had lasted eighteen months. During this period, the Steel Export Association endeavored to overcome obstacles to American collaboration with European groups and to make the steel cartel an effective instrument for control of world markets. Between the organization of the first international steel cartel and the end of the second, great strides were made in this direction. Everywhere steel producers were avoiding competition as a means of promoting their separate interests, and were turning to cooperative action as a means of promoting the interests of all. They sought refuge in economic collectivism.

Objectives of the Cartel

The cartel's objectives are clearly revealed in the circumstances which gave it birth, in the changes made in its structure and operation in response to experience, and in the opinions of its proponents. The immediate objective was to increase profits by controlling export prices. This required control over the flow of steel into world markets. It called for subordination of the immediate, separate interests of each seller to the longer-run, collective interests of all. It involved surrender of the discretion of individual sellers in the conduct of their business to a compact managerial group representing the whole industry. In brief, it called for centralization of power to make decisions governing steel production for, and sales in, world markets. Success of the effort to regulate prices depended largely on the extent to which such centralization of power was in fact achieved.

80. See *ibid.*, Ex. 1448, p. 11020.
81. *Ibid.* See also p. 10972. In defense of this policy, Mr. Bash testified: "We have done our utmost to get them to come in. . . . we went to the extent of offering them appreciably more than they had done in open competition. We not only asked them to come in, we pleaded with them to come in."

Influence of the First Cartel on Prices

The first steel cartel lacked adequate power. Its results are to be judged in the light of that fact. It had two serious defects: (1) its control over prices was remote; (2) its scope was narrow. It tried to control steel prices in export markets merely by limiting the domestic output of raw steel, and it left outside the organization two of the most important exporting countries. In spite of these shortcomings, steel prices immediately advanced on organization of the cartel.

The export price of steel billets in June 1926, before the cartel, was £4 5s. 3d. a metric ton. By December the price had advanced to £5 6s. The prices of merchant bars and structural shapes showed similar advances.[82] (See Figure 1.) However, the cartel was not solely responsible for this advance in prices. The British coal strike was doubtless an important contributing factor. British imports of steel increased substantially in 1926, while British exports declined sharply.

The advance in prices did not hold. With resumption of more normal operations in Britain and persistent production by German firms in excess of their quotas, steel prices declined in 1927 to about their pre-cartel levels. After Germany's national quota had been revised and the cartel placed on a more stable basis, prices stiffened. By June 1929, steel billets were selling at £5 8s. compared to £4 6s. 3d. in September 1927. Merchant bars had advanced in the same period from £4 13s. 9d. to £5 18s. 9d., while shapes had advanced from £4 10s. to £5 4s. 9d. Again, this price movement is not traceable wholly to cartel influence. Continued improvement in business conditions was probably a more important factor. In response to improved demand, world output of steel ingots and castings increased from 91,-790,000 tons in 1926 to 118,370,000 tons in 1929.

82. The greater stability in price of wire rods and steel rails reflects the influence of the pre-existing selling syndicates for these items.

The gold pound sterling prices in Figure 1 were prices actually quoted throughout the period, except in 1924 and 1925. After September 1931, of course, when England abandoned the gold standard, no settlement in gold pounds sterling was possible. But in terms of whatever currency a buyer discharged his obligations to a seller, the amount paid depended on the ratio of the gold equivalent of the particular monetary unit (as measured, for example, by its current exchange rate against a gold-convertible currency, such as Swiss francs or U.S. dollars) to the theoretical gold content of the English pound sterling. Since price quotations of steelmakers (or other businessmen) do not invariably reflect promptly and precisely fluctuations in exchange rates, the course of steel prices shown in Figure 1 probably does not accurately record changes in their net realization prices per ton of export sales. Nevertheless, Figure 1 probably gives a fair picture of the general movement of steel product prices.

FIGURE 1. CONTINENTAL EUROPEAN EXPORT PRICES OF SPECIFIED STEEL PRODUCTS, 1924–1939

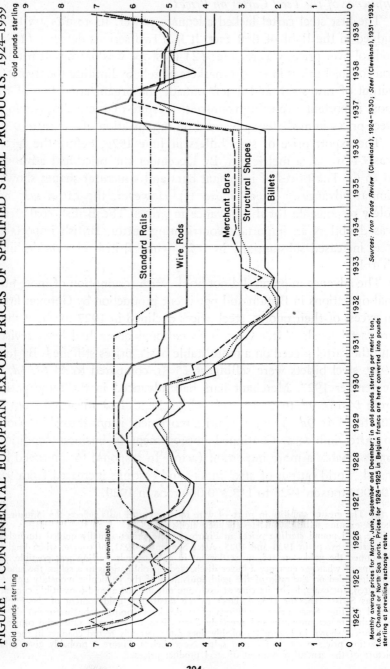

Monthly average prices for March, June, September and December; in gold pounds sterling per metric ton, f.o.b. Channel or North Sea ports. Prices for 1924–1925 in Belgian francs are here converted into pounds sterling at prevailing exchange rates.

Sources: *Iron Trade Review* (Cleveland), 1924–1930; *Steel* (Cleveland), 1931–1939.

When demand for steel fell off sharply with the depression, the cartel was unable to prevent sharp price declines. As world production of steel ingots and castings dropped from 118,370,000 tons in 1929 to 49,900,000 tons in 1932, the cartel collapsed.[83] The export price of billets, f.o.b. Channel ports, had dropped from £5 4s. 6d. in March 1929 to £1 19s. in June 1932. Prices of merchant bars and structural shapes showed a similar trend.

Influence of Second Cartel on Prices

Faced with such drastic declines in prices, cartel proponents undertook to re-establish the cartel and to make it more effective. A suitable instrument for effective control of the market could not be forged at one stroke. The cartel was reshaped and enlarged in response to experience and opportunity. Before World War II, the cartel had established seventeen closely knit selling syndicates, each operating in a relatively narrow market and following policies coordinated by the cartel itself. At the same time, the cartel membership was steadily enlarged until it included all important steel-exporting countries.

Under the second cartel the course of steel prices was upward, principally because of general business recovery and rearmament. Nevertheless, the cartel control at times apparently contributed to an increase in prices and at other times retarded price reductions. In June 1932, after the collapse of the first cartel, the f.o.b. Channel-port prices of billets, merchant bars, and structural shapes reached lows of £1 19s., £2 3s. 6d., and £2 6d. a metric ton, respectively. Prices stiffened when negotiations for re-establishment of the cartel got under way, and by December these products were selling for £2 3s., £2 18s., and £2 5s., respectively. The price of merchant bars advanced to £3 3s. and that of structural shapes to £3 1s. 6d. by the second quarter of 1934.

The price of bars remained unchanged until the middle of 1936, and the prices of billets and shapes until 1937. During the peak of business activity in 1937 (when annual world output of ingots reached a peacetime high of 131,300,000 tons) prices of billets, bars, and shapes advanced sharply. Between December 1936 and September 1937 the price of billets increased from £2 7s. to £5 7s. 6d.—

83. Hexner, *op. cit.,* Appendix VI, p. 324 f.

a rise of more than 100 per cent within nine months. During the same period prices of bars and shapes rose 85 per cent and 75 per cent, respectively.

Moreover, prices quoted by the cartel were minimum prices. Cartel members were free to sell for higher prices if they could obtain them. Since premiums above quoted prices were common at this period, realized prices probably increased even more than the quoted prices.

Certainly the cartel had not stabilized prices in the face of expanding demand. In the face of declining demand, however, the cartel apparently did exercise a temporary stabilizing influence. In the business recession of 1938, world output of steel ingots and castings decreased from the record high of 133,774,000 tons in 1937 to 107,687,000 tons.[84] This compares with an output of 121,720,000 tons in 1936. The prices of billets, bars, and shapes declined moderately as demand fell off in 1938, but they remained well above the levels of 1936 in spite of the much larger consumption in that year.

The cartel's success in maintaining higher prices than would have otherwise prevailed is even more clearly indicated in the case of wire rods and steel rails. Although the raw steel cartel collapsed during the Great Depression, the older and more firmly intrenched steel rail and wire rod *comptoirs* survived. Their stabilizing influence on prices in the face of a drastic decline in demand is shown in Figure 1.

The prices of these products fell sharply between 1929 and 1932, but the decline was relatively much less severe than that for other products over which all controls had been abandoned. From June 1929 to June 1932 the price of wire rods declined 29 per cent; steel rods, 15 per cent; bars, 65 per cent; and structural shapes, 61 per cent. During the revival of business after 1932, the price of wire rods and rails remained unchanged until 1937. The price of wire rods then advanced rapidly from £4 10s. to a high of £7 in June 1937. The quoted price of steel rails advanced only slightly.

The second steel cartel apparently succeeded in maintaining steel prices at levels somewhat higher than would otherwise have prevailed. Mr. Bash in his testimony before the Temporary National Economic Committee supports this conclusion. He said: ". . . of course, under the cartels the prices were good, otherwise there

84. *Steel*, January 1, 1940, p. 269.

wouldn't be any good reason to have a cartel." [85] Mr. Schroeder expressed a similar judgment: "Generally averaging over all products, [the cartel] has maintained a higher market price [than would otherwise have prevailed] in the foreign markets." [86]

Obstacles to Price Control

In spite of some success in controlling prices, the cartel had a difficult task. American participation was never complete, and the competition of nonmember American producers occasionally forced a reduction in prices by cartel members. Moreover, at times, particularly in periods of slack demand, individual cartel members made secret price concessions in violation of cartel regulations.

On the whole, however, they apparently appreciated the mutual advantages of cooperative action. Price concessions were likely to be discovered and quickly reported to cartel headquarters. Disciplinary action and market experience tended to develop standards of business behavior more conducive to an effective cartel. As the machinery for market control steadily improved, the price policies of cartel members became better integrated, coordinated, and standardized, and price competition became rarer.

Price Discrimination

Not only did the cartel tend to raise prices to consumers, but it practiced price discrimination among various buyers. The most easily detected discrimination was based on geographic location. The cartel customarily adjusted prices in particular areas to meet changes in a competitive condition, but it also adjusted prices to reserve specific export areas to particular national groups. Thus the quoted prices of particular steel products f.o.b. Channel ports frequently varied with the destination. Illustrating the first case, in November 1935 merchant bars were quoted generally at £3 3s. 9d. (gold), f.o.b. Channel ports. For shipments to South Africa, however, where competition from local producers was then severe, the price was £3.[87]

Discrepancies between domestic prices and export prices were not new to the industry, but they persisted during the cartel. Steel producers, except the Belgians and the British, generally sold their prod-

85. TNEC *Hearings*, Pt. XX, p. 10962.
86. *Ibid.*, p. 10979.
87. Hexner, *op. cit.*, p. 182.

ucts abroad at prices substantially lower than those charged in their domestic markets. Table 14 shows the relationship between the average prices of merchant bars for export and in the major domestic markets during 1927–1938 and for certain earlier years. German export prices varied over the twelve prewar years from a high of 97 per cent of domestic prices in 1937 to a low of only 45 per cent of domestic prices in 1932.

Tariff protection and cartel controls—both domestic and international—made possible this discrimination. Apparently the situation most conducive to this type of geographic price discrimination is one in which nation-wide monopolistic controls operate behind a tariff wall without benefit of cartel agreement with foreign sellers. When international cartel controls are added to domestic monopoly and tariff protection, the discrepancy between inland and export prices tends to diminish. As the first cartel gained in strength, from 1927 to 1929, this price differential was reduced; as the cartel weakened, in 1930 and 1931, it increased. (See Table 14.) After the breakdown of the international cartel, in 1932 the German national group (still functioning as a unit) was able to exact from domestic buyers of merchant bars more than twice as much as it charged foreign buyers of the same product.[88] With the reconstitution of the cartel, this price discrepancy steadily narrowed.

Relation of Controls to Prices

This record confirms two well-recognized economic principles. First, the firmer the monopolistic controls in a given market, the higher the prices. Second, monopoly prices are discriminatory prices. "Charging all the traffic will bear" does not mean that all the traffic will bear the same charge! In fact, it will not. But a clear-sighted monopolist will not let pass the opportunity to do business with some buyers or in some areas merely because the price he can obtain in those sales is less than he is getting elsewhere.

It has been estimated that German consumers prior to 1930 were forced to pay annually from 300 million to 400 million Reichsmarks

---

88. The influence of the tariff and the control of domestic markets was also evident in the relation between the British domestic and export prices. Until the adoption of import duties on iron and steel in 1932 and the cartelization of the domestic market, which shortly followed, British export prices had been about the same as domestic prices. Thereafter, domestic and export prices diverged, the former customarily exceeding the latter by a substantial margin.

TABLE 14

COMPARISON OF AVERAGE EXPORT PRICES OF MERCHANT BARS WITH
AVERAGE PRICES OF MERCHANT BARS ON MAJOR EUROPEAN
DOMESTIC MARKETS, 1913 AND 1925–1939

(Export Price at Port of Shipment as Per Cent of Domestic Price at Works)

Year	Germany	France	Belgium	England [a]
1913	95	66	95	b
1925	b	b	b	99
1926	b	b	b	94
1927	72	98	98	95
1928	82	102	98	98
1929	84	95	b	98
1930	70	92	b	100
1931	55	85	b	100
1932	45	57	b	93 [c]
1933	52	63	94	93
1934	58	70	100	87
1935	58	70	119	87 [d]
1936	59	70	114	89
1937	97	115	126	101
1938 [e]	93	127	110	90
1939	b	b	b	96

Sources: Data for Germany, France, and Belgium (and for England after 1927) were derived from Irvin Hexner, *The International Steel Cartel,* University of North Carolina Press, Chapel Hill, 1943, Table XIII, p. 195, and Table XIV, p. 196. English prices for the years 1925 through 1929 were obtained from the annual (January) "Market Review" of the *Iron Trade Review.*

a. The ratios of English export to domestic prices are based on June and December quotations.
b. Not available.
c. Britain levied import duties beginning this year.
d. British Iron and Steel Federation signed cartel agreement.
e. January to June only.

(equivalent to about $75-$80 million) more for steel than they would have paid had domestic prices been no higher than export prices.[89] However, this disparity between German domestic and export prices of steel gradually narrowed after 1932. First, the domestic prices remained unchanged through 1938. This facilitated the rearmament program of the Hitler regime. On the other hand, export prices rose under the influence of expanding demand and the increasing effec-

89. "Die Problematik der Stahl-Ordnung," *Frankfurter Zeitung* (Frankfurt), February 16, 1930; "Die Volkwirtschaflichen Kosten der Eisenverbande," *Magazin der Wirtschaft* (Berlin), December 5, 1929, pp. 1833-38.

tiveness of the international cartel. By 1937 they were 97 per cent of the German domestic prices.[90]

Nevertheless, continuously from 1932 through 1937 domestic consumers—not only in Germany but in the other major steel-exporting countries—paid more for domestically produced steel than foreign buyers paid for it. To the extent that domestic fabricators could pass the high price on to the ultimate consumer the latter's standard of living was impaired. To the extent that fabricators were themselves the exporters of products manufactured from high-priced domestic steel, their prospects of survival in international competition were also impaired.

German nonintegrated rolling mills, appreciating this disadvantage, opposed price increases made by the Rohstahlgemeinschaft soon after the cartel was organized. So emphatically did they protest the price discrimination that cartel members agreed to credit the finishing mills with the difference between the home and world prices on whatever steel the fabricators used in exported products.[91] In this way the final domestic consumers who were forced to pay higher prices for fabricated steel products in effect subsidized the export operations of steel producers.

Whether domestic consumers were more able than the producers to bear the burden of low prices in export markets is open to question. But there can be no disputing (1) that if they were not, the efficiency of the national economy as a whole was lowered by this policy, and (2) that regardless of whether they were or were not, the shift of the burden to their shoulders repudiated the basic principle of capitalism: that the penalties (losses) no less than the rewards (profits) of risk taking shall go to those who embark on a productive venture.

Relation Between National Groups and Their Governments

The steel cartel was a private business organization. The business groups that created it and managed it were undoubtedly trying to

90. But this did not mean that domestic consumers of German steel were relieved of the monopoly tax. Although the bulk of the German output was going into rearmament under the Goering Four-Year Plan, the part allotted to civilian uses still bore a price higher than that sold in export markets; but the discrimination in favor of foreign buyers grew gradually less.

91. See Tariff Commission, *Iron and Steel*, p. 374. The credits thus allowed were accepted as part payment for subsequent purchases of steel.

make international markets more profitable. The cartel was designed to advance the private interests of these groups by dividing markets among the members, by regulating the rate at which steel moved into these markets, and by controlling prices.

In spite of the private character of the cartel, however, the national groups affiliated with it, excepting the American group, were closely associated with their respective national governments. Every European national group looked to its government for support and cooperation in negotiations with other national groups. Promulgation of the first cartel in 1926 was contingent on a satisfactory commercial treaty between Germany and France. Parliament raised the tariff on iron and steel in 1935 at the request of the British Iron and Steel Federation to aid it in persuading continental members of the cartel to accept an import quota smaller than the normal continental exports to Great Britain.

Such close cooperation between the national groups and their governments tended to develop an identity of interest between them. This identity of interest was most marked in Germany. In May 1932 the Bruening government secretly acquired a controlling interest in Vereinigte Stahlwerke.[92] It paid for the stock about four times its market price. Vereinigte Stahlwerke had the only artillery munitions plant left in Germany under the Versailles Treaty, and produced about 50 per cent of German iron and steel. Although the government's ownership in Vereinigte was reduced through a later reorganization of the steel trust, the government remained the largest single shareholder.

The bond between the German steel trust and the government was even closer after the Nazis seized power in 1933. In fact, nazism was nourished by funds supplied by steel industrialists. Fritz Thyssen,

---

92. The government acquired its majority interest in Vereinigte through purchase of the Friedrich Flick shares in Gelsenkirchener Bergwerks.

Gelsenkirchener was one of the constituent concerns of Vereinigte, and after the merger it became the principal holder of Vereinigte stock. Flick owed large sums to a Dresdner Bank syndicate, secured by Gelsenkirchener shares. To liquidate the debt or to arrange a new loan with other creditors, it is said, Flick was negotiating with foreign interests. To forestall a possible shift in control of the leading German steel company to non-German hands, the government intervened. According to Bruno Wolff, "The government paid at a rate of about 90 per cent for approximately 110 Gelsenkirchener shares, on a day when the Gelsenkirchener shares were valued at 22 per cent on the stock market." See "Die Neugliederung des Stalvereins," in *Die Wirtschaftskurve* (Frankfurt), March 1934, Heft IV, pp. 358-67. See also *The Economist* (London), June 25, 1932, p. 140.

leading spirit in the trust, had cast his lot with Hitler as early as 1928, when he made a large gift to the National Socialist Party.[93] Dr. Albert Vogler, chairman of Vereinigte's Executive Board, in presenting a plan for reorganization of the trust on November 29, 1933, commented on the favorable political environment created by Hitler's accession to power:

> Wavering governments have been replaced by a firm state leadership. Together with peace and order also confidence has been established and thus the basis for a recovery of our economic system. With that the moment has come for the realization of all measures which form the basis for the future organic development of our industrial relationship. We can, therefore, today submit to you for determination the plan for the consolidation of the founder companies Gelsenkirchener, Phoenix, Van der Zypen and Vereinigte Stahlwerke . . . which has been so carefully prepared and examined in all details that it will work out favorably not only for our company but for the German economic system as well.

In an interim report for the period from April 1 to September 30, 1934 the management said: ". . . with the reorganization [of the Vereinigte Stahlwerke Aktiengesellschaft] 'a phase of development is complete which conforms to the basic principles of national socialist economics.' " [94]

Influence of German Group on Cartel Policy

As the Nazi program for controlling the national economy unfolded, the domestic steel cartel, in which Vereinigte Stahlwerke played a dominant role, became a quasi-public institution.[95] Though it was an agent of a government preparing for war, it represented the German national group in the international steel cartel.

Apparently this did not lessen the influence of the German national group in the cartel, although it obviously changed the role it played. The German industrialists at cartel meetings no longer acted exclusively in their private business capacity. They were representatives of their government as well, and as such were responsible for promoting the national interest of the Nazi state. These interests did not necessarily conflict; on the contrary, they were generally in har-

93. Fritz Thyssen, *I Paid Hitler*, Rinehart, New York, 1941, Pt. II, Chap. 5, p. 98.
94. *Scientific and Technical Mobilization*, Hearings before a Subcommittee of the Committee on Military Affairs, U.S. Senate, 78th Cong., 2d sess., pursuant to S.Res. 107, Pt. XVI, p. 1971. (These Hearings will hereinafter be cited: Kilgore, Pt. —.)
95. See Otto Nathan, *The Nazi Economic System*, Duke University Press, Durham, 1944, Chap. 3.

mony. However, the increasing, but concealed, influence of a Fascist regime in the affairs of the international steel cartel created a cleavage of interests, apparently not always recognized, between the German group and the national groups of democratic countries.

Three illustrations of how the German national group influenced cartel policy to promote German national interests follow:

1. In 1938 Stahlwerke Verband, representing the German national group in the international cartel, tried to prevent establishment of a sheet mill in Greece and thereby to retard the industrialization of Greece. It persuaded the other national groups in the cartel to refuse to sell semifinished steel to Greek buyers.[96] The German producers' effort to block Greek industrialization was apparently consistent with both their private and public interests. As the largest exporters of steel on the European continent their interest was to prevent development of competitive sources of supply. As representatives of a great power, their interest was to make secure Germany's position as supplier of manufactured goods to an agricultural hinterland and to forestall development in a potential enemy country of an industry basic to national armament.

2. The Nazi Government tried to advance Germany's national interest by subjecting the domestic supply of foreign exchange to political control. To reduce the adverse effects of exchange control on German exports, barter agreements were made with various foreign countries and foreign enterprises. The domestic cartels representing the leading German export industries were required to carry out the role assigned to them in these transactions. The Stahlwerke Verband was extensively engaged in operations of this type throughout 1934 and 1935.

As a result, the steel exports of the German national group persistently exceeded the quotas set by the cartel. As the Düsseldorf correspondent of the London *Iron and Coal Trades Review* reported:

Germany's success in expanding her iron and steel export trade has caused some difficulty, as she has exceeded her quotas in the international comptoirs. . . . The other members of the . . . Continental Steel Cartel are not unnaturally apprehensive regarding the use made by Germany of the primitive method of barter, which has been increasingly pursued during the past twelve months.[97]

96. See Kilgore, Pt. XVI, Ex. 531, pp. 2286-88.
97. "German Iron and Steel Industry in 1934," *Iron and Coal Trades Review* (London), January 11, 1935, Vol. CXXX, p. 90.

A year later Sir William Larke, director of the British Iron and Steel Federation, commenting on the same development, declared that German exports of steel had been

. . . artificially stimulated by such methods as subsidies, exchange manipulation and barter. . . . The latest policy, however, has been to refuse permits for barter transactions, except in so far as they encourage exports which could not have been secured by normal means, and which exports, in return, result in the importation of vital raw materials at reasonable prices.[98]

The German national group apparently was more concerned with implementing the Nazi rearmament program than with stabilizing the international markets for steel. Barter transactions economized in the use of Germany's limited stock of foreign exchange, and facilitated the stock-piling program essential to the German economy in wartime.

3. Later, when the Nazi rearmament program attained its full stride, it consumed so much of the German steel output that the Stahlwerke Verband was not in a position to authorize exports by its members even up to the quota limit. The German group insisted, however, that other national groups in the cartel, which had not exported more than their allotted tonnage, should compensate them at the rate stipulated in the cartel agreement for underselling quotas.

In 1938 and 1939 other national groups, including the American, paid substantial bonuses to the German group. Although this may have followed the letter of the cartel contract, it was not in accordance with its spirit. The purpose of the bonuses was to reimburse members who supported the international steel market by restricting exports or those who, because of slack demand, could not sell their tonnage allotment without reducing prices. By insisting on a bonus to compensate them for supplying steel to the domestic rearmament program in preference to selling abroad, the German steel companies were in effect demanding that the foreign producers, and indirectly foreign consumers, of steel subsidize the German rearmament program. This they did.

Epilogue

Although the steel cartel's formal operations ended in September

98. Sir William Larke, "The World Iron and Steel Industry," *Iron and Coal Trades Review*, January 17, 1936, p. 120.

1939, the cartel ties were not at once severed. When the British blockade prevented the German steelmakers from supplying their South American customers, they looked to the North American market for supplies to enable their South American subsidiaries to fill current orders. For many months German agencies in South America obtained a substantial tonnage from North American sources and were thus able to maintain their trade connections and good will. An incidental advantage of these arrangements to the German producers was to give them a certain amount of additional foreign exchange, representing the profit, or commission, on the American steel sold through the Germans' South American agencies.

This arrangement was eventually broken up. The steel cartel is dead; but the cartel idea survives. Allied bombings apparently did serious damage to German iron and steel plants. More important, the Potsdam program provides not only for the removal of industrial equipment but for severe restrictions on the output of Germany's basic industries. If this program is carried out the German iron and steel industry will count for little in world trade. But it is at least an open question whether the absence of a strong German steel industry will hinder the resumption of cartel activities. For though the cartel as an institution for controlling markets is indigenous to Germany, the will to control them has become increasingly universal.

Chapter 6

THE ALUMINUM ALLIANCE

OF ALL INDUSTRIES, the metal industries seem to be most readily adaptable to some form of concentrated control. Several influences account for this. The mineral deposits are in some cases highly localized, facilitating unified control by a few concerns or even engrossment by a single enterprise. In other instances, the ore deposits may be so widespread and cost conditions so variable that competition tends to become "ruinous." Moreover, in all these industries the element of chance in ore discoveries and the highly specialized character of the physical plant for recovery of the metal aggravate the risks of unrestricted competition. Or the explanation may be in some distinctive economic feature of the metal industries. In the process of ore extraction, reduction, or refining, the lowest unit cost may in some instances be realized only by a scale of operations so large that a few producers can most economically supply the effective demand.

Whatever the explanation, hardly a single commercially important base metal is not under concerted control of its producers. Iron and steel, copper, nickel, tin, zinc, lead, mercury, titanium, wolfram, chromium, cadmium, molybdenum, beryllium, and aluminum have all been subject to cartel controls of one type or another.

Of the two so-called "light metals" known to commerce, aluminum and magnesium, aluminum is the older and more important. Aluminum is a metallic element—one of the principal constituents of the earth's crust. Only oxygen and silicon are more abundant. Aluminum does not occur naturally in its pure form, but only in a wide variety of compounds. Of these, the most important are bauxite, feldspar, corundum, alunite, leucite, and common clays. With known techniques, however, only the higher grades of bauxite constitute a practical source of supply, though cryolite or some other fluorid is ordinarily used as a flux in the recovery process.[1] Bauxite is found on every continent in local deposits or "pockets" which vary widely in extent and quality.[2] The commercial grades range from about 35 to 70 per cent content of alumina, the normal aluminum salt. The grade depends also on the extent to which objectionable impurities are present. Of these, silicon is the most common and most significant. A few large aluminum companies have pre-empted almost all known deposits of bauxite of suitable grade.

Properties and Uses of Aluminum

Aluminum has three outstanding properties that have made a place for it in modern industry. First, it does not corrode easily and is not affected by many chemical reactions. Since it will not form a poisonous compound with any substance which is not itself a poison, and also because it is a rapid conductor of heat, it was early and widely adopted for household cooking utensils and also used in containers for chemicals, foods, and beverages. Nevertheless, to expand their market aluminum producers had to cultivate these demands and find new uses for the metal.

Second, aluminum is electrically conductive. Although its conductivity is only about 60 per cent of that of copper, forty-eight pounds of aluminum will replace one hundred pounds of copper in electric transmission lines because of its larger mass per unit of weight. Hence, whenever aluminum's price is less than twice that of copper, aluminum cable has an economic advantage. Not until about 1900 did this use for aluminum contribute much to market demand. It was only with the strengthening of aluminum cable by its construction around a steel core, after 1906, that it came into wide use, taking about one third of the output in some years.

Third, aluminum is one of the lightest metals. Among available substitutes, only magnesium is lighter. It is two sevenths as heavy as copper and one third as heavy as steel. Its relative softness and low tensile strength can be overcome readily by tempering, and by alloying it with other metals such as copper, manganese, and nickel.[3] The

1. W. Ashcroft, "Raw Materials and Aluminum Production," *Metallurgia* (London), February 1938, Vol. XVII, pp. 126-28.
2. The ore got its name from a town, Les Baux, in southern France, from the vicinity of which came much of this raw material in the early period of aluminum production.
3. Although the first electrolytically reduced aluminum was a copper alloy, the presence of the copper was inadvertent. The beginnings of intensive research in the heat

resultant combination of lightness with strength and durability has enabled aluminum, even at relatively high prices, to replace steel, copper, zinc, lead, and tin in a wide range of uses. These qualities give it a special advantage in the transportation industry. Aluminum was used in various automobile parts and accessories as early as 1910. For a time the automotive demand grew rapidly, but the consumption of aluminum per car has declined appreciably in the last quarter century.[4] Nevertheless, in peacetime the automobile industry takes more aluminum than any other industry.

In the late twenties, when aviation became popular, the transportation industries provided another boost to aluminum demand. Under the exigencies of war and the insistent demand for fast transportation, the aviation demand for the metal has "taken wing."[5] Moreover, the increasing use of aluminum in streamlined trains and motor buses—to reduce their weight—should insure an expanding market for it.

---

treatment and deliberate alloying of aluminum to improve its tensile strength came some twenty years later. The pioneer achievement was that of Wilm, a German metallurgist, who in 1910 obtained basic patents on his process for making "duralumin." See W. Y. Elliott and others, *International Control of Non-Ferrous Metals,* Macmillan, New York, 1937, Chap. 6, "Aluminum," by D. H. Wallace, p. 223. Development of an extensive series of alloys adapting the qualities of the metal to its special uses dates from the twenties. See Edwards, Frary, and Jeffries, *The Aluminum Industry,* McGraw-Hill, New York, 1930, Vol. II, Chaps. 1, 3, 4, 5.

4. At one time the average consumption of aluminum per car by Buick reached 240 pounds; by Hudson, 180 pounds; and by Studebaker, 110 pounds. But the persistent adherence to a high-price policy by Aluminum Company of America, coupled with the reluctance of the automobile manufacturers to become dependent on a single source of supply for a vital construction material, cut off much of the potential market in this field. The peak automotive consumption per car was reached about 1914, when aluminum was selling under 20 cents a pound for the first time, though there was a temporary upsurge in the early twenties during another dip in price.

See *U.S.* v. *Aluminum Company of America, et al.,* in U.S. District Court for the Southern District of New York (1937), Equity No. 85-73, Rec., pp. 4473-79 and 6262-72. (Because of the frequency with which the record in this case will be cited in the following pages, the citation will hereinafter be abbreviated to USAL and the various documents will be identified by the following symbols: Transcript of Record, Rec.; Exhibit, Ex.; Government Brief, Govt.Br.; Reply Brief, Rep.Br.; Answers of Aluminum Company of America to Interrogatories, Alcoa Int.; Answers of Aluminum Limited to Interrogatories, Alted Int.; Government Brief on Appeal, Govt.Br.App.)

The district court's decision in this case, 44 Fed.Supp. 97 (1944), was in favor of the defendant. The government appealed to the Supreme Court, which for want of a quorum filed the appeal in a suspended docket, 320 U.S. 708 (1943). Under an amendment of June 9, 1944 (58 Stat. 272) to the Judiciary Act, the Supreme Court certified the appeal to the Circuit Court of Appeals, 2d Circuit, 322 U.S. 716 (1944). The decision of the Circuit Court of Appeals, 2d Circuit, was handed down on March 12, 1945 (148 Fed. 2d 416), reversing the district court in part.

5. Within two years after the inception of the National Defense Program in May 1940, it was found necessary, to meet military requirements, (1) to expand domestic production facilities threefold, or from some 500 million pounds annual capacity to

Origins of Aluminum Industry

Aluminum was first produced commercially ninety years ago. It had been isolated in the chemical laboratory only thirty years earlier, in 1825. With the encouragement of Napoleon III, who anticipated that this new metal might be useful in military ordnance, one Henry Deville started production in a small plant near Paris in 1856. His process depended solely on chemical reactions, principally between aluminum chloride and sodium. It was so expensive that for a long time the chief market for the product was in jewelry. For forty years the original enterprise, or its successors, continued to produce aluminum by this costly process. The price gradually dropped with the accumulation of technical experience from about $12 a pound to about half that figure.

The signal developments in electrometallurgy during the eighties, after the invention of the dynamo, opened the way to a wide range of industrial and household applications for aluminum. These improvements reduced the cost of separating the metal from the aluminum oxide and enabled it to compete with other nonferrous metals. It is hard to say who first discovered a practicable method for overcoming the exceptional tenacity of the two elements in alumina— aluminum and oxygen. The basic invention was claimed in three separate patents. Americans made two of these inventions, Bradley in 1885 and Hall in 1886. A Frenchman, Paul Héroult, made a similar discovery about the same time.

Simply expressed, the process passes an electric current through a cell containing a "bath" of aluminous ores including with the alumina a solvent having a higher stability, so that when the alumina is decomposed, the oxygen moves in one current, toward the cathode, while the aluminum moves in the other current toward the opposite pole.[6] This was the gist of the process which all three inventors dis-

---

1,500 million pounds, (2) to curtail drastically civilian consumption of aluminum, and (3) to finance a large expansion of capacity in Canada by the Aluminum Company of America's affiliate, Aluminium Limited. (These companies will hereinafter be designated, respectively, Alcoa and Alted.) See series of reports of the Truman Committee, *Investigation of the National Defense Program,* Hearings before a Special Committee of the U.S. Senate, 77th Cong., 1st sess., pursuant to S.Res. 71, Pt. III (1941) and subsequent releases. (These reports will hereinafter be cited: Truman, Pt. —.)

By the end of the war, domestic capacity for the production of primary aluminum had increased about fivefold to 2,350,000,000 pounds. See *Aluminum Plants and Facilities,* Report of the Surplus Property Board to the Congress, Washington, September 27, 1945.

6. See Edwards *et al., op. cit.,* Vol. I, pp. 12 ff.

covered independently. It laid the basis for a great modern industry which in the last half century has brought significant changes in the conventional mode of living and, through its contribution to the development of aviation, helped to revolutionize modern warfare. That three men should have independently invented the process almost at the same time shows the cumulative character of technological advance. Each started with the problem which the Deville process left unsolved: how to get aluminum cheaply. Each tried to solve it by the new art of electrometallurgy.

Four Pioneer Companies

Each of these inventions became the basis of an independent business enterprise almost immediately. Bradley assigned his patent application to the Cowles brothers, who organized the Electric Smelting & Aluminum Company for the commercial development of the process. Though initially this concern produced only aluminum alloys, it succeeded, in 1891, a year before the issuance of the Bradley patents, in producing pure aluminum. The Pittsburgh Reduction Company acquired the Hall patent in 1888 and undertook the exploitation of the new invention. The Mellon family of Pittsburgh gave financial backing to the new enterprise and Arthur V. Davis, who became the outstanding leader for over fifty years in this industry, managed it with rare ability.

The Sweitzerische Metallurgische Gesellschaft, which was organized in 1887 by Héroult and an old Swiss metal-working concern,[7] first utilized the Héroult process commercially in Neuhausen, Switzerland. It acquired the patents on the Héroult process for all countries outside France. In 1888 this enterprise was reorganized as Aluminium Industrie A. G. (hereinafter, AIAG), with the substantial financial support of German capital. Allgemeine Elektrizitäts Gesellschaft (the German General Electric), more familiarly known as AEG, became a large shareholder in the new venture. In the same year, Héroult assigned the French patent rights on his process to a company originally organized in 1868, known as the Société Electrométallurgique Française. Because of its location, this company became known as the Froges enterprise.

7. For accounts of the early development of the industry, see: *ibid.*, Chaps. 1-3; D. H. Wallace, *Market Control in the Aluminum Industry*, Harvard University Press, Cambridge, 1937, Chaps. 1, 2, 5; and the article on "Aluminum," in *Encyclopedia Americana*.

Capitalizing Monopoly Privileges

Though each of these four pioneer enterprises held patent rights on the process which it used, to capitalize fully these monopolistic privileges they had first to settle conflicting patent claims, issues of priority, and like problems, either voluntarily or in the courts. Moreover, all these newcomers at the outset met the competition of the well-established French firm, Pechiney, usually identified by its location as d'Alais et Camargues, which was still producing aluminum by the old Deville process. Thus, keen competition broke out on the introduction of the electrolytic reduction process. The price of the metal in the United States sharply declined from more than $5 a pound in 1887 to about $3 in 1890 and to 75 cents in 1893. A similar drop occurred in European markets, though there the only actual competition was between the two Héroult process plants and the obsolete sodium process plant. For neither the Hall nor the Bradley techniques was licensed outside the United States before 1895.

Undoubtedly, this downward price movement reflected great cost reductions as production rose and steady progress was made in ironing out the kinks of the new electrolytic process. But another factor, particularly in the United States, was the commercial rivalry between the owners of the Hall and the Bradley patents. For either patentee to obtain the full advantage of his monopoly grant, it was necessary to eliminate the other. The test of the market might eventually have established the superiority of one process over the other. But after five years of active competition, which brought sharp price declines, one of the patentees apparently tired of the competitive struggle and sought a short cut to monopoly profits—through litigation.

In 1893 the Pittsburgh Reduction Company obtained an injunction against the Cowles brothers on the ground that production of aluminum by the Bradley process infringed the Hall patent.[8] Cowles produced no aluminum after that date, although after long litigation the courts upheld the Bradley patents and adjudged the Pittsburgh Reduction Company an infringer from the outset.[9] The parties then settled the controversy voluntarily. The Pittsburgh Company paid the Cowles brothers $1,429,907.94, partly as liquidated damages and

8. See USAL, Ex. 195.
9. *Electric Smelting and Refining Co.* v. *Pittsburgh Reduction Co.*, 125 Fed. 926 (1903).

partly in consideration of their promise to withdraw from the alumi-
num-refining industry.[10]

Alcoa Monopolizes Domestic Market

Thus the Aluminum Company of America (successor to the Pittsburgh Reduction Company as of January 1, 1907) became the sole
producer of aluminum in the United States. It successfully kept that
position until the outbreak of World War II. Moreover, as the Court
of Appeals has recently declared:

> This continued and undisturbed control did not fall undesigned into
> Alcoa's lap; obviously it could not have done so. . . . There were at least
> one or two abortive attempts to enter the industry, but Alcoa effectively an-
> ticipated and forestalled all competition and succeeded in holding the field
> alone.[11]

Alcoa's achievement in keeping, for nearly half a century, its position as the "single seller" of a basic material adapted to a wide range
of uses is unique in American industrial history. The methods by
which it accomplished this feat—fortified and preserved its domination of the domestic market—were varied and complicated. However,
our primary interest is in the international cartel arrangements by
which, mainly, the members of the industry, Alcoa included, safeguarded themselves from foreign competition. But since the cartel
effectiveness depended on the members' ability to control aluminum
exports, the general strategy of Alcoa, the largest single producer, in
keeping down domestic competition is significant. Just as the domestic strategy reinforced the cartel controls, so did the cartel reinforce
Alcoa's domestic monopoly.

Furthermore, the domestic development of the industry—specifically, the pattern of Alcoa's growth—makes it clear that this was not
a "distressed industry" trying to escape from "ruinous competition."
The industry had no problems of industrial maladjustment associated
with overinvestment, declining demand, advancing technology, or

10. USAL, Govt.Br., pp. 200-03. Another feature of the settlement was a special
price discount to Cowles on purchases of ingot.
   D. H. Wallace (op. cit.) gives a different account of this patent controversy—as of
several other episodes in the rise of Alcoa—from that given in the text above. Our interpretation of the development of monopoly in this industry is based very largely on
the facts of record in the 1937 Sherman Act proceedings against Alcoa cited above.
Doubtless the discrepancy between Wallace's account and that given here is partly due
to the fact that Wallace did not have access to the evidence presented in this case. The
proceedings were not instituted until after the publication of his book.
11. USAL, 148 Fed. 2d 416, 430 (1945).

shifting areas of production or consumption. Aluminum has never been a "chronically sick" industry, facing the necessity of industrial readjustment—salvaging or shifting excess resources—with all its costs and risks.

The Pittsburgh Reduction Company (Alcoa's predecessor) declared in its annual report to stockholders on September 17, 1895, "There has been no competition in the manufacture of aluminum during the past year, nor is there any prospect of such competition in the future, in this country." [12] Whether this was an avowal of policy or merely a report of facts, Alcoa could truthfully have repeated the first part of the statement in each successive annual report for the next forty-five years.

The program which enabled Alcoa to keep "continued and undisturbed control" of domestic aluminum production had both a positive and a negative side. On the positive side were its research and experimentation for improvement of technical processes, and also its exploration and development of potential market outlets. The qualities of aluminum which fitted it for certain uses had to be discovered and demonstrated. To introduce it successfully in competition with older and more familiar metals, it was often necessary to improve aluminum's qualities, as by alloying it to increase its toughness or tensile strength. Alcoa early attacked these problems with vigor, and by persistently pursuing them unquestionably kept itself technically and commercially in the forefront of the world aluminum industry.

Alcoa's Integration Program

Perhaps also mainly on the positive side was Alcoa's integration program. In 1896, it began the acquisition of bauxite deposits by purchasing certain mines in Georgia.[13] In a series of similar transactions culminating in the absorption ten years later of the General Bauxite Company, which held extensive acreage in Arkansas,[14] Alcoa became the owner of most of the known domestic deposits of high-grade bauxite.[15]

12. USAL, Ex. 478.
13. *Ibid.*, Alcoa Ints. 50, 51.
14. *Ibid.*, Rec., pp. 22498 and 23253 f.; and Ex. 121.
15. *Ibid.*, Rec., p. 23249 f.; and Alcoa Ints. 55, 56. In 1909 Alcoa strengthened its position still further by absorbing the Republic Mining & Manufacturing Company, which owned valuable bauxite deposits in Georgia, Alabama, and Arkansas. *Ibid.*, Ex. 122.

About the same time, it started integrating marketward by establishing its first sheet-rolling mill.[16] During the next fifteen years it successively undertook the manufacture of cooking utensils, cable, castings, and extruded products (for example, wire and trim). In 1901 Alcoa organized the United States Aluminum Company to fabricate kitchenware and the Aluminum Cooking Utensil Company to promote the distribution of these products. The next year it constructed an alumina plant for refining bauxite, preliminary to its electrolytic reduction. Finally, in 1906 Alcoa purchased the St. Lawrence River Power Company and began large-scale acquisition of riparian rights along the Long Saute of the St. Lawrence—its first move toward supplying its own hydroelectric power.[17]

Alcoa's management showed rare foresight and initiative in carrying out this integration program and in rounding it out in succeeding decades. As opportunity offered or occasion demanded, Alcoa bought up new sources of raw materials and power, introduced improved techniques, and extended its product lines.[18] By its aggressive integration policy, Alcoa not only freed itself from dependence on any outside interest but at the same time made it difficult, if not impossible, for an outsider to get a foothold in the industry.

Alcoa Keeps Out Competitors

The negative side of Alcoa's domestic strategy has been its efforts

16. USAL, 148 Fed. 2d 416, 435 (1945).

17. USAL, Alcoa Ints. 1, 110, 111. This project was never carried out, because of difficulties in obtaining the consent of the American and Canadian Governments. Eventually, Alcoa's properties, after being merged with others, in the Frontier Corporation, were sold to Niagara-Hudson Power Company. Ibid., Alcoa Ints. 112, 116, 123-28, 133-34.

Before 1906, Alcoa purchased all its power (mostly from Niagara Falls) under long-term contracts, and it has continued to depend on "outside" power, to some extent, since that date. Most of these contracts have stipulated that the supplier shall not furnish energy to any other aluminum producer. Ibid., Exs. 163, 165-67, 187-88, 191, 974, 1028. Though the restrictive clauses in contracts with Niagara Falls Power Company were cancelled by a secret agreement in January 1921, both the Department of Justice (ibid., Petition, par. 84) and the Power Authority of the State of New York (Brief, before the Federal Power Commission, March 1, 1940, In the Matter of the Application of the Niagara Falls Power Co., p. 24) contend that the restriction is still effective. See Charlotte Muller, "Aluminum and Power Control," Journal of Land and Public Utility Economics, May 1945, Vol. XXI, pp. 108-24.

18. For a fairly comprehensive survey of these developments, see USAL, Govt Br.App., pp. 16-115. Outstanding features of the record were: hydroelectric program in the Tennessee Valley, beginning in 1910; acquisition of bauxite deposits in South America (the Guianas), after 1913; elaboration and standardization of aluminum alloys, and improvement of die-casting and extrusion processes, after the war; purchase of Duke hydroelectric properties on Saguenay River, Canada, in 1925; and construction of reduction and fabricating plants on the Pacific Coast, in the thirties.

to exclude other enterprises from the aluminum industry. Whether or not one interprets Alcoa's integration and expansion program as, in part, a "pre-emptive" buying up of bauxite deposits and hydro-electric sites and an aggressive "buying out" of independent fabricators,[19] other features of its development support the view that Alcoa actively tried to block independent competitive enterprise in this field. And, in the main, it succeeded. During the early stages of its integration, Alcoa's general practice was to exact from sellers of properties which it acquired covenants not to compete afterwards, directly or indirectly, with Alcoa.[20] Similarly, it frequently required its suppliers not to deal with any other aluminum manufacturer.[21]

In 1912, as a defendant in antitrust proceedings, Alcoa accepted a consent decree which required it to abrogate these covenants in restraint of trade and to abandon such policies.[22] Thereafter Alcoa's obstructive tactics and its interference with actual and potential competitors were less conspicuous. But the Court of Appeals found in the recent antitrust case against Alcoa that the company had employed a "price squeeze" for several years to the prejudice of the competitive opportunities of independent sheet-rolling mills.[23] The

19. The Circuit Court of Appeals in the recent antitrust suit accepted the trial judge's finding that the evidence was insufficient to sustain the government's contention that Alcoa had "pre-empted" the field by its extensive acquisitions of bauxite deposits and water-power sites. USAL, 148 Fed. 2d 416, 432-33 (1945). But this judicial conclusion on a legal issue does not invalidate the economic judgment on the practical business consequences, expressed in the text above.

20. The General Bauxite and Republic Mining deals, cited above, included provisions of this character.

21. By a contract of January 1, 1907, with the Pennsylvania Salt Company, Alcoa agreed to buy a certain amount of alumina from Pennsylvania during the next five years and Pennsylvania undertook not to manufacture aluminum itself or to supply alumina to anyone else for aluminum manufacture. USAL, Ex. 123.

Alcoa's contracts with power companies likewise restricted them from supplying electricity to others for use in the production of aluminum. See citations above.

22. USAL, Exs. 1009 and 1010. These practices were also condemned, as evincing an "attempt to monopolize," by the Circuit Court of Appeals (2d Cir.) in *Baush Machine Tool Co. v. Aluminum Company of America,* 72 Fed. 2d 236, 242 (1934).

23. The "price squeeze" was a reduction of the margin between ingot prices and sheet prices. Independent fabricators charged that at times Alcoa reduced the margin to a level lower than the cost of rolling operations, and the government took the same position in its antitrust suit. USAL, Govt.Br.App., pp. 93 ff., esp. pp. 104-12.

While the margins on different classes of fabricated products (sheets, castings, rods, pipes, etc.) cannot be directly compared, analysis of the voluminous evidence on mill costs and selling prices of various aluminum intermediate products which the government introduced in the antitrust suit tends to confirm its contention that the changes in the profit margins on rolled sheet relative to those on other classes of products cannot be satisfactorily explained in terms either of relative demand changes or of technological developments affecting unit costs. The evidence suggests arbitrary and discriminatory price manipulation, for the purpose of getting rid of unwelcome competitors. Cf. *ibid.,* Ex. 1753. (*Footnote continued on next page.*)

court declared that this was "an unlawful exercise of Alcoa's power," and directed the lower court to enjoin the practice.[24]

In both their positive and negative aspects, Alcoa's successful efforts to maintain its dominant position in the domestic aluminum industry showed business acumen in its management. Seldom in the annals of corporate finance has any concern so clearly demonstrated ability to minimize risks and maximize profits. Alcoa may not have made itself invulnerable, but it substantially reduced the dangers of relying for market mastery on patent rights alone.[25]

Alcoa's "Foreign Policy"

Monopoly of domestic manufacture of a light product like aluminum is not enough to assure firm control of the market. Alcoa's opportunity to maximize profits depended also on fortifying its domestic position against invasion from abroad. Alcoa could not afford to ignore this possibility. Up to 1909 it was protected both by its basic patents and by a customs duty of 8 cents a pound. But it had to face the eventualities that Congress might lower the tariff wall and that when the Bradley patents expired no new patents of comparable importance would be available to it.

Meanwhile, of the three surviving "pioneers" in electrolytic aluminum reduction,[26] the two European producers by the Héroult process, AIAG and the Froges concern, were growing step by step with

---

Of eleven sheet-rolling mills which had been built by others than Alcoa before 1939, only seven remained independently in business in that year. Three sold out to other aluminum-fabricating companies in which Alcoa had a substantial stock interest. These were: Standard Aluminum Co. (1913–1916), Cleveland Metal Products Co. (1915–1918), and Bremer-Walz Corp. (1917-1919). One, the Baush Machine Tool Co., was liquidated in 1931, and Alcoa paid its owners $1,150,000 in settlement of a suit for treble damages under the antitrust laws. Of the remaining seven, only four sell sheet in the market; the others use their entire output in their own manufacturing operations. *Ibid.*, Govt.Br.App., pp. 93-112; Rec., pp. 2622-26 and 2674-77; and Exs. 79, 80, 83, 85, 86.

24. USAL, 148 Fed. 2d 416, 438 (1945).

25. Alcoa developed a rather strong patent position on fabrication processes after the expiration of its basic (Bradley) patents in 1909. However, it appears seldom to have had occasion to utilize this weapon, except in one or two fields, e.g., piston patents. Probably this was because of its strategic position as a single-seller in the virgin aluminum market. Quite apart from patent controls, no effective challenge to its policies could come from fabricators who had to look to it for supplies of ingot, sheet, etc.

26. The fourth, Cowles, ceased production in 1893. AIAG and Alcoa have preserved their separate identities since 1888. But the Froges enterprise merged in 1921 with the d'Alais et Camargues concern. Even before the merger, however, these two companies were linked, through Aluminium Française. This joint selling agency, organized in 1911, has since exercised monopolistic control of all aluminum produced by French interests anywhere. Edwards *et al., op. cit.,* p. 39; Wallace, *op. cit.,* p. 87 f.

Alcoa; and in 1895 a third enterprise, the British Aluminium Company, was licensed under the Héroult patents.[27] This situation plainly called for market aggression or market artifices—or both. Alcoa chose both. In 1895 it granted a license under the Hall patents to a small French concern, and these rights shortly thereafter passed to the well-established Pechiney firm, d'Alais et Camargues. This move was an open challenge to the Héroult-process group of producers, led by AIAG. They appear to have preferred a concord to a contest.

Early Aluminum Cartels

A bilateral agreement between AIAG and Alcoa in 1896 inaugurated the international cartel movement.[28] While the full text of this agreement is not available, one provision safeguarded each of the parties from the export of the product of the other to its own domestic and tributary market areas. Whether the contract settled the question of the respective patent rights of the parties, we do not know. This much is certain: the issue of priority between the Hall patents, on which Alcoa then relied, and the Héroult patents was never submitted to a judicial test either in this country or abroad.[29] It seems clear, thus, that the parties preferred a mutual accord to a competitive struggle for domination of the world aluminum industry.

Five years later, on November 2, 1901, just before the Héroult patents expired, aluminum producers organized a second and more comprehensive cartel.[30] It included not only the two parties to the 1896 agreement but also the other three European producers: the British Aluminium Company and the two French concerns, the Froges enterprise and the d'Alais et Camargues company. Each of the national groups reserved its home market for domestic producers exclusively and the agreement designated these areas "closed markets." The rest of the world, which at that time included Germany,[31] constituted the "open market." However, this open market was far

27. Wallace, op. cit., Chap. 2. After a poor beginning, this firm was reorganized in 1908, acquired water-power sites, and developed production facilities in Norway. It has grown to be an important, though secondary, factor in the world aluminum industry —with the help of British Government subsidies during and after World War I.
28. USAL, Rec., p. 19549; and Ex. 478.
29. Ibid., Rec., p. 5275.
30. Ibid., Ex. 268.
31. There was no independent production of aluminum in Germany at this time, though in 1897 the AIAG had constructed a small plant at the Rheinfalle. However, Germany was not treated as part of the home market of AIAG.

from being open to competition. The agreement fixed quotas for sales in it for each cartel member. For example, Alcoa's share of the open market—that is, of all sales outside the United States and Canada, France, Switzerland, and the United Kingdom—was 21 per cent.

To eliminate all price competition, the bylaws of the association authorized a governing committee periodically to establish prices for all sales in the open market. Finally, lest any member, by not charging all that the traffic would bear within its own market, should make it possible for third parties to buy up metal in a closed market for resale in the open market, the agreement required every member to maintain a domestic price not less than one cent higher than the cartel-fixed price in the open market.

These arrangements set the pattern for cartel controls in the numerous subsequent agreements, with only minor variations and with such adaptations as later political developments and industrial shifts necessitated. Alcoa's representative in this cartel was its wholly owned Canadian subsidiary, Northern Aluminum Company. Alcoa filed the application for this company's charter only two days before the agreement was signed.[32]

Cartel Experience

The course of the aluminum market during the five years 1901–1906, which was the specified term of the cartel, plainly discloses its monopolistic consequences whatever the association's objectives may have been. Although every member of the cartel had previously been operating under patent protection in its domestic market, prices everywhere advanced. The price advance was quicker and sharper in Europe, where pre-cartel market control—at least outside the aluminum-producing countries—was less tight than in the United States. The European members raised their prices 20 per cent within a few months, and by 1905 the increase had reached more than 100 per cent. On the other hand, Alcoa made no alteration in its scheduled

32. This device was evidently an attempt to relieve Alcoa of legal liability under the Sherman Antitrust Act. A. V. Davis, who negotiated the cartel agreement (USAL, Rec., p. 19584 f.), has testified that Alcoa was the real party in interest. *Ibid.*, p. 19578.

The corporate vehicle was at the outset called the Royal Aluminum Company. The title was shortly afterward changed to the Northern Aluminum Company, because in its haste to organize the instrument Alcoa had overlooked a recently enacted British statute which, in the absence of a special dispensation, forbade the use of the name "Royal" for a business enterprise in any of the British dominions.

TABLE 15

ALCOA'S AVERAGE ANNUAL PRICES OF ALUMINUM INGOT, 1893–1940

(In Cents Per Pound)

Year	Schedule Prices [a]	Year	Schedule Prices [a]	Net Realization Prices [b]
1893	78	1920	33.1	32.79
1894	61	1921	25.3	21.18
1895	54.4	1922	19.9	18.60
1896	47.8	1923	25.0	22.69
1897	36.1	1924	27.0	26.78
1898	33	1925	27.5	27.51
1899	33	1926	26.9	26.98
1900	33	1927	25.6	25.36
		1928	23.9	24.09
1901	33	1929	23.9	23.58
1902	33	1930	23.4	23.33
1903	33			
1904	33	1931	22.9	22.78
1905	33.1	1932	22.9	21.76
1906	36	1933	22.9	19.30
1907	38	1934	22.2	18.95
1908	29.3	1935	19.5	18.75
1909	24	1936	19.0	18.82
1910	22	1937	19.8	19.56
		1938	20.0	19.44
1911	20.3	1939	20.0	19.86
1912	20.2	1940	18.7	—
1913	21.2			
1914	18.8			
1915	24.5			
1916	35.3			
1917	37.5			
1918	33.5			
1919	32.8			

a. Computed from *U.S.* v. *Aluminum Company of America, et al.,* in U.S. District Court for the Southern District of New York (1937), Equity No. 85-73 (cited below as USAL), Answers of Alcoa to Interrogatories 27, 28, and from U.S. Bureau of Mines, *Minerals Yearbook,* Washington, 1938–1940. For the period prior to 1934, these prices differ somewhat from those shown in USAL, Exhibit No. 1638, though as a rule only by fractions of a cent. All of the prices in Ex. 1638 are for 99 per cent ingot; whereas prices shown here are for 98-99 per cent ingot up to 1934, after which date price quotations on this grade of ingot were withdrawn.

b. From USAL, Exs. 1637, 1701, 1744. These are the average net prices realized by Alcoa after making allowance for the part of freight charges absorbed (i.e., paid) by it. (Not available before 1920.)

"domestic" (United States and Canada) price of 33 cents a pound until 1905. Since Alcoa was the sole seller in the American market, this apparently was the price calculated to yield maximum net revenue.[33] Hence, initially, the brunt of cartel price manipulation fell chiefly on the European market, and Alcoa obtained direct advantages from the arrangement only in its export sales.

When the European open-market price rose to the equivalent of about 36 cents a pound, Alcoa got the association's approval for continuing the domestic price of 33 cents.[34] Whether fear that a price advance would impair its monopoly revenue or some other factor dictated Alcoa's domestic price policy in this period is not clear, but in 1906 (in compliance with obligations assumed under the agreement) Alcoa advanced its price to the cartel minimum.[35]

Both the European aluminum producers and Alcoa approximately doubled their productive capacity from 1901 to 1906. The course of prices reflects the failure of this rate of expansion to meet the mounting demand. Moreover, such data as are available on the trend of profits warrant a similar inference. While the European companies issued only sketchy financial statements, competent observers agree that the rates of return during these years were exceptionally high.[36] Alcoa's profits were not only high, they were steadily increasing.[37] Although as a single-seller in the American market in 1899 and 1900, it reported net profits on stockholders' equity of 11 and 15 per

33. Moreover, until 1905, no price increase here was required under the terms of the agreement. In virtue partly of its patent monopoly, and partly of its arrangements with the chief European aluminum exporter, AIAG, Alcoa was able to maintain a domestic price higher than the current price in the chief European open market (Germany) by more than the amount of the American tariff. The price differential in 1900 was 11 cents, while the tariff rate was only 8 cents a pound. Alcoa's domestic price was 10 cents a pound more than the cartel terms required it to maintain in its domestic market. See Table 15 for American prices. Wallace reports the course of European prices, based chiefly on Metallgesellschaft data for Germany, in Elliott et al., op cit., Chap. 6, pp. 226 ff.

34. USAL, Exs. 277-79; and Rec., pp. 19608-10.

35. It would be an error to deduce from these developments, however, that Alcoa was constrained, against its will, to follow a price policy which was engineered by the Europeans and which might readily have been regarded as extortionate. On the contrary, Arthur V. Davis, Alcoa's chief executive, took not only an active but a leading role in both the organization and administration of the cartel. See below.

36. See Wallace, Market Control in the Aluminum Industry, pp. 264-71, and other authors there cited.

37. Though Alcoa, then called the Pittsburgh Reduction Company, published no financial statements in these years, antitrust proceedings have recently brought to light extensive information on its investment and income accounts. See USAL, Exs. 1001, 1709, 1735-37. For certain computations based on data from these sources, showing the profitability of the enterprise, see Table 16.

TABLE 16

CAPITAL AND INCOME OF ALCOA, 1890–1939

Average of 5-Year Period	Stockholders' Equity [a]	Net Earnings [b]	Rate of Earnings [c]
50-year average	$71,512,490	$8,605,292	$12.03
1890–1894	926,914	34,519	3.72
1895–1899	1,289,717	76,709	5.95
1900–1904	2,724,879	437,839	16.07
1905–1909	9,342,810	2,742,842	29.36
1910–1914	26,405,810	4,704,458	17.82
1915–1919	73,144,840	19,372,863	26.49
1920–1924	106,521,424	4,310,215	4.04
1925–1929	158,222,029	21,332,858	13.48
1930–1934	166,032,477	4,689,319	2.82
1935–1939	170,514,000	28,351,298	16.61

a. Adapted from *U.S.* v. *Aluminum Company of America, et al.*, in U.S. District Court for the Southern District of New York (1937), Equity No. 85-73 (cited below as USAL), Exhibit No. 1709, col. D.
b. Before income taxes, but after deductions for all other taxes and for interest. From USAL, Ex. 1737, col. C.
c. Computed by division of net earnings by stockholders' equity.

cent, respectively, in each of the first two years of the cartel it earned 19 per cent. In 1905 and 1906 its profits were even higher: 26 and 35 per cent, respectively. Plainly, supply had not kept pace with demand.

Cartel Renewed

The aluminum producers had achieved an extraordinarily advantageous position by their mutual restraint and the pursuit of a common strategy. Their self-interest pointed to its retention. Accordingly, late in 1906 they concluded a revised cartel agreement.[38] This third scheme was, in effect, a renewal of the second.[39] It embraced the same parties, the four European producers and Alcoa. Alcoa's wholly owned Canadian subsidiary, Northern Aluminum Company, represented it in the cartel, as previously. The agreement incorporated similar provisions for dividing markets and fixing prices.

Though the 1906 agreement made minor readjustments in quotas,

38. USAL, Ex. 308.
39. *Ibid.*, Rec., p. 19643; and Alcoa Int. 460.

the most significant change was in tighter measures to enforce cartel commitments. Article XXX required each member to post a "guarantee deposit," proportioned to its sales quota in the "open market," which was subject to forfeiture as a penalty for any departure from the prescribed rules.[40] The agreement stipulated, also, that members should make regular reports to the association on volume of sales and prices realized in their respective "closed markets." This provision expressly applied to Alcoa's sales in the United States—as well, of course, as to those made locally by its subsidiary in Canada. Finally, to prevent dealers from circumventing the cartel-fixed price in open markets, the 1906 agreement expressly required Alcoa (whose own export sales were normally and regularly made solely through its Canadian subsidiary) to forbid its customers in the United States to resell the metal abroad.[41]

With more rigorous control of the market thus provided, the confederated producers undertook a tardy expansion of productive facilities.[42] During the next six years, through 1912, capacity expanded about threefold both in Europe and in the United States. In Europe, however, cartel members did not build all the additional facilities. Seven new aluminum enterprises were started there between 1906 and 1908. Evidently the high rate of profits, combined with the absence of patent barriers after the basic Héroult patents expired in 1903, provided an attractive opportunity for venture capital. The independent activities of these new entrants in the industry threatened the market dominance of the cartel group. With general business stagnation commencing late in 1907 and an internal dispute over

40. The deposit made by Northern amounted to $50,000 and it was specified that this covered liability for defection, *either* by Northern *or* by Alcoa. *Ibid.*, Ex. 308, Art. XXX.

41. *Ibid.*, Art. V.

42. Tardy, because, for one thing, Alcoa showed not only a larger *volume* of profits but a higher *rate* of return on stockholders' equity after the expansion of capacity than before it. Apparently prices under the cartel were at levels which prevented maximum returns on the investments. Between 1906 and 1908 there were protests within the cartel itself against the "high price policy" consistently being pursued, to the detriment, so it was alleged, of the European members' own interests.

In a letter of September 4, 1908 from A. Badin, head of the French group, to A. V. Davis, president of Alcoa, the writer characterized the cartel price policy, a policy long sponsored and vigorously defended by Alcoa, as *"la politique des très hauts prix."* He declared that such a policy was disadvantageous to his company, in that it limited sales drastically and encouraged potential competitors. *Ibid.*, Ex. 338. But Mr. Davis was unconvinced. So far from acceding to the plea for a reduction, he expressed the view that "The best thing would be to raise the price." *Ibid.*, Ex. 329. On another occasion he stated his position on this matter quite frankly: "So far as throttling competition is concerned, we do not believe that reducing prices will do it." *Ibid.*, Ex. 324.

continuing the "high price policy," this challenge led to dissolution of the third cartel on September 30, 1908.

Under the double impact of the cartel's end and business recession, ingot prices in Germany declined 50 per cent between mid-1907 and the end of 1908. Undoubtedly several of the new producers and some of the former cartel members were offering their output competitively in European markets for what it would bring. However, the end of the cartel did not mean complete disruption of organized market control everywhere.

Effects on American Markets

Consumers in the American market did not at once obtain the full benefit of a competitive price, partly because of a contract negotiated by Alcoa and AIAG in October 1908, immediately after dissolution of the third cartel.[43] Despite the rapid growth of French production, the Neuhausen firm was still the principal exporter of aluminum to world markets.[44] By this agreement, Alcoa and AIAG mutually pledged themselves not to invade the other's market. Thus, the American market did not feel the full brunt of the competitive pressure on prices for some time pending exploratory uncovering of trade lanes to this *terra incognita* by other European producers.

By 1909, however, the invasion of the American market was in full swing, imports reaching more than 900,000 pounds, some eight times the amount imported in the depression year of 1908 and nearly equal to imports in the boom year of 1907.[45] In 1910, encouraged by a reduction in the import duty from 8 cents to 7 cents a pound, imports again rose eightfold, amounting to more than 7.6 million pounds.

Unquestionably, much of this imported metal was competitively offered in the American market, and Alcoa was forced to lower its price steadily. A 25 per cent drop in 1908 from the average price of 1907 was followed by reductions of 20 per cent in 1909 and 10 per cent in 1910. The 1910 price of 22 cents a pound was the lowest at which aluminum had ever been offered to American consumers.

43. *Ibid.*, Ex. 343; and Alcoa Int. 476. Though Northern was nominally the "American" party to this contract, it was owned, 100 per cent, by Alcoa, and A. V. Davis, president of Alcoa, negotiated and signed the agreement. *Ibid.*, Rec. (printed), p. 773.
44. Wallace, *op. cit.*, p. 124.
45. See Table 17. References in the text to volume of imports exclude the metal imported from Canada by Alcoa.

TABLE 17

UNITED STATES IMPORTS OF ALUMINUM, 1900–1940

(In Thousands of Pounds)

Year	Total [a]	From Europe [b]	By Alcoa From Canada [c]	By Alcoa From Europe [d]
1900	183	183	—	e
1901	365	365	—	e
1902	558	375	183	e
1903	687	685	2	e
1904	363	363	—	e
1905	639	639	—	e
1906	614	614	—	e
1907	1,292	1,142	150	e
1908	113	113	—	e
1909	2,036	935	1,105	e
1910	12,387	7,612	4,775	e
1911	6,241	4,286	1,955	e
1912	14,803	5,197	9,606	e
1913	26,958	20,236	6,722	e
1914	15,964	11,148	4,816	e
1915	13,765	6,266	7,499	e
1916	8,200	52	8,148	e
1917	1,904	25	1,879	e
1918	1,503	5	1,498	e
1919	17,644	5,261	12,383	e
1920	40,074	27,771	12,303	—
1921	30,577	27,318	3,259	—
1922	39,951	32,415	7,536	717
1923	43,065	31,992	11,073	4,090
1924	29,394	23,445	5,949	5,177
1925	43,409	30,935	12,474	10,972
1926	74,878	55,529	19,349	23,822
1927	72,188	30,155	42,033	7,403
1928	37,895	14,660	23,235	9,327
1929	48,415	19,931	28,484	—
1930	24,498	12,724	11,774	—
1931	13,804	10,611	3,193	—
1932	8,005	5,265	2,740	—

TABLE 17 (continued)

UNITED STATES IMPORTS OF ALUMINUM, 1900–1940

(In Thousands of Pounds)

| Year | Total [a] | From Europe [b] | By Alcoa | |
			From Canada [c]	From Europe [d]
1933	16,710	14,552	2,058	—
1934	18,371	15,283	3,088	—
1935	21,075	15,862	5,213	—
1936	25,158	22,154	3,004	—
1937	44,701	19,096	25,605	400
1938	17,511	e	e	e
1939	28,060	e	e	e
1940	34,869	e	e	e

a. Total imports from all sources. Figures for 1900–1911, inclusive, represent "imports for consumption, by articles," from *U.S.* v. *Aluminum Company of America, et al.,* in U.S. District Court for the Southern District of New York (1937), Equity No. 85-73 (cited below as USAL), Ex. 453; for 1912–1933, inclusive, "general imports," from *ibid.,* Ex. 458; for 1933–1937, inclusive, "imports for consumption," from *ibid.,* Ex. 458; for 1937–1940, inclusive, "imports for consumption," from U.S. Bureau of Mines, *Minerals Yearbook,* Washington, 1940, p. 651. Before 1912, imports of aluminum ingots were not separately classified, but were grouped with "alloys of any kind of which aluminum is the component of chief value." Moreover, for this period there are no data available on the country of origin of such imports.

b. For 1912 and subsequent years from USAL, Ex. 458. For years prior to 1912, total imports minus imports from Canada, as shown in the third column.

c. For 1912 and subsequent years, from USAL, Ex. 458. For years prior to 1912, from *ibid.,* Alcoa Int. 15. Data given in the answer to this Interrogatory show the purchases of metal by Alcoa from its Canadian subsidiary, but in value terms only. These have been converted into physical units at the "declared" value of the imports. For most years, this basis of conversion probably results in a slight understatement of the actual volume of Canadian imports. This probability is based on two grounds: (1) the "declared" value per pound is computed from the values stated for *all imports,* i.e., imports from all sources, and hence the average value may well have been raised above the price that Alcoa actually paid its subsidiary for the metal; and (2) there may well have been imports in a small volume from Canada by others than Alcoa either on account of some extraordinary transactions between the Northern Company and a United States consumer, or on account of re-exports from Canada of some European metal. But the figures for 1912, the first year for which data on the country of origin of aluminum imports are available, indicate that the discrepancy between the actual imports from Canada and the estimated imports as computed above is so slight as to be practically insignificant.

d. USAL, Alcoa Ints. 16, 17, 18.

e. Not available.

Their response shows clearly how elastic was the demand for this new product and how mistaken had been Alcoa's judgment on the maximum-net-revenue-yielding price. Domestic consumption increased from 31 million pounds in 1909 to 47 million in 1910.[46]

46. Computed by adding imports, as shown in Table 17, to domestic production, as shown in Table 18. No data are available based directly on consumption of metal in fabricating processes.

TABLE 18

Production of Aluminum Ingot in United States, Canada, and World, 1893–1940

(In Thousands of Pounds)

Year	United States [a]	Canada [b]	World [c]	North American Percentage World Total [d]
1893	216	—	—	—
1894	494	—	—	—
1895	501	—	—	—
1896	1,002	—	—	—
1897	2,371	—	—	—
1898	2,993	—	—	—
1899	3,262	—	—	—
1900	5,062	—	—	—
1901	5,738	—	—	—
1902	5,763	1,714	—	—
1903	6,636	1,675	—	—
1904	8,100	2,161	—	—
1905	10,810	2,456	—	—
1906	14,125	3,667	—	—
1907	16,325	5,920	—	—
1908	10,679	972	—	—
1909	29,081	6,083	—	—
1910	35,402	9,648	—	—
1911	38,396	9,679	—	—
1912	41,806	12,028	—	—
1913	47,279	14,065	—	—
1914	57,973	14,551	—	—
1915	90,504	18,368	—	—
1916	115,107	21,185	—	—
1917	129,861	24,087	—	—
1918	124,725	23,535	—	—
1919	128,477	21,582	—	—
1920	138,042	22,384	276,169	58
1921	54,532	6,335	153,681	39
1922	73,633	12,341	192,236	44
1923	128,658	23,334	307,637	49

TABLE 18 (continued)

PRODUCTION OF ALUMINUM INGOT IN UNITED STATES, CANADA, AND
WORLD, 1893–1940

(In Thousands of Pounds)

Year	United States [a]	Canada [b]	World [c]	North American Percentage World Total [d]
1924	150,564	25,122	371,464	47
1925	140,116	28,907	398,552	42
1926	147,386	38,911	432,771	43
1927	163,607	82,735	486,055	50
1928	210,544	81,211	556,900	52
1929	227,973	63,440	593,880	49
1930	229,037	76,214	590,956	51
1931	177,545	68,101	483,841	50
1932	104,888	39,583	337,260	42
1933	85,125	35,528	311,740	38
1934	74,177	34,863	373,120	29
1935	119,295	46,341	569,580	29
1936	224,929	59,404	791,780	35
1937	292,631	93,810	1,059,300	36
1938	286,882	145,500	1,273,360	34
1939	327,090	164,524	1,467,400	33
1940	412,560	242,514	1,766,600	37

a. From U.S. Bureau of Mines, *Minerals Yearbook*, Washington, 1939, pp. 642-43.
b. From *U.S.* v. *Aluminum Company of America, et al.*, in U.S. District Court for the Southern District of New York (1937), Equity No. 85-73 (cited below as USAL), Exs. 459, 460, 721, Alted Ints. 169 and 173; and U.S. Bureau of Mines, *Minerals Yearbook*, 1941, p. 646.
c. U.S. Bureau of Mines, *Minerals Yearbook*, 1938, p. 589, and 1941, p. 646; and from USAL, Exs. 985 and 1647. We have corrected data from these sources to the extent that the official data on production in United States and Canada differ from the estimated output of these two countries as reported in the *Yearbook* of the American Bureau of Metal Statistics, on which the exhibits mentioned are based. Both the U.S. Bureau of Mines *Yearbook* and the American Bureau of Metal Statistics *Yearbook* derive much of the information on foreign production from the compilations made by Metallgesellschaft, of Frankfurt, Germany.
d. The quotient of United States plus Canadian production divided by world production.

Alcoa's earnings in 1909 were more than double those of the "boom year," 1907, and were at the rate of 41 per cent on stockholders' equity, the highest rate realized to this date. Despite the still lower prices in 1910, net profits were again higher than those realized at the height of the boom, this time by 50 per cent.

The emergence of even limited competition for a brief span in the international aluminum markets points to two consequences of cartel control.[47] First, it resulted in economic waste—underinvestment and socially uneconomic cost-price relationships. The cartel's high price policy stimulated "outside" competition. It brought abnormal returns to the older members of the industry, confederated in the cartel. Plainly, productive capacity had been restricted to a point far below the level to which resources could be economically employed in this industry.

Second, cartel control was not necessary to insure profitable operations. True, the ratio of Alcoa's net earnings to stockholders' equity declined from 31 per cent in 1907 to 11 per cent in 1908, which was a year of severe business depression. Throughout the prewar period, however, earnings represented a return on invested capital in the industry well above a normal competitive rate—certainly in America and probably in most instances in Europe.[48] Nevertheless, those who have tasted the fruits of monopoly are not easily persuaded that competitive gains afford adequate nourishment.

Fifth Aluminum Cartel Launched

Late in 1911, A. V. Davis of Alcoa began negotiations with the European producers to organize a new cartel.[49] The formulation of a new agreement patterned after the old, with home territories reserved to the several members, encountered two formidable obstacles. First, the American market had become by far the most attractive market in which to sell aluminum. The rapidly expanding automobile industry had surpassed all other outlets in importance. By 1912 it used perhaps a third of the domestic aluminum output, in cast parts where strength was relatively unimportant.

While consumption was expanding more rapidly in the United States than elsewhere, both production and capacity for a time ex-

47. Competition was "limited," because the two largest producers were, by agreement, not competing with each other.
48. The British Aluminium Company was an exception. It went through bankruptcy in 1908. But Wallace's view is that the British Isles are not well situated for aluminum production. In his opinion, the leading European companies were "enjoying reasonable profits" after 1908. From the scanty data available, they appear to us to have been not only "reasonable" but more than an ordinary competitive rate of return. See his chapter on "Aluminum" in Elliott et al., op. cit., pp. 229-30.
49. USAL, Rec., p. 18739.

panded more rapidly in Europe, under the stimulus of competition, than in the United States. Whereas in 1907, with production at full capacity in both spheres, Europe and America each produced about half the world output of 45 million pounds, the next year American production fell to half the domestic capacity. It was not until 1914 that American output again caught up with that of Europe. From 1908 to the outbreak of the war, aluminum productive capacity trebled on both sides of the Atlantic, but the increase abroad occurred mainly in the earlier part of this period.[50] With American consumption rapidly expanding after 1908 and with European production rapidly increasing, European aluminum pushed its way in increasing volume into the American market. When Mr. Davis went to Europe in 1911 to negotiate a new cartel, therefore, the European producers —with a foothold in the American market—were in a strong bargaining position.

The second obstacle to a new agreement reserving to Alcoa exclusively the American market was an investigation which the Antitrust Division of the Department of Justice had begun of Alcoa's practices and of its unrivalled position in the domestic industry. As president of Alcoa, Mr. Davis was negotiating with European producers for the re-establishment of collective control over the world's aluminum markets, and at the same time with the Department of Justice for a settlement of the issues which it had raised, among them Alcoa's participation in the earlier cartel arrangements. Eventually Alcoa accepted a consent decree, on June 7, 1912, which terminated the antitrust proceedings.[51] The cartel agreement was signed just five days later, on June 12, 1912.[52]

50. The rates of expansion of the aluminum industry in Europe and in America show a remarkable parallel, over the long term. In spite of temporary shifts in the relationship from year to year, capacities were virtually identical in 1907, 1914, 1921, 1927, and 1934. After Hitler came to power and undertook the rearmament program, German output rose rapidly and by 1938 had actually outstripped production in the United States. In that year Germany alone produced nearly as much as the United States and Canada together.

51. The formal complaint was filed May 16, 1912. See USAL, Exs. 1009 and 1010.

52. *Ibid.*, Ex. 143. This cartel followed the general pattern of the 1906 cartel. As previously, home markets were reserved and "open markets" were divided according to fixed quotas. A governing board periodically fixed a standard cartel price. To guarantee performance the agreement required members to post a deposit.

An added feature was the prohibition of members' dealing with nonmember aluminum concerns. Significantly, this did not apply to transactions between Northern, which was a signatory of the agreement, and its parent, Alcoa.

The 1908 Agreement Cancelled

In addition to abrogating certain covenants in restraint of trade, the consent decree cancelled the 1908 cartel agreement with AIAG (which had in fact expired), and enjoined Alcoa from taking part directly in similar arrangements in the future. In technical compliance with the court's orders, Alcoa itself abstained from signing the 1912 cartel agreement. Moreover, the agreement specifically provided that its restrictions applied solely to "sales of aluminum outside the United States." These facts are indubitable. It is likewise true that imports of European aluminum, which had declined sharply in 1911, increased by more than 20 per cent in 1912. Moreover, after the Democratic victory in that year, the duty on aluminum was reduced from 7 cents to 2 cents a pound, whereupon imports multiplied almost fourfold. They reached no less than 20 million pounds in 1913, equal to more than 40 per cent of Alcoa's domestic capacity.

In spite of these developments, it is not clear that the cartel contemplated that the American market would become a competitive battleground within which European producers might sell in such amounts and at such prices as they severally chose. For while Alcoa was not itself a member of the new cartel, its wholly owned Canadian subsidiary, Northern Aluminum Company, was a member.[53] By virtue of its membership, it had assumed certain restrictions on its operations in European markets.

What was the *quid pro quo*? It is possible, of course, that Alcoa regarded the benefits of collective action in European and Canadian markets as an adequate end in itself—even though the United States market were to remain not only "open," but competitive. On the other hand, a project was under consideration to organize a new company to produce aluminum in the United States, to be jointly owned by the European producers and by Alcoa through its Canadian subsidiary. This would give the Europeans an opportunity to participate to a limited extent in the profitable and expanding American market without exposing that market to the "disturbing" effects of their individual and uncoordinated competitive efforts. This device might "appease" the European producers and yet not endanger Alcoa's dominant position in the American market.

53. In the course of the consent decree negotiations, Mr. Davis disclosed to the Department of Justice Alcoa's intention to have Northern join the cartel.

The Strange Case of Southern Aluminium

At any rate, during the cartel negotiations the parties discussed a proposal to form such a company.[54] The project eventually took shape in the Southern Aluminium Company, nominally under French spon-

54. USAL, Ex. 1011. This exhibit consists solely of a letter dated February 17, 1912 from A. V. Davis, president of Alcoa, to J. A. Fowler of the Department of Justice, who was in charge of investigation of Alcoa and of the negotiations for a consent decree. It is so revealing of the undercurrents in the aluminum world at that time that we quote it in full:

Mr. J. A. Fowler   February 17, 1912
    Assistant to Attorney General
      Department of Justice
        Washington, D.C.
Dear Sir:

You are aware that the Aluminum Company of America owns the capital stock of the Northern Aluminum Company, Ltd., a Canadian corporation owning and operating a plant in Quebec. You will recollect that last November I described to you the deplorable state of the aluminum industry on the Continent and told you that the Northern Aluminum Company desired to cooperate with the continental aluminum manufacturers to improve the industry and to enter into an agreement with them by which each party to the agreement shall supply a given percentage of the aluminum market outside of the United States and subject itself to rules of sale as agreed upon by all the parties.

Inasmuch as you considered that no United States authority has jurisdiction over such an agreement, I went to Europe in December and met representatives from the three largest aluminum interests, one of which interests is in reality a syndicate representing the seven companies producing aluminum in France. I told the people with whom I met that the United States must be left out of the agreement altogether and that no written or implied agreement could be had with respect to importation into or exportation from the United States.

Accordingly a beginning was made upon such an arrangement and the relative market percentages were agreed upon for the four interests at this conference. It was further arranged that during the next two or three months the other producing companies should be interviewed and provided these other companies would agree to accept what seemed to be reasonable percentages that I should return in March and though I have not yet had definite information I am planning to go to Europe again about the first of March and, on the assumption that everybody is agreed with respect to the percentages, in order to complete the arrangements it will only be necessary to discuss rules of procedure, etc.

I desire to lay this matter fully before you partly with the idea of confirming by letter what I have said to you in conversation and partly with the idea that you will, I hope, be kind enough to guard against unintentionally wording the decree to be submitted to us so that it will prevent the Northern Aluminum making such arrangement.

It was suggested that, should such an arrangement be made by the producers outside of the United States, it would then be possible for them to enter actively into the development of new lines of consumption, which has never heretofore been possible, each company fearing that its missionary work would be taken advantage of by the others. As certain lines of such development will require investment of money it was suggested that all these producers outside the United States go together in such investments. As this seemed to be a good plan the Northern Aluminum Company expressed its willingness to participate in such investments. It further developed, however, that the French group or syndicate above referred to had decided to build an aluminum plant in the United States. Some dissatisfaction being expressed by the English and German companies that the French companies should do this to the exclusion of the other companies, the French companies stated that any company could join in this investment and then it was suggested that it would be better if all of the producers outside the United States should join in this investment the same as in the other contemplated investments. On the assumption that this is done, the Aluminum Company of America will find it-

sorship.[55] The company, incorporated in September 1912, started construction of a power plant and aluminum reduction facilities on the Yadkin River in North Carolina.[56]

From the outset Alcoa treated the Southern Company more as a foster child than as a rival suitor for the favors of American aluminum consumers. Shortly after its incorporation, Alcoa contracted to supply two thirds of the capital—more than $3 million—for a joint enterprise designed primarily to provide Southern with its alumina requirements.[57] This was an extraordinary transaction, viewed either from the standpoint of the Southern Company, exposed by such an arrangement to the mercy of its nominal rival, or from the standpoint of Alcoa, magnanimously lending a helping hand to a supposed competitor.

Alcoa-Southern Relations

A letter dated October 21, 1912, the same day this contract was signed, reveals the close working relationship between Alcoa and Southern. A. V. Davis of Alcoa wrote to A. Badin, managing director of L'Aluminium Française and president of Southern:

While both you and we hope that the American Nitrogen Company will be supplying the Southern Aluminium Company with its alumina within a very short time, we recognize with you that there may be some delay and that for the years 1913, 1914 and 1915, you may be dependent upon Bayer process alumina.

---

self in competition with a company in which the Northern Aluminum Company will be a small owner. I informed the people with whom I met that the Northern Aluminum Company could not participate in such an investment in case there was any objection to it by the Dept. of Justice of the United States.

If you approve such an arrangement, we would appreciate it if you would be kind enough to read the alternative under Section 7 of your proposed decree with a view of seeing that its wording does not unintentionally preclude such an arrangement.

Yours very truly,
President.

AVD/MC

55. *Ibid.*, Ex. 562.
56. *Ibid.*, Ex. 146; and Rec., p. 20388.
57. *Ibid.*, Ex. 179. The tentative name of this projected enterprise was the American Nitrogen Company, derived from the plans of its promoters (Alcoa and Southern, solely) to produce nitrates, along with alumina, by a new process invented by one Serpek. The Serpek patents belonged to an affiliate of L'Aluminium Française. However, the process proved to be uneconomical and the project never reached the stage of actual incorporation of the American Nitrogen Company. See *ibid.*, Alcoa Ints. 249 and 252.

We believe that we will have sufficient excess production in our East St. Louis plant to supply you with your requirements for these years and if so we shall be very glad indeed to do it and will quote you a price when the time comes, which will be a favorable one . . . But in order that you may have some positive assurance as to your supply, not dependent upon our having excess production, we will say to you that we will supply you, for your full requirements for these years from our East St. Louis plant with the provision that you will replace to us at our Shawinigan [Canada] plant, an equal tonnage with that which we supply to your Whitney plant.[58]

While this anomalous offer may not warrant the conclusion that Alcoa was responsible for the Southern venture, it throws great doubt on the competitive character of the project. A letter from Mr. Davis to Mr. Badin on May 10, 1913 raises further skepticism.

I trust you will appreciate it that it is our desire to cooperate with you people. . . . As to whether it is wiser to build at first one plant in the United States conjointly between Southern Aluminium Company and the Aluminum Company of America is to my mind rather a detail, and, if you prefer to have the Southern Company build its own plant at Whitney, while the Aluminum Company builds another for itself, I see no objection to that procedure.[59]

The conclusion is inescapable that the Southern Aluminium Company did not represent a genuine competitive threat to Alcoa. Indeed, the Circuit Court of Appeals, in a unanimous decision holding Alcoa a monopoly in violation of the antitrust laws, recently commented on this correspondence as follows:

. . . the correspondence . . . even though it may not justify the conclusion that the two were acting in conjunction, leaves no doubt that they were not to be competitors at arm's length. Perhaps, as the plaintiff argues, Alcoa did think that the new project [Southern] might be useful in persuading the plaintiff, whose attack had just ended in the decree of 1912, that the company was to be a real competitor. Be that as it may, the expected competition was not to be of the ordinary kind.[60]

The Southern Aluminium project was abruptly halted by the outbreak of the war in August 1914. A year later, after the French group had tried in vain to finance completion of the plants through Amer-

58. *Ibid.*, Ex. 563.
59. *Ibid.*, Ex. 564.
60. USAL, 148 Fed. 2d 416, 431 (1945).

ican banks,[61] Alcoa purchased all the assets of the nascent enterprise for $6,990,627.02—the exact amount expended by the European interests in the venture, including even organization expenses.[62] Thus Alcoa redeemed the investment made by the "friendly" European interests, and preserved their good will. Though it apparently paid far more for the property than it needed to, on a basis of arms-length dealing, it paid a small price for the benefits it obtained from the entire "deal" in 1912. For, whatever else it may or may not have been,[63] the Southern enterprise certainly was part and parcel of the 1912 "alliance." [64] The re-establishment of concerted control in the world aluminum market was unquestionably a real gain for Alcoa.

Life of Fifth Cartel Shortened by World War I

While United States imports of aluminum continued heavy until interrupted by World War I, they did not "break the market." Indeed, the price of ingot rose slightly in 1913.[65] Consumption expanded so rapidly that Alcoa itself undertook further additions to its production facilities, about 1912. On their completion in 1915 they more than doubled its domestic capacity and increased by 50 per cent its Canadian capacity.[66] Furthermore, throughout this period Alcoa found a ready market for every pound of aluminum it could produce.

61. USAL, Ex. 146. On the surface, it might appear odd that American capital hesitated to risk this venture, considering that the industry was known to have been exceptionally profitable for many years and that by early 1915 the war demand had pushed prices to higher levels. Yet, after all, it may not be so strange that outside bidders were conspicuous by their absence. For one thing, while the "money trust" which a short time previously had been the subject of congressional investigation may have been a myth, it would have been a venturesome banking group indeed which was willing to finance an invasion of the most prized industrial domain of the Mellon interests. In the second place, even more venturesome would have been the hardy enterpriser willing to risk the advance of substantial funds for completing a half-finished aluminum reduction works which had access, so far as was known, to no bauxite deposits whatever on this side of the Atlantic and which, in fact, was wholly dependent upon Alcoa for its alumina.

62. Ibid., Exs. 145 and 152; Rec., p. 20432.

63. On the basis of Judge Learned Hand's interpretation (148 Fed. 2d 431—see above), from the domestic angle the Southern enterprise was a Trojan horse.

64. The February 17, 1912, letter of A. V. Davis to Mr. Fowler, Assistant to the Attorney General, quoted in full in footnote 54, clearly shows this connection.

65. The annual average price of 21.2 cents a pound in 1913 was one cent higher than in 1912. While the price declined in 1914, this was a common incident of the general business recession and the initial impact of the war.

66. See Table 19. Alcoa's expansion of capacity at this rate does not show, of course, that it was not following a policy of monopolistic restriction. The growth of demand may well have made economical an even greater increase of investment in this industry. The fact that in the first two decades of this century Alcoa's output fell below its installed capacity in only a single year, 1908, indicates the persistence of restrictions on investment. Of course, domestic monopoly finds advantageous, and international cartelization facilitates, such a restrictive policy.

Thus, while the fifth international cartel differed from its predecessors in not reserving the American market to Alcoa, in some
ways it was an even more effective instrument of concerted action.
For it had achieved not simply an alignment for the time being of
the operating policies of aluminum producers; it brought about a
"firm alliance," as Alcoa's president put it.[67] It cemented their interests in a most intimate way, that is, financially. It led to the first development in this industry of internationally joint enterprise.[68]

The cartel voluntarily suspended operations on January 23, 1915.
During the war, governmental intervention—spurring output, controlling distribution, and (by war orders or otherwise) fixing prices
—displaced the familiar cartel controls. The outstanding developments in Europe during the war were the rapid expansion of productive capacity in Norway and in Germany. French and British interests, in the main, financed the Norwegian growth. The German
Government organized a state monopoly, Vereinigte Aluminiumwerke
A. G. (VAW), and provided the funds for a huge construction program. American productive capacity was likewise mounting in response to war demands. From 1914 to 1920 Alcoa again doubled its
capacity, thus keeping pace with the growth of the industry in Europe. Between 1914 and 1917 the domestic price of aluminum also
doubled, rising from 18.8 to 37.5 cents a pound.[69]

Aftermath of World War I

With the cancellation of large government orders after the war,
aluminum producers on both sides of the Atlantic faced the problem
of finding new markets to utilize their expanded capacities. In America the civilian demand picked up quickly and Alcoa, after briefly
quoting a one cent price reduction, restored the full wartime price.
With an import duty of only 2 cents a pound, a 33 cent price in the
American market offered tempting bait for European companies.

In the absence of cartel restrictions, Europeans offered metal in the
United States at prices below Alcoa's quotations, and imports once

67. USAL, Ex. 564.
68. Other instances of joint ventures than those discussed in the text above occurred
in Norway, for developing new productive facilities; in Britain, for buying out a trou-
blesome independent; and in France, for pre-empting bauxite reserves. Cf. Wallace,
Market Control in the Aluminum Industry, pp. 73 and 89.
69. The War Industries Board made arrangements with Alcoa late in 1917 which
stabilized the price for the duration of the war at 33.5 cents a pound.

TABLE 19

ALUMINUM PRODUCTIVE CAPACITY IN SPECIFIED REGIONS,
1890–1940 [a]

(In Millions of Pounds)

Year	United States [b]	Canada [e]	Germany [d]	World [d]	North American Percentage World Total [e]
1890	.06	—	—	—	—
1891	.14	—	—	—	—
1892	.20	—	—	—	—
1893	.20	—	—	—	—
1894	.48	—	—	—	—
1895	.50	—	—	—	—
1896	1.00	—	—	—	—
1897	2.36	—	—	—	—
1898	2.98	—	—	—	—
1899	3.26	—	—	—	—
1900	5.06	—	2	16	32
1901	5.72	—	—	—	—
1902	5.76	1.70	—	—	—
1903	6.62	1.70	—	—	—
1904	8.10	2.16	—	—	—
1905	10.80	2.46	—	—	—
1906	14.12	3.66	—	—	—
1907	16.32	5.92	2	50	44
1908	16.32	5.92	—	—	—
1909	29.08	6.08	—	—	—
1910	35.40	9.64	—	—	—
1911	38.38	9.68	—	—	—
1912	41.80	12.02	—	—	—
1913	47.28	14.06	10	144	42
1914	57.96	14.54	—	—	—
1915	90.50	18.36	—	—	—
1916	115.10	21.18	—	—	—
1917	129.86	22.08	—	—	—
1918	129.86	23.52	—	—	—
1919	129.86	23.52	—	—	—
1920	158.60	23.52	30	320	57

TABLE 19 (continued)

ALUMINUM PRODUCTIVE CAPACITY IN SPECIFIED REGIONS,
1890–1940 [a]

(In Millions of Pounds)

Year	United States [b]	Canada [c]	Germany [d]	World [d]	North American Percentage World Total [e]
1921	158.60	23.52	30	320	57
1922	158.60	23.52	38	320	57
1923	158.60	24.24	38	356	51
1924	158.60	27.24	48	400	46
1925	158.60	31.00	64	430	44
1926	163.00	38.90	72	450	45
1927	166.00	82.72	72	500	50
1928	200.00	82.78	78	546	52
1929	226.00	82.78	80	610	51
1930	250.00	82.78	80	616	54
1931	264.00	82.78	80	640	54
1932	268.00	82.78	80	640	55
1933	268.00	82.78	80	640	55
1934	268.00	82.78	120	640	55
1935	268.00	82.78	180	760	46
1936	268.00	82.78	240	880	40
1937	288.00	91.60	300	1,100	35
1938	288.00	110.00	370	1,300	31
1939	340.00	180.00	426	1,500	35
1940	430.00	280.00	500	1,800	40

a. Figures represent estimated annual capacity as of end of each year, under normal working conditions.

b. From *U.S. v. Aluminum Company of America, et al.,* in U.S. District Court for the Southern District of New York (1937), Equity No. 85-73 (cited below as USAL), Alcoa Int. 4; supplemented by data from U.S. Bureau of Mines, *Minerals Yearbook,* particularly for recent years, e.g., 1940, p. 646.

c. From USAL, Alted Ints. 162 and 169, supplemented by information from *ibid.*, Rec., e.g., pp. 14275 and 15318, and from report of the Truman Committee, *Investigation of the National Defense Program,* Hearings before a Special Committee of the U.S. Senate, 77th Cong., 1st sess., pursuant to S.Res. 71, Pt. III (1941), p. 929.

d. Estimates derived from various sources, including USAL, Exs. 985 and 1647; D. H. Wallace, *Market Control in the Aluminum Industry,* Harvard University Press, Cambridge, 1937, *passim;* R. J. Anderson in *Metallurgia* (London), July 1938, Vol. XVIII, pp. 57-90, and December 1938, Vol. XIX, pp. 65-68; and U.S. Bureau of Mines, *Minerals Yearbook,* for successive years.

e. Sum of United States plus Canada divided by world total.

more began to flow in large volume. In 1920 and again in 1921, more than 27 million pounds of aluminum were imported from Europe. Imports were equivalent to approximately 50 per cent of Alcoa's domestic production in the latter year. Prices steadily fell until, by the end of 1921, they were back at the prewar (1914) level of about 19 cents a pound. In that year, for the first time since 1897, Alcoa suffered an operating deficit amounting to slightly over $5 million, or nearly 5 per cent on stockholders' equity.

Confronted by an invasion of its domestic markets which had undermined its whole price structure, Alcoa responded by a countermove adapted to either of two alternative developments—a relentless competitive struggle with the European "interlopers," or resumption of "friendly cooperation" and re-establishment of cartel controls. Alcoa proceeded to expand its proprietary interests in European bauxite deposits, hydroelectric developments, aluminum reduction works, and fabricating facilities.

In meeting the challenge of the European producers by export of capital rather than by export of metal, Alcoa was obviously pursuing a common-sense, businesslike policy. By such a strategy it stood to achieve one or all of three possible objectives: (1) secure control of the source of American imports; (2) circumvent existing and potential tariff barriers to European markets; (3) place itself in position to exercise a more effective voice in prospective cartel controls. This counteroffensive was on a scale so extensive that the European producers could hardly fail to recognize it as a warning signal. In effect, Alcoa was asking them to choose between a regime of "every man for himself and the devil take the hindmost" and one of "live and let live"—with Alcoa's leadership undisturbed.

The restoration of substantial tariff protection for Alcoa's domestic market greatly facilitated this strategy. The Fordney-McCumber Tariff of 1922 raised the duty on aluminum to 5 cents a pound. In the same year Alcoa inaugurated the program of expanding its European investments—a program vigorously pursued for about five years, until the European producers were ready to come to terms in a new cartel.

Alcoa's European Expansion

In 1922 Alcoa purchased a 50 per cent interest in, and control of, the Norsk Aluminium Company, which Norwegian interests had organized during the war. This company was one of those which had exported considerable metal to this country at market-minus prices in the immediate postwar years.[70] In 1923 Alcoa acquired a third interest in Det Norske Nitrid, originally founded by the French, which had expanded greatly during the war.[71] It owned the largest plant in Norway. At the same time, on the suggestion of A. V. Davis, the French sold another third interest in this company to the British Aluminium Company. These transactions brought into partnership three concerns which, together, could dominate the European industry.

Two years later, after vainly trying to purchase a block of VAW stock, Alcoa reached a working agreement with this state-owned German aluminum monopoly. In consideration of the German company's undertaking to limit its sales to others in the United States to a definite volume at a stipulated price, Alcoa bought a substantial volume of metal from VAW for future delivery.[72] In the same year,

70. USAL, Exs. 21, 22, 162, 892, 907, 995. Alcoa agreed to purchase the stock in July 1921. The purpose of this contract was evidently to forestall its acquisition by Haskell, of Baush Machine Tool Company, who was then negotiating for it. Haskell had the promise of financial support from the automobile industry, in particular from Ford. *Ibid.*, Rec., pp. 2218-36.

71. *Ibid.*, Ex. 425; and Alcoa Int. 2.

72. *Ibid.*, Alcoa Int. 16. A. V. Davis has testified that in 1925 he made a trip to Europe to establish friendly relations with Mr. Von der Porten, managing director of VAW. They discussed several plans for participation of Alcoa in VAW, but the German Government refused to relinquish control and Alcoa finally abandoned the idea. *Ibid.*, Rec., pp. 20579-92.

A letter several months later from Mr. Von der Porten to Metallgesellschaft, selling agents of VAW, for the guidance of its American representative, the Ore & Chemical Corporation, supplies some information on the terms of the deal actually made. He said, "The agreement with the Americans provided specifically that we would be allowed to import into the United States in the year 1927 a total of 3500 tons of aluminum, and that we were authorized to sell at a half cent below the American prices. It was established in this connection that the American price would be 26 cents for 99 per cent metal and 25.8 cents for 98-99 per cent metal. Accordingly our prices were fixed at 25.5 and 25.3 respectively." *Ibid.*, Ex. 493.

The correspondence does not indicate whether the agreement on 1927 German exports to the United States was part of the 1925 purchasing contract or was a supplement or an extension of it. It is clear, however, that this agreement did not represent an isolated transaction. It indicates the path all European producers took in dealing in the American market during this period. Thus, on April 15, 1927, Ore & Chemical Corporation, referring to "arrangements with the other selling agents," wrote to its principal, Metallgesellschaft, "We to offer Bohn at the old price of 25.3 only 30,000 pounds, explaining that in view of the good demand in Europe, you are at present time sending very little aluminum to this country . . . The French were to offer Bohn 100/200 tons at the same price, the understanding being that the Swiss and English should not offer at all. On the other hand, we were to offer Doehler the 50,000 pounds for which he sent us an enquiry at 25.5, all of the others refusing to bid at all. Seligman [agent of the British] received a cable yesterday from his principals instructing him to protect the French by offering to Bohn a price of 25.5. . . ." *Ibid.*, Ex. 750. This correspondence shows that, if the other European producers were not privy to the agreement between Alcoa and VAW, they were operating under a similarly restrictive convention, tacit or explicit.

Alcoa also acquired half of the outstanding stock of Societa dell' Alluminio Italiano, a small-scale Italian producer previously owned by the French (AFC).[73] During 1925, also, Alcoa joined with French and Swiss producers (Neuhausen) in a Spanish enterprise, Aluminio Español S. A.[74]

Alcoa Buys Extensively

Supplementing its European acquisitions of metal reduction works, Alcoa was buying up extensive bauxite and water-power properties in Europe during this period. In 1921 it purchased mining rights in considerable acreage in Yugoslavia, along the Dalmatian coast, which it transferred to a subsidiary company, Jadranski Bauxit, organized in 1922. Alcoa later acquired other Yugoslavian deposits, and in 1925 organized a second company—the Primorski Bauxit—to hold and operate these. In 1924 Alcoa bought a 50 per cent interest in S. A. Mineraria Triestina (SAMT), which had extensive rights in Istrian bauxite. In 1926 Alcoa became the sole owner of this company. In that year, too, Alcoa organized the Société des Bauxites Françaises to take over certain additional leaseholds in French bauxite lands acquired after the war, besides those purchased earlier.[75]

At the same time, Alcoa was busily strengthening its European position by acquisition of water-power sites. Through its purchase of a majority of the stock (54.94 per cent) of Det Norske Aktieselskab Elektrokemisk Industri, in November 1924, Alcoa obtained control not only of a valuable undeveloped water-power site, Bjolvefos, but also of the Soderberg process patents held by Elektrokemisk.[76] In the same year, Alcoa acquired other undeveloped water-power properties

73. *Ibid.*, Alcoa Int. 2. In November 1928, Aluminium Limited, to which Alcoa had transferred its shares in Societa dell' Alluminio Italiano the previous June, acquired the remaining half of the Italian company's stock. Alted Int. 84.

74. *Ibid.*, Alcoa Int. 2; and Rec., pp. 4863 f. and 20634-34a. Alcoa was the dominant partner, with 50 per cent of the stock of the Spanish company, while AFC and AIAG each took a minority interest.

75. The foregoing transactions are recorded in *ibid.*, Alcoa Ints. 2 and 78, Alted Int. 196.

76. The Soderberg patents related to a process for the continuous operation of electrolytic reduction cells by means of constant replacement of carbon on the "head" of the anode as it is burned off the tip. Opinions differ widely upon the importance of this process. R. J. Anderson, reviewing the historical development of the aluminum industry in this century, suggests that the Soderberg process constitutes an outstanding technical achievement. He states (*Metallurgia*, February 1939, Vol. XIX, p. 146) that "it is considered more economical especially in the consumption of electricity. . . ." This judgment is not in accord, however, with that of A. V. Davis, based on Alcoa's experience. USAL, Rec., p. 20723.

in Norway through the purchase of A. S. Laate-Fas. Two years later, it purchased another Norwegian company, A. S. Kinservik, with similar assets.[77] In 1925 Alcoa acquired three undeveloped water-power sites in the south of France, with aggregate potential capacity of 60,000 horsepower. Titles to these properties rested in a wholly owned subsidiary, Forces Motrices de Berne.[78]

First Postwar Aluminum Cartel

By this series of maneuvers, Alcoa avoided trial by battle with the European producers and paved the way for a negotiated peace. Whether driven by the menace inherent in Alcoa's expansion program or persuaded by more positive business considerations, the European producers in 1923 organized the sixth international aluminum cartel. This was a simple gentlemen's agreement on prices.[79] It provided neither for quota distribution nor reservation of home markets. Although Alcoa did not subscribe to the convention,[80] after 1923 it entered into express agreements with major European aluminum interests regulating exports to the American market.

The course of prices shows the influence of these arrangements. In Europe, the price advanced about one third within three years, from about 18 cents a pound in 1922 to 24 cents in 1924. In the United States, the price rose by nearly 50 per cent in this period, or roughly from 19 cents to 27 cents a pound. This more rapid advance in the American price reflected a growing shortage of supplies, traceable in part to a booming demand for aluminum in the automotive and building trades and in part to Alcoa's stringent restriction of domestic production capacity.[81]

By 1925 the growing price differential between European and American markets had wiped out the additional tariff protection given to Alcoa in 1922. Imports, which had fallen off in the previous

77. Laate-Fas and Kinservik each held potential 100,000 H.P. development sites.
78. The foregoing were the principal, but not the sole, acquisitions of interest in European aluminum reduction works, bauxite deposits, and water-power sites by Alcoa in these years. For details of these several transactions, see USAL, Alcoa Ints. 2, 502, 506, 508, 509, 522; Alted Ints. 71 and 75; Rec., pp. 18444-47 and 19209-12.
79. See Benni, Lammers, Marlio, and Meyer, *Review of the Economic Aspects of Several International Industrial Agreements,* League of Nations Economic and Financial Section, Geneva, 1930, II, 41 (E 614), p. 26 f.
80. A. V. Davis has testified that Northern was invited to join, but that "we just simply thought we would be better off alone." USAL, Rec., p. 5184 f.
81. In the first half of the twenties Alcoa undertook no expansion of productive facilities in the United States and only a very small increase in Canada. See Table 19.

three years, began to rise. The "buying rush" carried aluminum imports to an all-time peak of 55 million pounds in 1926. Yet prices held firm, partly because 40 per cent of this record inflow of metal was purchased by Alcoa itself to meet the mounting demands of domestic customers which it could not supply from its own plants. In part, too, the explanation lies in the fact that the European producers who exported the other 60 per cent of American imports were not offering the metal competitively in this market.[82]

In response to the increasing demand, both Alcoa and the European producers undertook a belated expansion of productive facilities in the last half of the twenties. American capacity increased by 62 per cent in this period, and European by 25 per cent. Although a moderate readjustment of prices from the high level of 1926 accompanied this expansion—in Europe, a drop of 5 cents, in America, of 3.5 cents, by the end of the decade—profits did not suffer. In fact, Alcoa's average annual net earnings increased sharply—from 4 per cent on current stockholders' equity during the first half of the decade to 13.48 per cent in the last half. In Europe, too, aluminum company earnings were generally good, although those of one or two relatively inefficient firms declined slightly.[83]

Cartel Controls Strengthened

In spite of price recovery and mounting profits after formation of the 1923 cartel, its loose structure afforded an inadequate means of advancing the joint interests of its members. Accordingly, in 1926, the European producers re-established a full-fledged cartel on the lines of the prewar schemes.[84]

This seventh international aluminum convention imposed quota restrictions on all sales, domestic and export.[85] Moreover, the quota

82. As proved by the documents cited in footnote 72 above. See also, on the absence of competitive offerings, the testimony of American buyers: USAL, Rec., pp. 2310-12; 4313-17; 4434-61; 4527; 9462-65; 9489-90; and 9586-87. Of course, the acute shortage made it a "sellers' market" in any case. The Europeans had no need to undercut prices to dispose even of the large volume of metal they were shipping to this country.
83. Elliott et al., op. cit., p. 260 in Wallace chapter on "Aluminum."
84. See Benni et al., op. cit.
85. D. H. Wallace (Market Control in the Aluminum Industry, pp. 158-62) estimates that the quotas established by the 1928 agreement were: French, 30 per cent; German, 27 per cent; Swiss, 23 per cent; British, 20 per cent. These figures are, of course, exclusive of Alcoa's share in the world export trade represented by its Canadian affiliate's exports. Alcoa's stake in this field was substantial and the facts discussed below demonstrate that the European members of the cartel recognized this.

allocations applied both to ingot sales and to sales of metal in sheet or other semifabricated forms. Members were penalized if they exceeded their assigned quotas; they received compensation for underselling their quotas. To facilitate enforcement, members agreed to submit quarterly accounts to the association on sales volume, prices realized, output, and inventories. Finally, the association's executive committee periodically fixed standard delivered prices, uniform for all markets, closed or open. The original agreement fixed the term of the cartel at two years, but a supplementary accord of December 31, 1928 extended it for three years, with virtually no changes in mechanism or policy.

Alcoa was not formally a member of the 1926 cartel; nor did it join on renewal of the compact in 1928.[86] Indeed, since membership in such an arrangement had been specifically enjoined by the consent decree of 1912, Alcoa by joining would have become liable for contempt of court. However, on numerous occasions Alcoa cooperated with the cartel.[87] It observed its traditional policy of avoiding exports from the United States and it scrupulously followed the cartel-fixed prices in export sales through its Canadian affiliate.[88]

For example, when in 1929 an Italian subsidiary proposed to absorb part of the Italian customs duty in its domestic sales of aluminum, the European representative of the Canadian company counselled against such a policy, lest it give ground for suspicion that the North American companies were not loyally cooperating with the cartel. He cabled the head office in Pittsburgh that "If we pay duty in Italy, the Cartel will act as we being no longer cooperating and will follow

86. USAL, Rec., p. 16200.
87. This cooperation was chiefly in the regulation of imports to the United States and the maintenance of world prices. See *ibid.*, pp. 2292-93; 2310-12; 2316; 9489; 16311-13.
88. *Ibid.*, Alcoa Int. 23; Rec., p. 16311 f.; and Ex. 743. This exhibit reproduces a letter in which Alted's European representative stated (p. 3627), "We promise to follow the market prices fixed by the cartel."
In 1928 Alcoa made a change in its corporate setup. It formed a new company in Canada to represent it in all international arrangements and transactions. The name given this new unit was Aluminium Limited (Alted).
For convenience, in the next few text paragraphs dealing with the relationship between these two North American companies, on the one hand, and the 1928 cartel, on the other, we shall disregard legal technicalities, and treat Alcoa and Alted as simply separate organs of a single business enterprise. "Alcoa and its Canadian affiliate are unified in policy through ownership of controlling stock held by the same families or individuals." *Aluminum Plants and Facilities*, p. 19.

same procedure . . . elsewhere." [89] On another occasion Alcoa, through its Canadian affiliate, refused to sell alumina to a Swiss concern (Mermod) which was not a cartel member, because "it would irritate members of the cartel." [90] Again, by the terms of what was known as the Zurich Agreement of July 1930 for the division of the Japanese market, Alcoa, through Alted, obtained the right to supply 52 per cent of the total sales in that market, the remaining 48 per cent being divided among the cartel members—the French, British, German, and Swiss companies.[91]

Similar arrangements between Alcoa, represented by Alted, and the cartel were in effect after 1930 for assuring the American interests a fixed proportion of all metal sales to Russia and of total sales of certain fabricated products in India.[92]

Thus the absence of formal subscription to the cartel agreement by Alcoa made scarcely any difference in the effectiveness of the arrangement for control of international markets. The two groups steadily maintained harmonious relations.

89. *Ibid.*, Ex. 740; Rec., p. 16312.
90. Testimony of Mr. E. K. Davis, president of Alted, *ibid.*, Rec., p. 16322.
91. *Ibid.*, pp. 16306-10; and *Baush Machine Tool Company* v. *Alcoa*, 72 Fed. 2d 236, 240 (1930).
Furthermore, Alcoa's Canadian affiliate became the official sales agent of the Europeans, so that it alone could fix the price of all aluminum sold in Japan. This arrangement lasted until the outbreak of World War II, though the development of a domestic industry in Japan (actually in Manchuria) in the late thirties weakened Alted's (i.e., Alcoa's) dominant position in that market.
Two years after the Zurich Agreement, when the Japanese were laying plans for this Manchurian plant, they sought technical assistance from the European producers. Before refusing this request, the Europeans asked Alcoa and Alted to back them up in such a stand. Alted's European representative cabled the president of the company: "Am requested to ask if you also take engagement for yourself and for tributaries and friends as well to refuse technical assistance." Mr. E. K. Davis replied: "Accept engagement for ourselves and tributaries Stop Friends follow our example." USAL, Ex. 816, Items 5 and 6. At the trial, Mr. E. K. Davis identified the "friends" referred to in these cables as Alcoa. *Ibid.*, Rec., p. 15935.
92. USAL, Ex. 741; and Rec., pp. 16292-98, 16313-15, 16323. Alted's quota in the former case was one third and in the latter one half. In both instances the parties jointly agreed on the prices they would charge. The agreement for division of the Russian market continued in force through the thirties, though in March 1935 the parties revised quota allotments. *Ibid.*, Rec., p. 16301 f.
The president of Alted, E. K. Davis, a brother of A. V. Davis, gave the following explanation of the agreement relating to the Indian market: "The British Aluminium Company and Aluminium Limited were largely engaged in the manufacture and sale of aluminum electric cables. We are doing business in India, Australia, the United Kingdom and various other markets, all outside of the United States. In certain of those markets it was agreed as between the British Aluminium Company and my company that if one or the other happened to sell more than say, 50 per cent of the electrical conductors bought in India during a given period, that the party thus over-selling his agreed upon portion would buy from the other party a quantity of ingot to compensate for the dif-

Reorganization of Alcoa's Corporate Structure

Nevertheless, maintenance of bilateral relations with different producers in a number of separate markets had its drawbacks. And informal, multilateral accords always involve the risk of misunderstandings. It would clearly be more convenient all around if Alcoa could devise some expedient whereby, without itself becoming formally associated with the international cartel and thus openly infringing the terms of the 1912 consent decree and perhaps violating the antitrust laws, it could assume the obligations and reap the benefits of cartel membership. Eventually Alcoa found a way which it apparently regarded as at once safe and efficacious—a sort of corporate legerdemain enabling it to eat its cake and have it too.

On May 31, 1928 Alcoa obtained a Canadian charter for a company, Alted, which was thereafter to be its *alter ego* in international affairs.[93] Alcoa transferred to Alted on June 4, 1928 all its foreign properties, except its interest in four companies and certain mining rights, in exchange for 490,875 shares of the latter's stock.[94] Thus Alted at this stage was nothing more than a holding company for the management of Alcoa's foreign interests. But the mere exchange by Alcoa of its foreign properties for stock in Alted (the effect of which was simply to regroup a number of subsidiaries into one) left Alcoa in no less vulnerable a position under the antitrust laws than before the incorporation of Alted. For whatever a parent company could lawfully do through a single subsidiary it presumably could do through a number of subsidiaries and vice versa.

The next step provided at least a plausible basis for the contention that Alted was a separate and independent business unit—capable thus of making cartel arrangements without implicating Alcoa. Alcoa proceeded to distribute pro rata to its own stockholders the 490,875

ference and the price at which the ingot was dealt with in compensation was called settling price and it was changed from time to time in order to adjust it properly to market conditions." *Ibid.*, p. 16313.

93. USAL, 20 Fed.Supp. 13, 15 (1937).

94. All told, in this transaction Alted received from Alcoa the latter's shareholdings in thirty-three companies. USAL, Alcoa Int. 2; Alted Ints. 195, 196. Some of these companies were subsidiaries of others in the group. Thirteen were liquidated, merged, or sold within the next ten years, while in the same period Alted acquired a controlling interest in three other corporations from Alcoa, in addition to numerous "outside" acquisitions. Omitting steamship lines, the most important foreign property of which Alcoa retained ownership was the Surinaamsche Bauxite Company, holding land and mining concessions in Dutch Guiana.

shares of Alted's stock then in its treasury.[95] This was the crucial feature of the maneuver. It obviously resulted, *pro forma,* in two legally separate corporations. But inasmuch as initially they had identical stockholders, each of whom had the same proportionate interest in both companies, the legal fiction of Alted's "independence" could hardly be relied on to pass judicial scrutiny.[96] Not until at least a few minor changes in the stockholder lists of the two corporations had taken place could Alcoa colorably contend that Alted had "no connection at all with the American company." [97]

Alcoa and Alted Have Common Control ·

Though in time ownership of some Alcoa shares has passed to parties holding no Alted shares and vice versa, the control of the two companies has remained in the same hands as when Alted was a wholly owned subsidiary of Alcoa. Every one of the officers and directors of Alted was, of course, an "Alcoa man," when the company began business, that is, a person who had been employed by, or associated with, Alcoa.[98] Its chairman and president was E. K. Davis, a brother

95. The only effect of this distribution of Alted's stock received in exchange for Alcoa's foreign properties was to give each Alcoa stockholder two pieces of paper (stock certificates) in place of the one piece of paper he had theretofore, representing his identical proportionate share in the same corpus, or fund, of assets. In fact, the operation actually carried out was in all essential respects indistinguishable from the distribution of a stock dividend declared out of surplus. The only difference was that Alcoa stockholders, instead of getting additional shares of Alcoa stock, received their "stock dividend" in Alted stock.

96. Though the European producers renewed their cartel agreement on December 31, 1928, seven months after formation of Alted, Alcoa did not venture to have its affiliate join this cartel. The time was not yet ripe, evidently, for putting forward Alted as a genuine independent having "no connection at all with the American company." USAL, Alcoa Int. 584.

97. These are the exact words of Alcoa's contention. *Ibid.*

98. The roster of Alted's officers and directors as it stood in 1928 and as it stood in 1940 follows:

		1928	1940
President		E. K. Davis	E. K. Davis
Vice-Presidents		L. McCarthy	L. McCarthy
		E. Blough	E. Blough
		J. F. Van Lane	G. O. Morgan
			E. G. McDowell
Secretary		J. H. Alger	J. H. Alger
Treasurer		G. O. Morgan	J. F. Evans
Directors		E. K. Davis	E. K. Davis
		J. H. Alger	J. H. Alger
		E. Blough	E. Blough
		L. McCarthy	L. McCarthy
		A. Geoffrion	A. Geoffrion
		J. H. Price	E. G. McDowell
		J. F. Van Lane	R. E. Powell
			E. J. Mejia

Source: Moody's Manual of Investments (Industrials). On the Alcoa associations of the several individuals listed, see USAL, Rec., pp. 13750-82.

of A. V. Davis, who had previously been the general sales manager of Alcoa. Alcoa's management selected him for this new post, and he has remained the chief executive officer of the Canadian company.[99]

Moreover, changes in the stock ownership of Alcoa and Alted have not been great enough to disturb the common control of the two companies. The same small coterie which, through ownership of the majority of Alcoa's voting stock, exercised complete control of its affairs (including the Canadian and other foreign properties) before 1928, obtained a like control of the Canadian company through the pro rata distribution of Alted stock. Members of just three families, which have been identified with Alcoa from the start, the Mellons, the Davises, and the Hunts, composed this coterie, and they have not relinquished the joint control of the two companies since 1928.[100]

These majority stockholders could have had no interest, of course, in the emergence of any rivalry between Alcoa and Alted.[101] On the contrary, they have had every interest in insuring that the two companies are operated in harmony, along parallel or mutually supporting lines. In practice, the managements of Alcoa and of Alted, which hold office on sufferance of an identical majority group of stockholders, have consistently shown mutual solicitude for each other's interests.

Alcoa and Alted Operate Like a Single Enterprise

The two companies have operated precisely as though they were, in law, the single business enterprise which they obviously are in fact. For example, Alcoa made unsecured loans aggregating $3,225,000 to Aluminum Company of Canada during the two years after its "sale" to Alted.[102] Again, in the transfer to Alted on June 4, 1928, of Alcoa's 50 per cent interest in Societa dell' Alluminio Italiano, this

99. USAL, Rec., pp. 13690-91 and 13701-04.

100. At least they had not up to 1939, and probably have not since then. On January 2, 1939, members of the Mellon family, or trust frunds created for them, held 514,122 shares of Alcoa common stock and 228,163 shares of Alted common stock; Arthur V. Davis and Edward K. Davis together held 182,738 shares in Alcoa and 82,797 shares in Alted; Rov A. Hunt and Maria T. Hunt held 71,306 Alcoa shares and 33,431 Alted shares. Together these three groups held 768,166 Alcoa and 344,391 Alted shares, or 52.1 per cent and 50.9 per cent, respectively, of the total common stock of these companies outstanding on that date. Ibid., Ex. 774.

101. Even A. V. Davis testified in the first Baush case that Alcoa and Alted were "not set up for the purpose of competition." Ibid., Rec., p. 5347. See also testimony of Roy A. Hunt, president of Alcoa, that its management had no intention "to have competition" between the two companies. Ibid., p. 21770.

102. Ibid., Alted Int. 210. The Aluminum Company of Canada was the new title given in 1925 to the Northern Aluminum Company.

asset was appraised at $687,037.50. Five months later Alted acquired
the other half interest in the Italian company from the French company (AFC), for $941,850.[103] On July 1, 1931 Alted purchased
from Alcoa its interests in Prodotti Chemici Nazionali.[104] But for
eighteen months preceding this purchase—when it owned no Prodotti
stock—Alted advanced loans totalling $3,219,953.02 to Alcoa's sub-
sidiary.[105] Thereafter, up to December 31, 1937, it continued to make
advances for the expenses of this Italian concern, until the loans
reached $6,978,749.74.[106]

The terms on which Alcoa and Alted have transacted ordinary
commercial business with each other also indicate their continuing
identity of interest. For many years, Alted possessed no alumina
works and depended on Alcoa for its supply. Yet before 1934 no
written contracts covered these transactions. For six years, lacking six
weeks, Alted shipped bauxite to Alcoa for conversion into alumina,
for Alted's account, without any contractual commitments on either
side.[107]

103. *Ibid.*, Alted Int. 195. Actually, of course, Alcoa (or the body of its stockholders) was not a loser by the amount of the discrepancy between what it received and
what the French received for an identical interest. To the extent that Alcoa and Alted
had a common set of stockholders, it was a matter of indifference to them, severally or
collectively, whether the Italian subsidiary's stock was valued at $20,000 or $2 million
in the transfer to Alted. If the asset were overvalued, the Alted stock received in exchange would have been correspondingly reduced in unit value and vice versa. But if
Alted had been a bona fide purchaser, a genuinely independent corporate entity, Alcoa
(ultimately, its stockholders) would have been sacrificing more than $250,000 by this
single element of the deal.
104. *Ibid.*, Alted Int. 87. This "development company" experimented on the substitution of leucite, a mineral found in abundance in Italy, for bauxite in the production
of alumina.
105. *Ibid.*, Alted Int. 88. During the first six months of this eighteen-month period,
Alted loaned Prodotti $792,351.46 without even having in its possession a contract to
purchase Prodotti stock.
106. After Alcoa transferred the Prodotti stock to Alted on July 1, 1931 under a
contract of July 1, 1930, Alted reimbursed Alcoa to the last cent for its entire expenses
up to that date in underwriting "the leucite affair." However, aside from a small cash
payment, the reimbursement took the form of three notes for $500,000 each. After six
years, Alted still owed Alcoa a principal sum of $1.2 million on these notes, with ac-
crued interest. *Ibid.*, Ex. 382; Alted Int. 86. There is nothing to show whether Alted
has ever discharged this debt, though on December 22, 1936 it "wrote off" as worth-
less $6,330,092.04 of its investment in Prodotti. Alted Int. 214. Apparently Alcoa, al-
though it had an enforceable legal claim upon Alted for the full amount of the notes
plus interest, elected to forego a major portion of its claim and assume a share in the
loss sustained by Alted.
107. *Ibid.*, Alted Int. 137. Seven contracts covered these alumina transactions from
April 7, 1934 to December 31, 1937. But no contracts covered the previous exchanges.
This represents a rather unusual way of doing business. Quite aside from Alcoa's un-
wonted altruism in extending an accommodation of this nature to an "independent enterprise," potentially capable (under other ownership) of operating as a rival, it reveals
their indifference toward the terms of business transactions between themselves.

The Alcoa Power Company Deal

The Alcoa Power Company transaction affords perhaps the most striking example of this continued identity of interest between Alcoa and Alted. Alcoa organized this company to take over the undeveloped water-power sites on the Saguenay River it had acquired from the Duke interests in 1925.[108] For ten years after Alted's formation, Alcoa assumed the financial burden of carrying this unproductive asset and then, when its potential energy had been partly developed, turned it over to Alted on terms nicely adjusted to Alted's actual and prospective capacity to pay. These terms exhibit an absence of arms-length dealing between the parties.[109]

Thus in actual business practice the relations of Alcoa and Alted have followed the pattern of parent and subsidiary corporations.[110]

108. Alcoa acquired this power site from the Duke interests after they had formulated plans for the development of an integrated aluminum production enterprise. This acquisition eliminated the most powerful potential competitor that Alcoa had encountered in its entire history. It occurred shortly after the acquisition by Alcoa of a less formidable, but none the less substantial, venture promoted by the Uihleins, a Milwaukee family of brewers. By 1924, after six years of prospecting, negotiation, and extensive litigation with Alcoa, the Uihleins had obtained enough bauxite acreage in South America to supply an aluminum reduction works of economical size. *Ibid.*, Rec., p. 19999 f. They had also built a carbon plant at an expense of $2 or $3 million and, in search of a source of electric power, had approached James B. Duke, who owned the Saguenay site. These negotiations fell through and the Uihleins thereupon sold out to Alcoa (or to companies affiliated with Alcoa).

Shortly afterward, the Duke interests, after having financed George D. Haskell in an extensive survey of prospects for an aluminum enterprise, merged their prospective venture with Alcoa's going concern. In exchange for a substantial block of stock in Alcoa, the Dukes abandoned their independent aluminum project and turned over to Alcoa their huge undeveloped water-power site. *Ibid.*, Ex. 184; Rec., p. 20165. Subsequently Alcoa acquired a 53 1/3 per cent interest in the Duke-Price Power Company, which operated a 400,000 horsepower electric project on the Upper Saguenay. *Ibid.*, Alcoa Ints. 2 and 571; Exs. 258, 262, 263. After these acquisitions no competitive threat in the form of an integrated aluminum enterprise financed by private capital again confronted Alcoa until the Reynolds Metal Company's expansion during World War II.

109. *Ibid.*, Ex. 447. Both the original contract of purchase dated April 20, 1937 and the modified contract of February 23, 1938 stipulated a purchase price of $35 million, of which $20 million was to consist of long-term 4 per cent bonds. This price was about the amount of the book value of Alcoa's gross investment in the property plus accumulated interest. There is no evidence that it bore any close relation to current market value.

The second contract limited Alted's current obligations on the $15 million of unsecured debt to payments in the form of rental of electric power. The minimum annual rental fixed was $330,000, equivalent to 2.2 per cent interest on the unsecured debt. But if this $330,000 were credited to Alted as interest, of course, that would mean that the 165,000 horsepower delivered in exchange for the "rental" would, in effect, be furnished Alted without charge. On the other hand, if the rate of $2 per H.P.-year be taken as a reasonable charge for the power, in accordance with contemporary commercial standards, then, notwithstanding Alcoa's undertaking to credit these rental payments as interest it was, in effect, foregoing all interest on the unsecured debt.

110. An equally appropriate characterization of the relationship would be that it resembles two subsidiaries of a single holding company. Formally, this characterization is doubtless preferable, the Mellons, the Davises, and the Hunts being, as it were, the top

The background of this course of dealing helps one to understand it. Alcoa organized Alted, drafted its articles of incorporation, and paid its charter fee. The same small group of majority stockholders which controls Alcoa selected Alted's officers. Nevertheless, the appellate court held that "the existence of the same majority in the two corporations was not enough by itself to identify the two." Still the intercorporate business relations of the two companies at least cast doubt on Alcoa's contention that the Canadian company has "no connection at all with the American Company." [111]

But sidelights may be more illuminating than headlights. In a memorandum of March 15, 1937, Dr. Earl Blough, one of Alted's vice-presidents, reported the results of a conference held four days earlier in Pittsburgh on the subject of aluminum supplies for a projected aircraft engine plant to be built in China. He said: "The Aluminum Company of America *assured* Pratt and Whitney that they will be glad to cooperate ... *either directly or indirectly through Aluminium Limited,* as may be later developed." [112]

The European-American "Alliance"

Three years after Alted's formation the Great Depression had reached a stage that required sterner measures to stabilize markets. The way had been prepared for such a development. Minor changes had by this time occurred in the stockholder lists of Alcoa and Alted. Since together they controlled 50 per cent of the world's aluminum production capacity, it was manifestly important that one or the other of them should take a leading role in the play.

The idea of broadening and strengthening the 1928 cartel seems to have originated with Arthur V. Davis, then chairman of Alcoa's board. At any rate, in October 1930 he made a trip to Europe and in

---

holding company. On the other hand, historically the textual characterization, parent and subsidiary, seems better, since that was in fact the actual relationship at the outset.

As a representative of the Surplus Property Board states, "the two companies are commonly controlled and are in effect, twins." See *Aluminum Plants and Facilities,* p. 89.

111. Other features of the Alcoa-Alted intercorporate relations could be recounted, but they all point in the same direction. For example, though a large volume of trade in various forms goes on between Alcoa and Alted, virtually no dealings occur (1) between Alcoa and aluminum purchasers in Alted's sales territories, i.e., exports by Alcoa, or (2) between Alted and buyers in Alcoa's sales territory, i.e., sales in the United States by Alted. Also, the terms of this trade (in bauxite, alumina, aluminum, and fabrication services) are frequently discriminatory. USAL, Govt.Br. 705-715.

112. *Ibid.,* Ex. 385. Italics supplied.

a conference with M. Louis Marlio, chairman of the existing cartel, initiated the negotiations which culminated in the Aluminum Alliance of 1931.[113] On his return in November he broached the subject to his brother, president of Alted, who then began to draft the scheme for carrying out the project.[114] Throughout the following winter E. K. Davis was in frequent consultation with his brother, was advised by him upon the leading features of the plan,[115] and at his suggestion got the assistance of Alcoa's attorneys in formulating it.[116]

When a tentative draft was ready, Alted invited the European producers to America for a conference. In arranging the meeting, held in Montreal on April 15 and 16, 1931, Alted took care that Arthur V. Davis would be available for consultation with the European representatives.[117] Although he was not present at the Montreal conference, he and Roy A. Hunt, Alcoa's president, joined the party immediately thereafter. An excursion to various aluminum plants of Alcoa and of Alted during the next few days afforded ample opportunity for discussion of the terms of the proposed consortium with these Alcoa executives. After further negotiations in London and Paris that resulted in comparatively slight modifications in the major outlines of the plan drafted by E. K. Davis with the help of his brother,[118] every important aluminum-exporting company in the world signed the Foundation Agreement on July 3, 1931.[119]

113. *Ibid.*, Rec., pp. 4282-83 and 14667-68.
114. *Ibid.*, p. 14637.
115. *Ibid.*, pp. 14615-35 and 15084-87.
116. *Ibid.*, pp. 14652-55 and 15085-86. This legal firm, Smith, Buchanan & Ingersoll, had served as Alcoa's counsel for at least twenty years and continued to represent Alcoa thereafter. *Ibid.*, pp. 15164-65. In these circumstances, the government urged that this firm's acceptance of Alted as a client was evidence of the identity of interest between Alcoa and Alted. The trial court at first ruled that it was evidence of the connivance of Alcoa in the formation of the Alliance. *Ibid.*, pp. 15601-11. Later it reversed its position on this point. USAL, 44 Fed.Supp. 97 (1941). The appellate court concluded "that Alcoa was not a party to the Alliance." USAL, 148 Fed. 2d 416, 442.
117. USAL, Rec., pp. 14589-96 and 14638-41.
118. *Ibid.*, pp. 15208, 15309, 15374; cf. also pp. 15050-101, and Ex. 744.
119. That E. K. Davis recognized a unity of interest between Alted and Alcoa is clear from the following excerpt from a letter concerning the Alliance organization setup. In this letter, addressed to Henry Couannier, European continental representative of the North American companies, he said: "On account of pending litigation between the Aluminum Company of America and Haskell . . . under the title of Baush Machine Tool Company, it would be better to avoid letting my name appear as vice-chairman, substitute, alternate or what . . . If there is any likelihood of their registering the company, or letting the personnel be published in any manner, try and avoid having me mentioned as a vice-chairman." *Ibid.*, Ex. 777.

Structure and Functions of the Alliance

As the Foundation Agreement contemplated, the Alliance Aluminium Campagnie was incorporated in Switzerland in October 1931. (See Chart 3.) The company issued a total of 1,400 Class A shares of stock. The only subscribers were members of the cartel—one share for each hundred metric tons of their several annual capacities, as agreed upon in the Foundation Agreement.[120] The proportion of the total stock allotted to each company determined not only its relative voting power in the conduct of Alliance affairs, but also its quota in the total production as regulated quarterly or annually by the Alliance.[121] Alted received the right to subscribe for 400 shares. Hence its quota was 28.58 per cent of whatever aggregate production in any period the Alliance might sanction. Quotas of other members were: French, 21.36 per cent; German, 19.65 per cent; Swiss, 15.42 per cent; and British, 15 per cent.

However, the Alliance was more than a medium for restricting production and curtailing investment. The Foundation Agreement required the Alliance to remove from the market, at the outset, all accumulated stocks of members in excess of forty tons per Alliance share and to pay £55 a ton for them.[122] With excess stocks thus

120. *Ibid.*, Ex. 744, Clause 4. Actually, this clause specified the number of shares to which each signatory was entitled to subscribe. Whether the figure of 140,000 tons represented precisely the total existing annual productive capacity of the subscribers seems extremely doubtful. According to the data shown in Table 19, both the European and the North American productive capacity at that period were about 150,000 metric tons annually. Of the latter, Alcoa's United States capacity accounted for some 115,000 metric tons, and formally, of course, the cartel reckoning omitted this part of the North American capacity. Possibly the remainder (45,000 to 50,000 tons) of the discrepancy between the world capacity as shown in the table and the estimated annual capacity of the cartel members, as set forth in the Foundation Agreement, represents capacity of those small European producers who were not members of the cartel, including the Martigny Company in Switzerland and the three Italian enterprises.

But it is quite immaterial, of course, how close to, or how far from, the actual capacity of members was the "estimated capacity" which served as the basis of quota distribution. Whether the 140,000 tons represented fiction or fact, the number of shares each cartel member obtained in that total represented its proportion of the aggregate output which the governing board of the cartel determined that it was expedient to produce in each quarter.

In addition to the 1,400 shares issued to members, the Foundation Agreement authorized the issuance of 1,200 additional shares. These might be distributed to new members, or to old members on the acquisition of nonmembers or an expansion of capacity. But an addition to cartelized productive capacity in any one of these ways required the approval of the Board of Governors of the Alliance. *Ibid.*, Clause 6.

121. *Ibid.*, Clause 9.

122. *Ibid.*, Clause 17. The Alliance gave its members credit for the excess inventories thus pooled, and the members could use these credits to pay for their subscription to Alliance shares, up to 75 per cent of the subscription price. *Ibid.*, Clause 5. For that part of the tonnage transferred to the Alliance by any member, in excess of the

CHART 3. THE ALUMINUM ALLIANCE

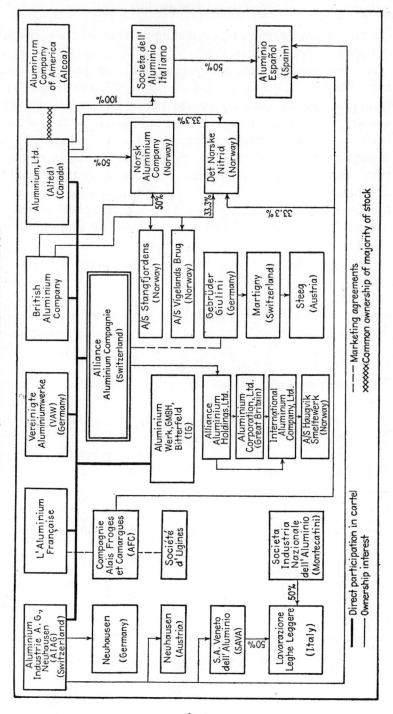

Direct participation in cartel
Ownership interest
– – – Marketing agreements
xxxxxx Common ownership of majority of stock

"frozen," a similar device for regulating prices in the ordinary course of business came into play.

Alliance directors periodically fixed minimum prices for aluminum, whether in ingot or in fabricated form.[123] To make these minimum prices effective, the Agreement authorized the Alliance to buy and sell metal. If a member could not sell his full quota in the market at the current minimum price, the Alliance stood ready to purchase the unsold portion at that price. Thus the Alliance "buying price" became an actual minimum price, since no member could have any incentive to sell aluminum in the market for a lower price than the cartel offered to purchase it—as long as the member's output was within his quota limits.[124] However, the Alliance could buy metal only from cartel members.

These were the main features of the Alliance cartel. Like the 1926 and 1928 agreements, it made no distinction between home and foreign markets. The Alliance regulated prices in all sales, wherever made, and since the plan provided for production restriction also, a firm control of the world market was assured. Unlike some previous ones, however, the 1931 Agreement made no express exception of the United States market. Such an exception would have been stultifying, for, unless the cartel members could count on Alcoa's cooperation, it was plain that the cartel hardly could have been effective if it limited its control of output and prices to the area outside the United States. Moreover, restriction of production by any producer anywhere necessarily affects that producer's ability to sell, and therefore, to export to the United States.[125]

---

amount eligible for credit on his Alliance stock subscription, the Alliance had to advance up to 90 per cent of the purchase price of the metal (represented by delivery warrants, c.i.f. Antwerp) at once and to make payment in full within three years. *Ibid.*, Clause 16. For these advances, the Alliance borrowed from the banks on the security of the delivery warrants.

123. *Ibid.*, Clause 16; Exs. 784 and 795; and Rec., pp. 15044-46.

124. If he had deliberately exceeded his production quota—for example, in an attempt to "beat the system" by selling over-quota output surreptitiously—the Alliance could confiscate the excess production. *Ibid.*, Ex. 744, Clause 9. Only marginal "over-runs," inadvertently made, were free of penalty. These could be deducted from an offending member's quota in the next period.

125. Of course, in theory, production-for-sale-in-the-United-States might have been exempted from the production restrictions imposed by the Alliance. But in practice any such exemption would, if genuine, almost certainly have made the restriction program an empty gesture. In any event, the Alliance made no such exception. *Ibid.*, Rec., pp. 15076 and 15334.

Alcoa's Relation to the Alliance

It seems to have been implicit, therefore, in this voluntary mutual curtailment of output by every important producer outside the United States (including the production in Canada under Alted's control) that cartel members would "respect" Alcoa's dominant position in the United States market.[126] It cannot be assumed that the cartel members undertook these self-imposed restrictions without some *quid pro quo*. The production controls directly affected the trading prospects of cartel members in the United States and in all other markets, domestic and export. The cartel managers were all practical businessmen, and they most certainly were not leaving the door "wide open" for Alcoa, their most formidable potential rival, to expand its business at their expense. They had ample ground for assurance on this vital point from (1) Alcoa's kinship with Alted, (2) Alcoa's record not only as a cartel cooperator but as a cartel leader for more than three decades, and (3) Arthur V. Davis' personal participation in the initiation and detailed elaboration of the Alliance scheme.

The actual operation of the Alliance bears out this interpretation of Alcoa's relationship to it as a "silent partner." Through the association of the brothers Davis, Alcoa frequently, if not regularly, obtained information regarding Alliance stocks and price policy, and even reports on its financial condition.[127] Moreover, as in the cartels before World War I, Alcoa through Alted apparently exercised a predominant influence in the conduct of the Alliance.[128] When E. K. Davis was asked in the Alcoa antitrust trial whether his group exercised a controlling influence in the Alliance, he frankly testified, "We

126. The appellate court, reversing the trial court, definitely held that the 1936 agreement, which superseded the Foundation Agreement, violated the Sherman Act. USAL, 148 Fed. 2d 416, 445. The court stated (p. 444), in discussing the bearing of the agreement on American foreign trade, that the "intent was to set up a quota system for imports."

Though the court exempted Alcoa from responsibility for formation of the Alliance, it did not rule on the question of whether the cartel operated to restrict American exports. But Clause 10 of the Foundation Agreement excepted from quota limitations metal produced under Alcoa-Alted tolling arrangements, and this might have wrecked the restriction scheme had Alcoa been free to sell tolled metal abroad. Were Alliance members so artless as to have overlooked this contingency?

127. USAL, Rec., pp. 14680-84. This information was confidential, never published by the Alliance.

128. Ludwig Braasch and George Hodson, who had long been in Alcoa's employ, were the manager and assistant manager, respectively, of the Alliance, constituting its entire executive staff from its organization until March 1939 and, presumably, to the present time. *Ibid.*, pp. 14678-79.

obtained the right which we asked for, to exercise a predominant influence over the administrative setup of the Alliance, and did so." [129]

Review of Alliance Policies

The cartel rigorously restricted output until the rearmament boom made restriction unnecessary.[130] So far as the depressed state of trade in the first half of the thirties permitted, the Alliance advanced prices. This was in line with Alcoa's own domestic policy and, of course, supplemented and reinforced that policy. The Alliance's initial "buying price" effective during the last quarter of 1931 was £55 (gold) a ton, equivalent to 12.33 cents a pound. However, this price applied only to metal transferred for credit against subscriptions to Alliance stock and to that transferred from members' previously accumulated "excess inventories." In effect, it was the buying price solely for purposes of Alliance organization. The first "operative" buying price, that is, a price determined with a view to controlling members' current market sales, was fixed simultaneously at £70 (gold) a ton, effective from December 31, 1931.

Because of unsettled monetary conditions and the general business depression during the first half of the thirties, the Alliance did not succeed entirely in "stabilizing" the world market for aluminum.

129. *Ibid.*, p. 14678. Alcoa has demonstrated on many occasions a sense of responsibility for cooperating with cartel members in carrying out the Alliance program. In one instance Alcoa cooperated directly with the Alliance, agreeing on its request to withhold technical assistance from the Japanese Government, which proposed to found an independent aluminum enterprise. *Ibid.*, pp. 15729-41. Another such instance was the attempt to bring the Giulini brothers' enterprises under cartel control. This concern controlled the two most important metal reduction plants outside the Alliance. By a contract executed in February 1934 in exchange for an Alliance undertaking that its members would purchase 12 per cent of their aggregate alumina requirements from Giulini, the latter agreed to operate under rigid restrictions and to observe the minimum selling prices fixed by the Alliance. *Ibid.*, Ex. 811. (For a similar arrangement for the preceding year, see Ex. 804, par. 10.)

Alcoa contributed to the execution of this deal by voluntarily foregoing the benefits of the arrangement previously prevailing between it and Alted, whereby Alcoa processed Alted's bauxite, in order that Alted might "do its share" in absorbing the Giulini alumina. Whereas before 1933 Alcoa supplied 100 per cent of Alted's alumina requirements; in 1933 no less than 90 per cent, and in 1934 about 80 per cent, came from Europe. *Ibid.*, Alted Int. 130 and Alcoa Int. 100. Since at this time Alcoa had unutilized alumina-refining capacity, this transaction indicates that Alcoa was making sacrifices to implement and strengthen the Alliance.

The decline in Alted's purchases of European alumina after mid-1934 reflects the assumption on May 24, 1934 by "the German group" (VAW and Bitterfeld) of all obligations of the Alliance under its contract of February 20, 1934 with the Giulini interests. *Ibid.*, Ex. 805, Sec. 6, par. 7. This deal was part of the German drive to obtain control of large supplies of alumina, in furtherance of the rearmament program.

130. See Table 20 showing annual production quotas fixed by the Alliance, and Table 21 showing successive changes in the buying price, from 1931 to 1938.

TABLE 20

ANNUAL PRODUCTION RATES FIXED BY THE ALUMINUM ALLIANCE,
1931–1938

Year	Metric Tons Per Alliance Share [a]
1931 (July 1 to December 31)	80
1932	53.75
1933	50
1934	55
1935	53
1936 [b]	70
1937	100
1938 (January 1 to March 31)	100

Source: U.S. v. Aluminum Company of America, et al., in U.S. District Court for the Southern District of New York (1937), Equity No. 85-73, Alted Int. 56 (c).

a. Equivalent to per cent of "estimated" capacity.

b. Beginning January 1, 1936, prescribed production rates were discontinued and production in excess of stipulated amounts was made subject to payment of a graduated royalty to the Alliance. Rates after this date are metric tons per Alliance share which could be produced, free of any royalty charge.

However, it kept the current "buying price" unchanged through 1932, and advanced it only £1 (gold) a ton for the next eighteen months. The pegged price then dropped to £68 (gold) a ton for the third quarter of 1934 and to £63 (gold) a ton for the final quarter of the year.

But the real price trend during this period was concealed by fluctuations in exchange rates and in the value of gold. Since British currency was not convertible into gold after September 1931, and since gold appreciated in terms of currencies of most aluminum-importing countries as well as of countries represented in the Alliance, a stable £ gold price was little more than a fiction. Perhaps the best index of the effect of cartel price regulation is the trend of net prices actually realized by Alted on ingot sales.

Effect of Exchange on Prices

Because Canada was still on the gold standard, Alted's average price declined nearly 2 cents a pound from 1931 to 1932. During 1933 and in early 1934 the Canadian Government pursued a policy of monetary depreciation to relieve trade depression and halt the fall

TABLE 21

ALLIANCE BUYING PRICES FOR MEMBERS' UNSOLD "QUOTA"
ALUMINUM, 1931–1938

Period	Swiss Fr. Per Metric Ton [a]	Pounds Sterling Per Metric Ton	Equivalent in Cents Per Lb.
Oct. 1, 1931–Dec. 31, 1931	1765.50	70	15.68
Jan. 1, 1932–Dec. 31, 1932	1765.50	70	15.52
Jan. 1, 1933–Mar. 31, 1933	1790.75	71	20.16
Apr. 1, 1933–June 30, 1934	1790.75	71	26.28
July 1, 1934–Sept. 30, 1934	1715.05	68	25.18
Oct. 1, 1934–Dec. 31, 1934	1589.00	63	23.30
Jan. 1, 1935–March 1938	1475.45	58.5	21.74

Source: U.S. v. *Aluminum Company of America, et al.,* in U.S. District Court for the Southern District of New York (1937), Equity No. 85-73, Alted Int. 53.

a. The figures in this column are computed from the prices in Swiss francs converted into United States currency at prevailing exchange rates as quoted in current *Federal Reserve Bulletins.*

in prices.[131] As the exchange value of the Canadian dollar fell in terms of the (theoretical) English gold pound and the (actual) Swiss gold franc, the yield in Canadian dollars of Alted's export sales—the bulk of its business—rose rapidly. From 1932 to 1934 Alted's annual average price for aluminum ingots rose more than 45 per cent, from 16.12 cents a pound to 23.47 cents. (See Table 22.) Thereafter internal monetary policy—under management of the Bank of Canada established in 1935—and external monetary policy, in particular the tripartite stabilization agreement of 1936, combined to stabilize both Canadian domestic prices and dollar exchange rates.[132]

In this situation, Alted, following Alliance prices, obtained an annual average of almost 21.5 cents a pound on ingot sales in both 1935 and 1936. Considering the general business recovery from the low levels of activity in 1931, this net price advance of 19 per cent in five years indicates that the Alliance price policy was businesslike but hardly "highhanded."

131. See Frank A. Knox, *Dominion Monetary Policy, 1929–1934,* a Study Prepared for the Royal Commission on Dominion and Provincial Relations, Ottawa, 1939, pp. 23-34. Although Canada prohibited the export of (monetary) gold on October 19, 1931, it was not until November 1932 that the government adopted a positive policy of depreciating the Canadian dollar.
132. See V. W. Bladen, *Money and the Price System,* University of Toronto Press, Toronto, 1942.

TABLE 22

ALUMINUM OPERATING RATES AND PRICES, 1931–1936

Year	Average Output Rate		Prices			
	Authorized by					
	Alliance	Alcoa	Alliance		Alted	Alcoa
	(Percent of Capacity)		(Swiss Fr. Per Metric Ton)		(Cents Per Pound)	
1931	80	67	1763.50	15.6	18.08	22.78
1932	53	39	1765.50	15.5	16.12	21.76
1933	50	32	1790.75	20.1	18.98	19.30
1934	55	28	1721.39	25.2	23.47	18.95
1935	53	45	1475.45	21.7	21.47	18.75
1936	70	84	1475.45	20.2	21.44	18.82

Sources: For Alliance data, U.S. v. Aluminum Company of America, et al., in U.S. District Court for the Southern District of New York (1937), Equity No. 85-73 (cited below as USAL), Exs. 791 and 804-805, and Alted Ints. 53 and 56 (c). For Alcoa data, operating rates computed from *ibid.*, Alcoa Int. 4, and U.S. Bureau of Mines, *Minerals Yearbook*, 1939, pp. 642-643; prices, from USAL, Exs. 1637, 1701, 1744. (The figures are the average net prices realized, after making allowance for the part of the freight charges absorbed, i.e., paid, by Alcoa.) For Alted data, *ibid.*, Alted Int. 166.

But for the violent fluctuations of exchange rates, the world market price might have conformed even more closely to the price resolutely maintained by Alcoa in the United States during the earlier years of the cartel.[133] In fact, the average Alliance buying price in Swiss (gold) francs a ton converted into United States cents a pound, from 1931 through 1934, was 19.1 cents, only 1.5 cents less than the average net price realized by Alcoa during the same period. But whereas Alcoa's prices were, on the whole, steadily falling during these years, the curve of world market prices was tending sharply upward.

These contrasting movements are probably partly a reflection of the growing rigor of world-market control from the formation of the Alliance up to 1935. Even more, however, they appear to reflect dif-

133. The most signal disturbances in exchange rates were those associated with the abandonment of the gold standard by Great Britain in September 1931, the suspension of specie payments by the United States in 1933 (followed by devaluation of the dollar in 1934), and the collapse of the gold bloc in September 1936. A comparison of the second and third from the last columns in Table 22—Alliance buying prices (converted into cents a pound at annual average exchange rates) and Alted's annual average net realization prices (likewise in cents a pound)—shows that these developments did not affect the actual net prices realized by cartel members in the same measure that they affected the exchange rates.

ferences in the course of general economic conditions in the United States and abroad. Though the Alliance had to impose a drastic reduction in output to make its prices effective in the first half of the thirties, it was not as drastic a curtailment as Alcoa found necessary during the depression. Similarly, the much later start of rearmament buying in Alcoa's market than in the markets of the formal members of the cartel helps to explain the earlier resumption of capacity output abroad and the maintenance of the world market price for aluminum in 1935 and 1936 at a level 14 per cent higher than that of the domestic price set by Alcoa.[134]

Removal of Restrictions on German Production

These cartel policies were obviously calculated to safeguard and advance the business interests of Alliance members and of their silent partner, Alcoa. The pattern was in no essential different from that of cartel policy generally. However, though well designed for the promotion of business interests, Alliance policies collided head on with the nationalistic interests of Nazi Germany, bent on regaining political ascendancy in Europe. When the Nazis attained power, foreseeing the paramount importance of aviation in modern warfare and fully aware of the necessity of unrestricted, indeed of greatly expanded, aluminum production to attain air superiority, they immediately took steps to release VAW from the cartel restrictions.[135]

Other members of the cartel opposed the special concessions sought by VAW. For example, E. K. Davis vehemently protested against the one-sided relaxation of restrictive policy. In a letter to Louis Marlio, chairman of the Alliance, he indicated the grounds for Alted's opposition. "We and the others who are about to be sacrificed to this cold-blooded scheme have carried in silence our respective burdens under the Alliance awaiting the time when we can enjoy some of the benefits of a strict application of the Association's rules." [136]

---

134. Computed on the basis of a comparison of Alted's average net realization price on ingot sales during these years with the average net price realized by Alcoa. See Table 22.

135. USAL, Rec., pp. 15507-08. As E. K. Davis summed up the situation: "The German producers stated that they were going to produce in excess of their production rights whether the Alliance authorized them or not. The Germans stated, in effect, that they considered themselves to be subjected to *force majeure* in the matter and asked to have their situation recognized, which was done."

136. *Ibid.*, Ex. 859. The date of this letter was February 13, 1934.

In various ways, the Alliance endeavored to supply the increased amounts of aluminum Germany demanded for her rearmament program, without relaxing its restrictions and without departing from the principle of proportional curtailment.[137] But the military "needs" of the Nazis and the monopoly strategy of the cartel were incompatible, and these efforts proved futile. Eventually, in consideration of VAW's undertaking not to export the enlarged German output [138] and thus impinge on the profit-making schemes of the Alliance, its non-German members withdrew their opposition to the removal of limitations on German production.[139]

The removal of all quota restrictions on VAW, as well as of the limitations on its expansion of production capacity, had implications for the national security of the non-German members and "friends" [140] of the cartel which they may have sensed, but which they did not permit to upset completely the general cartel strategy. During the three years from 1933 to 1936, the Nazis expanded the annual production capacity of this vital part of their arsenal some 160 million pounds, or 200 per cent. In the same period, North American capacity (all under a common control, and not yet subject to the impact of rearmament demands) remained constant. Other non-German members of the cartel expanded their aggregate annual capacity by 90 million pounds, or 40 per cent.[141]

By the end of 1936 the Germans were equipped to produce 90 per cent as much aluminum as was Alcoa, though three years earlier their capacity had been less than a third of the American. By the end of 1937 they had for the first time surpassed American productive capacity, and in 1938 the German output is reported to have exceeded the United States output by a small margin. What this record portended is now known to all men. Whether or not it was understood by those

---

137. See, for example, *ibid.,* Exs. 782 and 783; and Rec., pp. 15509-14.

138. Of course, VAW's engagement not to export represented no real concession by the Germans. They wanted increased supplies of aluminum as a means of implementing the Luftwaffe, not as a means of expanding their trade. Cf. R. J. Anderson, "Germany's Aluminum Economy," *Iron Age,* June 20, 1940, Vol. CXLV, No. 25, p. 40.

139. USAL, Rec., p. 15507.

140. This was the frequent designation of Alcoa among formal members of the cartel. See, e.g., *ibid.,* Ex. 740, Item 1; Ex. 816, Items 5 and 6; and Rec., pp. 15935-36.

141. See Table 19. According to the U.S. Bureau of Mines, which computes capacity in a different way from Alcoa, an increase of American capacity by 4 million pounds, or 2.3 per cent, occurred during these years. See *Minerals Yearbook,* 1938, p. 583.

who, like Alcoa executives, were aware of these developments as they occurred, they showed no concern over the prospects.[142]

Cartel Reorganizes but Alliance Survives

A revision of the cartel agreement followed shortly the release of the Germans from production restrictions. A resolution that became effective January 1, 1936 replaced the Foundation Agreement of 1931 with a new arrangement.[143] The Alliance continued to operate as the medium for joint regulation of output and prices. The principal modifications of the original scheme were two. First, Alted relinquished its special privilege of tolling arrangements with Alcoa in return for an express renunciation by the Europeans of their claim of privilege to exclude shipments to the United States from their production (and sales) quotas.[144] Second, the Alliance members adopted a new device for restricting production—outside Germany. Whereas before 1936 the Alliance had fixed over-all limits on output and subjected production in excess of a member's quota to forfeiture, thereafter it levied a graduated royalty tax on members that might elect to produce in excess of the recommended "running rate." [145] Similarly, the Alliance imposed a graduated tax on accumulation of stocks.

The world-wide boom in armament industries soon made output restrictions commercially inexpedient, as well as impolitic. Accordingly, after boosting the approved "running rate" to 100 per cent of "normal" capacity in 1937, and to 115 per cent thereof in the first quarter of 1938, the cartel suspended the royalty mechanism for curtailing output.[146] But the "buying price" mechanism remained in

142. G. R. Gibbons, senior vice-president of Alcoa, testified on May 14, 1941 that "We didn't start thinking about enlarging our stockpiles until you began thinking about whether you wanted to build a bombproof shelter, I expect . . . but we did start thinking about it in early 1940." Truman, Pt. III, p. 800.

It is not to be expected, of course, that private business, either competitive or monopolistic, will shape its production and investment policies to meet potential national emergency needs. On the other hand, had genuine competition prevailed in the American aluminum industry, capacity and output would probably have been nearer the levels which national defense required.

143. USAL, Exs. 789 and 830.

144. *Ibid.*, Rec., p. 16382. Incidentally, these "concessions" were more formal than real, on both sides. For Alted had under construction at the time an alumina plant of its own at Arvida. On the completion of this plant, shortly thereafter, it had alumina-refining capacity adequate for its metal reduction facilities. *Ibid.*, Alted Int. 133; and Rec., p. 16246. European exports to the United States three years before the "concessions" had been running at a steady rate of about 15 million pounds annually. This was barely half of the average annual imports from Europe in the twenties. See Table 17.

145. *Ibid.*, Rec., pp. 15725 f. and 16340-47.

146. *Ibid.*, Alted Int. 56; and Ex. 806.

effect, even though, after 1936, the minimum price had only nominal significance in view of the radically improved market conditions.[147]

After 1938 the Alliance remained comparatively inactive, as far as the public record discloses, to the end of the war. It was not dissolved, however, and it could again become a powerful instrument for controlling the world market now that the controls of belligerent governments are being relaxed. Aluminum was "drafted" for the emergency. In the United States, in Canada, in Europe, and doubtless in Asia as well, production capacity increased manyfold in the course of the war.[148] Now that the industry is being "demobilized" and permitted to "go to market" once more, if the resources and facilities available are to be utilized to the full limits of social economy, a definite program and a determined effort directed toward this positive goal will be necessary. For the strategy of restrictionism has behind it not only the ingrained habits of fifty years of persistent practice but the massive power of well-intrenched vested interests.

147. *Ibid.*, Ex. 373, Item 4; Alted Int. 53.

148. Much of this expansion, not only in Nazi-dominated Europe and in Soviet Russia but also in the United States, has been financed by governments. Over 80 per cent of the cost of the expansion of American aluminum reduction capacity has been met with public funds. Of the electric power requirements for operating this expanded plant capacity public works, chiefly those administered by TVA and Bonneville Power Authority, provide well over 90 per cent.

By the end of the war Alcoa and Alted together controlled 64 per cent of the world's primary aluminum capacity, according to the Surplus Property Board, and Alted had become the largest and lowest-cost producer in the world "because of subsidized war expansion in which the United States participated with other Governments." *Aluminum Plants and Facilities,* pp. 2 and 19.

Chapter 7

THE MAGNESIUM CARTEL

SILVERY WHITE MAGNESIUM is the lightest known metal that is malleable, ductile, and relatively inert under atmospheric conditions. Its specific gravity is only two ninths that of iron. Indeed, magnesium weighs barely two thirds as much as aluminum. The light metals, aluminum and magnesium, have other properties in common besides their weight. They resemble one another in color and in resistance to corrosion. Both are readily machinable and can be cast, extruded, rolled, drawn, or forged. In their pure form both have relatively low tensile strength, but when alloyed can be used for many structural purposes. Both also can be employed as a deoxidizing agent in a variety of metallurgical processes.

Moreover, both metals have been developed under international cartel arrangements in which a single company has played an important role. This is no accident. In refining processes, fabricating processes, and fields of application, the two light metals follow parallel lines. When two materials are potential substitutes for each other in a wide range of uses, and cost creates no great barrier, any program for "rationalizing," "stabilizing," or "monopolizing" one can be effective only if similar measures are adopted to control the other. The cartelization of magnesium, following on that of aluminum, illustrates the principle that in commercial organization no less than in technology "one thing leads to another."

Magnesium is derived from various magnesia salts, chiefly the chloride and carbonate compounds. Ordinary sea water or subterranean brines are common sources of magnesium chloride from which comes most of the metal produced in the United States, and before World War II all of it. Magnesium carbonate may be obtained from many ores, the most common being magnesite and dolomite. On calcination, it yields magnesium oxide. The metal is ordinarily purified by electrolysis,[1] although in recent years the thermal process has been introduced.[2]

Magnesium metal was first produced commercially in Germany about 1913. Using as a raw material the magnesium salts produced as a byproduct of the potash industry and refining them electrolytically, the Griesheim chemical concern supplied the entire prewar demand, not only in Europe but in America, at about $1.65 a pound. Magnesium's principal use then was for photographic lighting, the powdered metal yielding an intense white light on ignition.

When World War I cut off the customary source of magnesium, the price skyrocketed. In 1915 ingots sold in the United States for $5 a pound. In the form in which the metal was mainly used, powder or foil, it sold for $6.50 a pound. Although the military art of incendiarism had not sufficiently "advanced" to require a large amount of magnesium, judged by present-day standards, World War I increased its use somewhat, principally in flares and tracer bullets.[3]

Birth of the American Industry

This situation invited industrial experimentation. A favorable price, a variety of widely scattered raw materials, and the choice of several technically feasible production methods led to the development of a new industry. Beginning in 1915 the General Electric Company, the first American producer, turned out appreciable quantities of magnesium primarily for the photoflash bulbs it manufactured. Within two years at least seven other enterprises began magnesium

1. Sir Humphrey Davy was the first to isolate magnesium. In 1808 he produced comparatively pure metal both by electrolysis and by the reduction of magnesium oxide in a current of potassium vapor. For an account of the technical history and early development of the industry, see U.S. Geological Survey, *Mineral Resources of the United States,* 1915, Pt. I, pp. 735-41.

Deville, who played a prominent role in pioneering industrial development in this sphere, as in aluminum, produced a small amount of magnesium commercially about the middle of the nineteenth century. He used a thermal distillation process. However, its high cost was a bar to production except for laboratory purposes.

2. The Permanente, California, plant controlled by the Kaiser interests uses a thermal process which one Hansgirg developed, mainly in Austria. This plant with a capacity of 25 million pounds a year is one of the larger units in the war construction program begun by the federal government in 1941. See *Investigation of the National Defense Program.* Hearings before a Special Committee of the U.S. Senate, 77th Cong., 1st sess., pursuant to S.Res. 71, Pt. VII, pp. 2141-52, and Pt. XVII, Rept. No. 10. (These committee documents will hereinafter be cited: Truman, Pt. —.) See also U.S. Bureau of Mines, *Minerals Yearbook,* 1940, pp. 717-25; 1941, pp. 743-56.

3. Aviation was still so immature during World War I that even aluminum, the principal rival of magnesium as a light alloy base today, was used but little in aircraft construction.

production in this country and an eighth in Canada.[4] Total production from these sources increased rapidly, domestic output rising from 87,500 pounds in 1915 to 294,118 in 1918. After the war output declined sharply—to only 123,800 pounds in 1920.[5] Meanwhile the price had fallen to the prewar level of $1.60 a pound.

Shrinking demand and falling prices eliminated several of the pioneers. By 1920, only the American Magnesium Corporation (AMC), wholly owned subsidiary of the Aluminum Company of America (Alcoa), and the Dow Chemical Company [6] were producing magnesium. All others had been absorbed by rivals or had withdrawn from the field.

Moreover, Dow and Alcoa faced a renewal of European competition. Imports of 182,939 pounds supplied three fourths of the American market by 1922. Most, if not all, of this metal came from Germany or from German-controlled plants, the Griesheim interests having established subsidiary or affiliated enterprises in Great Britain and other countries which marketed their product under the trade name of Elektron. But an import duty of 40 cents a pound on magnesium plus 20 per cent ad valorem, under the Fordney-McCumber Tariff Act of 1922, abruptly ended this competition.

Competitive Position of Dow and Alcoa

Fortified by an insurmountable tariff wall, the domestic magnesium industry could develop the technical and commercial strength necessary to withstand foreign competition. Both Dow and Alcoa were well equipped to advance the art of production. Each had an important stake in the industry, but their stakes were not identical.

Dow's was a single interest—economical utilization of the raw materials of its chemical operations. Dow's principal business was the manufacture of chemical intermediate and end products for the pharmaceutical, soap, glass, textile, and metallurgical industries. Their

4. The pioneers in the order of their appearance were: Norton Laboratories, Rockport, New York; Electric Reduction Co., New York City; Rumford Metal Co., Rumford Falls, Maine; Shawinigan Electro-Metals Co., Shawinigan Falls, Quebec; Aviation Materials Corp., Niagara Falls, New York; American Magnesium Corp., Niagara Falls, New York; Dow Chemical Co., Midland, Michigan; Aluminum Company of America, Pittsburgh, Pennsylvania. However, not all the above enterprises operated simultaneously. See U.S. Geological Survey, op. cit., 1918, pp. 13-21.

5. See Table 23. Also, consult J. T. Rooney, "Present Status and Outlook of the Magnesium Industry," Chemical and Metallurgical Engineering, January 14, 1920, Vol. XXII, p. 60 f.

6. Hereinafter referred to as AMC, Alcoa, and Dow respectively.

TABLE 23

PRODUCTION OF MAGNESIUM IN SPECIFIED YEARS, 1915–1941

(In Pounds)

Year	United States	Germany	World
1915	87,500	—	—
1918	294,100	—	—
1920	123,800	—	—
1925	245,000	—	—
1926	322,000	—	—
1927	366,400	—	—
1928	521,000	—	—
1929	1,329,600	—	—
1930	1,173,500	—	—
1931	580,463 [a]	—	—
1932	791,699 [a]	—	—
1933	1,434,893 [a]	5,000,000	—
1934	4,249,838 [a]	—	—
1935	4,241,218 [a]	17,000,000	—
1936	3,903,312 [a]	—	33,000,000
1937	4,539,980 [a]	26,576,000	43,560,000
1938	6,415,000	31,020,000	52,800,000
1939	6,700,000	36,300,000	68,000,000
1940	12,521,726	55,000,000	98,780,000
1941	32,500,000	77,000,000	170,000,000

Sources: U.S. Bureau of Mines, *Mineral Resources of the United States,* Washington, 1920, Pt. II, pp. 17-20; 1930, Pt. II, p. 197; and Bureau of Mines, *Minerals Yearbook,* 1936, p. 1032; 1942 (preprint), p. 12.

As the Bureau notes, the information on German output is unofficial and highly speculative. However, the estimates here are believed to be conservative.

a. Produced and sold or used by the producer, that is, by Dow. Actual output not available for these years.

production required a large amount of brine and yielded a large surplus of magnesium chloride. Dow had either to find a market for this byproduct or dispose of it as waste. Disposal was costly, since magnesium chloride creates a public nuisance if it is simply dumped outside the plant. Thus Dow's raw material for the production of magnesium cost it "less than nothing." [7]

Alcoa's interest in developing magnesium was more complex. As a

7. See Dow Chemical Company, *Dow and Magnesium, A Statement filed by Willard H. Dow, President and General Manager of Dow Chemical Company, with the Special Committee of the United States Senate Investigating the National Defense Program (Truman Committee), at Washington on March 6, 1944,* Midland (Mich.), p. 2 f. This document is also published as Ex. 1165, Truman, Pt. XXIV, pp. 10683-709. It will hereinafter be cited simply: *Dow and Magnesium.*

single-seller of aluminum, it had a vested interest to protect. Development of magnesium—for many purposes an alternative metal—under controls in which it did not share would have jeopardized its aluminum monopoly. Moreover, magnesium and aluminum are complementary products for some alloys. Alcoa required an adequate and reliable magnesium supply at minimum cost. Finally, as an experienced metallurgist, it could profitably use its extensive "know-how" in the production and fabrication of magnesium.[8]

Thus both Dow and Alcoa had special incentives not only to participate in the industry's development, but to obtain a large share of the business. Moreover, both producers had ample resources, made available by their collateral trade interests, for research and development work in this new field. Neither was vitally dependent on the other for materials or basic patents. Under these salutary competitive conditions experimentation proceeded independently and fruitfully. During the first half of the twenties both firms made great improvements in refining, alloying, and fabricating processes.

Though technical progress occurred all along the line, it was not even nor was it parallel for the two companies. By 1927 Dow was apparently producing the metal more cheaply than AMC. In this branch of the business Dow had a distinct advantage from getting its raw material for "less than nothing," and it had added to this by the development of an efficient and simple reduction process.[9] On the other hand, AMC's close association with Alcoa gave it an advantage in fabricating and selling. Not only did it have access to Alcoa's metallurgical research facilities and experience, but in marketing it had ready at hand Alcoa's specially qualified sales organization. Moreover, its operations were more fully integrated on the whole, because of its parent company's large consumption of magnesium in aluminum alloys.

8. In its long and increasingly intimate relations with Dow, Alcoa repeatedly emphasized this point. For example, in an interoffice memorandum of September 13, 1932 from E. L. Cheyney to I. W. Wilson, reporting a conference with a Dow director, the writer said: "I pointed out to him that the Dow Chemical Company is essentially a chemist . . . whereas the Aluminum Company is essentially a metallurgist . . ." *Patents,* Hearings before the Committee on Patents, U.S. Senate, 77th Cong., 2d sess., on S. 2303, Pt. II, p. 1061. (Senator H. T. Bone was chairman of this committee; the Hearings will hereinafter be cited simply: Bone, Pt. —.)

9. AMC used the so-called magnesium oxide process, with magnesite ore as the basic raw material. This ore, found chiefly in the western part of the United States, had to be transported long distances for refining in the AMC plant at Niagara Falls. AMC's cheaper electric power did not compensate for Dow's costless raw material.

Magnesium's Selling Points and Handicaps

The task of Dow and Alcoa in making a place for the new metal was lightened by the great advantage the weight factor gave it in certain applications. This is very important in aircraft, in portable tools, in textile machinery—for example, "throwing beams"—and in automobiles. But the introduction of magnesium met serious obstacles. Besides the usual handicap of an "untried" material, magnesium had to contend with a popular prejudice grounded on its reputed inflammability.[10] Because in powdered form the stuff is easily ignited, the impression became widespread that the material was unsafe for ordinary uses to which metals are put.[11] Only a process of education could overcome this handicap.[12]

The decade after World War I was the experimental stage of the industry. It marked the transition of magnesium from, literally, a pyrotechnical flash to a dependable light metal alloy adapted for daily use in a wide variety of structural forms and decorative applications. The technical and commercial progress during this period is reflected in the growth of output, which reached 366,400 pounds in 1927, higher even than the wartime peak, and a steadily declining price—to a low of 55 cents a pound in that year. Roughly, between 1920 and 1927 output trebled and price fell by two thirds.

Alcoa Withdraws From Production

However, considering the comparatively heavy developmental cost, it is doubtful that either Dow or Alcoa realized a profit from its magnesium business before 1927.[13] Nor with two enterprises competing were the immediate prospects bright, even though these years laid the

10. In actual production processes—for example, in casting and heat treating—the inflammability of magnesium was a real difficulty. However, by research and experimentation the producers had substantially eliminated this hazard by the end of the twenties.

11. Willard H. Dow has stated that a Dow representative "had to put a stick of Dowmetal into a pan of flaming gasoline before the Army engineers could be convinced that it was even safe to have around." Truman, Pt. XXIV, p. 10291.

12. Probably Dow's advertising campaign for its product under the trade name of Dowmetal—instead of as magnesium alloys—helped to dissipate the popular prejudice.

13. This was the situation, at least, according to the assertions of the parties themselves. See *Dow and Magnesium*, p. 13 f. Also, Bone, Pt. II, pp. 934-1112; and *Scientific and Technical Mobilization*, Hearings before a Subcommittee of the Committee on Military Affairs, U.S. Senate, 78th Cong., 1st sess., on S.Res. 107 and S. 702, Pt. IV, pp. 391-402 (cited hereinafter: Kilgore, Pt. —).

The foregoing citations give the chief sources of the facts surveyed in this section and we shall refer to them only occasionally, for important documents or transactions.

foundation for a prosperous industry. If magnesium were to have the advantage of mass production, it seemed likely that it would involve severe competition and financial loss, temporarily at least, for the producers. However, as so frequently happens in a market of few sellers, an impending competitive struggle led to reconciliation of conflicting interests.

Whether the initial advances were made by Dow or Alcoa is not clear, but in December 1926 Dow offered to sell AMC its metal requirements at 55 cents a pound—20 cents less than the quoted market price.[14] Although this was less than AMC's cost of production,[15] it did not immediately accept the offer. In canvassing its advantages and disadvantages, H. E. Bakken, an Alcoa technical expert, pointed out that

> . . . there may be broader aspects of this problem than mere cost of production which might or might not control the decision as to whether or not we purchase metal from the Dow Company. If we purchase metal from Dow we presumably would eventually obtain an exclusive contract. In such an event we would remove from the present American market the price cutting competition. . . . If we do not obtain some sort of exclusive contract with the Dow Co. we accept severe domestic competition in a small volume business wherein the Dow Company holds an advantage in ingot sales of prob-

14. Bone, Pt. II, p. 992. See also U.S. Tariff Commission, War Changes in Industry Series, Report No. 10, *Magnesium*, Washington, March 1945, p. 38. (This report will hereinafter be cited: Tariff Commission, *op cit.*)

For annual average price data, see Table 24. The slight differences between Dow's current list prices and its "going prices" to AMC, as reported in the text, on the one hand, and on the other the prices shown in Table 24 are traceable mainly to two major factors. (1) The tabulated prices are annual averages, while the prices mentioned in the text frequently were changed during calendar years. (2) The tabulated prices are the average net prices realized by Dow on sales to the specified categories of customers, while the prices mentioned in the text are "quoted prices" or "contract prices." These may differ appreciably from Dow's net realization prices, because of (a) freight absorption, (b) special specifications for particular orders, (c) adjustments on account of defective material, tardy deliveries, etc.

For the convenience of the reader we have assembled a tabulated chronology of the changes in Dow's list prices and in its going prices to AMC, based on the sources cited *passim* in the text of this chapter. We believe this tabulation, shown in Table 25, to be substantially accurate.

15. AMC estimated that, including overhead expense, it could produce ingots at an average cost of 65 cents a pound and, exclusive of overhead, at 43 cents a pound. Bone, Pt. II, p. 992 f.

A later AMC memorandum explained the company's cost disadvantage as follows: "Whereas both Dow and ourselves have spent substantially equivalent amounts of money in process development, our scope has been much broader than Dow's. Dow has been content to spend most of his efforts on primary production of metal. We on the other hand have spread our efforts over the entire field from primary metal production to fabrication methods." *Ibid.*, pp. 997-98.

TABLE 24

DOW'S ANNUAL AVERAGE PRICES FOR, AND YEARLY SALES OF,
MAGNESIUM INGOTS, 1927–1943

(Prices: Cents Per Pound; Sales: Thousands of Pounds)

| Year | Prices | | | Sales | |
	To AMC	To Other Domestic Customers	To Foreign Customers	Foreign	Total
1927	55.09	73.12	66.81	60	116
1928	48.89	78.35	90.33	a	291
1929	49.44	80.54	50.43	44	682
1930	48.02	76.22	51.59	135	661
1931	41.58	54.06	39.41	56	353
1932	32.09	37.19	24.07	176	453
1933	28.01	34.70	24.04	276	557
1934	23.17	28.18	20.67	1,062	1,778
1935	18.98	28.17	20.45	2,846	3,543
1936	19.90	26.88	21.02	1,210	3,245
1937	20.11	27.00	23.59	448	2,551
1938	20.00	25.44	22.07	927	2,538
1939	19.04	25.51	20.29	3,796	5,644
1940	17.49	26.19	23.11	1,086	5,380
1941	16.05	26.14	28.61	1,531	6,104
1942	17.83	21.51	25.62	6,684	19,835
1943	21.03	22.14	25.09	6,988	17,735

Source: Adapted from Part XXIV, *Investigation of the National Defense Program,* Hearings before a Special Committee of the U.S. Senate (Truman Committee), 77th Cong., 1st sess., pursuant to S.Res. 71, Ex. 1177, p. 10720. The price data show the average net price realized by Dow.

a. Negligible.

ably .10 [$.10] per pound but in which we hold an advantage in fabrication sales because of our Aluminum Company connection.[16]

Dow and AMC Move Closer

During early 1927, AMC purchased small amounts of metal from Dow at the 55 cent price, which was lower than Dow had ever before sold it to any other customer. These transactions were apparently

16. *Ibid.,* pp. 994-95. As a counter consideration Mr. Bakken suggested that, if AMC could reduce its overhead by 50 per cent, it could produce magnesium at about the same cost as Dow. In this way it could assure Alcoa a "reliable source of supply" and at the same time keep "a foot in the door" until the future of magnesium was clearer.

TABLE 25

COMPARISON OF DOW'S LIST PRICES AND ITS PRICES TO AMC,
1927–1940

Period	List Price	Going Price to AMC	Special Discount	
				(Per Cent of List)
Jan. 1, 1927–July 15, 1927	$.75	$.55	$.20	27
July 15, 1927–Nov. 30, 1929	.80	.50	.30	38
Nov. 30, 1929–Mar. 10, 1930	.80	.45	.35	44
Mar. 10, 1930–Nov. 20, 1930	.65	.45	.20	31
Nov. 20, 1930–Aug. 24, 1931	.48	.38	.10	21
Aug. 24, 1931–Jan. 1, 1932	.30	.30	—	—
Jan. 1, 1932–June 1, 1933	.30	.28	.02	7
June 1, 1933–June 1, 1934	.30	.22	.08	27
June 1, 1934–June 1, 1935	.30	.21	.09	30
June 1, 1935–Jan. 1, 1938	.30	.20	.10	33
Jan. 1, 1938–Nov. 11, 1938	.30	.19	.11	37
Nov. 11, 1938–Jan. 1, 1939	.28	.19	.09	32
Jan. 1, 1939–June 1, 1939	.28	.175	.105	38
June 1, 1939–Sept. 1, 1940	.27	.175	.095	35

Sources: Based on sources cited *passim* in this chapter.

mutually satisfactory, and from AMC's standpoint they suggested the possibility of developing a closer relationship, or even community of interests. Dow had revealed to AMC its production costs, which indicated that Dow could produce magnesium for 20 cents a pound less than AMC's current cost and 8 cents less than AMC's "most optimistic hoped-for cost." [17] On the basis of these data, an AMC official recommended that the company withdraw from the production field, purchase its requirements from Dow, and specialize in the fabrication branch of the industry. "Metal can, I believe, be bought at such a schedule of prices based on yearly tonnage that we could as a selling and fabricating company resell ingot and fabricate *without domestic competition.*" [18]

In July 1927, AMC contracted with Dow to purchase substantial amounts of metal over the next eighteen months at 50 cents, a reduc-

17. *Ibid.,* Ex. 4, p. 999.
18. *Ibid.* Italics supplied.

tion of 5 cents a pound. This purchase contract covered, in fact, AMC's total magnesium requirements. At the time Dow reduced its price to AMC, it raised the price to others by a like amount—from 75 cents a pound to 80 cents. Hence the price differential in favor of Dow's former rival and new customer increased from 20 cents a pound in the first half of 1927 to 30 cents a pound in the last half of the year and in 1928.[19]

Since July 1, 1927 AMC has produced no magnesium metal. In 1928 Dow and AMC signed a new contract to run for five years, again granting AMC a preferential price. The parties renewed this contract with minor amendments in 1933 and again in 1938. Throughout this period AMC has bought its entire requirements from Dow at prices substantially lower than those offered any other domestic customer.

Alcoa and Dow Cross-License Patents

At about the time that AMC and Dow negotiated their first long-term purchase contract, they also signed a patent cross-licensing agreement.[20] The parties had conflicting patent applications on file for the heat treatment of magnesium-base alloys, and the Patent Office had begun an administrative inquiry to determine the respective rights of the applicants. To settle the controversy, each granted the other a nonexclusive, royalty-free license under any patents which might be issued to it on the applications in interference. But they went further than this: they also agreed to cross-license any other patents covering improvements in the process of heat treating magnesium-base alloys which either party might acquire during the five-year agreement. Moreover, the agreement authorized either party to grant sublicenses to third parties, but only on condition that the sublicensee should purchase from Dow or from AMC the metal used in practicing the licensed invention.

These contract and licensing arrangements strengthened both Dow and Alcoa, each in the field where it was potentially the stronger:

19. According to the price data Dow filed with the Truman Committee. The Tariff Commission in its report cited above gives different figures for "Annual Average Quoted Prices" from 1927 to 1942, inclusive. It obtained its data from the *Engineering and Mining Journal*. The discrepancies between the two lists are so wide in some years that it appears the *Journal* must have obtained its price quotations from some other source than Dow.

20. Bone, Pt. II, p. 999 f.

Dow in metal production, Alcoa in metal fabrication. Dow was assured an outlet for a large part of its magnesium production; Alcoa, of a cheaper source of metal supply. At the same time the arrangements made each more vulnerable in the field in which the other was currently stronger. But neither one had burned its bridges behind it. Dow retained the right to fabricate magnesium and to supply metal to other fabricators. AMC retained the right to resume metal production whenever it wished, or even to purchase part of its metal requirements elsewhere.[21] Nevertheless, the arrangements had eliminated competition in magnesium production, greatly weakened it in the fabrication of magnesium alloys, and placed all potential competitors in either field at a sharp disadvantage. Without making irrevocable commitments, the parties had agreed to "live together"— much as partners in a common-law marriage.

IG Plans to Re-enter American Market

Shortly after the 1927 Dow-AMC contracts had established Dow as the single seller of magnesium in the American market, competition threatened from another source. With the incorporation of I. G. Farbenindustrie in December 1925, the Griesheim concern, as one of its constituents, received strong financial support for aggressive development of its magnesium interests. IG promptly made plans to re-enter the American magnesium market. Profiting by the abortive attempt of Elektron Metals Corporation, which Griesheim had formed for a similar purpose in 1923, IG determined to utilize American business experience and to disturb existing business arrangements as little as possible.

In line with this policy, IG first sought to ally itself with Dow in metal production in the United States. Dow apparently regarded its technical and patent position as quite secure, and the negotiations came to nought. IG then approached other American firms. After consulting the Bohn Foundries and the Pennsylvania Salt Company in 1928, IG dropped consideration of these and other possible partners and began negotiations with Alcoa.

IG and Alcoa were not strangers. IG was half owner (with the Metallgesellschaft or Merton group) of the Bitterfeld aluminum

21. However, the minimum annual purchases stipulated (250,000 pounds a year, under the 1928 contract) were approximately AMC's current rate of consumption.

plant, which with Vereinigte Aluminiumwerke was a member of the aluminum cartel. Both Alcoa and IG had recognized the benefits of cooperative action in developing the light-metal markets. Moreover, Alcoa apparently appreciated the specific advantages of a magnesium tie-up with IG, which through Griesheim had originally developed magnesium metal and had produced it continuously since 1913. Thus its experience was greater than Dow's and Alcoa's combined.

At the same time, Alcoa had a wholesome respect for Dow as a potential competitor, and recognized the advantage of its taking part in any arrangement that might be made. Before committing itself, Alcoa sought some assurance of the alleged superiority of the technical processes and "know-how" which IG was offering as a *quid pro quo* for a stake in the American industry. On January 18, 1929 S. K. Colby of Alcoa wrote to William Von Rath of IG acknowledging "the desirability of an entente cordiale between our respective companies, but more particularly referring to the possibility of a mutual interest in the manufacture of metallic magnesium to which the Dow Chemical Company, of Midland, Michigan, *must* be a party." [22]

Joint Study of American Conditions

Alcoa, IG, and Dow agreed on an independent investigation of the commercial applicability of IG processes under American conditions, and of the comparative cost of the Dow and the IG processes, with a report "to the three parties in interest." Mr. Colby in confirming this project wrote to IG that "If the report . . . indicates that the German process is both technically and commercially superior to that now used in the United States, further conversations will be initiated looking to a community of interest."

The Fitzgerald Laboratories, specializing in electro-metallurgical problems, conducted the investigation and made its report on October 16, 1929.[23] On the basis of its study, the Fitzgerald Laboratories concluded that under

. . . conditions in the United States the German practice in the production of magnesium metal is superior to the American practice, in spite of a considerable advantage which the latter has in the skillful use it makes of its unique natural resources; that *ceteris paribus*, with the increased market for

22. Bone, Pt. II, p. 1002. Italics supplied.
23. *Ibid.*, pp. 1002-08.

magnesium in America which may reasonably be expected, the German practice would have an appreciable commercial advantage; that German practice
in the fabrication of magnesium is in advance of American practice; that a
combination of the specific advantages which the three companies possess
would be commercially more profitable than any one or even two working
alone.

These findings were more favorable to IG than Dow considered to
be warranted and it withdrew from the negotiations with the Germans. However, Dow was ready not only to continue its cooperation
with Alcoa in magnesium development, but even to supplement and
strengthen their existing ties. On the other hand, Alcoa apparently
reached the conclusion that IG had something substantial to offer, at
least from the strategic standpoint, which might enable Alcoa to keep
its "foot in the door." Accordingly, dual negotiations—Dow-Alcoa
and Alcoa-IG—proceeded simultaneously for several years, with
Alcoa occupying the intermediate position and playing, actually, the
role of mediator.

The negotiations reveal strikingly the technique of cartel diplomacy—the steady application of "pressure" and the resort alternatively to challenges and blandishments. The similarity to power politics in which trial by battle is a last resort is marked. The procedure
discloses the vast gulf between big business in practice and the patterns of behavior assumed in a regime of free competition. It shows
how the conference table superseded the market as the arena for decision making.

The Three-Sided Conflict of Interest

Dow made clear its attitude toward an IG hookup as well as toward a more definite understanding with Alcoa in a conference with
the latter in December 1929. As one of the Alcoa representatives reported this meeting:

. . . the Dow contingent were quite emphatic in questioning the Fitzgerald
report . . . it is a fair assumption . . . that the Dow Chemical Company
would only tie up with I. G. as a last possible consideration. They refused
absolutely to entertain a partnership or company-ownership relation with I. G.

Dr. Dow and his associates give no indication of being frightened by the
possible entry of I. G. into the American market.

After we had arrived at this point in our discussion, it was made perfectly plain to the Dow people that in view of their feelings toward I. G. only two courses were left open to us. One was to take a defensive and offensive position with the I. G. or take a defensive and offensive position with the Dow Chemical Company. Being Americans, for one thing, and recognizing past relations with the Dow people, it was the personal expression of both Mr. Colby and Dr. Jeffries that a tie-up with the Dow Chemical Company would probably be a desirable one, although for purposes of argument and otherwise it was pointed out that perhaps some of the officials of the Aluminum Company would doubtlessly look with favor on some sort of a tie-up with the I. G. . . . possible schemes were discussed briefly as to how the Dow Company and ourselves might cooperate.

The proposed plan of Dr. Jeffries wherein we continue somewhat along present lines, though in a much more purposeful and definite manner, appealed to Dr. Dow. This plan is based on the consideration that if the magnesium business does not exceed 5,000,000 pounds per year we have no great interest in it. If, however, it becomes a greater business than indicated by the above figure then we are interested not only in fabrication but also in production. . . . In the interim we would buy metal as a preferred customer and continue development of its use.

An interesting sidelight on the Dow Company's attitude was that they definitely stated that they were disappointed, not only at us in our development of the magnesium business, but in general they were disappointed at the slowness of the development . . . the Dow people are not entirely convinced that the Aluminum Company is putting quite enough effort on the development of the magnesium business, and it is my own opinion that if we could once convince the Dow people that we are earnestly seeking to develop the magnesium business as fast as we can and not merely keeping a safe position, that we would be over one of the most difficult obstacles standing between them and us in the way of satisfactory cooperative relations. Dow is inclined to think of us as standing beside the band wagon waiting for the band wagon to show trend and direction. If the band wagon goes strong then we step aboard; if it does not go so strong we stand to lose little. And that size-up is not far from right.[24]

Thus, although Dow was apparently willing to take part in a loose cooperative arrangement with its business rivals, if its primacy as an American magnesium producer were safeguarded, it preferred a struggle in the market to surrender at a conference table.

Alcoa apparently saw in the IG overture an opportunity to redress the balance of power between itself and Dow. While convinced that AMC had an advantage over Dow in fabrication processes, it was equally certain that its abandoned oxide process for metal production

24. *Ibid.*, pp. 1008-10.

was "entirely out of the running," indeed that it was "tottering on its last legs." [25] In Alcoa's view,

> The I. G. people are in a very strong position with regard to "know how" in production of metal. . . . The discussion . . . points to a union between ourselves and I. G. for we regard Dow greatly inferior to ourselves in the field of Fabrication and if we combine with I. G. we do not need the Production art known to the Dow Company.[26]

Nevertheless, Alcoa was extremely reluctant to embark on a venture which might lead to a competitive struggle with Dow. A confidential Alcoa memorandum of May 17, 1930 states that

> . . . any sort of combination or arrangement that might be suggested must be predicated upon avoiding, during the initial development of the magnesium business, destructive price-cutting competition. . . . The Dow Chemical Company, however, proposes to take and to hold the position of being *the* United States supplier of pig metal. They state that they are prepared for competition, and in effect wish to regard us as a preferred customer, in spite of the fact that we are consuming about half of their production. . . . So long as the magnesium business remains a small business, relatively speaking, that is . . . the Dow Chemical Company would be able to meet almost any kind of competition successfully. . . . To venture into the production of magnesium metal at present with I. G. Farbenindustrie, A.-G., or ourselves alone, does not, in the face of available facts, seem warranted. . . . Any attempt to sell the outside market would mean a price war with Dow, because under such conditions Dow would be minus the [AMC] business and would be forced to cut his selling prices to the core. . . .
>
> For the immediate present, with Dow as sole producer and ourselves and I. G. Farbenindustrie A-G. following up fabrication processes and fundamental research to increase the use of magnesium, *it is extremely doubtful whether anyone else would attempt to break into the magnesium business.* [Italics supplied.] . . . Even Dow . . . would, from a patent standpoint, find heavy weather. . . . Dow feels very secure in his ability to supply magnesium pig metal . . . at a lower cost than anyone else. We should state in general terms to I. G. Farbenindustrie A-G. the result of our investigation. We should propose a combination of interests based upon fabrication development . . . it should be suggested that actual production of metal be delayed until the market demands shall have increased sufficiently to warrant entering into competition with Dow Chemical Company. (It is, of course, not impossible for Dow Chemical Company to change its present policy . . . so that at a later date a union of ourselves and Dow . . . or all three companies may be practically possible.)[27]

25. *Ibid.*, pp. 1026 ff.
26. *Ibid.*
27. *Ibid.*, pp. 1097-99.

In the prolonged negotiations Alcoa, while never losing sight of the advantages of an alignment with IG, continued to show great respect for the strength of Dow's position. It hesitated to challenge Dow by cancelling its preferential purchasing contract and resuming metal production as IG urged, in partnership with it. An Alcoa inter-office memorandum of January 24, 1931 asserted unequivocally that

The patents of Dow, taken as a group, are the strongest group of patents on magnesium base alloys in this country. It appears that they will cover the newly developed alloys which may be important in future years. . . . It appears to be quite definitely indicated that a company formed by I. G. and ourselves should, for the present at least, purchase metal from Dow. . . . Finally, a development business such as the magnesium business promises to be for a number of years will thrive best in a noncompetitive situation.[28]

Alcoa and IG Reach Agreement

Alcoa continued its negotiations with IG. On October 23, 1931 they signed an accord, known as the Alig agreement.[29] Alcoa and IG pooled all their patents and technical knowledge on magnesium production and fabrication. To exploit this common fund, they agreed to organize a joint patent-holding company, sharing equally in its ownership. The Magnesium Development Corporation (hereafter MDC) was incorporated in March 1932 and the two shareholders transferred to it all their United States magnesium patents.

The governing body of MDC was a board of six directors, three chosen by Alcoa and three by IG. Either group of three directors, voting as a unit, could authorize the grant of sublicenses, for use in the United States, under MDC fabrication patents. Such sublicenses were subject to a royalty of one half cent a pound. However, with certain exceptions, sublicenses under production patents required the approval of a majority of the MDC directors. These were in all cases subject to a royalty of one cent a pound. The Alig agreement gave both Alcoa and IG a general license to utilize MDC patented fabricating processes royalty-free, but solely in the United States.[30]

28. *Ibid.*, pp. 1020 and 1029.
29. *Ibid.*, pp. 1036-52. A supplementary agreement of the same date makes certain interpretations of and minor changes in the main contract. One clause exempted Alcoa from liability if it should fail to procure for Alig an extension of the rights obtained by Alcoa from Dow under their 1927 cross-licensing agreement.
30. This privilege of royalty-free use of MDC fabricating processes was contingent on the market situation confronting the fabricator in purchasing metal, if and when

Either party to the Alig agreement had the right to organize a United States production company to exploit MDC's metal production patents provided it offered the other party equal participation in such an enterprise. But if either Alcoa or IG, or both jointly, thus engaged in production, the licensee company had to pay royalties to MDC of one cent a pound on all magnesium produced and sold.[31]

Privileges for IG

Although on the face of the Alig agreement Alcoa and IG shared equally in its benefits, in reality it reserved to IG important special privileges. First, by limiting the use of MDC's patents and "know-how" to the United States, it in effect excluded Alcoa and other possible American licensees from foreign markets.[32] Thus IG built a fence around the American magnesium industry, in so far as it was dependent on Alig patents and know-how. Second, the Alig agreement gave IG a preferential claim on all MDC earnings above 6 per cent a year on its paid-in capital, until such time as IG should have received one million dollars more than Alcoa from this joint enterprise. Third, IG could grant sublicenses to certain specified American firms for use of Alig's metal production processes without Alcoa's consent.

Finally, the Alig agreement limited the initial capacity of any production company which might be licensed, whether jointly or separately owned, to 4,000 tons annually and gave IG a veto over any increase. Apparently the object of this restriction was political rather than economic. From an economic standpoint, no reason is apparent for excluding Alcoa from the privilege of determining maximum domestic productive capacity. For presumably Alcoa would be no less assiduous than IG in the pursuit of maximum net revenue. In spite of these special concessions to IG, the Alig agreement strengthened greatly Alcoa's position in the American market.

---

either party (or both) organized a production company to operate in the United States. (See below.) In any event, the maximum royalty either Alcoa or IG would have to pay for using MDC fabricating patents was one half cent a pound.

31. If and when the company's inventory exceeded one half its annual capacity, it had to pay royalties on all magnesium produced.

32. While no express provision limited the *sales* territory of MDC licensees to the domestic market, export (to countries in which IG remained the sole owner of the patents on processes it had developed) of metal or fabricated products manufactured by Alig processes might have made the exporter liable for infringement. In those countries IG still reserved "the exclusive right to make, use, and vend" the patented device.

Dow Challenges the Alig Cartel

While the Alig agreement was being negotiated during the summer of 1931, Dow became aware of the prospective arrangement, which was certain to affect vitally its interests in the magnesium industry. Whether for bargaining purposes or otherwise, Dow made a drastic (37.5 per cent) reduction in the price of magnesium, from 48 cents to 30 cents a pound, in August 1931.[33] At the same time Dow withdrew the preferential price to AMC which from January 1927 to August 1931 had never been less than 10 cents a pound under the lowest list price at which it offered metal to other customers, regardless of quantity ordered. Whatever Dow may have meant by this gesture, Alcoa decided to avoid an outright competitive contest with Dow.

Alig Opens Negotiations With Dow

Shortly after it signed the Alig agreement, Alcoa opened negotiations with Dow looking toward a more definite hookup between Dow and the Alig cartel. Initially Dow welcomed these advances. An Alcoa memorandum on the first meeting, January 7, 1932, said that, after Alcoa had apprised Dow of the Alig agreement and the plans of the partners,

Mr. Dow stated that he felt this was a very constructive move and would be a great stimulus to the magnesium industry in the United States.

Dow asked if there would be an opportunity for Dow Chemical Company joining in the new company. Mr. Hunt stated that there seemed to be legal restrictions in this connection but Doctor Walter Duisberg, who would head the Magnesium Development Company, would be glad to discuss the possibility in a cooperative way. . . .

Mr. Dow expressed his opinion that the Magnesium Development Corporation would have some difficulty in collecting fabricating royalties and thought it might be good to have fabricating fees collected at the time the metal was sold. Mr. Hunt replied that no definite plans had been formulated.

Mr. Dow told Mr. Hunt that the present organization of the Dow Chemi-

33. See Table 25. The price was 32 cents a pound for l.c.l. shipments. An exact comparison of the list prices scheduled by Dow at different periods is difficult because the minimum quantities varied from time to time. While from November 20, 1930 to August 24, 1931 the lowest list price quoted to others than AMC was 48 cents a pound, this price applied to smaller orders than the 30 cents a pound price which went into effect on August 24, 1931. The latter price was available only to purchasers ordering fifteen tons or more in a single lot. Possibly Dow might have quoted a large-quantity purchaser a price somewhat less than 10 cents a pound above the price at which metal was being supplied to AMC during the period November 20, 1930 to August 24, 1931. That price was 38 cents a pound.

cal Company were ready to deal in the most friendly and cooperative spirit with the Magnesium Development Corporation and asked Mr. Hunt what the next step was. Mr. Hunt replied, as soon as the Magnesium Development Corporation is organized full discussions should be had with Doctor Duisberg.[34]

The position taken by the several parties at the outset clearly indicated wide differences in their views on the relative strength of Dow and the Alig partners. MDC first offered Dow an exclusive license under MDC production patents "in the brine field" and a nonexclusive license with the right to sublicense under MDC fabrication patents. The former license was to bear a royalty of 2 cents a pound on the first 500,000 pounds of annual output and one cent a pound on production beyond that amount. The offer did not specify the royalty on fabrication processes, but declared it would be the same as for other MDC licensees, except Alcoa and affiliated companies.[35] Dow summarily rejected this offer in a letter of March 31, 1932 to MDC.

We believe that Magnesium will be made by the Dow Chemical Company just as cheaply in this country as by any competitor.

The idea which was expressed that the Dow Chemical Company has no patents which are of interest to the Magnesium Development Corporation seems ridiculous to us. We have 37 issued patents and 31 applications relating to fabrication methods and alloy compositions and we regard them as of more value than the patents controlled by the Magnesium Development Corporation. Any proposal which does not take proper cognizance of the value of these Dow Chemical Company patents will not be of interest to us.[36]

On the other side, the correspondence between Alcoa and IG and between IG's American office and its home office shows that at the outset IG favored a metal reduction enterprise using its techniques to integrate with and strengthen the established fabrication business (AMC). An Alcoa memorandum of April 21, 1932 reported that Dr. Schmidt of IG

. . . appears to be reasonably assured that a satisfactory tie-up with Dow is very problematical, and on this assumption I believe he is going to recom-

34. Bone, Pt. II, pp. 1053-54. Dr. Duisberg was a son of the chief "architect" of IG, but he was a native American. He was the first president of MDC.
35. *Ibid.*, p. 1056.
36. See *Dow and Magnesium*, p. 27.

mend to M. D. C. that serious consideration be given to the establishment of a producing company and a fabricating company all under one roof, so to speak. . . . It is, of course, realized that Dr. Schmidt was tremendously disappointed in what he saw of the Dow efforts to fabricate magnesium products, and since Dr. Schmidt is so convinced that the Dow methods are doomed to failure and since he also has such faith in the know how and patent strength of M. D. C., he feels reasonably sure that if we were to produce metal and fabricate products from it, we would be able to sell those products at a profit; whereas Dow would find himself in a position where practically his entire outlet would be limited to ingot sales.[37]

Eventually, however, IG appears to have swung around to the Alcoa view. In an IG interoffice memorandum of January 14, 1933 Dr. Duisberg stated:

The value of the Dow patents in the fabrication field cannot be minimized. It must be said frankly that the patent situation of M. D. C. is not what could be called an invulnerable monopoly position. . . . As for [metal production], Alcoa has always taken the attitude that it would be glad to begin production immediately if the cost of production would enable us to compete with Dow . . . One must realize, however, that the [cost] calculations were never such that there was a direct stimulus to invest money in the magnesium production.[38]

But IG was dissatisfied with its share of the benefits from the Alig agreement. It pointed out to Alcoa that it was not a beneficiary under Alcoa's preferential purchase contract with Dow, that AMC, as a subsidiary of Alcoa, paid no royalties to MDC, and that the existing arrangements were proving more profitable to Alcoa than to itself. IG expressed the opinion that the

Dow situation can be clarified only either through a contest or through an agreement providing for closest cooperation by taking in Dow as a partner in the sphere of interests of Alcoa and I. G. . . . We feel that the development of the M. D. C. has come to a turning point and that a decision must be made.[39]

Alcoa responded to IG pressure by offering to sell it a half interest in AMC, and thereby assure IG of some share in Alcoa's earnings

37. Bone, Pt. II, p. 1054. On another occasion an Alcoa official declared that the IG "people express contempt for Dow." *Ibid.,* p. 1009.
38. *Ibid.,* p. 1079.
39. *Ibid.,* p. 1066 f., letter of IG Secretariat to Dr. Duisberg, December 23, 1932.

from its magnesium business. IG accepted the offer and became a partner in the fabricating company on February 8, 1933.[40]

Alcoa, as a preferred purchaser of Dow metal, a royalty-free user of MDC fabrication patents, and with access to IG's production patents if it should choose to use them, was reluctant to break off relations with Dow and begin metal production. The Alig partners decided, therefore, to test the relative strength of their and Dow's patent positions by a contest in the courts. In doing so they recognized that merely starting a suit might "bring Dow to terms." [41]

Alig Partners Unsheath the Sword—and Wave the Olive Branch

MDC filed a patent infringement suit against Dow in December 1932. Even after this move, however, Dow continued to supply Alcoa (AMC) with all its requirements of metal, under the 1928 contract. Moreover, to the end of the contract period (June 1933) Dow continued to give AMC the small (2-cent-a-pound) preferential discount which it had granted its biggest customer from January 1, 1932 when Alcoa opened the negotiations for binding Dow more closely to the cartel. On the expiration of the 1928 contract, while the patent controversy was still pending—in fact six months before its amicable settlement—Dow and AMC signed a new five-year metal-purchase contract.

The contract terms substantially restored the preferential position of the Alig group among Dow's customers. While the minimum amounts to be delivered annually and the minimum for the five-year period of the contract remained the same as under the 1928 contract, AMC obtained a "prior claim" on Dow's output.[42] The base price to AMC was to be 24 cents a pound, as against 30 cents then quoted to other customers buying in large lots.

But this was not the whole of the price advantages for the Alig group. First, Dow agreed to maintain a price differential in favor of AMC in selling to other customers except the Ford Motor Company. The guaranteed discount to AMC was 4 cents a pound under the price accorded other buyers purchasing less than 30,000 pounds in a

40. *Ibid.*, p. 1069 f.
41. Alcoa's patent attorney suggested that MDC had "two objects in view, the first object being to bring Dow to terms, the second object being to actually prosecute the suit to its logical end." *Ibid.*, p. 1059.
42. For full text of contract, see *ibid.*, p. 1072 f.

single order. Only if another Dow customer agreed to buy more magnesium than AMC during the same period could he get the same price. Second, Dow was to reduce its base price as it increased its total annual sales. Regardless of whether Dow quoted a price lower than 28 cents a pound to any other customer (except Ford), the 24 cent price to AMC was to be progressively reduced as Dow's annual sales increased from 325 tons up to 4,000 tons or more, when a minimum price of 19 cents a pound became effective. Finally, the contract required Dow, in supplying even its own fabricating department with magnesium alloys, to set a price no lower than the current price to AMC.

According to evidence presented to the Truman Committee, the actual discount to AMC below the list prices quoted to other Dow customers under this contract ranged from 27 per cent to 37 per cent in different periods between June 1933 and November 1938. (See Table 25.) Dow has defended this price discrimination on the ground of the commercial advantages of having a "steady quantity purchaser." [43] Both the law and business have long recognized the propriety of quantity discounts. But since 1914 the Clayton Act has banned price discrimination "when the effect may be to substantially lessen competition or tend to create a monopoly." [44] And since 1936 the Robinson-Patman Act has recognized such quantity discounts as legal only if they represent a saving in cost, and the law places the burden of proof of such a saving on the seller.[45]

On its face, the price discrimination under the Dow-AMC contract is difficult to justify on such grounds.[46] The contract guaranteed AMC a price differential of at least one cent a pound even though some other customer agreed to purchase as much as 1,499,999 pounds over

43. *Dow and Magnesium,* p. 28.
44. Act of October 15, 1914, C. 323; 38 Stat.L. 730; U.S. Code, Title 15, c. 1, Sec. 13.
45. Act of June 19, 1936, C. 592; 49 Stat.L. 1526; U.S. Code, Title 15, c. 1, Sec. 13a.
46. From August 24, 1931, when Dow made its countermove on hearing of the Alig deal, until June 1, 1933 when the new contract went into effect, Dow had forced AMC to pay for its metal supplies virtually the full list price charged to other domestic magnesium fabricators. Indeed, for four months out of the period AMC received no special, i.e., discriminatory, discount whatever. For the remaining seventeen months it received a special discount of only 2 cents a pound. This compares with a price differential in its favor which from June 1927 to August 1931 had never been less than 10 cents a pound and which from June 1, 1933 to September 1, 1940 was at no time less than 8 cents a pound. Evidently the extent of the quantity discount allowed to AMC depended on other factors than cost saving to the seller.

a five-year period—or within one pound of the minimum which AMC agreed to take. It also guaranteed AMC a reduction in its price as Dow's total sales increased, exclusive of sales to Ford, even though the increase might come from purchases made by AMC's competitors. In brief, the contract gave AMC a lower price as its competitors did more business.

Alcoa Gets "Favored Nation" Treatment

This was not all. Another part of the agreement, which Alcoa called the "favored nation clause," was truly "the heart of the contract," from the Alcoa standpoint.[47] It required Dow in selling fabricated products to compute its prices according to a prescribed formula. One element in this formula was the cost of metal. Dow was required to charge its own fabricating department for magnesium ingots the same price at which it was supplying AMC. Another element in the formula was the "fair cost of fabrication." The contract defined this concept and specified its accounting components in detail. The pricing formula even included a provision for profit at a specified rate. Moreover, Dow agreed to submit its cost accounts to check by independent auditors. Thus the Alig partners got assurance that in pricing its fabricated products Dow would include the same cost elements which AMC used.

This new five-year purchasing contract supplemented and bolstered the Alig agreement of October 1931. On one hand, Dow preserved its position as the sole producer of magnesium metal in the United States. On the other hand, Alcoa and IG through their jointly owned subsidiary had an assured source of metal supply for five years—at a price substantially lower than that at which AMC had ever before obtained metal, either by production or by purchase from Dow. Moreover, the price was certainly lower than that at which any competing fabricator could obtain his supplies.

But the price terms were far from all the benefits accruing to Alcoa and IG. The "favored nation clause" prevented any serious competitive "disturbance" of the magnesium market. Since the patent controversy was still outstanding, however, full consummation of the cartel scheme remained to be achieved.

47. Bone, Pt. II, p. 1085.

Dow and Alig Partners Join Hands in Patent Pool

To this end the parties promptly resumed negotiations, and on January 1, 1934 Dow signed a cross-licensing agreement with MDC and AMC.[48] MDC waived all damage claims for alleged past infringement of its patents and agreed to withdraw its suit. Dow and MDC granted to each other nonexclusive licenses under all their respective magnesium fabrication patents—and under no others. Thereby, in effect, the Alig group conceded Dow's primacy in metal production. Each party might grant licenses to others under its own patents and sublicenses under the licenses received from the other. Dow agreed to pay MDC a royalty of one cent a pound on all the magnesium metal it sold.[49]

The cross-licensing agreement stipulated that Dow and AMC should collect a royalty of 1.5 cents a pound from their sublicensees. Dow was to remit two thirds of the royalties which it collected to MDC, and AMC was to remit one third of the royalties which it collected to Dow. However, either party might grant royalty-free sublicenses on condition that the sublicensee buy his entire metal from the licensor. Actually the sole royalty revenue which either of the principal parties has obtained has been the one cent a pound royalty which Dow has paid MDC on all its metal sales to fabricators. AMC granted no sublicenses before the war, and the twenty-four sublicenses Dow granted were royalty-free. This was because Dow restricted its sublicensees, in the use of the licensed inventions, to metal purchased from Dow.[50]

Shortly after the May 1938 decision of the Supreme Court in the *Leitch* v. *Barber* case, holding such practices illegal, Dow omitted the clause formally imposing this restriction from its sublicense contracts, but, according to former Assistant Attorney General Arnold,[51] actual

48. *Ibid.*, pp. 1087-91.
49. *Ibid.*, Art. IV. This general rule of royalty liability had two exceptions. Dow was exempt from royalty (1) on metal exports, and (2) on magnesium in forms in which it would lose its identify on first use. Similarly, AMC agreed to pay Dow a royalty on all the magnesium it sold with the same exceptions, providing a royalty on the metal had not been paid to MDC at its source. In view of the purchase contract between Dow and AMC this obligation was purely nominal, of course, so long as AMC continued to refrain from engaging in metal production or from patronizing an "outside" (equivalent to foreign) source of supply.
50. *Ibid.*, pp. 1103-06.
51. *Ibid.*, pp. 981 and 1110.
In *Leitch* v. *Barber*, 302 U.S. 458 (1938), the Supreme Court ruled that clauses in patent licenses obliging the licensee to purchase from the licensor material used in the practice of the licensed invention were invalid. On May 11, 1939 Dow and MDC exe-

restriction continued none the less. The following excerpt from a
letter of April 8, 1940 from Dow's sales manager to a prospective
magnesium customer shows how Dow contrived to maintain the
restriction after dropping the restrictive clause from licenses.

> We are enclosing a proposed sales contract in duplicate covering your
> requirements for 12-month period starting April 1, 1940. If this contract is
> satisfactory to you please sign and return one copy. Upon receipt of this
> signed sales agreement, we will forward you our standard license for sand
> casting.

Furthermore, these standard licenses reserved to the licensor (Dow)
a one-year cancellation option. This gave assurance that if the licensee
failed to renew the contract for purchase of his annual metal requirements from Dow he could be deprived of the privilege of using the
pooled patents in fabricating magnesium purchased from any other,
i.e., noncartel, source. Thus, those fabricators whom Dow licensed
to use the pooled patents were as effectively tied to the use of Dow
magnesium as they had been under the "exclusive use" clause of the
original license contract.

Anomalously, though only fabricating patents were licensed or
sublicensed under the January 1934 cross-licensing contract, MDC
has received no royalty revenue whatever at any time from any one
directly for the use of its fabricating patents, admittedly its chief
stock in trade.[52] Dow has paid MDC a royalty of one cent a pound
on all the magnesium it has sold to fabricators or has fabricated itself. In this way, the fabricating patents provided a leverage which
enabled the cartel to levy a tax on magnesium *metal production.*

Though this tended to curtail Dow's operations in magnesium
production, precisely as would an output tax levied by the government, it fortified Dow's monopoly position as the sole domestic supplier of the metal. For, in effect, the agreement assured Dow that
only those fabricators purchasing their metal supplies exclusively
from it could use the MDC patented fabricating processes. More-

---

cuted an amendment to the 1934 cross-licensing agreement which required the use of a
uniform sublicensing contract. In this revised form they dropped the restrictive stipulation regarding the metal to be used. See Kilgore, Pt. IV, p. 398, and accompanying
Exs. 49, 50, 51.
    52. The legality of this aspect of the 1934 cross-licensing agreement, simply by itself
and independently of other features of the cartel scheme, is an issue beyond the scope
of the present study.

over, the cross-licensing agreement resulted in the withholding of
MDC's production patents from use in the United States, though IG
was using them in Germany to produce more magnesium before
World War II than the combined output of all other countries.

Dow Agrees Not to Compete With IG in Europe

There still remained one feature of Dow's operations not covered
by the tie-up with the Alig cartel in the five-year purchase agreement
and in the cross-licensing agreement. Dow was free to embark on an
aggressive export policy. A fully implemented international cartel
required some restriction on Dow's freedom to sell metal abroad.
The parties took care of this by a contract which Dow and IG signed
on September 5, 1934.[53]

The term of this contract was from August 1, 1934 to January 1,
1938. During this period, Dow undertook not to compete with IG
in European markets. Specifically, Dow agreed "to confine its sales in
Europe to IG" except for sales of not over 300,000 pounds annually
to an old Dow customer, the British Maxium concern. The contract
stipulated that Dow must charge Maxium 4 cents a pound more than
its price to IG.

Since the agreement imposed no reciprocal obligation on IG not to
compete with Dow by selling metal in the American market, one
must look elsewhere for Dow's reward. Dow asserts that ordinary
commercial advantages on both sides explain the deal.[54] On its face,
and apart from the one-sided restriction, the contract was a simple
sales agreement. IG undertook to purchase for the first sixteen
months of the contract, September 1, 1934 to December 31, 1935—
a minimum of 950 tons of magnesium metal, at 21 cents a pound,
c.i.f. Hamburg. This was probably equivalent to a domestic price of
not more than 20 cents a pound. Thus IG obtained a price concession
of 10 cents a pound below Dow's current list price on domestic deliveries to other buyers than AMC, and 5 cents below its "average
realized price" on domestic deliveries including sales to AMC.

In Mr. Dow's testimony before the Truman Committee on March
6, 1944, he contended that "the Dow Group was determined to
make a position for magnesium in the United States by taking the

53. Bone, Pt. II, p. 1111 f.
54. Dow and Magnesium, p. 29 f.

metal out of the specialty and putting it into the commodity class. This could be done only through the price reduction of volume production. . . ." [55] He asserted that the sales to IG under the 1934 contract "helped Dow to get into larger production." [56] Doubtless this is correct, particularly since the actual volume of deliveries to IG ran well above the minimum amounts specified in the contract—reaching a total in the three years 1934–1936 of 3,952,966 pounds, equal to 45 per cent of Dow's entire output in these years.

But the price advantages of the larger production were confined to members of the cartel. During this entire period, or indeed from August 1931 to November 1938, Dow made no reduction in list price to other domestic fabricators—despite the alleged advantage to the domestic industry of larger production.

Dow Defends Price Discrimination

In defense of the discriminatory price to IG, Mr. Dow declared that "the Germans in 1934 and 1935 were buying the metal that Americans would not buy." No one can say definitely whether Americans would have bought an additional 4 million pounds of magnesium in those years at the price at which Dow supplied it to IG. For the metal was never offered to them at that price. In current business conditions, probably they would not have done so. The large German purchases represented part of the Nazi rearmament program.[57] Domestic demand was still based on civilian uses without the stimulus of large government orders.

Nevertheless, had Dow offered magnesium to domestic buyers at the same low price it gave IG, it would have stimulated search by American manufacturers, particularly in the aviation and automotive fields, for ways to substitute magnesium for aluminum. For they would then have been able to buy magnesium at a lower price per pound than aluminum,[58] and because of magnesium's lighter weight

55. *Ibid.*, p. 15 f.
56. *Ibid.*, p. 59.
57. One could hardly account otherwise for the rapid expansion of German production between 1933 and 1938, when output increased sixfold or from 5 million pounds to 31 million pounds. See Table 23. See also H. Alwicker, "Use of Magnesium Alloys in the European Automotive Industry," *Journal of the Society of Automotive Engineers,* September 1939, Vol. XLV, No. 3, p. 9.
58. Alcoa's average scheduled price of aluminum ingots in 1934 was 22.2 cents a pound, 19.5 cents in 1935, and 19 cents in 1936. This gives an average price for the three years of 20.2 cents a pound for aluminum, as compared with the set price of 20 cents a pound which Dow realized on its sales of magnesium to IG during these years.

it would "go half as far again" as aluminum, pound for pound. The higher costs—in the current state of the art—of fabricating magnesium than of fabricating aluminum would certainly have cancelled part of magnesium's advantage in price and lighter weight. The opportunities for technical advance in the relatively undeveloped art of fabricating magnesium were probably greater, however, than those for improving aluminum fabrication processes. Moreover, non-discriminatory competitive pricing in the domestic and international magnesium markets would eventually have lowered the prices of both magnesium and aluminum. In the long run, this would undoubtedly have expanded the use of both metals.

It does not follow that the magnesium and aluminum industries would have been more prosperous under a competitive regime. The cartel arrangement whereby magnesium was produced and sold in the American market by a single seller was probably commercially sound—from the short-run viewpoint, at any rate.[59] But even granting this, it was not primarily on account of the commercial soundness of the arrangement that Dow remained a single-seller. It was because of the mutual commitments among Dow and the Alig partners defining their respective rights and obligations in a market control scheme.

Series of Contracts Fit Into Cartel Pattern

In a loose cartel of this kind, the whole is greater than the sum of its parts. Judged separately, the Dow-AMC contract of June 1933 might appear to be nothing more than a simple purchase contract—although a discriminatory one—providing for Dow a steady customer for a large part of its output; and for Alcoa, an assured supply at the lowest price. The MDC-AMC-Dow contract of January 1934 and the Dow-IG contract of September 1934 have the same innocent appearance, viewed separately. The parties have defended the MDC-AMC-Dow contract as an arrangement to insure the unimpeded development of magnesium fabrication by making available to each fabricator the best techniques without danger of patent infringement suits.[60] Perhaps they could make out a defense for even the Alig

59. For an illuminating discussion of the long-run interests of business in a low-price policy, see Edwin G. Nourse, *Price Making in a Democracy*, The Brookings Institution, Washington, 1944.
60. For example, *Dow and Magnesium*, p. 28.

agreement of 1931 on similar grounds, considering it alone. But when one views all these arrangements as parts of an organic whole, takes account of their restrictive features, and considers their avowed objectives, it is small wonder that they looked to the Department of Justice like a combination in restraint of trade.

In fact, on January 30, 1941 a federal grand jury returned indictments against Alcoa, Dow, MDC, AMC, and IG and certain of their officers alleging that they had unlawfully conspired and combined to restrain interstate and foreign trade in magnesium products.[61] On April 15, 1942 the Attorney General filed a civil complaint in the same jurisdiction setting forth similar charges.[62] The defendants chose not to contest the criminal action and entered pleas of *nolo contendere* and paid fines. The court then entered a consent decree in the civil case. The decree cancelled all patent licenses and licensing agreements among Alcoa, IG, Dow, AMC, and MDC. It threw open to the public the royalty-free use of their magnesium fabrication patents for the full terms of the patents, and of their production patents until six months after the end of the war. Thereafter the production patents must be licensed to any applicant on payment of reasonable royalties.

CONCLUSIONS

This record does not provide a judicial finding that the cartel arrangements reviewed are illegal under the antitrust laws. But the members of the cartel by their pleas of *nolo contendere* chose in open court not to dispute the government's contentions as to the illegality of their business arrangements. The Supreme Court has declared that such a plea of *nolo contendere* "admits guilt for the purposes of the case." [63]

But the legal significance of these cartel arrangements is of only collateral, or incidental, concern from the standpoint of the present study. Their economic significance is "writ large" in American experience. That the cartel tended to retard magnesium developments

61. See *U.S.* v. *The Dow Chemical Company, et al.,* in the U.S. District Court for the Southern District of New York, Criminal Action No. 109-191, and *U.S.* v. *American Magnesium Corporation, et al., ibid.,* No. 109-90.
62. *U.S.* v. *Aluminum Company of America, et al.,* in the U.S. District Court for the Southern District of New York, Civil Action No. 18-31.
63. See *Hudson* v. *U.S.,* 272 U.S. 451, 455 (1926).

by its discriminatory policies seems clear. The restrictions on the growth of the magnesium industry in this country are shown in the "stabilization" of output at a level of about 4.5 million pounds annually in the five years 1934–1938.[64] German output increased sixfold in that period; but this may be traced primarily to the influence of rearmament orders. However, general business activity was on the upgrade in the United States and conditions were favorable for an increasing demand for magnesium.[65]

It was not until 1939, when Dow's magnesium inventory had fallen to less than half a million pounds—less than a quarter of the amount that the single-seller himself declares was "needed to meet emergencies"—that the industry undertook any significant expansion of productive capacity.[66] Within two years, partly with the financial aid of the British Government, the industry finally laid plans for increasing domestic magnesium capacity to 36 million pounds, a sixfold increase over the 1938 output. In the next two years, to relieve the serious shortage, the American Government had to provide funds for a tenfold expansion of capacity. By the end of the war, domestic magnesium productive capacity had risen still further, to 586 million pounds a year.[67]

Thus, the cartel scheme, by cultivating a philosophy of restrictionism and a habit of discriminatory dealing, tended to retard domestic magnesium production and, inadvertently, to handicap national defense. The development of the magnesium industry on a noncompetitive basis before the war points to the need of some better means of insuring industrial expansion in the interests of the common welfare and a dynamic economy.

64. See Table 23. Actually, the only figures available for the first four of these years are, as shown in the table, for "primary metal produced and sold or used by the producer." The comparable item for 1938 is 4,819,617 pounds. These data conceal inventory changes, but we know from Dow's testimony before the Truman Committee that inventories sharply declined over this period as a whole. See Truman, Pt. XVII, Rept. No. 10, p. 7.

65. As an index of general business activity, national income rose 37 per cent from 1934 to 1937, and 25 per cent from 1934 to 1938. Indicating the magnitude of the rise in potential demand, the expansion of output in the domestic aviation industry in these five years was 127 per cent. While value figures of aircraft production are not available for 1938, apparently the growth of the industry was even more rapid, measured on this basis. See U.S. Department of Commerce, "Air Commerce Bulletins," and *Aviation*, Vol. XXXVIII (1939), No. 2.

66. See *Dow and Magnesium*, p. 36.

67. See *Magnesium Plants and Facilities*, Report of the Surplus Property Administration to the Congress, Washington, December 7, 1945, p. 29.

Chapter 8

THE INCANDESCENT ELECTRIC LAMP CARTEL

PHOEBUS IS the allegorical name given the international electric lamp cartel on its birth in 1924. But this prodigy had worthy forefathers, an acquaintance with whose exploits and characteristics throws more light on the cartel than its name.

Although the industry was nearly a half century old when the cartel was born, the business had developed from the outset on a monopolistic rather than a competitive pattern. The cartel was the culmination, not the inauguration, of a program to avoid competition in the manufacture and sale of electric lamps.

Early Patent Monopolies

Basic to the success of any international cartel is the organization of domestic markets. The electric lamp industry began in every major industrial country as a legal monopoly based on patent rights. The United States Bureau of Patents issued to Thomas A. Edison on January 27, 1880 a patent covering the first commercially successful incandescent electric lamp.[1] In England at about the same time, the British Government granted a patent for a similar lamp to Joseph W. Swan. When these patents ran out toward the close of the cen-

1. Patent No. 223,898. Edison's lamp consisted of four basic features: (1) a high resistant filament of carbon, (2) suspended in a vacuum, (3) enclosed in a glass bulb, (4) through which an electric current could be passed by lead-in wires of platinum. These elements were old. The British Government had granted the first patent on the incandescent lamp more than a generation earlier to Frederick De Moleyns. See John W. Howell and Henry Schroeder, *History of the Incandescent Lamp*, Maqua Company, New York, 1927, p. 29. Edison's patent was justified on the ground that it covered a combination of old elements to produce a new thing. See *Edison Electric Light Co.* v. *United States Electric Lighting Co.*, 52 Fed. 300 (1892). "But the degree of difference between carbons that lasted one hour and carbons that lasted hundreds of hours seems to have been precisely the difference between failure and success, and the combination which first achieved the result 'long desired, sometimes sought and never before attained,' is a patentable invention. . . . Finally and principally, by the substitution [of a carbon filament for platinum], there was presented the complete combination of elements, which for the first time in the art produced a practical electric light." *Ibid.*, p. 308.

tury, the industry became highly competitive in both countries. In Germany, where the courts held the patents invalid, competition had developed earlier. The leading producers of these countries promptly sought new ways to stabilize their markets.

General Electric Takes the Lead

In the United States the General Electric Company assumed leadership in this program. This company, formed by a consolidation in 1892 of Edison General Electric Company and the Thomson-Houston Company,[2] controlled the basic Edison patent, and until its expiration two years later had a virtual domestic monopoly in electric lamps.

When the basic patent expired and new producers entered the field, General Electric took two steps which tended to stabilize the domestic market. First, it entered into a cross-licensing patent agreement with its chief rival, Westinghouse Electric & Manufacturing Company,[3] providing for a "recognition of patents of each company by the other and the right, subject to certain exclusions, to a joint use thereof."[4] Second, it organized the Incandescent Lamp Manufacturers, an unincorporated association consisting of six independents which entered the field when the Edison patent expired. The association fixed prices, divided business, and allocated customers among its

2. Edison General Electric had been organized in 1889 to consolidate the several Edison companies engaged in the promotion and sale of electrical power and equipment. See J. W. Hammond, *Men and Volts*, Lippincott, New York, 1941, p. 156. Thomson-Houston Company, organized in 1884, was an aggressive rival of the Edison company and held valuable patents covering the production of alternating electric current.

3. On January 27, 1941 the government filed a complaint in the U.S. District Court for the District of New Jersey against the General Electric Company; International General Electric Company, Incorporated (a General Electric subsidiary); six of its licensees, including Westinghouse Electric & Manufacturing Co.; Corning Glass Works and two subsidiary patent-holding companies; and N. V. Philips Gloeilampenfabrieken, a Dutch concern operating on an international basis. The suit was brought under the antitrust laws. Trial of the case, which was begun in the spring of 1943, was suspended because of the war, after 7,344 pages of documentary evidence had been introduced by the government. It was resumed after the war's close, but by the summer of 1946 the case had not been decided. (This proceeding will hereinafter be cited: *U.S.* v. *G.E.,* Civil Action No. 1364.)

Westinghouse, incorporated in 1889, was successor to the Chartier Improvement Company, organized in 1872. Shortly after its incorporation Westinghouse Electric & Manufacturing Company acquired Westinghouse Electric Light Company, which had previously acquired Consolidated Electric Light Company and Sawyer-Man Electric Company. In 1893 after protracted litigation, the Edison Electric Light Co., a subsidiary of General Electric, got an injunction under its patent No. 223,898 against Sawyer-Man. See *ibid.,* Answer of Defendant Westinghouse Electric, par. 32.

4. General Electric Company's Fourth Annual Report to Stockholders, January 31, 1896.

members. It brought new producers into the arrangement as they entered the market.[5] Although Westinghouse was not a member it was a party to the price-fixing agreements.

General Electric Tightens Its Control

General Electric tightened its control over the industry by acquiring in 1901 a 75 per cent stock interest in the National Electric Lamp Company, which in turn acquired control of all members of the Incandescent Lamp Manufacturers Association. By 1911 National, which continued to acquire business rivals as they appeared, controlled eighteen subsidiaries in the lamp industry. Even though General Electric actually controlled them, National and its subsidiaries advertised themselves as separate and competing concerns.[6]

During the next decade General Electric took further steps to prevent competition in the sale of electric lamps. Together with other lamp manufacturers it made exclusive contracts with the manufacturers of lamp-making machinery and of bulbs and tubing, binding them to sell goods exclusively to General Electric and the companies associated with it, or to sell to competing companies only at discriminatory prices. Through tying contracts, it forced distributors to buy all their carbon filament lamps (on which the basic patent had expired) from General Electric and associated companies if they were to obtain lamps of improved design manufactured exclusively by General Electric and its associates. It also engaged in local price discrimination to drive rival manufacturers out of business.

In this way, General Electric maintained control of the domestic market for a decade and a half almost as effectively as it had under its basic Edison patent. Seventeen years after that patent had expired, wholly independent companies produced only 7 per cent of the entire

5. *U.S.* v. *General Electric Company, et al.,* No. 113, Supreme Court, October Term, 1926, Transcript of Record, p. 807 f. This was an antitrust suit involving the patent cross-licensing agreement between General Electric and Westinghouse and their marketing policies designed to maintain the resale price of lamps. The lower court opinion, in favor of the defendant, is reported in 15 Fed. 2d 715 (1925) and the Supreme Court opinion, affirming the judgment of the lower court, in 272 U.S. 476 (1926). (This proceeding will hereafter be cited: *U.S.* v. *G.E.* (1926).)

6. U.S. Tariff Commission, Report No. 133, Ser. II, *Incandescent Electric Lamps,* Washington, 1939, p. 33; and *U.S.* v. *G.E.* (1926), Transcript of Record, p. 808 f. See also, *U.S.* v. *General Electric, et al.,* U.S. Circuit Court for the Northern District of Ohio, Eastern Division, in Equity No. 8120, Final Decree. This was also an antitrust case. It never came to trial, however, being settled by a decree, entered by the court on October 12, 1911. It will hereafter be cited: *U.S.* v. *G.E.* (1911).

American output of incandescent lamps. General Electric produced directly 42 per cent and controlled through National 38 per cent more. Westinghouse produced 13 per cent,[7] but under its cross-licensing agreement with General Electric its price policy conformed to that of the industry's leader.

Court Finds Arrangement Illegal

In October 1911 a federal court held that General Electric, Westinghouse Electric & Manufacturing, Westinghouse Lamp Company, Corning Glass Works, National Electric Lamp Company, and twenty subsidiaries and five independents had violated the Sherman Antitrust Act. The court enjoined these companies from continuance of their unlawful practices.[8] It ordered the National Company to dissolve and General Electric to acquire its assets and those of its subsidiaries. This made clear to the public General Electric's relation to the bogus independents, but it did not disturb General Electric's dominant position in the industry. It merely consolidated General Electric's 42 per cent and National's 38 per cent control to give General Electric direct control of 80 per cent of the nation's lamp output. But the court did forbid the lamp manufacturers from collectively fixing prices and from making price maintenance contracts with lamp distributors.[9]

Though its decree was inadequate, the court apparently intended to create a commercial and legal environment favorable to the development of competition. Technological developments and General Electric's discovery of effective means for keeping a preponderant share of the business without violating the decree prevented this outcome. General Electric has continued to dominate the domestic market and to exert a stabilizing influence in world markets.

General Electric's Improvement Patents

After 1911 General Electric's control of the domestic market

7. Tariff Commission, *op. cit.,* p. 33; *U.S.* v. *G.E.* (1926), Transcript of Record, p. 858.

8. *U.S.* v. *G.E.* (1911), Final Decree. The court found "upon the petition that defendants are and have been engaged in unlawful agreements and combinations in restraint of trade and that the doing of the acts set forth in the petition and hereinafter enjoined are unlawful."

9. It recognized, however, the right of each defendant "to grant or receive from others appropriate manufacturing licenses under such patents [as the licensor lawfully owned] upon terms and conditions fixed by the licensor." *Ibid.*

rested largely on three improvements in the incandescent electric lamp: (1) the use of tungsten instead of carbon as a filament; (2) a process for drawing tungsten filaments economically and efficiently; and (3) the use of gas instead of a vacuum in the bulb. These made the electric lamp more efficient, cheaper, and more lasting. No producer who failed to use these improvements could compete effectively with those who did. But their use was promptly restricted by patents owned by General Electric.

Two Viennese scientists, Alexander Just and Franz Hanaman, invented a lamp using tungsten as a filament about 1910.[10] General Electric soon acquired American rights in their invention and on February 27, 1912 obtained Patent No. 1,018,502. In 1913 General Electric obtained the Coolidge patent covering drawn tungsten filament and in 1916 the Langmuir patent covering the use of gas. General Electric's scientists had developed both these improvements in the company's research laboratories.[11]

Cross-Licensing Agreements

Using to the full the bargaining strength these patents gave it, General Electric from time to time made cross-licensing patent agreements with its competitors. These agreements divided domestic markets, fixed prices at which its leading competitor sold lamps, and regulated exports.[12] They have varied in their details but they have generally recognized two classes of licensees—A and B, with different rights. Westinghouse is the only A licensee. The B licensees are Consolidated Electric Lamp, Hygrade Sylvania (now Sylvania Electric),

10. Just and Hanaman were poorly paid laboratory assistants in the Technical High School in Vienna. Howell and Schroeder, op. cit., p. 94.

11. U.S. v. G.E. (1926). In the language of the court, "These three patents cover completely the making of the modern electric lights with the tungsten filaments, and secure to the Electric Company the monopoly of their making, using and vending." (272 U.S. 476 at p. 481.)

12. In U.S. v. G.E. (1926) the Supreme Court affirmed the validity of the patent-licensing agreement between General Electric and Westinghouse. Nevertheless, after the government instituted the current antitrust suit, U.S. v. G.E., Civil Action No. 1364, General Electric drastically modified its licensing policy. On August 1, 1945 the parties cancelled the Westinghouse cross-licensing agreement, and replaced it with a new agreement providing for exchange of nonexclusive licenses on a royalty-free basis. See Business Week, August 11, 1945, p. 84; March 16, 1946, pp. 20-22. When the so-called "B" licenses (except that of Consolidated) expired on December 31, 1944, the parties did not renew them. Instead, a temporary arrangement took their place, pending the outcome of the current antitrust action. This took the form of a simple grant of immunity from patent infringement suits. Ibid., March 16, 1946, p. 24.

Chicago Miniature Lamp Works, Tung-Sol Lamp Works, and Ken-Rad Tube & Lamp (recently absorbed by Westinghouse).

Under the last agreement of record with Westinghouse, dated January 1, 1927 and executed June 15, 1928, each company gave the other a nonexclusive license on all its present and future United States patents covering improvements in electric lamps and machines, appliances, or processes for the manufacture of electric lamps.[13]

The agreement further provided for complete and continuing interchange of information "as to new inventions and developments (after patent applications have been filed) and as to technical and manufacturing methods and costs, machinery and processes employed . . . in the manufacture of electric lamps . . ." (Paragraph 23.) It also authorized General Electric to grant nonexclusive sublicenses on Westinghouse patents to its *B* licensees, provided they adhered to the same restrictions as General Electric imposed on them under its own patents.

The agreement provided that Westinghouse pay royalty of only one to 2 per cent on sales of tungsten lamps up to 25.4421 per cent [14] of the combined sales of General Electric and Westinghouse, but 30 per cent on sales in excess of this proportion. This in effect limited Westinghouse sales to this fixed proportion. Also, Westinghouse had to sell lamps at prices and on terms set by General Electric.

Each recognized the validity of the other's patents throughout the life of the agreement. Westinghouse was authorized to use General Electric's trade-mark "Mazda," a privilege denied to all other licensees.[15] The agreement covered domestic patents only and permitted sale of lamps abroad by Westinghouse only where General Electric was authorized to sell under its several agreements with foreign firms.

13. (Paragraphs 7 and 11.) The licensing agreement between General Electric and Westinghouse is reproduced in *U.S.* v. *G.E.*, Civil Action No. 1364, Ex. 25-G.

14. Payment of minimum royalties was applicable to sales by Westinghouse up to 22.4421 per cent of combined sales for 1927. Thereafter the percentage of combined sales carrying the minimum royalty increased annually at the rate of one per cent until it reached 25.4421.

15. Howell and Schroeder explain the significance of the Mazda trade-mark as follows: "Persian mythology gives to their ancient god of light the name of Ahura Mazda, and to the Persians, light was knowledge. Mazda service, therefore, very fittingly stands for the accumulation and transmission to lamp manufacturers of the knowledge which enables them to produce the best light." *Op. cit.*, p. 101. Joint use of a trade-mark by nominal competitors is good sales practice, too.

The agreements with the *B* licensees differed from that with Westinghouse in these particulars: They provided for smaller production quotas, larger minimum royalties, and smaller penalty royalties; restricted licensees to the production of either small or large lamps as specified in a particular agreement;[16] prohibited licensees from using General Electric's marks, "Mazda," "G.E.," or "National"; prohibited all export of lamps produced under the licensed patents. They did not require *B* licensees to conform to General Electric's prices.[17]

Nature of Patents Rights Granted to Licensees

General Electric's control over the American industry is based largely on its patents. The first *B* license was granted in 1916 after the Just and Hanaman patent was upheld by the Second Circuit Court of Appeals.[18] Following the expiration of the Just and Hanaman, Coolidge, and Langmuir patents, however, General Electric's control over its licensees has had a less secure patent foundation. In 1939 a General Electric official admitted the weakness of the patent structure when he wrote: "I presume the 'B' Licensees are growing restive under decreased patent protection that is available to them under our license in so far as incandescent lamps are concerned." [19]

General Electric officials had recognized as early as 1926 that the expiration of their basic patents would weaken their control of the industry. In April of that year George F. Morrison, who was then vice-president of General Electric, wrote:

The Vacuum Lamp . . . is covered by the Just and Hanaman and Coolidge Patents which expire . . . on February 27, 1929 and December 30, 1930, respectively. I believe there are no other patents owned by the General Electric

16. Incandescent lamps, of which there are approximately 9,000 sizes and types, vary from the tiny "grain of wheat" surgical lamp to the giant 10,000-watt lamp used for outdoor lighting. The purpose for which it is designed as well as its size determines whether a lamp be classified as large or small. Large lamps are used primarily in homes and in commercial and industrial establishments on 110- or 120-volt circuits and ordinarily vary in wattage from 7½ to 1,500. Small lamps are used in automobiles, toys, flashlights, radio panels, etc., on extremely low voltages.
17. The *B*-licensing agreement forms are reproduced in *U.S.* v. *G.E.*, Civil Action No. 1364, Ex. 29-G and Ex. 30-G.
18. *General Electric Co.* v. *Laco-Philips Co.*, 233 Fed. 96 (1916). See also *U.S.* v. *G.E.*, Civil Action No. 1364, Pre-Trial Brief for General Electric Co., p. 32.
19. *U.S.* v. *G.E.*, Civil Action No. 1364, Ex. 219-G, letter from M. L. Sloan to J. E. Kewley, October 3, 1939.

Company which would prevent others making this type of lamp when the Coolidge patent expires.[20]

Two years later another General Electric official expressed a more optimistic outlook. He said:

I believe we can establish the value of our patent property promptly . . . I think we would be considerably ahead even if more than half of our patents were invalidated, provided that the remaining portion were validated in such a manner that we could secure preliminary injunctions.[21]

In 1933 this same official wrote:

With the so-called basic patents all expired and with our decision not to take the Fink leading-in wire patent to court, there are three patents on which we now mainly rely.[22]

These three patents were: the Mitchell and White No. 1,423,956, July 25, 1922, for tipless bulbs; the Pacz No. 1,410,499, March 21, 1922, on nonsag filament; and the Pipkin No. 1,687,510, October 16, 1928, on frosted bulbs. Although these patents did protect General Electric's position for many years, ultimately two of the three were held invalid.

Patents and the Courts

The Pacz patent, which was to expire in 1939, was found invalid by the Supreme Court in 1938. In the language of the Court, "The claim is invalid on its face. It fails to make a disclosure sufficiently definite . . . Congress requires of the applicant 'a distinct and specific statement of what he claims to be new, and to be his invention.' . . . The limits of a patent must be known for the protection of the patentee, the encouragement of the inventive genius of others and the assurance that the subject of the patent will be dedicated ultimately to the public." [23]

On the implications of this decision for General Electric's patent position, a Hygrade Sylvania representative has commented:

20. *Ibid.*, Ex. 64-G. This letter is quoted in full on pp. 327-28, n. 75.
21. *Ibid.*, Ex. 208-G, Memorandum from Zay Jeffries to T. W. Frech, December 21, 1928.
22. *Ibid.*, Ex. 211-G, Memorandum from Zay Jeffries to T. W. Frech, October 19, 1933.
23. *General Electric Co. v. Wabash Appliance Corp., et al.*, 304 U.S. 364 (1938), at pp. 368-69.

The Court clearly shows that undue broadening of the scope of a patent will not be permitted; yet the G. E. cannot maintain its position without such broadening.[24]

The Pipkin inside frost patent was declared invalid in the latest court decision. It had previously experienced a varied court reception. By 1939 it had been "twice found invalid by lower courts, and twice found valid by Courts of Appeal . . ." [25] On December 9, 1942 it was again declared invalid by a district court which held that: "It is obvious that there was nothing new in either the interior mat surface defined by Pipkin in his claim, or the process identified therein as the method of producing it." [26]

The Court of Appeals of the Third Circuit upheld the district court's decision. This court held that the Pipkin patent was a product patent and as such did not disclose anything new. On November 7, 1945, the Supreme Court affirmed this decision.[27] The patent would normally have expired in October 1945, yet for sixteen years General Electric had enjoyed its almost uninterrupted protection.

Of General Electric's three most important patents since the expiration of the Langmuir patent, only the Mitchell and White product patent on tipless lamps passed court test. Although General Electric owned over 400 lamp patents, its patent position was apparently very weak. In 1937 J. W. Greenbowe, reporting to Westinghouse the results of a study of both Westinghouse and General Electric patents, concluded: "The picture presented is clear as to the patent values and leaves no doubt as to the actual lack of fundamental patent protection in either company." [28] After expiration of the so-called basic patents, therefore, General Electric maintained industry control by license agreements based on relatively unimportant patents or patents which were ultimately found invalid.

General Electric Controls Prices to Consumers

When it made the Westinghouse agreement, General Electric also

24. *U.S.* v. *G.E.*, Civil Action No. 1364, Ex. 215-G, Memorandum by Laurence Burns to J. Wooldridge, dated May 24, 1938.

25. *Ibid.*, Ex. 202-G, Memorandum by L. Burns to R. M. Zabel, April 5, 1939.

26. *General Electric Co.* v. *Jewel Incandescent Lamp Co., et al.*, in U.S. District Court for the District of New Jersey, Equity No. 5482; 55 USPQ, pp. 474 ff.

27. *General Electric Co.* v. *Jewel Incandescent Lamp Co., et al.*, 146 Fed. 2d 414 (1944); 67 USPQ, pp. 155 ff.

28. *U.S.* v. *G.E.*, Civil Action No. 1364, Ex. 213-G, letter from J. W. Greenbowe to D. S. Youngholm, dated July 30, 1937.

set up a plan to control wholesale and retail prices, although the 1911 decree had forbidden resale price maintenance contracts. Under the new plan, which the Supreme Court upheld, General Electric designates its wholesale and retail distributors as commission agents and requires them to sell lamps at such prices as General Electric determines. Westinghouse adopted an identical plan at the same time.[29]

In recent years General Electric and Westinghouse together have produced about 80 per cent, by value, of all the large lamps sold in the United States and General Electric alone has determined the prices at which these lamps are sold, both to first buyers and to ultimate consumers.[30] With General Electric's B licensees, they have supplied about 90 per cent. General Electric, its B licensees, and Westinghouse have also produced about 90 per cent, by value, of the domestic output of miniature lamps.[31] Twenty-two relatively small, high-cost, so-called independent companies, mostly located around New York City, handle the remaining 10 per cent. The export business in lamps is almost exclusively in the hands of General Electric and Westinghouse.

General Electric's Integration and Affiliations Facilitate Control

General Electric's links with allied industries and its integrated operation have strengthened its control of the domestic industry and helped it to stabilize international markets. Both General Electric

29. For the method of distribution, see *ibid.*, Answer of Defendant General Electric, pp. 29 ff., particularly pp. 29-38. General Electric has three major types of consumers: large customers (such as central stations, manufacturers, and railroads) to whom General Electric sells lamps directly; large consumers (such as manufacturers, mining companies, railroads, etc.) to whom General Electric's agents supply lamps under contracts between the customers and General Electric which the "agents" have negotiated; and general customers, to whom the agents supply lamps. Agents fall into various categories, most important of which are the wholesale and the retail groups. General Electric designates the distributors in each group and negotiates with each an agency contract. No agent (e.g., a wholesaler) determines the price at which any other agent (e.g., a retailer) shall sell the lamps handled by it. In 1941 approximately 15 per cent of General Electric's sales were to consumers of the second class; and approximately 58 per cent to general consumers. Under this method of selling, General Electric determines the price which ultimate consumers must pay for every lamp of its manufacture purchased. The Supreme Court upheld this arrangement in *U.S. v. G.E.* (1926).

30. This indicates that General Electric has lost ground relatively since 1911 when it acquired the business of National. At that time it alone handled about 80 per cent of domestic business.

31. *U.S. v. G.E.*, Civil Action No. 1364, Complaint, par. 102, and Answer of Defendant General Electric, par. 102.

and Westinghouse are producers of a full line of electrical machinery, equipment, and appliances.[32] General Electric makes in its own plants virtually all the parts and materials used in the production of lamps. So does Westinghouse—to a lesser extent. The manufacture of an incandescent lamp is essentially an assembly process, although "assembly" is now performed largely by automatic machinery. A lamp's more important parts are glass bulb, tungsten filament, stem, and base. The Corning Glass Works is the only domestic maker of glass bulbs for sale to manufacturers of large incandescent lamps and it is the principal source of glass tubing and rods for miniature bulbs.[33] General Electric is the only manufacturer of large lamps that also makes bulbs and is the sole domestic producer of a complete line of lamp bases. All other domestic lamp manufacturers, except Westinghouse, buy their bases from General Electric.

General Electric and Corning have been closely affiliated for more than three decades. The government alleges that they have pooled patents, restricted output by accepting quotas, and jointly fixed prices of glass bulbs and tubing.[34] Obviously, if independent manufacturers buy their bases from General Electric and their bulbs from Corning at prices set by arrangement with General Electric, they cannot compete effectively with General Electric either at home or abroad.

The manufacture of lamps in recent years has become a highly mechanized process. General Electric's influence over the market has been enhanced by restrictive patent-licensing agreements with manu-

32. As full-line suppliers of electrical machinery and equipment to electric light and power companies, which are important distributors of electric lamps and equipment, General Electric and Westinghouse start with a tremendous marketing advantage over smaller, specialized lamp manufacturers.
33. With the Corning ribbon machine, bulb making has become an almost completely automatic and amazingly high-speed process—800,000 bulbs a day being turned out by a single machine. Tariff Commission, *op. cit.,* p. 10.
34. The arrangements for these activities include the license agreements of January 9, 1914, and January 28 and March 30, 1922. General Electric, Corning, and Empire Machine (a glass-machinery-patent-holding company in which Corning had a controlling interest) granted to American Blank Company exclusive licenses under their United States patents covering the production of glass bulbs and tubing and glass-making machinery. In return, Corning and General Electric received from American Blank nonexclusive rights to the use of such patents. Other arrangements include the sales agreements of January 1922, February 1929, and November 1935 between General Electric and Corning which fixed the percentage of the former's glass bulb and tubing requirements to be supplied by the latter. These agreements also regulated Corning's prices, not alone in its sales to General Electric but also in its sales to General Electric's competitors. See *U.S.* v. *G.E.,* Civil Action No. 1364, Complaint, pars. 7, 8, 71-74, and 181, and corresponding paragraphs in defendants' Answers. See also Exs. 555-G to 571-G.

facturers of lamp-making machinery, who together with General Electric make most such machinery produced in the United States.[35]

Thus General Electric has controlled the American electric lamp industry through its own and acquired patents, through aggressive leadership directed toward price stabilization and output regulation, through absorbing trade rivals, through patent pooling, and through restrictive cross-licensing agreements. This control kept other American producers from disturbing world markets, in which General Electric had a large stake and which it wanted to stabilize.

Early Development in Germany

Outside the United States, Germany took the lead in the lamp industry, and before World War I had become the world's leading exporter. The German industry was indirectly associated with the American Edison interests. The German Edison Company (Deutsche Edison Gesellschaft), predecessor of (German) General Electric (Allgemeine Elektrizitäts Gesellschaft, commonly known as AEG), was licensed by the Edison Continental Company of Paris in 1881 to manufacture incandescent lamps under the Edison patents on a

---

35. A case in point is the agreement reached between General Electric and Alfred Hofmann & Company (one of the two more important independent manufacturers of lamp-making machinery) dated April 26, 1924. When this agreement was made the world's leading producers were negotiating the world cartel. The Hofmann agreement apparently was designed to promote the cartel by preventing the export of American-made lamp-making machinery which might disturb the cartel arrangements. In a letter dated January 21, 1924, George F. Morrison, vice-president of General Electric, wrote with respect to the importance of controlling the manufacture and sale of lamp-making machinery as follows: "Our purpose, of course, . . . is to get the manufacture of our lamp making machinery under control with a view to protecting our foreign as well as our domestic interests." Ibid., Ex. 338-G, p. 1770. On April 9, 1921 J. M. Woodward, the European representative of International General Electric, wrote as follows: "In Paris there is an agency representing Alfred Hofman . . . whose catalogue contains illustrations of patented G. E. lamp making machinery, which are offered for sale in France . . . to the great disturbance of the situation *which we are trying to establish.* . . . Will you please consider stopping this infringement at the place where it is easiest to stop it." Ibid., Ex. 330-G, p. 1754 f. Italics supplied.

The outcome was the agreement negotiated by General Electric with Hofmann. It provided: that General Electric would grant Hofmann a royalty-free license to manufacture lamp-making machinery under its patents and patent applications and to sell such machinery only to domestic licensees of General Electric for their own use within the United States; that Hofmann would grant General Electric a royalty-free nonexclusive license to use its patents and product improvements; that Hofmann would admit the validity of General Electric patents and patent applications; that Hofmann would not export or sell for export lamp-making machinery without specific permission from General Electric; and that Hofmann would transmit to General Electric a report on sales of and inquiries concerning lamp-making machinery. See ibid., Ex. 327-G. This agreement was terminated in February 1930 with the payment of $65,000 to Hofmann by General Electric in settlement of claims for damages. Ibid., Ex. 328-G.

royalty basis. The German Edison subsequently agreed with Siemens & Halske, a leading rival manufacturer of electrical equipment, to share Edison patent rights and divide markets.

The German companies ended the agreement with Edison Continental in 1887 because of patent difficulties. During the next decade such rigorous competition developed that the price of incandescent lamps declined from 5 marks in 1886 to 1.6 marks in 1894. Out of this struggle three full-line electrical equipment companies emerged as the leading German producers of lamps—AEG, Siemens & Halske, and the German Incandescent Gas Burner Company (Deutsche Gasglühlichtgesellschaft).

Trend Toward Cartelized Control

In 1903, AEG and Siemens & Halske took the lead in organizing the first European electric lamp cartel, Verkaufsstelle Vereinigter Glühlampenfabriken. The cartel, which established uniform prices for all its members, included the eleven leading manufacturers of Germany, Austria, Hungary, Italy, Holland, and Switzerland. Although the cartel continued to operate until March 31, 1914, technical developments in manufacturing undermined its effectiveness.

In 1902 the German Incandescent Gas Burner Company placed on the market the first lamp utilizing a metallic filament (osmium wire) instead of carbon. A few years later Siemens & Halske produced a tantalum filament lamp. Meanwhile Just and Hanaman had developed the tungsten filament, and AEG had secured the German rights to General Electric's tungsten wire-drawing process. Thereupon AEG, Siemens & Halske, and Auergesellschaft (successor to the German Incandescent Gas Burner Company) organized the Drahtkonzern, popularly known as the Filament Trust, under which the three German concerns pooled their principal lamp patents.

A sharp rise in sales and uncertainty about patents on metal filaments and the wire-drawing process brought many new firms into the field. However, when a Reich court in 1917 upheld the tungsten wire-drawing patent, most of the newcomers had to quit. Among those that survived were Julius Pintsch A. G., which had developed its own process for making "crystal" filaments, the Bergmann Elektrizitäts Werke, operating under a license from Siemens & Halske, and the

Wipperfürth Radio-Electric Company.[36] In the same year these three companies and the Filament Trust entered into a cartel price-fixing agreement. Later important central European manufacturers joined this cartel.

Postwar Developments in Germany

World War I further centralized control of the German industry, but it also impaired Germany's position in world markets. By the close of the war, German exports had disappeared, foreign branch factories had been seized, and "Osram," the trade-mark under which the foreign business had been largely conducted, had passed into foreign hands.[37] In several countries new domestically owned factories had been opened, old plants had been expanded, and tariff protection of home markets had been granted.

So in 1919 the Germans took steps to regain their lost markets and establish a more rigorous control of the domestic market. The three leading German lamp manufacturers, AEG, Siemens & Halske, and Auergesellschaft, which had previously pooled their lamp patents and sold lamps at uniform prices, segregated their lamp businesses from their other operations and consolidated them into a single enterprise. They merged patents and trade-marks, technical experience, inventories, and manufacturing facilities and sales organizations under the common ownership of Osram G. m. b. H., Kommanditgesellschaft, a business partnership which also had the advantage of limited liability.[38]

Just before this, Auergesellschaft had acquired the lamp business of the Wipperfürth Radio-Electric Company. Now Osram acquired the Augsburg Wolfram Lamp Company,[39] and then the lamp division of the Bergmann Electric Works. Of the more important lamp manufacturers only Julius Pintsch A. G. remained as a separate concern. With control over the domestic market tightened, Osram turned its attention to Germany's lost foreign markets.

36. League of Nations, *Review of the Economic Aspects of Several International Industry Agreements*, Geneva, 1930, p. 68.
37. The trade-mark "Osram" is a contraction of osmium and wolfram, the ore from which tungsten is obtained.
38. This corporate exercise in cake eating and having was achieved by confining the unlimited liability of the partnership to a single partner (as German law permits) and making this partner a limited liability company.
39. League of Nations, *op. cit.*, p. 69.

The Dutch Industry

In this effort Osram was confronted at the outset by the vigorous rivalry of the N. V. Philips Gloeilampenfabrieken of Eindhoven, Holland, which alone produced far more than all other Dutch lamp manufacturers combined.

N. V. Philips stems from a small business established in 1891 by Frederick Philips, a banker, and his son, Gerard, a chemical engineer. It acquired its present corporate name in 1912. Since 1920 it has been controlled by a holding company, N. V. Gemeenschappelyk Bezit van Aandeelen Philips Gloeilampenfabrieken. The holding company owns 96 per cent and 86 per cent, respectively, of Philips' outstanding preferred and common stocks. It in turn is closely controlled by the holders of only ten preferred shares, representing six thousandths of one per cent of the paid-in capital stock of Bezit. These shares are believed to be owned exclusively by the Philips family.

The Philips company grew and prospered greatly during World War I. Before the war it had imported all its glass bulbs and argon gas from Germany and Austria. With these sources cut off, Philips built its own plants to make these items.[40] Holland's neutrality enabled Philips to expand its export of lamps to continental Europe and to other foreign markets at enormous profit.[41]

By 1929 Philips had become the world's largest exporter of incandescent lamps.[42] It was an almost completely integrated company, making its own glass bulbs, tungsten wire, argon gas, and other materials. While it purchased its lamp bases from Holland's single base manufacturer, Philips had a stock interest in this concern. In addition, Philips owned about thirty factories in England, Norway, Czechoslovakia, Poland, Italy, Spain, Switzerland, Argentina, and, with Anglo-American interests, in Australia.[43]

The British Industry

Osram's second most important competitor was the British indus-

---

40. Arthur Balink, "The City of Light; Story of Dr. Anton F. Philip II," *Knickerbocker Weekly* (New York), June 21, 1943, Vol. III, No. 17, p. 20 f.

41. Between 1912 and 1919 Philips' dividends on common stock were increased from 7 to 151 per cent. *Moody's Manual of Investments* (Industrials), 1940, p. 2406.

42. Tariff Commission, *op. cit.*, p. 61. In 1929 the Netherlands exported lamps valued at $11,171,000 (practically all of which were exported by Philips) while Germany exported lamps valued at $8,927,000. By 1937, German exports exceeded in value exports from the Netherlands.

43. *Ibid.*, p. 72.

try.[44] Although concentration in the control of the industry had not gone so far, pre-1914 developments in Great Britain had broadly paralleled those of the United States and the major European countries. The industry had begun in Britain as a legal monopoly. The Edison-Swan Electric Company, Ltd., with patents covering the carbon filament lamp, was the sole British producer of electric lamps until the basic patent expired.[45] Thereafter competition promptly developed and remained vigorous until the introduction of the tungsten filament lamp.

In 1907 General Electric Company, Ltd., acquired British patent rights for the tungsten filament lamp from both the Austrian and German patent holders and erected the first English factory for metal filament lamps.[46] In 1909 the British Thomson-Houston Company acquired British rights to (American) General Electric's drawn tungsten filament lamp, and in 1913 to its gas-filled lamp. Soon after, (British) General Electric entered into a contract with the Philips company to build an argon plant in England.[47]

Centralized Control Established

To eliminate patent conflicts, promote technological improvement, and control the market, British Thomson-Houston, (British) General Electric, Edison-Swan Electric, and Siemens Brothers, Ltd. (the British branch of Siemens & Halske) organized the Tungsten Lamp Association in 1913.[48] This setup provided for an exchange of patents and for division of the market on a quota basis.

During the war as demand expanded, the Association relaxed its

44. The value of British exports of metal filament lamps in 1929, according to the Tariff Commission, was $3,218,000. *Ibid.*, p. 61.

45. This company was an amalgamation, in 1883, of the Edison Electric Light Co., Ltd., and the Swan United Electric Light Co., Ltd. See *Stock Exchange Official Intelligence* (London), 1885 and 1895.

46. See Sub-Committee appointed by the Standing Committee on Trusts, Parliamentary Report, Command Paper 622, Findings and Decisions on the Electric Lamp Industry, London, 1920, p. 3. (This work will hereinafter be cited: Standing Committee on Trusts.)

General Electric Co., Ltd., was originally strictly an English company and not an offshoot of the American firm of the same name. In fact the British firm first used the words "General Electric" in its corporate title in 1886, three years before the American company was incorporated. Originally a merchandising concern solely, apparently it was not until it had developed manufacturing interests on an extensive scale, after the turn of the century, that it had any corporate relationship or connection with the American company. See Adam G. Whyte, *Forty Years of Electrical Progress*, E. Benn, Ltd., London, 1930.

47. Standing Committee on Trusts, p. 3.

48. *Ibid.*, p. 4.

enforcement of market quotas. In 1917 the Association's control of the market was impaired when British courts declared invalid the patents on which British Thomson-Houston claimed exclusive control of the drawn tungsten patents.[49] Faced with insecurity in their patents and more vigorous competition at home and overseas, the members of the Association established a closer relationship by incorporating as the Electric Manufacturers' Association of Great Britain, Ltd., and pooling patents. Besides British Thomson-Houston, (British) General Electric, Siemens Brothers, and Edison-Swan, the new association included six smaller concerns. Association members produced 90 to 95 per cent of all incandescent lamps manufactured in Great Britain.

The major companies pooled about one hundred patents,[50] and licensed the other companies on a royalty basis. Licensees agreed not to dispute the validity of the patents during the life of the agreement. They continued to buy their drawn wire exclusively from British Thomson-Houston, even after its patent was held invalid by the House of Lords.[51]

The Association has enforced a common price policy among its members, and has controlled the prices paid by consumers through resale price maintenance contracts supported by black lists and discriminatory discounts.[52] Through the Association the British industry was prepared to present a united front in its struggle for postwar markets. Moreover, concentration of control in the British industry went further. In 1928 British Thomson-Houston, Edison-Swan, Metropolitan Vickers Electrical Company, Ltd. (controlled by Westinghouse), and Ferguson Company amalgamated as the Associated Electrical Industries, Ltd. After this step Associated Electrical, (British) General Electric, and Siemens were the big three in England.[53]

The French Industry

France's part in the postwar international trade in electric lamps was not so important as that of American, German, Dutch, and Brit-

49. *Ibid.*, p. 11. The case was an infringement suit, *British Thomson-Houston* v. *Messrs. Duram, Ltd.* It was carried through the High Court of Justice, the Court of Appeals, and the House of Lords. All found for the defendant.
50. Committee on Industry and Trade (Balfour Committee), *Survey of Metal Industries*, London, 1928, Pt. IV, p. 319 (hereinafter cited: Balfour Committee).
51. Standing Committee on Trusts, p. 11.
52. *Ibid.*, p. 5.
53. See League of Nations, *op. cit.*, p. 72.

ish producers. France as a net importer of lamps was the best European market for surplus domestic output of the other countries. Imports of metal filament lamps into France in 1929 exceeded in dollar value those of any important lamp-manufacturing country.[54] At the same time France ranked fifth in dollar value of lamp exports.

The French industry after World War I was dominated largely by two full-line electrical machinery and equipment companies—Compagnie Française Thomson-Houston and Compagnie Générale d'Électricité. These two companies and a third, the Établissements Larnaude, merged their lamp departments in 1921 to form the Compagnie des Lampes. After the merger, Compagnie des Lampes still further concentrated control of the industry by acquiring the stock or assets of competing companies.[55]

Community of Interest Among Leading National Groups

The postwar era found the world's leading lamp manufacturers closely organized on a national basis. A considerable community of interest also had developed among the more important national groups through exchange of patents and through stock ownership. General Electric from the outset had promoted its interests in foreign markets by an exchange of patent rights with foreign corporations under which each exploited separate markets.[56]

General Electric had entered into at least three such patent agreements with foreign companies as early as 1905. Within less than a year after its organization, it made an agreement with the French company, Compagnie Française pour l'Exploitation des Procédés Thomson-Houston, in which General Electric owned a stock interest. In 1904 it made a similar agreement with a Japanese concern, Tokyo Electric Company, Ltd.,[57] and the next year it acquired a controlling interest in that company.

54. Tariff Commission, *op. cit.*, p. 61. French imports in 1929 were valued at $2,429,000 while French exports were valued at $860,000.

55. The two most important companies thus acquired were Compagnie Lorraine des Lampes and Société Lacarrière. Compagnie des Lampes has also expanded its operations in foreign countries through subsidiaries. League of Nations, *op. cit.*, p. 71 f.

56. "The General Electric Co. as leader in the industry generally has been able to obtain from foreign companies cash payments variously described as 'royalties,' 'service charges,' or 'retainers' that partake of the nature both of charges for services and information and royalties for the use of patents." Federal Trade Commission, *Electric-Power Industry, Supply of Electrical Equipment and Competitive Conditions*, S.Doc. 46, 70th Cong., 1st sess., Washington, 1928, p. 140.

57. *Ibid.*, p. 145.

On May 25, 1905 General Electric signed an agreement with British Thomson-Houston (in which it also owned a controlling stock interest) providing for an "exchange of patents, information and selling rights in specified territories." [58] The agreement recognized North America and the colonies and protectorates of the United States as General Electric's exclusive territory, the United Kingdom as the exclusive territory of British Thomson-Houston.

General Electric early adopted the policy of acquiring stock interest in foreign firms with which it made patent agreements. On January 31, 1894 when General Electric made its second annual report to its stockholders, it owned a stock interest with a par value of $163,000 in Union Elektrizitäts Gesellschaft of Germany. General Electric's ownership interest in this German firm continued until 1904. On AEG's absorption of Union in that year, General Electric obtained a financial stake in the German consolidation. [59] AEG was the successor to Deutsche Edison Gesellschaft established in 1883. According to Liefmann, General Electric had "stood godfather" at AEG's founding. [60] General Electric's total investment in foreign companies as reported to stockholders had increased from $530,743.63 in January 1893 to $4,423,294 (par value) in January 1906. [61] It owned a stock interest with a par value of $125,950 in British Thomson-Houston as early as 1896. [62] General Electric increased this interest from time to time until by 1902 it had acquired control of the British company. [63]

Germans Cooperate Internationally

Before World War I the "big three" German producers had begun to apply to foreign markets the principle of cooperation which they had developed in their home market. AEG, Siemens & Halske, and Auergesellschaft, all with British branches, concluded an agree-

---

58. *Ibid.*, p. 142.
59. League of Nations, *op. cit.*, p. 67.
60. Robert Liefmann, *Cartels, Concerns and Trusts*, Methuen & Co., London, 1932, p. 248.
61. The first figure represents the value of "rights in foreign countries under patents of Thomson, Rice and others including contracts for delivery of $100,000 stock of Canadian General Electric and substantial interests in other manufacturing and exploitation organizations in foreign countries." See First Annual Report to Stockholders, January 31, 1893. The latter figure is the par value of stocks owned in "sundry foreign companies." See Fourteenth Annual Report, January 31, 1906.
62. Fourth Annual Report, January 31, 1896.
63. See General Electric's Tenth Annual Report to Stockholders, January 31, 1902.

ment in 1912 with British manufacturers for exchange of patents in England.[64] In the same year they signed a contract with Compagnie Française Thomson-Houston (in which General Electric owned a substantial stock interest and with which it had a patent exchange agreement) covering the exploitation of the Thomson-Houston processes. In 1913 they concluded similar agreements with the Philips company in Holland, with the Watt Company of Vienna, and with United Incandescent Lamp & Electricity Company of Hungary.[65]

World War I Suspends International Cooperation

World War I upset the community of interest among the important national groups which had lessened competition in world markets. By the warring nations' seizure and sale of alien enemy property, lamp manufacturers lost the foreign properties through which they had shared in the domestic business of enemy countries. The war severed international business connections and impaired personal business relationships among the nationals of the leading industrial countries. It also dislocated customary channels of world trade.

The Central European countries had lost most of their foreign markets. Producers in neutral countries and in the more fortunately situated Allied countries had seized the war-given opportunity to expand their foreign trade and put it on a firmer footing. This had contributed to an increase in productive capacity far beyond customary requirements. According to the Balfour Committee, world demand for electric lamps at the close of the war could have been supplied by half the existing capacity.[66]

Before the war Germany had customarily exported more than 50 per cent of her output of incandescent electric lamps.[67] As Osram set out to regain its foreign markets it encountered the competition of its former rivals and of its own former foreign subsidiaries as well. It also met higher tariff walls. Rather than try to export over these barriers, Osram built new plants abroad or bought an interest in existing plants. Between 1919 and 1924 Osram either acquired a share in going concerns, or established new subsidiaries in Czechoslovakia,

64. League of Nations, *op. cit.*, p. 68.
65. *Ibid.*
66. Balfour Committee, p. 59.
67. League of Nations, *op. cit.*, p. 69.

Sweden, Poland, Switzerland, and Austria.[68] Germany's re-entrance into world markets aggravated the problem of overcapacity. Unless conflicting interests could be reconciled, a vigorous postwar competitive struggle was imminent.

Technology Intensifies Competition

Technological developments also tended to intensify competition and increase its hazards. The manufacture of electric lamps had emerged from the handicraft stage and had become a highly mechanized and largely automatic process. It involved comparatively large investment of fixed capital in extremely specialized plants with a relatively high proportion of overhead costs and low labor costs per unit of output.

Standardization of lamps had contributed to the industry's mechanization. A reduction in the number and size of lamp bases and sockets was the first step in standardization. Since 1900, in residential installations in the United States, a standard socket and base has replaced 175 sizes. Most lamps produced in this country now use only seven standard bases.[69] Introduction of the tungsten filament made possible the second major step toward standardization. Tungsten lamps can be manufactured more closely to voltage specifications than carbon filament lamps. This permits standardization of circuit voltages. More than 90 per cent of the lamps used for general lighting in the United States now are made for only two voltages; four voltages cover 99 per cent of the output. Standardization during the twenties reduced from forty-five to six the number of lamp types for general lighting, in the wattage range from fifteen to one hundred.[70]

Simplification and standardization made feasible automatic machinery and mass production. Eighty-six technological innovations from 1907 to 1931 reduced tremendously the labor time per unit of output.[71] Between 1920 and 1931 the number of man-hours per lamp declined by 77.2 per cent—from 0.099809 to 0.022743. In 1920 domestic assembly plants produced 362,140,000 electric lamps with an

68. Ibid., p. 69 f.
69. Tariff Commission, op. cit., p. 40.
70. Ibid., p. 41.
71. Witt Bowden, Technological Changes and Employment in the Electric Lamp Industry, Bulletin 593, Bureau of Labor Statistics, U.S. Department of Labor, 1933, pp. 30-32.

average labor force of 17,283; in 1931 they produced 503,350,000 lamps with an average labor force of only 5,817.[72] Mechanization, accompanied by an increase in the ratio of fixed to variable costs, increased the most economical scale of production. But it also increased the financial hazards of unrestricted competition; large-scale producers were increasingly unwilling to risk their stakes in free markets.

Demand for Electric Lamps Is Inelastic

The mechanization of the industry and the postwar surplus capacity promised, in the absence of a control program to prevent it, a sharp increase in the output of electric lamps. Unfortunately they did not promise a compensating expansion in the market for electric lamps. In the technical language of economists, the demand for incandescent lamps is inelastic. A decrease in price will not be accompanied, other influences remaining unchanged, by a proportionate increase in expenditures for lamps.

This is true for four main reasons: Expenditures for electric lamps constitute a relatively small part of total family or business budgets; the need for them has through habit become urgent but it is virtually a fixed, or constant, need; there are no satisfactory substitutes for electric lamps; and the demand for them is a joint demand, being a demand for lamps, lamp fixtures, and electricity.

The cost of electricity is more important than the cost of lamps. Once electricity is available and lighting equipment has been installed, lamp prices will exert but little influence on the use of lamps. Total sales of lamps will respond only slightly to changes in their price. A 50 per cent reduction in the price of a 20 cent electric bulb built to last 1,000 hours is unlikely to affect noticeably the owner's use of the bulb or his promptness in replacing it when it is worn out.

An increase in the importance of fixed capital in the production process, plant capacity in excess of normal requirements, and an inelastic demand, all made competition more hazardous and cartelization more attractive to the postwar incandescent electric lamp industry.

General Electric Is Interested in Protecting Its Domestic Market

General Electric, the world's largest manufacturer of electric lamps, with a domestic market which absorbed 50 per cent of the world's

72. *Ibid.*, p. 1.

annual output, had a definite stake in stabilization of world markets. The magnitude of the American market would inevitably attract mass producers from other countries unless barriers were erected to keep them out. Officials of International General Electric (hereinafter International), General Electric's subsidiary in control of the company's foreign interests, were apparently fearful of the threat of competition from abroad.

During negotiations preceding the formation of Phoebus in the spring of 1924, J. M. Woodward, in charge of International's European incandescent lamp business, warned A. W. Burchard, president of International, of the danger of competition in the American market from the Philips company. Under Anton Philips' leadership it was expanding greatly the scope of its operations. Mr. Woodward wrote Mr. Burchard in part as follows:

But I may again say by way of emphasis that I desire to effect an arrangement which will be to the absorbing interest of the Philips Company throughout as much of the remaining "useful life" of Anton Philips as possible. He, and practically he alone, constitutes a danger to our American profits. Should our patent protection at any time become weak in all or part of America he will be our greatest menace, the least vulnerable and the most resourceful of our competitors. He is insanely anxious to get into England, and for my part, if I could arrange it on a sound basis and without losing all my personal friends locally, I would get him there in short order. England is the greatest bait, carefully handled, which can be held out to him, and if we exercise the ordinary principles involved in poker, I am satisfied that we can make arrangements which will be profitable and satisfactory for a long time to come.[73]

In a letter written soon after Phoebus was formed, an International official expressed the same fear to another official of the same company. He advised that it was necessary

. . . to establish with our European associates a patent holding company that would control, insofar as possible, all of the patents and rights in connection with machinery and applications dealing with the modern manufacture of incandescent lamps. This policy . . . anticipated in addition to the perpetual control of patents on such machines remaining in the hands of the General Electric Company and its associates, the protection of the business of our several interests in their respective fields of activity, not the least im-

73. *U.S.* v. *G.E.*, Civil Action No. 1364, Ex. 2112-G.

portant of which is the domestic business of the General Electric Company.[74]

General Electric officials frequently have placed on record their fear of impending competition and their intention to use cross-licensing patent agreements to build a market structure so stable that the expiration of General Electric's basic patents could not shake it. For example, on April 28, 1926, before negotiation of a new patent-licensing agreement with Westinghouse, George F. Morrison, then vice-president of General Electric, wrote to Gerard Swope, then president of General Electric, calling attention to the early expiration of the three basic patents covering the tungsten lamp on which General Electric's control of the market primarily rested. Mr. Morrison acknowledged the stabilizing influence that General Electric's license agreements at home and abroad had exerted and indicated that an agreement with Westinghouse was essential to prevent encroachment upon General Electric's American market by either domestic or foreign competitors.[75]

74. *Ibid.*, Ex. 387-G. Formation of the cartel did not dispel General Electric's fear that uncontrolled foreign markets would constitute a threat to its domestic operations. In 1937, commenting on the possible termination of International's contracts with Osram, an International official indicated that while he did not fear exports of lamps by Osram to the United States, unless it were aided by a government subsidy, he realized that "There is very real danger Osram might sell lamp making equipment to unlicensed manufacturers in the United States who are in great need of efficient machinery." For this and other reasons, the official indicated that "we would view with considerable alarm the cancellation of Osram contract." *Ibid.*, Memorandum by Philip Reed, Ex. 72-G.

75. *Ibid.*, Ex. 64-G. This letter throws so much light on the major objective of General Electric's patent-licensing program that we quote it in full.
"The important patents on which our Lamp Agreement with the Westinghouse Electric & Manufacturing Company is based are as follows:
"The Just and Hanaman Patent, covering broadly all kinds of tungsten filament lamps; expiring February 27, 1929.
"The Coolidge Patent, covering an incandescent lamp having a filament or [*sic*] drawn tungsten wire, either vacuum or gas-filled; expiring December 30, 1930.
"The Langmuir Patent, covering all commercial forms of gas-filled or Type 'C' Lamps; expiring April 18, 1933.
"The Vacuum Lamp, which represents 54% of our Lamp business in dollars and 70% in numbers, is covered by the Just and Hanaman and Coolidge Patents which expire, as stated above, on February 27, 1929 and December 30, 1930, respectively. I believe there are no other patents owned by the General Electric Company which would prevent others making this type of lamp when the Coolidge patent expires.
"It is unnecessary to enumerate here the many advantages that have accrued to the General Electric Company, the Westinghouse Company and the lamp industry as a whole, both in this country and in foreign lands, in the way of standardization, simplification and stabilization of the lamp industry as a result of our Lamp License Agreements. In view of the short time that will elapse before the expiration of these important patents it behooves us to at this time give very serious and careful thought to the

General Electric's Foreign Business Consolidated

To consolidate and supervise its foreign business and to extend its licensing program abroad General Electric in 1919 organized a wholly owned subsidiary, the International General Electric Company, Incorporated.[76] General Electric promptly made an agreement with In-

working out of a plan that will insure the continuance of the very satisfactory license agreements and to co-operative arrangements which have contributed so much in the past to the development of the electrical industry as a whole, and made possible such satisfactory profits to those engaged in the business.

"I think we have the necessary material, in the way of important process patents, to form the basis of an agreement that would extend for many years beyond the expiration of the present agreements.

"The first step in this direction would be to take up negotiations with the Westinghouse Company for an extension of their present agreement, . . . Just how far we would have to go in this direction would be a matter of negotiation.

"On various occasions during the past three years I have discussed this matter with Mr. Cary [vice-president of Westinghouse Lamp Company] and taken the position that we would not expect in any new arrangement to give the Westinghouse Company a participation in excess of 20%. This of course was not satisfactory to him, and he has mentioned a figure of 30%. We no doubt could compromise on 25%. Perhaps we could satisfy them with a smaller percentage, but I doubt it. I believe that we would be justified in going this far if we could make an arrangement that would permit them to reach this increased figure over a period of years, they getting a larger percentage of the growth in the business than we during the period agreed upon—say a growth of 1% per year during five years. Under our present agreement they pay us 1% royalty on their net sales up to their allotment, and for sales in excess of this they pay us 1% plus 10%. In a new arrangement permitting them a larger allotment I would insist that upon sales in excess of this allotment they pay a higher royalty than the 10% they now pay on their excess. In fact, I would make the excess royalty so high that there would be no incentive for them to go beyond their allotment, say, a 25% royalty.

"Whether or not we would be successful in getting the Westinghouse Company to pay us an increased royalty on the increased business allotted to them, over their present allotment of 17.25%, is problematic. We might try on something like this.—They are running now at about 20%. We might let them continue to do 20% on the present royalty basis of 1% and increase the royalty by one-half of 1% for each percent they increase over 20% and up to the new percentage agreed upon, say, 25%. Personally I would not be so keen about increasing their present royalty on the increased allotment above their present allotment as I would be about fixing a high royalty for any excess done beyond the percentage agreed upon.

"The Westinghouse Company, of course, is the key to any lamp license arrangement in this country, and we must get them in line before making any arrangement with the other Licensees. In fact, it is necessary to get the Westinghouse Company in line if we are to be successful in working out arrangements with the foreign lamp manufacturers. You are familiar with the work that has been done and the plans that we have been developing in foreign countries during the past twenty-four years, all for the purpose of protecting our domestic lamp business against foreign encroachment when our important patents expire. That time is rapidly approaching. No better stimulus to the necessity of continuing these activities could be given than frequent reviews of what is going to happen to our lamp business when these important patents expire. The fact that we have had in this country such a satisfactory plan of co-operation between the various manufacturers has been helpful in getting the co-operation of the foreign manufacturers. It is of the utmost importance, therefore, that we have our house in order here, and as I have stated in the foregoing, the first step in this direction is to get the Westinghouse Company lined up in a new agreement."

76. A small portion of its preferred stock is owned by General Electric Employees Securities Corporation, all of whose stock is owned by General Electric. See *ibid.*, Answer of Defendant General Electric, par. 4.

ternational providing that General Electric would confine itself to the United States, its possessions, colonies, territories, and dependencies (exclusive of the Philippines, Puerto Rico, and the Virgin Islands), and that International would cover the rest of the world. General Electric made International its sole agent abroad, and gave it power of attorney "to deal with, cancel, modify, carry out" all business arrangements in foreign countries, including the right "to vote all shares owned by General Electric in any foreign company." [77]

General Electric assigned to International all its trade-marks and trade names for use in foreign countries, and each company agreed to assign to the other all its patents, present and future, and rights under patent applications, for exclusive use in their territories. Each agreed to keep the other fully informed on its "patent situation," and General Electric agreed to give International "access to its factories at all reasonable times, and shall furnish all data, drawings, etc., as requested by the International Company or by those designated by it."

International Makes Patent Agreements With Foreign Companies

Armed with these broad powers, International negotiated agreements with the world's principal manufacturers to exchange patents and technical experience and to delimit exclusive and nonexclusive sales areas. Under these agreements, the home country of each party constitutes its exclusive sales territory. Within it the domestic producer secures the sole right to manufacture and sell electric lamps under all patents of both parties.

These agreements protect General Electric from the competition of all major foreign producers, their subsidiaries and affiliates (except the Russian industry and numerous small Japanese companies) in the manufacture or sale of electric lamps in the United States. They, in turn, bar International from doing business in the principal markets of these foreign companies.[78]

77. The agreement is reproduced in full in *ibid.*, Ex. 386-G.
78. From 1922 to 1939 International made agreements with the following companies: General Electric, Ltd. (1922); Societa Edison Clerici Fabrica (1926); General Electric Sociedad Anónyma (1926); Compagnie des Lampes (1927); Osram (1929); China General Edison (1929); Compañía Mexicana de Lámparas Eléctricas (1930); Philips (1931); Vereinigte Glühlampen und Elektrizitäts A. G. (1938); Associated Electrical Industries, Ltd. (1939); Tokyo Shibaura Denki K K (1939). These companies agreed to apply the terms of the agreements to their affiliates also. Many of these agreements superseded earlier contracts.
Under these agreements International was barred from doing business in the follow-

Since the licensing agreement between General Electric and Westinghouse prohibits each party from exporting lamps to those countries from which either is barred under its agreements with foreign concerns, and since General Electric's agreements with other domestic producers (its *B* licensees) prohibit them from exporting any lamps, the foreign and domestic agreements fit into a general plan which protects General Electric's home market from the competition of the principal foreign producers and the home market of the principal foreign producers from the competition of the major American producers.

Osram and International Promote World Cartel

While General Electric was making these moves Osram took the lead in a program to stabilize prices in European markets. With seven other continental lamp manufacturers, it organized in 1921 Internationale Glühlampen Preisvereinigung, a price-regulating cartel.[79] This simple price-fixing agreement proved inadequate, and the cartel "broke down utterly during February" of 1924.[80] Then Osram and International undertook to create a more permanent and effective organization. They conducted extensive negotiations with other leading European producers throughout 1924. International's Mr. Woodward has recorded the course of negotiations and the role which he played in them. On April 7, he reported to Mr. Burchard:

> As a result of this [the cartel's] breaking down, Meinhardt [of Osram] became convinced that *our arguments* as to the uselessness of a price schedule *by itself* are well founded [italics supplied]. He therefore proposed to Philips a basis for syndication. The upshot was an agreement for the division of their commercial profits, making adjustments out of the increase of the present business, in the usual manner, to bring the relations to a 2 to 1 basis. . . . It was not at that time Meinhardt's hope to bring the American affilia-

---

ing countries: Austria, Belgium, Brazil, Bulgaria, China, Czechoslovakia, Denmark, Estonia, Finland, France, Germany, Great Britain, Greece, Holland, Hungary, Irish Free State, Italy, Japan, Latvia, Lithuania, Luxemburg, Mexico, Norway, Poland, Portugal, Roumania, Spain, Sweden, Switzerland, Turkey, and Yugoslavia. In many instances, International was also barred from the dependencies, colonies, and protectorates of these countries.

For text of these agreements, see *ibid.,* Exs. 39-G ff.

79. League of Nations, *op. cit.,* p. 70.

80. *U.S.* v. *G.E.,* Civil Action No. 1364, Ex. 2112-G. This is a letter from J. M. Woodward, European representative of International, to A. W. Burchard, president of that company, dated April 7, 1924.

tions in. On the contrary I have reason to think it was his hope to use the strength of this syndicate in order to force the hands of the American group in the matter of issuing a price schedule [apparently for overseas markets]. When he approached me and found that we are not at all hostile to the syndicate and approve of exactly the sort of association proposed, it was a matter of a few minutes to come to an arrangement on the principles.

Mr. Woodward also said in this communication:

Circumstances and luck having brought about almost the precise situation which we have from the beginning desired, and the proposition having been made, I have given my adherence to it in the belief that you would approve it. . . .

In anticipation of the present turn of events I have avoided coming to a conclusion of the license agreements with any of the English manufacturers except Hirst. It always has been my intention to use the license for the purpose of inducing co-operation between themselves first and the Continental manufacturers later, should the occasion arise, as it now has.[81]

On September 19, 1924, Mr. Woodward reported to his chief that "It may require considerable maneuvering to get a formula adopted which will be accepted by the Germans and Philips, as their interests are exactly opposite . . ." [82]

Cartel Agreement Is Signed

On December 23, 1924, Mr. Woodward reported success in his efforts to secure a more comprehensive and effective arrangement for stabilizing world lamp markets, or as he expressed it "to develop the affair into a living partnership." [83] Next day the world's leading

81. *Ibid.*
82. Philips had expanded its foreign markets greatly during the war and early postwar period largely at the expense of the German industry. Osram was interested in recapturing Germany's lost markets, Philips in retaining those already won.
83. *U.S.* v. *G.E.,* Civil Action No. 1364, Ex. 2117-G, a letter from J. M. Woodward to A. W. Burchard. The letter reads in part as follows: "Every party manufacturing 500,000 lamps or over has been negotiated with by one party or another and we know precisely the terms on which they will sign. . . .
"He [Woodward's associate] has worked with me continuously in every negotiation with every party since you left and is as familiar with the meaning of the various articles . . . as I myself or as any other person who has taken the responsibility of making the decisions. . . .
"The process has been one of education, and as that education progressed I have taken advantage of the entire freedom of action which you left me, to develop the affair into a living partnership. For a long while it appeared as if the only thing which it would be possible to achieve would be a naked agreement between the parties as to quota. Specially did this seem to be true at the time when the personal relations became strained to the point of passing very strong epithets back and forth. Gradually the Euro-

lamp manufacturers signed the Convention for the Development
and Progress of the International Incandescent Electric Lamp Industry. Mr. Woodward, outstanding promoter of the cartel, resigned
his position as European representative of International to become
general counsel for Phoebus.

The cartel's leading members included Osram, Philips, Tungsram,[84]
(British) Associated Electrical Industries, Compagnie des Lampes,
International General Electric of New York, Ltd. (London), and the
so-called Overseas Group. These consisted of General Electric's subsidiaries: in Brazil, the General Electric Sociedad Anónyma; in China,
the China General Edison Company; and in Mexico, the Compañía
Mexicana de Lámparas Eléctricas.[85]

---

pean owners and managers came to like the idea of a permanent relationship . . . and
we took advantage of every opportunity offered to advance this idea. . . .
    "Also they have become impressed, some more than others, with the fact that they
must cooperate in what we call the Business Development program, and have become
educated not so much in the morality of this cooperation as in the necessity for it, as
well as in the necessity for keeping faith wherever it is attempted. . . . I think this is
going to be one of the most helpful factors in cementing the relationship which we
have established. . . . I may say without being misunderstood that the European parties
are entirely amateurish, for reasons which arise from their historic division of interest.
They realize this, and that realization coupled with their still active mistrust of each
other has caused them to accept our leadership and to invite its continuance. This situation gives us an opportunity which I do not think we can neglect. The entire group can,
in my opinion, with careful and intelligent handling on our part, be ultimately organized into at least an inseparable coalition and probably into something better still,
within the next nine or ten years at our disposal. This result does not depend upon the
chance of actual mergers between the component parts since it can be reached otherwise
by taking hold of the enterprise in its beginning and never letting it get away from us
through slack or indifferent manipulation."
    Earlier, Mr. Woodward had written, "To be perfectly frank I think we should come
to an agreement at the earliest date possible, since from this time on our position will
become less favorable in most quarters. . . .
    "The intention is to leave the business of any important country in the hands of the
organization of that country if it is in position to hold a substantial portion of it. . . .
It is obvious what this may mean to us if we are skilful in expanding the idea in the
years to come." *Ibid.*, Ex. 2112-G.
    84. Popular designation for the leading Hungarian producer, Vereinigte Glühlampen
und Elektrizitäts A. G.
    85. International General Electric of New York, Ltd., is a British company wholly
owned by General Electric. *U.S.* v. *G.E.*, Civil Action No. 1364, Ex. 59-G. International General Electric Company subdivided with International General Electric of New
York, Ltd., the foreign rights which it received under its agreement with General Electric. The arrangement bars the subsidiary incorporated in Great Britain from selling
lamps in continental European countries and their colonies, Japan and its colonies,
Brazil, Mexico, China, Great Britain and Northern Ireland, Eire; the Isle of Man,
Gibraltar, Cyprus, Rhodesia, and other British possessions in Africa north of Rhodesia.
It assigns all other areas to this British subsidiary, which did not manufacture lamps but
"supplied lamps for sale," obtaining them from other companies. *Ibid.*, Exs. 49-G and
2137-G.
    Mr. Woodward, representing International, initially signed the cartel agreement, sub-
ject to the approval of his principals, but International in its corporate capacity saw fit

Cartel Structure and Administration

To administer the cartel its members organized a Swiss corporation, Phoebus S. A. Compagnie Industrielle pour la Développement de l'Éclairage. (Chart 4 shows in simplified form the structure and organization of the cartel.) Members subscribed to Phoebus stock in the proportion that the lamp sales of each bore to the total lamp sales of all during the base period, July 1, 1922 to June 30, 1923.[86] A General Assembly, which as a rule met twice a year, had final authority over policy matters. Voting power in the General Assembly, based on the amount of stock held, was distributed in this order: Osram, Philips, Tungsram, (British) Associated Electrical Industries, Compagnie des Lampes, and the Overseas Group of International subsidiaries.[87]

The cartel's most important permanent administrative agencies were the Administrative Board and the Board of Arbitration. The Administrative Board issued rules and regulations for applying the terms of the agreement and carried out the policies of the Assembly. The Board of Arbitration, consisting of a Swiss professor of law, a Swiss federal judge, and a technical expert on international cartels, arbitrated all disputes among cartel members, particularly patent claims, royalty payments, and the like.[88]

Under the Administrative Board were four major administrative

---

not to become a party to the cartel. Mr. Woodward wrote Mr. Burchard on December 23, 1924, in part as follows: "Having made all of the decisions in this case since your departure, I naturally took the responsibility of signing the contracts under the same terms as the other parties present, that is to say subject to approval in due course of our principals." *Ibid.*, Ex. 2117-G. At another point in this communication the writer states, "It can be quite easily arranged that a foreign corporation can take over our international lamp trade, and this will be especially convenient as a mechanical matter in view of the close and constant contact we must maintain with the organization set up under the General Agreement."

86. Information from an official of a cartel member.

87. One vote was allowed for each million unit lamps sold during the base period (lamps of varying size and power are reduced for purpose of calculating voting privileges to a standard unit). Small producers which sold less than a million lamps grouped themselves for voting purposes. See League of Nations, *op. cit.*, p. 74. As noncartel companies were acquired by cartel members and as sales quotas were modified through purchase by certain members of the quotas of others, voting power in the General Assembly was modified from time to time. At the outbreak of World War II, voting power is said to have been distributed among the more important members as follows: Osram about one third of total; Philips about one fourth; Tungsram about one sixth; (British) Associated Electrical Industries about one tenth; Compagnie des Lampes about one twentieth; Overseas Group (International) about 3 or 4 per cent; the balance of about 7 per cent was scattered among a number of smaller concerns.

88. *Ibid.*, pp. 73-74.

CHART 4. INTERNATIONAL INCANDESCENT ELECTRIC LAMP CARTEL, 1935–1939

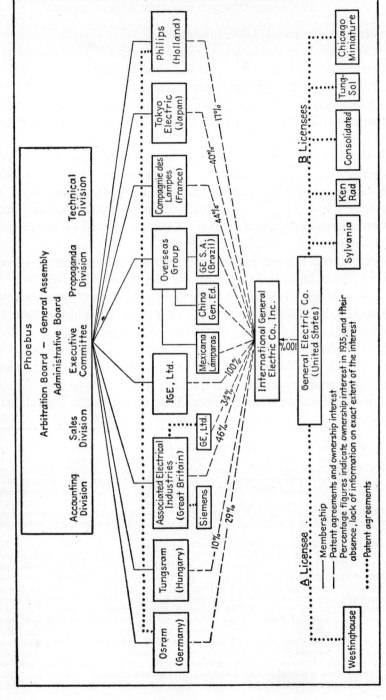

divisions: accounting, sales, propaganda, and technical. The accounting division determined allowable sales for each member under its quota and made monthly reports to enable members to adjust their actual sales to their allowables. The sales division administered price policies, cooperating with national assemblies in each area. The propaganda division strove to increase the use of electric lamps, and members' lamp sales at the expense of those of non–cartel members. The technical division supervised the work of standardization and exchange of technical information. Phoebus conducted a laboratory for testing lamps as a part of its program of standardizing quality.

Functions of the Cartel

The cartel had two acknowledged major functions: exchange of patents and technical information, and division of markets.[89] Proponents of the cartel highlight the former and dim the latter.

The cartel agreement provided that each member might use the patents and know-how of all other members during the life of the agreement at fees agreed on between the parties or determined by the arbitration board. Each member was required to throw open his plants and research laboratories to the inspection of any member. Since the cartel gave protection to rival sellers by insuring each a share in the market, the incentive to demand patent rights and know-how was apparently weakened, particularly where royalties were charged for the use of patents.

Market Areas

The agreement established three types of market areas: home territories, British overseas territories, and common territory. The home territory consisted of twelve countries in each of which one or more cartel members had important manufacturing facilities and larger sales than other members. According to Mr. Woodward the cartel endeavored "to leave the business of any important country in the hands of the organization of the country if it is in a position to hold

89. The cartel agreement stated the general purpose of the cartel as follows: "The aim and purpose of this agreement is to secure the cooperation of all contracting parties in order to insure a more profitable use of their manufacturing facilities in the production of bulbs, to secure and sustain an equally high quality of bulbs, to increase profits in distribution, to increase the effectiveness of electric lights and to increase the use of lights for the benefit of the consumer." See Dr. Wm. Meinhardt, *Der Weltglühlampenvertrag,* C. Heymann, Berlin, 1932.

a substantial portion of it." [90] The British overseas territory consisted of the British Empire exclusive of Great Britain and Canada and was dominated by the British group. However, they shared this market with Philips, the Overseas Group, Tungsram, and Osram, in the order named. The common territory, when the cartel was organized, consisted of the balance of the world, except the United States and Canada.[91]

With minor exceptions, the cartel gave to each member a sales quota within each of these three market areas based on the ratio of its sales to total sales during the base period, July 1, 1922 to June 30, 1923.[92] The quota system insured to each member a dominant position in its domestic market and a fixed share in other markets. A member was free to distribute its sales in common territory as it chose, providing sales in the whole of that territory were kept within its quota limitation. However, a member was not permitted to transfer unused portions of its quota in one market area to another type of market area, for example, from home territory to common territory. Each market area was a separate unit for purposes of quota allocation and administration. Common territories were subdivided from time to time and members given quotas in the new subdivisions.[93]

90. *U.S.* v. *G.E.,* Civil Action No. 1364, Ex. 2117-G. The home territories and the dominant cartel members of each were: Germany, Osram; Great Britain, Associated Electrical Industries; Holland and Belgium, Philips; Hungary, Tungsram; France, Compagnie des Lampes; Austria, Osram and Tungsram; Italy, Osram and Philips and Tungsram; Spain, Osram and Philips and Compagnie des Lampes; Brazil, General Electric S. A. (a General Electric subsidiary); China, General Edison (a General Electric subsidiary); Japan, Tokyo Electric Co., Ltd.

91. While nominally the American and Canadian markets were outside the scope of the cartel, actually prior commitments reserved them to General Electric.

92. In some instances the cartel departed from this practice. German exporters had not regained their prewar position in some foreign markets by 1922–1923 and insisted on quotas more closely approaching their relative prewar sales. Their quotas were increased largely at the expense of Philips; Philips in turn was compensated by a larger share in the British home and overseas markets. Quotas have been bought and sold among cartel members. Quota transfers required approval of the General Assembly.

93. The purpose of such subdivision apparently was to insure each member a proportionate share of the better markets without competing for them or to avoid a member's being forced to give up a portion of sales in a market in which he was well established because he wished to inaugurate a developmental campaign in some other area. The most important subdivision of the common territory was that of 1933, when the common markets were subdivided into European common territory and overseas common territory. The purpose of this particular division apparently was to separate the portion of the common territory in which International was interested from that in which it was barred under agreement with the several European producers. In the European common territory Osram is said to have had approximately 35 per cent of total sales, Philips a slightly smaller percentage, and Tungsram about a fourth. The balance was scattered. In the common overseas territory, International had about one third and was followed by Philips, Osram, and Tungsram in the order named, with the balance scattered.

Under the cartel no limit was placed on total sales of all members. Nor was any cartel member bound to limit its individual sales. However, substantial penalties were exacted of those members which exceeded their quotas. The penalty varied with the amount of sales beyond the quota: an excess of 25 per cent or more in any year entailed a forfeiture of all profits on the excess. Penalties were distributed among those cartel members which sold less than their quotas.[94] Payment of penalties was guaranteed by the deposit of indemnity funds by the members.

National Groups Fix Prices

The cartel did not directly fix the specific prices at which members sold lamps. Price competition was ruled out indirectly—by insuring each member a stipulated portion of the market. Nevertheless, prices were not left entirely to the discretion of particular members. Within home markets national assemblies, comprised of the quota participants for the given market, customarily determined them. In fixing prices, however, national assemblies had the advice of the Phoebus sales committee.[95] In brief, Phoebus advised on price policy; the national assemblies fixed prices.

General Electric's Cartel Participation

General Electric's affiliation was through its wholly owned subsidiary, the International company incorporated in Great Britain, and its local subsidiaries in Brazil, China, and Mexico. It goes virtually without saying that General Electric adjusted its operations to the cartel program. Nor were the express commitments of these subsidiaries the only ties binding General Electric to Phoebus. By separate contractual arrangements between International, its subsidiary, which is an American corporation, and the principal cartel members, General Electric had woven its operations into the cartel pattern as effectively as though it were an outright member. International's agreements with individual cartel members conform closely in scope and purpose to the scope and purpose of the cartel. Those agreements made before 1924 may be regarded as forerunners of the cartel; those after that date as supplementary to it. Although the agree-

94. League of Nations, *op. cit.*, p. 73.
95. *Ibid.*, p. 74.

ments-differ in detail, they all contain two basic features: exchange of patent rights and division of markets.

The patent exchanges cover all existing patents and those acquired during the life of the agreements, on electric lamps, lamp parts, machines and processes for making lamps, and all technical information and "know-how." [96] This fund of potential and unpatented technical knowledge made available to International licensees throughout the world includes not only inventions and improvements developed by General Electric but also those originating among its American licensees. Under the cross-licensing agreements with the American companies, General Electric has the right to sublicense, under the foreign patents of American companies, developments which it is licensed to use domestically.

But International's agreements with cartel members are far more than patent-licensing agreements and agreements to exchange technical information. They are agreements to eliminate all competition between the parties in the manufacture and sale of electric lamps in the exclusive territory of each. For example, the agreement between Osram and International (signed July 11, 1929 and to last until June 30, 1970) provides that during its life neither party will

become interested, directly or indirectly, in the manufacture of lamps in or the sale of lamps for use in the exclusive territory of the other; and each party will cause such of its controlled companies as have not at this time an agreement with it of contrary effect to observe the same obligation.[97]

This provision apparently applies to all electric lamps whether patented or unpatented or whether made by patented or unpatented processes. It is a simple agreement of the parties to refrain from competition. Other International agreements contain similar provisions. In general, they establish North America, Central America, and United States possessions and dependencies (except the Philippines) as the exclusive territory of International (and hence of General Electric), and reserve to the other contracting party its home and colonial markets as exclusive territory.

Although the agreements designate the South American markets as nonexclusive, they in effect recognize them as the proper spheres

96. The agreement with Philips specifically excludes glass-making machinery, but General Electric and Corning have similar agreements with Philips covering bulbs, tubing, and glass-making machinery.
97. U.S. v. G.E., Civil Action No. 1364, Ex. 39-G, Art. III, pp. 403-04.

of influence of General Electric. For example, a provision of the Osram-International agreement gives International the right to fix minimum prices and conditions of sale at which Osram may sell its patented products in South American markets. This provision apparently applies to all articles coming potentially within the agreement whether produced under Osram or International patents.[98] International's agreement with Philips gives International similar authority over the prices and conditions of sale at which Philips must sell.

Phoebus Plus General Electric—a World Cartel

Since the cartel provided for unrestricted exchange of patent rights and the International agreements embraced all major cartel members, together these arrangements create practically a world-wide patent pool. Virtually all patents and technological information on electric lamps, wherever developed, are funded. Moreover, the process by which they have been assembled in a common pool limits their use to firms that faithfully adhere to a concerted business policy. Access to the funded patents is not conditioned on actual technical contribution to the pool. It is conditioned, rather, on the promise to contribute any technological developments which may be made, and to follow "sound business policy" in the use of the patents, as conceived by the well-entrenched enterprises dominating the cartel.

Taken together, the International agreements, under which North American markets are reserved for General Electric, and the Phoebus agreement, under which a formula for sharing the remainder of the world markets is provided, transform an international cartel into a world cartel. The two sets of arrangements complement each other. The several International agreements are basic; they are essential to keep European producers out of American markets and General Electric out of the European markets.[99] The cartel simply provides for

---

98. *Ibid.*, Art. IX.

99. Both International and General Electric have recognized that the agreements made by International are basic to the security of domestic markets. See letter of April 28, 1926, from G. F. Morrison to Gerard Swope, quoted in full on pp. 327-28, n. 75.

A year earlier Mr. Burchard had written to Mr. Morrison in part as follows: "The only important lamp manufacturer in the world who has not taken a license, or recognized these patents [International's patents in foreign countries] is the Westinghouse Lamp Manufacturing Co. . . . it is only proper to request the Westinghouse Lamp Manufacturing Company to consider the situation with a view to giving like recognition to our rights. Protracted delay in this matter is likely to be quite embarrassing to the International General Electric Co. in its relationships with its licensees." *Ibid.*, Ex. 2124-G.

the manner in which the areas not reserved to General Electric shall be divided.

The whole arrangement was rounded out by General Electric's domestic agreements under which the *B* licensees could not sell in foreign markets and the *A* licensee (Westinghouse) was limited to sales in countries in which General Electric is authorized to sell lamps. These domestic licenses have prevented American producers not themselves parties either to the International agreements or to the Phoebus agreement from disturbing the arrangement.[100]

General Electric's influence over the cartel has not been limited to these agreements. The company has made important financial commitments that facilitated the cartel's organization and insured its effectiveness. When the cartel was formed General Electric agreed to lend more than $1.5 million to Osram. Osram was to use these funds to construct plants and to acquire with International certain patents and an interest in certain Austrian plants.[101]

General Electric Acquires Stock Interest in Cartel Members

General Electric continued its policy, initiated long before Phoebus' birth, of acquiring stock interests in foreign companies making

100. An official of Sylvania characterized this arrangement as follows: ". . . you spoke of a possible license from the G.E. to export lamps to certain countries. I don't know whether I explained the situation to you, but the fact is that in the world at large the more important electrical interests, such as the G.E., Siemens [Osram] of Germany, Philips of Holland, etc., are closely bound together in a cartel with the result that they have entered into binding agreements, apportioning world markets between the respective companies. Accordingly, you can see that if the G.E. broke their agreement and allowed us to export into a foreign country which was assigned under the cartel agreement to a European manufacturer, that European manufacturer would have a claim to enter the American market in competition with us and probably could not be restrained from doing so. This is something which would probably not be to our advantage." *Ibid.*, Ex. 113-G.

101. Letter from J. M. Woodward to Owen D. Young, September 19, 1924, *ibid.*, Ex. 2115-G. Mr. Woodward wrote Mr. Young in part as follows: "All parties are committed to observe the prices established in the usual way and expressly agree that not to do so would be unfair . . .

"This necessitates some serious aid and assistance to various parties who admit that their present position has been built up by disregard of the rights of others."

Consolidation of a plant in Vienna belonging to Tungsram, one belonging to Osram and Philips, and the Kreminezky plant was planned. "In this consolidation it is expected that the General Company will participate to the extent of one fifth of the total value, requiring an investment of about $650,000 some of which, probably about $150,-000, would be regained . . ."

Mr. Woodward continued: ". . . it is proposed to buy the Westlake patent rights for all purposes for all continental Europe. . . . this contemplates an investment by us of $250,000 . . . with a loan to the Osram Syndicate of $750,000, . . ." In addition this letter indicated that International advanced $32,500 to enable Tungsram to purchase the Justam Co. in Budapest. This sum International hoped to regain from the liquidation of Justam assets.

lamps. By 1935 General Electric owned about 29 per cent of the outstanding stock of Osram, 17 per cent of Philips, 44 per cent of Compagnie des Lampes, 10 per cent of Tungsram, 46 per cent of (British) Associated Electrical Industries, 34 per cent of General Electric Co., Ltd., and 40 per cent of Tokyo Electric Co.[102]

General Electric's connections with Osram and Philips have been particularly close. These concerns, the three most important lamp manufacturers in the world, operated jointly a bulb factory in Shanghai. International and Osram jointly organized two Swiss companies to acquire the continental rights to automatic glass bulb-blowing machines and glass tube-making machines. In Brazil, a local subsidiary of International supplied Osram and Philips with all their lamp requirements. In Mexico, International and Osram operated a jointly owned factory for the manufacture of lamps. International's sales in the Argentine market were supplied from Philips' plants in Holland until Osram's projected plant in Argentina could provide them. International, Osram, Philips, Tungsram, and Westinghouse operated a joint selling agency in Argentina, Compañía de Lámparas Eléctricas S. A. (known as Laco).[103]

102. *Ibid.*, Ex. 59-G, Memorandum by W. C. Duncan entitled "Total Participation of G.E. Co. in Lamp Business of the World, by its Own Sales and by Share Ownership, Direct and Indirect, in Other Companies (Confidential)." General Electric's percentage of stock ownership in some of the companies had decreased by 1940.

103. These joint operating arrangements were based upon a series of special agreements among these so-to-speak "Class A" members of the cartel. The more important of these agreements were between: Osram and International, effective July 1, 1929 (*ibid.*, Ex. 39-G); International and Philips, effective March 14, 1931 (Ex. 40-G); Osram and Philips, about the same date. The 1929 agreement between International and Osram provided for the acquisition by International of a 16 2/3 per cent interest in Osram and for cross-licensing arrangements broadening the exclusive territory of each concern. International's exclusive territory, originally the United States and Canada, was broadened to include North America and Central America; Osram's exclusive territory, originally Germany, was broadened to include Austria, Czechoslovakia, Denmark, Germany, Hungary, Norway, Poland, Sweden, Switzerland, Roumania, Bulgaria, Yugoslavia, Turkey, Finland, Estonia, Lithuania, Latvia, Lichtenstein, Memel, and Danzig, and after October 1, 1939, Italy. This meant that other European companies operating in these areas must look to Osram for licenses under International patents. International reserved the right to grant Philips nonexclusive licenses in the Scandinavian countries, Switzerland, Poland, and after October 1, 1939, Italy. International's agreement with Philips assigned as exclusive territory to Philips, Holland, Belgium, and Luxemburg. The International-Philips agreement indicated that a similar agreement between Osram and Philips was in process of negotiation. At the time the International-Philips agreement was concluded, the following statement by A. F. Philips was attached to and formed part of the International agreement: "We have in process of negotiation with Osram G.m.b.H. . . . a lamp license agreement of substantially the same scope as that of our lamp license agreement with you . . ." (*Ibid.*, Ex. 40-G.) Osram and Philips entered into similar agreements with other members of the cartel designed to supplement and fortify the cartel. In some instances, market quotas were redistributed and markets in common territories were subdivided.

The Cartel as an Instrument for Controlling the Market

The international lamp cartel represented an attempt to substitute privately administrated, centralized control for the forces of the market in determining who should produce lamps, by what processes and where they should be produced, where and at what prices they should be sold. Under the guidance of its dominant associates and its "sleeping partner," the cartel has functioned as a sort of international planning agency for the control of the lamp industry. How have the industry and the public fared under this control? How has the cartel affected prices, profits, costs, the use of resources, the art of lamp making, and the quantity and quality of lamps produced?

The cartel's influence has been limited by its failure to extend its control over the entire industry. A General Electric official estimated in 1934 that in countries outside the United States served by cartel members independents did about 40 per cent of the business, and that in the United States their share amounted to approximately 10 per cent.[104] Independents multiplied for several reasons. During the life of the cartel, patented technology was not coextensive with the art of lamp manufacture and access to the industry was never completely barred. Cartel price policy made entrance into the industry attractive. Conflicts of judgment and of interest among cartel members tended to weaken cartel control. The cartel arrangements were subject to legal attack in certain jurisdictions, particularly the United States. Important patents expired from time to time. These factors tended to weaken the cartel. Its effectiveness apparently declined during the thirties. Nevertheless, the cartel did not collapse and no doubt has served to bolster temporarily the position of its members.

Influence of the Cartel on Prices

Under the cartel, members had little incentive to get business through the time-honored custom of selling for less. Profit margins, not turnover, became the key to higher earnings. A Westinghouse official in February 1937 expressed the matter as follows:

104. *Ibid.*, Ex. 2143-G, letter from M. L. Sloan to C. H. Minor, Sept. 27, 1934. This letter does not indicate how the independents' share of the business was distributed among different sizes and types of lamps. However, it is probable that, at least in the United States, their sales at this time were concentrated largely in Christmas tree and other miniature lamps. See Tariff Commission, *op. cit.*, pp. 29-30.

In all countries . . . where we do business in the Common Territory we invariably have a larger percentage of the market than our [allowable] percentage in the Common Territory, consequently, if the growth of business is greater in those countries than in the Common Territory as a whole, the position becomes more embarrassing for us as regards exceeding our permissible sales. Unless one can purchase units at a very reasonable figure—and it is not always easy to do this—it becomes most unprofitable to exceed one's permissible sales. The goal therefore to be aimed at is to make as much money as possible out of those units we are permitted to sell. In other words, it is much more advantageous for us to make a profit of 5¢ per unit on 4,000,000 units than 2½¢ per unit on 8,000,000 units.[105]

That the cartel has made prices higher than they would have been under free competition is shown by what happened when competition broke out. In 1928 the Swedish Cooperative Union (Kooperativa Förbundet), convinced that cartel prices were unreasonably high, laid plans to build a lamp factory. Phoebus promptly met this move by a substantial cut in lamp prices and by the threat of patent suits.[106] Undismayed, the Cooperative Union proceeded with its plans. On May 28, 1931, the Northern Luma Cooperative Society, an international cooperative sponsored by Swedish K. F. and owned by cooperative wholesale societies in Sweden, Denmark, Finland, and Norway, began production. Luma sold lamps cheaper than Phoebus, and at a profit.

As a General Electric representative summed it up: "The policy among the Phoebus group is to maintain relatively high prices on lamps."[107] In general, prices have been highest where market control

105. *U.S.* v. *G.E.*, Civil Action No. 1364, Ex. 2146-G, memorandum from Westinghouse International files. Westinghouse officials recognized the benefits of avoiding price competition, although apparently some were dissatisfied with Westinghouse's share of the export market. On December 2, 1938, W. E. Downer of the London office complained to J. W. White of the New York office: "It is perfectly true that we are the second largest lamp manufacturers in the world . . . , but we only have a participation, outside of the U. S. and Canada, of approximately 1.2% of the licensed Lamp Manufacturers' business, which is probably about 0.6% of the world business outside the U. S. and Canada. I agree this is definitely lousy." *Ibid.*, Ex. 2156-G.

106. Marquis Childs gives an account of these developments in *Sweden, the Middle Way*, Yale University Press, New Haven, 1936, pp. 37-42. According to Childs, the cartel reduced prices on certain types of lamps from the equivalent of 37 cents to 27 cents while the cooperative factory was under construction.

107. *U.S.* v. *G.E.*, Civil Action No. 1364, Ex. 2143-G, a letter from M. L. Sloan to C. H. Minor, September 27, 1934. A Westinghouse representative in 1938 characterized cartel price policy as follows, "with the patent monopoly in 1924 prices were very high, and the profit spread was enormous. With lots of jam everybody was happy, but since then, prices have dropped tremendously, with the result that there is little jam, and consequently more dissatisfaction." *Ibid.*, Ex. 2156-G, W. E. Downer to J. W. White.

was most completely centralized and where the cartel found a friendly legal environment. The home markets of Philips and Osram most nearly conform to these conditions.[108] In 1938 retail prices of 25-watt, 40-watt, and 60-watt metal filament lamps in Holland were 32, 59, and 70 cents, respectively, in American money. Similar lamps sold in Germany for 30, 36, and 48 cents. In Sweden lamps of this type sold for 23, 27, and 33 cents, respectively, while in the United States all three types sold for the same price, 15 cents.[109]

Association Domination

Although Great Britain had long been more favorable to free enterprise than either Holland or Germany, the Electric Lamp Manufacturers' Association exercised such complete control of the market that the subcommittee of the British Parliamentary Standing Committee on Trusts reported in 1920: "the determination of what is a reasonable price for electric lamps sold to the general public . . . [rests] with the Electric Lamp Manufacturers' Association." [110] The Committee found that lamps sold to the public at 3s. could have been sold at 2s. with a "satisfactory working profit" both to manufacturers and distributors. One and a quarter million half-watt lamps, purchased in Holland at 3s. a lamp, were resold at 12s. 6d., although a price of 8s. would have left "ample margins for the importers and distributors." [111]

General Electric has stated its policy on lamp prices as follows: "We have always tried to price our lamps in such a way as to give to the public a part of the reductions in cost resulting from improvements in methods and of course to maintain the business we are doing in relation to the total business done in the United States." [112] Lamp prices in the United States have been lower than anywhere else in the world, with the possible exception of Japan, and the trend has been persistently downward. Between 1920 and 1938, 60-watt lamps

---

108. Not only is the business in Holland and Germany largely concentrated in the hands of Philips and Osram, respectively, but the Dutch and German Governments by means of tariffs and import quotas have aided and abetted the cartel in carrying out its restrictive programs.

109. Tariff Commission, *op. cit.,* p. 49. Lamps of the same wattage produced in different countries may be unequal in quality. Quality differences could account for part of the lamp price variation noted above.

110. Standing Committee on Trusts, p. 7.

111. *Ibid.,* p. 20.

112. *U.S.* v. *G.E.,* Civil Action No. 1364, Ex. 98-G.

TABLE 26

RETAIL PRICES IN THE UNITED STATES FOR INDICATED SIZES OF DOMESTIC
INCANDESCENT METAL FILAMENT LAMPS AND CHRISTMAS TREE
LAMPS FOR SPECIFIED DATES, 1920–1938

Size in watts or lamp style	50	60	75	100	Christmas tree
Date of introduction	July 1916	November 1907	July 1916	April 1915	
Original list price	$0.28	$1.75	$0.65	$1.00	
Date			Retail Price		
Jan. 1, 1920	$0.35	$0.40	$0.70	$1.10	a
Jan. 1, 1925	.27	.32	.45	.50	$0.12
Jan. 1, 1929	.22	.22	.35	.35	.10
Jan. 1, 1930	.20	.20	.35	.35	.10
Jan. 1, 1931	.20	.20	.35	.35	.10
Jan. 1, 1932	.20	.20	.35	.35	.05
Jan. 1, 1933	.20	.20	.35	.35	.05
Jan. 1, 1934	.20	.20	.20	.25	.05
Jan. 1, 1935	.20	.20	.20	.25	.05
Apr. 1, 1935	.15	.15	.20	.20	.05
Jan. 1, 1936	.15	.15	.20	.20	.05
Oct. 1, 1937	.15	.15	.20	.20	.05
Apr. 1, 1938	.15	.15	.15	.15	.05

Source: U.S. Tariff Commission, Report No. 133, Ser. II, *Incandescent Electric Lamps,*
Washington, 1939, p. 47 f.
a. Not available.

declined from 40 to 15 cents, 75-watt lamps from 70 to 15 cents, and
100-watt lamps from $1.10 to 15 cents.[113] (See Table 26.)

This downward price trend reflects lower production costs resulting from product standardization and increased mechanization of

113. An exhibit prepared by General Electric and submitted in connection with the
pending antitrust proceedings indicates a reduction of 50 per cent between 1921 and
1928 in General Electric's list prices for "all types and services of large and miniature
lamps" and from the same base a reduction by 1939 of approximately 70 per cent. This
exhibit indicates reductions of more than 10 per cent from prices of the previous year
in each of the years 1922, 1923, 1924, 1928, and 1935 (*ibid.*, Ex. 2110-G). We have
used the Tariff Commission data because they are broken down by lamp sizes and hence
permit price comparisons between types of lamps in the sale of which competition has
from time to time developed. The Tariff Commission's data on large lamps covering the
period January 1929 to January 1933 were secured from the Edison Electric Institute
Bulletin, August 1933, Vol. I, No. 5, p. 147. The data on large lamps for the period
January 1, 1934 to April 1, 1938 and the data on small lamps for the entire period
were secured from the General Electric Co.

productive processes. These have permitted mass production, and the world's largest domestic market has supplied the requisite demand.[114]

Influence of Japanese Competition

The scale and timing of price reductions were influenced by other factors. Competition, potential or actual, may be largely responsible for them. The Just and Hanaman patent covering tungsten lamps expired February 27, 1929, and the Coolidge patent on drawn tungsten wire expired December 30, 1930. General Electric, recognizing that the expiration of these patents might open the door to competition, made new contracts with potential competitors at home and abroad to fortify its position in the market. Probably General Electric's price cuts of January 1, 1929 were a part of this same strategy. Whatever the objective, the price reductions of 1929 were inadequate to avert threatened competition.

The expiration of the Just and Hanaman and Coolidge patents was followed by a large increase in Japanese output. This has perhaps been a greater influence on world markets than any other peacetime development since Phoebus was organized. Between 1925 and 1935 Japanese production in plants employing five workers or more increased almost sixfold (see Table 27). Most of this increase came after the Just and Hanaman patent expired. During that decade Japan became next to the largest producer of electric lamps, second only to the United States. Much of this expansion was in small plants operated by firms not in the world cartel.[115]

The large number of small producers prevented effective control of price and output. With low labor cost and a favorable exchange position, Japanese lamps pushed their way increasingly into world markets. Since they met import quotas as well as tariff barriers in most continental countries, they flowed in increasing volume into the Americas and Great Britain.

---

114. According to an exhibit presented by General Electric in the antitrust proceedings, its output of lamps per man-hour increased from thirty in 1926 to ninety in 1939. See *U.S.* v. *G.E.,* Civil Action No. 1364, Ex. 2110-G.

115. Of 310 factories producing incandescent lamps in Japan in 1933 only 12 employed more than 100 workers and more than 250 employed fewer than 30 each. The largest producer was the Tokyo Electric Company (in which General Electric owned a 40 per cent stock interest). Tokyo Electric was a member of Phoebus. Eleven other companies organized themselves into a domestic cartel in 1933. In addition to 298 relatively small factories, most of which did not belong to the cartel, Japan had thousands of shops employing fewer than 5 employees. Tariff Commission, *op. cit.,* pp. 60-65.

TABLE 27

JAPANESE PRODUCTION OF INCANDESCENT ELECTRIC LAMPS IN PLANTS
EMPLOYING FIVE OR MORE WORKERS, 1924–1935

(In Thousands)

Year	Number	Value	
		Yen	U.S. Currency [a]
1924	55,123	17,277	$7,116
1925	57,063	17,089	7,013
1926	63,631	15,225	7,174
1927	87,255	26,315	12,476
1928	97,550	24,327	11,290
1929	134,183	17,064	7,866
1930	114,812	15,192	7,503
1931	202,054	18,037	8,811
1932	286,653	19,685	5,534
1933	340,393	21,971	5,635
1934	310,750	19,998	5,942
1935	308,683	21,210	6,089

Source: U.S. Tariff Commission, Report No. 133, Ser. II, *Incandescent Electric Lamps,*
Washington, 1939, p. 64.

a. Yen converted to United States currency on basis of the annual average rates of exchange as shown in the *Federal Reserve Bulletin.* The annual average value of the yen in United States currency varied from a high of 47.4113 cents in 1927 to a low of 25.646 cents in 1933. Because of such sharp fluctuations in exchange rates, the converted figures fail to show satisfactorily the actual changes in volume of business.

United States imports of large lamps increased from 947,000, with a value of $41,000, in 1929 to 22,224,000 in 1937, with a value of $373,000. During the same period imports of miniature lamps increased from 3,416,000 with a value of $86,000 to 100,089,000 with a value of $538,000. (See Table 28.) Almost all these imports came from Japan. Most of them were either miniature or common household-type lamps of 60 watts or less. Prices of the 60-watt lamp declined during this period from 22 cents to 15 cents, or by about one third; of the miniature lamp from 10 to 5 cents, or by 50 per cent.

General Electric met this foreign competition in 1932 when household lamp imports were at the peak by introducing a so-called D-type household lamp retailing for 10 cents and by reducing the price of Christmas tree lamps by 50 per cent. Mr. Swope stated in a letter of June 9, 1932 that General Electric's price policy was designed to

TABLE 28

United States Imports for Consumption of Metal Filament Incandescent Electric Lamps, 1925–1938

Year	Large Lamps			Miniature Lamps			Total		
	Quantity	Value	Unit Value	Quantity	Value	Unit Value	Quantity	Value	Unit Value
	(In Thousands)			*(In Thousands)*			*(In Thousands)*		
1925	4,875	$325	$0.066	2,269	$52	$0.023	7,144	$374	$0.052
1926	4,918	381	.077	1,351	35	.026	6,269	416	.066
1927	1,879	144	.076	2,301	50	.022	4,180	194	.046
1928	1,299	97	.075	2,143	47	.022	3,442	144	.042
1929	947	41	.044	3,416	86	.025	4,363	127	.029
1930	11,651	391	.034	17,938	351	.019	29,590	743	.025
1931	21,191	697	.033	48,179	675	.014	69,370	1,372	.020
1932	32,788	627	.019	80,722	533	.007	113,509	1,161	.010
1933	19,343	299	.015	97,274	465	.005	116,617	764	.007
1934	25,595	486	.019	67,245	352	.005	92,840	838	.009
1935	32,241	544	.017	72,170	432	.006	104,411	976	.009
1936	25,280	427	.017	117,255	653	.006	142,535	1,080	.008
1937	22,224	373	.017	100,089	538	.005	122,313	911	.007
1938	10,260	187	.018	55,998	299	.005	66,258	487	.007

Source: U.S. Tariff Commission, Report No. 133, Ser. II, *Incandescent Electric Lamps,* Washington, 1939, p. 50.

"maintain the business we are doing in relation to the total business done in the United States." In this letter he explained the 1932 price adjustments on the specific ground that "our percentage of the business was being reduced by manufacturers who were infringing our patents in the United States and by manufacturers abroad, principally Japan, whose product was coming into this country." [116]

Voluntary Cooperation Weak

Although lower cost may account in part for General Electric's price reductions, it does not tell the whole story. The price adjustments reflect the weakness of any private cartel which is necessarily dependent on voluntary cooperation. Dominant producers somehow must meet the competition of non–cartel members. Thus even a little competition influences cost-price relationships, though the market be as closely controlled as the domestic electric lamp market.

These price reductions were made without seriously impairing General Electric's profit position.[117] General Electric has earned from its sale of lamps and lamp parts in every year for which data are available not less than 20 per cent on its average capital investment in that department of its business.[118] The rate of earnings in 1930 was 34.39 per cent; in 1935, 23.38 per cent; 1936, 27.00 per cent; 1937, 29.94 per cent; 1938, 20.46 per cent; 1939, 22.83 per cent.

Persistence of such high rates of earnings indicates that the consumer would have been even better served if additional resources had been used to produce lamps or if existing facilities had been more fully employed. The public welfare would have been promoted if the supply of electric lamps had been increased enough to lower prices to levels that would yield a more nearly competitive rate of return on capital invested in the production of lamps.[119]

116. *U.S.* v. *G.E.*, Civil Action No. 1364, Ex. 98-G.

117. *Ibid.*, Ex. 2110-G, Financial Data Relative to Lamp and Lamp Parts Business.

118. General Electric computed these earning rates on a basis of its federal income tax returns. Capital investment included investment in affiliated companies and miscellaneous securities at their adjusted tax value rather than book value (cost rather than market value) and fixed assets (plant accounts) at cost less depreciation allowed for tax purposes. Income excluded unrealized gains and losses and included an allowance for depreciation at rates authorized by the corporation income tax law. Because of the varied character of General Electric's operations, its statement represents an estimate rather than a precise calculation. No data were presented for 1931–1934. *Ibid.*, Ex. 2110-G.

119. Even though the demand is inelastic, public interest in an enterprise system demands that resources be so effectively utilized that rates of return, with due allowance for risks, be equalized among all industries. The 20 to 30 per cent made by General Electric is obviously in excess of a competitive rate.

Several factors prevented Japanese competition from reducing earnings to a competitive level. Import duties of 20 per cent and public preference for the American product handicapped Japanese imports. Moreover, General Electric launched a vigorous program to combat them. It resorted to both commercial devices and the law, particularly the patent infringement suit. A General Electric official reported on its program as follows:

Next, I might mention different lines of action [in addition to the low-priced D lamp] against the Japanese lamps.

Apparently the efforts to invoke the anti-dumping provisions of the tariff against these lamps were not successful.

Instructions have been issued by the Customs officials not to admit lamps that obviously are marked so as to imitate closely the markings on standard American lamps.

It is probable that our patent situation is strong enough to justify the Government in placing an embargo on imported lamps that infringe our patents. However, for policy reasons, we have not attempted to have this done.

The most effective measure has been suit against or notification of our intention to sue distributors of imported lamps that infringe our patents. This line of action has been followed on the Pacific Coast with desired results and I understand will be followed elsewhere. The principal patents are the inside frosting, non-sag filament wire, tipless construction and the Langmuir gas-filled lamp patent. (I understand the last mentioned expires in a month or so.) . . .[120]

Influence of Cartel on Cost of Production

Cartel proponents contend that the cartel has reduced costs by improving techniques and spreading this knowledge among cartel members. It is impossible to verify this. There is no direct evidence that the cartel has stimulated research. But the evidence suggests that

---

120. *U.S.* v. *G.E.*, Civil Action No. 1364, Ex. 221-G, letter from W. C. D. to C. H. Minor, dated March 10, 1933. (W. C. D. presumably is W. C. Duncan, an official of International.) Dr. Meinhardt has described the relative influence of tariff barriers and the cartel in protecting the domestic markets of cartel members as follows: "the problem of the tariff protection of the domestic industry substantially loses its influence by the establishment and development of the cartel. By virtue of quotas the domestic industry secured its percentage of the business. By the same quotas the interest of the importing country is secured. If the domestic industry should try to deprive importers of their business they would exceed their quota and would be forced to pay fines exceeding their profits. Therefore the domestic industry does not need tariff protection provided no outsiders appear to disturb the situation, a danger which any manufacturer must always keep in mind if he makes any kind of cartel agreement." Meinhardt, *op. cit.*, Chap. 3.

General Electric's jealous safeguarding of its technical pre-eminence tended to discourage independent research by its licensees. General Electric's attitude is indicated in the complaint of a Sylvania official that "We feel that G. E. is definitely taking a narrow point of view on their stand that only they in the industry need to promote new developments." [121]

A representative of another B licensee, Tung-Sol Company, declared that ". . . a lamp licensee has no inducement to develop new inventions if General Electric Company can freely take whatever they develop." [122]

The loss to the industry and the public resulting from General Electric's tactics is suggested by the following excerpt from a memorandum by another Sylvania official:

> The G. E. should exchange engineering information with us on new technical developments. If we were permitted earlier knowledge of developments, we might be able to influence their trend toward more practical directions. For example, in the case of reflector lamps, we could have brought G. E.'s attention to the advantages of flashed aluminum seven years ago; in the case of sterilizing lamps, we could have contributed much to the G. E. five years ago; and in the case of fused lamps, we could have saved the industry money by base fusing at least a year and a half earlier than we did. In the case of hot air coiling, we could even now launch a general improvement in coiling.[123]

Possibly also the major producers put more and more trust in restrictive arrangements to protect their respective market positions and so came to regard research as less urgent, especially since a technological advance made by one cartel member became readily available to all the others and since research was costly.[124]

On the other hand, an originator of a novel process or a product

---

121. *U.S.* v. *G.E.*, Civil Action No. 1364, Ex. 200-G, Memorandum by R. M. Zabel to F. J. Healy, August 18, 1939.

122. *Ibid.*, Ex. 197-G, letter from Richard Eyre to H. W. Harper, dated September 13, 1935.

123. *Ibid.*, Ex. 198-G, Memorandum by O. H. Biggs, dated April 25, 1938.

124. In the summer of 1939, Westinghouse discontinued some of its research activities for these reasons. At any rate, Sylvania reports as follows on this: "Second in line of profit are the B licensees because of their lower expenditure for development cost and third in line of profits is Westinghouse because they have neither the high volume nor the extensive parts manufacturing and they have been, until recently at least, carrying a high overhead in development cost. Mr. Sloan [of General Electric] stated that because of this profit situation Westinghouse had recently been discontinuing some of their extensive development work." *Ibid.*, Ex. 199-G, Memorandum by R. M. Zabel to F. J. Healy, August 15, 1939.

improvement might benefit more than the others since there was nothing in the cartel agreement to prevent a member from exacting royalties from other participants for the use of an invention developed by him. Moreover, the leading cartel members, who were also leading domestic producers in their home markets, no doubt recognized that the cartel's life was always uncertain and appreciated the competitive disadvantage in which they might find themselves if they slackened their own research activities.

A representative of International General Electric has indicated that European producers were more interested in keeping prices high than in lowering costs. On March 23, 1927 Mr. Woodward wrote from Europe to an International official in New York:

> His [a European manufacturer's] feeling is that the larger companies here have the policy of keeping everything as cumbersome and as expensive as possible in order to keep the smaller companies at a disadvantage. This matter is of deep concern to us not only because of the lamp investments which the IGE has in Europe and which must be made to pay as much as possible but because of the further fact that the present prices in certain markets are a constant incentive to the creation of new factories.[125]

The Quota System and Costs

Moreover, the market quota system probably tended to raise costs. Efficient producers apparently preferred to share the market on an agreed basis with less efficient rivals than to compete with them. Cartel penalties and subsidies protected weaker producers and tended to raise average costs. In 1924 Mr. Woodward advised Owen D. Young that to prevent their bankruptcy the cartel would assign larger quotas to some of the weaker companies than they could fill. The bonus which they received for not filling their quotas apparently was a subsidy to inefficiency.[126]

Non–cartel members doubtless also had higher costs than they would have had if they could have used the cartel's patents, even at a reasonable royalty. In America, for example, General Electric's access to processes and machines not generally available gives it a cost advantage over most, if not all, other American producers. The largest single item of cost in making lamps is the glass bulb. Patent control resting, not on General Electric's own patents, but on its con-

125. *Ibid.*, Ex. 2129-G.
126. *Ibid.*, Ex. 2115-G.

tractual arrangements with Corning prevents any other producer from making large bulbs by the most efficient processes or from getting them except from a single-seller at discriminatory prices.

Similarly, General Electric is the sole source of lamp bases for all American manufacturers except Westinghouse. General Electric's rivals, buying their globes and bases from monopolists, have higher costs on these items than General Electric incurs in manufacturing them.[127] Finally, those manufacturers not licensed by General Electric must use obsolete production processes or risk expensive infringement suits which may or may not be well founded. In these circumstances, their costs are probably higher than those of General Electric or of its licensees.

Outside of America, Phoebus fought independents wherever they arose. It advertised Phoebus members' products, and set up "fighting companies" to drive out competition. These campaigns probably raised costs both to the independents and to the industry as a whole.

Influence of Cartel on Lamp Quality

The cartel and its members tried to standardize lamps. The General Assembly had final jurisdiction over quality standards. Standards could be changed only by the Assembly. To insure that members would comply with these standards, a testing laboratory was maintained in Switzerland to which cartel members were required to send sample lamps. The cartel agreement provided that Phoebus should "insure and sustain an equally high quality [of lamps] . . . increase effectiveness of electric lights, and . . . increase the use of light for the benefit of the consumer." But in practice the cartel's standardization program apparently also had other objectives not altogether compatible with its announced purposes. These unavowed objectives were: (1) limitation of, and on occasion a reduction in, the life of lamps, to increase sales; and (2) elimination of quality competition in the sale of lamps.

127. The manufacture of both bulbs and bases is highly mechanized. The optimum scale of production under existing techniques is very large. Probably the scale of production made possible by concentrating the demand for glass bulbs and bases upon single-sellers results in lower costs than could be achieved if each lamp manufacturer undertook to produce his own bulbs and bases. Probably also if all producers of lamps had access to the techniques of bulb and base making either of two results would follow: (1) the techniques would be adapted to smaller, less costly machines; or (2) the price of bulbs and bases would sink to a cost-of-production level and lamp manufacturers would have no incentive to make their own.

Some of the cartel's policy-makers have admitted that an increase in sales was one of the primary objectives of the lamp standardization program. Mr. Woodward, in reporting to Owen D. Young on September 19, 1924 concerning the cartel negotiations, stated:

All manufacturers are committed to our program of standardization, as well as the adoption of our formulae for arriving at the economic life of lamps. . . . This is expected to double the business of all parties within five years, independently of all other factors tending to increase it.[128]

A General Electric engineer sent a memorandum to his superior officer in 1932 concerning the company's tactics in building sales by shortening the life of flashlight lamps. In this revealing document, he observed:

Two or three years ago we proposed a reduction in the life of flashlight lamps from the old basis on which one lamp was supposed to outlast three batteries, to a point where the life of the lamp and the life of the battery under service conditions would be approximately equal. Sometime ago, the battery manufacturers went part way with us on this and accepted lamps of two battery lives instead of three. This has worked out very satisfactorily.

We have been continuing our studies and efforts to bring about the use of one battery life lamps. . . . If this were done, we estimate that it would result in increasing our flashlight business approximately 60 per cent. We can see no logical reason either from our standpoint or that of the battery manufacturer why such a change should not be made at this time.

Messrs. Parker and Johnson now have this matter up with the battery manufacturers and I would urge that every assistance be given them to put it over.[129]

But as we have seen, the cartel's control of output was achieved indirectly through quota allotments and payment of penalties by members whose sales exceeded their quotas. Apparently the program of increasing sales by shortening the life of lamps clashed with the endeavor of individual firms to avoid penalties for overselling their quotas. Concerning this problem the Tokyo Electric Company, Ltd., wrote Phoebus in 1927 as follows:

128. *U.S.* v. *G.E.*, Civil Action No. 1364, Ex. 2115-G.
129. *Ibid.*, Ex. 1860-G, letter from L. C. Porter to M. L. Sloan, *et al.*, November 1, 1932. Shortening the life of a lamp may improve its efficiency, i.e., the number of lumens yielded per unit of electricity consumed. In some circumstances, the increased efficiency may offset the reduced duration. See text below.

. . . we are succeeding step by step to deprive the customers of infringers from their hand on account of our very best endeavors in recommending high efficiency lamps and good illumination to the public; we have shortened the life of our lamps from 3000 hours to 2000 hours for vacuum lamps and from 2500 hours to 1600 for gas-filled lamps; we could increase the sales of gas-filled lamps and high watt lamps so much that in the basic period our sales billed of gas-filled lamps was only 5% of the total sales billed, while in the second fiscal period it amounted to 25%.

We are quite ready to continue and strengthen our endeavor to do everything possible to deprive the outsiders of their business to the general advantage of the parties of the Agreement, and to bring our lamps to agreement with the Phoebus standard in all connections of life and others regardless of the considerably difficult local conditions. But, if the increase in our business resulting from such endeavors directly mean a heavy penalty, it must be a thing out of reason and shall quite discourage us.[130]

Depression Intensifies Competition

During the Great Depression, after the basic patents had expired, competition among lamp producers became keener, both within and without the cartel. Apparently some cartel members could not resist appealing to consumer preferences by offering longer-lived lamps. One way of doing this was to make lamps for a voltage higher than that for which the ordinary circuit is wired, as suggested by the following excerpt from a 1934 communication from A. F. Philips, head of the Dutch company, to Mr. Minor of International.

The Phoebus Development Department has recently circulated the usual voltage statistics for the various countries covered by the General Agreement. From these figures it appears that unfortunately there seems to exist in various territories a growing tendency to supply lamps for higher voltages than in the past, which therefore leads to the conclusion that in a great many cases such lamps are being underrun.

This, you will agree with me, is a very dangerous practice and is having a most detrimental influence on the total turnover of the Phoebus Parties. Especially with a view to the strongly decreased prices in many countries, this may have serious consequences for Phoebus and after the very strenuous efforts we made to emerge from a period of long life lamps, it is of the greatest importance that we do not sink back into the same mire by paying no attention to voltages and supplying lamps that will have a very prolonged life.[131]

130. *Ibid.,* Ex. 2131-G, letter from O. Pruessman to C. F. Johnstone, May 2, 1927 The Tokyo Company's memorandum was enclosed in this letter.
131. *Ibid.,* Ex. 2140-G, letter dated January 30, 1934.

An official of General Electric described the situation confronting his company in the spring of 1933 as follows:

A situation exists in respect to the quality of lamps, regarding which we feel that you must do something personally.

First of all, we are being pushed very hard by non-Mazda competition. Most of these lamps are at somewhat lower efficiency than ours and inherently have a longer life. It is very difficult to convince the typical consumer that efficiency of the lamp is the important thing. He is prone to judge quality by life alone. We realize that the constant reduction of lamp life that we have been in the process of carrying on has kept the volume of business up, but cannot refrain from giving a word of warning and a suggestion that it is about time to call a halt on this in view of the competitive situation.[132]

If the cartel's program to shorten the life of lamps had increased the efficiency of lamps and decreased the cost of lighting, the cartel would have promoted both producer and consumer interests. The former would have sold more lamps; the latter would have paid less for lighting. General Electric contends that by persistent research

. . . electric lamps have been increased greatly in usefulness and efficiency, rendered of more uniform high quality and their cost of manufacture has been decreased, with the result that the highest quality lamps have been supplied the public at greatly reduced prices . . .[133]

Efficiency v. Economy

The problem of securing efficient and economical electric illumination is a complex one. Its correct solution requires considerable technical knowledge and control of several variable factors that affect efficiency and economy.[134] The consumer's interest in economical lighting may conflict with his interest in efficient lighting. Efficiency may be purchased at the cost of economy, although it need not be. The efficiency of a lamp is expressed in terms of the light units (lumens) which it yields for each watt of power consumed. Efficiency depends primarily on two factors: (1) the temperature attained in the filament as the current flows through it; and (2) the

132. *Ibid.*, Ex. 1862-G, letter from R. G. Morison and A. L. Powell to H. B. Myrtle, May 19, 1933.
133. *Ibid.*, Answer of Defendant General Electric, p. 63.
134. For a nontechnical discussion of the relation between the length of life and the efficiency of electric lamps, consult Bowden, *op. cit.*, pp. 60-62; for a more technical discussion, consult John A. Kraebenbuehl, *Electrical Illumination*, Wiley, New York, 1942. Chap. 12.

quality of the materials and workmanship built into a lamp.[135] Efficiency increases rapidly with an increase in temperature. An increase in temperature makes for both a whiter light and a more efficient lamp—more lumens for each watt of power consumed. Better materials and workmanship also increase efficiency by insuring against mechanical failure and blackening.

Efficiency may be achieved at the expense of longevity, although it need not be. The life of a lamp depends on the same factors which determine its efficiency; viz., (1) the temperature of the filament, and (2) the quality of the materials and workmanship. But in this instance the relation between temperature and longevity of the lamp is directly opposite to the relation between temperature and efficiency. The higher the temperature, the shorter the life of the lamp. Longevity, like efficiency, however, varies directly with the quality of the materials and workmanship.

An increase in efficiency from an increase in temperature, if accompanied by compensating improvement in quality, would yield a more efficient lamp with no shortening of its life. If efficiency is achieved at the expense of longevity, whether it is at the expense of economy will depend on the relative price of lamps and the cost of current. A given number of light units (lumens) may be provided either by burning a low-wattage lamp of relatively high efficiency or a higher-wattage lamp of a lower efficiency.[136] Which is the more economical way of securing a desired amount of light will depend chiefly on (1) the cost of lamps, and (2) the cost of electric current.

Where lamps are relatively cheap and electric current is expensive, a desired degree of illumination can be gotten most economically by using efficient lamps of relatively low wattage. They will have to be replaced more frequently than lamps of lower efficiency, but it costs

135. Temperature, in turn, depends on: (1) the applied voltage—the greater the voltage, the higher the temperature; (2) the size and configuration (concentration) of the filament—the smaller the diameter and the greater its concentration, the higher the temperature at the same voltage; (3) the extent of loss of heat through radiation and convection; and (4) the presence or absence of gas. The suspension of the filament in argon or other inert gas, instead of in a vacuum, tends to preserve the life of a tungsten filament by lessening evaporation. The use of argon gas will give a longer life at the same temperature, but it will require more electrical energy; or it will insure the same life at a higher temperature (thereby increasing efficiency), but again it requires more electrical energy.

136. It may also be secured by variations in the rated voltage for which the lamp is designed compared to the voltage of the source of current by which it is supplied. Thus a lamp designed for 120 volts and operated on a 115-voltage circuit will give longer life and less efficiency than it will if operated on a 120-volt circuit.

relatively little to replace them. They will give more light per unit of electricity paid for (kilowatt hours) than would a less efficient, longer-lived lamp. They will also require less current to insure the desired degree of illumination. It pays to use relatively more of the low-priced element in illumination (lamps) and relatively less of the higher-priced element (electric current).

On the other hand, where lamps are high in price and electricity is cheap it may pay to secure the desired illumination by using less efficient, longer-lived lamps of higher wattages. To replace a lamp will be relatively expensive, but replacements will be necessary only at long intervals. The lamps will give less light per unit of electricity paid for than would a more efficient, shorter-lived lamp, and will require more current to give the same amount of light. But again it pays to use more of the low-priced element (electrical current) and less of the higher-priced element (lamps).[137]

The Cartel and the Consumer

Without knowledge of all the variables in a particular situation, neither the layman nor the engineer can deny or affirm that the cartel's reduction in the life of lamps gave the consumer more efficient lamps and more economical lighting. It is clear, however, that consumer preferences did not determine producers' policy.[138] Some

137. A third consideration may be the cost of labor in replacing lamps. Ease of access and cheap labor make replacing lamps inexpensive, and hence add little to the cost of lamps. Difficulty of access and high-wage labor add more to the cost of lamp service. It should be noted, also, that where lamps have to be replaced frequently, the danger of being temporarily without any light is greatly enhanced. These may be important factors in certain types of industrial operations, commercial (advertising) installations, and maritime (navigation aid) uses. In the ordinary residence, store, office, or factory, however, such factors are of little importance.

138. In selling him lights, General Electric has apparently followed a policy of keeping the consumer in the dark. For example, in 1934 International opposed a proposal made by Phoebus representatives that lamps be marked in lumens instead of watts. Although lumen marking would have permitted more intelligent buying by the public, it might have curtailed the use of electricity to the disadvantage of the public utility companies. On this ground International opposed the plan, pointing out that in the United States public utilities were privately owned, used Mazda lamps exclusively, and were important purchasers of power-producing equipment made by General Electric and Westinghouse. "They appreciate that even today their largest single item of income is derived from their lighting load, and they cooperate whole-heartedly in all efforts to increase current consumption from this source. . . . it is vital that the lamp manufacturer at least not decrease the income-producing load of the central station in the United States . . . The future expansion of the business of the large electrical manufacturers of the United States depends primarily upon the creation of an increase in power consumption. The use of lumen marking, with its potential power-consumption

producers made a deliberate effort to conceal their reductions in the life of lamps. A General Electric official in 1937 wrote to an official of the Champion Lamp Works:

Decision has just been made to change the life of the 200-watt 110-120 volt PS30 bulb lamp from 1000 hours. design and published to 750 hours design and published. This change will be made on clear, white bowl and inside frost finished lamps, but the silver bowl and the daylight lamps will be continued at 1000 hours design and published.

We do not know just when this change will go into effect, and we are giving no publicity whatever to the fact that the change is contemplated. I am giving you this advance information today, just as we are giving it to our own factories, so that you, too, can start building up some 750-hour stock in contemplation of the ultimate change.[139]

Again, in 1939, a General Electric official wrote to one of the company's licensees, Tung-Sol Lamp Works, as follows:

In conformity with our practice of notifying you of impending changes in our lamp product, we are calling to your attention a change which has been approved:

1. The design life of the 2330 Lamp has been changed from 300 back to 200 hours, the change to take effect as soon as manufacturing facilities will permit. It is understood that no publicity or other announcement will be made of the change.[140]

Cartel Discourages Quality Competition

The cartel's standardization program had another object besides increasing sales by shortening lamp life—to eliminate competition in

decrease, retards the expansion of an industry in which we must be vitally interested, . . ." *U.S.* v. *G.E.,* Civil Action No. 1364, Ex. 2143-G, a letter from Mr. Sloan to Mr. Minor, September 27, 1934.

General Electric representatives manifested a similar solicitude for the public utilities, at the expense of the consumer, in their early promotion of fluorescent lighting. After conferences with representatives of the Edison Electric Institute, whose membership consists of more than a hundred public utility companies, they agreed to avoid advertising the fact that fluorescent lighting (which is far more efficient than incandescent lighting and hence uses less current to obtain a desired illumination) will reduce lighting costs, and on objections from public utility representatives they discontinued a fluorescent lighting display at the New York World's Fair in 1939, because it demonstrated to the consumer fluorescent lighting's greater efficiency as compared with incandescent lighting. See Hearings before the Committee on Patents, U.S. Senate, 77th Cong., 2d sess., on S. 2303 and S. 2491, Pt. IX, *passim,* but particularly Ex. 23, p. 4849; Ex. 49, p. 4916; and Exs. 50 and 51, p. 4917.

139. *U.S.* v. *G.E.,* Civil Action No. 1364, Ex. 190-G, letter from D. C. Hughes to D. H. Marsh, April 9, 1937.

140. *Ibid.,* Ex. 193-G, letter from D. C. Hughes to L. Rieben and A. W. Gast, dated December 22, 1939.

quality. For example, after General Electric licensees had been induced to make their lamps conform to Mazda lamps in length of life and in efficiency, they were encouraged to avoid comparative tests of quality and to rely on company good will and prestige to promote sales. A General Electric official described this strategy in 1933 as follows:

> Now that the Licensees have come to the use of efficiencies and design lives which are the same as for Mazda lamps there will be much less likelihood of tests and test results being utilized in commercial practice than was the case before. They have all agreed that tests should not form the basis for acceptability of a product except in a very general way.[141]

General Electric not only sought to prevent competition based on quality, but it investigated compliance with its program and when departures from its policy were uncovered rebuked the "offender." A General Electric official wrote to an official of Consolidated Electric in 1938 criticizing portions of Consolidated's advertising booklet:

> 1. The curve on page 7, showing the average life which is some substantial percentage in excess of the rated life. This chart seems to me to be somewhat in violation of our policy to use the same efficiency and the same rated life, and the disclosure of a margin over and above this rated life seems to call for argument as to how much margin other manufacturers have, and tends to create discussion on quality differentials. I am sure you did not have this in mind when the chart was printed, and yet I think you will see the point I have in mind.
> 2. Questions and Answers, particularly question #2 on page 18 and answer #13 on page 21. These two answers are directed to the proposition that quality can and should be disclosed by individual tests whenever a customer desires such proof. We have all found the difficulty of depending upon occasional tests as a rival measure of quality, and we have all rather come to the conclusion that in dealing with specifications and acceptability of lamps, it is far better to secure acceptance of our product on institutional confidence rather than to urge a general or broad program of testing of individual lots.[142]

Apparently General Electric licensees were not the only offenders. Licensees sometimes had occasion to rebuke General Electric for itself resorting to quality competition in the sale of lamps. In July 1938 an executive of Hygrade Sylvania wrote to General Electric:

141. *Ibid.*, Ex. 187-G, letter from Mr. Sloan to C. O. Brandel, February 21, 1933.
142. *Ibid.*, Ex. 191-G, letter from M. L. Sloan to D. H. Marsh, dated February 18, 1938.

I realize that it is difficult to control matters such as this 100% but because of other information I have as to claims by your salesmen that G.E. lamps are at least 3% better than Hygrade lamps, I am a little bit confused as to whether you are still in favor of the policy of the four Government lamp contractors not engaging in a competitive way in proving detailed superiority of individual brands.[143]

CONCLUSIONS

Freedom of enterprise in the manufacture and sale of incandescent electric lamps has been restricted from the very beginning of the industry. Not simply patents, but the use made of patent privileges has contributed greatly to this result. Competitive forces have been severely hampered, and sometimes stifled, in organizing the production of, and regulating the market for, this modern everyday "necessary." The dominant producers have rejected competitive enterprise as a way of ordering the industry. They have tried to abate the risks of a system in which each producer boldly and independently pursues his own advantage in a free market. On the contrary, lamp manufacturers have, in the main, conducted their business in accordance with mutually negotiated, deliberately concerted, and jointly administered policies.

The cartel has functioned as a sort of international planning agency for the industry, controlling it primarily for the benefit of cartel members. The controls have been by no means completely effective. In a dynamic democratic society it is indeed difficult to keep in harness the forces of competition. As competition in the lamp industry has developed from time to time, or as it has appeared imminent, it has forced the producers to pass on to consumers some of the gains of an advancing technology. While the achievements of technical research have made possible improved quality and lower costs and prices, there is no evidence that the cartel itself has stimulated technical progress. On the other hand, the dominant producers have discouraged independent research by small companies and have used their control of technology to perpetuate their preponderant position in the industry.

Privately administered cartel controls in the lamp industry, to the extent that they have worked, have tended to keep prices up and in-

143. *Ibid.*, Ex. 192-G, letter from E. J. Poor to M. L. Sloan, dated July 22, 1938.

vestment down. The cartel, by denying the public the advantages of competitive cost-price relationships, has tended to block an economical use of resources in lamp production. A vigorously enforced standardization program has shortened the life of lamps partly at least in order to increase profits. The cartel has placed producers' interest first.

Perhaps this was to have been expected. But it is a question whether the best interests of the producers themselves have in fact been served. That they have profited from Phoebus can scarcely be denied. But businessmen have a stake in a free private enterprise system which extends far beyond their short-run profit interest. A profit-making system that is not at once held in check by free competition and galvanized by spontaneous enterprise simply does not make sense.

Chapter 9

THE CHEMICAL INDUSTRIES: AN INTRODUCTORY
SURVEY

Development and Scope of Chemicals Manufacture

THE CHEMICAL INDUSTRIES have no hard and fast boundary lines. The domain of industrial chemistry—the science which treats of the composition and transformation of matter—is potentially as broad as the whole field of manufacture. Few branches of industry today do not, in some stage of their operations, use one or more chemical processes or a product of such processes to "work up" materials on the way toward finished products.

Finished or semifinished products which are the direct outcome of chemical operations made up perhaps 40 per cent of American manufactures by value in 1939.[1] But these goods were highly diversified and were made in a great variety of ways. Most are not commonly regarded as chemical products, nor the industries which produce them as chemical industries. They include metals, fuels, sugar, paper, soap, glass, fertilizer, ceramics, ink, drugs, cement, alcoholic beverages, photographic supplies, textiles, leather, glue, paints, rubber, and other products. The manufacturers of these products employ chemical processes, but most of them are primarily consumers rather than producers of chemicals. They refine or utilize chemicals, instead of manufacturing them. A suitable term for these lines of business would be "chemical processing industries," as distinct from chemical industries.

The primary job of chemical industries is production of chemicals.

1. An estimate of this kind depends a great deal on the estimator's criterion of "chemical operations." Using the standard suggested by the specimen list of chemically processed products in the text below, something like 45 per cent of the $56.8 billion total value of manufactured products in 1939 falls in this category. Making some allowance for the very broad definition of chemical processing industries used in this computation, the proportion can safely be put at 40 per cent. A computation on the "value added by manufactures" basis gives about the same result. See *Statistical Abstract of the United States,* 1943, pp. 773-800.

The scope of this cartel study is as broad as the activities of the concerns that have come to be known as chemical companies. However, these activities themselves are not neatly defined or clearly delimited. Chemical companies have followed the paths and bypaths projected by chemical technology: numerous and not always clear. The chemical industries have not advanced along a narrow course, but on a wide front. They have sprawled over a great many fields, some of them previously occupied by other producing interests.

Chemistry Works a Second Industrial Revolution

Chemical technology is so charged with vitality, so cumulative, so pervasive, that the boundaries between chemical industries and other industries are artificial and fluid. The young and powerful chemical giants today challenge the nonchemical industries of yesterday; they constitute a competitive threat to vested business interests in the "mechanical" and handicraft fields. Synthetic fibers have revolutionized the textile industry; during the war, synthetic rubber virtually supplanted natural rubber; synthetic plastics have made serious inroads into the markets for metals and wood; synthetic motor fuels have proved superior to gasoline. The products of the test tube and the laboratory simulate leather and supplement hides for leather-using industries. Indeed, chemistry in the industrial arts has wrought a second industrial revolution. No part of our economy has been free from its influence.

The threat of industrial chemistry to vested business interest—its corrosive action on long-established economic boundaries—has given powerful impetus to unified control in the chemical industries. To protect customary markets from the capricious onslaughts of chemical technology and insure development of new techniques and new products in an orderly manner—from the standpoint of their business interests—chemical companies have resorted to various expedients. These range from comprehensive written agreements, perpetual patent pools, and intercompany exchange of stocks, to casual gentlemen's understandings, nebulous codes of business ethics, and friendly favoritism in commercial relations. Thanks partly to one or another of these devices, and partly to mere rational self-restraint in perspicacious recognition of the mutuality of the interests at stake and of the obstacles which differences in marketing techniques and control of raw materials interpose, the major "chemical companies" generally do not engage in the manufacture of fuels, metals, glass, soap, paper, and alcoholic beverages.[2]

Nevertheless, the line of demarcation between chemical processing industries and chemical industries is by no means fixed and impenetrable. The scope of chemical companies' activities is broad and tends constantly to expand. Chemical companies number their products by the thousands, and the number grows daily. Chemical products are used in virtually every branch of industry and agriculture and come to the consumer in almost every product he consumes; yet, because they are primarily industrial raw materials which have lost their identity, the average consumer is unaware of them. To him even their names are meaningless.

Heavy Chemicals

Two major divisions of the chemical industries are those producing heavy chemicals and organic chemicals, although these product groups are not mutually exclusive.[3] The heavy branches of the chemical industries belong in the group of so-called "heavy" industries, because their products—like iron and steel, nonferrous metals, lumber, and cement—are bulky and their prices, in relation to weight or bulk, are low. As Kreps puts it:

The heavy chemical industries in general include all those enterprises which turn out bulky chemicals cheap per unit of weight. The consumption of raw

2. This generalization applies more accurately to the American industry than to the European. Probably technological considerations have also been a factor in deterring chemical companies from extending their sphere of operations into the chemical processing industries. But this factor does not appear to have been decisive. Neither Imperial Chemical Industries, Ltd., in Great Britain, nor I. G. Farbenindustrie A. G., in Germany, limits its activities as narrowly to the "chemical" field as American companies generally do. For example, both these giant chemical companies produce synthetic fuels on a large scale. In the United States, petroleum companies occupy this field. Both the above foreign concerns also produce and fabricate metals on a large scale, as does the Montecatini firm in Italy. In the United States, production of metals by "chemical companies" is the exception rather than the rule.

3. This classification is neither entirely logical nor exhaustive. In strict logic, heavy chemicals contrast with fine chemicals—chemicals produced in relatively small quantities, of high quality and purity and relatively high value per unit of volume. Analytical chemicals for laboratory testing, pharmaceutical and photographic specialities, and the like, are frequently called fine chemicals. However, a great number of items usually classified as organic chemicals qualify under this definition as fine chemicals. On the other hand, many so-called fine chemicals are now produced in such quantities as to qualify them as heavy chemicals. The classification of chemicals as "heavy" and "organic" is convenient, even though not entirely logical. It conforms to common usage and embraces the majority of chemicals produced.

materials and the output of finished products normally run into thousands and millions of tons and into the tens and hundreds of millions of dollars.[4]

Heavy chemicals are raw materials for manufacturing and for agriculture. They include sulphuric and other inorganic acids; the alkalies—soda ash, caustic soda, sodium bicarbonate; fertilizers—mainly compounds of nitrogen, phosphorus, and potassium; chlorine and its derivative bleaching and disinfecting compounds; calcium carbide and its derivative, acetylene; industrial gases—oxygen, carbon dioxide, argon, neon; white lead; cyanides, and numerous other products.

Sulphuric acid is the most important single heavy chemical. Large quantities go into the production of other chemicals—superphosphates, sulphate of ammonia, rayon, alum, salt cake, Glauber's salts, copper sulphate. It is widely used, also, in metallurgy ("pickling" steel), in petroleum refining, in tanning of leather, and in textile dyeing. The alkalies are basic raw materials for the production of glass, soap, paper, and certain kinds of rayon; they have many uses also in the textile industry, in petroleum refining, and in the preparation of various foods and drugs. American production of the three most important heavy chemicals—sulphuric acid, soda ash, and caustic soda—amounted to about $57 million, $45 million, and $37 million, respectively, in 1939.[5]

Organic Chemicals

Organic chemicals are the compounds of carbon, though business usage sometimes restricts the term to compounds of carbon and hydrogen. They are called organic because scientists once believed that these compounds could be produced only by the "vital force" in living organisms. Friedrich Wöhler dissipated the idea in 1828 when he unwittingly ushered in the age of synthetic organic chemistry by accidentally synthesizing urea. Today chemists can artificially make hundreds of thousands of organic compounds, most of which are not duplicated in nature.[6]

4. Theodore J. Kreps, "Heavy Chemicals," *Encyclopaedia of the Social Sciences*, Macmillan, New York, 1937, Vol. VII, p. 300.
5. Bureau of the Census, Sixteenth Census of the United States, *Manufactures*, 1939, Vol. II, Pt. I, pp. 827, 829. Soda ash was the source of almost 60 per cent of the caustic soda produced.
6. Edwin E. Slosson, *Creative Chemistry*, Century, New York, 1921, p. 62.

In this field the chemical companies have confined their operations chiefly to making synthetic products. For example, they have not generally engaged in the distillation of hardwood (yielding wood alcohol, acetic acid, acetone), or in the fermentation and distillation of natural carbohydrates (yielding alcoholic beverages), or in the production or refining of natural oils, fats, waxes, sugar, starches, natural resins (shellac, rosin), or turpentine. Although these are all organic chemicals, they are not synthetic. Their manufacture involves such physical or biochemical processes as milling, fermentation, distillation, refining. Ordinarily the enterprises which make these products are separate from chemical companies. Other concerns than chemical firms specialize in the processing of particular natural raw materials such as hardwood, or producing a line of closely related end-products, such as essential oils.

Production of organic chemicals depends especially on coal, though other source materials, such as air, water, and cellulose, are used. On destructive distillation, coal yields large quantities of byproduct ammonia in addition to coke, various combustible gases, and coal tar. Chemical companies generally purchase the coal-tar byproduct of municipal gas works and of iron and steel plants, rather than produce it themselves.

Coal tar, which for a hundred years was a waste product or found limited use as roofing material, has become the most versatile raw material of modern chemistry:

It is one of the strategic points in war and commerce. It wounds and heals. It supplies munitions and medicines. . . . The chemist puts his hand into the black mass and draws out all the colors of the rainbow. This evil-smelling substance beats the rose in the production of perfume and surpasses the honey-comb in sweetness.[7]

Further distilled, coal tar yields about a dozen primary products or "crudes," the most familiar of which are benzol (benzene), toluol (toluene), xylol (xylene), phenol (carbolic acid), naphthalene, anthracene, and the final residue, pitch.

These coal-tar crudes have laid the basis of an important sector of the chemical industries. From them chemists have learned to produce hundreds of "intermediates" by rearranging, adding, and subtracting

7. *Ibid.*, p. 61.

molecules in a highly intricate and complex manner. And from these extraordinarily versatile intermediates in turn they produce many thousands of finished, completely synthetic dyestuffs, pharmaceuticals (aspirin, the sulfa drugs, atabrine), perfumes, food flavors, poisons, and plastics. Moreover, coal-tar chemicals are indispensable constituents of many other products: explosives, antiknock motor fuels, all kinds of rubber goods.

The Role of Petroleum

As chemists have become increasingly proficient in handling molecules, they have found that other hydrocarbons besides coal tar may serve as raw material for organic chemicals. Of these the most promising are petroleum and natural gas. The chemical laboratory has almost erased the economic boundaries between coal or lignite and petroleum. Leading industrial countries such as Germany and England produce part of their motor fuel from coal. On the other hand, petroleum derivatives have increasingly supplemented coal tar as the starting point in chemical synthesis. Today ethylene glycol (a major constituent of antifreeze mixtures) and several commercial plastics and synthetic rubber are produced mainly from raw materials derived from petroleum or natural gas. It is technically and commercially possible to obtain glycerin, formaldehyde, acetic acid and anhydride, and the major alcohols from these same sources, and in recent years part of the supplies of all these widely used chemicals has come from oil and gas.[8]

These developments are transforming the manufacture of fuels and lubricants, the traditional domain of petroleum refining, into a synthetic chemical industry. Originally the processing of crude oil involved primarily separating its natural constituents by fractional distillation and purifying the resultant fractions. Today this process has become truly chemical. By increasingly refined and scientifically controlled methods of "cracking," oil refineries systematically alter the chemical composition of the various crude fractions to yield, in the desired proportions, a variety of new motor fuels and chemicals. Petroleum cracking now produces large quantities of toluene, one of the components of TNT. It also yields butadiene, the major in-

8. See Reginald L. Wakemen, "Plastics and Chemicals from Petroleum Base," *National Petroleum News*, July 23, 1941, pp. R226-32.

gredient of the leading synthetic rubbers. The high-octane motor fuels developed in recent years are completely synthetic products, chemically tailor-made to specifications.

Another basic raw material of industrial organic chemistry is cellulose, the chief constituent of the solid framework (cell walls) of all plant life. The major industrial sources of cellulose are wood and cotton. Salt, lime, and sulphur, which have to be paid for, and water and air, which are practically free, just about complete the materials base of big-tonnage chemicals. Modern alchemists have transmuted these commonplace materials into cellophane, rayon, films, plastics, explosives, lacquers, imitation leather—and the end is not yet.

This brief sketch of the main roots, stems, and branches of modern industrial chemistry may give a clearer notion of the scope of the present study. Enterprises commonly known as chemical companies are customarily producers of one or more of the following classes of goods or of the intermediate materials from which they are made: dyestuffs, explosives, fertilizers, artificial textile filaments and fibers, paints, synthetic lacquers, plastics, synthetic rubber, synthetic fuels, pharmaceuticals, perfumes, glue, photographic film, and dry-cleaning and disinfecting products.

Few chemical companies produce all these products, but most chemical companies produce several of them. They also produce a wide range of heavy and organic chemicals, partly for their own use but often mainly for chemical processing industries. These include, besides such widely used items as caustic soda, chlorine, and sulphuric and acetic acids, materials more specifically adapted to particular processing industries, such as paint and varnish ingredients, photographic chemicals, antifreeze ingredients, rubber chemicals, tanning materials, food preservatives, alcohols and other solvents.

Evolution of the Chemical Industries

The ancient Greeks manufactured white lead; the Chinese, gunpowder and porcelain; the Phoenicians, glass. All these were chemical operations. However, the emergence of a genuine chemical industry awaited the transformation of the empirical arts of handicraft into a scientifically directed technology. The major stimulus to the science of chemistry and the most signal advances in its industrial application came with the Industrial Revolution.

During the eighteenth and nineteenth centuries, industrial needs for chemicals rose so rapidly that the crude methods of time-honored practice could no longer supply them. The transformation of textile manufacture, especially, from handicraft trades to mass-production industries was the crucible from which emerged a whole series of new chemical industries. The reactants were the insatiable demand for detergents, dyes, and bleaching compounds and the soaring prices for these materials, obtainable in larger quantities from traditional sources only with increasing difficulty.

In this situation, a revolutionary development was Nicolas Leblanc's discovery in 1791 of a method of synthesizing soda ash (sodium carbonate) from sulphuric acid, common salt, and limestone. Leblanc's process increased the already mounting demand for sulphuric acid, which was also used in the dyeing of textiles and in the rapidly growing metallurgical industries. The continuous chamber process, perfected in 1810, made possible large-scale production of sulphuric acid.

Great Britain, cradle of the Industrial Revolution, promptly assumed world leadership in the production of heavy chemicals. During the nineteenth century its exports of soda ash, caustic soda, bleaching powder (a byproduct of the Leblanc process), Glauber's salts (an intermediate Leblanc product), and other heavy chemicals such as sulphuric and nitric acids dominated world markets and ran into millions of pounds sterling annually.

Toward the end of the nineteenth century, when the Industrial Revolution entered its chemical phase, other industrial countries, particularly the United States and Germany, challenged British leadership. They were aided by important technological developments. As early as 1863 Ernest Solvay, a Belgian, invented the ammonia-soda process for the manufacture of soda ash. The Belgian Société Solvay (later Solvay et Cie.) and its associates promptly extended their operations throughout the industrial world. By the first decade of the twentieth century the Solvay process had largely supplanted the Leblanc process, had reduced the price of soda ash by more than 70 per cent, and had enabled the leading industrial countries to become independent of the British alkali industry, although Great Britain by itself adopting the Solvay process still remained the largest exporter of alkalies.[9] The British lead in heavy chemicals was further cut when about 1905 German chemists perfected the contact process for the direct manufacture of sulphuric acid.

More important than either of these developments to the eventual eclipse of British chemical supremacy was the discovery of the almost unlimited chemical potentialities of coal tar and its derivatives. Though this development originated in England, Germany quickly took the lead. By World War I Germany produced between 75 and 80 per cent of the world's dyestuffs and German chemical companies controlled another 5 per cent made in foreign plants. In addition, these companies supplied to non-German dyestuffs makers more than half the coal-tar intermediates they consumed.

The only other important exporters of dyestuffs were the Swiss, who were largely dependent on German coal-tar crudes and intermediates. Although the United States was the world's leading chemical producer—chiefly heavy chemicals for the domestic market—American dyestuffs manufacturers supplied only about 10 per cent of the domestic consumption. Even for this small output, they imported about 90 per cent of their intermediates. Both British and American dyestuffs establishments were in reality little more than assembling plants.[10]

German Leadership in Chemicals

German predominance in modern "creative chemistry" stemmed chiefly from three basic factors. First, Germany made an early start in adapting its educational system to the practical needs of modern industry, grounded on exact science. In particular, it developed technical high schools which served as a training ground for industrial

9. See Williams Haynes, *Chemical Economics*, Van Nostrand, New York, 1933, Chap. 6 and pp. 176-79; Kreps, *op. cit.*, pp. 300-04; Stephen Miall, *A History of the British Chemical Industry*, Benn, London, 1931, Chap. 1.

10. U.S. Tariff Commission, Report No. 125, Ser. II, *Dyes and Other Synthetic Organic Chemicals in the United States*, 1936, p. 1; U.S. Bureau of Foreign and Domestic Commerce, Trade Information Bulletin No. 605, *German Chemical Developments in 1928*, p. 27; League of Nations, Publications, Ser. II, *The Chemical Industry*, 1927, No. 4, pp. 28, 84; Sub-Committee appointed by the Standing Committee on Trusts, Parliamentary Report, Command Paper No. 1370, *Report on Dyes and Dyestuffs*, London, 1921, p. 4. (Hereinafter cited: Standing Committee on Trusts.)

From 1900 to 1910, of 819 United States patents issued for organic colors, no less than 685 went to German, and 113 to Swiss, inventors. Only 9 went to Americans and 5 to British subjects. Kreps, "Dye Industry," *Encyclopaedia of the Social Sciences*, Vol. V, p. 302 f.

technicians of high calibre.[11] These schools were not mere adjuncts to the educational system at the secondary level, providing a sort of apprenticeship training in arts and crafts. They were thoroughly integrated in an educational process which culminated in the great German universities. The capstone of the whole structure, on the side of the physical sciences, was the Kaiser Wilhelm Institute. The prestige of these institutions of higher learning and of scientific research and their solicitous cultivation of exacting standards of scholarship permeated technical instruction at every level and stimulated a wide interest in scientific achievement.[12]

Second, the German homeland was comparatively deficient in many important natural resources, notably iron, copper, and oil. To make up for deficiencies of its endowment, Germany created new resources by painstaking industrial research.[13] Moreover, for this task such raw materials as Germany possessed in abundance, notably coal and various mineral salts, provided a promising base for chemical developments.

A third factor contributing to German pre-eminence in industrial chemistry consisted of certain traits of German character. Chief among these are a penchant for systematization and a vaulting nationalistic ambition.[14] While these are not peculiar to the German people, they rest on ethnographic and historical grounds which have made them so common and so pronounced a feature of the German mind as to warrant calling them national traits.

Technology the Handmaid of Industry

These factors help to explain the outstanding success of German scientists in pushing forward the boundaries of chemical technology. German businessmen have made this prolific technology the hand-

11. Cf. Theodore J. Kreps' article in the volume of essays honoring Professor F. W. Taussig, *Explorations in Economics*, McGraw-Hill, New York, 1936, pp. 152-53.

12. In contrast, English universities like Oxford and Cambridge trained relatively few chemists: "Their students, trained in the classics for the profession of being a gentleman, showed a decided repugnance to the laboratory on account of its bad smells." Slosson, *op. cit.*, p. 80.

13. In the United States, where natural resources are more abundant and population density is far less than in Europe, Yankee ingenuity has been directed toward devising and introducing labor-saving techniques. These factors help to account for American leadership in the development of machine processes and mass production.

14. Though imperialism has not been entirely unknown in the history of Anglo-Saxon countries, it has generally been associated with commercial rather than political ambitions. Moreover, at least in the last half century, it has increasingly been subordinated to peaceful pursuits.

maid of industry. They built extensive, well-equipped laboratories and hired doctors of philosophy (in chemistry) by the hundreds. They assembled large, well-trained sales staffs and taught consuming industries how to use the new chemical products these technicians were developing. Meanwhile, according to an "official" historian of the British chemical industries, "The majority of . . . English firms had just enough vitality to keep them from putrefaction." [15] More than any other nation, Germany perceived in chemistry "the wave of the future" and determined to harness it in the interests of business and empire.

The German Government has shaped its tariff and patent laws to meet the needs of its industrialization program. German businessmen have been quick to use patents, both at home and abroad, to fortify their leadership in industrial chemistry.[16] On occasion they have also engaged in wholesale bribery of dyers, "full-line" forcing, dumping, and local price cutting to eliminate actual or potential competition in

15. This statement was made in a book sponsored by the British Society of Chemical Industry to commemorate its 50th anniversary; Miall, *op. cit.*, p. 85.

16. German firms, in applying for patents, have followed the practice of blocking out as large a monopoly area and disclosing as little technical information as possible. Frank A. Howard, of Standard Oil Company of New Jersey, has described the patent policy of I. G. Farben as follows: "The I. G. patent policy is to disclose in the patent as little as possible, the whole idea being to get protection and at the same time reveal as little as may be of the unprotectable technical knowledge required for the successful production of the invention." At the same time Mr. Howard recognized the danger of this practice. He stated: "I have already assumed the right to advise the I. G. that the policy was a dangerous one. [Presumably because patents which give information inadequate to permit of successful practice by anyone skilled in the art are legally invalid.] In the U.S. we are, at the present time, adding materially to the disclosures of many of the patents with this in mind." Letter to E. M. Clark, March 19, 1930, in *Patents*, Hearings before the Committee on Patents, 77th Cong., 2d sess., on S. 2303 and S. 2491, Pt. VII, p. 3674. (Hereinafter referred to as Bone, Pt. —.)

German industrialists have followed this policy pertinaciously. During World War I American companies were unable to make either salvarsan (the specific for syphilis) or synthetic ammonia using the methods described in the confiscated German-owned American patents.

In World War II another Standard Oil employee appraised IG's patent policy as follows: "I have been particularly impressed both by the thoroughness with which the I. G. have covered the field and the clever way in which the claims have been drawn. So far, the patents issued to others have only brought to light a very limited number of omissions of any consequence.

"Even if some of the I. G. claims should be too broad to make it possible to enforce them, the patent structure as a whole is so impressive that it may well serve as a guide to us in our own efforts to build up a strong position on butyl rubber." Again, on the same subject:

"By covering themselves in so many different directions . . . it would seem that they have gone a long way toward eliminating competition as far as this specific type of synthetic rubber is concerned." *Technological Mobilization*, Hearings before a Subcommittee of the Committee on Military Affairs, U.S. Senate, 77th Cong., 2d sess., on S. 2721, Pt. II, p. 501.

particular areas.[17] The temporary losses or expenses incurred by the use of such tactics may be more than offset, in the long run, by the monopoly revenue they help to make secure.

World War I—a Catalyst

World War I awakened the Allied countries to the fact and significance of German leadership in coal-tar chemistry. They saw German dyestuff plants converted to the production of explosives and poison gases. They saw German industrialists fix nitrogen from the air and produce explosives without Chilean nitrate. Lacking essential experience, the Allies were forced to hasty, clumsy makeshifts.

However, these fumbling efforts were the beginning of independent modern chemical industries outside Germany. Between 1914 and 1919 the number of American dyestuffs manufacturers increased from seven to ninety, their output from $3 million to $67.5 million.[18] The United States, France, Great Britain, and other industrial countries made great progress in chemical technology, most signally perhaps in the manufacture of dyestuffs and synthetic nitrogen. They expanded enormously their capacity for recovering such basic coal-tar crudes as toluol and phenol, for manufacturing the explosives TNT and picric acid. They learned to produce phenol synthetically. With the help of sequestered German patents, they developed a process to produce acetone, used in the manufacture of the smokeless powder, cordite, and as "dope" for airplane wings.

After the war, the war-born infant chemical industries were nurtured by protective tariffs.[19] They were also the beneficiaries of the

17. U.S. Alien Property Custodian, Report 1918–1919, pp. 30-37; *Dyestuffs*, Hearings before the Committee on Finance, U.S. Senate, 68th Cong., 2d sess., on H.R. 8078, pp. 85, 98-101, 509 f. See the excellent discussion in Charles A. Welsh, *The World Dyestuffs Industry* (unpublished doctoral dissertation, New York University, April 1944), pp. 46-65.

18. Bone, Pt. V, p. 2058.

19. Although they had managed to meet the minimum needs of wartime, American dyestuffs makers had only a limited experience. Both the limited range and the high prices of their products indicated that a renewal of German competition would soon have wiped out most of them. U.S. Alien Property Custodian, *op. cit.,* p. 39 f.; Standing Committee on Trusts, pp. 6-7, 17-18, 20-21.

American dyestuffs producers organized the American Dyes Institute to campaign for popular support and congressional action to protect the industry from foreign competition. They lobbied extensively, arranged speeches by Army officials and resolutions by American Legion meetings, and planted newspaper stories describing the horrors of gas warfare, the "plans" of German dyemakers to ruin American industry, the intention of the French and British Governments to protect their respective industries, and the like. See Hearings before a Special Committee Investigating the Munitions Industry,

confiscation of enemy properties, particularly the valuable German-owned patents.[20]

In Peace or War—an Onrushing Technology

Since World War I the chemical revolution has continued at a quickening pace. By 1939 the United States, Great Britain, and to a lesser extent France, Italy, Japan, and the USSR, had become virtually self-sufficient in the production of most dyestuffs, pharmaceuticals, and other coal-tar products, and in the synthesis of nitrogenous fertilizers and explosives. They were still deficient, however, in many relatively complex or recently developed products.[21]

The rapid development of the world's chemical industries after World War I was greatly spurred by the growth of rayon and plastics and the development of aliphatic chemistry, but preparation for World War II was also a factor, particularly in Germany and Japan. In particular the German and Japanese Governments heavily subsidized their chemical industries for war purposes.[22] Government subsidies, direct or indirect, spurred German developments in synthetic rubber and plastics, synthetic fuels, light metals, and various other substitutes for natural materials.

However, the world's chemical industries would have grown

U.S. Senate, 73d Cong., Pt. XI, pp. 2397-2417; Pt. XII, pp. 2754-74 et seq.; *Report* (74th Cong., 2d sess., S.Rept. 944), Pt. III, pp. 270-73. (These Hearings will hereinafter be cited as Nye, Pt. —, or Nye, *Report*, Pt. —, after the name of the committee chairman.)

20. On December 12, 1918, the United States Alien Property Custodian sold at public auction the sequestered pharmaceutical and dyestuffs assets of the (German) Bayer company. These assets consisted chiefly of the capital stocks of (American) Bayer & Company, the Synthetic Patents Company, and the Williams & Crowell Color Company, and some 1,200 drug and dye patents. Sterling Products Company, with a bid of $5,310,000, was the purchaser. It later sold the dyestuffs assets to Grasselli Chemical Company, which in 1925–1926 sold them back to IG.

The Alien Property Custodian transferred the remaining 4,700 sequestered German chemical patents to a nonprofit corporation, the Chemical Foundation, which it had organized in cooperation with a number of American chemical companies. The contract required the Foundation to license the patents on uniform terms to all American applicants. See *Report of Alien Property Custodian, 1917–1922*, Cong. Doc. 7981, 67th Cong., 2d sess., 1922; and *U.S. v. The Chemical Foundation*, 5 Fed. 2d 191 (1925), affirmed in 272 U.S. 1 (1926).

21. The average price of dyestuffs produced within the United States in 1936 was 54 cents a pound, and that of dyestuffs exports only 35 cents. The average value of dyestuffs imports, in contrast, was no less than $1.51. This indicates the concentration of the American industry on volume production of the cheaper dyes, like indigo and sulphur black, while leaving to the Germans the more restricted market for special-purpose, high-priced dyes. Tariff Commission, *op. cit.*, p. 2.

22. See Bureau of Foreign and Domestic Commerce, Trade Promotion Series, No. 189, *Synthetic Organic Chemicals*, p. 136 f.; Trade Information Bulletin No. 823, *World Chemical Developments in 1934*, pp. 13-24, 28, 36.

rapidly without artificial encouragement. The advance of scientific knowledge has gone on unremittingly, and in one way or another these advances would have found practical application. The increase in population, development of higher living standards, expansion of industry generally, and the particularly rapid growth of automobile, rayon, paper, and petroleum industries, have greatly stimulated the demand for industrial chemicals.

The chemical industries have passed through three phases. The first was characterized by relatively simple, large-scale production of heavy chemicals; the second by the introduction, in relatively small quantities, of a great variety of highly complicated, specialized, synthetic chemicals of the coal-tar family. In the third phase, which began about 1914, synthetic chemicals are rapidly taking rank with inorganic acids and the alkalies in the group of heavy-chemical industries—witness the annual production of hundreds of thousands of tons of rayon, synthetic ammonia, synthetic rubber, and plastics, and tens of millions of gallons of synthetic industrial alcohols, synthetic fuels, and synthetic finishes.

Mass production of synthetics has utilized basic techniques of creative chemistry for the initial development of which before 1914 German technicians were mainly responsible, though in their subsequent elaboration and extension American chemists have played an outstanding role.[23] Germany's head start has been a big factor in her continued leadership. Greater experience, more technicians, intensive research, aggressive patent and sales policies, and governmental subsidies have proved important advantages to German chemical manufacturers whether in competitive markets or in cartel bargaining. These advantages enabled them to outdistance all others in export markets before World War II.[24] In total output, however, the Ameri-

23. Synthetic alcohols, all the aliphatics, most of the plastics, nylon, and Neoprene are distinctively and exclusively American developments.

24. Before World War I Germany accounted for 28 per cent of all chemical exports. Despite the almost complete loss of her foreign markets and many of her foreign properties, in less than a decade Germany again accounted for 28 per cent of world exports of chemical products, according to estimates presented to the 1927 International Economic Conference. Great Britain followed with 16 per cent, next Chile with 15 per cent, and then the United States and France with 10 per cent each. League of Nations, *op. cit.*, p. 12. In 1938 Germany still led the world with exports provisionally estimated at $263 million, followed by the United States ($159 million), the United Kingdom ($132 million), and France ($91 million). Bureau of Foreign and Domestic Commerce, Trade Promotion Series, No. 193, *World Chemical Developments in 1938*, p. 12; see also Trade Information Bulletin No. 753, *German Chemical Developments in 1930*, p. 5.

can industry, with its much larger domestic market, far exceeded the German before the war.[25]

Relation of National Industrial Concentration to Cartelization

Although all the major industrial countries and a multitude of business units participate in the world trade in chemicals, the forces of free competition do not rule the world markets. The techniques of business diplomacy frequently supplement and in some instances have supplanted independent decision making by separate producers in response to free market forces.[26] The geographic and industrial areas within which particular companies will operate, the scale of their output, the prices of their products, the use or nonuse of their technology, have increasingly become objects of negotiation, subjects of national and international agreement. More and more the conference table has been taking the place of the market as a regulator of the chemical industries.

Cartelized control within domestic markets is a prerequisite to an international cartel. Domestic market controls need not take the form of monopoly. The national unit in an international cartel is usually an association or company authorized to speak for the whole of the domestic industry. Before firms can effectively take part in an international cartel—accept joint obligations, impose mutual restraints, apportion benefits in the world market—they must be in a position to limit the volume and fix the selling terms of exports from their own country. To do this they must set up some form of cooperative or unified control within their national area.[27]

25. Rough estimates indicate that the United States accounted for 34 per cent and Germany for 24 per cent of the world's total chemical production in 1913, and 43 per cent and 17 per cent, respectively, in 1929. Great Britain and France followed in 1929 with respective shares of 11 and 7 per cent. Bureau of Foreign and Domestic Commerce, Trade Information Bulletin No. 690, *German Chemical Developments in 1929*, p. 1; see also League of Nations, *op. cit.*, p. 21.

During the thirties the United States probably lost ground relative to other countries, notably Germany, Japan, and the USSR, where production policies were shaped to war needs. However, it undoubtedly retained its leadership in output, and has regained much or all of the lost ground since 1939.

26. The complexity of chemical processes, combining possibilities of infinite variations in some directions with the necessity of meticulously exact uniformity in many specific processes, the exceptional importance of joint products and byproducts, the large scale of production required to get the most economical results, and the extremely specialized character of plant equipment, all tend to impede competitive adjustments. These factors practically rule out even a passable approach to pure competition in these industries.

27. In the words of Sir Alfred Mond (Lord Melchett), one of the founders of the

On the other hand, international cartels speed the concentration of control within national areas. Cartels enable their constituent members, the national units, to rule their respective domestic markets without fear of foreign competition. Moreover, membership in international alliances may give the organized producers an advantage over nonmember domestic competitors, because it often puts at their disposal the combined patent rights and technical resources of their foreign cartel partners.[28]

A few gigantic chemical companies, each the product of vertical integration, horizontal combination, and circular expansion, have a preponderant share of, and exert a pervasive influence in, international chemical markets.[29] Each of these big companies produces a wide range of chemical products. In the American domestic market, control is somewhat less concentrated. In many industrial areas closely related to or allied with the chemical industries, a large number of relatively small and specialized companies continue to operate. Many independent concerns manufacture glass, paper, ink, matches, fertilizers, alcohol, pharmaceuticals, paints and varnishes, and so forth. The chemical processing industries also include numerous independent enterprises making special grades or types of chemicals or chemi-

---

great British Imperial Chemical Industries: "You cannot discuss big problems of industry with other countries until your own industries are organized first. Only recently I had occasion to talk with the leaders of big organized industries on the Continent, in Germany and in America, and I discussed this subject. These people want to talk to one or two men who represent industry in England, and if I heard one complaint made it was the impossibility of carrying on any negotiations with some great English industries, because they have not yet solved this problem and there is nobody to talk to. There is simply nobody with authority, and however big any individual company may be, it represents only a small fraction of the industries of the nation, and therefore a representative of it cannot speak in an authoritative manner." *Industry and Politics*, Macmillan, London, 1928, pp. 249-50.

28. For example, in 1930 du Pont wrote to Mitsui on the subject of releasing patent rights on the former's ammonia oxidation process: "We are receiving from time to time inquiries from Japanese concerns, and in view of our happy relations with Mitsui & Co. we think it preferable to refer such matters to your concern because we feel that it would be of mutual benefit for all these inquiries to pass through one central office." Nye, Pt. V, p. 1350. Because of the "happy relations" between these two companies, all Japanese producers became dependent upon Mitsui for access to du Pont rights and know-how in ammonia oxidation.

29. Vertical integration means linking technically successive processes under a single management. Horizontal combination means bringing together under unified control—whether or not by a single management—two or more enterprises producing goods of the same kind. By circular expansion we mean the addition of cognate lines of products to those already being made by a firm; the techniques may or may not be similar, the products may or may not be complementary.

cal products, such as plastics, which may be directly competitive with some part of the output of the big combines. These independents are often not formally associated with the combines in a direct and intimate way.

INTEGRATION AND CONCENTRATION IN AMERICAN CHEMICAL INDUSTRIES

Separate companies producing chemicals and allied products in the United States run into the thousands.[30] The field is vast, complex, and rapidly growing. The variety of products, some new and some old, and the variety of processes, some complicated and some simple, insure room for many producers, large and small. A small firm may bring on the market some new drug, patent medicine, fine chemical specialty, or new plastic material, and, with or without patent protection, build up and hold a secure place in its specialized field. Abundant opportunities created by a rapidly expanding market and constantly changing technology encourage individual enterprise, particularly in this country where individualism and the tradition of economic independence remain strong. The enormous size of the American market, the great dispersion of raw materials, and the protection afforded by laws against unfair competition and monopolistic encroachments—all have encouraged and sustained a great number of producers.

By custom, moreover, many of the chemical processing industries, involving relatively simple operations and producing primarily for the ultimate consumer, remain outside the sphere of the major companies. They use well-known techniques. Stable technology keeps these fields open to the old-fashioned enterpriser.[31]

30. The Census of Manufactures reported 9,203 "establishments" in "chemical and allied products" in 1939. According to the Census Bureau's definition of an "establishment," however, two or more departments of a single factory may be treated as separate establishments. Moreover, when a single enterprise owns several plants each of them may be classed as an "establishment," especially if they are located at a distance from one another. The number of separate chemical companies is undoubtedly much smaller than the number of manufacturing "establishments" in the industry.

31. Of the 9,203 separate plants reported in the field of chemicals and allied products by the Census of Manufactures in 1939, such groups as drugs, medicines, toilet preparations, insecticides, paints, varnishes and colors, hardwood distillation and naval stores, fertilizers, animal and vegetable oils, cleaning and polishing preparations, and soap and glycerin, together accounted for some 6,800.

Technology Makes for Integration

Despite the continued existence of a large number of small independent firms, a few giant companies have come to exert a pervasive influence in the chemical industries. The nature of the technology helps to explain why chemical manufacturers have expanded their operations horizontally, vertically, and circularly. Even though it embraces and permeates many disparate fields of industry, viewed from the standpoint of end-products, chemical technology has an inherent unity and homogeneity. However much processes may differ in detail, the fundamental techniques for transforming a few basic raw materials—air, water, coal, petroleum, wood, metallic ores, and salts—into a great variety of useful commodities are relatively few. Basically, therefore, no field of chemical industry is alien to any large chemical company which possesses sufficient capital, research facilities, and skilled chemists.

Chemical technology is not only fundamentally homogeneous, it is also enormously complex. The possible permutations and combinations of atoms are virtually infinite, and the scientific process of exploring them recognizes no artificial boundary lines between industries. From the same raw materials the chemist can produce fuels, fertilizers, beverages, drugs, and explosives. Chemical research often converts waste products of one operation into raw materials for another. It may develop a new manufacturing process or a new use for a particular chemical, the commercial success of which depends on the production of a variety of other chemicals. In no other group of industries are the interconnections so complex.

It is economical for chemical companies to broaden and diversify their operations, in particular to make the most of joint products and byproducts. This "spreads the risks"—risks which are especially great in an industry so subject to radical technological changes. It also spreads the overhead costs of plant and equipment, administration, sales, and research. Research especially has become so great an expense with the advance in chemical technology that only a company with a wide range of interests can afford to maintain the staff and laboratory facilities required to keep abreast of technical developments. Reflecting this advantage of size, a relatively few large business organizations have made, and acquired exclusive rights in, an increasing proportion of the outstanding advances in chemical "know-how" in recent years.[32] A progressive technology, the traditional mainspring of individual enterprise, has contributed to concentration of control in the chemical industries.

In 1939 the total assets of forty major American chemical companies, thirty-eight of which are registered with the Securities and Exchange Commission, were about $2,060,000,000.[33] Three companies, E. I. du Pont de Nemours ($735.8 million), Union Carbide & Carbon ($336.8 million), and Allied Chemical & Dye ($236.7 million), together accounted for about 64 per cent of this total. Six additional companies, American Cyanamid ($77.3 million), General Aniline & Film ($61.5 million), Monsanto Chemical ($54.8 million), Hercules Powder ($49.1 million), Air Reduction ($44.2 million), and Dow Chemical ($41.9 million), accounted for another 16 per cent.[34] Some of the latter group are even more diversified than the "big three"; and most of them are highly integrated concerns engaged in a wide range of operations.

Du Pont's Premier Position

These corporate giants are the outcome both of internal growth and of combination. Du Pont, founded in 1802, remained exclusively a manufacturer of explosives throughout the nineteenth century. In the last decades of the century, it embarked on a program of "trust building." By 1912 it had absorbed about a hundred other explosives companies and had achieved almost a complete domestic monopoly. In that year, as a result of an antitrust suit, a federal court ordered its dissolution. The decree required division of its assets among three "successor companies": a reorganized du Pont company and the

32. Effective research in industrial chemistry nowadays requires heavy investment in laboratory and library facilities and large financial reserves to carry the losses from "negative result" experiments. The really fruitful experiments are comparatively "few and far between." Moreover, chemical science has reached a stage in which significant advances are more and more dependent on the combined efforts of a corps of research workers, each specializing in some relatively narrow segment of the field. The outstanding case of teamwork in technology is the development of the atomic bomb, a research experiment which cost $2 billion. This figure is somewhat misleading, however, since all (other) cost considerations were sacrificed in the interest of time.
33. Securities and Exchange Commission, *Survey of American Listed Corporations,* "Chemicals, Fertilizers," Report No. 6, November 1941, p. 5. In our computation, data for two omissions from the SEC list, American Cyanamid and Diamond Alkali, are added from *Moody's Manual of Investments* (Industrials).
34. These percentages would be somewhat higher if we omitted from the SEC list several companies, notably the Koppers Company ($109.9 million), many of whose products are nonchemical.

Hercules and Atlas Powder Companies. Du Pont had already begun to expand into other fields, however, and in less than a decade it was bigger than before the dissolution.[35]

World War I gave du Pont both opportunity and incentive for further large-scale expansion. Munitions manufacture yielded tremendous profits which both spurred and helped to finance a great increase in du Pont's explosives-producing capacity. It found peacetime outlets for this capacity in lacquers and artificial leather, both nitrocellulose products. Du Pont acquired, chiefly during the war or immediately before, a number of companies producing nitrocellulose (pyroxylin) plastics, lacquers, coated fabrics (Fabrikoid), acids, and other heavy chemicals, pigments, colors, paints, and varnishes. With German competition temporarily eliminated from the organic chemicals field, it invested $50 million in dyestuffs development.

Even after this expansion in chemical fields, du Pont had enough war profits left over to purchase $47 million of General Motors stock, roughly a 25 per cent interest that gave it working control of the corporation. This investment assured a market for du Pont finishes, Fabrikoid, and certain chemicals used in all "leaded" gasoline.[36] The expansion of General Motors in refrigerator manufacture also broadened the market for du Pont chemicals.[37]

With the close of the war, du Pont expansion in chemical fields continued.[38] It had previously acquired nitrate properties in Chile to supply nitrogen for explosives, and in the twenties began production of synthetic nitrogen and nitric acid. By 1940 it was producing rayon, nylon, cellophane, photographic film, several kinds of plastics, seed disinfectants, automobile antifreeze, synthetic rubber, and a wide range of inorganic and organic chemicals.[39]

35. For the long and interesting history of "the powder trust," see the article with that title by W. H. S. Stevens, *Quarterly Journal of Economics*, 1912, Vol. XXVI, pp. 444-81.
36. The Ethyl Corporation is owned jointly, in equal shares, by General Motors and Standard Oil of New Jersey.
37. General Motors purchases its refrigerant chemicals from Kinetic Chemicals, Inc. This company is a jointly owned subsidiary of du Pont and GM, each of which has a 50 per cent stake in the enterprise.
38. See Nye, *Report*, Pt. III, pp. 21-23, 58, and Hearings, pp. 1022-80; *Moody's Manual of Investments* (Industrials); du Pont Company, Public Relations Dept., *The Du Pont Company and Its Activities*, 3d ed., 1940; Haynes, *op. cit.*, pp. 273-78; William S. Dutton, *Du Pont, One Hundred and Forty Years*, Scribner's, New York, 1942.
39. Outside the chemical field, besides its 25 per cent interest in General Motors, du Pont has large stockholdings in the United States Rubber Company and Remington

Measured by the scope and scale of its manufacturing operations, its patent holdings and research activities, and its communities of interest with other leading chemical companies, du Pont had become the outstanding factor in the domestic chemical industries. Indeed, considering its extensive financial interests beyond the borders of its primary industrial interests, it ranks among the principal foci of power in the American economy.[40]

Union Carbide & Carbon

Union Carbide & Carbon (UCC) was organized in 1917 as a merger of four companies in the carbon, carbide, industrial gas, and electro-metallurgical fields. Several of its constituent companies, notably the National Carbon Company, were the outcome of horizontal consolidation within one or another of these fields. Since its organization, UCC has expanded greatly by acquiring control of other companies for cash or through exchange of stock. As of December 31, 1940, it controlled about twenty-five subsidiaries in the United States and Canada and forty-two in other countries.[41] Its major products fall into five groups: ferroalloys; carbide and carbide derivatives; carbon electrodes and batteries; organic chemicals; and plastics.

The principle of technological continuity and affinity governed the original merger and its subsequent expansion. Both carbide and ferroalloys are electric-furnace products, and carbon electrodes are used in operating the furnaces. Coke is a raw material for both carbide and electrodes. UCC's work in carbon led to the manufacture of brushes for electric motors and of electrodes for lamps and bat-

---

Arms Co. It owns 60.17 per cent of Remington's common stock. SEC Registration Records, 1939; *Moody's Manual of Investments* (Industrials), 1945, p. 1750. Du Pont's stockholdings in U.S. Rubber are not directly reported. By far the largest U.S. Rubber stockholder is Rubber Securities Company. This is a du Pont family holding company, and its interest in U.S. Rubber, supplemented by that of individual members of the family, is sufficient to give the du Ponts working control of the rubber company. See R. W. Goldsmith and R. C. Parmelee, *The Distribution of Ownership in the 200 Largest Non-Financial Corporations*, TNEC Monograph No. 29, Washington, 1940, pp. 121-22.

40. A du Pont vice-president who had a few years before been chairman of the Democratic Party's National Committee wrote to another du Pont vice-president in 1934: "You . . . are in a position to talk directly with a group that controls a larger share of industry through common stock holdings than any other group in the United States. When I say this, I mean that I believe there is no group, including the Rockefellers, the Morgans, the Mellons, or anyone else that begins to control and be responsible for as much industrially as the du Pont Company." Nye, Pt. XVII, p. 4426.

41. See *Moody's Manual of Investments* (Industrials), 1944.

teries. From the production of its major carbide derivative, acetylene —an important industrial gas—it branched into the manufacture of other industrial gases, notably oxygen. UCC also expanded into the manufacture of a general line of organic chemicals. It has been particularly active and successful in aliphatic developments, and eventually it entered the related plastics field.

Allied Chemical & Dye

Allied Chemical & Dye comes nearest to being the "grand merger" in American chemical industries. It represents an amalgamation of five companies: General Chemical, Barrett, Solvay Process, Semet-Solvay, and National Aniline & Chemical. Each of these predecessor companies was a predominant factor in its particular field. General Chemical was itself the result of a merger in 1899 of twelve producers of sulphuric acid, who banded together largely to meet the threat of the contact process, developed by the German Badische Anilin Company. Later it developed its own contact process and also acquired American rights to the Badische process.

The Barrett Company operated as an agent for the sale of most of the domestic output of byproduct ammonia.[42] It was also the country's leading purchaser of coal tar and manufacturer of coal-tar products. Solvay Process was the American partner in a world-wide network of companies set up to exploit the Solvay soda ash process, and was by far the leading American producer in this field. Through its affiliate, Semet-Solvay, it manufactured and installed coke ovens and produced coal tar and its derivatives.

In 1910 General Chemical, Barrett, and the two Solvay companies jointly organized the Benzol Products Company to manufacture aniline oil. Semet-Solvay, General, and Barrett segregated their dyestuff business in 1917 and merged it with the business of Benzol Products and that of a number of other American manufacturers of dyestuffs and intermediates to form National Aniline & Chemical Company. National Aniline produced considerably more than half the dyestuffs consumed in America in 1919.[43] Finally, in 1920, these five com-

42. In 1924 it marketed about 85 per cent of the byproduct ammonia output of coke oven plants. Tariff Commission, Report No. 114, Ser. II, *Chemical Nitrogen*, Washington, 1937, p. 210. See Chapter 4 for a more complete discussion of Barrett's operations.
43. Alien Property Custodian, Report 1918–1919, p. 39; see also *Moody's Manual of Investments* (Industrials), 1920, p. 800.

panies merged to form the largest and most imposing aggregation of chemical interests in the United States at that time. The alliance covered the basic chemical fields—acids, alkalies, and other heavy chemicals, and coal-tar byproducts and derivatives.

Since its formation, Allied has extended its operations and financial interests, though less spectacularly than du Pont or UCC. About 1928 it began producing synthetic ammonia, and is today the largest American producer. It is the only producer of synthetic nitrate of soda. Allied has also become an important producer of electrolytic chlorine and caustic soda. It has substantial stockholdings in Air Reduction, United States Steel, and Owens-Illinois Glass.[44] Allied produced in 1937

. . . some 28 percent of the sulfuric acid made for sale, 29 percent of the caustic soda, 38 percent of the coal tar, 40 percent of the aluminum sulfate (alum), 45 percent of the soda ash, 66 percent of the ammonium sulfate and benzol, and all of the sodium nitrate made in the United States.[45]

Though du Pont and UCC have surpassed it in size, Allied continues to occupy a prominent position in virtually all branches of basic chemical manufacture. Unlike its two largest rivals, it sticks closely to this field. It has followed the conservative policy of not competing with its customers; it produces no plastics, rayons, lacquer, film, explosives, medicinals, aliphatic chemicals, or solvents.[46]

American Cyanamid

Organized in 1907 to exploit a new process for fixing nitrogen from the air in the form of calcium cyanamide, American Cyanamid confined itself for several years primarily to the field of fertilizers. In the late twenties it branched out rapidly into plastics and resins, dyestuffs, pharmaceuticals, and a wide range of industrial chemicals. By 1936, fertilizers constituted only about 10 per cent of its gross sales.[47]

44. Its holding in Air Reduction was 90,000 shares, as of December 31, 1934. New York *Times*, March 15, 1936. This had increased to 270,000 shares ten years later. *Moody's Manual of Investments* (Industrials), 1945, p. 1615. It held 150,000 shares of U.S. Steel stock at the beginning of 1945. *Ibid.*
45. Clair Wilcox, *Competition and Monopoly in American Industry*, TNEC Monograph No. 21, p. 201.
46. Haynes, *op. cit.*, pp. 262-68.
47. *Moody's Manual of Investments* (Industrials), 1944; Bone, Pt. V, pp. 2517-20.

American Cyanamid has been particularly aggressive in purchasing other firms, whether directly competitive or in "adjoining" fields. Its major acquisitions since World War I include: Selden Company, specializing in phthalic anhydride (1927); Calco Chemical Company (1929) and later nineteen other dyestuff manufacturers; Kalbfleisch Corporation (1929), a leading producer of acids and other heavy chemicals; Lederle Antitoxin Laboratories, and Davis & Geck, Inc. (1930), in the field of pharmaceuticals and medical supplies; General Explosives Corporation (1933); and H. A. Metz & Co. (1937), manufacturer of textile and tanning chemicals. Altogether, American Cyanamid acquired a controlling interest in about thirty-five previously independent companies during this period.

Major Chemical Companies Recognize Special Interest Fields

The existence of a few giant American chemical companies does not indicate the full extent to which centralized administrative control has replaced competition as a regulator of American chemical markets. Although the sprawling activities of the major companies overlap in the production of both heavy and organic chemicals, each has its distinctive major interests. For example, none of the other leading chemical companies duplicates du Pont's production of rayon, cellophane, nylon, synthetic fabrics, or auto waxes and polishes.[48] In most other fields in which du Pont is primarily interested, its rivals among the leading chemical companies are few: in explosives, Hercules, Atlas, and American Cyanamid; in synthetic ammonia, Allied and Dow;[49] in photographic chemicals and film, Eastman Kodak and General Aniline; in antifreeze mixtures, Commercial Solvents, Shell, and UCC; in acetic acid and anhydride, UCC and Tennessee Eastman; in synthetic finishes, Monsanto, Hercules, and Atlas.[50]

Similarly, UCC has few or no rivals in its major fields, electric-

48. However, in none of these fields except cellophane and nylon, which are protected by dominating patents, does du Pont occupy the position of a single-seller. In the production of rayon and auto waxes and polishes, in particular, du Pont is only one among many producers.
49. Du Pont owns 25 per cent of Dow's Midland Ammonia Corporation.
50. These generalizations apply mainly to the relationships between the leading chemical companies. As we have previously noted, numerous specialized companies not generally recognized as chemical companies operate in one or more of the chemical fields. For example, Eastman Kodak is not only the leading manufacturer of cameras but also an important producer of photographic film and, through its subsidiary, Tennessee Eastman, of acetic acid. Similar illustrations can be found in the fields of batteries, rayon, antifreeze, acetic anhydride, and ferroalloys.

furnace ferroalloys, industrial gases, electrodes, carbons, and batteries. UCC and Air Reduction dominate the market for industrial gases, mainly acetylene and oxygen. Allied Chemical is the only major chemical company which sells ammonium sulphate and synthetic nitrate of soda fertilizers; and though it shares with several smaller producers the market for alkalies, it is the recognized leader in this field.[51] And Dow remains predominant in its original and still major field of brine derivatives.

Apparently the large chemical companies recognize and respect each other's major fields of specialization.[52] Du Pont has elected not to make alkalies, ferroalloys, or coal-tar crudes for sale; Allied does not manufacture rayon, or acetylene and its derivatives; Union Carbide keeps out of the field of explosives. Du Pont does not produce nitrogenous fertilizers on a large scale, even though it is a major producer of synthetic ammonia, the basic raw material.

Mr. du Pont remarked that they are not producers of fertilizer as such but only produced ammonia which they sold to others for conversion into fertilizers; that they have had no experience whatever in the fertilizer end of the business and that that market seemed to be well taken care of by American Cyanamid, Allied, and others.[53]

51. See "Allied Chemical & Dye," *Fortune*, October 1939, Vol. XX, No. 4, p. 50.
Several of the "majors" produce some alkalies—caustic soda, for example—either directly for their own use or as byproducts for sale to customers with whom they are closely associated (e.g., Dow-Corning), or indirectly through the medium of jointly owned subsidiaries, in which glass companies are frequently their partners (e.g., American Cyanamid–Pittsburgh Plate Glass).
See *Moody's Manual of Investments* (Industrials), 1944, pp. 853-54, 1729, 2271.
52. "Chemical companies traditionally don't go out of their way to compete directly with each other in the same markets." *Business Week*, November 25, 1944, p. 86. This is even more true of the smaller chemical companies. Mathieson Alkali, Commercial Solvents, Columbian Carbon, Diamond Alkali—all companies with total assets of $20 million to $30 million at the end of 1939—remain essentially those indicated by their titles. No doubt this is sound business practice. In some instances it may represent nothing more than what the economists call "rational" business behavior. However, where the number of sellers remains small, for whatever reason, their behavior may be quite different from what it would be in competitive markets.
53. Memorandum of conversations between representatives of IG, Standard Oil Company of New Jersey, and du Pont, March 6, 1930. *Investigation of the National Defense Program*, Hearings before a Special Committee Investigating the National Defense Program, U.S. Senate, 77th Cong., 1st sess., pursuant to S.Res. 71, Pt. XI, p. 4646. (Hereinafter referred to as Truman, Pt. —.)
Du Pont entered the nitrogen field primarily to supply its own requirements for explosives manufacture. Allied Chemical's entry into nitrate of soda fertilizer production followed General Chemical's experiments with the Haber process at Muscle Shoals during World War I. Building on this experience, after General Chemical's merger in 1920 with Solvay, whose major interest was in sodium compounds (alkalies), and Barrett, the leading seller of byproduct sulphate of ammonia, Allied's stake in the fertilizer field steadily expanded.
Since 1930 du Pont has gone into the production of nitrogenous fertilizers in the

Du Pont also stays out of alkali markets, although it produces alkalies for its own use. It has entered the field of ex-carbide products only to manufacture its own requirements, leaving to UCC production for market sale.[54]

The field of calcium carbide (and acetylene) derivatives is generally recognized as "belonging" to Union Carbide.[55] In the United States it shares this field with Air Reduction. When, in 1941, du Pont decided to expand greatly the production of its synthetic rubber, Neoprene, it turned to Air Reduction to obtain its basic raw material, acetylene. To meet this demand Air Reduction erected a new calcium carbide plant adjacent to du Pont's new Neoprene plant.[56]

Direct Collaboration in Joint Enterprises

Nearly all chemical companies consume large quantities of industrial alcohol. All are capable of producing it. Nevertheless, in this as in other fields, they generally respect established trade interests. When du Pont went into the production of ethyl alcohol, it joined with National Distillers Products to set up Eastern Alcohol. To avoid conflict with vested interests in the solvents field, they entrusted the marketing of Eastern's surplus to United States Industrial Alcohol (now United States Industrial Chemicals), one of the four large alcohol producers which together dominate the American market. Union Carbide consumes most of its rapidly expanding output of synthetic alcohol in its own operations. It markets a part of the remainder through United States Industrial.[57]

United States market. *U.S.* v. *Allied Chemical & Dye Corporation, et al.*, in U.S. District Court for the Southern District of New York, Civil Action No. 14-320, Complaint and Consent Decree, May 29, 1941. However, du Pont still consumes the bulk of its ammonia output in its own special fields, e.g., the manufacture of explosives. It confines its fertilizer business to the sale of its own urea preparations. Thus Allied's percentage of the market for synthetic ammonia products undoubtedly greatly exceeds its share of total national production. See Wilcox, *op. cit.*, p. 137.

54. Du Pont's stake in acetic acid differs in form though not in substance from its stake in other ex-carbide products. But no more in this special case than elsewhere in the ex-carbide field is UCC's dominance thereby impaired. See below.

55. See text below.

56. *Standard Corporation Records,* 1941. Calcium carbide is produced by the reaction of coke and limestone in an electric furnace. Carbide is the primary source of acetylene, which it yields by reaction with water.

57. See Harrison E. Howe, "Industrial Alcohol," *Encyclopaedia of the Social Sciences,* Vol. VII, pp. 681-82. According to Howe, writing in the early thirties, USI itself produced 40 per cent of the American supply of industrial ethyl alcohol. Air Reduction, which with UCC dominates the ex-carbide field, owns about 25 per cent of USI's stock, which it acquired "with a view to closer cooperation with it in . . . developments that

Commercial Solvents, a leading domestic producer of alcohol and other solvents, apparently recognizes du Pont's primacy in the manufacture of pigments, while du Pont, in return, leaves the solvents market to the large solvents manufacturers. Thus, Commercial Solvents sold out its pigments business in 1931 to du Pont's subsidiary, Krebs Pigment & Color Company.[58]

Joint action in adjacent or overlapping areas has frequently supplemented the policy of recognizing chemical spheres of influence. Du Pont and National Distillers set up a joint subsidiary to manufacture industrial alcohol for du Pont's needs. In the synthetic nitrogen field Dow and du Pont join hands—du Pont owns 25 per cent of Dow's subsidiary, Midland Ammonia, which produces ammonia from hydrogen generated as a byproduct of Dow's chlorine manufacture. Du Pont and UCC have a joint subsidiary in the acetic acid market— an ex-carbide field.

Division of fields is common practice not only within the chemical industries proper, but also between them and closely related lines of industry. When Standard Oil of New Jersey, whose major field is petroleum refining and the production of fuels, became the junior partner of I. G. Farben in the chemical field, Standard endeavored to avoid competition with du Pont and agreed to consult with du Pont whenever its chemical operations threatened to impinge on the latter's domain.

We have been working under a sort of indefinite understanding with Mr. Irenee du Pont to the effect that they were interested in the chemical business and would confine their relations with the I. G. strictly to that business whereas we were interested in the fuel business and would confine our relations to the fuel business. . . .

My definite suggestion, therefore, is that we make every effort to convince the du Pont people that our backing of the I. G. in the chemical business in the United States is not directed against them . . . and that we believe that if we can maintain, as in the past, the closest and friendliest relations with

naturally fall within the scope of the activities of both companies." *Moody's Manual of Investments* (Industrials), 1932, p. 832; 1942, p. 2734. These companies have several of the same officers and directors. USI also holds some Air Reduction stock.

58. The du Pont interest in pigments was largely built up from its acquisition during the twenties of two old and well-established firms in this field, Harrison Bros. and the Krebs enterprise. In 1942 the Krebs corporation was dissolved, and all du Pont's pigments business has since been conducted directly by the parent company. See E. I. du Pont de Nemours & Company, "Annual Report for the year 1942," Wilmington, 1943, p. 8.

them, we will be in an advantageous position to serve both them and the
I. G. in the United States in matters where there might otherwise be unnecessary conflict of interests on both sides.[59]

The chemical additives used in making "antiknock" gasoline fall
into a borderline field between industrial chemicals and petroleum
fuels. In the United States, two chemical companies, an oil company,
and an automobile manufacturer, each the leader in its field, cooperate in producing and distributing Ethyl fluid. General Motors did the
pioneer work in this development. It joined with Standard Oil of
New Jersey to form the Ethyl Corporation, to which they gave the
exclusive right to make and sell the patented Ethyl mixture. Du Pont,
the major stockholder in General Motors, supplies Ethyl Corporation
with tetraethyl lead under a long-term contract. The Ethyl-Dow
Chemical Company, a joint subsidiary of the Ethyl Corporation and
Dow, the leading domestic producer of bromine, supplies the former
with its ethylene dibromide, another important component of Ethyl
fluid.[60]

Again, Standard Oil developed a process for the synthetic production of toluol from petroleum. Coal tar had previously been the sole
source of this important chemical. When Standard approached du
Pont as a possible customer for its new synthetic, du Pont was reluctant to aid in this encroachment on the steel industry's domain:

Mr. Stewart says that their company [du Pont] is in a rather peculiar
position as they have a close working arrangement with the U. S. Steel Corporation which at the present time produces about one-half of the Toluol in

59. Standard memorandum, June 21, 1928, Truman, Pt. XI, pp. 4645-46. A Standard
director expressed solicitude for the interests of Commercial Solvents, as well as du
Pont: "If S. were now to ally itself with I. G. . . . in the manufacture of chemicals,
solvents, etc., it would be competitive with D. and C. S. Such competition on the part
of S. in a field entirely apart from the petroleum business . . . would undoubtedly be
resented by D. and C. S. and impair the existing cordial relationship. . . . It is believed
that for I. G. to enter into these various fields in the United States successfully it must
be done in a constructive way and one that will not bring about a competitive condition
that would yield no profits, or that would destroy existing United States interests."
Ibid., p. 4643.
In the same way, when Standard sought a scheme for development of synthetic rubber
production in the United States in the late thirties, it decided upon an "orderly"
division of the field between rubber and oil companies, licensing the former only for
production of the rubber itself, licensing the latter only for the production of raw
materials. The Rubber Reserve Company, although a government agency, adopted the
same policy in its synthetic rubber program, rather than upset vested business interests.
Ibid., p. 4487 f.
60. Ibid., p. 4642; Dutton, op. cit., p. 293; and Moody's Manual of Investments
(Industrials).

the United States. In order to protect this position, while the du Pont Company privately wish to see synthetic Toluol produced, they cannot openly encourage such production as they are fearful of jeopardizing the preferred position that they hold with the steel corporation.[61]

Intercorporate Stockholding Promotes Unity

Nor have the steel companies, despite their manufacture of coke byproducts, seen fit to enter the chemical market. Such mutual recognition by producers in different fields of their respective vested interests is sometimes coupled with intercompany ownership. For example, Allied Chemical, which through its Barrett subsidiary was the chief American distributor of coke byproducts, owned some 150,000 shares of United States Steel common stock in the years 1937–1941.[62]

Glass and soap companies are important consumers of chemicals. Some glass companies have gone into the production of alkalies to supply their needs for soda ash, which constitutes by weight approximately one fifth of their raw materials. However, Pittsburgh Plate Glass in doing so cooperated with American Cyanamid. Together in 1931 they organized Southern Alkali, Pittsburgh Plate taking 51 per cent and Cyanamid 49 per cent of the company's stock. Owens-Illinois, Allied Chemical's biggest soda ash customer, has from time to time threatened to produce its own supplies; Allied's ownership of more than 200,000 shares of its stock may have deterred it from such a venture.[63]

When du Pont obtained the rights to a new cleansing agent for textiles in 1932, it invited Procter & Gamble to participate in the enterprise. They formed the Gardinol Corporation for this purpose. Meanwhile IG had worked out a broader cartel arrangement with the largest British producer, Unilever, covering the use of detergent chemicals (with certain exceptions) in the soap industry. Similarly,

---

61. Truman, Pt. XI, p. 4649. The document does not explain the nature of du Pont's "preferred position." For a brief period during 1927 and 1928, du Pont owned 114,000 shares of U.S. Steel common stock representing about one per cent of that company's total outstanding voting stock. The Federal Trade Commission, in an investigation of this acquisition, concluded in 1929 that du Pont, General Motors, and U.S. Steel were all loosely connected, though it found no violation of the antitrust laws in their relationships. Du Pont controlled GM directly; GM was a heavy purchaser of steel from U.S. Steel; and all had close financial relations with J. P. Morgan & Co., which was represented on U.S. Steel's and GM's boards of directors. *Report on du Pont Investments*, February 1, 1929, pp. 5-7.
62. *Moody's Manual of Investments* (Industrials).
63. "Allied Chemical & Dye," *Fortune*, October 1939, Vol. XX, No. 4, p. 50.

Jasco, Inc. (the joint IG-Standard chemicals venture), enlisted Procter & Gamble's cooperation in the synthesis of fatty acids from paraffin wax for use in soap manufacture.[64]

Business Diplomacy in Chemicals

The general practice of delineating fields, both within and around the chemical industries, is obviously not the casual result of unilateral decisions made in competitive markets. Nor is it wholly a historical accident. Moreover, it is not traceable simply to rational behavior by independent producers even in imperfectly competitive markets. It is rooted in business psychology. It reflects a wide consensus that maintaining "friendly relations," and avoiding conflict, is "good business." It is part of a modern code of business behavior which has evolved from business experience and been formed by business diplomacy.

"Not treading on others' toes" may be sound business policy from the viewpoint of the companies which adhere to it. However, when chemical companies, out of regard for vested interests and prior equities, habitually abstain from fully exploiting the revolutionary potentialities of their technology, the practice tends to undermine the rule of a freely competitive market.[65] Thereby the transmission of the fruits of technical progress to the general public is retarded, and such gains in living standards as do materialize are "purchased" at an unnecessary sacrifice.

This aspect of cartelization of the world chemical industries is as important as the blocking out of geographic market areas. The consequences are scarcely distinguishable. Such a taboo on trespassing in another firm's recognized field, however sound it may be as a business practice, if persisted in can scarcely avoid strait-jacketing the American chemical industries. It will limit their growth, mobility, and vitality—much as did the archaic custom of Chinese women in voluntarily binding their feet.

64. Bone, Pt. V, p. 2350; Pt. VI, pp. 2667, 2904.
65. The bare fact of the eclipse of competition, whether in this or in any other field of trade, need not be occasion for dismay though it sometimes is. After all, the competitive market is essentially only a device for ordering the economy. To the extent that the real ends of economic activity—production of wealth, promotion of welfare, provision of opportunities for creative self-expression in a workaday life—can be realized more certainly and at less cost by some alternative device for ordering the economy, or a segment of it, nothing but sentiment would stand in the way of discarding it. And probably sentiment could not long block the change. The question remains whether cartels offer such a method.

Constricted Sources of Supply of Chemicals

Thus, in spite of abundant resources and technical competence, only a very few American manufacturers are producers of some of the most important chemicals. According to the Temporary National Economic Committee:

Among 200 chemical raw materials manufactured by some 600 companies covered in a survey made by a trade journal in 1939, there were 35 with 5 producers, 21 with 4, 11 with 3, and 7 with only 2; thus 74, more than one-third of those in the group, were made by less than 6 concerns. Among 75 chemicals included in the Bureau of Foreign and Domestic Commerce study of concentration of output in 1937, there were 11 where the 4 leading firms produced between 40 to 70 percent, 17 where they produced between 70 and 100 percent, and 10, including products as important as synthetic methyl alcohol and calcium carbide, where they produced 100 percent. In 37 cases, including soda ash, chemically pure glycerin, nitrocellulose (pyroxylin), and cellulose acetate, information was withheld because the degree of concentration was so high that it could not be revealed under the census disclosure rule. Among 212 items in a group of chemicals and allied products, for which figures were given showing the share of the leading firm, there were 112 where this share was over 35 percent, 41 where it was over 50 percent, and 13 where it was over 65 percent.[66]

Moreover, the sellers of industrial chemicals are frequently fewer than the manufacturers. For some manufacturers produce certain chemicals only for their own consumption; their output does not enter the market. In two major fields in which concentration of production in a few chemical establishments is impracticable—byproduct coking and hardwood distillation—single sales agencies have taken over most domestic output and restricted marketing competition.[67]

66. Wilcox, *op. cit.,* p. 201.
67. Steel and gas companies produce most of the sulphate of ammonia and coal tar in the United States, as byproducts. The Barrett Company early took over the marketing of most of these chemicals. Moreover, it went far to eliminate competition between byproduct ammonia and other sources of nitrogen by an arrangement involving the importer of Chilean nitrates, and by its exclusive agency for marketing of the synthetic nitrogen produced by its parent company, Allied Chemical & Dye.
The wood chemical industry is composed of a number of relatively small distillers operating plants in or near the forests, remote from their major markets. The William S. Gray Company, a sales agency, has eliminated "the dangers and difficulties of individualist [i.e., competitive] marketing" of their crude methanol and acetate of lime. Haynes, *op. cit.,* p. 191. Haynes states that Gray and the Wood Products Company, organized originally by a number of wood distillers to take over their crude methanol for refining and marketing but later absorbed by USI, "in the main controlled the market with the view of stabilizing supply and price." *Ibid.,* p. 192. The United States Government has brought suit against Gray and twenty hardwood distillers under the

Du Pont, Allied Chemical, General Aniline, and American Cyanamid together account for about 80 per cent of the dyestuffs produced in the United States; du Pont, Hercules and Atlas Powder, about 80 per cent of the explosives; Union Carbide and Air Reduction, about 85 per cent of the oxygen and acetylene. United States Industrial Chemicals and Commercial Solvents each makes roughly 25 per cent of the domestic output of industrial ethyl alcohol. UCC, du Pont, and Monsanto, all large alcohol producers, consume most of their own output. Du Pont, UCC, Commercial Solvents, and Cities Service, through a subsidiary, account for about 90 per cent of national production of synthetic methanol. Here, too, du Pont and UCC consume a large part of their output in their own operations. Allied Chemical provides about 40 per cent of America's annual supply of soda ash; Allied and five other producers account for virtually the entire domestic output.[68]

During 1937–1939, Niacet Chemical Company, du Pont, and Carbide & Carbon Chemicals Corporation (CCCC), a subsidiary of UCC, accounted for about two thirds of the domestic output of synthetic acetic acid. However, Niacet, the joint subsidiary of Shawinigan Chemicals, Ltd., of Canada, UCC, and du Pont, alone made about 95 per cent of the total open-market sales. Other producers consumed virtually all their output in their integrated operations. Similarly, before the war, Celanese, du Pont, Tennessee Eastman, and CCCC produced virtually the entire national output of acetic anhydride; yet the amounts marketed by the first three, all heavy users of this chemical, were so small that CCCC alone accounted for well over 90 per cent of domestic sales.[69]

---

antitrust laws. It claims that the defendants produce about 95 per cent of the crude methanol output and that by their arrangements with Gray they have allotted production quotas among themselves and fixed exorbitant prices. The government quotes statements to this effect by Gray and other defendants. *U.S.* v. *William S. Gray & Co., et al.,* in U.S. District Court for the Southern District of New York, Indictment returned April 5, 1944; Complaint (Civil Action No. 27-145) filed August 29, 1944. In the criminal case all defendants except two plead *nolo contendere* and paid fines. The indictment was dismissed against two defendants, one of whom had died. The civil case has not yet come to trial.

68. Data from Standard & Poor Corporation, "Chemicals," *Industry Surveys,* Pt. II, January 7, 1944, pp. 8, 11 f., 16, 18; see also Bone, Pt. V, p. 2481.

69. Although other companies have developed competitive processes for synthesizing acetic acid and anhydride, UCC still manufactures these chemicals from calcium carbide. These marketing arrangements mirror the general recognition of Union Carbide's dominance in the ex-carbide field.

Technological Rivalry and Business Stability

Thus, despite the complexity of the American chemical industries and the explosive quality of chemical technology, chemical products go to market in an "orderly" manner. The major chemical companies generally respect each other's vested interests; they shun price-cutting or aggressive selling tactics; they try to avoid industrial conflict. As youthful members of a mature business community which has largely freed itself from the nineteenth century tradition of rugged individualism, the chemical industries have readily adapted their practices to the modern business principle of live and let live. As a family reared in an era when cartelization was rapidly becoming the accepted norm of business conduct, they habitually identify price competition with "chiselling."

In general, the deportment of the principal manufacturers in the chemical trades is "ethical"; their attitude toward one another, "cooperative." [70] This sector of industry is shot through with cartel arrangements—many of them loose and informal, most without official machinery for enforcement. But diverse and often nebulous as are these conventions, they weave the threads of many divergent interests into a business pattern resembling but slightly that of a free market.

Two competent students of the chemical industries have described this behavior pattern as follows:

Competition within the chemical industry has been keen, but for the most part it has been remarkably orderly, one can truthfully say, gentlemanly. Competition is really technical competition or competition between different processes or between products competing for the same end use. Hardly ever is the competition between two or more producers of the same material by the same process.

Competition between technical, scientific and engineering skill is as keen as lightning flashes, but pressure-selling, price-cutting and labor-sweating are not generally practiced in the industry. Selling methods are apt to be on the

---

70. Allied Chemical is said to be an exception to this generalization. Its management is generally secretive; it makes no such broad agreements for technical cooperation as do most other large chemical companies; it joins in no form of trade association activity; it refuses even to countenance participation by its technical staff in professional meetings. This attitude is generally attributed to the dominant influence of the late Orlando Weber, a businessman of the old school. See "Allied Chemical & Dye," *Fortune,* October 1939, pp. 148, 150, 152. Nevertheless, this company does not ignore completely the general rule of "live and let live."

conservative side, and sales are based usually on the quality of the product for the specific use intended rather than on price alone.[71]

Fortune has given a somewhat more picturesque, but none the less accurate, characterization:

. . . the chemical industry, despite its slowly lowering curve of real prices, is an "orderly" industry. It was practicing "cooperation" long before General Johnson invented it in 1933. It has seldom been bedeviled by overproduction, has had no private depressions of its own, and has not often involved itself in long or bloody price wars. The alcohol sector of the industry has frequently been guilty of disorderly conduct, and alkali made by the Solvay process has got into some nasty brawls with electrolytic alkali. But by and large the chemical industry has regulated itself in a manner that would please even a Soviet Commissar. . . . Its gentlemanly instincts are all against pushing and crowding. . . . The industry . . . is . . . the practioner of one definite sort of planned economy. . . .

Today the whole chemical picture has an air of financial stability that is unusual in so new an industry. There is no evidence of fighting among its companies for position: price structures are steady . . . This is the unique industry that knows its costs and refuses to sacrifice profits for the sake of volume. Competition is chemical . . . but the surface, the financial surface, is serene. And it will probably continue to be: new developments seek outlets through established chemical industrial channels, for there lie the talent and the money for development, one as vital as the other for any new process.[72]

Research Cuts Two Ways

Even the elaborate research laboratories of the major chemical companies are not a single-edged fighting instrument of business rivalry. They cut two ways. Patents may be used to promote and protect a product; they may also be used to delineate and fortify an industrial sector or a market area. They are devices for fostering trade in new directions or by improved methods; but they are also instruments for controlling an industry. A patentee may use his exclusive privileges to advance his own individual interest at the expense of business rivals. But he may find his patent even more profitable if he joins with other patentees to use all their patents to protect their established business interests against newcomers.

71. George E. P. Smith, Jr., and Henry F. Palmer, "Chemical Industries as the Basic Growth Industry of the Future," *Chemical and Metallurgical Engineering*, October 1944, p. 117.
72. "Chemical Industry: I," *Fortune*, December 1937, pp. 157, 162. See also Edward H. Hempel, *The Economics of Chemical Industries*, Wiley, New York, 1939, p. 37.

Rival chemical companies strive, of course, to discover new and better products, cheaper and more efficient processes. They try to reduce costs by converting wastes into salable byproducts, by increasing volume of production through finding new uses or new market areas for their output, and by many other means. They attempt to make secure their position in the industry by assuring themselves of adequate raw materials and dependable trade outlets, through integration or otherwise. In a dynamic industry they would soon "drop out of line" if they neglected such measures. Chemical manufacturers have found, however, that profits may suffer not only from lack of an aggressive policy in pushing forward their separate business interests, but also from pressing too far the advantage which a new product or a new process might temporarily yield them. They use their inventions and discoveries for their own gain, of course, but part of that gain they find in greater security.

The major companies may use their patent rights to bargain with other producers, whether major or minor, foreign or domestic. Each may seek to increase its share in the collective power over the industry, to cement its relations with other "going concerns," and to fortify itself and them against outside attack. In sum, chemical companies try to prevent technological progress from upsetting business stability and jeopardizing established interests. The behavior of chemical prices reveals the practical effect of these stabilizing policies.

Administrative Price-Making in Chemicals

Chemical prices are relatively stable. Their behavior reflects administrative rather than competitive determination. Wilcox has summarized the statistical evidence for TNEC as follows:

The "orderliness" of the trade is reflected in the behavior of its prices . . . From January 1926 to December 1933, the prices of more than half of 51 chemicals included in the Bureau of Labor Statistics index changed less than 12 times; those of 11 changed less than 5 times; those of calcium carbide and coal tar (indigo) changed only twice; the price of liquid carbon dioxide did not change at all. In February 1933, the prices of 12 of the industry's products, including nitric acid, sulfuric acid, aqua ammonia, calcium carbide, and coal tars, stood exactly where they had in June 1929; the price of 9 had risen. . . . The prices of seven chemicals were the same in 1929, 1932, and 1937.[73]

73. Wilcox, *op. cit.*, p. 202.

Even the price record of one of the two "disorderly" groups cited by *Fortune* reflects relative stability. Electrolytic caustic soda has been the chief disturbing factor in alkali markets. It is produced as a joint product with chlorine. As the demand for chlorine has mounted, surplus supplies of soda have weighed on the market and precipitated sporadic price wars that reduced its price, which had been constant for three years, from $2.95 per hundred pounds in 1930 to an annual average of $2.52 in 1931, and $2.30 in 1938. Soda sold for $2.55 through most of 1932; for $3.00 from December 1932 through May 1933; for $2.60 through 1934, 1935, 1936, and part of 1937. When the low of $2.30 was reached in 1938, it remained unchanged thereafter for five years.

These price movements do not reflect the erratic behavior of free competition, but the studied adjustments of administrative price-making in a "troubled" situation. They indicate how discretionary price control may be tempered by the march of technology and changes in basic economic forces.[74] "Price wars" broke out, were terminated by "armistices," recurrently flamed up again, and finally settled into a long siege. And enduring peace is not yet in prospect.

Industrial chemical prices are clearly not the prices of a free competitive market. The number of sellers is too few, the scale of their operations too large. Where single-sellers can influence the market by their production policies, they can set their prices administratively. In doing so no seller can ignore the effect of his price policies on his rivals' price policies.[75] To the extent that particular industrial chemicals are homogeneous, the products of different sellers tend to be equally acceptable. Though the advantages of established trade connections (including assured access to supplies of other chemicals) may make buyers comparatively indifferent, for a brief period, to

74. Industrial ethyl alcohol prices—*Fortune's* other "disorderly" market—changed frequently between 1929 and 1939. Prices declined rapidly during the depression years 1929 to 1933. A large excess of productive capacity accounted for these "frequent price upsets" (Standard & Poor Corporation, *op. cit.*, p. 12). Industrial alcohol is generally considered a sick industry suffering from "competitive excesses." It is not under the control of the so-called "chemical" companies. In contrast, prices of synthetic methanol experienced no such "upset." They reflected the influence of the major chemical companies and of the common sales agency, Gray, in whose hands sales are concentrated.

75. If the price-cutter's product is produced jointly with some other products, an expansion of output of the price-reduced product might flood the market or build up costly inventories of the jointly produced product. In the chemical industries, where joint costs play an important role, the effect of a price cut and increased output of one product on the output and price of a jointly produced item may exert as much influence on a seller's price policy as the anticipated reaction of rival sellers will exert.

price inducements on a particular product offered by other sellers than their usual supplier, no seller can long continue to sell a staple chemical for more than a rival gets.

In such product lines, the "potential" demand for each seller's "potential" output (measured by his current productive capacity) tends to be quite elastic. Each, by lowering his price, could gradually attract the bulk of the business—providing other sellers did not follow suit. Each by raising his price could exclude himself from the market—under the same assumption. But since rival sellers are apt to follow the lead of a price-cutter to avoid losing patronage, a price cut by one tends to lower the prices of all. Therefore each seller of an undifferentiated chemical product must carefully consider the reaction of business rivals in formulating his price policies. In striving to enrich himself he will try to avoid a price policy which might impoverish all. He is tempted to follow a policy of live and let live.

Role of Demand in Pricing Chemicals

The belief of chemical producers that the total demand for their products is inelastic has strengthened their disposition to follow a live-and-let-live policy. The chemical companies appear to have reasoned along these lines. Their most important customers are other industries. In most cases, the cost of chemicals consumed is a relatively small portion of the selling price of the buyer's final product —steel rails, a house, an automobile, or an article of clothing. Consequently, industrial consumers of chemicals are not likely to vary their total purchases of chemicals very much on account of changes within an ordinary range of price fluctuation—at least before a considerable period has elapsed. Since demand for industrial chemicals is inelastic, a uniform price reduction would not appreciably increase the industry's total sales, but would reduce total revenues. Hence, if one company were to cut its prices, it could gain in sales volume primarily by drawing customers away from other companies. And if the others were to meet its lower prices, all would be losers.

Whether or not chemical industry executives have consciously reasoned in this way, all are loath to disturb good relations by undercutting each other's prices. The basis for this hesitancy is only partially sound. The demand for many specific chemicals is apparently highly elastic. Price reductions will often be accompanied by a more than proportionate increase in the amount purchased, with a consequent increase in the sellers' total revenues. This is likely to be true particularly where one chemical can be substituted for another. In their choice of chemicals, industrial consumers naturally pay close attention to price and quality. Indeed, the enormous expansion of the chemical industries in recent decades has been largely due to the substitution of new, cheaper, and superior synthetic chemical products, such as rayon, plastics, and synthetic fertilizers and dyestuffs, for competitive "natural" materials. These accomplishments, to which chemical companies point with pride, refute their frequent claims that the demand for chemical products is inelastic.

However, producers' aversion to price competition is not entirely groundless. The substitutability of one chemical for another may make the demand for either one extremely elastic; but the industrial demand for the two chemicals taken together may nevertheless be relatively inelastic. This qualification does not apply, of course, to new products with completely new uses, or having outlets not previously filled by the chemical industries. But usually an expansion in the market for a chemical product resulting from a decrease in its price is at the expense in part of some other chemicals which it displaces. Since the major chemical companies generally produce a wide range of products, they are reluctant to initiate price cuts, which may spread to other sectors of the chemical field.

Role of Cost

Rational decisions of chemical manufacturers—made in pursuit of their own interests, but not without consideration of the interests of the group as a whole—are based on the cost characteristics of chemicals no less than on the conditions of demand. Production conditions are extremely diverse. Because of the technical interdependence of the varied productive operations of chemical companies and the profusion of joint products and byproducts, determining the cost of a particular chemical is often an arbitrary matter. When the same operations yield several products, it is impossible to distribute total costs among these products on any scientific basis.[76] The customary practice is to distribute them among the jointly produced goods accord-

76. Cf. Theodore J. Kreps, "Joint Costs in the Chemical Industry," *Quarterly Journal of Economics*, 1930, Vol. XLIV, p. 416.

ing to an estimate of what their respective markets will bear. The joint cost conditions affecting a given chemical may vary greatly, moreover, among different producers. For example, coal tar shares its joint costs with coke, ammonia, and gas differently when the producer is primarily interested in coke production than when his main product is gas. The major chemical companies themselves do not produce precisely the same range of products or use the same processes.

In such conditions of supply it is extremely difficult for one seller to judge the probable response of a competitor to the seller's price changes. A manufacturer's price reduction on one product might result in quite an unexpected retaliatory price cut by rival manufacturers on some item in a wholly different line of products. More important, it might disrupt the entire scheme of the division of fields which the industry has come to recognize. The likelihood that price competition at one point will lead to price competition at every point makes producers hesitant to inaugurate independent price changes.[77] It also encourages them to find a way of insulating price-making from the vagaries of the market. It leads to cooperative action.

Network of Explicit Agreements Also Promotes Price Manipulation

In the anxiety of chemical companies for security they have often jointly fixed prices. Since 1940 the federal government has brought antitrust suits alleging price fixing in at least twelve separate chemical and pharmaceutical fields. These include dyestuffs, nitrogen fertilizers, bichromates, oxalic acid, formic acid, muriatic acid, chromic acid, sulphuric acid, hormones, insulin, retail and wholesale drugs. In seven of these suits the defendants pleaded *nolo contendere,* paid fines, and accepted consent decrees enjoining price fixing in the future. Among the defendants were the country's leading chemical producers: Allied Chemical, du Pont, American Cyanamid, Dow, Monsanto, and others. The remaining cases are still pending. In addition, the Federal Trade Commission issued cease and desist orders in 1937 and 1938 against price fixing in the sale of liquid chlorine, flake calcium chloride, and rayon.

77. The depressed state of business throughout the early thirties doubtless influenced price policies in the chemical industries, as it did elsewhere. With a temporary surplus of plant capacity, price cutting may have been more than ordinarily tempting; but it was also more than ordinarily hazardous. Later, in a generally expanding market, the philosophy of increasing profits through enlarging output and sales at lower prices seems to have made more headway.

The extreme diversity in markets for particular chemicals also creates a strong incentive to monopoly practices. For example, the manufacture of embalming fluid calls for comparatively small quantities of formaldehyde. Since formaldehyde is only an insignificant part of the undertaker's costs, this market can bear a high price per unit. On the other hand, large quantities of formaldehyde go into the manufacture of certain plastics, and the use of these particular plastics, in preference to competitive materials, may hinge upon a few cents difference in prices.[78]

Similarly, methyl-methacrylate has a low-price, large-quantity market for ordinary commercial plastic products and a potentially high-price, low-quantity market for the manufacture of dentures. Clearly, all the producers of formaldehyde and of methyl-methacrylate would benefit if they could treat these markets separately, charging what the traffic will bear in each—a low price in the one, a high price in the other. Such price discrimination would be impossible in a free market. It requires complete discipline and organization at the supply end. The manufacturers of dentures and of embalming fluid must not have access to the cheap market; competing producers must not be permitted to undercut prices in, and hence destroy, the high-price market.

In part because of a series of patent agreements with each other and with foreign producers, two companies, Röhm & Haas of Philadelphia and du Pont, are the only American producers of methyl-methacrylate plastics. By informal, verbal agreement, also, they have pursued a uniform price policy.[79] They marketed methyl-methacrylate in the form of molding powders, for a variety of industrial uses, at 85 cents a pound. To licensed dental laboratories they supplied, at more than $22 a pound, prepared mixtures consisting of methyl-

78. See Haynes, *op. cit.*, pp. 60-64, 101.
79. Mr. Haas, who runs the American firm, described his agreement with du Pont to Dr. Röhm, head of the German Röhm & Haas, as follows: "We arranged that in the case of products where we compete we shall consult with each other on prices, etc., in order to avoid destructive price cutting. A matter like this cannot be put into the contract, because it would be against the law. We have to rely on our verbal assurances and our experience with DuPont during the last fifteen years has proven that they can be relied upon to live up to an arrangement of this kind." Bone, Pt. II, p. 826. In testimony before the committee, a representative of Röhm & Haas denied any such agreement, stating that "this letter was written merely to calm Dr. Röhm down." *Ibid.*, p. 905. However, he admitted that du Pont regularly followed and conformed to Röhm & Haas published prices: "We are the price leaders" (p. 906). See pp. 703-04, 706-07, 714, 717.

methacrylate powder (polymer) and liquid (monomer), both essential to the manufacture of dentures. At the same time they refused to sell the monomer in any other form to any other buyer. In this way they apparently planned to force the dental trade to rely exclusively upon them for supplies. The enormous price spread attracted "bootleggers" who found that they could "crack" the commercial powders back to the liquid, and sell the polymer and monomer together at a profit to the dental trade.[80] To combat this practice, at the suggestion of a licensee, Röhm & Haas considered adulterating the cheap commercial powders so that, for use in dentures, they would come under the ban of the Pure Food and Drug Administration. The licensee suggested that:

A millionth of one percent of arsenic or lead might cause them to confiscate every bootleg unit in the country. There ought to be a trace of something that would make them rear up.[81]

Although Röhm & Haas thought this was "a very fine" suggestion, there is no evidence that they put it into effect. They continued, however, to police the trade, to report on the activities of bootleggers, to exact from their customers a guarantee that they would not use their commercial powders in the manufacture of dentures or sell them for such use, and to cut off sales to purchasers who did not keep that promise.[82]

By agreements with the foreign patent owners, du Pont and Gen-

---

80. *Ibid.*, p. 718.

81. *Scientific and Technical Mobilization*, Hearings before a Subcommittee of the Committee on Military Affairs, U.S. Senate, 78th Cong., 1st sess., on S.Res. 107 and S. 702, Pt. VI, p. 947; see pp. 729-30. (Hereinafter referred to as Kilgore, Pt. —.) To this ingenious suggestion Röhm & Haas replied: "We agree with you that if we could put some ingredient in our commercial molding material which would disqualify it under the Pure Food and Drug Act, this would be a very fine method of controlling the bootleg situation. We shall take this matter up with our development department and advise you whether any such material could be used." *Ibid.*

82. Bone, Pt. II, pp. 724 f., 865. A letter from Imperial Chemical Industries to du Pont in 1941, asking du Pont not to market its product in a way that would disturb the high prices charged the dental trade for vinylite resins, attests the complete artificiality of these prices: "Vinylite resins are now marketed in the U. S. at $40 per pound . . . These prices are, of course, wholly artificial: but nevertheless they are actually realizable and it is clearly of the highest importance to preserve the situation. It is, therefore, essential to us that your company, when it comes to marketing a similar product, avoids the making of any arrangements which might in any way tend to lower the price of Resin M for dental work . . ." C. D. Edwards, *Economic and Political Aspects of International Cartels,* Monograph No. 1 of the Subcommittee on War Mobilization, Committee on Military Affairs, U.S. Senate, pursuant to S.Res. 107, 78th Cong., 2d sess. (Washington, 1944), p. 13.

eral Aniline have shared exclusive American rights to the newly developed "Monastral" colors, suitable for use both in paints, a low-
price field, and in textile dyeing, a high-price field. Both companies
ran a series of experiments and held conferences to determine the
practicability of "adding contaminants to 'Monastral' colors to make
them unsatisfactory on textiles but satisfactory for paints," to prevent leakage from the low-price to the high-price market.[83]

Fraternization Helps to Keep the Peace

Not only a diversity of industries but also a variety of companies
of different size and bargaining strength make up the market for
chemicals. Chemical companies usually sell a large part of their output to other chemical companies, some of which could readily produce the required materials themselves. This situation invites price
discrimination to prevent competition. It contributes to the development of friendly relations among potential competitors, helps to block
off "spheres of interest," and to place outsiders under a competitive
handicap.

When Röhm & Haas and du Pont discontinued sales of methyl-
methacrylate liquid monomer in an effort to fence off the high-price
denture market, they made an exception in sales to CCCC, although
this company was a direct competitor in this field. CCCC manufactured its own denture base of vinylite and methacrylate. They decided,
however, to meet CCCC's request because:

As a large and powerful corporation they could undoubtedly find some
way to make a denture commercially acceptable and they might even find a
way to make their own monomer.
By selling them we should retain a reasonable degree of cooperation and
good will, whereas in refusing to sell them the opposite would be true.[84]

83. Kilgore, Pt. VI, p. 730 f. They considered the following devices:
"Such substances as ground glass and carborundum were suggested for incorporation
with the pigment. While these materials would undoubtedly scratch printing rolls, there
is considerable doubt as to their effect in paints and lacquers."
"*Deteriorate cotton.*—Compounds might be incorporated into CPC which when
applied to textiles and followed by bleaching or heating treatment might increase the
deterioration of the cloth. . . .
"Irritating substances—It is known that certain resins and solvents are irritating to
the skin, often causing dermatitis. It might be possible to formulate a CPC composition
which will make textile materials irritating to the skin." *Ibid.,* pp. 948, 950.
84. Bone, Pt. II, p. 856. The "powerful corporation" refers to Union Carbide, CCCC's
parent.

Again, du Pont supplied methanol to Standard Oil of New Jersey in 1937–1941 at a heavy discount—about half the market price—to keep Standard from going into production itself.[85]

The dyestuffs industry most clearly exhibits a cartel pattern colored by the practice of intercompany purchases and sales. Lacking a monopoly, no single producer could readily manufacture the complete range of dyestuffs. For the limited number which they produce, even major manufacturers depend on their competitors for certain intermediates. Du Pont's 1939 sales of dyes and intermediates to General Dyestuff, sales agent for General Aniline, amounted to $1,450,000 and its purchases from that company to $756,000. By general consent, some companies specialize in certain intermediates and supply other manufacturers at a discount from published prices.[86]

These reciprocal customer relationships facilitate cooperation among the leading companies in other ways. Such contracts often provide not only for intercompany sales at special prices, but for interchange of patent licenses and technical information.[87] In some instances they have even stipulated uniform sales prices for dyes produced under the contract. By such practices the dominant producers have virtually eliminated price competition in dyestuffs markets. They consult with each other on prices; they exchange samples; they make laboratory tests to determine the strength of each other's products; and they exchange reports on the tests so that price differences will correspond to differences in dye potencies.[88] The small, independent producers keep their prices in line for fear of the disfavor of the large companies on which they depend for some of their intermediates. Moreover, independents are at a competitive handicap because

85. See Chapter 11.
86. Du Pont, National Aniline (Allied Chemical), and American Cyanamid have frequently arranged to have which ever one of them was the purchaser supply the seller with the raw materials for the items desired. The former party retains title throughout the conversion of the crudes into intermediates, paying a "processing fee." This method of doing business may possibly circumvent the legal prohibition of price discrimination in the Robinson-Patman Act. Bone, Pt. V, pp. 2491-93, 2502-15.
87. See the many cross-licensing contracts between du Pont and General Aniline (or General Dyestuff) reproduced in *ibid.*, pp. 2521-65.
88. See *ibid.*, pp. 2130-34, and accompanying exhibits. Representatives of American manufacturers and of I. G. Farben conferred in 1938, in an attempt to reach an agreement on sales prices in Argentina. According to one of the conferees, "the I. G. were reluctant to even considering [*sic*] the suggestion claiming . . . because there were so many classes of concentrations it would be extremely difficult if not impossible to calculate a Standard. Mr. Kinsman [of du Pont] stated the problem had been solved in the States, therefore he could see no reason why it could not be solved here." *Ibid.*, pp. 2417 f.

of the discriminatory prices which they are forced to pay for these materials.[89]

INTEGRATION AND CARTELIZATION ABROAD

Cartelization of chemical industries has gone much further abroad than in the United States. In no other major producing country is the demand for chemicals so large, the market area so wide, or the tradition of economic individualism so strong as in this country. In most branches of American chemical manufacture, two or more separate producers operate, and despite a variety of cooperative arrangements, formal and informal, and the existence of patent monopolies on a number of specific products, effective competition has not entirely disappeared. Though trade rivalry may have been sublimated, it has not evaporated altogether. By contrast, European chemical markets are far more closely controlled. If American chemical industries are oligopolistic, British, German, French, Italian, indeed European, chemical industries are monopolistic.

British Chemical Industries

Before 1926, the four leading British chemical companies were Brunner Mond, United Alkali, Nobel Industries, and British Dyestuffs. Brunner Mond, organized in 1873 to exploit the Solvay process in England, promptly took the lead in alkalies. In the next half century it expanded the scope of its operations by acquiring rival manufacturers and by adding new lines until it became Britain's largest producer of heavy chemicals. Shortly after World War I it acquired Castner-Kellner Alkali, which had introduced an electrolytic process for producing caustic soda and chlorine, and with government aid completed the great synthetic ammonia plant at Billingham of which it later acquired full ownership.

United Alkali represented a merger in 1890 of about fifty soda ash producers utilizing the Leblanc process and facing severe competition from the Solvay process.[90] By steady expansion it held its place, second only to Brunner Mond, as a producer of heavy chemicals.[91] Al-

---

89. *Ibid.*, pp. 2126, 2129-31.
90. It was a comparable situation which led to the formation of General Chemical in the United States in 1899.
91. Besides branching out into acids, United Alkali profited from the growing chlorine trade, though the advent of electrolytic processes affected adversely this source of revenue. Chlorine was a byproduct of the Leblanc, but not of the Solvay, process.

though the two companies competed vigorously for a time, they eventually joined hands to the extent that United marketed its exports through Brunner Mond's world-wide selling organization.

The Nobel Dynamite Trust and the other leading British explosives manufacturers merged in 1918 to form Explosives Trades, Ltd., predecessor to Nobel Industries. By investment in leading foreign companies in the same industry and by cartel agreements, this company obtained a complete monopoly of explosives in Empire markets. Having secured this monopoly, Nobel, like du Pont, branched out to become a leading producer of artificial leather, paints, and lacquers. Its manufacture of ammunition also led it into the large-scale production of nonferrous metals.

British Dyestuffs was the outcome of Great Britain's World War I effort to attain self-sufficiency in dyestuffs. In 1918 the two leading producers, British Dyes, Ltd., organized jointly by the dyers and the government in 1915, and Levinstein, Ltd., for decades the leading independent British manufacturer, merged to form British Dyestuffs Corporation. The merger controlled about 75 per cent of the domestic output of dyestuffs. Although competitors sprang up after the war, eight years later British Dyestuffs still controlled more than two thirds of the domestic output.

England Goes "Imperial"—in Chemicals

In 1926, under the leadership of Sir Alfred Mond (later Lord Melchett) and Sir Harry (later Lord) McGowan, Brunner Mond, United Alkali, Nobel, and British Dyestuffs merged, to form Imperial Chemical Industries, Ltd. (ICI). In spite of the assertions of its founders that the merger would result in increased technical efficiency, the commercial advantages of unification appear to have been the principal factor in this consolidation. Centralization of research and unification of selling and administrative organizations may have reduced overhead appreciably. But consolidation of these four big chemical companies, each already operating on a mass-production scale and at least three of them in quite distinct fields, afforded no great opportunity to increase plant efficiency and lower production costs. ICI has continued to produce dyestuffs, explosives, alkalies, and general chemicals in separate plants managed by separate operating companies.

The main object of the ICI merger was unquestionably commercial power, power to control the market. One giant corporation with an issued capital of £56 million,[92] dominating the chemical industries of an empire, could more effectively insure stability in domestic markets and greatly increase the bargaining power of the British chemical industries in dealing with foreign chemical manufacturers. In the words of Sir Alfred Mond, the formation of ICI

. . . would enable the British chemical industry to deal with similar large groups in other countries on terms of equality. The amalgamation of interests would enable them to speak with a united voice, and . . . would give them all the authority and prestige and advantages of a great combination.[93]

ICI was a mechanism for market control, an instrument of industrial power. It undoubtedly enhanced the earning capacity of British chemical industries. It provided a lever for obtaining a larger part of the national income and a greater share in world markets without the necessity of competing for them. The whole was no doubt greater than the sum of its parts.[94]

ICI's Ambitions

The avowed aims of ICI's founders extended beyond the British Isles or even the British Empire. Considering themselves apostles of a "new industrial order," they aspired ultimately to organize the chemical industries of the entire world. They proposed to substitute for the "chaotic" rule of competition in the market a "modern" and "civilized" rule by negotiation, conference, and agreement.[95] A du Pont official recorded for its confidential files an account of Sir Harry McGowan's plans:

Sir Harry . . . went on to give me a general picture of what he and Sir

92. By the end of 1939 ICI's issued capital was £74.2 million, its net worth £87 million and gross assets more than £100 million.
93. *Op. cit.*, p. 214 f.
94. The organizers of ICI evidently capitalized the expectation of higher profits at about £18 million. This was the amount by which ICI's original capitalization of £56.5 million exceeded the combined market value of the shares of its constituent firms. Patrick Fitzgerald, *Industrial Combination in England,* Pitman, London, 1927, p. 101. The promoters were not disappointed. Besides writing off large amounts from plant and equipment accounts and accumulating a substantial surplus, ICI paid an average annual dividend out of profits of 7.2 per cent in the period 1927–1936, on its inflated capital. Even in its worst year, 1931, it paid dividends of 4.5 per cent. ICI *Proceedings* at the Tenth Annual General Meeting, April 29, 1937, p. 2 f.
95. See Mond, *op. cit., passim.*

Alfred Mond had in mind in the matter of international agreements . . . Sir Harry explained that the formation of ICI is only the first step in a comprehensive scheme which he has in mind to rationalize chemical manufacture of the world. The details of such a scheme are not worked out, not even in Sir Harry's own mind, but the broad picture includes working arrangements between three groups—the I. G. in Germany, Imperial Chemical Industries in the British Empire and du Ponts and the Allied Chemical & Dye in America. The next step in the scheme is an arrangement of some sort between the Germans and the British.[96]

Not only has consolidation at home made for successful bargaining abroad, but ICI's participation in international cartel agreements has helped it consolidate its domestic monopoly. ICI has become increasingly predominant in the chemical industries of the British Empire because of its financial strength and prestige, its extensive research facilities, and its highly integrated operations, and also because of the exclusive patent rights and "know-how" which it has received from foreign companies. Cartel arrangements have given it exclusive British rights to manufacture nylon, Duco, and Dulux finishes, artificial leather, and gasoline from coal.

Since its organization, ICI has expanded the range of its activities and increased its market control by absorbing more than forty companies, some in competitive and some in noncompetitive lines. Moreover, by agreement with Lever Bros., Ltd., and Courtaulds, Ltd., which dominate the fields of soap and rayon respectively, ICI has marked off its domain from these adjacent provinces. It has buttressed its monopoly-hold on the heavy chemicals by not entering these chemical processing fields.[97] While independents continue to operate in

96. Bone, Pt. V, p. 2245 f. ICI's success in its cartelization program is shown in Chart 5.

97. Brunner Mond sold its soap interests to Lever in October 1919 and agreed thenceforth to stay out of the manufacture of soap in exchange for an exclusive and permanent contract to supply Lever's soda ash requirements. At the time, half of Brunner Mond's domestic sales of soda ash, its chief product, were to soap manufacturers, of whom Lever was by far the largest. Fitzgerald, *op. cit.*, p. 80.

ICI apparently has some sort of understanding with Courtaulds. Courtaulds purchases its heavy chemicals requirements from ICI; ICI refrains from the production of rayon. When, in 1939, ICI obtained from du Pont the British Empire rights to nylon, it chose to share with Courtaulds the exclusive right to manufacture fibers and yarns. A jointly owned subsidiary, British Nylon Spinners, Ltd., is the vehicle by means of which the two companies collaborate in this field. Moreover, the United States Government alleges that Courtaulds and Canadian Industries, Ltd., the largest Dominion chemical company, a joint subsidiary of du Pont and ICI for manufacture in Canada, have a definite understanding to stay out of each other's field. See text, p. 458.

CHART 5. ICI'S MAJOR INTERNATIONAL CARTEL CONNECTIONS, 1934–1939

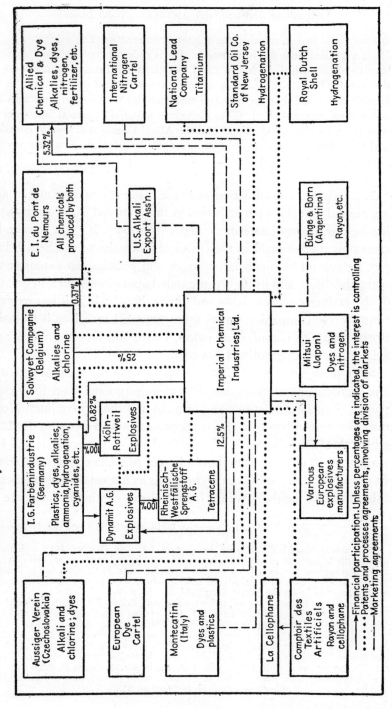

various chemical fields, they do so under the protection of ICI's market stabilization policies.[98]

The German Chemical Industries

The German chemical industries came as close to complete cartelization as the combined efforts and organizational talents of German business and a Nazi state could achieve—and that was close indeed. Even before 1933 industrial syndicalization had progressed far, perhaps farthest of all in chemicals. Fascism merely completed the program and integrated the entire structure. Permeating and dominating Germany's cartelized chemical industries has been the Interessengemeinschaft Farbenindustrie A. G. (literally, Dyestuffs Industry Community of Interests, Inc.—hereafter IG), incorporated in 1925.

The "big six," who founded and constituted virtually the entire German coal-tar chemical industry, had been linked in a community

---

98. See Fitzgerald, *op. cit.*, pp. 79-101; Pierre Damade, *Le Mouvement de réorganisation industrielle en Grande-Bretagne*, Recueil Sirey, Paris, 1938, pp. 83-99; Haynes, *op. cit.*, pp. 241-48; ICI *Proceedings* at the Annual General Meetings.

Like du Pont, ICI has become an important world power, not merely in the chemical industries but in national and international industrial finance. A du Pont official stated in 1928 that, apart from its own subsidiaries and joint companies, ICI had a 12.5 per cent financial interest in the German Dynamit A. G. (successor to the German partner of the Nobel Dynamite Trust), .82 per cent in I. G. Farben, 5.32 per cent in Allied Chemical & Dye, .37 per cent in du Pont, and an unspecified share in Deutsche Solvay Werke. Nye, Pt. V, pp. 1297-99. Outside the chemical field, ICI has had substantial investments in, and directors on the boards of, both General Motors and International Nickel Company (Canada). ICI *Proceedings* at the Fifth Annual General Meeting, April 14, 1932, p. 5.

By expansion and consolidation, ICI has gone far afield from its original interests. It is a large manufacturer of such diverse products as carburetors, airplane tanks, radiators, motorcycles, glass containers, and animal feeds, besides being the most important manufacturer of salt and holding a dominant position in several nonferrous metals.

Only a few basic chemical activities, such as the production of byproduct sulphate of ammonia, sulphuric acid, and coal-tar crudes, remain partially outside its direct control. These cannot be amalgamated into ICI largely because of their close byproduct relationship to other industries. However, these branches of chemical production are well organized in various trade groups, such as the National Sulphuric Acid Association, Ltd., the British Sulphate of Ammonia Federation, Ltd.—a joint sales agency the owners of which accounted in 1927 for more than 90 per cent of domestic sulphate of ammonia production and used this cooperative agency to make cartel agreements with similar associations in European countries—the National Benzol Association, the Fertilizer Manufacturers' Association, and the Association of Tar Distillers. All these groups are members of the over-all Association of British Chemical Manufacturers, and their activities are thus probably well coordinated with those of ICI in overlapping fields. For example, ICI is a member of the Sulphate of Ammonia Federation. Again, a central agency markets all nitrogen products, including byproduct sulphate of ammonia and ICI's synthetic ammonia. Fitzgerald, *op. cit.*, pp. 84-86; League of Nations, *op. cit.*, p. 96 f.

Although several independent companies manufacture synthetic resins and other plastics, most producers belong to the British Plastics Federation, Ltd. Tariff Commission, Report No. 131, Ser. II, *Synthetic Resins and Their Raw Materials*, p. 79.

of interests long before they gave it corporate form. In 1904 Farb-werke vorm. Meister, Lucius & Brüning, of Höchst, acquired the bulk of the stock of its competitor, Leopold Cassella & Co., of Frankfurt, and in 1908 the combined group purchased the stock of Kalle & Co., of Biebrich. Also in 1904, Badische Anilin und Sodafabrik, of Lud-wigshafen, Farbenfabriken vorm. Friedrich Bayer & Company, of Elberfeld-Leverkusen, and Aktiengesellschaft für Anilinfabrikation (Agfa), of Berlin, made a fifty-year agreement to exchange infor-mation and patent licenses, to supply each other with materials, to market abroad cooperatively, and to pool profits.

In 1916 these two groups joined in a fifty-year agreement, mod-elled on the Badische-Bayer-Agfa consortium, and took in two other chemical companies, Weiler-ter-Meer and Griesheim-Elektron. By 1925, when IG was incorporated, the activities of the associated com-panies extended far beyond the dyestuffs field. They produced a full line of synthetic organic chemicals, including pharmaceuticals and photographic supplies, and a variety of electrochemical products, in-cluding light metals.[99]

Since 1925, IG has enormously expanded the compass and volume of its operations and its control over German chemical industries.[100] On its own, IG began to manufacture, or greatly expanded its manu-facture of, rayon filaments and fibers, synthetic nitrogen, fertilizers, light metals and alloys, industrial gases, synthetic gasoline, synthetic rubber, and plastics. It has also increased greatly its production of basic synthetic organic chemicals and heavy chemicals. It has ex-tended its control back to sources of power and raw materials, nota-bly by acquiring 45 per cent of the shares in the Rheinische Stahl-

99. See Standing Committee on Trusts, pp. 4-5, 18-19; Welsh, op. cit., pp. 55-61, 68-69; Haynes, op. cit., pp. 233-36.
100. Bureau of Foreign and Domestic Commerce, Trade Information Bulletin No. 605, German Chemical Developments in 1928, p. 24; Trade Information Bulletin No. 753, German Chemical Developments in 1930, pp. 28-29, 38-40; Trade Information Bulletin No. 795, German Chemical Developments in 1931, p. 35; and Haynes, op. cit., pp. 236-38, 258. The Nazi regime merely increased the scope, coverage, authority, and rigidity of the cartel system, and integrated it into the totalitarian program. The Minister of National Economy, exercising his authority under the compulsory cartel law of 1933, compelled the chemical industries to organize into nineteen branches, all under central-ized supervision. Robert A. Brady, Business as a System of Power, Columbia University Press, New York, 1942, Chap. 1; Bureau of Foreign and Domestic Commerce, World Chemical Developments (annual publication). The German "free enterprise" system of the twenties, which had already surrendered much of its freedom, evolved gracefully and naturally into the totalitarian system of the thirties. The discussion in the text below refers solely to the situation before World War II.

werke, a large producer of coal and coke. In 1930 IG controlled the entire German production of dyes, nearly all the explosives, 90 per cent of mineral acids, 65 to 85 per cent of synthetic nitrogen, 40 per cent of pharmaceuticals, 30 per cent of rayon. Before World War II it controlled some 40 per cent of total German chemical output.[101]

Through its investments IG controls the major explosives manufacturers, Dynamit A. G., Vereinigte Köln-Rottweiler Pulverfabriken, and Rheinisch-Westfälische Sprengstoff. Köln-Rottweil is also an important producer of rayon. IG acquired a 50 per cent interest in Dr. Alexander Wacker Gesellschaft für Elektrochemische Industrie, a company with which it divides the market for electrochemicals, the most important of which are carbide derivatives.

Moreover, IG has close working relations with the other German chemical manufacturers big enough to warrant consideration. For example, it dominates the nitrogen syndicate to which all producers belong. It is a joint owner with Ruhrchemie A. G., of Chemische Fabrik Holten G. m. b. H., a company which they organized for commercial use of waste gases from their synthetic nitrogen plants. In 1937 IG owned a large block of the German Solvay company's stock. Solvay is the largest producer of alkalies on the European continent. Because of IG's size and power, it apparently dominates most or all of the syndicates in which the various branches of chemical manufacture, like other parts of the German economy, are organized.[102] In

101. Bureau of Foreign and Domestic Commerce, Trade Promotion Series, No. 195, *World Chemical Developments in 1938*, p. 35. Its percentage of control depends, of course, upon how narrowly one defines the chemical industries. The publication cited shows the gross earnings of thirty-four representative German chemical companies (p. 36); all the major producers seem to be included. IG's gross earnings, together with those of Dynamit A. G., which IG controls, amount to 62 per cent of the total. Omitting the major potash producers, since potash production is essentially extractive rather than chemical in character, the ratio is about 67 per cent.

102. Though developments during the war and under AMG are outside the scope of this study, the situation in 1943 as General Eisenhower summarized it in one of his reports as Supreme Commander in the American Zone of Occupation indicates the continuance of the concentration tendency, and IG's expansion, up to that date. His report states that, of the total German output, "I. G. Farben produced in 1943 100% of synthetic rubber, methanol, sera, and lubricating oil; 95% of poisonous gases, and nickel; 92% of plasticizers; 90% of organic intermediates; 90% of plastics; 88% of magnesium; 84% of explosives; 75% of nitrogen; solvents, 75%; gunpowder, 70%; calcium carbide, 61%; x-ray film, 50-60%; pharmaceuticals, 55%; insecticides and fungicides, 55%; synthetic resins, 53%; chlorine, 46%; high octane gasoline, 46%; compressed gases, 45%; sulphuric acid, 35%; synthetic gasoline, 33%; spun rayon (1939), 28%; artificial silk (1938), 24%; gasoline total, 23%; aluminum, 8%." New York *Times*, October 21, 1945, pp. 1 and 12 (Section 1).

The report adds that IG had stock interests in 613 corporations, including 173 in foreign countries, piled up assets of 6 billion Reichsmarks, and "operated, with varying degrees of power, in more than 2000 cartels."

addition, IG has invested heavily in foreign chemical companies and entered into alliances with almost all the world's great chemical companies.

IG Interests Not Confined to Chemicals

IG is the largest industrial corporation in Europe. According to the Department of Justice, it is the largest chemical company in the world.[103] Through cartels, patent pools, and similar arrangements, its power extends far beyond its broad field of manufacturing operations and its extensive financial interests. It is one of the largest coal producers in Germany [104] and a leader in the German coal syndicate.

With the great German rayon trust, Vereinigte Glanzstoff, IG owns Aceta G. m. b. H., which produces acetate rayon. It cooperates with Metallgesellschaft, the dominant nonferrous metals concern, in the manufacture of light metals. Through its substantial output and exclusive control of synthetic gasoline and lubricants, it occupies a strategic position in German markets for oil products. Through rayon and dyestuffs, it is closely associated with the textile industries; through pharmaceuticals, with medical supply firms; through fertilizers, with agriculture. It operates its own agricultural research laboratories and experiment stations.[105] Finally, through its heavy exports,[106] its large financial interests abroad, and its alliance with many foreign chemical companies, IG occupies a commanding position in the world's chemical industries.

As early as 1904 Dr. Carl Duisberg, one of its founders, predicted that IG would emerge a veritable "state within a state." [107] Its politi-

103. *U.S.* v. *Allied Chemical & Dye Corporation, et al.,* in U.S. District Court for the District of New Jersey, Indictment (Criminal Action No. 753c) returned May 14, 1942, par. 30.

104. Helmut Wickel, *I.-G. Deutschland,* Der Bücherkreis, Berlin, 1932, p. 148.

105. Robert A. Brady, *The Rationalization Movement in German Industry,* University of California Press, Berkeley, 1933, pp. 235-37, 241-42; Bureau of Foreign and Domestic Commerce, Trade Information Bulletin No. 605, *German Chemical Developments in 1928,* pp. 6, 35-39.

106. Its exports of dyestuffs alone amounted to at least $40 million in 1939 (at the official exchange rate). Bureau of Foreign and Domestic Commerce, Trade Promotion Series, No. 211, *Chemical Developments Abroad,* p. 7. In addition, it controlled several large foreign producers. Before the depression, IG's total exports amounted to $150 million. Haynes, *op. cit.,* p. 238.

107. Wickel, *op. cit.,* p. 185. An American businessman in Germany wrote in 1929: "Six weeks in Germany have convinced me that I. G. Dyeworks is the real octopus embracing almost everything in the economic, and a large part of the political, life of post-war Germany. Whenever you mention the name of I. G. Dyeworks to anybody in Germany, he registers awe, fear, admiration . . ."

cal power and influence became great indeed. IG officials supported the Nazi revolution and IG played a central role under the Hitler regime in organizing and administering the German chemical industries along totalitarian lines. It cooperated with the Nazi state in preparation for war, in the conduct of economic warfare, and in administration of industry in conquered territories.[108]

In France, It's Kuhlmann

France in the twentieth century has played a secondary role in the chemical field, in which Frenchmen contributed so much to science and technology in the days of Lavoisier and Leblanc and in which the country was a commercial leader before the decline of the natural dyestuffs and drugs industries. In certain branches of chemical technology, France has continued to make significant advances, notably in electrometallurgy, in the synthesis of ammonia, and in rayon and cellophane manufacture. But by and large it has become a "borrower" rather than a "lender" in this field.

Information on the organization of the French chemical industries is scanty. It is clear, however, that a relatively small number of producers, or groups of manufacturers, has come to dominate large areas of this industrial field and has greatly restricted the play of free competition. In 1930 a major group of some twenty financially interrelated companies centered about the Établissements Kuhlmann.[109]

Kuhlmann was originally a manufacturer of heavy chemicals. In 1923 it purchased, from the French Government, Cie. Nationale de Matières Colorantes, which had taken over German dyestuffs plants confiscated during World War I. By subsequent acquisitions, Kuhlmann extended its control to an estimated 70 per cent of French dyestuffs production in 1930. In addition, it had working agreements

108. "I. G. Farben has participated vigorously in carrying out 'Grossraumwirtschaft' (continental-economy) plans which require the Balkans to furnish Germany with more foodstuffs, raw materials, oil, and minerals, in return for which they receive from the Reich larger amounts of chemicals, fertilizers, pharmaceuticals, and cosmetics, in addition to machinery and technical and engineering services.

"In doing this, I. G. Farben has gone *far beyond* the normal operations of an industrial concern and has not only become an instrument for carrying out German policies in this area but sometimes even *formulates* them." Karl Falk, "I. G. Farben 'Adds the Balkans to the Reich,'" *Foreign Commerce Weekly* (Department of Commerce), October 17, 1942, p. 4; see also pp. 4-9 ff., and *ibid.*, October 24, 1942, pp. 8-11 ff.

109. Maurice Fauque, *L'Évolution économique de la Grande Industrie chimique en France*, University of Strasbourg, Strasbourg, 1932, pp. 204-05.

with the only other large dyestuffs producer, which controlled about 24 per cent of domestic output. All manufacturers belonged to a national dyestuffs cartel.

Directly, and through financial affiliations, Kuhlmann has an important stake in other chemicals as well. In 1930 it owned an estimated 40 per cent of the domestic synthetic nitrogen capacity and more than half the nitric acid and nitrate salt capacity. Kuhlmann and the Société de Saint-Gobain, the second largest French chemical company, with major interests in heavy chemicals and fertilizers, accounted for about two thirds of the French production of superphosphates in 1930 and most of the sulphuric acid output.

Other important French chemical companies operate for the most part in specialized fields. For example, several manufacture fertilizer from potash and phosphate, drawing their raw materials from the rich French deposits. Even those concerns which are financially independent of Kuhlmann and St. Gobain are linked with them through international cartels or in the comprehensive trade association, the Comité des Industries Chimiques de France. The committee

. . . has had a far-reaching effect in unifying the direction and efforts of the industry as a whole. It consists of approximately 20 of the leading chemical companies in France. The main objectives are the elimination of uncoordinated effort by these concerns . . .[110]

In Italy, Montecatini

In Italy, as in Germany, a highly centralized and syndicalized industrial organization antedated fascism. Montecatini, Societa Generale per l'Industria Mineraria ed Agricola of Milan, "the largest chemical and mining firm of southern Europe," has long been "the outstanding factor and . . . the largest part of the Italian chemical industry . . ."[111] It is also the largest industrial corporation in the

110. Bureau of Foreign and Domestic Commerce, Trade Information Bulletin No. 652, *The French Chemical Industry and Trade in 1928*, p. 4. See the corresponding publications for 1929, pp. 3, 21, and for 1930, pp. 2-5, 20-22 and *passim* (Bulletins No. 726, 781). Also Fauque, *op. cit.*, pp. 180-85, 195-224; *Moody's Manual of Investments* (Industrials); L. Ballande, *Essai d'étude monographique et statistique sur les ententes économiques internationales*, Paris, 1936, pp. 75-78; League of Nations, Publications, Ser. II, *Review of the Economic Aspects of Several International Industrial Agreements*, 1930, No. 41, pp. 42, 52.
111. Bureau of Foreign and Domestic Commerce, Trade Promotion Series, No. 169, *World Chemical Developments in 1936*, p. 75; see p. 76.

country.[112] Its mining, quarrying, and metallurgical activities include copper, aluminum, sulphur, zinc, lead, lignite, and marble. It is a large producer of hydroelectric power.

Montecatini's chemical products, including those of its subsidiaries and affiliates, cover virtually the entire field, embracing explosives, synthetic fertilizers, dyestuffs, plastics, rayon, synthetic fuels, and almost all heavy and organic chemicals. Moreover, Italian chemical industries have been organized into a great number of cartel-like groups, first autonomously and voluntarily, later by law. Either Montecatini itself or the domestic chemical associations hold membership in many international cartels. In this way and through financial interpenetration—Montecatini's investments abroad and the reverse flow of capital from foreign chemical and metallurgical companies—Italian chemical industries have been firmly integrated into the mosaic of world chemical cartel controls.[113]

Chemical Industries in Other European Countries

The same cartel pattern prevails in other industrial countries. In Belgium the Union Chimique Belge and Solvay et Cie., which appear to be closely related, exercise a preponderant influence.[114] Belgian chemical trade associations, supervising "almost every aspect of the industry," had come by 1938 to embrace 100 per cent of the heavy chemical branches of the industry "and about 80 per cent of the numerous small and scattered allied chemical factories." [115]

In Czechoslovakia the dominant company is the Aussiger Verein (Verein für Chemische und Metallurgische Produktion, of Aussig), whose relative importance and breadth of interests approximate those

112. Bureau of Foreign and Domestic Commerce, Trade Information Bulletin No. 705, *Italian Chemical Developments in 1928 and 1929*, pp. 4, 8, 50; Brady, *Business as a System of Power*, p. 72.
113. Bureau of Foreign and Domestic Commerce, Trade Promotion Series, No. 195, *World Chemical Developments in 1938*, p. 48; *The European Chemical Industry in 1932*, pp. 31, 38, and *Italian Chemical Developments in 1928 and 1929*, pp. 3-9 (Trade Information Bulletins No. 813 and 705, respectively).
114. When Union Chimique Belge (UCB) was organized in 1928 it absorbed S. A. Fours à Coke, Semet-Solvay & Piette, among other companies. M. Piette is one of several officers of Solvay et Cie. who are also officers of UCB. Moreover, *Moody's Manual of Investments* (Industrials) reported in 1928 that "Mutuelle Solvay" owned 50 per cent of UCB's preferred stock.
115. Bureau of Foreign and Domestic Commerce, *World Chemical Developments in 1938*, p. 18; see also *World Chemical Developments in 1936*, p. 29 f.; Trade Information Bulletin No. 708, *The Chemical Industry in Czechoslovakia*, pp. 4-7, 24-25; Haynes, *op. cit.*, pp. 250-51, 258; Karl Falk, *op. cit.*, *Foreign Commerce Weekly*, October 17, 1942, pp. 7-8.

of Montecatini in Italy. Aussiger Verein participated before the war in 150 cartels, 50 of them international in scope. It had various foreign investments in partnership with Solvay et Cie. and with IG.

In Japan the chemical industry has been organized along totalitarian lines under the leadership of the Zaibatsu (family overlords of industry) who sought "to eliminate needless competition." [116]

CARTELIZATION OF THE WORLD CHEMICAL INDUSTRIES

International trade in chemical products is not free. Nor have tariff barriers and arbitrary controls set up by major industrial countries between the two world wars been the sole obstacles to free trade. Within the area circumscribed by governmental regulation, the world's leading chemical manufacturers set up their private controls. They divided markets; they marked off industrial fields; they established export quotas; they exploited specified fields and markets cooperatively. Joint control of the market became the general rule; free competition, the exception.[117]

Cartel control arrangements in the chemical field have two aspects. They are not mutually exclusive, but supplement and reinforce each other. First, these controls may be looked at as arrangements governing the marketing of particular chemicals or classes of chemicals. Some chemical cartel relationships consist of nothing more than concerted commitments of designated companies covering sales of specified products for a definite term. But this does not exhaust the whole scope of cartelization developments in the chemical field.

Or, secondly, these controls may be considered from the standpoint of chemical company relationships. Arrangements for exchange of stocks among major chemical companies in different countries or for exchange of patents, processes, and "know-how" in all or a wide range of chemical manufacturing lines are obviously cartel arrangements. Their express terms and provisions are not always concerned with the marketing of chemical products. Nevertheless, they surely affect the marketing policies of the companies concerned.

116. Bureau of Foreign and Domestic Commerce, Trade Information Bulletin No. 823, *World Chemical Developments in 1934*, p. 17. See also Brady, *Business as a System of Power*, Chap. 3.
117. One of the most encyclopedic handbooks of international cartels states that "international economic agreements, very numerous in the chemical industry, affect every category of product." Ballande, *op. cit.*, p. 40 and *passim*.

Viewed from this second standpoint, chemical cartel controls embrace specific commodity agreements, but they also embrace much more: a whole series of tangible and intangible relationships, nebulous and specific arrangements, amorphous and settled conventions which elude precise definition but which have had a real and potent influence in shaping the development of the world's chemical industries and in regulating chemical markets. These intercorporate relationships may establish "friendships" more enduring and more significant than formal "alliances." They may rest in part on accredited standards of business behavior. But as a rule they find concrete expression now and then, here and there, in explicit contracts covering specific chemical products, processes, or market areas.

Major chemical companies manufacturing a wide range of products on a mass-production basis have felt the need of a "foreign policy" for their own security, and foreign policies cannot function in a vacuum. As a result a pattern of intercorporate relationships among these great chemical companies supplementing the specific commodity cartels has grown up that confines business rivalry within a framework of informal conventions, gentlemen's understandings, and administrative controls. Cartel controls of this type promote a recognition of joint as well as separate interests and put financial stability ahead of individual prowess, national pride, and even technological rivalry.

There are also many cartel controls in the form of definite contracts committing the parties to a common policy in the sale of particular chemical products. Separate cartels regulate the sale of zinc white, nitrates, soda ash, Glauber's salts, chloride of lime, magnesium sulphate, superphosphates, cyanides, dyestuffs, calcium carbide, bromine, tanning extracts, tartaric acid, a great number of drugs, acetic acid, white lead, glue, and numerous other products.[118]

Significance of Cartel Controls

The existence and vitality of cartel controls of the less formal type, alongside these contractual arrangements or in the background, does not mean that all chemical companies have eliminated all conflicts of interest and found a way to live together as one big happy family. They have not abandoned all rivalry in the quest for markets.

118. See Bureau of Foreign and Domestic Commerce's annual world chemical surveys.

Chemical companies usually decide who shall sell what, where, how much, and on what terms in foreign markets by negotiation rather than by competition, because they believe cooperation "pays." They reach their decisions by driving hardheaded bargains. Each party tries to obtain the best terms for itself. Thus these decisions reflect the relative bargaining power of the parties involved. This depends on many factors, including the efficiency of their processes, strength of their patent positions, quality of their products, extent of their financial resources, and support of their governments. In the final analysis, the issue turns on the comparative readiness of the several parties for a competitive "war" if negotiations break down.

This kind of business rivalry differs from effective competition in that the bulk of its benefits are likely to go to the cartel members rather than to the consumers. Cartelization does not eliminate intercompany rivalry, but it affords less assurance than genuine market competition that the consumer and society will benefit from it. Often producers "fight it out" by dickering around a conference table, rather than by improving quality and lowering prices.

The maintenance of "peaceful" cartel relationships of this type requires skilled use of all the arts of diplomacy known to statecraft. "International order" in the chemical industries may be conceived as a product of the diplomatic relations among a few Great Powers, each on the lookout for its own interest. In general, the major chemical companies are committed to a policy of collaboration, pacific settlement of disputes, and equitable division of spheres of influence. They endeavor to maintain friendly relations with their rivals. They make nonaggression pacts, pledging mutual respect for each other's borders and "sovereign" domains. They enter into permanent or temporary alliances for mutual assistance in defense of vital interests against attacks from any quarter.[119]

119. In 1929 Standard and IG cemented a series of agreements with an expression of their mutual desire to cooperate in all eventualities. The statement read in part: "Both parties agree that in the event of an attack by a third party brought against either of them directly or indirectly, in attempted derogation of the title to patent rights transferred hereunder, they will cooperate loyally in defense of such attack." Bone, Pt. VII, p. 3467. Du Pont and ICI similarly cemented their alliance with pledges of enduring cooperation and loyalty. In the following exchange of correspondence between Sir Harry McGowan and Lammot du Pont, the two companies agreed to respect each other's territories, even should national governments seek to restore freedom of trade: "My dear Lammot . . . The growing realization of the necessity to modify that accumulation of trade restrictions and barriers which the countries of the world have built up . . . should eventually bring about altered trading conditions and freedom from restrictions both in

But occasionally an excess of zeal or a lapse of prudence leads to an "unfriendly act." [120] This is likely to bring threats of reprisals and warlike preparations. Usually, however, the business diplomats working feverishly in an atmosphere charged with "growing tension" can "find a formula" which avoids an open breach.

The language of diplomacy should not be allowed to obscure the plain unvarnished fact, well recognized in the chemical industries, that any company may provoke a showdown if it considers that the ultimate gains of conflict outweigh its inevitable losses. The British Committee on Trusts has epitomized the situation neatly:

... We are ... impressed ... with the degree to which international competition in dyes (as also to some extent competition within the national frontiers) is a conflict of commercial 'Great Powers' exhibiting all the characteristics of militant diplomacy carried on with financial and commercial brute force in the background, rather than a simple economic matter of striving to offer, in competition with others, the most acceptable article at the most favourable price. In this 'haute politique' of large-scale industry the unassociated group of small concerns though severally and jointly more efficient as regards mere production, may be at the mercy of the aggressive and predatory policy of the less efficient but financially more powerful rival.[121]

Continuing Insecurity of Major Chemical Companies

Adjustments of conflicting interests among chemical companies, as

---

Europe and in the States. . . . Whatever the changes may be, and however they may affect our individual concerns, on one thing you may rely, they will not be allowed to disturb the harmony of the relations between our two concerns . . . I have warned my people that no fiscal alterations in the U.S.A. must be allowed to affect the interpretations to be placed on our patents and processes agreement and the working out of the cooperation for which that agreement provides."

"Dear Sir Harry: . . . I am much interested in what you say and heartily approve your attitude . . . I feel the same; namely, that our relations have been so happy and have produced such satisfactory results that we should let nothing in the way of international agreements interfere in any way with the progress we have made, or may make in the future." Nye, Pt. V, pp. 1112-13, 1117.

120. An official of Standard Oil (N.J.) complained to representatives of Socony-Vacuum, which had developed a product competitive with one which Standard was then marketing: "Mr. Howard told them that we did not regard their act of bringing out this material as a friendly one and thought that they should have raised this subject with us. . . . He said that he felt that this was only a question of reputable business practice and that he was very much surprised that they would take any other attitude." Bone, Pt. IV, p. 1761. One du Pont official wrote to another about IG's reported plans to open a synthetic ammonia plant in the United States: ". . . you may think it wise to point out that this is inconsistent with their declared policy and an unfriendly act to the du Pont interests." Nye, Pt. XII, pp. 2874-75.

121. Standing Committee on Trusts, p. 20. The British committee favored a centralized organization of the British dyestuffs industry, to make it possible to bargain with and compete on equal footing with foreign industry.

among sovereign states, is a ticklish problem. Political and commercial developments and technological changes are constantly shifting the balance of power. When a company's strategic position has improved, it ordinarily demands a greater share in world markets. Negotiations are often marked by bickering, bluffing, flexing of muscles, and caustic debate before a bargain is struck. A formal settlement, if and when reached, may be short-lived. Still, whether by enduring treaty or uneasy armistice, the leading "powers" have established a *modus vivendi*. They maintain it by periodic adjustment and renegotiation.

The major chemical companies adjust their affairs on the principle that bona fide competition does not pay. Occasionally independents, or even cartel members, may resort to the methods of industrial conflict. They may cut prices or duplicate productive facilities in a market admittedly not large enough to support additional capacity at existing prices. Or they may "invade" each other's sales territory. But such tactics are generally frowned upon as "unethical." They are more often threatened than practiced.[122] When used, they are usually temporary expedients for obtaining a better bargain or bringing "rugged individualists" into line. They are preliminaries to diplomatic action, paving the way to a negotiated peace.

Prolonged competitive struggles, fights to the finish, among the chemical giants are less likely to occur than "total" war among nations. Businessmen recognize that a struggle for complete supremacy tends to be self-defeating. The relationships between the major American and British chemical companies, on the one hand, and their German and Japanese counterparts, on the other, illustrate the greater reluctance of these business groups than of national governments to resort to trial by battle.

American and British companies remained essentially free of political control during the thirties. In the totalitarian countries, governments were intent on world domination. Big chemical companies not only played a vital role in abetting these aggressive designs, but

---

122. The following memorandum from the files of the Remington Arms Co. illustrates these tactics: "*Export prices.*—When Mr. Pickard [a du Pont official] talks with I. C. I. and R. W. S. [a German firm] he will probably draw them out on how best Remington can cooperate with them toward a higher level of prices in the foreign field. R. W. S. are bad offenders, so far as prices are concerned on center-fire metallics in Latin America, and should be made to realize that unless they raise their prices ours can very readily be reduced." Nye, Pt. V, p. 1195.

shaped their own business strategy on a similar model. Thus between the two wars ICI and du Pont were unable to reach completely amicable over-all agreements with either IG or Mitsui. They attained a workable degree of collaboration, but the aggressive thrust of IG and Mitsui for a greater share in the control of world chemical markets was unmistakable.[123] They frequently presented their rivals in the democratic countries with a choice between industrial conflict and "appeasement."

Nevertheless, neither IG nor Mitsui "declared war" on the American and British chemical industries. Moreover, when World War II broke out, IG and Mitsui on the one hand, and du Pont, ICI, and Standard Oil on the other, did not completely sever "diplomatic relations." Although direct communication was disrupted by the war, the companies merely "suspended" their collaboration. The general understanding was that they would take up again at the close of the war where they had left off, in an atmosphere of mutual concord and cooperation.[124]

123. IG and the Japanese chemical manufacturers were often brusque, quick to take offense at real or fancied transgressions by others. They blew alternately hot and cold, but constantly strove to obtain a greater share and better position in world markets. Du Pont and ICI, on the other hand, were generally conciliatory and polite; their tactics were often defensive and conservative; their policy, one of appeasement.

Sir Harry McGowan, then chairman of ICI, spoke the language of diplomacy in stating the problem which Japanese competition raised: "The . . . problem of Japanese competition has to be solved . . . through measures of co-operation with Japanese producers. I refuse to believe that there are not ways of reasonable development for Japan which do not involve any material or permanent damage to British trade, provided British manufacturers adjust themselves to the new conditions. The leaders of British and Japanese industry must talk more and more with one another." ICI, *Proceedings* at the Seventh Annual General Meeting, April 19, 1934, p. 7.

"I feel sure that in the course of time Japanese concerns will be convinced that it is to their own best interests to work in friendly co-operation with the manufacturers of other countries." ICI, *Proceedings,* at meetings held May 1, 1935, p. 5.

When Mitsui began to compete with foreign dyestuffs producers in the Japanese market, the foreign interests took the initiative in seeking an agreement. The far eastern representative of National Aniline (an Allied Chemical subsidiary) described the temporary agreement reached in 1934 as merely "an *armistice* during which a status quo will be preserved by mutual consent in Japan." Bone, Pt. V, p. 2092. (Italics supplied.) Later agreements provided for Mitsui a steadily increasing share of the Japanese market. In 1939, however, it refused to negotiate further in this field, its government having agreed to ban dyestuffs imports henceforth.

Meanwhile Mitsui began independent moves abroad. National Aniline's representative reported in 1934 that "a Mitsui *invasion* of the China indigo market may be expected soon," and proposed negotiations in an effort to reach "an amicable arrangement." *Ibid.,* p. 2089. (Italics supplied.) Agreements were reached, but only at the cost of constant concessions to Mitsui's demands for an ever larger share, first in China, then in other Asiatic countries. *Ibid.,* pp. 2088 ff.

124. In numerous cases American companies awaited permission from their cartel partners before shipping to markets which the latter could no longer supply. They took over such markets only for the duration of the war. In some cases the American com-

Technological Competition

In spite of—indeed partly because of—the tendency among the leading chemical companies to settle market conflicts by diplomatic procedures, they vie strenuously to advance their separate interests through laboratory research. A chemical company must search constantly for new products and more efficient processes to survive. Otherwise the march of technology would soon pass it by.

New and better chemical processes and products are constantly supplanting or supplementing the established ones. Synthetic nitrogen, dyestuffs, acetic acid, methanol, textile fibers, have all wholly or partly replaced natural sources of supply. The synthetic product developed by one company meets in the market the synthetic product which a rival company makes by a different process. Hydrogen may be produced in a number of ways. Hydrogen and nitrogen may be combined to make ammonia by several different processes. Acetic acid, butadiene, high-octane gasoline, may be synthesized by various techniques. Interprocess competition is supplemented by interproduct competition: witness the recent profusion of plastics and rubber-like materials developed by rival companies. Cellulose acetate displaced celluloid in safety glass, and cellulose acetate in turn gave way to vinyl resins. Rival rayons compete in the textile market. Du Pont's antifreeze, Zerone, has UCC's Prestone as a market rival, and its Duco meets the competition of other lacquers.

Nevertheless, "technological competition" operates within a general framework of market cooperation. The most striking instances of product displacement are those in which the product superseded was produced by "outsiders"—nitrate miners, indigo planters, hardwood distillers, cultivators of silk and cotton.[125] Though displace-

---

panies used the familiar German packages and trade-marks to preserve customer good will for the German products. In other cases, cartel partners agreed to terminate exchanges of technical information temporarily but to resume it at the end of the war. Many American and German companies assigned to each other the patent rights which each owned in the other's country, in an attempt to carry out the spirit of the prewar agreements, and to avoid confiscation of the patents because of their ownership by enemy nationals. Except where government action has compelled abrogation of such understandings relating to postwar resumption of cartel relations, available evidence does not indicate that the entrance by the United States into the war altered them. Some agreements explicitly provided that conflicts in the political field would not terminate them. See Edwards, *op. cit.*, pp. 62-70, 74-75.

125. Technical advances have resulted in literally hundreds of product displacements, of course, within the various branches of the chemical industries. Some of these shifts

ments perhaps no less radical have occurred among the products of major chemical companies, generally the same company has had a large stake in both the new product, or the product of a novel process, and the product or process rendered obsolete by its introduction. In few cases has one major's development of a new product rendered obsolete a principal product of another. "Business ethics" and "friendly relations" generally block such extensive encroachments by one company on the recognized domain of others.[126]

When a few large, fully integrated concerns produce a myriad of joint products, utilize complicated and rapidly changing techniques, and employ capital on a vast scale, market behavior is inevitably unlike that when the number of sellers is large, the product homogeneous, the processes simple, and the capital investment of any single producer relatively small. The size, financial strength, and technical resources of such companies as du Pont and ICI make them unwilling to engage in a real competitive struggle. None is likely seriously to consider trying to supplant the others in world markets, even though at the moment it may have a specific or general competitive advantage.

A company which, because of a superior process, may today have other companies at its mercy may find one of its own processes obsolete tomorrow and some part of its capital investment in jeopardy. A

---

have been no less radical than those mentioned in the text, e.g., chlorine for bleaching powder, brimstone for pyrites. It may be that changes within the chemical industries are less "striking" than those which involve outsiders principally because the burden of technological obsolescence is in the latter case more evident. If a technical advance displaces a large body of laborers from accustomed lines of employment, it is more likely to arrest popular attention than in the event its main incidence is on invested capital.

On the other hand, it may be that internal displacements have been less spectacular because the pace of the change-over has been deliberately regulated to temper its adverse effects. By smoothing out the transition, the cost of obsolescence can be moderated. This appears to have occurred in the gradual displacement of wood alcohol by synthetic methanol.

126. For example, in 1935 IG required Jasco, the joint IG–Standard Oil chemical venture, to close down its plant using IG's superior arc acetylene process and to offer the process to the two major American companies interested in this field, UCC, the dominant producer, and du Pont, a major consumer of acetylene in its manufacture of synthetic rubber, acetic acid, and anhydride. UCC objected to this offer to du Pont:

"Mr. Rafferty said that his firm was not at all interested in synthetic rubber and that they had no objection in this regard. Since his firm, he said, was the largest manufacturer of Anhydride Acid in the United States, it would not be a matter of indifference . . . if such an important consumer as Du Pont should disappear from the market.

"A discussion followed about the border lines between Carbide and Carbon, on the one hand, and Du Pont, on the other, and it appeared that it was not easy to delineate these border lines and that, in the course of time, there might be changes." Bone, Pt. III, p. 1462.

large chemical company, tempted to manufacture products for which it supplies some important constituent material, has good reason to think twice before doing so. On second thought it may realize what might happen to its profits if the chemical companies that buy supplies from it should retaliate. For, if a company were vigorously to press its momentary advantage based on a particular product or process, its relative efficiency would not necessarily determine the outcome of the ensuing struggle. Competitors might be able to meet its lower prices indefinitely, offsetting their losses by income from other operations. They might readily retaliate by price cutting in lines in which the initial "upsetter of the applecart" was more vulnerable, and a general price war might ensue.

But if the chemical markets do not conform to competitive markets either in structure or behavior, neither do they conform strictly to the typical market which the theorists of imperfect competition have analyzed. Business executives of chemical companies are seldom willing to rely on independent rational behavior to insure market stability. They have developed a set of business principles, policies, and procedures to protect and promote their mutual interests and to give security to their investments.

Technological Cooperation

A dynamic technology is a constant threat to vested interests. An effort to use it for individual advantage may impair the financial position of the entire group. But, through cooperative control, it may be made to promote the interests of all. In Lord Melchett's words:

As there is no monopoly in inventions, nobody can say whence the next great idea will come . . . This fact implies that at any moment it might be within the power of any one country to project a new idea which would at once disconcert the whole world balance of industry. This instance gives rise to the natural desire . . . to co-operate with all those working on similar ideas, so as to pool the results of invention and research and to bring to bear . . . the economic rate of production.[127]

The nature of chemical technology encourages cooperation among chemical companies. Invention is a cumulative process. Today it is more than ever a group process. New processes or products are not

127. *Op. cit.*, p. 212. Apparently the author conceives the "economic rate of production" as that which will disturb least the existing "world balance of industry."

isolated inventions. They not only grow out of all that has gone before, but they depend on a great many closely related discoveries. In the modern industrial laboratory they are developed by the sustained, cooperative efforts of teams of trained, salaried professionals. If conflicting patent rights and business interests impede the free flow and use of technological ideas, they retard technological progress. They may enable some company to block off a narrow channel in a developing art and exclude others from it. Ownership of a particular patent may give a veto power over subsequent developments based on the innovation in which the patentee has exclusive rights. Thus, the obstructive power of patents may be great indeed.

Through pooling their knowledge, experience, and monopoly privileges, chemical companies can eliminate costly litigation, increase the fruitfulness of their research, and gain a tremendous advantage over "outside" would-be innovators. Patent pools need not be discriminatory, of course. They may be employed primarily to broaden knowledge and insure its free use. All who contribute to the pool may be free to use the funded patents without restriction.

Such pools are rare in the chemical industries. When chemical companies exchange patent licenses and technical information, they usually do so subject to restrictions. These reservations may apply to the industrial fields in which the knowledge may be used, or to market areas or prices. Thus patent pools may be devices to control markets rather than to disseminate knowledge. Exchange of patents affords a means of "ordering" an industry, a means which has been freely used in the chemical field.

In a patents and processes agreement between du Pont and ICI, du Pont licenses, or agrees upon request to license,[128] ICI to use all its present and future patents and secret "know-how" for the manufacture and sale within the British Empire of, for example, dyestuffs and explosives, and ICI licenses du Pont similarly for the United States. This is a cartel agreement in fact, whatever may be its legal

128. In form, most of the du Pont patents and processes agreements are not themselves cross-licenses, but merely agreements or arrangements to cross-license patents in a specified field upon future request by either party. The terms of exchange are often left to subsequent negotiation. Du Pont officials have stressed this feature in denying that these agreements are in restraint of trade within the meaning of the antitrust laws. See, e.g., Nye, Pt. V, pp. 1204-05. As a test of market control, this technicality seems unimportant. If the agreements mean anything—and apparently they mean much—they are the means of eliminating competition between du Pont and its business rivals.

status. Each of the parties has the right to use both its own and its licensee's patents and processes only in its allotted territory. When the licenses are exclusive, as they often are, neither party may use even its own patents and processes in the allotted territory of the other. Such agreements limit competition between the contracting parties, and fortify each in competing with independents.

Agreements Lessen Competition

On their face, agreements of this kind apply only to processes and products covered by patents and secret inventions. Legally the parties are free to compete in the sale of all products not covered by patents and secret processes. However, in practice, such agreements not only lessen the will to compete, they make competition difficult if not impossible.[129] In the chemical industries technological change is so rapid that a division of market territories for products coming within the scope of all patents and secret processes in a given field usually entails a complete division of territories for all related products. As a du Pont official has explained:

It is obvious that when one company has given the other licenses in that company's exclusive territory that it becomes more and more difficult for the granting company to carry on business in the territory of the grantee, as the granting company gradually loses its rights to use the various improvements which keep its product abreast of the times. It also follows that it would not be good business practice to maintain agents in these territories who would only be free to sell products not covered by patents or secret processes. There is no obligation to get out of any territory, although it is obviously necessary from a common sense viewpoint to gradually withdraw from the exclusive territories of the other party.[130]

American companies have urged the legality of these arrangements. As du Pont has explained in connection with its agreement with the British Levinstein:

The sole object and purpose of this agreement was to afford a working basis for exchange of technical information between Levinstein, Limited, and the Du Pont Company, and to enable each to use the patents and the secrets of the other in the respective territories where such property rights were owned.

It is common knowledge that territorial restrictions in the case of letters

129. As the parties themselves have declared. See quotation below.
130. Edwards, op. cit., p. 7.

patent and secret processes are in very common usage in practically every country throughout the world, and have received the universal sanction of the courts.

This contract is just such an ordinary business document. It deals, as its title indicates, only with patented and secret processes, placing no restrictions, territorial or otherwise, upon the sale of products not embodying the secrets of patents referred to in the contract.[131]

Unquestionably, du Pont and Levinstein each sought to improve its market position by exchanging patented technology. Unquestionably, also, this agreement greatly reduced or eliminated competition between the two companies. Moreover, the agreement bound the parties to exchange in the future techniques which at the time the contract was signed were not their property, might not even have been discovered, and to which, therefore, the special privileges granted by the patent laws to patentees could not possibly apply. But, in any case, the legal status of such agreements is irrelevant to this study.

In their intercorporate dealings, large and powerful chemical companies use patents and secret processes as counters in a never-ending bargaining process. They "swap" them for equivalent benefits from others. They trade them for the right to a larger share in existing markets or for participation in new fields. They use them as chips in a poker game in which the stakes are world markets. While patents and "know-how" may promote the industrial arts, they also are unquestionably a source of business power.

But patents are, after all, only one instrument of business power, and perhaps not even the most important one even in the chemical industries. Of equal if not greater importance is the "spiritual atmosphere" in which business goes on, the prevailing attitude toward each other of the great companies with world-wide interests. Sir Alfred Mond has described this as follows:

The old idea of the heads of great businesses meeting each other with scowls and shaking each other's fists in each other's faces and . . . trying to destroy each other's business may be very good on the films, but it does not accord with any given facts. The alliance of great companies operating on huge scales with every kind of interest and working in harmonious co-operation renders it possible to have exchange of information as regards methods of business and new ideas, and we all do better by working in that manner . . .[132]

131. Nye, Pt. XXXIX, p. 13429.
132. ICI, *Proceedings* at the First Annual General Meeting, May 31, 1928, p. 7.

Chapter 10

ALKALIES, EXPLOSIVES, AND THE GRAND ALLIANCE

THE ALKALI CARTEL

ONE OF THE OLDEST chemical cartels centers around the network of companies set up by the Solvay brothers and their foreign partners in the leading industrial countries to exploit their newly developed ammonia soda process for making alkalies. In 1872 Ernest Solvay and Ludwig Mond organized Brunner Mond in Great Britain and the Solvay brothers granted it an exclusive license for the British Empire. In 1881, Brunner Mond and Solvay et Cie. jointly organized the Solvay Process Company of New York, with exclusive rights to the United States market. Solvay Process and Brunner Mond then formed a joint subsidiary, Brunner Mond of Canada. From time to time thereafter the original Solvay company (Solvay et Cie.), whose exclusive territory was the European continent, established subsidiaries in Germany, Holland, France, Italy, Russia, and, in partnership with Aussiger Verein, Czechoslovakia, Poland, Yugoslavia, Hungary, and Roumania.[1]

These companies were linked not only financially but by patent licenses and marketing agreements providing for exchange of technical information, price fixing, and division of sales territories.[2] Except for the American company, each still produces all or most of the soda ash and a major part of all alkalies in its home territory.[3]

The structure and power of the Solvay cartel remained substantially unchanged until World War II. Besides controlling affiliated European companies, the Belgian Solvay company was linked with

1. Karl Falk, "I. G. Farben 'Adds the Balkans to the Reich,'" *Foreign Commerce Weekly,* October 17, 1942, p. 8.
2. Theodore J. Kreps, "Heavy Chemicals," *Encyclopaedia of the Social Sciences,* Macmillan, New York, 1937, Vol. VII, p. 304.
3. U.S. Bureau of Foreign and Domestic Commerce, Trade Information Bulletin No. 813, *The European Chemical Industry in 1932,* pp. 33, 47; Trade Information Bulletin No. 781, *French Chemical Industry and Trade in 1930,* p. 6; Trade Information Bulletin No. 708, *The Chemical Industry of Czechoslovakia,* p. 6; Trade Information Bulletin No. 705, *Italian Chemical Developments in 1928 and 1929,* pp. 22-23; Trade Information Bulletin No. 605, *German Chemical Developments in 1928,* p. 24.

I. G. Farbenindustrie, both holding stock in Aussiger Verein [4] and in the German Solvay company, the most important continental producer of alkalies. Both IG and German Solvay were members of the German Soda Syndicate. The Belgian Solvay company also owned about 25 per cent of the stock and held directorships in both Imperial Chemical Industries and Allied Chemical & Dye. ICI inherited from Brunner Mond a substantial, though smaller, investment in Allied, and for a brief period Sir Alfred Mond was a member of Allied's board of directors.[5]

Solvay's Influence Extends Beyond Alkalies

The community of financial and commercial interests built originally about the Solvay process has helped to link some of the outstanding chemical giants of recent years—ICI, IG, Allied Chemical, Solvay et Cie., and Aussiger Verein. The relations of ICI and Belgian Solvay are exceptionally close. They regularly exchange technical information and scrupulously respect each other's market territories in the general field of alkalies and related products.[6] The control by these two companies of their American offspring, Solvay Process, was weakened somewhat by dilution of their financial interest when Solvay Process was merged in Allied Chemical & Dye in 1920. Moreover, Allied has a reputation for secretiveness in technical matters and for jealously guarding its "birthright" as an American-controlled enterprise.[7]

4. Falk, *op. cit.,* p. 7.

5. ICI, *Proceedings* at the First Annual General Meeting, May 31, 1928, pp. 2, 7. ICI later sold its shares in Allied to Belgian Solvay. Also, it sold its controlling interest in Brunner Mond of Canada to Allied. See Hearings before a Special Committee Investigating the Munitions Industry, U.S. Senate, 73d Cong., Pt. V, p. 1298; Pt. XII, p. 2869. (These Hearings will hereinafter be cited as Nye, Pt. —, after the name of the committee chairman; the *Report* [74th Cong., 2d sess., S.Rept. 944] as Nye, *Report,* Pt. —.)

6. See Nye, Pt. V, p. 1299. For list of agreements covering these activities, see Schedule A, appended to the Agreement of June 30, 1939, between du Pont and ICI. A copy of this Agreement appears as Exhibit 2 in the complaint filed January 6, 1944 in the antitrust suit, *U.S. v. Imperial Chemical Industries, Ltd., et al.,* in U.S. District Court for the Southern District of New York, Civil Action No. 24-13. This case will hereinafter be cited: *U.S. v. ICI.* References to the complaint will cite the numbered paragraphs; and references to the defendants' answers, which have corresponding paragraph numbers, will be abbreviated to: ICI Answer, par. —, or du Pont Answer, par. —; or where they agree, simply: Answers, par. —. Though the courts have not yet adjudicated this case and thus from the legal standpoint certified the existence and determined the significance of all the facts bearing on the issues involved, for present purposes we treat as established facts government allegations which the companies in their answers admit to be true. For these, citation will be simply: *U.S. v. ICI,* par. —.

7. See text, p. 395, n. 70, and W. Haynes, *Chemical Economics,* Van Nostrand, New York, 1933, p. 269.

Nevertheless, American collaboration in the world alkali cartel did not end when Solvay Process became a subsidiary of Allied. Through an American alkali export association, Allied cooperated with ICI and Belgian Solvay until 1941 in regulating export markets. Allied has also helped to stabilize world markets for two of its other major lines, nitrogen and dyestuffs, in both of which ICI has a big stake and is a leading member of the international cartels.

Electrolytic Process Threatens Solvay Cartel

When the electrolysis of brine, yielding caustic soda and chlorine, threatened the world-wide Solvay alkali monopoly, this conflict of interest was eventually reconciled under the leadership of companies closely associated with Belgian Solvay. ICI—the Solvay process licensee—became the leading electrolytic producer by acquiring exclusive British Empire rights in the pioneer Castner-Kellner process. In Germany, IG became the leading electrolytic producer and joined with German Solvay and all other domestic alkali producers in the soda ash and caustic soda cartels. These domestic German cartels fixed prices and production quotas and marketed their members' output. In Italy the Solvay company itself became the leading electrolytic producer. In Czechoslovakia the dominant producers of caustic soda were Nestomitzer, the joint Belgian Solvay–Aussiger Verein subsidiary, and Aussiger Verein itself.[8]

During the thirties ICI, Solvay et Cie., IG, and Aussiger Verein, the major continental producers of alkalies by both the electrolytic and Solvay processes, reaffirmed and consolidated their community of interests in a formal cartel agreement.[9] The cartel provided for exchange of technical information and patent licenses and for parcelling out exclusive marketing territories.

Rivalry between Solvay and electrolytic producers was keener in

8. See p. 430, n. 3.
9. The 1939 du Pont–ICI Patents and Processes Agreement (Schedule A) lists an agreement, dated December 1938, between these four companies, providing for "exchange of technical information and patents on electrolytic chlorine manufacture and principal derivatives." *U.S.* v. *ICI,* Complaint, Ex. 2. Presumably this cartel divided markets by assigning to each member the patent rights for its allotted territory. The long-standing financial ties and close relations in the alkali field among these four companies unmistakably point to a cartel arrangement antedating the formal 1938 agreement. The complaint (par. 48) in the antitrust suit, *U.S.* v. *United States Alkali Export Association, Inc.* (filed March 16, 1944 in U.S. District Court for the Southern District of New York), alleges that this cartel was in existence before 1936. (This case will hereinafter be cited: *U.S.* v. *Alkasso.*)

the United States than in Europe. In the late nineties electrolytic producers began to make sharp inroads on Solvay's caustic soda market.[10] As several different techniques for electrolytic production developed, and as the demand for chlorine grew rapidly, electrolytic caustic soda relentlessly pushed its way into the market.

Allied Chemical was not the only American producer of caustic soda with foreign affiliations. Some of the electrolytic producers also had working arrangements with European cartel members. The (American) Castner Alkali Company operated under a Castner-Kellner license which presumably restricted its operations to the United States, just as ICI's license to use this process restricted it to the British Empire. In 1937 Solvay et Cie. and ICI each agreed separately with Pennsylvania Salt and Michigan Alkali, leading American electrolytic producers, to supply them with information necessary to set up electrolytic chlorine–caustic soda plants using processes the European companies had developed.[11] Pennsylvania Salt is a member of the association of American alkali exporters, which has an agreement with ICI for division of markets. It also has had an agreement with IG whereby "I. G. receives option on exclusive right to use Gibbs cell [electrolytic process] in all European countries with the exception of Great Britain." [12]

American Producers Join World Alkali Cartel

The principal American electrolytic and Solvay producers have indirectly taken part since 1924 in the world alkali cartel. The channel for cooperation, on the American side, has been the United States Alkali Export Association, Inc. (Alkasso), a Webb-Pomerene association which was formed in 1919. The California Alkali Export Association (Calkex), formed in 1936, has cooperated with it in regulating American foreign trade in this line.[13] According to the

10. Haynes, op. cit., pp. 185-86.
11. Schedule A of the 1939 du Pont–ICI Agreement, loc. cit. Pennsylvania Salt had been using another electrolytic process in its Wyandotte (Michigan) plant since 1903. Haynes, op. cit., p. 182.
12. Patents, Hearings before the Committee on Patents, 77th Cong., 2d sess., on S. 2303 and S. 2491, Pt. V, p. 2350. (Hereinafter: Bone, Pt. —.) The development of the Gibbs cell was an important factor in the steady growth of electrolytic production. Haynes, op. cit., p. 147.
13. TNEC Monograph No. 6, Export Prices and Export Cartels (Webb-Pomerene Associations), pp. 169, 224. The cooperation takes the form of sharing jointly with Alkasso the latter's cartel privileges and obligations.

United States Department of Justice in its antitrust suit, these two associations included all important American producers and together controlled more than 95 per cent of American alkali exports until the resignation of Solvay Process in 1941.[14]

On the European side, the channel of cooperation between the American producers and the cartel has been ICI, which has made a series of agreements with Alkasso.[15] Confirming the agreement of 1929, ICI concisely stated its purpose: "It is understood there will be complete co-operation between us in order to avoid competition in any part of the world . . ." [16]

The antitrust complaint states that the parties fixed uniform selling prices, used common selling agents, accepted both percentage and absolute quota limits on exports to specific markets, and established fixed ratios between their alkali exports.[17] The government alleges that, as part of the general understanding between the parties, ICI recognized the United States as Alkasso's exclusive market and agreed to stop exporting alkalies to this country.[18]

Alkasso Assumes Responsibility for All American Exports

Alkasso agreed to include in its quota computations exports of independent American companies. ICI indicated that it expected Alkasso also to control the export prices of American independents:

> We confidently expect . . . that, apart from your responsibility for the tonnage of U. S. A. exports, you will take the necessary steps to control Inyo and any other makers of alkali products in the U. S. A., so that by the stabilization of prices we may achieve some benefit from our arrangement with you.[19]

14. *U.S.* v. *Alkasso,* Complaint, par. 40. The complaint states that, as a result of war conditions and the resignation of Solvay, the share has dropped to 75 per cent.

15. In 1924 the British party was Brunner Mond, which acted for United Alkali as well as for itself. In general, we shall hereinafter disregard the distinction between ICI and its constituent concerns.

16. *U.S.* v. *Alkasso,* Complaint, Ex. B. Copies of the agreements are appended to the complaint as exhibits.

17. ICI conceded to Alkasso a steadily rising share until 1932 but then refused to make further concessions. *Ibid.,* Exs. B and C.

18. *Ibid.,* pars. 41, 43. It is likely that Alkasso and ICI did reach some such informal understanding, leaving it out of the written agreements because of its clear violation of the Sherman Act. It is difficult to believe that the American and British producers would have eliminated competition between themselves all over the world, as they did, while continuing to compete actively in the United States, or that Alkasso would have accepted limitations on its exports without some assurance of freedom from foreign competition at home. In any event, American imports of alkalies were relatively small, before as well as after the 1924 ICI-Alkasso agreement.

19. *Ibid.,* Ex. B. The 1933 agreement also implies Alkasso's continued responsibility for nonmember exports. See Article XI of that agreement.

The success of the ICI-Alkasso agreements depended not only on Alkasso's ability to restrain American independents, but also on ICI's ability to speak for other foreign manufacturers. ICI could not have guaranteed Alkasso exclusive territories or a fixed share of designated markets, had not Belgian Solvay and IG agreed to respect these decisions. IG and Solvay, in turn, would scarcely respect Alkasso's allotted markets unless Alkasso could keep American alkalies out of Solvay and IG territory—the continent of Europe.[20]

When, during the mid-thirties, independent American producers on the Pacific Coast exported alkalies to Europe, both IG and Solvay protested, according to the Department of Justice, and threatened to retaliate by exporting into the exclusive and joint territories of ICI and Alkasso. The Department alleges that Alkasso responded by taking the lead in organizing the Pacific Coast producers in Calkex.[21]

Shortly after the formation of Calkex, Alkasso entered into a new agreement with ICI and Solvay et Cie.[22] Like its predecessors, this agreement divided markets with, roughly, Europe as Solvay's exclusive territory, the British Empire (except Canada) as ICI's domain, and North America outside the United States as Alkasso's preserve.[23] The parties agreed on sales quotas for joint ICI-Alkasso territories, mainly China, Japan, and South America. Each party assumed responsibility for, and agreed to include in its quota, all exports from its "exclusive territory" and each agreed also to try to prevent shipments into the others' exclusive markets.

The organization of Calkex made it possible for Alkasso to give such assurance to its cartel partners. A 1937 memorandum which outlined the "cooperative export program" of Calkex and Alkasso indicates quite plainly that Calkex integrated the export operations of its members with those of Alkasso and the world alkali cartel.[24] A

20. *Ibid.*, par. 48.
21. "Alkasso caused the three Pacific Coast companies to organize defendant Calkex." *Ibid.*, par. 55.
22. The Department of Justice states that this agreement was supplementary to a similar agreement in which IG was included. *Ibid.*, par. 48.
23. The government asserts that in a broader understanding IG, ICI, and Solvay also agreed to refrain from exporting to the United States. *Ibid.* It appears anomalous that the European producers should undertake to restrict their exports to Alkasso's "exclusive territory," which, in terms, excluded the United States, in exchange for Alkasso's undertaking to control exports *only* from Canada and Mexico!
24. *Ibid.*, Ex. E. The government complaint in the Alkasso case describes in some detail the alleged manner in which Alkasso and Calkex maintained control over almost all American exports of alkalies. It alleges that they exercised constant surveillance over

new agreement in 1941 between ICI and Alkasso temporarily adjusted previous agreements to wartime conditions, indicating that the war did not prevent "business as usual."

These agreements between Alkasso and ICI and Solvay et Cie. are clearly designed to establish joint control of world markets, to eliminate competition among leading exporters, and thereby to increase their profits. Elimination of competition among domestic producers in export sales no doubt has weakened competitive forces in the domestic market and contributed to the rigidity of alkali prices in the United States. Producers who learn to cooperate successfully in selling abroad are unlikely to compete aggressively at home.

Temporary price declines in the American market have been of brief duration and apparently have reflected the market strategy of dissatisfied cartel members. In 1930–1931, for example, Allied Chemical precipitated a price war apparently to increase its domestic sales and thereby strengthen its claim to a larger share in export markets.[25] The government alleges that the association persistently pursued a policy of supporting domestic prices by demanding progressively higher export quotas from its cartel partners, by offering especially favorable export quotas to domestic electrolytic producers, and by "dumping" abroad their byproduct caustic soda.[26]

Cartel Encounters Difficulties

From time to time new competitors, frequently encouraged by their governments, seriously threatened the cartel's control over world markets. Local manufacturers arose to demand a share in the Chinese, Brazilian, and Argentine markets. Exports from Japan, the USSR, and western United States competed with cartel exports. Cartel members met these threats in several ways. To discourage local manufacture they cut prices in the threatened markets. Sometimes

---

all exports, that they kept a record of sales by independents, and that they have persistently harassed "bootleggers" by local price discrimination, cutting off their sources of supply, and propagandizing against their products, while at the same time making them a standing offer to act as their agent. *Ibid.*, pars. 53, 58-61.

25. "Allied Chemical & Dye," *Fortune*, October 1939, pp. 50-51.

26. *U.S.* v. *Alkasso*, Complaint, par. 62. Presumably Solvay producers could more easily curtail their output to their restricted export quotas than electrolytic manufacturers, whose caustic soda output is a byproduct of chlorine. Hence the offer of higher export quotas to the latter at the expense of the former would decrease the supply offered in America.

they established local plants, or acquired control of local ventures, with minority participation by local capital.

For example, in their 1924 compact, ICI and Alkasso agreed to sell alkali at preferential prices to a Brazilian company, Matarazzo, which was contemplating manufacture. In Argentina, du Pont and ICI persuaded a local paper company which had decided to manufacture its own alkalies to do so in collaboration with their local subsidiary, which offered participation in the new venture to IG and Solvay.[27] The following letter (evidently from Alkasso) to Calkex, explaining a price reduction in Latin America, clearly illustrates the cartel strategy when threatened by competitive local manufacture:

> The main factor was the apparent need for some temporary price action in the face of unusual pressure for the erection of local industries, particularly in Mexico, Brazil, and the Argentine, and with special reference to caustic soda and soda ash—and where government assistance was being sought.
>
> In Brazil the problem has been met by the formation of an exploratory company . . . to circumvent action by others, satisfy government, and seeking government concessions to carry on this work estimated to take almost two years before any production could be contemplated—if found desirable and economical.
>
> In the Argentine ash prices were also reduced as a temporary measure, first, because of interest of government in the entire alkali picture, and second, owing to considerable interest by local groups in such a venture. . . . Under the circumstances, it was considered good strategy to reduce prices for a temporary period.[28]

When these devices failed, cartel members drew the new competitors into their community of interest. For example, ICI shared the Chinese market with a local producer according to predetermined quotas, and the Solvay group, for a consideration, granted the USSR concessions in Asiatic markets.[29]

Thus, technological developments and national interests have

27. See pp. 462-63.

28. Corwin D. Edwards, *Economic and Political Aspects of International Cartels*, Monograph No. 1 of the Subcommittee on War Mobilization, Committee on Military Affairs, U.S. Senate, pursuant to S.Res. 107, 78th Cong., 2d sess. (Washington, 1944), pp. 47-48. A statement by ICI, evidently to Alkasso, reflects the same policy: "We should like to make it clear that our object, when we considered the manufacture of soda ash in Brazil, was primarily to control or preserve our present joint control of the market and to safeguard your, as well as our, future import business. It was for this reason that we intended to limit the size of the projected plant to 20,000 tons." *Ibid.*, p. 47.

29. Bureau of Foreign and Domestic Commerce, Trade Information Bulletin No. 823, *World Chemical Developments in 1934*, p. 3.

limited the cartel's ability to play fast and loose with the consumer. The electrolytic process forced down alkali prices. "Younger" countries, previously dependent entirely on imports for their supplies, have obtained temporary price concessions by encouraging domestic manufacture or as a result of threats of their nationals to start competitive enterprises. However, the cartel has frequently either stifled such local ventures by price cutting or has brought them into the cartel. By these tactics it has maintained its effectiveness as an instrument for regulating world trade in alkalies.

THE EXPLOSIVES CARTEL

Brunner Mond was the link connecting ICI with Allied Chemical, Solvay, and IG in the alkali field. Similarly, Nobel Industries paved the way for ICI's "grand alliance" with du Pont,[30] a relationship only slightly less intimate than an outright partnership. The original alliance was limited to explosives, the field in which both companies were mainly interested until after World War I.

In 1886 Alfred Nobel created the famous Nobel Dynamite Trust Company, Ltd., which dominated the international explosives trade until World War I.[31] The Nobel Trust made agreements in 1897, and again in 1907, with Vereinigte Köln-Rottweiler Pulverfabriken, a large German manufacturer, and du Pont and associated American manufacturers, dividing world markets among themselves.[32] In 1914 the same companies drew up a new agreement which divided markets through an exchange of exclusive patent licenses. Because of the war, they never put it into effect.

30. Du Pont reached an agreement with Levinstein, Ltd., in the field of dyestuffs during World War I. See text, p. 428; also Nye, Pt. XXXIX, pp. 13423-30. It is not clear whether this agreement remained in effect after Levinstein merged into British Dyestuffs, or after Dyestuffs became part of ICI. In any case, it seems to have had little influence on du Pont–ICI relations, probably because both companies were far more concerned at this stage about their relations with IG, the major power in this field, than with each other.
31. Eckart Kehr, "Munitions Industry," Encyclopaedia of the Social Sciences, Vol. XI, pp. 129-30. The Trust owned Nobel Explosives Co., Ltd., and Alfred Nobel Company of Hamburg, which were respectively the leading English and German producers.
32. W. H. S. Stevens, "The Powder Trust," Quarterly Journal of Economics, Vol. XXVI (1912), pp. 466-67. The original contract provided for price fixing, but this was later dropped because of the Sherman Act. The 1907 agreement also provided for pooling of profits. Nye, Pt. VI, p. 1299, and Report, Pt. III, p. 222. Most of the information developed in this chapter on du Pont–ICI relations is based on legal documents in the antitrust proceeding, U.S. v. ICI.

Meanwhile, Nobel's Hamburg subsidiary split off from the Trust and merged in Dynamit A. G. (DAG). After the war IG, by obtaining control of both DAG and Köln-Rottweil, became the dominant German explosives producer.[33] In Britain, Nobel Industries, Ltd.,[34] emerged from an amalgamation of Nobel Explosives and other important British concerns, with a virtual monopoly in its field.[35]

Renewal of du Pont–Nobel Ties After World War I

By a general explosives agreement in 1920, du Pont and Nobel resumed their prewar relationship.[36] They agreed to exchange exclusive licenses under present and future patents and secret processes in the field of explosives. Du Pont obtained the United States, Mexico, most of Central America, Colombia, and Venezuela as its exclusive territory, while Nobel got Europe, Asia, Africa, and Australasia. For the rest of South America they exchanged nonexclusive licenses.

By concurrent special compacts, the two companies eliminated any possibility of competition between them in nonexclusive markets. Under the South American Pooling Agreement, they agreed to pool and share profits from sales of commercial explosives in all South American countries, except Chile, and to exchange information on all governmental requests for bids on military explosives. To take care of the important Chilean "commercial" market, in 1921 they organized Cia. Sud-Americana de Explosivos (CSAE), giving Atlas Powder Company an allotment of 15 per cent of CSAE's stock.[37]

As early as 1910, du Pont and Nobel Explosives had acquired an equal interest in, and joint control of, Canadian Explosives, Ltd. (CXL).[38] To this joint subsidiary, later renamed Canadian Industries, Ltd. (CIL), they gave royalty-free, nonexclusive licenses under

33. Köln-Rottweil is an IG subsidiary. IG has exercised complete control over DAG. It has taken DAG's earnings and has guaranteed to DAG's stockholders dividends equivalent to its own. Moreover, it has an option to buy them out. See IG's yearbook, *I. G. Farbenindustrie Aktiengesellschaft,* for 1937, p. 57; also Nye, Pt. V, pp. 1201-03; *U.S.* v. *ICI,* par. 18.

34. The original merger was Explosives Trades, Ltd., but it soon changed its name to Nobel Industries.

35. In 1924, "Sir Harry [McGowan] stated that he anticipated no difficulty in dealing with the small U. K. concerns not under Nobel control." Nye, Pt. XII, p. 2866.

36. By about this date both companies had already acquired their substantial stockholdings and directorates in General Motors.

37. Atlas' share was roughly equivalent to its proportion of current total sales in the Chilean market; du Pont and Nobel divided the remainder of the stock equally between themselves. See *U.S.* v. *ICI,* par. 36.

38. *Ibid.,* ICI Answer, par. 37.

their patents to produce specified explosives and other chemicals in Canada and Newfoundland. In 1925 they made the licenses exclusive, at the same time restricting them to explosives and their raw materials.

Significance of "Patents and Processes" Agreements

These du Pont–Nobel explosives agreements set the pattern for later du Pont–ICI collaboration over a much wider range of subjects. On their face, they were merely an exchange of rights to use patented or secret technology. In practice, however, they virtually eliminated all competition in explosives between the two companies throughout the world. They prohibited each company from selling its products manufactured under the cross-licensed patents or by secret processes in the other's exclusive territory, even though it might have produced them by its own patented or secret processes. Both companies remained free to sell unpatented products or products made by nonpatented or nonsecret processes in the territory of the other. However, complete cooperation in all protected lines was scarcely consistent with real competition in the unprotected ones, and in fact such competition has not developed.[39]

Even if du Pont were guided solely by independent commercial considerations in deciding whether or not to compete in ICI (or Nobel) territory by selling products not covered by patents or secret processes, Nobel could generally count on du Pont's decision not to compete. For it would scarcely pay du Pont to set up export sales facilities for the limited range of products still free, particularly since such products might at any time be supplanted by new ones to which its British associate would have the *exclusive* right—even though du Pont should bring forth these new developments! In short, the agreements are not mere patent and process licensing agreements to promote and protect the technological interests of the two parties. They

39. Du Pont, anxious to establish the legality of its agreements, maintains that they exerted restrictive influence on trade only in products covered by patents or secret processes: "To the extent that du Pont has not exported to the British Empire products, other than products made under patents or secret processes licensed by ICI as hereinafter admitted, or has not exported products to other countries, this has been because of its own decision independently arrived at . . ." *Ibid.*, du Pont Answer, par. 28.

"To the extent that this [du Pont's failure to export explosives into Nobel's exclusive territory] was not the result of licenses granted under the General Explosives Agreement, du Pont so refrained because it believed such exports would prove commercially unprofitable to it . . ." *Ibid.*, par. 38.

represent a sort of partnership arrangement providing for joint exploitation of world markets.

Special arrangements later made by du Pont and ICI (or Nobel) covering military explosives illustrate and confirm this analysis. By separate agreements in 1925, 1926, and 1928, du Pont obtained a specified share in the European market for military powders. Under the 1928 contract, ICI and du Pont each obtained tonnage quotas for specified types of explosives sold to European governments. They also allotted particular government customers to one or the other's sales organization, which took orders for either company's products.[40]

Under a 1926 agreement, du Pont and Nobel cooperated in the same way in selling military explosives in South America. Later they extended this plan to all three major joint territories, Europe, Asia, and South America. This agreement set forth "the commissions to be paid by each company to the other for assistance in obtaining business." [41] The following cable of November 11, 1932 from du Pont to its Paris sales office indicates that these sales arrangements provided a covert method of sharing profits under the guise of paying "commissions":

Replying to your letter no. 2511 if 50/50 arrangement on all sales decided upon for Europe there is no occasion for setting up a clause providing how profits are to be determined. In the meeting with H. J. Mitchell [ICI executive] it was agreed that we would do as we had in the past in South America. We accept each other's figures without question. Payments are called commissions, and no mention should be made of profits in agreement. Any chance setting up methods of determination of commissions extremely dangerous to both of us. This agreement based on mutual confidence and should be so regarded.[42]

40. According to du Pont, the purpose of this arrangement "was to minimize selling and administrative expenses and to avoid duplication of work in connection with the sale of the products covered thereby . . ." *Ibid.*, du Pont Answer, par. 43. Whatever the motive, the effect undeniably was to eliminate competition.
In the absence of competition, consumers apparently were offered a poor product at a high price. The minutes of du Pont's foreign relations committee, in 1928, report as follows: "This arrangement is meeting with difficulties in the case of N.C. [nitrocellulose] powders because Mr. Smith [the ICI agent] is selling not at all in his territory, and Colonel Taylor [the du Pont agent] is having difficulty in securing Nobel's 30 percent proportion because of the high price and poor quality of their product. This is causing dissatisfaction on Colonel Taylor's part as he feels he could sell du Pont powders in cases where he is turned down in offering Nobel's, and on Nobel's part because they are not getting any N.C. business." Edwards, *op. cit.*, p. 15.
41. *U.S.* v. *ICI*, par. 159.
42. Nye, Pt. V, p. 1094. In spite of this cable, du Pont and ICI deny that these arrangements were profit-sharing schemes. *U.S.* v. *ICI*, Answers, pars. 42, 159.
However this may be, the close working relationship between du Pont and ICI is

Explosives Cartel Re-formed

The return of German producers to world markets after the war provided both the occasion and the incentive for re-establishing an explosives cartel on a world-wide basis. By 1925, DAG had made substantial inroads in Nobel's and du Pont's markets for commercial explosives.[43] Accordingly, Nobel and du Pont took a series of steps early in 1926 that brought DAG (and Köln-Rottweil, for which it acted) into the cartel and virtually eliminated all competition in the commercial explosives field.

First, they acquired stock in DAG.[44] Although both deny that they did this as part of a "conspiracy . . . to eliminate competition," as the United States Government alleges,[45] Sir Harry McGowan made it clear in urging Nobel's directors to sanction the purchase that a primary consideration in making it was to establish a "binding community of interests." [46]

Second, du Pont, DAG, and Köln-Rottweil entered into an in-

---

indicated in this instance by ICI's admission that it and du Pont, "being desirous of discouraging as much as possible the erection of factories for the manufacture of military explosives," agreed not to build any in South America, China, or Europe without mutual consent. *Ibid.,* ICI Answer, par. 160.

43. The Versailles Treaty prohibited German export of military explosives, but the Germans were ignoring this ban. Both du Pont and Nobel knew this. Du Pont officials did not request the government to protest since the United States was not a signatory to the treaty. They expressed the opinion that Nobel could stop such exports by calling them to the attention of the British Government, but that in the interests of maintaining or re-establishing close and friendly relations with the German manufacturers, it would not do so. Nye, Pt. IX, pp. 2264-65; Pt. XII, p. 2799; *Report,* Pt. III, pp. 246-56.

44. In 1934 du Pont reported that it held 8 per cent of DAG's total stock outstanding, and ICI, 12.5 per cent. Nye, Pt. V, pp. 1283, 1298. In a statement issued on November 15, 1945, du Pont denied that it then held any stock interest in DAG. It declared that it "has no investment whatever in IG, or any of its subsidiaries" (of which DAG is one). But in the press release, du Pont admitted that in 1933, when it began to dispose of the DAG stock, its investment in the IG subsidiary amounted to $2,395,-316. New York *Times,* November 16, 1945.

45. *U.S.* v. *ICI,* Complaint and Answers, pars. 45-46.

46. He said: "The above deals with the financial aspect, but the second and, to my mind, even more important point than obtaining 5% return is the fact that by the introduction of this money we secure a closer and more binding community of interests than is practicable by any other form of cooperation. In our negotiations for trading understandings we have found the German people very reasonable, and we have succeeded in securing agreement to their total abstention for a period of five years from competition with us in any of the British markets, and I feel sure that we shall get agreement—provided we join financially with them—to making that period ten years. They have also expressed their willingness to leave the African Company's territory alone and to work jointly with us in those markets in which we are both interested. Further, agreement has been reached that they will refrain from doing anything likely to prejudice the interests of the various companies in which we are interested in the Balkan States. All these undertakings will, I am sure, substantially strengthen our position in the various export markets and will enable us to make our business there far more remunerative than would be possible in competition." Nye, Pt. XII, pp. 2867-68.

formal agreement providing for exchange of licenses under all commercial explosives patents and secret processes, present and future.[47] Under this arrangement, du Pont was to get exclusive rights for the United States and most of Central America, the Germans to get similar privileges for various continental European countries, and both parties to exchange nonexclusive rights in South America.[48]

Third, Nobel and DAG made a similar cross-licensing agreement.[49] Under this deal, which the parties faithfully executed before the war, Nobel obtained exclusive rights in British Empire markets and DAG in certain continental European markets. Other markets were to be exploited jointly, except in certain cases—Spain, France, Belgium, and Italy—where they were closed to both by prior commitments to other companies. By giving Nobel the right to sublicense du Pont under DAG's Canadian and Newfoundland patents, the agreement implemented the du Pont–Nobel joint enterprise in this region, CIL.

Fourth, du Pont and Nobel signed a new patents and processes agreement.[50] This in effect amended the explosives agreement of 1920 so as to accommodate it to their new commitments to DAG. The new agreement removed from Nobel's exclusive territory those European markets which the separate arrangements between du Pont

47. This agreement was reduced to writing but was never signed. It appears as an exhibit in the Nye Hearings, labelled "Unsigned—in effect as gentleman's agreement." *Ibid.*, Pt. V, pp. 1367-72. Du Pont has recently denied that the agreement was carried into effect. *U.S.* v. *ICI;* du Pont Answer, par. 48. Lammot du Pont testified in 1934, however, that du Pont had notified the Germans that du Pont would be bound by it.

"This agreement . . . was informally agreed to but was not executed. It, therefore, is not in effect, I believe, legally, but we have notified the Germans, I think informally, that we were satisfied to be bound by it, that is, we would agree to the agreement verbally, informally, but we have not executed it.

"Senator Clark. The point I am making is that you . . . are actually proceeding under that agreement at the present time, are you not?

"Mr. Lammot du Pont. Yes, sir." Nye, Pt. V, pp. 1203-04; see also Pt. XII, p. 2790, and Bone, Pt. V, p. 2264.

48. At about the same time DAG agreed to reduce its sales to Mexico and to stop them altogether after May 1930, which it did. The du Pont Answer, par. 49, denies any connection between this Mexican agreement and the "gentleman's agreement" with DAG, but offers no other explanation for this act of self-abnegation by DAG in withdrawing from a lucrative market which it had just agreed to quit, in a contract which du Pont alleges was never carried into effect.

49. ICI admits that both parties to this arrangement carried it out but denies that they signed a formal contract. *U.S.* v. *ICI,* ICI Answer, par. 50.

50. *Ibid.*, par. 51. The government complaint alleges that the purpose of this 1926 agreement was to adjust the relations of the parties in the light of their concurrent arrangements with DAG and to implement a tripartite understanding to eliminate competition in the sale of explosives. Du Pont and ICI deny any such purpose or understanding, but offer no other explanation of the pattern into which the actions fit. *Ibid.*, Answers, par. 51.

and DAG and between Nobel and DAG allotted to the German company.

Fifth, for the old du Pont–Nobel South American Pooling Agreement, du Pont, Nobel, and DAG substituted a tripartite cooperative arrangement for exploiting South American markets, exclusive of Chile and Bolivia. They formed Explosives Industries, Ltd. (EIL), du Pont and ICI each taking 37.5 per cent of its issued stock and DAG 25 per cent. They also agreed that in EIL territory they would either sell through the joint agency or at prices approved by it.[51] In either case, each bound itself not to sell more proportionately than its share in EIL. If DAG sales fell below its 25 per cent quota, EIL was to give it cash compensation.[52] Finally, through their subsidiary, CSAE, du Pont and ICI guaranteed DAG 25 per cent of the combined CSAE and DAG explosives business in Chile and Bolivia.[53]

Explosives Cartel a Model for the "Grand Alliance"

These actions shaped the broad outlines of the world explosives cartel. By allotting exclusive market territories, by establishing quotas, fixed price schedules, or joint enterprises, the three big producers, American, British, and German, effectively bridled competition in commercial explosives throughout the world.

But the arrangements did more than this. Their significance reached beyond their immediate objective. They bound together the world's three greatest chemical companies, du Pont, ICI, and IG, in an enduring alliance. This alliance underwent little change until the outbreak of World War II. Du Pont sold its stock in EIL to ICI and DAG in 1938, and in 1939 the British Alien Property Custodian took over DAG's shares, thus making EIL a 100 per cent ICI subsidiary. But competition did not result. Du Pont and ICI thenceforth sold commercial explosives in South America through their joint subsidiaries, the Duperial companies, which divided their purchases 50-50 between du Pont and EIL (ICI).

Although on the outbreak of war du Pont and ICI suspended

51. *Ibid.*, pars. 54-55. Du Pont states that the quotas did not apply to blasting powder and that it did not clear its prices with EIL. *Ibid.*, du Pont Answer, pars. 54-55.
52. "Senator Clark. Which in effect is a contribution, 75 percent of it, from du Pont and I.C.I.
"Mr. Lammot du Pont. Correct." Nye, Pt. V, p. 1218; see p. 1217.
53. Du Pont asserts that this 25 per cent guarantee applied only to sales of blasting explosives and detonators. *U.S. v. ICI*, du Pont Answer, par. 59.

CSAE's guarantee to DAG of a 25 per cent share in the Chilean and Bolivian markets, they instructed CSAE to cooperate with DAG's local agents so as to "assuage . . . any feeling on the part of DAG that you might be taking advantage of their present position of being unable to supply." [54] Thus even the outbreak of war did not entirely disrupt the continuing community of business interests.

While the du Pont–ICI–IG (DAG) relationships provide the basic framework of the world explosives cartel, they do not reveal all its details. ICI has many contracts with, and frequently a financial interest in, local companies operating in territories not reserved to du Pont or DAG. It inherited from Nobel numerous agreements with French, Spanish, and Belgian companies each of which reserved to the contracting parties their respective domestic and empire markets as exclusive territory. Nobel obtained from DAG as part of their 1926 understanding a commitment that it would not sell in these markets.

Nobel had agreed to pay to the Spanish company half its profits on sales to Mozambique and Angola; similarly, it had agreed to pay an indemnity to the Belgian company for confining its sales to Belgium and its colonies.[55] To exploit its own exclusive territory of South Africa, Nobel joined with the diamond trust, De Beers Consolidated Mines, Ltd., to form a subsidiary, African Explosives & Industries, Ltd.[56] This jointly owned company has since become one of the world's largest commercial explosives firms, supplying the enormous demands of the South African and Rhodesian mining industries.

Nonaffiliated American Companies Cooperate in World Markets

In America, du Pont's two major domestic competitors in explosives, the Hercules and Atlas Powder Companies, have at times joined with it in regulating international markets. Atlas joined Nobel and du Pont in CSAE, for exploitation of the Chilean market.[57] In 1926 Atlas sold to CIL (then CXL), the joint subsidiary of du Pont

---

54. *Ibid.*, par. 168. The du Pont and the ICI Answers admit they instructed CSAE as quoted but denied that CSAE followed their recommendation.

55. *U.S.* v. *ICI*, pars. 176-78; Nye, Pt. XII, p. 2860. ICI's various commitments in Europe explain the prohibition in 1933 of du Pont's constructing any factory for military explosives on the continent or selling any military explosives in Spain, Portugal, or Czechoslovakia without ICI's consent. *U.S.* v. *ICI*, ICI Answer, par. 160.

56. ICI, *Proceedings* at the First Annual General Meeting, May 31, 1928, p. 17.

57. See p. 439. In 1942 du Pont acquired Atlas' interest in CSAE. *U.S.* v. *ICI*, par. 169. On Atlas' deals with CIL, see *Moody's* (Industrials), 1929, p. 75.

and Nobel, two Canadian explosives companies which it had acquired during World War I. In exchange it received about 9 per cent of CIL's stock. In 1928 ICI and du Pont bought out Atlas' stockholdings in CIL, and Atlas has since kept out of the Canadian explosives market.

Again, according to evidence presented at the Nye Hearings, Atlas and Hercules assured du Pont that they would not disturb the cartel's control in the Colombian market:

> *Explosives Industries, Ltd.*—Atlas and Hercules activities.—The activities of these two companies, particularly in Colombia, were discussed, and Mr. Brown [of du Pont] stated that in conversations he had had with their representatives he had been informed that neither company intended to institute more aggressive measures, and that he felt they would be content with a share of the market not in excess of their present proportions.[58]

In 1925 du Pont and Hercules jointly purchased the property of a Mexican explosives manufacturer, and combined their Mexican business in a new company, Cia. Mexicana de Explosivos (CME). In the same year they induced DAG to withdraw from sales in Mexico.[59] Since these arrangements, CME has supplied virtually the whole of the Mexican explosives market.

European Outsiders Are Bought Off

From time to time DAG also has brought into line independent explosives producers whose competition has threatened the cartel. In 1925 DAG obtained from two small German manufacturers agree-

---

58. Nye, Pt. V, p. 1374.
59. See p. 443, n. 48. The agreement with DAG, like other cartel agreements, was the outcome of a balancing of power and a weighing of the respective abilities of the participants to wage a war. Originally DAG requested a quota in Mexico: "Mr. Irenee du Pont called attention to the fact that Mexico is . . . at the back door of Hercules and du Pont and that these companies could undoubtedly meet German prices while the plant to be built in Mexico could do even better. . . . The attention of the Germans was called to the fact that this business could in all probability be secured by Hercules and du Pont at a higher price than offered by the Germans and that the American group was willing to go to any price in order to retain this business. . . . The Hercules representatives called attention to the fact that their principal export market so far had been in Mexico; that there had been serious inroads in their business in that country and that if they could not recover their position it might be necessary for them to become aggressive in other export markets. It was pointed out that their plant at Hercules, California, is nearer to the markets of the West Coast of South America than any other plant . . . also that their plant at Hercules is operating at only 40 percent of capacity." Edwards, *op. cit.,* pp. 10-11. This was a clear threat to DAG's Chilean business.

ments (in return for an annual indemnity payment) to limit their exports of explosives; and from a Finnish company, an undertaking to forego exports entirely.

In 1927 DAG disposed of a more serious threat to the cartel—an ambitious export program by the Westfälische-Anhaltische Spreng-stoff A. G. (Coswig), a Stinnes enterprise, which until then had confined its sales largely to associated coal mines.[60] In behalf of the cartel, DAG obtained Coswig's agreement to restrict its exports to certain continental European countries, Chile, Bolivia, and the Dutch East Indies, to limit sales in the last three markets to a specified amount, and to observe DAG's prices. To compensate Coswig for limiting its operations, DAG agreed to pay it £5,000 a year for ten years. Since the other major cartel members, du Pont and ICI, were co-beneficiaries of this arrangement, they assumed part of DAG's indemnity obligation.[61] The parties renewed this agreement in 1936,[62] and du Pont, ICI, and DAG continued to make similar agreements, minus the indemnity feature, with other explosives firms as occasion demanded.[63]

Moreover, cartel members have in recent years extended their control to the closely related ammunition field. In 1933 du Pont acquired a majority of the stock of Remington Arms Company, Inc., one of the largest American manufacturers, and then brought Remington's business into line with its ICI partnership by means of a Remington-ICI patents and processes agreement signed in 1935. In the same year, Remington made an agreement with a du Pont–ICI Argentine ammunition subsidiary, giving the latter exclusive rights in, and confining its sales to, the Argentine market.[64] ICI and Remington in

60. DAG and Coswig had an agreement on prices, but it covered only the domestic market. Nye, Pt. XII, pp. 2864, 2866.

61. The parties estimated that half the £5,000 was payable on account of Coswig's cooperation in joint South American territory. Du Pont and ICI agreed to contribute to this £2,500 in proportion to their shares in EIL. This came to £937 10s. each per year. U.S. v. ICI, par. 61.

62. When du Pont withdrew from EIL in 1938, it turned over to ICI and DAG £3,900 to liquidate its obligations in the Coswig deal.

63. Agreements limiting exports and fixing prices were made with the (Norwegian) Norsk Spraengstofindustrie A/S in 1929, with the (Swedish) Bofors Nobelkrut A.B. in 1930, and with two Belgian companies in 1939. On the Bofors agreement, see Nye, Pt. XII, pp. 2802-03 and 2880. Bofors is a subsidiary of the famous German munitions firm of Friedrich Krupp. Scientific and Technical Mobilization, Hearings before a Subcommittee of the Committee on Military Affairs, U.S. Senate, 78th Cong., 2d sess., on S.Res. 107, Pt. XVI, p. 2080. (Hereinafter: Kilgore, Pt. —.)

64. As part of this deal, Remington got a share of the Argentine company's profits. U.S. v. ICI, par. 183. The defendants say that because of Argentine Government restrictions they never carried out this contract.

1936 jointly bought out their most important Brazilian competitor.[65]
The dominant members of the explosives cartel have also strengthened their control over the ammunition industry by acquiring patent
rights in tetracene, a superior sensitizer used in the priming composition of ammunition.[66]

THE "GRAND ALLIANCE": DU PONT AND ICI

Like du Pont, Nobel branched out rapidly into other chemical
fields after World War I. The substitution of "Industries" for "Explosives" in the corporate titles of both Nobel and the du Pont–Nobel
Canadian affiliate reflects the broadened scope of activities. By a
series of steps du Pont and Nobel (after 1926, ICI) extended their
collaboration to cover virtually all chemical products manufactured
by both. This process of commercial integration culminated in the
comprehensive du Pont–ICI Patents and Processes Agreement of
1929.

As early as 1916, du Pont and Nobel officials had discussed cooperating in dyestuffs, artificial leather, and celluloid.[67] Their 1920 and
1926 explosives agreements (which provided for exchange of patents and secret processes and for division of markets) also provided
for bringing new products under similar arrangements by mutual consent. Indeed, Nobel's chairman indicated that his understanding of
the 1920 agreement was that it was not confined to explosives, or
even to patents and secret processes, but embraced all products in the
sale of which the two companies, save for the agreement, would have
been competitors.

> Sir Harry [McGowan] said . . . that they did not feel that the Agreement
> was complete in itself but that it was "a camouflage" to cover all relationships
> between the two companies and that Mr. P. S. du Pont had assured him
> recently that the Agreement represented the spirit of the understanding be-
> tween the two companies, applicable to all questions.[68]

65. *Ibid.*, pars. 185-87. Remington then turned over its Brazilian business to this
company, receiving $125,000 from ICI in compensation, and the partners agreed to have
the joint company take over the entire Brazilian ammunition business as soon as it was
capable of handling it.
66. A DAG subsidiary purchased all patent rights in this German invention and
through patent exchange agreements distributed them to "friendly" ammunition manufacturers in various countries, subject to marketing restrictions. See Bone, Pt. I, pp.
521-626.
67. Nye, Pt. XXXIX, pp. 13426-28.
68. *U.S.* v. *ICI*, du Pont Answer, par. 34. Sir Harry made this statement in 1923.

Although du Pont, in writing, promptly rejected this interpretation of the compact, it has since admitted that, in practice, "in a few instances du Pont and ICI, without formally bringing new products within the terms of the Agreements, cooperated [on them] as if they had been included. . . ." [69] A du Pont vice-president reported in 1924 that

> . . . we have proceeded with respect to *many* of these [new products] much as we would have done had they been included in the agreement on explosives. . . . This has been based on *general policy,* and we believe the results have been satisfactory and of benefit to both parties.[70]

During the twenties du Pont formed several subsidiaries in foreign countries to manufacture its new Duco lacquers. For the British Empire market it chose Nobel as its partner and they organized a joint subsidiary, Nobel Chemical Finishes, Ltd. (NCF).[71] To NCF, Nobel transferred its existing business in cellulose finishes and du Pont its

69. *Ibid.,* par. 67. The ICI Answer admits this was done "as a matter of policy." Some of the "new products" on which the parties cooperated were not patented products but were made by secret processes. Whether a producer's proprietary right in an unpatented secret process carries with it a legal power to impose restrictions on its use by a licensee comparable to those which a patent licensor may impose is uncertain. In any case, the antitrust laws recognize no distinction between agreements concerning the marketing of products made by secret processes and those on products which anyone is free to produce.

70. Nye, Pt. XII, p. 2861. Italics supplied. In rejecting Sir Harry's interpretation of the 1920 agreement, Irenee du Pont said in 1924: "The Agreement did not in fact and never was intended to cover products in respect of which there did not exist any such patented or secret process; and further that the du Pont Company had not at any time and could not now admit any interpretation which carried or even implied any restraint on their unfettered rights to sell any non-patented or non-secret product in any part of the world." See minutes of conference of April 24, 1924, *U.S. v. ICI,* du Pont Answer, par. 34.

In the light of the American antitrust laws, obviously du Pont "could not . . . admit" Sir Harry's interpretation without compromising itself under the law of the land. The issue of whether or not the agreement between du Pont and Nobel was in fact broader than its language, as contended by Sir Harry, only the courts can settle.

But regardless of the outcome of this test, the arrangements have apparently eliminated competition between du Pont and ICI. Du Pont may be legally free under its various contracts with ICI to sell or refrain from selling products not made by patented or secret processes wherever it chooses. But "the business necessities of the moment . . . the best interests of the respective parties" have in fact led them generally not to compete. To forego competition in the sale of unpatented products is doubtless as sound a business principle as to forego competition in the sale of patented processes. Moreover, an agreement not to compete in the sale of patented products both facilitates and makes more attractive the practice of not competing in the sale of unpatented products.

71. *U.S. v. ICI,* par. 68. Du Pont states in its Answer that it decided to manufacture finishes in Great Britain because of a prohibitive British tariff. However, the way in which it carried out its decision—by merging with Nobel all of its British Empire business in finishes and offering control of the joint enterprise to Nobel (Nobel owned 51 per cent and du Pont 49 per cent of NCF)—suggests a broader understanding between the two. Whatever may have been its moving purpose, the arrangement had the effect of stopping all competition between du Pont and Nobel in the finishes field.

exclusive rights to Duco for the British Empire, outside of Canada. Du Pont agreed not to sell Duco within the Empire. NCF undertook not to export it.[72] In 1927 du Pont stopped selling artificial leather cloth (Fabrikoid) and related products in Great Britain, apparently in line with its general policy of avoiding competition with ICI. In the same year, du Pont and ICI formed a joint subsidiary to manufacture these products for the Australian market.[73]

Du Pont and Nobel also broadened their collaboration in Canada. On January 1, 1926, they signed a patents and processes agreement with CIL, exchanging exclusive licenses for the manufacture of certain chemicals other than explosives. The agreement reserved the Canadian market to CIL and the rest of the world to du Pont and Nobel. Other chemicals could be brought under the agreement by mutual consent. At the same time, du Pont and Nobel agreed to exploit new products in Canada through CIL.

Chemical Affinity—the 1929 Formula

When Nobel became part of ICI, du Pont and ICI officials undertook to define the future relations between the two companies. The result of their deliberations was the basic 1929 treaty which formally bound them in virtual partnership. The contractual vehicle of this relationship was the Patents and Processes Agreement,[74] covering sub-

---

72. Du Pont and Nobel modified these export limitations in 1927 to permit du Pont and NCF to make limited sales in each other's exclusive territory under a profit-sharing arrangement. The government complaint (par. 69) attributes this relaxation to NCF's inability to supply all Empire requirements.

73. *U.S.* v. *ICI*, par. 70. Du Pont and ICI assert that they cooperated in this fashion because the market was not large enough to accommodate more than one factory. This looks much like concerted planning: du Pont did not erect *one* plant, independently, because it knew the market was not large enough (at existing prices) for *two*. Under the circumstances, resort to the device of a jointly owned subsidiary was probably sound business policy. If, at the same time, some assurance of adequate protection for consumer interests could be found, the procedure adopted might even be justified on general welfare grounds.

74. Appended to *ibid.*, Complaint, as Exhibit 1. Before signing this Agreement on July 1, 1929, du Pont and ICI prepared a general statement of principles, known as the "London draft." This provided that each company would have its own exclusive license territories—which the other would respect—and would make every effort to avoid "conflicting developments" in joint territory. This was a clear and simple statement of intention to exploit world chemical markets in concert. Du Pont and ICI have since stated that they never formally ratified this compact. They assert that their relationship involves nothing more than an interchange of patent licenses and secret processes. But the settled course of dealings between the parties before 1929, the language of the London draft, and the actual consequences of the 1929 Agreement, all indicate that du Pont and ICI decided to eliminate *de facto* (whatever the arrangement might signify *de jure*) any substantial trade competition between themselves.

stantially all the chemical products both companies then produced. These included: nonmilitary explosives,[75] cellulose derivatives (plastics, film, and lacquers), paints and varnishes, pigments and colors, acids, fertilizers, synthetic ammonia, synthetic products of the hydrogenation of coal and oil, dyestuffs and other organic chemicals, alcohols, insecticides, fungicides, and disinfectants. The major exceptions were rayon and cellophane (both produced by du Pont, but not by ICI), military explosives (here the two had separate arrangements already described), and alkalies (produced by ICI but not by du Pont). Those products not covered by the Agreement, and manufactured by only one of the two partners, were generally subject to separate contractual arrangements with other parties.

In this broad sector of the chemical industries, the 1929 Agreement became the lodestone for du Pont's and ICI's "foreign relations." The companies agreed to exchange technical information and exclusive licenses to make, use, and sell under all their patents and secret inventions, present and future. Du Pont received exclusive rights for North America except Canada, and ICI for the Empire with the same exception. They agreed to exchange nonexclusive licenses for the remainder of the world, again excluding Canada. Each undertook to license no other companies in nonexclusive territories without first informing the other. In a contract so broad, no precise formula for determining royalties was practicable, and the royalty provisions were in very general terms:

Licenses granted as aforesaid shall be subject to adequate and justifiable compensation to be agreed upon by separate negotiations, but it is understood that such compensation will be determined under *broad principles* giving recognition to the mutual benefits secured *or to be secured hereunder,* without requiring detailed accounting or an involved system of compensation.[76]

75. The 1929 contract left the previous special agreements on this line of products in full force.
76. *U.S.* v. *ICI,* Complaint, Ex. 1, par. 2 (g). Italics supplied. Such broad criteria, designed to meet unforeseen contingencies and assure lasting benefits from the partnership in all its reaches, precluded a strictly businesslike, arms-length bargaining over specific royalties. Indeed, the parties' own language in this paragraph shows plainly that they shied away from the problem of assessing the relative value of their respective detailed contributions to the common fund of technology. This suggests that what each was seeking in this deal was not merely, or even primarily, a "good bargain" for release of its own technical developments and for access to those of the other, but also a means of avoiding competition.
The government alleges that such royalty payments as were made represented a further attempt to camouflage an illegal conspiracy to monopolize, under the guise of a

Some exceptions to this general outline of the arrangement were specifically authorized. Either company might continue an established trade in the exclusive territory of the other until the latter developed productive capacity adequate to meet the demand in that territory. Du Pont might continue to export dyestuffs to India pending later agreement. Application of the general provisions to the entire dye-stuffs field was subject to negotiations by both parties with IG, which dominated the dyestuffs markets of the world.[77] Finally, all the licenses were subject to existing relationships and commitments of du Pont and ICI to other parties. On expiration of any of these external contracts, each party agreed to try to make new contracts in conformity with this basic 1929 Agreement.

How the Alliance Was Implemented

Such, in broad outline, was du Pont's and ICI's plan for cooperative exploitation of world chemical markets. Having laid down the general framework within which they would cooperate, they implemented it from time to time by specific measures. In 1931, du Pont transferred to ICI its East Indian dyestuffs business, and ICI sold du Pont all the stock of its American sales agency, the Dyestuffs Corporation of America.[78] In 1935 du Pont sold to ICI its shares in their jointly owned British subsidiary, NCF, and also in their joint Australian subsidiary, Leathercraft Proprietary, Ltd.[79] Thus each company withdrew from the other's exclusive domain.

---

mere exchange of licenses, and were actually compensations to each party for its losses of export business as a consequence of having to withdraw from the other's exclusive territory. Du Pont and ICI assert that the payments were the result of an honest, arms-length consideration of the advantages accruing to each company under its licenses. Obviously one advantage was the elimination of competition between the two companies. *Ibid.*, Complaint and Answers, pars. 87, 104.

77. Each party agreed that in entering an agreement with IG it would "use its best efforts to extend same to include the other party hereto." *Ibid.*, Part III of Exhibit 1.

As another exception to the general scheme, Germany, Italy, and France became du Pont's exclusive territory for the manufacture and sale of paints, varnishes, lacquer, and coated textile products. In these countries du Pont had already arranged with local interests to exploit its developments in these fields, particularly Duco and Fabrikoid.

78. See Bone, Pt. V, pp. 2283-85. Du Pont states that it continued to export dyestuffs to India, through ICI. *U.S. v. ICI*, du Pont Answer, par. 101. Even so, with ICI serving as du Pont's sales agent, no intercompany competition in India was possible.

79. *U.S. v. ICI*, pars. 102, 103. ICI maintains that the NCF deal was "occasioned by difficulties which arose because of ICI's other activities, in defining the actual products which were to be treated as falling within the Agreement made by ICI and Du Pont on the organization of NCF, and consequent differences on matters of policy which arose between ICI and Du Pont in the operation of NCF." *Ibid.*, ICI Answer, par. 102. In

In 1934 du Pont and ICI modified their Patents and Processes Agreement to permit each company to sell within the other's exclusive territories products embodying solely its own inventions. In the antitrust case, the government contended that this alteration was purely formal, that du Pont and ICI had made it in the hope that it would validate their Agreement under the American antitrust laws, and that they had no more intention of entering each other's exclusive market territories after 1934 than before. The following incidents lend support to this view.

When du Pont and Röhm & Haas were negotiating their 1936 cross-licensing agreement covering acrylic acid derivatives, Röhm & Haas was reluctant to sign the contract because ICI, which had important patents in this field, retained the right under the 1934 amendment to sell in the American market. According to the president of Röhm & Haas, du Pont officials assured him repeatedly that the 1934 amendment had no practical importance, and that "there is not the slightest possibility of the ICI's coming into the American market . . ." [80] As Mr. Haas reported:

> For certain legal reasons, which I do not understand . . . I.C.I. reserves to itself the right to sell in the United States in emergency cases, but Mr. Wardenburg [of du Pont] assured me that although this has been in force for many years, such an emergency has never arisen.[81]

A similar situation arose under cartel agreements among du Pont, National Lead, and IG, governing throughout the world the exploitation of the pigment titanium. When IG complained of du Pont's unwillingness to give it more than a nonexclusive license for its allotted market territory, National Lead assured IG that, for all practical purposes, it might consider the license exclusive:

---

short, the problem of defining the activities of the joint ICI–du Pont company within ICI's recognized market led du Pont to withdraw from that market entirely, even in this special field where du Pont had made especially important technical contributions. This action demonstrates how complete was the collaboration and division of markets which resulted from the 1929 Agreement.

80. Mr. Haas continued this report as follows: "but du Ponts are afraid to write a letter to this effect because in the case of an investigation of their firm by politicians, the politicians might make capital of such a statement, i.e., they might attempt to point out that the world was divided up between I.C.I. and du Ponts." Bone, Pt. II, p. 824.

81. *Ibid.*, p. 823. To quiet Mr. Haas' fears, Mr. Wardenburg agreed to, and did, write a letter stating that du Pont happened to know that ICI's developments had been of such a nature as to preclude any possibility of its attempting to enter the American market. *Ibid.*, pp. 688-90, 822-25.

In regard to the phrase "nonexclusive license" to which you call our attention . . . we have to refer to the United States antitrust laws which absolutely forbid the granting of exclusive licenses between two manufacturers in the United States as such a practice would tend to create a monopoly. Therefore, the use of this phrase "nonexclusive license" is simply to comply with the United States laws and in practice the licenses under each other's patents will undoubtedly prove to be, to all intents and purposes, exclusive.[82]

Du Pont and ICI deny the government's allegations concerning the purpose and import of the 1934 amendment, and du Pont denies that it ever gave Röhm & Haas any such assurance.[83] In any event, since only one of the parties had the patent rights of both (as well as the rights granted by other companies in similar, dovetailing cartel agreements) in its assigned territory, and since the two companies cooperated closely in exchanging technical information and licenses and in joint exploitation of common territories, the 1934 amendment could scarcely have had much practical effect. There is no evidence that either du Pont or ICI has actually taken advantage of the privilege it conferred and offered its products in competition with its partner's in that partner's exclusive territory.

The Alliance Is Renewed

When the 1929 Patents and Processes Agreement (as amended in 1934) expired in 1939, du Pont and ICI replaced it with a similar contract. The major change was the inclusion of new products, many of which were already being treated as though they were included—notably certain chlorine products, antiknock compounds, synthetic resins and plastics, pharmaceuticals, Neoprene (du Pont's synthetic rubber), and nylon.

Both du Pont and ICI have pointed out that even with these inclusions the 1939 Agreement covered only 50 to 60 per cent of their production.[84] Among its major products not covered, du Pont lists military explosives, nylon, cellulose acetate plastics, rayon, cellophane, and photographic film. However, both military explosives and nylon

---

82. Kilgore, Pt. VII, p. 966. These arrangements failed in their purpose, a United States district court having decided that the agreements were in violation of the antitrust laws. *U.S.* v. *National Lead Company, et al.,* in U.S. District Court for the Southern District of New York, Civil Action No. 26-258, Opinion filed July 5, 1945. (Hereinafter referred to as *U.S.* v. *National Lead.*)
83. *U.S.* v. *ICI,* Complaint and Answers, par. 106.
84. *Ibid.,* du Pont Answer, par. 110; ICI Answer, par. 194.

came within the compass of the du Pont–ICI partnership, explosives under special agreements previously described, nylon under an agreement of March 1939 in which du Pont gave ICI exclusive rights for the British Empire and nonexclusive rights in certain other countries.[85] The rest are products which ICI does not make and most are subject to agreements between du Pont and other foreign companies. Similarly, ICI lists among its major products not covered by the agreement alkalies, lime and building materials, nonferrous metals, and fuels and other products made by hydrogenation of coal or oil.[86] But du Pont manufactures none of these products, except zinc, which it produces solely for its own consumption.

Though these excepted fields are important, their exclusion from the alliance in no way weakens it. For wherever the business interests of du Pont and ICI overlap, the alliance assures that neither need fear competition from the other, that they will work together as partners do. Thus their alliance has strengthened the position of both parties in bargaining with outsiders, be they consumers, trade customers, or (and perhaps especially) potential competitors.

Business Implications of the Alliance

In conducting their business ICI and du Pont not only have scrupulously observed their division of fields, but they have shown a solicitude for each other's interests more characteristic of partners than competitors. When ICI received an order from an American firm in 1934, it first inquired whether du Pont would approve such action even though it was anxious to make the sale. Thereupon du Pont's London representative cabled his home office:

Advise Hercules Powder Co., Rotterdam, Holland, inquiring prices delivery 50 tons diphenylamine for shipment to New York, N.Y. I.C.I. London naturally anxious consummate business suspecting inquiry placed because of your inability supply. However, do not wish to disturb your market and before offering request you to advise if any reason you prefer they do not quote and secondly at which price per ton c.i.f. New York, N.Y., you consider I.C.I. London justified quoting. Cable immediately.[87]

85. This agreement is listed in Schedule A of the 1939 Patents and Processes Agreement. Moreover, the agreement itself explicitly includes nylon. *Ibid.*, Complaint, Ex. 2, Art. III (T).
86. Hydrogenation was included in the 1929 Agreement, but it was subsequently removed to permit ICI to come to terms with the major powers in this field, IG, Standard Oil, and Royal Dutch Shell.
87. Nye, Pt. V, p. 1157.

When the United States Government undertook a public works project in 1932 for deepening the channel of the Detroit River, du Pont obtained the contract for supplying the explosives. The contract specified that only American labor and materials should be used. Since some of the explosives were used in the Canadian portion of the river, du Pont felt obligated, despite this provision, to remit part of its profits to CIL, the du Pont–ICI joint Canadian subsidiary.

Because of the specific provisions of the Patents and Processes Agreements, and because of joint use of a common technological fund, it became necessary for du Pont and ICI to consult before concluding agreements with other companies, even in fields only remotely related to those covered by their Agreement. In negotiating with third parties, their problem was to frame agreements so that they would not conflict with their grand alliance. As du Pont explained, when ICI sought an agreement with the Anglo-Persian Oil Company:

> In the first place, I.C.I. has no right to make an agreement with any third party anywhere in the world (British Empire included) which would involve disclosure to such third party of any patents or secret information obtained from us. If they should form a Subsidiary Company which they control, they would have such rights in the British Empire, but even then, they would have to take precautions satisfactory to us against disclosure to any minority interests of such patents and secret processes. In the second place, I.C.I. have no right to make any exclusive agreement with a third party in nonexclusive territory, as we have nonexclusive rights to I.C.I. patents and information in North America, exclusive of Canada and Newfoundland. . . .
>
> From the above it is evident that I.C.I. are not free to proceed with the Anglo-Persian Company without our consent . . .[88]

In effect, the two companies have acted as one in "foreign policy" matters. To deal with one was to deal, directly or indirectly, with the other.

Du Pont and ICI have abandoned all pretense of business rivalry in numerous major foreign markets, including Canada, Argentina, and Brazil. There they do business as a single, unified concern through jointly owned local companies. By this procedure not only have they eliminated competition between themselves, but they have succeeded

---

88. Edwards, *op. cit.*, p. 4. At another time du Pont asserted its right to prevent ICI from exchanging know-how with Röhm & Haas of Germany on the ground that such an agreement might permit du Pont information to leak to unauthorized third parties. *Ibid.*, pp. 34-35.

in cartelizing these tributary chemical markets, thanks to their combined power and prestige.

How the Alliance Works—in Canada

In Canada, CIL is the corporate vehicle of their joint enterprise.[89] Originally limited to the explosives business, it later extended its field to other chemicals. By 1929 the three parties had agreed in principle "that Du Pont's and ICI's manufacturing operations in Canada . . . and their export trade to Canada . . . would be conducted through CIL." [90] Accordingly, they turned over to CIL their Canadian subsidiaries in the ammonia and heavy chemicals field and agreed to give it the Canadian rights under all their patents and processes without charge, in exchange for a similar grant to them by CIL for the rest of the world.[91] They also agreed that in exporting to Canada each would, as a general rule, quote CIL prices on the basis of a prearranged price formula. In buying dyestuffs for resale, they agreed

89. Du Pont and ICI together own more than 80 per cent of CIL's common stock. Probably their CIL shareholdings are approximately equal. See Report of Commissioner, Combines Investigation Act, *Canada and International Cartels*, Department of Justice, Ottawa, October 10, 1945, p. 19. Despite their controlling interest in the company, ICI denies "that they exercise any power of control . . . except on matters of major policy . . ."! *U.S.* v. *ICI*, ICI Answer, par. 12.

90. *U.S.* v. *ICI*, par. 115. The partners and their subsidiary eventually embodied this oral understanding regarding their relationships in a formal Tri-Party Agreement, signed on December 1, 1936. *Ibid.*, par. 116; *Canada and International Cartels*, p. 20.

Du Pont declares that they also agreed that "this would apply only insofar as practicable and that . . . either principal would be free in individual cases, where its interests would be better served, to adopt other procedures." *U.S.* v. *ICI*, du Pont Answer, par. 115. However, Mr. Lammot du Pont had earlier (December 11, 1933) summed up his company's view of the position of CIL as follows: "We regard CIL as the vehicle of industrial effort for ICI and du Pont in Canada. The Canadian minority stockholders are investors who wish to place their money or allow it to remain, with the ICI–du Pont combination. The theory back of this CIL operation, so far as ICI and du Pont are concerned, is expressed in the old saying 'Canada for Canadians,' meaning—the industrial operations of the partners in Canada are intended to be conducted through CIL. *CIL was not set up to do anything else and has, we believe, never been considered so.*" *Ibid.*, par. 115. Italics supplied.

91. *U.S.* v. *ICI*, pars. 73-75 and 117. The grant to CIL of exclusive Canadian rights in du Pont's and ICI's patented inventions did not mean, however, that CIL was free to exercise these rights regardless of the interests of its parents. Its development of Canadian manufacturing facilities was contingent upon, or subordinate to, the overriding interests of du Pont and ICI in exporting to Canada. The minutes of a tripartite meeting in Montreal in 1930 bring this out clearly: "It is very undesirable that CIL should provide manufacturing capacity in Canada if, from a family viewpoint, Canadian requirements can be more profitably supplied by the existing capacity owned by one of the major stockholders." *Canada and International Cartels*, p. 20.

The report by the Canadian Combines Investigation Act Commissioner notes that one of the consequences of this arrangement was that "Because of the restrictions on its operations CIL was unable to cooperate in the efforts made by the Canadian Government to expand trade with the West Indies. . . ." *Ibid.*

CIL should apportion its purchases equally between them. A Canadian official says that one effect of the agreements is that "CIL is to confine its operations to Canada and is not to engage in any export trade." [92]

CIL has expanded the range and volume of its chemical activities to become one of the largest chemical producers in the country. It is the Canadian beneficiary of such privileges and rights as its principals acquire in cartel agreements with foreign producers. These, together with the prestige of its principals, have given it a tremendous bargaining power which it has used to negotiate many domestic cartel agreements with other chemical manufacturers. In this way it has been able to cartelize the Canadian market and integrate it into the broader pattern of world cartel controls.

A number of CIL agreements have apparently delimited the various chemicals and related fields, preventing the encroachment of one group on the interests of another. In its antitrust suit, the government alleges that some time before 1936 du Pont and ICI through CIL agreed with Courtaulds, Ltd., the British rayon trust, not to produce rayon in Canada, in exchange for Courtaulds' promise not to manufacture caustic soda, sulphuric acid, and similar chemicals for its own use.[93] The government alleges a similar agreement between CIL and the Canadian International Paper Company, in which the latter agreed to refrain from manufacturing chemicals (presumably chemical raw materials used in paper manufacture) in return for CIL's commitment not to enter the paper field.[94] Again, CIL and Procter & Gamble, Ltd., the soap company's Canadian subsidiary, jointly own the Gardinol Corporation of Canada, Ltd., which manufactures special detergents for textiles. This arrangement parallels that of du Pont and Procter & Gamble in the United States.

Apparently CIL also cooperates with Shawinigan Chemicals, Ltd., the other major Canadian chemical manufacturer. This company is a

---

92. Du Pont and ICI deny any rigid limitation on CIL's exports. *U.S.* v. *ICI*, Answers, par. 122.

The Commissioner of the Canadian Combines Investigation Act also declares that "In handling products made by both major stockholders CIL is required to divide the business as far as possible on a 50/50 basis between ICI and du Pont." But he adds that "In actual practice it has not been possible to maintain equality." *Canada and International Cartels*, p. 20.

93. *U.S.* v. *ICI*, Complaint, par. 131.

94. *Ibid.*, par. 130.

subsidiary of the Shawinigan Water & Power Company, a very large producer of hydroelectric power. Shawinigan is one of the world's principal producers of calcium carbide—the economical production of which requires large quantities of cheap electricity—and its many important derivatives. Whether by agreement or otherwise, Shawinigan confines its operations largely to this field which, in general, CIL avoids. In its antitrust suit the government alleges that ICI, du Pont, and Shawinigan are parties to an understanding whereby CIL refrains from manufacturing acetylene and its derivatives in return for Shawinigan's promise to confine itself to that field.[95]

Another cartel in which CIL participates, thus helping its parents to round out the international scope and to solidify the power of the market controls established, is in titanium pigments. CIL and the National Lead Company, du Pont's American cartel partner in this field, organized a joint company to manufacture and sell titanium in Canada.[96] Finally, in 1939, CIL and the Stauffer Chemical Company, a leading American producer of carbon disulphide and IG's exclusive licensee in this field for the United States and Canada,[97] jointly formed Cornwall Products, Ltd., to manufacture this chemical in Canada. Du Pont–Stauffer cooperation in the United States parallels Stauffer-CIL cooperation in Canada. In 1928, du Pont and Stauffer formed a joint subsidiary, Old Hickory Chemical, to manufacture carbon disulphide in the United States. Thus in many directions CIL has helped its parents to weld cartel controls on the chemical industries, and to maintain or strengthen their position in these market-regulating mechanisms.

95. *Ibid.,* par. 129. For a time, one of the directors of CIL was also a director of Shawinigan's parent company. Regardless of whether such an understanding existed as the government alleges, in practice the general rule seems to have been that Shawinigan and CIL have kept their major operations in separate fields. An exception is that CIL manufactures chlorinated hydrocarbons, which are acetylene derivatives. These include Neoprene, the du Pont synthetic rubber. Both du Pont and ICI have agreements in the field of chlorinated acetylene derivatives with Dr. Alexander Wacker G.m.b.H., the major continental producer. See Schedule A of the 1939 du Pont–ICI Patents and Processes Agreement, *ibid.,* Ex. 2; and Bone, Pt. V, p. 2266. As we have seen, IG owns 50 per cent of Wacker.

ICI is a fellow member with Shawinigan in the international acetic acid cartel. *Ibid.,* p. 2235. Du Pont is also associated with Shawinigan and Union Carbide in Niacet, each having a one-third interest in this joint subsidiary. Niacet dominates the United States market for acetic acid. IG has cooperated with Niacet and other cartel members by prohibiting its American licensees, the Shell Chemical Company and Jasco, from exporting acetic acid. *Ibid.,* Pt. III, pp. 1376, 1380-82, 1405-07.

96. *U.S.* v. *ICI,* par. 132.

97. IG reserved the right, however, also to license Pennsylvania Salt for this territory. Bone, Pt. V, p. 2351.

How the Alliance Works—in South America

The du Pont–ICI South American policy is similar to its Canadian policy. To avoid conflict of interests, to strengthen their combined position in the markets, and to counteract the growth of local manufactures encouraged by economic nationalism,[98] du Pont and ICI organized Duperial Argentina in 1934 and Duperial Brazil in 1936. The partners share ownership in both companies equally. They transferred to these companies their local factories and sales agencies and gave them exclusive rights to manufacture and sell certain lines of chemical products in their respective territories.

In general they agreed to conduct all their Argentine and Brazilian business in chemicals, including their exports to these areas, exclusively through these two subsidiaries. In turn, they bound the Duperial twins to purchase from du Pont and ICI chemicals (with certain exceptions) which the twins did not themselves manufacture locally. In established lines of trade, Duperial purchases were to be so apportioned between the parents that each would retain its existing volume of export business. Of new business, the subsidiaries were required to give each of the parent companies an equal share. In all lines the parents were to fix jointly Duperial purchase prices and resale prices. The parents also defined the sphere of Duperial manufacturing and trading operations, in terms of both products and market area.[99]

Through Duperial Argentina, whose market territory includes also Uruguay and Paraguay, ICI and du Pont have not only ended competition between themselves, but brought both local and foreign competitors into many cartel arrangements designed to stabilize the markets for particular chemical products. One of Duperial's chief business rivals from the outset was a rich, powerful, and aggressive local commercial house—Bunge & Born (B. & B.). When B. & B. learned of du Pont's and ICI's plans to pool their business in Argentina, it requested a share in the enterprise. After participation in Duperial was refused it, B. & B. began drafting plans for independent manufacture of chemicals in several lines directly competitive with major interests

98. These were the reasons stated by an ICI director. *U.S.* v. *ICI,* du Pont Answer, par. 136.
99. Du Pont and ICI admit these agreements, but assert that they did not adhere to the provisions governing purchases and price determination, except "in certain cases." *Ibid.,* Answers, pars. 135-39, 152-54.

of the Duperial partners. For this expansion program, B. & B. had ample funds and the support of local sentiment for home industries.

Du Pont and ICI met this challenge by both conciliatory and war-like tactics, as the strategy of the moment dictated. To discourage B. & B. from producing sulphuric acid, Duperial cut sulphuric acid prices and at the same time made a rather flattering offer to guarantee B. & B. a substantial proportion of the tartaric acid market—in which B. & B. was already an important factor and Duperial had little interest, except for bargaining purposes.

We then proceeded to tell Bunge & Born that . . . our shareholders had decided that our existing share in the sulphuric-acid market would be protected quite irrespective of the level to which prices might decline during the ensuing period of competition. We explained that this information was being proffered in order that Bunge & Born might visualize the effect on their own prospective returns from sulphuric acid manufacture, but that, quite apart from the effect of their entry into the sulphuric acid field, it is now our definite policy to bring about a reduction in acid prices . . . to the point where that business would no longer provide a constant invitation to others to enter the same field. Having so defined our future policy on sulphuric acid, we felt that Bunge & Born might see grounds for reconsidering the proposal made . . . some months ago . . . for their surrendering any idea of making sulphuric acid and, in part compensation, accepting what we had to offer on the tartaric acid side.[100]

Similarly, to dissuade B. & B. from manufacturing carbon disulphide, Duperial offered to supply it with 25 per cent of its own output, for resale by B. & B.[101]

Duperial a Link With Other Chemical Companies

Duperial proved a convenient instrument for coordinating with the trade of its parents the Argentine sales activities of various foreign chemical companies as well as of those of local competitors. For example, Duperial sold anhydrous ammonia in Argentina not only for du Pont and ICI but also for various European exporters. This arrangement for common use of a joint sales agency effectively ruled

100. Edwards, op. cit., p. 11.
101. The record does not indicate the outcome of these negotiations. According to the Department of Justice, B. & B. obtained a market quota in the sale of tartaric acid and accepted Duperial's offer to supply it with carbon disulphide for resale. Du Pont and ICI, while not denying that Duperial made the carbon disulphide offer, deny that B. & B. accepted it. They deny any agreement on tartaric acid. U.S. v. ICI, Answers, pars. 146-47. See also Edwards, op. cit., p. 48.

out competition. Duperial contracted in 1935 to purchase the by-product anhydrous ammonia output of Cia. Primitiva de Gas, the largest local producer of manufactured gas.[102] The objective of this deal was apparent.

In 1935 Duperial organized Ducilo S. A. to erect a local rayon factory. Du Pont and ICI offered 15 per cent of the shares of Ducilo to the dominant French rayon manufacturer, Comptoir des Textiles Artificiels, in exchange for the Argentine rights to its patents and processes. Du Pont had long cooperated with Comptoir in the rayon field.[103] B. & B. again made a bid for recognition, with a project for building an independent rayon plant. To block this, du Pont and ICI offered B. & B. 15 per cent participation in Ducilo. B. & B. accepted with the understanding that it would not engage in competitive production before 1955. To make room for their new partner, Duperial and Comptoir reduced proportionately their subscriptions to Ducilo stock.

These same companies worked out a similar deal for the production of cellophane. Du Pont had originally gone into the manufacture of cellophane under license from Comptoir's subsidiary, La Cellophane. In 1936 du Pont and La Cellophane agreed to permit Ducilo to manufacture cellophane in Argentina. In this way du Pont and Comptoir integrated the Argentine rayon and cellophane markets into their cartel relationship, and extended the cartel to include a potential local competitor.

Another deal on much the same pattern helped to safeguard the du Pont–ICI interests in alkalies. During the thirties, a large Argentine paper manufacturer, La Celulosa Argentina S. A., ventured to build an electrolytic plant for supplying its caustic soda and chlorine requirements. This gesture of independence by an important customer of the principal chemical companies with vested interests in alkali manufacture—and in the Argentine import trade—did not go unheeded. Both IG and ICI promptly sought "to get the situation in hand." Eventually ICI, with a stake larger by far than that of any other alkali importer in this particular market, succeeded through Duperial in bringing La Celulosa to terms.

102. *U.S.* v. *ICI*, par. 142. Bureau of Foreign and Domestic Commerce, Trade Promotion Series, No. 195, *World Chemical Developments in 1938*, p. 113.
103. See text, p. 512.

Duperial and La Celulosa organized a new company, Electroclor S. A. Argentina, each taking 50 per cent of its stock. In accordance with previous agreements between ICI and its continental allies, according to the Department of Justice, Duperial in turn offered 22.2 per cent of its Electroclor stock (11.1 per cent of the total) to IG and 11.0 per cent (5.5 per cent of the total) to Solvay et Cie and Duperial and La Celulosa agreed thenceforth to stay out of each other's primary field of manufacture.[104] Moreover, another part of the deal prohibited Electroclor from exporting; on the other hand, du Pont and ICI, "as a matter of business policy," refrained from selling in Argentina the types of products manufactured by Electroclor.[105] Duperial Brazil has played a role similar to that of its Argentine twin in eliminating competition in Brazilian chemical markets.

This brief review of how the du Pont–ICI alliance works at home and abroad in strictly chemical fields and in "adjacent" lines of industry, in technological matters and in business affairs, makes clear the intimate relationship, analogous to partnership, which has evolved from their Patents and Processes Agreement.

Scope of the Alliance's Influence

Thus the influence of the du Pont–ICI "partnership" extended far beyond the immediate scope of activities common to both companies. (See Chart 6.) All other cartel agreements to which either party subscribed had to fit into the general pattern of their patents and processes compact and conform to its specific provisions. These auxiliary agreements, in turn, became a part of the superstructure steadily being constructed on the foundation of the general Agreement. They helped to "stabilize" all those branches of chemical manufacture in which either du Pont or ICI was engaged and to reinforce the power of the alliance.

Not only du Pont but all the other major chemical companies have come to recognize the British Empire as ICI territory. Similarly, not

---

104. War broke out before Duperial had actually transferred the stock to IG, and the British Government prohibited the transfer. However, du Pont, in view of its "moral commitment" to IG, promised to use its good offices to have the transfer consummated after the war. As evidence of its good intentions, Electroclor contracted to make IG's Argentine subsidiary, Anilinas Alemanas S. A., the sales agent for a portion of its output, in accordance with the terms of the basic ICI-IG accord. At the insistence of the United States Government, du Pont has prohibited the performance of this contract. *U.S.* v. *ICI*, par. 151.

105. *Ibid.*, Complaint and Answers, par. 150.

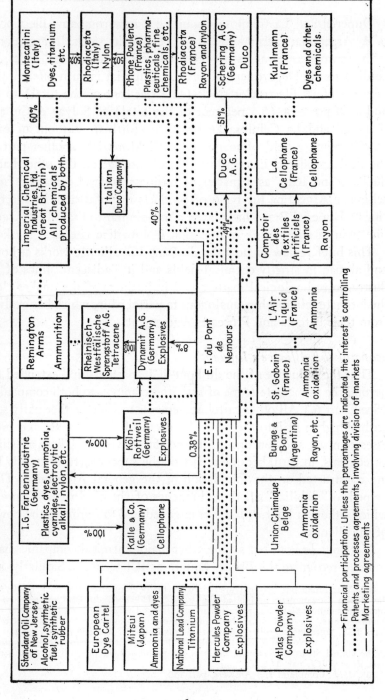

CHART 6. DU PONT'S MAJOR INTERNATIONAL CARTEL CONNECTIONS, 1934–1939

→ Financial participation. Unless the percentages are indicated, the interest is controlling
⋯⋯ Patents and processes agreements, involving division of markets
— — Marketing agreements

only ICI but other foreign companies generally recognize the primacy of du Pont in the American market, in the fields of its special interests. Du Pont and ICI agreements with other companies reinforce their own agreement to recognize each other's exclusive territory. Their mutual obligations and privileges are intertwined with similar obligations and privileges growing out of scores of collateral agreements with third parties.

All these agreements fit into a pattern. IG is no more likely to give du Pont operating rights in the British Empire, or ICI rights in the United States, than are either of these companies to license IG for the other's exclusive sphere. When du Pont says that its decisions not to export to the British Empire were based on factors other than its agreements with ICI, it points out:

> Some of du Pont's products were covered by patents or secret processes under which it was licensed by third parties and such licenses did not confer rights for certain territories, including, among others, the British Empire . . .[106]

The quasi partnership of du Pont and ICI is but part, although an extremely important part, of a system of interlocking cartel arrangements which jointly and severally help to police the world's chemical industries and to reconcile the opposing interests of major chemical companies.

106. *Ibid.*, du Pont Answer, par. 28.

Chapter 11

THE ROLE OF I. G. FARBEN

IG Strategy

I. G. Farben has played a leading role in world chemical cartels. But more than du Pont and Imperial Chemical Industries (ICI), it has chosen to play a lone hand. Possessing superior technical resources and a head start in several directions over other producers, benefiting also from greater governmental assistance, IG has been unwilling to merge its interests in a genuine, equal partnership with any other company. Instead, it has tried to use its advantages to achieve comprehensive international dominion in the chemical realm. It has granted to other companies use of its precious "know-how" and patents only in narrowly defined fields of chemical manufacture, subject to rigorous market restrictions, and then only in return for substantial benefits, frequently greater than it has given. When it has engaged in joint ventures, it has generally insisted on retaining ultimate control, either directly through the corporate setup or indirectly through specific contracts.

A shrewd bargainer, with strong nationalistic interests, IG has played the game of cartelization not merely as a way of living with its business rivals, but as a means of supervising, circumscribing, and, wherever possible, controlling their activities. It has used cartel agreements as instruments of economic aggression. By such agreements, it has frequently checked competitive production abroad and circumvented nationalistic trade restrictions and subsidies designed to promote domestic enterprise.

The breadth of its chemical interests has led IG into agreements with every major world chemical producer, covering together virtually every branch of chemical manufacturing. (See Chart 7.) These agreements, meticulously drafted, have tended to "stabilize" the chemical markets. At the same time, they have insured to IG a large measure of control and direction over the world's chemical industries.

IG's Position and Policy at the End of World War I

When World War I ended, IG still held a commanding position in two major chemical fields: high-pressure synthesis (the most important product of which was synthetic ammonia) and coal-tar derivatives. In both fields the "specifications" in the confiscated IG patents had been drawn so cleverly that even with their aid non-German producers were so seriously handicapped that they demanded tariff protection from their governments. Lacking IG's "know-how," they generally found such subsidies inadequate, particularly in dyestuffs. American, British, and French producers were unable to produce many dyestuffs at all, and only a few of the most common at competitive prices.[1]

Convinced of their disadvantage in world markets as IG's competitors, du Pont, British Dyestuffs, Brunner Mond, and the Compagnie Nationale des Matières Colorantes sought its cooperation. Yet, with one minor exception—a temporary agreement between IG and Compagnie Nationale, lasting only from 1922 to 1923, and not renewed until 1927 [2]—none of these companies obtained an agreement either in nitrogen or dyestuffs, in the decade after the world war. Confident of its ability to regain its prewar dominance, IG demanded terms which the foreign companies, however great their need, were unwilling or unable to accept.

Du Pont Fails to Reach a Permanent Agreement With IG

Du Pont pursued a double-barrelled strategy in seeking to establish itself as a leading chemicals manufacturer. On the one hand, it conducted an intensive campaign for tariff protection and subsidy, arguing that such assistance was necessary to establish strong and independent American chemical industries. On the other hand, almost immediately after the Armistice it negotiated with Badische (of IG) to bring about permanent collaboration between the two companies. Du Pont apparently sought tariff protection not only for its general advantages to the domestic industry in the home market, but more

1. The British Dyestuff Import Regulation Act of 1920 permitted imports in those cases in which domestic dyers could not otherwise obtain their requirements at reasonable prices. This exception to the general embargo permitted heavy German sales in the British market.

2. U.S. Bureau of Foreign and Domestic Commerce, Trade Information Bulletin No. 532, *German Chemical Developments in 1927,* p. 1.

CHART 7. I. G. FARBEN'S MAJOR INTERNATIONAL CARTEL CONNECTIONS, 1934–1939

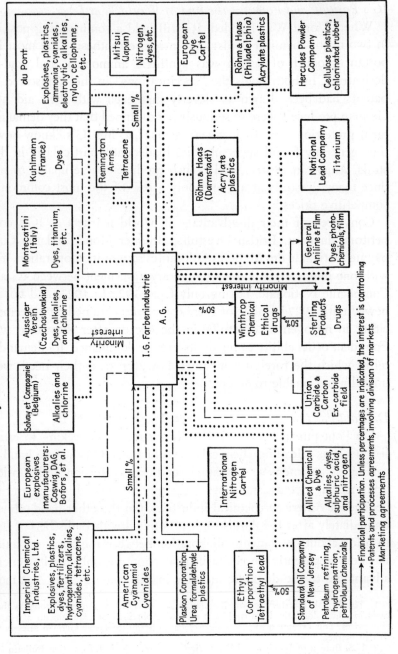

→ Financial participation. Unless percentages are indicated, the interest is controlling
••••• Patents and processes agreements, involving division of markets
----- Marketing agreements

specifically to strengthen its own hand in bargaining with IG.[3]

Du Pont and Badische reached a tentative agreement in 1919 "to form a company for the world exploitation of the Bosch-Haber ammonia process." Du Pont was to supply the capital and Badische was to obtain, in exchange for its technical experience, 25 per cent of the new company's stock.[4] The parties never carried out this plan, and relations between them deteriorated rapidly. Badische was apparently offended by du Pont's efforts to obtain a high American tariff on dyestuffs. Du Pont's foreign representative reported that Dr. Bosch, head of IG, "could not understand how we could try to make arrangements with the Badische for the ammonia process and at the same time make everything possible to exclude the German dyes from America."[5]

IG Is Truculent

Undoubtedly IG's withdrawal from the deal reflected increasing confidence in its ability to regain its former dominant position in world markets without concessions to foreign companies involving sacrifice of German control.[6] IG frequently complained to du Pont of "unfriendly acts," and used such incidents as pretexts for declin-

3. See Hearings before a Special Committee Investigating the Munitions Industry, U.S. Senate, 73d Cong., Pt. XI, pp. 2571-73. (These Hearings will hereinafter be cited as Nye, Pt. —, after the name of the committee chairman.)

Since one faction in the IG management still believed it could "bully the U. S.," du Pont's representative pointed out, "you can see the importance of everlastingly turning the regulatory screw in America both as to control of imports and future protective legislation." The writer thought that confiscation of German patents and their sale to the Chemical Foundation had had a salutary effect equal to that of the tariff. He said: ". . . this evidence of America's power has been a great factor making it possible to deal with them" [that is, with IG's management].

4. Ibid., pp. 2573-74. This joint enterprise was to have had the entire world as its market, except Germany and prewar Austria-Hungary (Badische's exclusive domain), France (where Badische had prior commitments), and the British Isles. This last exception was contingent on Badische's reaching a separate agreement with the British.

5. Ibid., Pt. XXXIX, p. 13433. Another factor may have been IG's resentment at a suspected attempt by du Pont secretly to hire some of its chemists. A du Pont interoffice communication reports Dr. Bosch's ire over this supposed attempt to entice IG's employees. "He added that he was very glad not having made any arrangement with us in regard to ammonia after the experiences he had had the last months of our way of doing business. He was furious and added that they—the Badische—would go ahead in America next year as soon as peace had been officially restored . . . and that they had lots of prominent friends there." Ibid., p. 13439.

The German Government supported Badische in this episode by arresting four German chemists who had allegedly been hired by du Pont. German newspapers carried headlines characterizing these men as "traitors," and the whole incident as an "American plot" against Germany. Ibid., pp. 13438, 13444-47; and Charles A. Welsh, The World Dyestuffs Industry [unpublished doctoral dissertation, New York University, April 1944], pp. 152-61.

6. See, for example, Nye, Pt. XXXIX, p. 13437.

ing to participate in joint enterprises unless du Pont would concede to IG ultimate control or veto power in such projects.[7] Repeatedly du Pont proposed to IG during the twenties that they organize a jointly owned company to exploit one or another chemical field—in particular, dyestuffs or nitrogen. Du Pont always insisted, however, on controlling any American subsidiaries, and conceded to IG control of any German ventures. IG consistently rebuffed du Pont, holding out for at least a 50 per cent share in any joint enterprise. Despite its eagerness to cooperate with IG, du Pont stubbornly refused to make such a concession. Consistent refusal by du Pont, unlike some other American companies, to acknowledge IG's pretensions and grant it an equal share (and hence the power to veto du Pont policies) in any American venture apparently prevented these companies from working out a broad, general agreement under which they could cooperate as partners in world markets.[8]

Similarly, British Dyestuffs encountered IG's determination to regain control over the world dyestuffs industry. In exchange for its technical information, IG demanded that the British company limit its sales to the United Kingdom and give the Germans half its profits. The British, with a governmental mandate to build a strong, independent coal-tar chemical industry, could not accept such a subservient position.[9]

Du Pont and ICI, failing to obtain satisfactory agreements with IG permitting their independent growth, turned to each other. Although seeking strength in partnership, they did not throw down the gage of battle to the German leviathan. They left the door open for collaboration. Specifically, they made their 1929 Patents and Processes Agreement, in its application to dyestuffs, subject to any later agreements between either party and IG.

7. For example, when du Pont sought to exploit its Duco development in Germany, it first approached IG. IG not only disclaimed interest but said that it had "no objection to du Pont going ahead with Duco in Germany in competition with them." *Patents,* Hearings before the Committee on Patents, 77th Cong., 2d sess., on S. 2303 and S. 2491, Pt. V, p. 2250. (Hereinafter: Bone, Pt. —.) Accordingly, du Pont formed a joint German manufacturing subsidiary (Duco A. G.) with Schering A. G. Later IG officials said that they "resented the du Pont Company entering the German market and taking up the manufacture of Duco there." Nye, Pt. XXXIX, p. 13451.

8. See Bone, Pt. V, pp. 2071-74, 2249-61; Corwin D. Edwards, *Economic and Political Aspects of International Cartels,* Monograph No. 1 of the Subcommittee on War Mobilization, Committee on Military Affairs, U.S. Senate, pursuant to S.Res. 107, 78th Cong., 2d sess. (Washington, 1944), p. 8.

9. Bone, Pt. V, pp. 2244-45; Bureau of Foreign and Domestic Commerce, Trade Information Bulletin No. 605, *German Chemical Developments in 1928,* p. 2.

IG Aggressively Re-enters American Markets

Meanwhile IG, trading mainly on its patents and know-how and resorting to financial penetration and cartel agreements with relatively weaker or more complaisant concerns, sought independently of du Pont to re-establish itself in the American chemical industries.[10] IG's first step was to regain its prewar dominance in dyestuffs, pharmaceuticals, and photographic chemicals. To achieve this, it set about reassembling the more vital parts of the prewar mechanism which had been broken into fragments.

One of the most important prewar German subsidiaries in America was the Bayer Company, a leading producer of dyestuffs and pharmaceuticals—notably, Bayer aspirin. The parent company, Bayer of Leverkusen, was one of the German "big six." The Alien Property Custodian seized Bayer (of New York) in 1917, and later sold it to Sterling Products, Inc. Sterling retained the pharmaceutical business, but turned over the dyestuffs assets (along with the skilled staff of dyemakers) to Grasselli Chemical Company, an old American firm.

Grasselli did not long retain its independence. In 1924 it offered the Germans a share in its dyestuffs business in exchange for freedom from their competition and access to their patent rights and techniques. Thereupon Bayer of Leverkusen and Grasselli jointly organized Grasselli Dyestuff Corporation, to which Grasselli transferred its dyestuffs business and both partners granted exclusive licenses under their dyestuffs patents in the United States and Canada and agreed to grant similar licenses and give technical assistance in future. Grasselli Chemical received 51 per cent of the joint subsidiary's stock, and Bayer of Leverkusen 49 per cent with an option on another one per cent.[11]

In 1925 certain other German chemical companies—which later in the year merged with Bayer to form IG—became stockholders in

10. A du Pont official, reviewing in 1926 "several incidents which might indicate growing aggressiveness on the part of the I. G. and perhaps a hostile attitude toward the du Pont Co.," noted "what seems to be the policy of the I. G. to take up manufacturing in the United States. I would not be surprised if they looked forward to the time when their interests in America are as great as in Germany." He concluded, however, that IG was not motivated by hostility to du Pont: "The I. G. is very aggressive and is particularly seeking to establish itself in the United States . . . but . . . it is 'not proven' that these different moves of the I. G. are actuated by hostility to the du Pont Company. Some things indicate this. My feeling is rather that they are seeking their own interests and feel strong enough and sure enough of themselves to go it alone." Nye, Pt. XXXIX, pp. 13450-52.
11. The contract appears in Bone, Pt. V, pp. 2140-44.

Grasselli Dyestuff through contracts with Grasselli Chemical. This transaction reduced the American share in the joint subsidiary to 35 per cent. In 1928, before its merger with du Pont, Grasselli Chemical sold to IG its remaining shares in Grasselli Dyestuff. Thus, in ten years Bayer's American dyestuffs properties had reverted completely to IG ownership.

Grasselli Dyestuff was renamed General Aniline Works, Inc., in 1929, and IG exchanged its General Aniline Works stock for shares of American IG Chemical Company, a holding company for IG's American interests. In 1939 American IG Chemical became General Aniline & Film Corporation.[12] Another IG subsidiary was General Dyestuff Corporation, which IG made its exclusive American dyestuffs selling agent, for both dyes manufactured here by its subsidiary, General Aniline, and imported dyes made by IG. General Dyestuff in 1939 and 1940 supplied 26 and 28 per cent, respectively, of the total value of dyes sold in the United States.[13]

Sterling Products, which had retained Bayer's pharmaceutical business, also soon established close intercorporate relations with IG. In trying to regain control of its former American Bayer properties, IG held important bargaining weapons. It not only possessed valuable technical information and patent rights on new developments, but still held unimpaired rights throughout most of the world to its famous trade-mark, the Bayer cross. Armed with these weapons, IG worked out a series of agreements which enabled it to recover its dominant position in American, indeed in world, pharmaceutical markets.

South American Markets Relinquished to IG

Within a year after its purchase of the Bayer Company (N.Y.) from the Alien Property Custodian, Sterling agreed to pay to the former German parent company no less than 50 per cent of its profits on all sales in Latin America in exchange for rights to IG's patents, proc-

---

12. *Ibid.*, pp. 2061-65, and accompanying exhibits. IG and its American allies tried to conceal the ownership of American IG and General Aniline & Film stocks. However, ultimate control and ownership undoubtedly rested with IG and its agents. See analysis based upon public hearings before the Securities and Exchange Commission, *ibid.*, pp. 2566-77.

13. *Ibid.*, p. 2481. See also *U.S.* v. *General Dyestuff Corporation, et al.*, in U.S. District Court for the Southern District of New York, Indictment (Criminal Action No. 11-135) filed December 19, 1941, *passim.* (Hereinafter referred to as *U.S.* v. *General Dyestuff.*)

esses, and trade-marks in the United States market. In 1920 Sterling surrendered to Bayer of Leverkusen the entire Latin American market except for aspirin, and agreed to give the German company 75 per cent of its profits on these sales.

In 1923 Bayer of Leverkusen obtained the right to half the profits of the Winthrop Chemical Company, a Sterling subsidiary producing ethical drugs, in exchange for its agreement to leave the United States and Canadian markets exclusively to Winthrop. Winthrop agreed not to export from those markets. Sterling also gave the German company a voice in management and half the profits of Sterling's British subsidiary, which had acquired the Bayer trade-marks for Britain. Three years later IG obtained half of Winthrop's stock, which, like Bayer's shares in Grasselli Dyestuff, eventually passed into the hands of General Aniline & Film. At the same time it acquired full control of the British subsidiary.

In the 1923 contract, to run for fifty years, Bayer and Sterling divided the world pharmaceuticals market into exclusive territories for each, and Sterling agreed to pay the German company half its profits in the Cuban market, part of the "Sterling area." [14] By 1937 American IG itself had a substantial investment in Sterling Products.[15]

When the British blockade cut off IG from its South American markets in 1939, Sterling agreed to have Winthrop ship pharmaceuticals to IG's South American agents without identifying labels. The agents then affixed IG labels, thus preserving IG customer good will. As late as November 1940, the president of Sterling assured IG of his continuing desire to protect IG interests: "You know that whatever we do, we are going to do for your interest, just as we always have." [16]

Another American market to which IG returned soon after World War I was the photographic field. In 1928 IG and Ansco Photoproducts, Inc., an American manufacturer of photographic equipment and supplies, formed Agfa Ansco Corporation, IG receiving 60 per cent

14. Most of these agreements are reproduced in *U.S.* v. *The Bayer Company, Inc. (New York), et al.,* and *U.S.* v. *Alba Pharmaceutical Company, Inc., et al.,* in U.S. District Court for the Southern District of New York, Civil Actions No. 15-364 and 15-363, Complaint and Consent Decree, September 5, 1941. See also Edwards, *op. cit.,* pp. 20, 49-51, and Joseph Borkin and Charles A. Welsh, *Germany's Master Plan,* Duell, Sloan & Pearce, New York, 1943, pp. 138-42.
15. This was disclosed in hearings before the Securities and Exchange Commission. American IG also held stock in du Pont and Eastman Kodak. Bone, Pt. V, p. 2574.
16. Edwards, *op. cit.,* pp. 66-67.

of its stock and Ansco 40 per cent. Under this arrangement Agfa
Ansco's activities were restricted to the American market, in which
it obtained exclusive rights to a carefully defined portion of IG's
photographic supplies, patents, and techniques. The rest of the world
was reserved to IG. Eventually Agfa Ansco became a part of General Aniline & Film.[17] In 1940 General Aniline also absorbed the
Ozalid Corporation, organized by IG interests about 1933 and receiving exclusive American rights in the field of photographic printing
chemicals.[18] According to the Department of Justice, in 1941 General
Aniline accounted for about 15 per cent of the photographic materials manufactured and sold in the United States.[19]

Technique of Piecemeal Penetration

The second method used by IG in returning to the American market was to renew and extend its cartel agreements with financially
independent American chemical manufacturers. Whether by design or
otherwise, this was a piecemeal process. IG's American cartel affiliations are legion. Few American chemical companies do not have some
form of agreement or understanding with IG for reconciling conflicting interests and for cooperating in chosen spheres of the world
chemical markets. Without exception these compacts are of a specific character, limited to the regulation of some particular chemical
field distinguishable on a basis of the raw material, the process, or
the product. While they differ widely in both importance and scope,
even one as extensive and intimate as the so-called "marriage" contract between Standard Oil of New Jersey and IG has nothing like
the range of the du Pont–ICI alliance. It is narrowly focused on the
relations between chemical and petroleum technology.

IG's cartel compacts with American firms have several other features in common besides their specialized character. Without exception they restrict American exports and reserve to IG important sectors of the world market. They provide for an exchange of technical

17. See Bone, Pt. V, p. 2352; Bureau of Foreign and Domestic Commerce, Trade Information Bulletin No. 753, *German Chemical Developments in 1930*, p. 40; *U.S.* v. *General Aniline & Film Corp., et al.*, in U.S. District Court for the Southern District of New York, Indictment (Criminal Action No. 111-136), December 19, 1941 (hereinafter referred to as *U.S.* v. *General Aniline*).
18. *U.S.* v. *Dietrich A. Schmitz, et al.*, in U.S. District Court for the Southern District of New York, Indictment (Criminal Action No. 111-137), December 19, 1941.
19. *U.S.* v. *General Aniline*, par. 20.

information and cross-licensing of patents, present and future. IG has apparently had two major objectives in making these agreements: participation in the American market without disturbing its stability or losing control of basic "know-how" and patent rights, and protecting itself from competition in other markets.

Since the range of its chemical manufacturing activities is broader than those of the American concerns with which it is affiliated, IG has been in a better position than its several American partners to treat each particular contract as part of a larger framework of controls. It could view the development of chemical technology as an integrated whole, and thus use it most effectively as an instrument of industrial control. Of course, the advantages of these arrangements were not wholly one-sided. The American companies which negotiated them frequently obtained from IG techniques and "know-how" which gave them opportunities for growth in new directions and sometimes "opened doors" to further technical advances. But they obtained these advantages at a high price.

IG's cartel contracts with its American colleagues have limited the scope of their individual activities both directly, in manufacturing and trading, and indirectly, in research. The cramping, restrictive influence of IG's penetration of the American market is evident in its numerous cartel contracts with American firms, both those with companies having a minor stake in some small sector of the chemical industries and those with the "big three"—Allied Chemical, Union Carbide & Carbon (UCC), and du Pont.

Thus, illustrating IG's connections with minor firms, the agreement of 1934 between IG and Röhm & Haas of Philadelphia is restricted to acrylic acid derivatives. But this is not all. With the avowed objectives "to avoid as far as possible any patent controversies between themselves . . . and to regulate the conditions of manufacture and sale," the basic agreement narrowly limited the use of the patent rights exchanged, even in this small field. Specifically, it prohibited their use for the preparation or improvement of photographic articles, celluloid-like masses or products made therefrom, dyestuffs, artificial rubber, pharmaceutical articles, or abrasives.[20] Only in the manufacture of acrylate plastics, in the development of which it had made important contributions, was Röhm & Haas free to use the techniques

20. Bone, Pt. II, p 749.

acquired—and even there only for products sold in the American market.

With growing experience and continuing research, Röhm & Haas' interest in the exploration of new commercial outlets steadily quickened. This was in itself a salutary development, and doubtless the cross-licensing arrangements with IG were a stimulating factor. But increasingly the company found it technologically and commercially inexpedient to stay within the narrow boundaries to which IG had restricted it. It repeatedly complained of the severity of the restrictions under which it operated and requested IG to ease them. Eventually, in 1940, Röhm & Haas got IG's permission under its license to manufacture and sell acrylates in certain additional, but still carefully defined, product fields.[21]

Significance of IG's American Affiliations

IG has made cartel agreements on this model with General Aniline in dyestuffs, with Agfa Ansco in film, with Sterling and Winthrop in drugs and pharmaceuticals, with Standard Oil in the overlapping domains of the petroleum and the chemical industries, with Röhm & Haas in acrylate plastics, with the Unyte Corporation [22] in urea formaldehyde plastics, with Hercules Powder Company in cellulose plastics and in chlorinated rubber, with Dow and the Aluminum Company of America in magnesium, with American Cyanamid in cyanides,[23] with Ethyl in tetraethyl lead and iron carbonyl,[24] with

21. *Ibid.*, pp. 758-60.
22. *Ibid.*, Pt. V, p. 2341; U.S. Tariff Commission, Report No. 131, Ser. II, "Synthetic Resins and Their Raw Materials," p. 34. IG organized Unyte with American interests owning important patents in this field. Unyte later became a part of the Plaskon Corporation.
23. See p. 485. IG reported a 1936 agreement with American Cyanamid wherein the latter granted to IG manufacturing rights for "phosocresol Aerofloat": "I. G. obligates itself not to participate for the duration of the agreement in any way, directly or indirectly, in the manufacture or the sale . . . in North and South America. I. G. will pass on to ACCO inquiries with respect to the phosocresol sale in these territories." Bone, Pt. V, p. 2342.
24. In 1935 Ethyl furnished IG with "know-how" and engineering assistance for constructing a tetraethyl lead plant in Germany, under joint IG-Ethyl ownership. Apparently part of the inducement to make this disclosure was an IG offer of technical information on some related subject, which is not specified in the published record. Another part of the consideration was Ethyl's participation in the prospective profits from this enterprise for supplying Germany with antiknock motor fuel, an important element in its rearmament program.
A du Pont official objected to Ethyl's making this bargain. He wrote to the president of Ethyl Corporation on December 15, 1934: "It would seem, on the face of it, that the quantities of Ethyl lead used for commercial purposes in Germany would be too small

Pennsylvania Salt, Stauffer Chemical, and Koppers in particular fields.[25]

All these IG arrangements with American companies limit the latter to specific chemical fields. Such limitations, imposed for business reasons, are frequently contradictory to technological realities and tend to inhibit the progress of the chemical industries subject to them. They may have promoted the business interest of IG, and even in a certain measure those of its American colleagues or affiliates, but they interfered with the economical use and development of technology. The growth of the organic chemical industries in the last century would not have been possible had such restrictions been persistently placed upon them.

Moreover, these cartel contracts also limit the American companies to specific market areas, and most of them explicitly recognize IG's prior claim to markets outside the United States, in exchange for IG's cooperation within the United States. Finally, and perhaps even more significantly, they provide for exchange of technical information and

to go after. It has been claimed that Germany is secretly arming. Ethyl lead would doubtless be a valuable aid to military aeroplanes.

"I am writing you this to say that in my opinion under no conditions should you or the Board of Directors of the Ethyl Gasoline Corporation disclose any secrets or 'know how' in connection with the manufacture of tetraethyl lead to Germany." *Scientific and Technical Mobilization,* Hearings before a Subcommittee of the Committee on Military Affairs, U.S. Senate, 78th Cong., 1st sess., on S.Res. 107 and S. 702, Pt. VI, p. 939.

A month later the president of Ethyl informed the Army Air Corps that "there is no technical data of military importance known to us which would be involved in the building of such a plant that has not already received wide publicity, or is of common knowledge in the aviation field." On the basis of this assertion, Ethyl obtained governmental approval for the project. The same letter revealed positive grounds for Ethyl's readiness to proceed with the job. The writer frankly stated that Ethyl was anxious to carry out its agreement with IG because its parent companies, General Motors and Standard Oil, both had important business interests in Germany, and Ethyl did not wish to run the risk of reprisals. *Ibid.,* pp. 939-44.

AMG has recently released a document found in the captured files of IG which reveals how greatly this disclosure contributed to Germany's war potential. In this report to the Gestapo, IG was justifying its "marriage" with Standard Oil. It claimed that the Ethyl "know-how" and license had been conveyed "at the urgent request of Standard Oil to comply with our wish." The report continued: "It need not be pointed out that without lead tetraethyl modern warfare could not be conceived. Since the beginning of the war we have been in a position to produce lead tetraethyl solely because, a short time before the outbreak of the war, the Americans had established plants for us ready for production and supplied us with all available experience. In this manner we did not need to perform the difficult work of development because we could start production right away on the basis of all the experience that the Americans had had for years." New York *Times,* October 19, 1945, p. 9.

In iron carbonyl, Ethyl settled a patent interference with Badische by recognizing the IG patent, agreeing not to sell this product for antiknock purposes outside the United States and Canada without IG's consent, and agreeing to purchase its entire requirements for marketing within those countries from IG. Bone, Pt. V, p. 2341.

25. See Bone, Pt. V, pp. 2333-53.

cross-licensing of patents, both present and future. In this way IG used temporary advantages to entrench itself permanently. It secured rights to future technological developments of its American partners in the designated fields, however important they might be, on prearranged terms. No other chemical company in the world has drawn unto itself, and made tributary to its own technical and commercial advancement, the fruits of research in so many different directions.

IG and Allied

IG eventually established working relations or reached understandings with each of the "big three." It succeeded first in eliminating competition between itself and Allied Chemical in alkalies through its firmly cemented relations in this field with Solvay and ICI and the latter's agreements with Alkasso, of which Allied's Solvay subsidiary was the leading member. Similarly, through its General Aniline subsidiary, IG has cooperated closely with Allied's National Aniline in the United States dyestuffs market. In world markets the two companies have entered into quota and price-fixing agreements.[26] Apparently Allied has also cooperated with IG in the international nitrogen cartel.

Finally, under a 1936 patents and processes agreement with Allied's General Chemical, IG agreed not to manufacture sulphuric acid in North America, or to license anyone else to manufacture it, except dyestuff producers for their own use.[27] By these several arrangements, IG has found a way to cooperate with Allied in all its major fields: alkalies, dyes, nitrogen and nitrogenous fertilizers, and sulphuric acid.

IG's Relations With Union Carbide

In its basic agreement with Grasselli Dyestuff, IG explicitly excluded from its licenses the manufacture of "carbide and carbide derivatives and products from carbide derivatives, as for example, acetic acid, acetic acid anhydride, acetone, acetaldehyde." [28] This is UCC's

26. See text, pp. 405-06.
27. This agreement may represent an outgrowth of an old agreement between General Chemical and Badische Anilin, covering rights to the latter's contact sulphuric acid process.
28. Bone, Pt. V, p. 2233.

field. IG's cartel agreement with Shawinigan of Canada recognizes the North American ex-carbide market as the latter's exclusive domain. This arrangement amounts to virtually the same thing as would a reservation of the United States market for these products to UCC in a direct cartel agreement between it and IG. For Shawinigan and UCC cooperate closely, in fact are partners, in this field; their joint American subsidiary is Niacet, their joint Canadian subsidiary, Canadian Resins & Chemicals, Ltd.[29]

That IG and UCC have established working relations effectively preventing competition between them is clearly shown by the intriguing history of the venture in acetylene manufacture. Jasco, a joint subsidiary of Standard Oil and IG, built a plant at Baton Rouge in the early thirties to make acetylene from refinery gases by IG's arc acetylene process. IG permitted Jasco to use the acetylene to manufacture acetic acid, but only enough to meet the requirements of Standard's subsidiary, Standard Alcohol. It kept UCC constantly informed of the development, and assured UCC that Jasco sales of surplus acetic acid would not disturb the market. To insure this it arranged to sell the acid through Niacet.

IG's American representative reported its negotiation of this arrangement to IG with the following comment: "We believe that in entering into this agreement we have acted in the interests of I. G., in order to maintain good relations with U. C. C." [30] IG persistently rejected Standard's proposals to expand the plant, lest such a move should get it "into difficulty with Niacet." [31] It finally forced Jasco to stop production and to offer to sell out to UCC, although Standard's cost estimates indicated that the subsidiary's operation would prove profitable.[32]

IG had several formal agreements directly with UCC covering fields of mutual interest. In one, the parties "define the limits of their respective interests concerning sales on [sic] the field of glycols" [33] and related products, recognizing the United States and Canada as

29. On the Niacet setup, see text above. UCC has a 51 per cent voting stock interest in Canadian Resins & Chemicals. *Moody's Manual of Investments* (Industrials), 1945, p. 2415.
30. Bone, Pt. III, p. 1439.
31. *Ibid.*, p. 1464.
32. *Ibid.*, pp. 1373-79, 1382-87, and accompanying exhibits.
33. *Ibid.*, Pt. V, p. 2345. Prestone antifreeze, one of UCC's most important products, presumably comes under the scope of this agreement since it is composed of ethylene glycol.

UCC's exclusive sphere. Furthermore, IG and UCC's subsidiary, Carbide & Carbon Chemicals Corporation (CCCC), exchanged patent licenses and know-how in a number of fields—including certain cellulose products, alcohols, aldehydes, ketones, glycols, other solvents, and polyvinylchloride.[34] Some of these agreements grant exclusive rights to each party in its reserved territory; others are on a nonexclusive basis.

IG and du Pont Draw Together

Thus, IG's invasion of the American market, after failure to reach a comprehensive agreement with du Pont, did not result in effective competition either in the numerous chemical markets in which both were important factors or in other lines. On the contrary, IG created cartels everywhere it went. Although the two companies did not reach a general understanding defining their respective spheres of operations and reconciling all their divergent interests, both have recognized the benefits of cooperation and have persistently sought it by conciliatory negotiation.

In its relations with du Pont, as in its relations with other American chemical companies, big and little, IG has followed the same piecemeal procedure, fencing in one field at a time. The difference between the du Pont–IG relationship and the others is only in the greater number of the successive compartmental contracts these two parties have made. During the interval between the two world wars, they entered into a score or more of specific arrangements for the cooperative development of particular fields.[35] We have already discussed two notable instances of such collaboration: the comprehensive explosives agreements between du Pont, ICI (Nobel), and IG's subsidiaries, Dynamit A. G. (DAG) and Köln-Rottweil, and the formation in 1938 of Electroclor by du Pont and ICI (through Duperial), Solvay, IG, and La Celulosa, for joint exploitation of the Argentine electrolytic chemicals field.

IG and du Pont have also cooperated, through the former's American partner in the pharmaceutical field, Winthrop Chemical, in the formation of a joint subsidiary to manufacture seed, soil, and plant

34. *Ibid.*, pp. 2349, 2353.
35. These arrangements were no doubt facilitated by du Pont's investment of more than one million dollars in IG stock during the twenties. This holding amounted to 0.38 per cent of the total IG stock outstanding. Nye, Pt. V, p. 1283.

disinfectants.[36] To this company, Bayer-Semesan, they assigned exclusive American and Canadian patent rights in this field. Since these included, on du Pont's side, not only its own patents and processes but also those obtained from ICI, and on Winthrop's side, not only IG's developments but also those of its other parent, Sterling Products, Bayer-Semesan represented an aggregation of overwhelming power in its limited field.

In 1929, du Pont and Kalle & Co., one of the original "big six" of IG, concluded a cellophane agreement, exchanging patents and processes whether patented or not. Both du Pont and Kalle had similar agreements with La Cellophane, so that by a three-way exchange of licenses they divided world markets among themselves.[37]

Even in the two major fields in which they had failed to reach an all-inclusive agreement—nitrogen and dyestuffs—du Pont and IG have collaborated since the twenties. IG seriously considered constructing a nitrogen plant in the United States; indeed, by 1930 it had formulated definite plans for such a project. After discussing the project with du Pont officials, however, IG abandoned its plans.[38] Later, IG representatives indicated that they had done so in deference to du Pont's prior claims in this field. They reported after a conference with du Pont officials: "We pointed out . . . that we had been very considerate of Du Pont's interests in the field of nitrogen (we had renounced the manufacture of nitrogen in Baton Rouge; had refused to give a license to the Hercules Powder Corporation) . . ." [39]

IG Consults du Pont

In 1933 and in 1936, Hercules requested a license from IG to use certain ammonia processes. With reference to the 1936 request, IG's American agent wrote to the home office:

We have conferred with Wardenburg, general manager of Du Pont's ammonia department. Du Pont takes the position that I. G. is free to enter into an agreement with Hercules and that Du Pont could not be sore at I. G. if I. G. entered into such an agreement.

Wardenburg, himself, however, expresses the opinion that in order to reach the understanding between Du Pont and I. G. which he and other

36. Bone, Pt. V, p. 2265.
37. Ibid., pp. 2264, 2339.
38. Nye, Pt. XII, pp. 2874-75; Bone, Pt. V, p. 2261.
39. Bone, Pt. V, p. 2261.

Du Pont executives desire, it would be better if I. G. were not burdened by commitments in the United States.

At the present time Hercules is negotiating with Du Pont about a new contract for the purchase of ammonia and Du Pont is willing to supply Hercules at the lowest possible price. Wardenburg further remarked that he felt that Hercules had calculated on too low a cost price for ammonia, considering the capacity Hercules needs.[40]

IG replied: "In view of Du Pont's position, we think it is expedient to reject the Hercules proposal." [41] The IG agent reported du Pont's reaction to this decision as follows: "Mr. Wardenburg thanked me very much and remarked that Du Pont greatly appreciated I. G.'s decision in this matter." [42]

IG evidently recognized and respected du Pont's nitrogen interests in the United States market. Du Pont apparently reciprocated in the world markets, where the nitrogen cartel, dominated by IG, held sway. The government's antitrust suit against the world's major nitrogen producers alleged restraint of United States commerce in nitrogenous fertilizers and included du Pont among the defendants.[43] Du Pont's Patents and Processes Agreement with ICI included nitrogen, and ICI was a charter member of the nitrogen cartel. Duperial Argentina was the local sales agent not only for its parents but also for the European nitrogen cartel. Finally, du Pont licensed IG to use its patent covering oxidation of ammonia (into nitric acid) for certain European countries. It also licensed the leading chemical manufacturers in other countries for their respective markets—St. Gobain, Union Chimique Belge, Mitsui, Chimstroy (USSR), and, in the United States, Hercules and Atlas.[44]

40. *Ibid.*, Pt. IV, pp. 1861-62.
41. *Ibid.*, p. 1862.
42. *Ibid.*
43. This suit was settled by a consent decree on May 29, 1941, and du Pont was enjoined from engaging thenceforth in restraints of trade in nitrogen and nitrogenous fertilizers. *U.S.* v. *Allied Chemical & Dye Corp., et al.*, in U.S. District Court for the Southern District of New York, Civil Action No. 14-320, Complaint and Consent Decree, May 29, 1941.
44. Schedule A of the 1929 du Pont–ICI Patents and Processes Agreement, appended as Exhibit 1 to *U.S.* v. *Imperial Chemical Industries, Ltd., et al.*, in U.S. District Court for the Southern District of New York, Civil Action No. 24-13, Complaint. This Schedule lists "Lurgi" as the German licensee. See also Nye, Pt. XII, p. 2890. Lurgi's precise relation to IG is not clear. The *Handbuch der Deutschen Aktiengesellschaften,* 1937, lists three so-called "Lurgi" companies as wholly owned subsidiaries of the German metal trust, Metallgesellschaft. IG had very close relations with Metallgesellschaft; three of IG's leading officials were also Metallgesellschaft directors. In any case, IG stated in 1936 that du Pont had licensed it under a German ammonia oxidation patent,

Du Pont Cooperates With IG's American Subsidiaries

While unable to agree upon a joint American dyestuffs venture, du Pont and IG officials nevertheless in the late twenties "agreed that the sales departments of the two companies should establish as frank and friendly relations as possible." [45] Later, IG representatives reported having pointed out to du Pont that

> . . . an amicable cooperation existed in the field of dyestuffs, consisting on the one hand of understandings about foreign markets; and on the other of amicable settlements of all patent litigation in the U. S. A. We further called to their attention that there had been a uniform sales policy and that the General Aniline Works had made big purchases from Du Pont of heavy chemicals and intermediate products.[46]

In the domestic market, the scope and character of this cooperation between du Pont and IG's General Aniline and General Dyestuff have been described above. Indicating the prevailing attitude and the principal channel of their intercourse, a du Pont official wrote in 1937: "As you perhaps know, it is our policy, as far as possible, to settle patent conflicts with G. A. W. [General Aniline Works] by agreement." [47]

In exchanging patent licenses the parties imposed restrictions on marketing territory and on products to be manufactured, similar to the restrictions which IG itself imposed on its American licensees. Several of these agreements reserved to the licensor the right to fix the sales prices charged by the licensees. These provisions continued until 1940 and 1941, when du Pont and General Aniline each waived the contract right to fix its licensees' sales prices.[48] Furthermore, du Pont and IG's American dyestuffs subsidiaries have been important customers of each other for materials and intermediates, usually at preferential prices.

---

and a du Pont memorandum in the same year reported a receipt by du Pont of $6,617 in royalties from IG during the preceding year, from an ammonia oxidation license. Bone, Pt. V, pp. 2342, 2266.

45. Bone, Pt. V, p. 2261.
46. *Ibid.* This quotation is from a 1935 IG memorandum.
47. *Ibid.,* p. 2266.
48. General Aniline changed its policy "after consultation with our lawyers and on their advice . . ." *Ibid.,* p. 2577. Du Pont in explaining its waiver stated: "While such a provision may be legally proper it is contrary to the policy of the du Pont Company." *Ibid.,* pp. 2534, 2546.

Du Pont and IG Collaborate in World Markets

In foreign dyestuffs markets, du Pont (along with the other major American producers) has cooperated fully with IG, the cartel leader.[49] When du Pont withdrew from India under its 1929 agreement with ICI, it renounced competition with IG, the major supplier in this large export market.[50] During the thirties, du Pont, National Aniline (of Allied Chemical), the European cartel (dominated by IG), and Mitsui divided the Chinese market by allotment of quotas, and fixed sales prices.[51] In Argentina and Brazil, du Pont (later the Duperials), National, and IG collaborated in fixing uniform selling prices during most of the thirties.[52]

IG recognized du Pont's vested interests in the American chemical field most clearly and fully in the arrangements it worked out with Standard Oil. By their basic agreements, IG and Standard of New Jersey agreed to produce in partnership chemicals derived from petroleum or natural gas but not closely related to the oil business. But in the Jasco partnership, Standard occupied the position, to use Walter Teagle's term, of a "junior partner." In every joint venture in which Jasco actually engaged, IG exercised ultimate control. In practical effect, Standard had signed a nonaggression pact not only with IG, but with all those chemical companies throughout the world with which IG had cartel relations. If the Standard-IG combination had "committed trespass" in the chemical field, under these arrangements, primary responsibility would have rested on IG, not Standard.

Both partners took pains, however, promptly to assure du Pont that their joint venture was not intended, and would not be permitted, to menace du Pont interests. In 1930 the three parties agreed on a policy to govern their relations. This policy was recorded in the minutes of a joint conference of du Pont, IG, and Standard officials:

49. *Ibid.*, pp. 2086-2101, and accompanying exhibits.
50. Before du Pont withdrew, it evidently cooperated with IG and Allied Chemical in fixing sales prices. Allied's general manager, in writing to its president concerning division of the Indian market, mentioned du Pont's "usual plans of agreement on price." *Ibid.*, p. 2094.
51. *Ibid.*, pp. 2086-94. National, Mitsui, and the European dye cartel made similar arrangements for Japan and India.
52. In 1937 du Pont called its Brazilian agent's attention to complaints that the agent was selling certain dyes at less than half the prices quoted by European manufacturers. Du Pont reminded him of "our Company's policy to establish selling prices which are in line with those already in effect," and suggested that he "take immediate steps to rectify the situation." Edwards, *op. cit.*, pp. 14-15.

If . . . products or chemicals will be produced that are now commercially manufactured by the du Pont interests, the Standard and I. G. would discuss same with the du Pont Co. and endeavor to find a way in which the commercial exploitation of such processes and products would best be carried on to the greatest benefit of each of the three parties. . . .

Mr. du Pont expressed himself as pleased and well satisfied with the discussion, and said that the du Ponts would welcome the opportunity to become associated with the I. G. and Standard in any enterprise in which the interests would be mutual.[53]

IG Defers to du Pont's Established Trade Interests

The story of synthetic rubber in the United States reveals clearly IG's solicitude for du Pont's interests in chemicals coming under the Standard-IG partnership. Standard tried strenuously for six years to persuade IG to release its Buna techniques for American exploitation. It was a vain effort. Standard never did obtain IG's Buna "know-how." Whatever other factors may have lain behind IG's stalling tactics, one consideration was its determination not to upset du Pont's profitable monopoly in the specialty synthetic rubber field.

IG also used its veto power under the partnership agreement with Standard to protect du Pont's interests in cyanides and methanol. In 1937 Röhm & Haas asked Jasco to supply it with acetylene for conversion into cyanide products. IG refused Jasco permission to fill this order because of its cartel obligations to du Pont and American Cyanamid. IG recorded its position as follows:

Since du Pont is attempting at the moment to manufacture hydrocyanic acid . . . and since, moreover, we have offered du Pont a license . . . we cannot open negotiations with Röhm & Haas. We cannot do so for the additional reason that it would be contrary to the spirit of the Cyan agreement . . . for I. G. to lend its aid in putting up an additional cyanide plant. The American parties to this agreement, namely, American Cyanamid Company and du Pont, will be very much interested in supplying a large consumer such as Röhm & Haas. . . .

As regards vinylchloride, it would not be desirable to have Röhm & Haas begin to manufacture this product because it is the basic material for artificial fabrics about which we are negotiating with du Pont at the moment. We, therefore, ask you to give a negative answer to Röhm & Haas' inquiry.[54]

53. *Investigation of the National Defense Program,* Hearings before a Special Committee of the U.S. Senate, 77th Cong., 1st sess., pursuant to S.Res. 71, Pt. XI, p. 4647. (Hereinafter: Truman, Pt. —.) See also Bone, Pt. V, p. 2250.

54. Bone, Pt. III, p. 1501.

Du Pont's and IG's failure to "find a formula" for jointly producing synthetic ammonia was also a failure to establish effective collaboration on synthetic methanol—an alternative product. Nevertheless, IG continued to recognize du Pont's interests in this field and its preferred position in the American market. When Standard sought rights to IG's methanol processes, IG insisted upon, and Standard acknowledged, an obligation to consult du Pont before exploiting them commercially. Both partners were anxious to avoid direct conflict with du Pont.

Although Standard obtained a license from IG in 1936, it did not immediately manufacture methanol. Instead, it contracted to purchase its requirements from du Pont.[55] Howard of Standard reported this transaction, by cable to IG, as follows:

> We have made contract with du Pont for one year's supplies beginning next Summer and are at same time discussing with them our estimated investment and operating costs with understanding that if they are willing to give us supplies at price level not showing satisfactory return on our investment we will take from them. They seem entirely satisfied with our position.[56]

Thus both Standard and IG evinced their business solidarity with du Pont. On the other hand, du Pont showed its appreciation by supplying Standard with methanol at 17.5 cents a gallon, about half the market price.[57]

IG's solicitude for du Pont's interests during the thirties—its refusal to license Hercules in nitrogen, and its restrictions on the activities of Standard and Jasco—marks a definite change of attitude. During the twenties, IG had persistently rebuffed du Pont's proposals to cooperate and aggressively invaded the American market in fields exploited by du Pont. By the thirties it had changed its tune.

55. A Standard official reported du Pont's suggestion that "we name a figure at which we would be willing to purchase our supplies from them rather than engage in manufacturing ourselves." *Ibid.*, Pt. VIII, p. 4630. See pp. 4592-93 and accompanying exhibits.

56. *Ibid.*, p. 4647. This 1936 contract (for 1937 supplies) was renewed for two more years. Standard produced no methanol until mounting war demands made it difficult for du Pont to supply it. Thus, Standard chose to use patent rights acquired from IG, not to supply a general market in competition with du Pont, but to obtain a price advantage in its own purchases.

57. Frank Howard stated in 1940 that the market price was 25 cents; according to the Bureau of Labor Statistics, it was 30 to 33 cents. *Ibid.*, pp. 4602-03. The Robinson-Patman Act forbids such price discrimination, but Howard suggested a means of evading this proscription. *Ibid.*, p. 4633.

Reason for IG's Change in Tactics

Several factors may have contributed to this change. First, its commitments to du Pont may have served IG as a cloak for retarding American chemical development. At any rate, IG frequently cited its commitments to du Pont as a ground for blocking developmental programs of its other American partners. At other times it blocked du Pont's efforts to go ahead in other fields, using its commitments to other companies as a reason. Playing off one American ally against another helped to keep world chemical markets under IG's dominance.

Second, IG may have come to realize that it could not rule the world's chemical industries alone. Du Pont had emerged as the leading factor in the American chemical industries; it was now a power to be reckoned with in world chemical markets. Strategy called for collaboration. It must have become apparent to IG that du Pont was unwilling to countenance any resumption of IG's pre–World War I discretionary control of the American chemical market in which du Pont had acquired a stake, and that it was in position to block any such strategy. Finally, du Pont had some patents and processes that IG wanted.

IG was anxious, during the thirties, to obtain rights to du Pont's original synthetic rubber developments. IG had a high regard for Neoprene and even after it had gone ahead with Buna, its interest continued in the initial processes of Neoprene manufacture, notably the transformation of acetylene into monovinylacetylene (MVA), as a source of butadiene.[58] IG took the initiative in seeking an agreement with du Pont in this field, and negotiations continued for many years. Du Pont wanted the American rights to other IG processes in exchange for its MVA, but IG had made so many other commitments in the United States that the parties found difficulty in agreeing upon a suitable *quid pro quo*.[59] In particular, IG's prior commitments to Jasco in Buna rubber and to Unyte (Plaskon), General Aniline, Röhm & Haas, Hercules Powder, and others in the various fields of plastics in which du Pont was interested, severely limited IG's ability to meet du Pont's demands.[60]

58. See Chapter 3.
59. Bone, Pt. V, p. 2261.
60. See *ibid.*, pp. 2341, 2348, 2352-53.

Pattern of IG–du Pont Relations

Nevertheless, out of these negotiations du Pont and IG made their nearest approach to a general trade agreement. While the understanding was only tacit, a du Pont official has expressed his conception of it as follows:

> The I. G. and du Pont have an informal agreement that when we have German patents which seem to us might be profitably exploited in Germany, and when these patents cover subjects on which we have no prior commitments or moral obligations to discuss with anybody else, we will bring them first to the attention of the I. G. and they will do the same for the United States.[61]

On the basis of this general accord, du Pont and IG reached several specific agreements for cooperative development of new products and processes by exchange of patent rights and techniques. In 1938 du Pont granted IG German rights to MVA and related products for use in making Buna rubbers, and in 1939 the German rights to nylon, two extremely valuable concessions. Du Pont also apparently recognized IG's prior rights (in America, vested in its subsidiary, Unyte Corporation) in the field of urea formaldehyde resins, and confined itself to supplying raw materials for their manufacture by Plaskon (into which Unyte merged) and American Cyanamid. Du Pont obtained the American rights to polystyrene plastics from IG in 1938, and in 1940 IG agreed, at least in principle, to give du Pont American rights to vinylchloride polymers.[62]

Du Pont and IG were not in partnership; they had neither a broad alliance like that of du Pont and ICI, nor a narrow one like that of IG and Standard. Neither party gave anything to the other for nothing, nor merely in the interest of friendship and good will. Their relationship was a hard-boiled one, largely based on opportunism; they were friendly or unfriendly depending, mainly, on the urgency of IG's need for du Pont's cooperation.

Nevertheless, their collaboration involved something more than a

61. *Ibid.*, p. 2265.
62. The MVA, styrene, and nylon agreements are listed in Schedule A of the 1939 du Pont–ICI Patents and Processes Agreement, *loc. cit.* See also Edwards, *op. cit.*, p. 63; and Bone, Pt. II, pp. 819-22, 836-38.

All these agreements took the form of an exchange of patent rights and information, partly on an exclusive, and partly on a nonexclusive, basis. All carefully limited the market territories and chemical fields for which rights were granted.

series of unrelated agreements covering individual products and processes. IG took numerous steps to protect du Pont interests, and granted to du Pont numerous valuable rights. Du Pont did the same for IG; it would be difficult to tie specific *quids* to specific *quos* in these many bargains. Both companies gave heed to strategic considerations favoring some kind of understanding; each either had something the other wanted or could at least harm the other's interests. Both realized the hazards of seriously antagonizing each other, and, above all, the folly of upsetting the market. This was the nature of their gentlemen's agreement: they would cooperate wherever possible, and in any event they would act like gentlemen. Neither proposed to engage in "senseless price competition," or take action which would injure the other if it could help it.

IG and ICI

Like du Pont, ICI was either unable or unwilling to merge its interests with those of IG by a detailed, all-inclusive, mutual interchange of technology and markets. However, its collaboration with IG was both more extensive and more intensive than that of du Pont.[63] ICI and IG were not impeded in their dealings by antitrust statutes. They were not limited in suppressing competition between themselves to patents and processes exchange agreements. They could, if they desired, make simple contracts to divide markets, fix prices, or restrict output, while keeping their patents and "know-how" to themselves.

As we have seen, ICI and IG have completely eliminated competition between themselves in nitrogen and nitrogenous fertilizers, alkalies, and explosives by participating in international cartels. In 1931 ICI joined the European dye cartel, of which IG was the leading member. The two companies eliminated the last vestiges of market rivalry in dyestuffs in 1938 by setting up a jointly owned corporation, Trafford Chemicals, Ltd., to manufacture certain dyestuffs in Britain—presumably those which IG had continued until then to sell there because of ICI's inability to duplicate them.[64]

IG and ICI participated in many other specific chemical cartels,

63. Like du Pont, ICI made the friendly gesture of purchasing IG stock in the twenties. Its purchase amounted to about $2.5 million, or 0.82 per cent of the total. Nye, Pt. V, p. 1298.
64. Schedule A, 1939 du Pont–ICI Agreement, *loc. cit.*

directly or indirectly, before World War II. Both were members of a
sodium cyanide cartel, along with the Deutsche Gold und Silber
Scheideanstalt and others. Scheide and American Cyanamid had an
agreement in the field of hydrogen cyanide or hydrocyanic acid,[65] and
IG, du Pont, and American Cyanamid were among the members
of an international cyanide cartel. These agreements were undoubtedly
interrelated. ICI has been a member of the European Salt Cake Association, which divided markets and allotted export quotas to its
members. Another leading participant was the German sulphate
syndicate, in which IG plays an important role. The list of prior
commitments appended as Schedule A to the 1939 du Pont–ICI
Patents and Processes Agreement includes several agreements between IG and ICI to exchange patent licenses, and some of these
agreements also provide for other forms of cooperation.

IG and ICI cooperated, also, with Standard Oil and Royal Dutch
Shell, in controlling the synthesis of gasoline from coal. IG, ICI, and
Shell had jointly owned the International Bergin Company, which
held the original Bergius hydrogenation patents. When IG turned
over to Standard Oil and Shell its world-wide hydrogenation rights,
except for Germany (and the United States, which went exclusively
to Standard), ICI received a favored position, partly because of its
share in International Bergin.

Through International Hydrogenation Patents Company, Ltd.
(IHP), Standard and Shell gave ICI the exclusive license for hydrogenation of coal in the British Empire. The license permitted ICI to
produce up to 25 per cent of the total consumption of petroleum
products in the Empire, and no more; IHP promised to give no licenses for the hydrogenation of petroleum in the Empire in excess
of the remaining 75 per cent. ICI agreed in turn to offer IHP exclusive rights under all its relevant patents and processes, to market
exclusively through Standard and Shell or companies named by them,
to purchase all its crude oil requirements from Standard and Shell,
and to pay stipulated fees (tantamount to royalties) for engineering
assistance and other services to International Hydro Engineering &
Chemical Company (IHE), which Standard and Shell set up for this
purpose. Du Pont apparently gave its consent to ICI's acceptance of

65. Bone, Pt. V, pp. 2338, 2340.

this contract.[66] Thus ICI took its place in the IG-Standard world hydrogenation cartel.[67]

THE STANDARD-IG "MARRIAGE"

IG considered itself too strong to "take unto itself" any chemical partner except as a weaker half. Neither ICI nor du Pont would accept such a subordinate position. Accordingly, IG selected for its mate, not a chemical company, but one of the world's most powerful industrial combinations—Standard Oil Company of New Jersey.

The agreements of 1929 and 1930 between Standard and IG [68] represented, first, a simple mutual commitment not to compete, by recognizing the primacy of the one in petroleum and of the other in chemicals. In chemical developments relating to production of the ordinary products of oil refining, such as motor fuels and lubricants, Standard was to have a majority interest but was to offer IG a minority interest. In developments relating to the production from oil or natural gas of chemicals not ordinary or necessary products of oil refining, IG was to have a controlling interest but was to offer Standard a minority share.[69]

To Standard, these agreements promised, first, ownership and control, outside Germany, of IG's hydrogenation processes and any future IG processes for making synthetically products having similar uses to those of the customary petroleum refinery products, from whatever raw material they might be derived;[70] and, second, a junior partnership with IG, outside Germany, in the manufacture of new chemical products derived from petroleum or natural gas. In this way Standard (and Shell) removed the threat of competition from

66. ICI contemplated constructing a hydrogen plant, for use both in ammonia synthesis and hydrogenation. Under ICI's obligation to transmit all operating information relating to hydrogenation to IHP, there was danger that du Pont "know-how" relating to the manufacture of hydrogen, transmitted to ICI for use in ammonia synthesis, might flow improperly to IHP and IG. Hence ICI had to ask du Pont's consent. See the letter of Sir Harry McGowan to Lammot du Pont. Nye, Pt. XII, pp. 2895-96.

67. Bone, Pt. VII, pp. 3337, 3350-52.

68. See Chapter 3, pp. 92-94.

69. Among the exceptions to the general arrangements was the reservation to IG of the German market. Standard obtained no rights to participate in, much less to control, the exploitation of new IG chemical or petroleum-refining developments in Germany.

70. Standard was to have exclusive ownership and control of such processes in the United States; in the rest of the world, outside Germany, it was to share control with Shell. For the international development, Standard and Shell organized two corporate subsidiaries, IHE and IHP. Bone, Pt. VII, pp. 3349-50.

IG in the oil business, and IG in turn fortified itself against any serious menace to its designs for international leadership in chemicals from oil.[71]

How Standard Benefited From Its Union

Standard's use of its exclusive rights to IG's processes in the oil industry shows clearly that its main object in acquiring them was to strengthen its control over the oil industry. For the purpose, the IG agreements performed a dual function—defensive and offensive. Acquisition of the hydrogenation rights eliminated the most serious threat ". . . which has ever faced the company since the dissolution," according to Frank Howard, the Standard official who played a leading role in the negotiations with IG.[72] Once these rights were safely acquired, Standard and Shell showed little disposition to use them, or to encourage others to use them, in actual productive operations.[73] Their acquisition forestalled the threat to the oil industry of liquid fuels and lubricants from coal. On the positive side, Standard persistently used the rights it obtained from IG, both as an inducement and as a lever, to bring other petroleum-refining companies into comprehensive patent pools, extending far beyond the scope of the specific patent rights which it had obtained, and giving Standard a perpetually favored position in the use of the pooled technology. In this program it achieved considerable success.

Standard and Shell did little to encourage widespread synthetic production of liquid fuels and lubricants from coal. They had acquired these processes primarily to protect their own vast interests in petroleum. Standard summarized its policy as follows:

I. H. P. [International Hydrogenation Patents Company] should keep in close touch with developments in all countries where it has patents, and should be fully informed with regard to the interest being shown in hydrogenation and the prospect of its introduction . . . *It should not, however, attempt to stir up interest in countries where none exists.* If the Management decides that in any country the interest in hydrogenation is serious, or that developments in such country are likely to affect I. H. P.'s position adversely,

71. See Chapter 3.
72. See Chapter 3, n. 67.
73. Shortly after Standard acquired the patent rights, the opening up of the prolific East Texas oil field upset supply-demand relationships in the oil industry and put off the day of threatened oil shortage. This may have been a factor in Standard's withholding them from use.

then I. H. P. should discuss the matter actively with the interested parties, and attempt to persuade them that its process should be used. . . .

If coal, tar, etc., hydrogenation be feasible from an economic standpoint, or if it is to be promoted for nationalistic reasons or because of some peculiar local conditions, it is better for us as oil companies to have an interest in the development, obtain therefrom such benefits as we can, and assure the distribution of the products in question through our existing marketing facilities.[74]

Standard and Shell pursued precisely the same policy with other competitive processes.[75] Walter Teagle, Standard's president, wryly attested to the success of these policies in discouraging the adoption of hydrogenation:

The IHP has very large investment [*sic*] in hydrogenation on which, up to date, it has secured a very inadequate return. There is little doubt in our minds but what, if other than oil companies had dominated the situation, the management's conduct of the business would have been along lines better calculated to secure the maximum return on the capital invested.

In view of the rapid development of late in nationalism it is, of course, unfortunate that at its inception the IHP did not adopt a more active policy, as during the intervening time these other processes have, stimulated in part by the spread of nationalism and the disinclination of IHP to grant licenses, been now developed to the point where they are actually competitive.[76]

Standard Brings Other Major Oil Companies Into the Family

Soon after acquiring ownership of hydrogenation, Standard formulated a program for bringing other American petroleum companies into a joint venture to exploit these processes. It organized Hydro Patents Company to administer the American rights and "invited" eighteen major American oil companies to take shares in the company and licenses from it.[77] Some of them, faced with the risk of pay-

74. Bone, Pt. VII, pp. 3354-55. Italics supplied. See also pp. 3357-58.
75. An I. G. Farben memorandum written in 1932 indicates that it had given IHP the right to manufacture and sell methanol for use in motor fuels. Standard and IG agreed on the correct policy for IHP to follow: "Such general line would seem to be not to push the licensing of the process but not to refrain from granting licenses in cases where people would otherwise go ahead themselves . . ." *Ibid.*, Pt. VIII, p. 4622.

In Standard's efforts to participate in control of the Fischer hydrocarbon synthesis process, which was competitive with hydrogenation, the motive was revealed alike by its actions and by statements of its officials. In these negotiations Frank Howard twice urged the desirability of Standard being in position to *"guide or restrict"* or "guide *or limit* commercial developments under such processes." Italics supplied. *Ibid.*, Pt. VII, pp. 3700-01.

76. *Ibid.*, p. 3731.
77. *Ibid.*, p. 3341; Truman, Pt. XI, p. 4724.

ing higher royalties as outsiders, took the invitation as a command. They accepted, despite the substantial cost to themselves, despite the unwillingness of Standard to give more than the vaguest information until they actually joined, [78] and despite the admittedly onerous terms offered them, simply because they were afraid to stay out. As Frank Howard reported:

Kingsbury [of Standard Oil of California] says frankly that he thinks the plan rather tough on him since, if used on a very large scale, it will result in very large royalty payments . . . but that, in view of the potentialities of the process, he cannot justify staying out and therefore expects to come in. He says he believes that, if the other people speak with equal frankness, they will tell the same story and I think he is exactly right. All of these great companies are going to kick like steers at the prospect of paying any substantial running royalties. . . . My hope is, however, that they will all feel just as Kingsbury does, i.e., that they cannot afford to be left out.[79]

Standard's proffered hydrogenation licenses contained numerous restrictive features at which the oil companies complained violently but helplessly. To render engineering services and manufacture catalysts, Standard organized Hydro Engineering & Chemical Company. The proffered licenses required that the oil companies (1) use Hydro Engineering's services at a fixed fee, (2) buy their catalysts from it, and (3) transfer to it the exclusive rights under any patented catalysts which they might themselves develop. No matter what its contribution in the engineering and catalyst field, every licensee was bound to make its technical developments available to Hydro Engineering, and hence to Standard, without recompense, while continuing to make regular payments to HE and Standard.

The oil companies also protested the restriction on licensees to produce only the ordinary products of petroleum refining.[80] At the same time they complained about the breadth of the definition of hydrogenation, within the petroleum field. They contended that the field

78. "Only the briefest and most general information on the methods employed and the results obtainable will be given at this time. Those who take the small initial participation will be regarded as having evidenced a bona fide desire to investigate the process with a view to becoming permanently identified with its ownership and the pioneering of its commercial use." Bone, Pt. VII, p. 3521.

79. *Ibid.*, p. 3519. At least one other company, Cities Service, felt the same way; see *ibid.*, pp. 3519-20.

80. They were particularly agitated by their exclusion from the production of chemicals from oil, a rapidly developing branch of petroleum technology. Of course, Standard was not in position to modify this restriction. It was a vital part of its bargain with IG.

of these licenses and of the compulsory cross-licensing on all subsequent developments was far broader than the patents which Standard had obtained from IG. On this point, Howard frankly admitted:

> The definition of the term "hydrogenation process" is not an effort to
> define the scope of any patents which we own, but rather an effort at defining
> the field of our present and future inventions, within which field all parties
> must cross-license one another.[81]

Standard Buttresses Its Control

When the Fischer process for hydrocarbon synthesis emerged as a
powerful competitor of hydrogenation, Frank Howard wrote: "We
must face the fact that the IHP has definitely lost its complete control over the production of synthetic oils." He urged that "if we are
to do anything in the way of trying to guide or restrict the development of the Fischer process outside of Germany, the time to do so
is now." [82] The interest in these several processes shown by various
countries, anxious to secure a domestic source of motor fuel, made
action by Standard urgent. Howard kept prodding his associates:

> . . . We must try to move our Fischer negotiations as fast as we can if we
> expect to have a part in this picture. In my opinion we ought to have a part
> in it. If we let the foreign government[s] proceed . . . without any co-opera-
> tion on our part the outcome will be that we shall wind up in a very large
> proportion of our markets with the governments actively interested in the
> oil business in competition with us rather than in co-operation with us.[83]

After long negotiations, Standard, Shell, and IG obtained a major
share in the world rights to the Fischer process, averting a competitive threat to their entrenched position. As Howard reported in
1938:

> The high points of the matter are that Jersey and Shell acquire sufficient
> effective control of the hydrocarbon synthesis process in the world outside
> of the U. S. so that their position as leaders in the entire field of synthetic
> petroleum production is assured.[84]

Standard's most ambitious attempt since the 1911 dissolution to
unify the American petroleum industry under its leadership centered

81. Bone, Pt. VII, p. 3536. See pp. 3342-45 and accompanying exhibits.
82. *Ibid.*, pp. 3700-01.
83. *Ibid.*, p. 3733.
84. *Ibid.*, p. 3816. See pp. 3355-63 and accompanying exhibits.

about the catalytic cracking of petroleum. Many oil companies were experimenting in this general field, and it was clear in the late thirties that, by the proper use of catalysts, petroleum refiners could eventually alter the composition and quality of their products almost at will. Catalytic cracking has given us 100-octane gasoline, butadiene, and toluene from petroleum and a far higher direct yield of gasoline than from any previously known method. Standard's claims in the field were based largely on hydrogenation and on hydroforming, a method which it discovered of cracking petroleum in the presence of hydrogen. Hydroforming obtains the benefits of catalytic cracking without actual hydrogenation, that is, without absorption of the hydrogen by the petroleum fractions.

Standard took the lead in negotiating a series of agreements for uniting most of the companies active in the catalytic-cracking field in a community of interests known as CRA (Catalytic Research Associates). Its strategy in trying to effect this combination varied from time to time; at times it attempted to convince its associates in Hydro Patents of the desirability of including the entire field of catalytic cracking, or at least of hydroforming, within their hydrogenation agreements. Eventually it was forced to make separate agreements in this far broader field. However, the major strategy remained always consistent: to use the leverage of its own and IG's patents and the prestige of its leadership to effect a permanent power bloc and obtain a favored position in a highly dynamic and extremely broad sector of petroleum technology.[85]

Standard's effort to share in the control of sulphuric acid alkylation, an important process for making high-octane gasoline, shows this strategy at work. A vice-president of Standard Oil Development Company outlined it in a letter to Frank Howard as follows:

I hope that you will be having discussions with Anglo-Iranian on the catalytic cracking matter and it seemed to me there was some chance that if Anglo-Iranian . . . held out for a participation in foreign catalytic cracking royalties you might be able to accede gracefully to a small participation and accept as a partial quid [pro] quo either a free ride under Anglo-Iranian's alkylation patents world-wide or even a participation with them in an attempt to exploit the field jointly.[86]

85. *Ibid.*, pp. 3375-3424.
86. *Ibid.*, p. 3871; see pp. 3366-71 and exhibits.

The strategy succeeded. Despite an admittedly weak position in sulphuric acid alkylation, by the use of its patents and prestige in catalytic cracking Standard obtained not only "a free ride" but a 20 per cent control in world rights to the new process.

Standard's Tactics

Standard took other steps to further its control of petroleum technology. In 1931 IG discovered a new synthetic oil product, Paraflow, which Standard found had the properties of a pour-point depressant —that is, upon mixture with oil it lowered the temperature at which the oil ceased to pour or flow. In 1932 Standard obtained from IG the exclusive American rights to this product and by continued research added complementary patents of its own. Standard used these exclusive privileges to eliminate competing pour-point depressants from the American market, regardless of whether they infringed its patents.

To do this it resorted to a variety of tactics. It bought out competing manufacturers. By full-line forcing and tying arrangements, it persuaded customers to buy their pour-point depressants exclusively from it. By granting to other pour-point depressant manufacturers preferential discounts on Paraflow, and even in one case a special license to make and use Paraflow, Standard got them to withdraw their products from the market.[87]

At least one of these competing products, Santopour, was a more effective and economical pour-point depressant than Paraflow. Unless its price was raised or its quality deteriorated, Santopour threatened to displace Paraflow. After Standard had come to terms with the manufacturer of Santopour, it was embarrassed about the possible adverse reaction of the trade to the withdrawal of Santopour from the market. In discussing the proper policy to pursue, a Standard official reasoned as follows:

If Santopour of present quality is continued on the market as a competitor of Paraflow and at the same price, there will be a substantial shift in business from Paraflow to a smaller volume of Santopour due to the greater potency of the latter in many oils. This will result in a very substantial decrease in the total volume of pour depressants sold and a proportionate decrease in gross dollar income. . . .

87. *Ibid.*, Pt. IV, pp. 1756, 1767.

If Paraflow and Santopour are both to be marketed without loss of total income it is apparent that Santopour would have to be adjusted to the same cost per unit of pour reduction as Paraflow. This could be done by either making a substantial increase in the price of Santopour or diluting it to a considerable extent. . . .

We would have to tell a rather embarrassing story to explain the marked change in either price or potency of Santopour, and the real reason for the change would be obvious to the trade.

Our conclusion is, therefore, that the best policy is to retire Santopour as quickly and as quietly as possible, and to market only Paraflow of present potency.[88]

Standard Defends Its Cartel Tactics

Standard has vigorously denied that its contracts with IG have retarded chemical developments in the United States. It has claimed that under these contracts it obtained the rights to valuable IG processes and developed other processes from them, of which American industry would not otherwise have had the benefit.[89] Standard actually obtained discretionary use of IG's patents and processes only in the field of petroleum refining—mainly the manufacture of liquid fuels and lubricants. Here Standard has indeed put into practice important new processes based in part on rights acquired from IG: hydrogenation, the subsidiary methane steam process for the manufacture of hydrogen from natural gas, various other kinds of catalytic cracking, and the production of Paraflow. However, it does not follow that these processes would not have been introduced into the United States by some other means had not Standard and IG made their restrictive covenants of 1929.

First of all, for ordinary business reasons IG could scarcely have afforded to refrain altogether from exploiting its techniques in the rich American market. Had it not found a partner willing to accept such restrictive terms on its operations in the chemical field as those imposed on Standard, it doubtless would have found other means of entering the American market. If the world-wide rights to IG's developments in the chemistry of petroleum were worth the $30 million to $35 million which Standard paid for them, it is not likely that IG would have permitted them to lie idle.

88. *Ibid.*, p. 1824.
89. See *ibid.*, Pt. IX, pp. 5033-5358, and Truman, Pt. XI, pp. 4359-4497, 4830-34, *passim*.

Moreover, Standard had obtained a *nonexclusive* license from IG for the hydrogenation of petroleum in the United States in 1927.[90] Consequently, the introduction into the United States of the basic elements of this process, and of the important processes and products which Standard itself developed in the hydrogenation field—e.g., methane steam improvements, catalytic cracking (hydroforming), 100-octane gasoline, and toluene—did not depend on the restrictive covenants of 1929. Standard obtained additional powers and benefits in 1929: *exclusive* control of hydrogenation, for coal and oil alike, in the entire world outside Germany, and a junior partnership in petroleum chemicals. But while Standard obtained far more under the 1929 contract, the American petroleum and chemical industries gained little more, from the technological standpoint, than they should have obtained, and might readily have developed, under the 1927 contract.[91]

Did American Petroleum Technology Gain?

Finally, and most important, it is reasonably certain that without undue delay the American petroleum industry would have developed virtually all these processes independently—or others of equal worth —even if IG had never released them to Standard or any other American company. In fact, American technicians have developed alternative processes for cracking petroleum which are in some ways superior to IG's techniques, though of course it cannot be assumed that American alternatives would have been discovered as early as they were, without the stimulus of IG's developments. For all the publicity attending the hydrogenation development, and despite Standard's organization of all the major American oil companies to exploit it, only Standard and Shell, both of which had a proprietary interest in the process, have ever actually employed it, and they have done so only on a very small scale. The consensus of the oil industry is that it is uneconomical.

In catalytic cracking the contributions of IG and Standard, although important, were neither indispensable nor basic. In spite of Standard's leading role in the campaign to bring all catalytic refiners

90. Bone, Pt. VI, pp. 2853-59.
91. We say "should have obtained" because the 1927 license called for continuing disclosure to Standard of IG's new technical developments in "the hydrogenation field," as they occurred. *Ibid.*

together in CRA, the Standard-IG patents by no means covered the field. The Houdry process was already in commercial use. Indeed, Standard urged the organization of CRA primarily as a means of developing and exploiting catalytic processes competitive with the pioneer Houdry process.[92] Other major companies had made important developments in the field, and were negotiating with foreign patent owners. The American oil industry not only would have had, but actually did have in the Houdry process, a revolutionary development in catalytic cracking without the IG processes obtained by Standard.

Standard has pointed out that, on the basis of these hydrogenation and catalytic-reforming techniques, it has developed processes for obtaining toluene and butadiene directly from petroleum. These processes are extremely important; but, as Standard itself concedes, it did not get them from IG. Standard developed them itself. Moreover, its access to the basic techniques was not contingent on the 1929 "marriage" to IG. Standard developed the toluene and butadiene processes out of the IG hydrogenation techniques, for which it had obtained a simple license in 1927. Even if Standard had treated these processes as "chemical developments," under the 1929–1930 contracts, and offered them to Jasco for joint exploitation, it is difficult to see how the 1929 partnership arrangement could have speeded their development. In truth the negotiations to determine their status might well have retarded it.[93]

Another important process which Standard acquired from IG was methane steam. Standard obtained this process only for uses subsidiary to its petroleum operations (hydrogenation and hydroforming). Hence, valuable as it was, the contribution of the process to technological progress in the American chemical industries was nil; and, in the oil industry, it was no greater than that of the petroleum operations to which it was subsidiary. This contribution was not crucial. In the chemical field, as we shall see, IG steadfastly resisted the introduction of the methane steam process. On the whole deal, Standard

92. *Ibid.*, Pt. VII, pp. 4066-68, 4072; *Fortune*, February 1939, pp. 56-57.
93. A tentative memorandum of agreement concerning catalytic cracking between Standard and IG in 1939 stated: "If the products produced or the procedure used to produce them are unusual or abnormal for the oil industry . . . [and] if the products made . . . are used for purposes other than the main purposes of the oil industry, notably as raw materials for the chemical field, no license . . . can be claimed . . ." Bone, Pt. VII, pp. 4061-62.

may or may not have obtained its money's worth in purchasing from IG patent instruments for control over the world petroleum industry, valuable rights to participate in important new petroleum-refining developments, and protection against synthetic motor fuel derived from coal. But the American economy apparently obtained relatively little that it would not have obtained without such restraints on trade.

How IG Used Its Standard Partnership

While Standard used its rights obtained from IG to strengthen its position as a petroleum refiner and to consolidate control in the oil industry, IG used its Standard hookup to fortify its world leadership in the chemical industries and to guide and at times restrict chemical developments in the United States. Among the major chemical products and processes of which the American rights flowed to Standard or Jasco were synthetic rubber, the arc acetylene process, ammonia, and methanol.

Under one pretext or another, often contrary to Standard's urgent requests, IG obstructed American development in all these lines. In doing so, IG undoubtedly was motivated partly by business reasons. Its American interests were broad and diverse, its alliances with American firms numerous and complex. They frequently overlapped. To protect its cartel interests and obligations at one point, it had to restrict the operations of its cartel partners at another.

Apparently, however, IG's motives were also partly political. After the Nazis came to power, IG's relationship to the German Government became more intimate. In the controls which the Nazi state set up over German industry, it was often hard to determine where state control ended and cartel control began. Totalitarianism ultimately involved almost complete unification of business and state. It became increasingly difficult throughout the thirties, therefore, to distinguish between IG's purely business objectives and the political aims for which it served as a Nazi instrument.[94] In its cartel activities it merged business and politics: which of these factors predominated in shaping IG policy is perhaps relatively unimportant. What is sig-

94. See *Elimination of German Resources for War*, Hearings before a Subcommittee of the Committee on Military Affairs, U.S. Senate, 79th Cong., 1st sess., on S.Res. 107 and S.Res. 146, Pt. VII (December 1945), pp. 943-44 et seq.

nificant is that its patent controls and cartel relationships permitted IG to exercise a restrictive influence on the American chemical industries which was incompatible with American economic and political interests.

We have seen how IG withheld essential "know-how" from Jasco and refused to let it develop Buna rubber in the United States. We have also seen how IG forced Jasco to close its Baton Rouge "E" plant (the acetylene and acetic acid project).[95] IG had used its commitments to du Pont as one excuse for its delaying tactics on synthetic rubber. In closing the Baton Rouge plant, IG pleaded its obligations to UCC on acetylene derivatives.

Standard repeatedly urged the continuance, or the reopening, of the Jasco E plant to produce other products than acetic acid; but its pleas were always rebuffed, IG offering its cartel commitments to other American chemical companies as an excuse. In refusing Jasco permission to produce monochlor acetic acid, IG cited its agreements with the American dyestuff producers, du Pont, National Aniline, and Dow, which made this product for use in the manufacture of indigo.

IG refused Standard permission to let Jasco produce butyl alcohol (butanol) because of its "friendly relations" with UCC and Commercial Solvents. It also blocked Jasco's manufacture of: (1) acetaldehyde, because as an IG representative expressed it, ". . . we do not wish to disturb the market"; (2) vinylchloride or its raw materials, because it wanted to reserve this plastic as a bargaining counter for du Pont's Neoprene or MVA; (3) acetylene for sale to Röhm & Haas for the manufacture of cyanides, in deference to du Pont and American Cyanamid; and (4) acetic anhydride, because "U.C.C. . . . would probably regard it as very disagreeable. . . ."[96]

IG Plays Fast and Loose With American Partners

IG persistently played off one American cartel partner against another, using its commitments to one as a pretext for limiting its favors to others. In this way it could use most effectively its patents and techniques as instruments for controlling American chemical developments.

95. See Chapter 3, n. 78.
96. Bone, Pt. III, pp. 1497, 1505; see also pp. 1392-1402 and exhibits.

When du Pont could no longer supply Standard's methanol requirements in 1941, Standard decided to construct its own plant under patent rights which it had received from IG in 1936. Standard met the same delaying tactics, however, that it had encountered in synthetic rubber. In licensing Standard to produce methanol, IG reserved the privilege of supplying the necessary catalysts, which it made under a secret formula. Howard reported in 1937 that Standard was free to produce the catalyst itself if IG was unable to supply it, but: "It is clearly understood . . . that the I. G. cannot give us any of the very special technique and experience which they have developed for the preparation of this catalyst." [97]

After the outbreak of war, IG agreed to leave with its American patent attorneys full instructions on the preparation of the catalyst, to be turned over to Standard only in case of emergency. In November 1940, when a methanol shortage seemed imminent, two Standard officials requested Howard to ask IG for this information. When Howard did so, IG replied that it could still supply the catalyst and suggested Standard place an order. Howard replied that Standard had been trying unsuccessfully to obtain shipments of catalyst from IG since November 1939, and could not afford further unnecessary delay. Not until April 1941 did IG's representatives grant Standard the information which Standard had so urgently requested.[98]

Another Jasco venture definitely contemplated by Standard and IG was the manufacture of synthetic ammonia (nitrogen). As we have seen, IG vetoed this project, claiming later (in 1935) that it had done so in deference to du Pont. IG used its predominant influence in the Standard-IG chemical partnership to retard American production of nitrogen in still another way. IG owned the basic patents on the methane steam process for manufacture of hydrogen, an essential step in the synthesis of ammonia. Standard obtained the methane steam rights for use solely in hydrogenation leading to the ordinary products of petroleum refining. After acquiring additional patents and techniques in the early thirties, Standard built two large methane steam plants, and in 1937 imparted its methane steam "know-how" to IG for use in the synthesis of ammonia.[99] But in the United States,

97. *Ibid.*, Pt. VIII, p. 4668.
98. *Ibid.*, pp. 4604-07.
99. See *ibid.*, Pt. IV, pp. 1769-75; Pt. XI, p. 5048.

IG neither used its methane steam rights and technical knowledge, nor permitted others to use them, to produce hydrogen for ammonia synthesis or for general chemical purposes.

IG repeatedly refused methane steam licenses to American chemical companies although they were willing to pay substantial royalties for this process, which they regarded as the best and cheapest method of producing hydrogen.[100] IG turned down Hercules Powder's requests for a license in 1933 and 1936 for use in nitrogen manufacture when du Pont objected.

Political Factors in IG's Strategy

Political motivation became unmistakable in IG's methane steam license negotiations with Atlas Powder. When Atlas asked for a license, IG's American agent wrote to IG as follows:

> The project of Atlas Powder Company is analogous to the project of Hercules. It will be carried out irrespective of whether or not you will give Atlas a license and technical advice.
> We do not know whether under these circumstances you would still refuse to promote in any way the building of basic nitrogen plants in the United States.[101]

Later, in urging IG to license Atlas, the same agent argued that "by refusing to grant such licenses you will not seriously hamper a nitrogen program that may be divised [sic] by the U. S. A. Government," because alternative processes would be used.[102] Thus advised, IG resumed negotiations with both Atlas and Hercules. But IG abruptly terminated negotiations with Atlas when it learned that Atlas was planning to construct an explosives plant under contract with the British Government.[103]

IG's power over American chemical developments is reflected in the fact that, while IG was granting a license to Hercules and denying one to Atlas during 1940, Standard had already secured control of all these patents, IG having transferred them to Standard

---

100. *Ibid.*, Pt. IV, pp. 1783-84; Pt. XI, p. 5097.
101. *Ibid.*, Pt. IV, p. 1862.
102. *Ibid.*, p. 1866.
103. Atlas protested that it had not helped the British but had really hampered them by refusing to fill their orders until they advanced capital for constructing the plants. Even Atlas' offer to confine its use of the methane steam process to production of hydrogen for commercial explosives manufacture was unavailing.

under the Hague Agreement in 1939. In spite of Standard's public
declaration that the Hague Agreement "terminated all the rights between IG and Standard at that time," [104] IG patently retained substantial interest in a process purportedly assigned to Standard. The
fact that IG no longer had possession of the methane steam patents
did not prevent it from continuing to use its influence to hamper
American nitrogen production.[105]

THE DYESTUFFS CARTEL

IG pursued the same policy of cartelization in world chemical markets generally that it did in American chemical markets, but elsewhere it was unhampered by antitrust laws. In no other branch of the
chemical industries was this policy more effective than in dyestuffs.
In dyestuffs IG achieved its initial greatness, kept its pre-eminent
position the longest, and fostered the most thorough cartelization of
the world industry.

The community of interests in the German dyestuff industry before
World War I was in itself an almost complete cartelization of the
world industry. The rise of domestic dyestuff industries in many countries after the war, heavily subsidized and protected though they
were, created at once an opportunity and, from the business standpoint, a strategic need for an extension of that community of inter-

104. Bone, Pt. IX, pp. 5066-67.
105. *Ibid.*, Pt. IV, pp. 1776-86. The real situation was that IG retained a valid claim
to the legal title in these patents. As the court declared in *Standard Oil Co.* v. *Markham*
(*op. cit.*, p. 659): under the "real agreement" made at the Hague in 1939, "Standard-
IG should have the nominal legal title to the Class B Standard-IG patents [which
included methane steam] and the Jasco patents, subject, however, to an obligation to
reconvey at the end of World War II or on demand to IG." The court added that in
these patents Standard-IG obtained only "the licensing and royalty rights specified
in the Four-Party Agreement."
   Standard officials took substantially this position in their testimony before the Bone
Committee in 1942. Bone, Pt. IX, pp. 5209-13. But they took a contrary position in
the Markham suit. (See also Bone, Pt. IX, p. 5067.) A letter written in 1940 by
Standard's chief patent attorney indicates how the parties arranged the trick of having
their cake and eating it too:
   "These patents are now assigned to I. G. on the records of the United States Patent
Office. We have, however, in our files an assignment of these patents from I. G. to
Standard-I. G., bearing date in September 1939. Accordingly, if I. G. now issues a
license to Atlas Powder Company and we subsequently file our assignment, it will be
apparent to anyone who investigates the matter that I. G. granted a license under the
patents after title had passed to Standard-I. G. . . .
   "Mr. Joslin [IG's attorney] and I agreed that there would be no harm in I. G.
granting the license to Atlas Powder Company. If we record the assignment from I. G.
to Standard-I. G., we should probably then execute an agreement authorizing I. G. to
grant this license as of the date when it was granted." *Ibid.*, Pt. IV, p. 1860.

ests. The inexperienced foreign producers welcomed alliances with IG as a means of obtaining its technical assistance and as an avenue of escape from its competition.

But major chemical companies like ICI, du Pont, and Kuhlmann were unwilling for a time to accept the onerous terms on which alone IG was willing to form alliances, and for several years after the war they had no dyestuffs agreements with IG. Indeed, none of these leaders ever found a mutually acceptable basis for complete technical and commercial collaboration with IG, although all of them eventually established friendly relations facilitating the coordination of their dyestuff marketing policies, and even concluded specific agreements on particular products or for limited market areas.

The European Cartel

As early as 1927, a syndicate of French dyestuff producers, led by Kuhlmann and representing virtually the entire French production, reached a cartel agreement with IG. In broad outline the parties agreed to respect each other's home markets, to sell jointly or on prescribed quotas in other markets, and to collaborate in fixing sales prices. In 1929 a syndicate comprising three Swiss producers—Gesellschaft für Chemische Industrie, of Basle (Ciba), J. R. Geigy, and Chemische Fabrik vorm. Sandoz, both also of Basle—which controlled the great bulk of that country's output, joined the European dye cartel.[106] The three countries represented in the 1929 cartel accounted for more than four fifths of the total value of world dyestuff exports.[107] ICI joined the cartel in 1931,[108] and the leading producers of most other European countries soon followed suit. During the thirties, the European dye cartel controlled 60 to 70 per cent of the world's total output of dyestuffs and a still larger proportion of total exports.[109]

106. Ciba, Sandoz, and Geigy already had created a community of interests, pooling profits, conducting research and foreign sales through joint agencies. Together with a smaller local manufacturer, Durand & Huguenin, they produced about 90 per cent of Swiss output in 1937. Durand & Huguenin was an IG subsidiary until 1939, when Ciba took it over. As such, it participated indirectly in the cartel. Bureau of Foreign and Domestic Commerce, Trade Promotion Series, No. 189, *Synthetic Organic Chemicals*, p. 105; see pp. 104-07; Bone, Pt. V, pp. 2061, 2124-25.
107. Bone, Pt. V, p. 2328; see pp. 2327-32.
108. As previously mentioned, ICI and IG later eliminated any remaining competition between themselves in dyestuffs by organizing Trafford Chemicals, a joint enterprise.
109. See L. Ballande, *Essai d'étude monographique et statistique sur les ententes*

The only important producing countries not formal members of the European cartel were the United States, Japan, and the USSR. Russia, which had had a bilateral agreement with IG during the twenties, became substantially independent of imports, and as it used almost its entire dyestuffs production at home the cartel connection seems to have been allowed to lapse. As the Japanese industry expanded during the thirties under the stimulus of national subsidies, the European cartel members and American producers reached a series of market-sharing agreements with their far eastern rivals. The aggressiveness of the Japanese made these agreements little more than temporary makeshifts. From time to time they broke down; but they were as often renewed on revised terms, which invariably represented concessions to the Japanese. In this manner the parties managed to preserve a mechanism of control, however weak, in oriental markets, and to forestall forthright competition.

Relations Between American Dyestuffs Producers and Cartel

American dyestuff manufacturers cooperated both among themselves and with members of the European dye cartel in regulating world markets. This collaboration took various forms, many of which we have already described in connection with the sketch of intercorporate relationships among the outstanding leaders of the world's chemical industries. A brief review follows of these collaborative devices in so far as they relate to dyestuffs, to show how they formed a consistent pattern of cartelization.

1. Five companies—General Dyestuff, du Pont, National Aniline (of Allied Chemical), Calco Chemical (of American Cyanamid), and Cincinnati Chemical Works—together accounted for 90 per

économiques internationales, Paris, 1936, pp. 75-78; League of Nations, Publications, Ser. II, *Review of the Economic Aspects of Several International Industrial Agreements*, 1930, No. 41, pp. 41-43.

The Italian dyestuffs industry came under the joint control of IG and Montecatini around 1930, when these two acquired the stock of the dominant producer, Aziendi Colori Nazionali Affini (ACNA), and another, smaller manufacturer. The remaining Italian producers were closely affiliated with foreign cartel members, and all ultimately became associated both in a domestic dye consortium and in the European cartel. Bureau of Foreign and Domestic Commerce, *Chemical Developments in Foreign Countries, 1934*, p. 6; *German Chemical Developments in 1931*, pp. 34-35; *Italian Chemical Developments in 1928 and 1929*, p. 8 (Trade Information Bulletins No. 824, 795, and 705, respectively); see also Nye, Pt. XII, pp. 2855-56. The Czech firm, Aussiger Verein, which also joined the cartel, had a virtual monopoly of domestic dye production. Williams Haynes, *Chemical Economics*, Van Nostrand, New York, 1933, p. 250.

cent, by value, of the dyestuffs sold in the United States in 1939.[110] Of these five companies, three were American and two were direct subsidiaries of members of the European dye cartel. General Dyestuff is the exclusive American selling agent for both IG, whose 1939 dye exports from Germany to this country amounted to 5.7 per cent of total American domestic sales, and for General Aniline, IG's American subsidiary, which produced 20.6 per cent, by value, of total 1939 American dyestuffs.[111] Cincinnati is the joint subsidiary of the Swiss

TABLE 29

RELATIVE POSITIONS OF UNITED STATES DYESTUFF SELLERS IN 1939 [a]

Seller	Percentage Shares in Domestic Products Sold		Percentage Shares in Domestic Sales	
	Quantity	Value	Quantity	Value
Total	100.0	100.0	100.0	100.0
General Dyestuff	13.1	20.6	16.1	26.3
Du Pont	24.5	29.6	23.5	25.5
National Aniline	29.5	21.1	24.5	15.9
Cincinnati Chemical	8.8	9.0	11.3	14.5
Calco Chemical	10.6	9.2	10.7	7.9
Others	13.5	10.5	13.9	9.9

a. Compilation by du Pont's Organic Chemical Department, reproduced in *Patents,* Hearings before the Committee on Patents, 77th Cong., 2d sess., on S. 2303 and S. 2491, Pt. V, p. 2481. The figures for 1940, *ibid.,* are very similar. The first two columns deal with sales of domestically produced dyestuffs, and thus include exports and exclude imports. The last two columns deal with sales in the United States market, and hence exclude exports and include imports.

companies, Ciba, Sandoz, and Geigy. The difference between its 9 per cent share in American 1939 dyestuff production and its 14.5 per cent share of total American sales represented, as in the case of General Dyestuff, imports from its parent companies. Hence 29.6 per cent of American dyestuff production and 40.8 per cent of domestic sales were under direct control of full-fledged members of the dye

110. See Table 29. The percentage was the same in 1940.
111. IG was still exporting sizable quantities of higher-priced dyestuffs from Germany to the United States in 1939 and 1940. This is indicated by General's considerably greater share in the total *value* of domestic *sales* than in the quantity of domestic *production.*

cartel.[112] Before World War II, the German and Swiss parent companies limited the sales of their American subsidiaries to the United States and Canadian markets, and gave them exclusive rights there.[113]

2. The large American dyestuff manufacturers cooperate closely in the domestic market: they consult on prices; exchange samples; buy and sell in large quantities among themselves, often at discriminatingly favorable prices; and settle patent conflicts by cross-licensing. In this fashion, du Pont, National, and Calco have largely eliminated competition among themselves and with the local agents and subsidiaries of the formal cartel members, in the American market. Moreover, National and Calco have entered patent-pooling agreements directly with IG,[114] and du Pont and General Aniline regularly cross-license each other under numerous dye patents, amicably settling all their potential controversies.[115]

3. After ICI signed its 1929 Patents and Processes Agreement with du Pont and joined the European dye cartel, it withdrew from the American market, du Pont withdrew from British Empire markets, and both companies cooperated in common markets throughout the rest of the world.[116]

4. National (Allied Chemical) in effect adhered to the du Pont–ICI Agreement as far as its dyestuffs trade was concerned, by following a policy of staying out of British markets as long as ICI remained out of the American.[117] This understanding consummated ICI's program for reserving control of British markets to itself. The other elements previously described were: ICI's membership in the European cartel, its joint ownership with IG of Trafford Chemicals, and its alliance with du Pont.

5. This leaves only one major member of the European dye cartel, namely the French firm Kuhlmann, not definitely linked with the American industry. However, circumstantial evidence points to an understanding between the French dyemakers and the leading Ameri-

112. IG wrote, with reference to the application of the European cartel agreement to the United States: "Sale to and export from the U. S. A. fall within the contract." Bone, Pt. V, p. 2339. The percentages are in terms of value.

113. Both the Swiss and IG subsidiaries in the United States have refused foreign orders, except in Canada, stating specifically that they were not permitted to export. During the war, the foreign parents relaxed this restriction temporarily, because of their own inability to reach their foreign customers. *Ibid.*, pp. 2117-23 and exhibits.

114. *Ibid.*, pp. 2342, 2349, 2351.

115. See text, pp. 405-06; and Bone, Pt. V, pp. 2130-32.

116. See pp. 450-56.

117. Bone, Pt. V, pp. 2103-04.

can producers, wherein the Americans would stay out of the French home market,[118] and Kuhlmann would limit its exports to the United States.[119]

6. Finally, du Pont and National, the major American exporters, participated throughout the thirties with the members of the cartel and Mitsui in market-sharing and price-fixing agreements in the leading foreign markets, China, Japan, India, Brazil, and Argentina.[120]

IG Retains Leadership in Dyestuffs

IG has retained undisputed leadership in the world dyestuff industry by its intensive research, aggressive patent policies, and energetic selling methods.[121] Since IG, with its unique advantage of a "full line" of dyes, and trading on its prestige, could outsell its rivals in most export markets in any event, and since the latter in negotiations with IG had few bargaining weapons, IG's cartel partners have accepted extremely small export quotas as the price of immunity from IG competition in their domestic markets. For the most part, their exports are confined to low-cost bulk dyestuffs. This explains why most of the cartel agreements providing for market quotas apply to the Far East and Latin America. These are the leading export markets for the cheaper dyes. In higher-priced and more lucrative specialties, IG has retained an even more complete monopoly.[122]

118. In 1935 Kuhlmann proposed to National that National accept compensation in other markets for withdrawal from the French market: "The suggestion emanates from the fact that your confreres in the U. S. A., because of our excellent relations with them, refrain from sale in France. On our side, we have until now, renounced any desire to install a plant in the U. S. A. for the manufacture of dyestuffs." *Ibid.*, p. 2356.

119. A letter written by Geigy in 1937 indicates that Kuhlmann had been allotted a quota of $300,000 dyestuff sales in the United States. *Ibid.*, p. 2357. The letter does not state who gave the French this quota. However, in a cross-licensing agreement of the same year, General Aniline gave to a syndicate of French producers (including Kuhlmann) "permission" to sell, but not to manufacture, in the United States certain dyes covered by specified patents. *Ibid.*, pp. 2578-80.

120. See text, p. 484.

121. The factors mentioned are not put forward as a complete catalogue of the "causes" of IG predominance. Other factors which have probably contributed to the outcome include, besides its "running start," the comparative advantages of dyestuffs manufacture in Germany over opportunities in other lines of production there, and the comparative disadvantages of dyestuffs manufacture in some other countries in which alternative lines of production offer better profit prospects. In the language of economists, this latter factor represents the working of the law of comparative advantages. Just how much it may have had to do with IG's continued leadership, we do not pretend to know—or venture to guess.

122. See Chapter 9, n. 21. As Table 29 shows, General Dyestuff accounted for only 16.1 per cent of the total quantity of dyestuffs sold in the United States market, lagging far behind National and du Pont. However, in dollar value it led all others with 26.3 per cent of the total.

Thus IG retained the lion's share of world trade in dyes. In 1939 it alone accounted for well over half the total, which amounted to about $90 million.[123] Moreover, IG expanded its direct stake in foreign dyestuff industries, notably in the United States (General Aniline), Italy (ACNA), and Great Britain (Trafford). However, IG achieved and maintained its position in an "orderly" manner; competition has not "disrupted" dyestuff markets.

ROUNDING OUT THE PICTURE

The leading chemical companies have developed a pattern of control through a series of intercorporate arrangements to which they have adjusted their diverse operations. Since the manufacturing fields of chemical companies are not coterminous, these arrangements are numerous; and, since each is limited and circumscribed by all the others, they are varied and complex. In some cases one or another of the major companies has expressly excluded specified products from the coverage of more general agreements. But, with or without such an explicit reservation, most big companies have chosen, at one time or another, for one reason or another, to treat some particular line of products as a case apart.[124]

Thus du Pont has accorded separate treatment to Duco and nylon. These are not only original inventions but creative achievements of the first rank, which du Pont developed independently. In disposing of rights to them, du Pont has tried to obtain suitable compensation, benefits, or advantages. Although it made separate arrangements for these products abroad, it generally turned first to established chemical companies with which it had previously made other agreements.

In the case of Duco, du Pont set up separate companies in various countries to which it granted the local rights. It took in, as junior partners: in Great Britain, Nobel; in Italy, Montecatini;[125] and in

123. Bureau of Foreign and Domestic Commerce, Trade Promotion Series, No. 211, *Chemical Developments Abroad*, p. 7.

124. This does not necessarily mean, in fact it almost never means, that the special arrangements made for the given line of products are of a type suitable to a competitive development. It does mean simply that the terms of control for that line of products are independently negotiated, and as a rule the arrangements include one or more "outside" parties, that is, participants who would not have "a place in the picture" were the development handled along customary lines.

125. Montecatini supplied the Italian Duco company with its solvents. Bureau of Foreign and Domestic Commerce, *Italian Chemical Developments in 1928 and 1929*, pp. 3, 50; Nye, Pt. XVII, pp. 4351-52.

France, Société Central de Dynamite.[126] Du Pont offered the German rights to IG, which declined them. Du Pont's eventual associate in the German Duco enterprise was Schering A. G., a subsidiary of Kokswerke und Chemische Fabriken A. G.[127] Similarly, du Pont sold local foreign nylon rights to IG, ICI, the Rhodiaceta company (a French rayon manufacturer with whom, and with whose parent, Société des Usines Chimiques Rhone Poulenc, du Pont had close working relations) and Rhodiaceta Italiana, a joint subsidiary of Montecatini and Rhone Poulenc.[128]

When du Pont decided to manufacture rayon filaments and fibers, it obtained American rights to a French Comptoir process. The Comptoir also licensed du Pont to manufacture cellophane in the United States. In both cases Comptoir received in return a substantial bloc of stock in the separate du Pont companies organized for these ventures.[129] In the case of cellulose acetate rayon and plastics, du Pont obtained exclusive North American rights from Rhone Poulenc and Rhodiaceta, in patents and processes agreements which limited each party to its allotted geographic market.[130]

The Rayon Cartel

The manufacture of rayon filaments and fibers (the only branch of the industry treated here) is quite distinct from the manufacture of rayon fabrics. It is in a sense a "special" field, because most of the world's great rayon manufacturers are not chemical companies. However, the big rayon companies have very close intercorporate financial ties, and the industry is highly cartelized. Moreover, the relations between rayon and chemical companies—both those which produce rayon, like du Pont and IG, and those which do not, like ICI—are extremely close and friendly.

We have noted the close cooperation of ICI with Courtaulds, the British rayon trust. Courtaulds has working arrangements with the French rayon combine with which du Pont is allied. Courtaulds is

126. Nye, Pt. XII, p. 2811.
127. Bone, Pt. V, p. 2250; Schedule A of the 1939 du Pont–ICI Patents and Processes Agreement, loc. cit.
128. Schedule A, 1939 du Pont–ICI Patents and Processes Agreement, loc. cit.
129. Du Pont later acquired all the stock of these companies and made them integral departments of its own business organization.
130. Schedule A, 1939 du Pont–ICI Agreement, loc. cit.; Nye, Pt. XI, p. 2899, Pt. XVII, p. 4352.

also closely associated with the German "big business" unit in this sphere, Vereinigte Glanzstoff. They have a joint subsidiary. They own a large, if not a controlling, portion of the major Italian producer, Snia Viscosa. Moreover, Courtaulds owns stock in the Dutch Algemeene Kunstzidje Unie (AKU) group, a combination of the Dutch Enka interests and Glanzstoff. IG participates in a division of markets agreement for Germany with Glanzstoff; IG and Glanzstoff jointly own Aceta G. m. b. H., an acetate rayon producer. IG has agreements with Glanzstoff's subsidiary I. P. Bemberg A. G., eliminating competition between them throughout the world in cuprammonium rayon.

Four companies or groups dominate the United States rayon market, producing 81 per cent of American output in 1938: American Viscose, a Courtaulds subsidiary; du Pont; a group of closely related subsidiaries of Glanzstoff-AKU (American Enka, North American Rayon, and American Bemberg) ; and, in the acetate field, Celanese Corporation of America controlled by the Swiss Dreyfus brothers, who also control the British and Canadian Celanese companies. The stability and uniformity of their prices indicate that these four dominant producers, the European principals and associates of which are so closely linked by cartel ties, have managed to maintain an "orderly" market in America.[131]

The Titanium Cartel

The world-wide cartel in titanium, a superior white pigment developed in the past three decades, represents a submerging of the separate interests of the leading chemical companies in the field. During the twenties, the National Lead Company, leading American manufacturer of white pigments, acquired control of the American and Norwegian companies organized to exploit two of the three basic titanium inventions, and split the world market between them.

In 1927 National Lead and IG organized a joint subsidiary, Titan-

131. In 1937 the Federal Trade Commission after hearings issued a "cease and desist" order directing du Pont, Viscose, and other companies to discontinue a conspiracy to fix prices. *Viscose Co., et al.*, Complaint No. 2161, order issued July 3, 1937; see Commerce Clearing House, *Trade Regulation Service*, Vol. II, p. 17211. See also Clair Wilcox, *Competition and Monopoly in American Industry*, TNEC Monograph No. 21, pp. 202-05; Ballande, *op. cit.*, pp. 83-88; League of Nations, *International Industrial Agreements*, pp. 49-56; Bone, Pt. V, pp. 2337, 2343; Bureau of Foreign and Domestic Commerce, *German Chemical Developments in 1927*, pp. 5, 9.

gesellschaft, and assigned to it several continental European countries and China and Japan as its exclusive sphere. IG in turn made an export quota agreement, on behalf of Titangesellschaft, with a French company which owned world rights in the Blumenfeld patents—the third group of basic titanium inventions. Similarly, National Lead's own subsidiary for the foreign field, Titan Company, Inc., organized in Britain Titan Products, Ltd., in conjunction with ICI and two other local companies, to serve as their exclusive agent in that market. Later, National Lead and CIL organized Canadian Titanium Pigments to exploit the Canadian market.

Meanwhile, du Pont, Montecatini, Aussiger Verein, Laporte of Great Britain, and others had acquired the Blumenfeld rights in their respective countries.[132] Within a few years, these two competing international groups of companies joined forces. Du Pont and National Lead agreed to exchange patent rights and technical information for the United States, Central and South America. Du Pont's London manager characterized this agreement as follows: "We look upon this patent pool as a definite advance in cooperation and the strengthening of both parties' position to the exclusion of outsiders." [133] As a result, these two companies and their two domestic licensees, small companies with output restricted under their licenses, monopolized the American titanium market.

Aussiger Verein and Montecatini both likewise came to terms with the National Lead–IG–Titan group, eliminating competition between them. Also, Titan Products, Ltd., reached an accord with Laporte, dividing the large British market between them. In return Laporte agreed to stay out of Canada. IG and National Lead, together with a Japanese manufacturer and the French (Blumenfeld) company, organized a joint subsidiary to take over the Japanese market. Thus the titanium cartel represented a merger of all the important interests, a

132. We have previously mentioned the merger in 1931 of the pigment business of du Pont and Commercial Solvents in the newly formed Krebs Pigment & Color Corporation. It was in this merger that du Pont obtained its entree into the titanium field, as Commercial Solvents put into Krebs the titanium rights and business of its subsidiary, Commercial Pigments Corporation. *Moody's Manual of Investments* (Industrials), 1944, p. 1805.

133. *U.S.* v. *National Lead Company, et al.*, in U.S. District Court for the Southern District of New York, Civil Action No. 26-258, Opinion filed July 5, 1945, p. 43. The court recognized that this official lacked the authority to make this statement, but concluded that it was a fair description of du Pont's attitude. The court found du Pont as well as National Lead guilty of violating the antitrust laws.

pooling of all competing patent rights. The president of National Lead has described it with refreshing bluntness:

> May I call the proposed combination, for simplicity, a cartel? The whole purpose of the cartel is to obtain a monopoly of patents, so that no one can manufacture it excepting the members of the cartel, and so can raise the prices by reason of such monopoly to a point that would give us much more profit on our present tonnage, but also prevent a growth in tonnage that would interfere with their greater profits in lithopone.[134]

CONCLUSIONS

No single cartel controls world trade in all chemicals. Neither does free competition regulate the flow of capital into the chemical industries and the flow of products to consumers. The independent, rational decisions of a multiplicity of business rivals do not alone determine what chemicals shall be produced, where, in what amounts, and at what prices they shall be sold. Independent decision making has been supplemented, and in many spheres replaced, by joint administrative action adjusted to a network of cartel arrangements which chemical producers have worked out over a long period of time. Business rivals, anxious to escape the risks and insecurity of competition, have sought through collective action to subject their markets to administrative discipline. They have contrived these controls on an empirical basis. They have adjusted them to meet particular situations.

The numerous chemical cartels differ in their details. In a few instances rival concerns have eliminated all competition between themselves by coordinating their activities through quasi partnerships. More frequently a number of companies have developed an interrelated group of compacts blanketing some major chemical field. Supplementing these "grand alliances" are a host of specific agreements which, taken together, involve virtually all important producers of chemicals, and affect almost every chemical product. The agreements vary in coverage from single products to the whole range of operations of the companies concerned. They vary in form from informal understandings among financially independent concerns to corporate consolidations or even outright mergers.

134. *Ibid.*, p. 22 and *passim*. Lithopone is a competing white pigment, produced by du Pont and others. See also *Scientific and Technical Mobilization*, Hearings before a Subcommittee of the Committee on Military Affairs, U.S. Senate, 78th Cong., 1st sess., on S.Res. 107 and S. 702, Pt. VII, pp. 959-77; Ballande, *op. cit.*, pp. 59-60.

We have sketched only the major outlines of these highly complicated industrial arrangements and described in detail only a few
parts of the whole complex. They fit together, however, like the parts
of a jigsaw puzzle, to give outward unity and inward consistency to
the picture. These arrangements tend to cluster about, and to adjust
themselves to, the strategic exigencies of a few relatively large companies. Chief among these are IG, du Pont, and ICI—the big three.

The relationships of every chemical company with its rivals are
necessarily conditioned and shaped by the entire range of external
policies and commitments of all the others—but particularly of these
three. Du Pont cannot take on another general partner in British Empire chemicals markets; it already has ICI. Standard Oil was not free
to merge its interests in the petroleum chemical field with du Pont
after having taken IG for its spouse. True, du Pont can and does
have hundreds of agreements with other producers covering products
in which it has made no commitments under its ICI partnership or
applying to markets, domestic or foreign, not reserved to ICI. The
same is true of its understanding with IG.

The Pattern of Cartel Control

But all these individual agreements must be mutually compatible.
Du Pont can offer to no more than one company the exclusive rights
to a particular geographic market for a specific product or process.
When du Pont grants to a third party a license involving rights
which it has received from ICI, it must incorporate all the limitations
which ICI placed upon the original grant. When ICI agrees with a
third company to exchange technical information in a field in which
it has obtained information from du Pont, it must have du Pont's
consent and must protect du Pont's rights.

Thus, every agreement both helps to shape, and itself fits into,
a logical pattern of cartel control. By defining for each company its
area of operation, its duties and its rights, an agreement makes it
possible for all companies to plan, individually and in concert, with
some assurance of how each will behave. By limiting and regulating
the activities of chemical companies, cartel agreements get rid of the
uncertainties of a freely competitive market. The cartels provide a
relatively stable framework within which conflicting interests may be
reconciled by maneuver, bargain, and compromise.

Our account of these complicated cartel arrangements by which business has sought to reconcile conflicts, establish "order," and "stabilize" markets describes the situation as it existed before the war. Moreover, it is necessarily incomplete. Many of these arrangements have never been made public. And from those that are of public record we have had to choose. For to treat all in detail would extend the study too far. It would exhaust the reader. But almost every major chemical company has some kind of cooperative working relationship and understanding with one or another of the "big three" that directly or indirectly links it with all other chemical companies.

Cartelization of the world's chemical industries is the outcome of a process of business diplomacy. New problems are constantly arising; new products and processes and companies threaten the balance of power and the stability of markets in this dynamic field. The function of business diplomacy is to adjudicate these issues, to adjust existing relationships to them. This process of constant adjustment by negotiation, rather than by free competition in the market, or by authoritative decisions of a unified administrative mechanism (as in the tin, rubber, and several other industries), is the distinctive characteristic of the cartel system in the world's chemical industries.

INDEX

Sugar industry (*Continued*)
  Cuban: competition between American and native owners, 23; in dilemma, 30-39; income from, 30; importance to economy, 31; organization of, 23; prices, 28, 34; production costs, 23; single seller, 33-34; U.S. tariff preference, 22, 26, 42
  Czechoslovakian, 36
  German, 36
  Government assistance: cartel quota enforcement, 38; subsidies, 42
  Hawaii, 26, 30
  Javanese: dumping, 21; planting, 27; price discrimination, 21-22; sales area, 21; single seller, 21
  Organization of, 14, 24-25
  Philippines, 26, 30
  Poland, 36
  Puerto Rico, 26, 30
  Technology, effect of, 25
  United States: importing, 18; sugar control measures, 41-43; tariff, cost to consumer, 50
  See also Sugar
Sulphuric acid, 366, 384; *see also* Chemicals
Surinaamsche Bauxite Co., 255
Surplus capacity, *see specific industries*
Swedish Cooperative Union, 343
Sweitzerische Metallurgische Gesellschaft, 220
Synthetic Ammonia & Nitrates, Ltd., 131
Synthetic ammonia processes, *see* Ammonia, synthetic
Synthetics, 87-89, 364-69; *see also* Chemicals

TARAPACA Y ANTOFAGASTA (CIA. SALITRERA DE TARAPACA Y ANTOFAGASTA), 140
Tariffs: American: on chemicals, 374, 469, on lamps, 350, on nitrogen, 144, on sugar, 17, 22, Fordney-McCumber (1922), 22, 226, 228, 233, 240, 248, 251, 276, Smoot-Hawley (1930), 22, 37, 42; British, on iron and steel, 211; dyestuffs, 505
Technology, 87, 129-31, 134, 219, 223-24, 277-78, 350-52, 364-69, 395-97; *see also* Chemicals
Thomson-Houston: processes, 320, 322; *see also* British Thomson-Houston Co.; Cie. Française Thomson-Houston
Thyssen group, 175
Titangesellschaft, 514

Titanium, *see* Chemicals industries
Tokyo Electric Co., Ltd., 321
Trafford Chemicals, Ltd., 489, 509, 511
Tung-Sol Lamp Works, 351, 359
Tungsram (United Incandescent Lamp & Electricity Co.), 323, 332

UCB (UNION CHIMIQUE BELGE), 417, 482
UCC (Union Carbide & Carbon Co.), 459, 478-79, 502; division of fields, 386-88, 394, 425; formation, 381, 383-84; IG relations, 96, 109; intercorporate relations, 389
Union Carbide & Carbon, *see* UCC
Union Chimique Belge, *see* UCB
Union Elektrizitäts Gesellschaft, 322
United Alkali Co., Ltd., 142, 406
United Incandescent Lamp & Electricity Co., of Hungary, *see* Tungsram
United States Alkali Export Association, *see* Alkasso
United States Industrial Chemicals, *see* USI
United States Steel Corp., 151, 199
United States v. *The Chemical Foundation*, 375
United States, Hudson v., 302
United Steel Works (Vereinigte Stahlwerke): organization of, 175, 211; rate of return, 177
Unyte Corp., 476, 487
USI (United States Industrial Chemicals), 388-89, 394

VAW (VEREINIGTE ALUMINIUMWERKE A.G.), 245, 249; agreement with Alcoa, 249; release from aluminum cartel commitments, 270-72
Vereenigde Javasuiker Producenten, *see* VJP
Verein für Chemische und Metallurgische Produktion, of Aussig, *see* Aussiger Verein
Vereinigte Aluminiumwerke A.G., *see* VAW
Vereinigte Glanzstoff, 513
Vereinigte Köln-Rottweiler Pulverfabriken A.G., *see* Köln-Rottweil
Vereinigte Stahlwerke A.G., *see* United Steel Works
Verkaufsstelle Vereinigter Glühlampenfabriken, 316-17
VJP (Vereenigde Javasuiker Producenten), 21

WACKER, DR. ALEXANDER, G.M.B.H., 459
War: War of the Pacific, 120; World War
I effect: on aluminum market, 244-45,
on chemical production of Allies, 374-
75, on electric lamp cartel, 316-17,
323, on magnesium output and prices,
275-76, on nitrate industry, Chilean,
120, 125, on steel industry, 171-72,
on sugar supply, 18-19, 24; World
War II effect: on aluminum capacity,
273, on chemical production, 377, on
explosives cartel, 444-45, on magnesium output, 303, on nitrogen industry, 141-42, 158, 162, 168-70
Watt Co. of Vienna, 323

Webb-Pomerene Act, 199
Webb-Pomerene ass'ns., 199, 200-01, 433
Welsh Plate and Sheet Mfrs. Ass'n., 198
Westfälische-Anhaltische Sprengstoff A.G.,
see Coswig
Westinghouse Electric & Mfg. Co.: agree-
ment with GE, 305, 308-09, 327-28,
330; cartel participation, 341; organi-
zation of, 305
Wheeling Steel Corp., 201
Winthrop Chemical Co., 472-73, 476, 480
Wipperfürth Radio-Electric Co., 317

ZAIBATSU, 418
Zurich Agreement, 254-55